PERSONALITY

THEORY AND RESEARCH *Tenth Edition*

Daniel Cervone
University of Illinois at Chicago

Lawrence A. Pervin
Rutgers University

BICENTENNIAL
1807
WILEY
2007
BICENTENNIAL

John Wiley & Sons, Inc.

VICE PRESIDENT AND PUBLISHER	Jay O'Callaghan
EXECUTIVE EDITOR	Christopher T. Johnson
ASSISTANT EDITOR	Maureen Clendenny
EDITORIAL ASSISTANT	Eileen McKeever
MARKETING MANAGER	Jeffrey Rucker
PRODUCTION MANAGER	Kelly Tavares
PRODUCTION EDITOR	Lea Radick
DESIGNER	Hope Miller
ILLUSTRATION EDITOR	Sandra Rigby
PHOTO EDITOR	Ellinor Wagner
COVER IMAGE	Warhol, Andy (1928–1987). Mona Lisa, 1963. Synthetic polymer paint and silkscreen ink on canvas, 125 3/4 × 82 1/8 in.
BICENNTENIAL LOGO DESIGN	Richard Pacifico

This book was set in New Aster by Laserwords Private Limited, and printed and bound by R.R. Donnelley. The cover was printed by Phoenix Color.

To order books or for customer service please, call 1-800-CALL WILEY (225-5945).

ISBN 13: 978-0-471-74241-8

Printed in the United States of America

10 9 8 7 6 5 4 3 2

To Bobbie, David, and Levi (LAP)

To Jenny and Nicholas (DC)

PREFACE

This text introduces students to the two interlocking sides of personality psychology. One is the field's research side. Research on personality and individual differences is a vibrant, multi-national enterprise. We have worked to ensure that our book introduces readers to the field's latest research methods and findings. These span an amazingly wide range. Molecular genetic techniques and brain imaging methods shed light on the biological bases of personality. Research on personality and culture illuminates the connections between individual development and sociocultural settings.

We also introduce readers to the field's other side: theory. In any science, a field's greatest intellectual achievements are its comprehensive theories. We remember Newton, Darwin, and Einstein not because of any particular experiment or scientific observation of theirs, but because they provided theoretical frameworks of breadth and explanatory power. This book presents the major theoretical frameworks that have guided the contemporary science of personality.

Throughout the text, coverage of theory and research is intertwined. We evaluate classic and contemporary theories in light of current research evidence. However, in addition to chapters that combine theory and research, two of our chapters are specifically devoted to research advances in key areas of study. Chapter 9 reviews research on biological foundations of personality. Students learn about advances in the study of temperament, genetics, neuroscience, and evolutionary psychology. Chapter 14 reviews research on personality in context. We cover work on interpersonal relationships, cultural and socioeconomic factors, personality development across the life span, and the application of personality theory to questions of social change.

There are not many ways in which textbooks are likes wines. But there is at least one: Good ones have "balance." Different elements of the total product are shown in their best light. No one element overwhelms the others. We have tried to present a textbook that is balanced in two respects. First, as just noted, we balance coverage of theory versus research. Second, and of equal importance, is that we provide balanced coverage of the field's alternative theoretical perspectives. We strive to present each theory in its best light. Although we also analyze each theory critically (primarily in critical evaluation sections at the end of chapters), our overarching aim is to present students with the fundamental insights and scientific strengths of each approach.

Many students who use this book may have little formal background in scientific psychology. Most, of course, will not go on to a career in the field. We have taken account of this in the text. It is easily accessible, even to the student with little or no background beyond a standard intro psych course. We believe that we have achieved accessibility without sacrificing any of the intellectual depth that has been the "backbone" of this text since its first edition.

This tenth edition of *Personality: Theory and Research*, then, aims to:

1. *Present the major theoretical perspectives on personality.* We cover the field's major theoretical perspectives in depth. This, we feel, is vastly better than alternative strategies. Some textbooks cover a very large number of theories, including minor perspectives that have little relevance to the contemporary scientific fields. Such volumes commonly provide students with only superficial knowledge of important theories that should be understood deeply. They also commonly fail to provide adequate coverage of the field's many advances in research. Others adopt the opposite strategy. Authors organize coverage around research topics while presenting little coverage of the field's major theoretical perspectives. For the student being introduced to the personality psychology, this approach is terribly costly. The student fails to appreciate the ways in which theories have shaped the research enterprise throughout the field's history. Understanding personality psychology's major theories is also an important part of a broad liberal arts education; a number of the theories we discuss have influenced other fields of study and society at large.

   We focus somewhat more on theoretical *perspectives* than on particular "great theorists." We do present the student with much information about classic theorists (e.g., Freud, Rogers) and their contributions. However, the contemporary science of personality is guided primarily by broad perspectives to which multiple theorists and researchers contribute. Our coverage reflects this fact.

2. *Integrate theory and research.* Our aim here is to show the student how theory and research inform one another. Theoretical developments spur research, and research contributes to the development, modification, and evaluation of personality theories.

3. *Integrate case material with theory.* By necessity, theory and research deal with abstractions and generalizations, rather than with specific and unique individuals. To bridge the gap between the general and the specific, we present case study material that illustrates how each theory assesses and interprets the individual. We follow one case throughout the book to show how the various theories relate to the same person. Thus, the student can ask: Are the pictures of a person gained through the lens of each theory completely different from each other, or do they represent complementary perspectives? Our inclusion of case material also enables the student who is interested in clinical psychology to see connections between personality psychology and clinical practice.

4. *Treat each theoretical approach objectively and even-handedly.* We present each theory on its own terms and only then evaluate it in relation to standard criteria. Each of the theories of personality provides insights and intellectual tools that are unique, and our most important task it to present these to the reader. We evaluate the theories critically only after these presentations. Our evaluations are not designed to persuade students of the merits of a particular approach, but to broaden their understanding of the theories and to enhance and encourage their own critical thinking skills.

5. *Present the complex scientific field in an accessible manner.* There are actually two goals here. They differ, but they do not necessarily conflict.

One is to teach students about the field of personality psychology as it really exists—including some of its nuances and complexities. Even the introductory student deserves to have more than a "watered-down" approach that, e.g., merely presents one or two key ideas from each theory. The other goal is to make the material easily accessible. We relate scientific theories and research findings to students' own interests and concerns. We avoid jargon as much as possible. We have aimed for a straightforward writing style.

We hope that *Personality: Theory and Research* will enable students to appreciate the complexity of personality, the capacity of case studies and empirical research to shed light on this complexity, and the scientific and practical value of systematic theorizing about the individual. We also hope that students may discover a particular theory of personality that makes personal sense to them and is useful in their own lives.

Note to instructors (Students may read it too, of course!). For those of you familiar with prior editions of this text, your first question may be how this edition differs from the previous ones. There are three things to say in response to this question:

— The overall format of the text remains the same. The ordering of chapters, and their interweaving of theory with research, was judged in past editions to be a strength of the book and thus has been retained.

— The presentation of material within individual chapters has been improved. In particular, we have provided greater uniformity of coverage across chapters. Each time we introduce a theory we discuss, in order, a) the *view of the person* explicit or implicit in the theory, b) the *view of science* embraced by the main theorists, c) the *structure and process* elements of the theory, and d) how the theory addresses *growth and development*. Then, each time we evaluate a theory, we consider five criteria in order: a) quality of the *scientific observations* on which the theory rests; the degree to which the theoretical concepts are b) internally coherent and *systematic*, c) *testable*, and d) *comprehensive* with respect to the issues of personality psychology; and e) whether the theory has fostered valuable *applications*. These five criteria are introduced in Chapter 1. They are applied to each individual theory in critical evaluation sections that conclude the coverage of each approach. They are then applied to the field of personality psychology as a whole in Chapter 15, which concludes our text. This consistent structure should make it easier to organize classroom lectures around recurring sets of questions.

— We have updated and expanded our coverage not only of recent research, but of theories. We did so thanks in large part to feedback from professional reviewers. We'll explain. One natural tendency when revising a textbook is to focus primarily on research findings that have been published since the preparation of the previous edition. A risk is that, after a couple of revisions, a textbook's coverage may become tilted toward research at the expense of theory. If so, the book no longer serves the needs of introductory students, who need a *textbook* not a professional research handbook. Reviewers of the 9th edition informed us that we had done a perfectly sufficient job of updating our coverage of research but that, as we prepare the 10th edition, we should bear in mind that students also need thorough coverage of theories. More than any other course in the standard curriculum offered by a psychology department, personality psychology introduces students to broad theories of human nature. These theories have long rich intellectual histories. The personality course is the place for students to learn about these theoretical frameworks and to relate them to other courses in the undergraduate curriculum, as well as to experiences in their own lives. In response to this feedback from reviewers we have, at a great many junctures of the book, expanded and deepened our coverage of the theories of personality and the intellectual traditions within which they developed. One particularly extensive example of this extension is found in Chapter 6, which includes new material on intellectual trends past and present, especially existentialism and the positive psychology movement.

ACKNOWLEDGEMENTS

We thank the Psychology staff at John Wiley and Sons for their continued support. Their valuable suggestions that have made this book a better classroom product for both instructors and students. We also thank our many students and colleagues whose constructive suggestions have improved our coverage of personality theory and research. In particular, we are grateful to Dr. Tracy L. Caldwell for suggesting the "toolkit" metaphor that appears in our first chapter and reappears in the text's concluding passages.

DANIEL CERVONE
University of Illinois at Chicago
LAWRENCE A. PERVIN
Rutgers, the State University

This text benefited from input from outside reviewers whose scholarly feedback enhanced the final product. Reviewers included: Michael Firmin, Cedarville University; Randall Jorgensen, Syracuse University; Christopher Leone, University of North Florida; Michael Stevens, Illinois State University; Tamara Towles-Schwen, Buffalo State College.

SUPPLEMENTAL MATERIALS

Included with the text is access to an electronic Instructor's Manual and Test Bank (IMTB) authored by Dr. Tracy L. Caldwell. The IMTB can be found on the web at www.wiley.com/college/cervone. It includes Chapter Overview and Objectives, Suggested Lecture Topics, Instructional Aids (including recommendation for films, tapes, demonstrations, and, most of all, websites that are relevant to the text and lectures), Questions for Thought and Discussion, and a Test Bank that includes multiple-choice, True/False, and Essay items.

The 10th edition of the Instructor's Manual and Test Bank (IMBT) also provides, for the first time for this book, detailed PowerPoint presentations of material covered in the text. The slides are sequenced according to the text's coverage of material and maintain the text's chapter headings and subheadings so that instructors who wish to depart from the text's coverage can very easily identify corresponding slides.

Resources for the student include Flashcards designed to increase students' "personality vocabulary."

CONTENTS

CHAPTER 2

CHAPTER 3

CHAPTER 4

FREUD'S PSYCHOANALYTIC THEORY: APPLICATIONS, RELATED THEORETICAL CONCEPTIONS, AND CONTEMPORARY RESEARCH, 111

CHAPTER 5

CHAPTER 6

CHAPTER 7

TRAIT THEORIES OF PERSONALITY: ALLPORT, EYSENCK, AND CATTELL, 235

CHAPTER 8

TRAIT THEORY: THE FIVE-FACTOR MODEL; APPLICATIONS AND EVALUATION OF TRAIT APPROACHES TO PERSONALITY, 267

CHAPTER 9

CHAPTER 10

CHAPTER 11

CHAPTER 12

SOCIAL-COGNITIVE THEORY: BANDURA AND MISCHEL, 449

CHAPTER 13

SOCIAL-COGNITIVE THEORY: APPLICATIONS, RELATED THEORETICAL CONCEPTIONS, AND CONTEMPORARY RESEARCH, 493

CHAPTER 14

CHAPTER 15

PERSONALITY THEORY: FROM EVERYDAY OBSERVATIONS TO SYSTEMATIC THEORIES

1

My friend is not very self-confident. She's my friend but she always tries to show that she's better by trying to take my boyfriends away from me. She's a fake friend, obviously. She could be fun to hang out with, until there is a guy on the way. She would try to do everything to show that she's better, because, really, she's got low self-esteem. She always has to have a guy by her side, to feel good. Otherwise she feels worthless.

This person I know is extremely insecure about himself. This insecurity has embodied itself in bizarre behavior patterns, which ultimately describe a sad, paranoid soul who has undergone many hardships, not necessarily digesting the origin of such mishaps. Instead of recognizing himself as the instigator he has chosen to blame others for his actions.

I can be selfish, but I believe it is because I try to be perfect. Perfect in the sense I want to be an "A" student, a good mother, a loving wife, an excellent employee, a nourishing friend. My significant other thinks I try too hard to be "Mother Theresa" at times—not that that is a bad thing. But I can drive myself insane at times. I have led a hard childhood and adulthood life; therefore I believe I am trying to make up for all the bad times. I want to be productive, good—make a difference in my world.

I'm a real jackass. I'm intelligent enough to do well in school and study genetics, but have no idea when to shut up. I often am very offensive and use quite abrasive language, although I'm shy most of the time and talk to few people. I'm sarcastic, cruel, and pompous at times. Yet I've been told that I'm kind and sweet; this may be true, but only to those I deem worthy of speaking to with some frequency. I'm very fond of arguing and pretty much argue for fun.

My friend is an outgoing, fun-to-be-with person. Although when he feels that something is not right, I mean according to his standards, he is a perfectionist in an obsessive manner. If he feels that someone is not capable of completing a job he takes over and does it himself. Behind closed doors his temper is unbelievable, loud, and never happy. In a social environment he is Mr. Happy-Go-Lucky.

This person is shy at times. They tend to open up to some people. You never know when they're happy or sad. They never show their real feelings and when they do it's so hard for them. They did have a trauma experience that closed them up—where they seem to be afraid to let their real self show. They are funny and do have a lot of fun and are fun to be around but at times it's hard to know if they're really having a good time. The person is loved by a lot of people, and is an extremely giving person, but they don't like "seriousness."

These sketches were not written by professional psychologists or by advanced students in the field. They were written by people just like you: students enrolled in a course on the psychology of personality, who were writing on the very first day of class. When we, the authors of this textbook, teach this course, we commonly begin by asking class members to describe their own personality, as well as that of a friend. Students' descriptions are insightful and richly detailed—so much so that one is forced to ask: Is the class filled with "personality theorists"?

In a sense, the answer to this question is "yes." We are all personality theorists. We all spend countless hours asking questions about ourselves ("Why am I depressed?" "Why do I become so anxious when I have to speak in public?") and other people ("Why are my parents so weird?" "If I introduce Maria to Mike, will they hit it off?"). In answering these questions we develop ideas—rich, complex, sophisticated ideas—about why people act the way they do. We develop our own theories about personality.

The fact that we think so much about people raises an important point for you to consider now, at the outset of your course in personality psychology. The point is the following: You already know a lot about the subject matter of this course. You probably know more about the subject matter of this class, at its very beginning, than you do about any other course you could possibly take in college. By comparison, imagine what would happen if a professor in a different course asked students to do what we ask: to write a description of the course's main subject matter on the first day of class. Consider a math, history, or chemistry course: "Please describe integral calculus." "Outline the causes of the Bolshevik Revolution." "Describe your favorite chemical bond." Such requests would be absurd. Whereas these courses are designed to *introduce* you to the subject matter, this course is different. Personality "needs no introduction." You already know, and can describe in detail, a great many "personalities." You have ideas about what makes people tick and how people differ from one another. You use these ideas to understand events, to predict future events, and to help your friends handle the stresses, bumps, and bruises of life. You already possess, and use, your own theory of personality.

"But"—you may be asking yourself—"if I already know so much about personality, why should I take this class? What can I learn about personality from professional personality psychologists? What are the personality theorists who are discussed in this book accomplishing that I'm not?" This chapter addresses these questions. Specifically, it introduces the field of personality psychology by considering the following three questions.

1. How do scientific theories of personality differ from the ideas about persons that you develop in your daily life?

2. Why is there more than one personality theory? In what general ways do the theories differ and how can one evaluate their relative merits in furthering a science of personality?

3. What are personalists and researchers trying to accomplish? What aspects of persons and individual differences are they trying to understand and what factors are so important that they must be addressed in any personality theory?

QUESTIONS TO BE ADDRESSED IN THIS CHAPTER

Everybody wants to know about personality. What is my friend really like? What am I really like? Can people change their personality—and if so, how? Is there a basic human nature—and if so, what is it? Asking these questions is not hard. Providing solid, scientifically credible answers is. One group of people who tries to provide answers are psychologists working in the field of personality psychology. This book introduces you to this field of study: its research methods, primary findings, and most important theories.

In many ways, personality psychology may seem familiar to you. The professional psychologists' questions about persons resemble questions that you already ask. Yet there are big differences between most people's day-to-day, informal thinking about personality and the formal scientific theories developed by personality psychologists. The differences are not so much in the questions that are asked but in how answers are sought. Let's begin, then, by considering some of these differences.

Think for a moment about how you develop ideas about people. You observe and interact with friends and family. You reflect on yourself. You get ideas from books, songs, movies, TV shows, and plays. Somehow, from this mix, you end up with beliefs about the nature of persons and the main differences between individuals. This mix of information is information enough *unless* one is trying to develop a formal theory of personality. Personality theorists are charged with studying persons scientifically. This charge has five implications; specifically, to develop a scientific theory of personality, theorists must pursue five goals that typically are not pursued in everyday, informal thinking about persons.

FIVE GOALS FOR THE PERSONALITY THEORIST

The five goals the personality theorist pursues involve both theory (the ideas used to understand persons, their development, and the differences among them) and evidence (the scientific observations that become the database for the theory). As you read this book, you can think of these five goals as five criteria for evaluating the theories. The various theories differ considerably in their success in achieving each of these five goals. The five are:

OBSERVATION THAT IS SCIENTIFIC

Good scientific theories are built on careful scientific observation. By observing people scientifically, the personality psychologist obtains systematic descriptions of universal human tendencies and differences among people. These descriptions then need to be explained by a scientific theory.

In personality psychology, there are three key requirements for scientific observation. First, one must study a large and diverse group of people. Psychologists cannot base theories of personality on observations of small numbers of people whom they happen to run into in their daily life. People may differ from one social or cultural setting to another, and the psychologist must be aware of these differences. Second, one must ensure that observations of people are *objective*. Psychologists must eliminate from scientific observations any preconceptions or stereotypes about people. They also must describe their research methods in enough detail that someone else can replicate the research in order to verify that their results are reliable. Third, psychologists use specialized tools to shed light on specific thinking processes, emotional reactions, and biological systems that contribute to personality functioning. They observe persons just as you do, but supplement these observations with scientific measures and methods unique to their field. Chapter 2 of this book presents the research methods of personality psychology.

THEORY THAT IS SYSTEMATIC

Once the psychologist has good descriptions of personality, he or she can formulate a personality theory. Ideally, the theory will provide some understanding of what people are like.

Here, too, the difference between you and the professional psychologist involves *how* the psychologist formulates ideas. Before you take this class, you already have developed lots of different ideas about different people. Yet there is something that you probably have not done. You probably have not related all your ideas to one another in a systematic, logical way. Suppose that one day you say "my friend is depressed because her boyfriend broke up with her" and another day you say "my mother is depressed just like her mother was; she must have inherited it." If so, you usually do not have to relate these statements to each other systematically; nobody asks you to spell out the relations between interpersonal factors (e.g., relationship breakup) and biological ones (inherited tendencies). But this is what the scientific community asks the personality theorist to do. The theorist must relate his or her ideas to one another in a logical, coherent way. The personality psychologist must create theory that is systematic.

THEORY THAT IS TESTABLE

If you tell a friend that "My parents are weird," your friend is not likely to say "Prove it!" But the scientific community says "Prove it!" any time a scientist says anything. The personality psychologist must develop theoretical ideas that can be tested by objective scientific evidence. This is true of any science, of course. But in personality psychology, attaining the goal of a testable theory can be particularly difficult. This is because the field's subject matter includes features of mental life—goals, dreams, wishes, impulses, conflicts, emotions, unconscious mental defenses—that are enormously complex and inherently difficult to study scientifically.

THEORY THAT IS COMPREHENSIVE

Suppose you are renting an apartment and are contemplating inviting in a roommate to share rent costs. When thinking about people you know, trying to decide who to invite, there are a lot of questions you might ask about their personalities: Are they fun-loving? Conscientious? Open-minded? And so forth. Yet there also are a lot of questions about personality that you are *not* likely to ask. For example: If they are fun-loving, is it primarily because they inherited this quality or learned it? If they are conscientious now, are they likely to be more or less conscientious 20 years from now? If they are open-minded, is it primarily because of cultural experiences through which they learned to think about the world or because of a universal human tendency toward open-minded thinking that evolved through the eons and thus is part of everyone's bio-psychological make-up? If a personality psychologist burst into your room and started asking you these questions you'd likely say—after getting over the surprise of having a personality psychologist burst into your room—"Who cares about these questions? I don't care if they evolved this, or learned that, or what they'll be like in 20 years. I just want a decent roommate."

When thinking about persons, you can be selective. You can think about qualities of personality that interest you and ignore the others. But the personality psychologist cannot do this. Personality psychologists must think of everything; they are charged with developing theory that is comprehensive. A personality theory should address all psychologically significant aspects of persons. Later in this chapter, we consider the wide range of questions that need to be addressed in a comprehensive theory of personality.

APPLICATIONS: FROM THEORY TO PRACTICE

As the quotes from students that open this chapter ("Chapter Focus" box, above) make clear, you formulate insightful ideas about personality prior to ever studying the field of personality psychology. Yet it is rare that people convert their personal insights into systematic applications. You may recognize that one friend's problem is a lack of self-confidence and that another's is an inability to open up to people. Yet, you probably do not then devote your time to designing therapy methods that anyone can use to boost people's confidence in themselves or enable them to open up. However, many personality psychologists do this. They aim not only to develop testable, systematic theory, but to convert their theoretical ideas into beneficial applications. You will learn about many such applications throughout this book.

In summary, this text introduces you to a field of study whose goal is not merely to say something interesting and insightful about people. The personality psychologists' goals are (1) to observe people scientifically and to develop theories that are (2) systematic, (3) testable, (4) and comprehensive, and (5) to convert this data-based theory into practical applications. It is these five features that distinguish the work of the personality psychologist from that of the poet, the playwright, the pop psychologist—or the student writing personality sketches on the first day of class. The poet, the playwright, and you the student may each provide insight into the human condition. But the personality psychologist is uniquely charged with developing a comprehensive, testable, systematic theory, basing that theory on scientific observation, and developing theory-based applications that benefit individuals and society.

Throughout this book, we evaluate the personality theories by judging their level of success in achieving these five aspects of a formal scientific theory of personality. We do so in "critical evaluation" sections that conclude our presentation of each theory. In our final chapter, we judge how successful the field of personality psychology as a whole has been in achieving these five goals.

The present chapter introduces you to the field by discussing what a personality theory is, what questions a theory of personality should answer, and what functions the theory should serve. We also preview the personality theories you will learn about in detail in later chapters. Chapter 2 introduces the research methods through which personality psychologists develop and test their theories. The material in these first two chapters provides intellectual tools that you can use to evaluate the ideas you will learn about throughout your course in personality psychology.

WHY STUDY PERSONALITY?

Why take a course in personality? One way to answer this question is to compare the material in this course with that of other courses in psychology. Consider intro psych—the typical "Psych 101." Students often are disappointed with its content. The course does not seem to be about whole, intact people. Instead one learns about parts of people (e.g., the visual system, the autonomic nervous system, long-term memory, etc.) and some of the things people do (learning, problem solving, decision making, etc.). "But where in psychology," one reasonably might ask, "does one learn about the whole, intact person?" The answer is here, in personality psychology. Personality theorists address the total person. They try to understand how all the different aspects of an individual's functioning are related to each other (Magnusson, 1999). One reason for studying personality psychology, then, is that it is addresses psychology's most complex and interesting topic: the whole, integrated, coherent, unique individual.

Another reason for taking a course in personality psychology involves the wider intellectual world. The personality theories we will discuss have been influential not only within the confines of scientific psychology—they have influenced society at large. The ideas of the personality theorists are part of the intellectual tradition of the past century. As such, these ideas already have influenced your own thinking. Even before taking a course in personality, you might say that someone has a big ego, call a friend an "introvert," or believe that a seemingly innocent slip of the tongue reveals something about the underlying motives of the speaker. If so, you *already* are using the language and ideas of personality theorists. This course, then, provides insight into some foundations for your own ways of thinking about people—ways of thinking you have acquired by living in a culture that has been influenced by the work of personality theorists.

DEFINING PERSONALITY

The field of personality addresses three issues that are difficult to reconcile: (1) Human Universals, (2) Individual Differences, and (3) Individual Uniqueness. In studying universals, one asks: What is generally true of people; what are universal features of human nature? When studying individual differences, the main question is: How do people differ from one another; is there a set of basic human individual differences? Finally, regarding uniqueness, one asks: How can one possibly explain the uniqueness of the individual person in a scientific manner (since science often strives for general principles rather than portraits of unique entities)? Personality psychologists address dozens of more specific questions, as you will see throughout this book, but the specific issues generally can be understood in terms of overarching questions about universal properties of personality, individual differences, and the uniqueness of the individual.

Given this three-part focus, how are we to define *personality*? Many words have multiple meanings, and *personality* is no exception. Different people use the word in different ways. In fact, there are so many different meanings that one of the first textbooks in the history of the field (Allport, 1937) devoted an entire chapter merely to the question of how the word *personality* can be defined!

Rather than searching for a single definition of the word *personality*, it is useful to learn from philosophers, who teach that if one wants to know what a word means one should look at how the word is used—and, while looking, one should bear in mind that the one word may be used in a number of different ways (Wittgenstein, 1953). Different people indeed use the word *personality* differently. The general public often uses the term to represent a value judgment: You like someone who has a "good" personality or "lots of personality." A boring person has "no personality." In this casual usage, the word means something like "charisma." Personality scientists, however, use the word differently. The book in your hands is most definitely *not* a book about "Charisma: Theory and Research." The personality scientist is not trying to provide value judgments about the goodness of individuals' personalities. He or she is trying to advance objective scientific inquiry into persons. Let's consider, then, the scientist's definition.

Different personality scientists employ subtly different definitions of the word *personality*. The differences reflect their differing theoretical beliefs. As you work through this book, you will see that some of these differences are quite important. But for now, in Chapter 1, you can think of the differences as being subtle. These is a strongly shared sense of what *personality* means among personality scientists. All personality psychologists use the term **personality** to refer to *psychological qualities that contribute to an individual's enduring and distinctive patterns of feeling, thinking, and behaving*. Having stated that definition, let's elaborate on it a bit.

By *"enduring,"* we mean that personality characteristics are qualities that are at least somewhat consistent across time and across different situations of a person's life. This becomes clear by counter-example: Suppose you're at a sporting event with a friend who's usually calm and quiet, but at one point during the game he starts yelling angrily at a referee. After the game, he is his usual calm self. Most personality psychologists would *not* say that, during the game, his personality had changed. Instead, they would explain his unusual behavior of yelling angrily by referring to the situation he was in, not to his personality traits. His relatively consistent tendency to be calm would be seen as a feature of his personality.

By *"distinctive,"* we mean that personality psychology addresses psychological features that differentiate people from one another. Again a counter-example is instructive. If someone asks you to describe your personality you do not say, "I tend to feel sad when bad things happen, but happy when good things happen." You don't say this because *everybody* tends to feel sad/happy when bad/good things happen. These psychological tendencies are not distinctive. Even when personality psychologists study universals (i.e., aspects of mental life shared by all persons), they generally use their understanding of universals as a foundation for studying differences among individuals.

By *"contribute to,"* we mean that the personality psychologist searches for psychological factors that causally influence, and thus at least partly explain, an individual's distinctive and enduring tendencies. The key distinction here is the one between the two scientific tasks of *description* and *explanation*. Much work in personality psychology, as in any science, is descriptive. In personality psychology, researchers may describe trends in personality development, the main individual differences in a population of people, or patterns of behavior exhibited by a particular individual in different situations. However, the personality theorist hopes to move from such description to scientific explanation by identifying psychological factors that causally contribute to the patterns of development, individual differences, and individual behavior that are observed. One should bear in mind that many factors other than ones we call personality also contribute to enduring patterns of behavior. Imagine yourself in a classroom lecture. It is likely that the person in the room who is doing the most talking is the professor. But one would not explain this in terms of the professor's personality. There exist powerful social role requirements that call for professors in lecture rooms to talk and for students to be quiet (except when asking questions or contributing to a class discussion). The professor's talkativeness and the students' relative quietness, then, would be explained in terms of social roles and norms in the lecture setting, not personality factors.

Finally, by saying "feeling, thinking, and behaving," we merely mean that the notion of personality is comprehensive; it refers to all aspects of persons: their mental life, their emotional experiences, and their social behavior. Personality psychologists strive to understand the whole person.

QUESTIONS ABOUT PERSONS: WHAT, HOW, AND WHY

With a definition of personality in hand, we can ask a new question: When developing a theory of personality, what types of questions is the personality theorist trying to answer? Questions about people generally are of three types. We want to know *what* they are like, *how* they became that way, and *why* they behave as they do. Thus, we want a theory to answer the questions of what, how, and why.

The *"what"* refers to characteristics of the person and how these characteristics are organized in relation to one another. Is the person anxious, persistent, and high in need for achievement? If so, is she anxious and persistent because she is high in need for achievement? Or is she persistent and high in need for achievement because she is anxious?

The *"how"* refers to the determinants of a person's personality. How did genetic influences contribute to the individual's personality? How did environmental forces and social learning experiences contribute to the person's development? How did biology and environment interact? How do people, through their own choices and efforts, contribute to their own personality development?

The *"why"* refers to causes of, and reasons behind, an individual's behavior. Answers generally involve questions of motivation: Is the person motivated by a desire for success or a fear of failure? If a child does well in school, is it to please parents, to develop skills, to bolster self-esteem, or to compete with peers? Is a mother overprotective because she is highly affectionate, because she seeks to give her children what she missed as a child, or because she is compensating for feelings of hostility she feels toward the child? A complete theory of personality should yield a coherent set of answers to these three types of questions (what, how, and why).

ANSWERING QUESTIONS ABOUT PERSONS SCIENTIFICALLY: UNDERSTANDING STRUCTURES, PROCESSES, DEVELOPMENT, AND THERAPEUTIC CHANGE

To answer the *what*, *how*, and *why* questions reviewed above, the personality psychologist usually addresses four distinct topics: (1) personality *structure*—the basic units or building blocks of personality, (2) personality *process*—the dynamic aspects of personality, including motives, (3) *growth and development*—how we develop into the unique person each of us is, and (4) *psychopathology and behavior change*—how people change and why they sometimes resist change or are unable to change. We introduce these topics now and return to them throughout this book.

STRUCTURE

The concept of personality **structure** refers to stable, enduring aspects of personality. People possess psychological qualities that endure from day to day and from year to year. The enduring qualities that define the individual and distinguish individuals from one another are what the psychologist refers to as personality structures. In this sense, they are comparable to parts of the body, or to concepts such as atoms and molecules in physics. They represent the building blocks of personality theory.

Units of Analysis

As you will see throughout this text, different personality theories provide different conceptions of personality structure. A more technical way of saying this is that different theorists provide different basic variables, or different **units of analysis**, in their scientific models of personality structure. The idea of units of analysis is important for understanding how personality theories differ, so we will take a moment to illustrate the concept.

As you read this text, you may be sitting in a chair. If we ask you to describe the chair, you may say that it "weighs about 9 pounds." Another person may say that "it probably cost about 50 dollars." Someone else may describe the chair by saying that it is "fairly well made." Each of these units of analysis—pounds, dollars, degree of "well made"—tells us something about the chair. Even though the things they tell us may be systematically related—e.g., poorly made chairs may weigh and cost less—the units of analysis clearly are distinct; if you heard someone say "the chair probably cost about 50 dollars" you wouldn't argue "no, you're crazy, it weighs about 9 pounds!"

The general idea, then, is that virtually anything can be described in more than one way—that is, via more than one unit of analysis—and each of the various descriptions may provide some valid information about the thing being described. People are no exception. The different theories of personality you will learn about in this book use different units of analysis to analyze personality structure. The resulting analyses may each be correct, in their own way. Yet each may provide different types of information about personality. Let as consider, then, some of the different units of analysis used by personality theorists.

One popular unit of analysis is that of a personality **trait**. The word *trait* generally refers to a consistent style of emotion or behavior that a person displays across a variety of situations. Someone who consistently acts in a way that we call "conscientious" might be said to have the trait of "conscientiousness." A term that is essentially synonymous with *trait* is *disposition*; traits describe what a person tends to do, or is predisposed to do, and thus can be thought of as psychological dispositions to act in one or another manner. You probably already use trait terms to describe people. If you say that a friend is "outgoing," "honest," "disagreeable," or "open-minded," you are using trait terms. There is something implicit—something that "goes without saying"—when you use these terms. If you say that a friend is, for example, "outgoing," the term implies two things: (1) the person tends to be outgoing *on average* in his own daily behavior (even if, on occasion, he does not act this way), and (2) the person tends to be outgoing *compared to other people* (if you think the person is less outgoing than most other people, you probably would not call him "outgoing"). If you use trait terms this way, then you are using them in the same way as most personality psychologists do.

One last feature of the units of analysis that are trait variables deserves mention. Traits usually are thought of as continuous dimensions. People have more or less of a given trait, with most people being in the middle and some people falling toward either extreme.

A different unit of analysis is **type**. The concept of type refers to the clustering of many different traits. For example, some researchers have explored combinations of personality traits and suggested that there are three types of persons: (1) people who respond in an adaptive, resilient manner to psychological stress; (2) people who respond in a manner that is socially inhibited or emotionally overcontrolled; and (3) people who respond in an uninhibited or undercontrolled manner (Asendorpf, Caspi, & Hofstee, 2002). Psychologists interested in the development of personality in childhood have suggested that child-parent relations can be understood as consisting of three or four distinct types (Bakermans-Kranenburg & Van Ijzendoorn, 1993). The key notion associated with a type construct that makes it different from a trait construct is that alternative types are seen as qualitatively distinct categories. In other words, people of one versus another type do not simply have more or less of a given characteristic, but have categorically different characteristics. This is most easily explained with an analogy outside of psychology. Height clearly is not a type variable. Even though we call some people "tall" and others "short," we recognize these words do not identify distinct categories of people. Instead, height is a continuous dimension. In contrast, biological sex is categorical. Unlike "tall" and "short," "man" and "woman" identify qualitatively distinct categories of persons.

Many psychologists use units of analysis other than trait or type concepts. One prominent alternative is to think of personality as a **system**. A system is a collection of highly interconnected parts whose overall behavior reflects not only the individual parts, but their organization; colloquially, one might say that in a system "the whole is greater than the sum of the parts." Theorists who view personality as a system recognize that people have distinctive characteristics that are well described by personality trait and type constructs. However, they tend not to use trait or type concepts as their basic units of analysis for explaining a person's behavior. In these approaches, a trait term such as "conscientiousness" does not correspond to a structure that a person has; instead, it functions merely as description of what a person does. An analogy may be helpful to understand this reasoning. You may know that the weather in the city of San Francisco is very "pleasant." But you would not say that "pleasantness" is a structural feature of San Francisco in the way that, for example, hills are a structural feature. San Francisco does not "have"

The four basic personality types

hills in the same way that it "has" pleasantness of weather. If we were in the science of meteorology, we would not explain the weather in San Francisco by saying that the city "has pleasantness" that caused the pleasant weather. The term "pleasantness" is a *description* of qualities that are *explained* in terms of a complex system of meteorological forces. Similarly, many personality psychologists would not explain a person's conscientiousness by saying that the person "has conscientiousness" but by exploring a system of emotional and thought processes that produce the behavior that we describe as conscientious. The units of analysis in the scientific explanation would be the emotional and thought processes and the interconnections among them.

Hierarchy

In addition to the issue of units of analysis, there is another consideration in the study of personality structure. It involves the notion of **hierarchy**. Many theories of personality view the structures of personality as being organized hierarchically.

In general, two things are related hierarchically if one of them is an example of the other or serves the purpose of the other. The relation between "trees" and "plants" is hierarchical in that trees are an example of plants. "Jogging" and "getting in shape" are related hierarchically in that jogging serves the purpose of getting in shape (whereas getting in shape does not serve the purpose of jogging). Interestingly, the notion of hierarchy can be applied to different types of units of analysis in the study of personality. For example, people's goals are related hierarchically. Broad, high-level goals (e.g., be successful, be a good person) are linked to more specific, lower-level goals (e.g., get a promotion at work, be kind to strangers; Carver & Scheier, 1998). Personality

Motivation: Personality theories emphasize different kinds of motivation (e.g., tension reduction, self-actualization, power, etc.)

traits can be understood hierarchically. High-level traits (e.g., extraversion, conscientiousness) organize narrower, lower-level tendencies (e.g., sociability, punctuality; John, Hampson, & Goldberg, 1991); there is a hierarchy here in that the lower-level traits are simply a way of exhibiting the higher-level characteristics (e.g., being punctual is a way of being conscientious).

In contrast, some personality theorists do not explicitly posit a hierarchy of personality structures. Instead, they see different systems of personality as influencing each other in a mutual, back-and-forth manner that is not necessarily hierarchical (e.g., Bandura, 1999).

PROCESS

Just as theories can be compared in terms of how they treat personality structure, they can be compared in terms of how they treat personality processes. Personality **process** refers to psychological reactions that change dynamically, that is, that change over relatively brief periods of time. Even though you are the same person from one moment to the next, your thoughts, emotions, and desires often change rapidly and dramatically. One moment you are studying. The next, you are distracted by thoughts of a friend. Next, you're hungry and getting a snack. Then you're feeling guilty about not studying. Next, you're feeling guilty about over-eating. This rapid, dynamic flow of motivation, emotion, and action is what personality psychologists attempt to explain when studying personality processes.

Just as in the study of personality structure, one finds that, in the study of personality processes, different theorists employ different units of analysis. The differences commonly involve different approaches to the study of motivation (Pervin, 2003). Personality theorists emphasize different motivational processes. Some highlight basic biological drives. Other theorists argue that people's anticipations of future events are more important to human motivation than are biological drive states experienced in the present. Some theorists emphasize the role of conscious thinking processes in motivation. Others believe that most important motivational processes are unconscious. To some, the motivation to enhance and improve oneself is most central to human motivation. To others, such an emphasis on "self processes" underestimates the degree to which, in some cultures of the world, self-enhancement is less important to motivation than is a desire to enhance one's family, community, and wider world. In their explorations of motivational processes, the personality theorists you will read about in this book are attempting to bring contemporary scientific evidence to bear on classic questions about human nature that have been discussed and debated in the world's intellectual traditions for more than two millennia.

GROWTH AND DEVELOPMENT

Personality theorists try to understand not only what individuals are like in the here and now. They also want to know how the person got this way; more formally, they strive to understand personality development. The overall study of personality development encompasses two challenges that are relatively distinct. One is to characterize patterns of development that are experienced by most, if not all, persons. A theorist might, for example, posit that all individuals develop through a distinct series of stages, or might propose that certain motives or emotional experiences are more common at one versus another age for most persons. A second challenge is to understand developmental factors that contribute to individual differences. What factors cause individuals to develop one versus another personality style?

In the study of individual differences, a classic division of possible causes separates "nature" from "nurture." On the one hand, we may be who we are because of our biological nature, that is, because of biological features that we inherited. On the other hand, our personality may reflect our nurturing, that is, our experiences in our family and in society. In a joking manner, we might say, If you don't like your personality, who should you blame: Your parents, because of the way they nurtured you? Or your parents, because of the genes they passed on to you that shaped your biological nature?

At different points in its history, psychological research has tended to highlight either nature or nurture as causal factors. In the middle parts of the 20th century, theorists focused heavily on environmental causes of behavior and devoted relatively little attention to genetic influences. Starting in the 1970s (Loehlin & Nichols, 1976), investigators began systematic studies of similarity in the personalities of twins. As we will discuss in detail in a later chapter, these studies provided unambiguous evidence that inherited factors contribute to personality. In recent years, however, there has been a third trend. Researchers have begun to identify interactions between genetic and environmental factors. They have recognized that nature and nurture are not separate influences. Instead, they interact dynamically. For example, environmental experiences activate genetic mechanisms so that certain types of experiences can alter the biology of the organism (Gottlieb, 1998). Increasingly, then, both psychologists and biologists (Ehrlich, 2000; Grigorenko, 2002; Lewontin, 2000) recognize that the problem with the traditional nature versus nurture question was the word *versus*. Biological and environmental factors are not competing forces, but factors that interact, often in complementary ways, in the development of the persons (Plomin, 1994; Plomin & Caspi, 1999; Plomin, Chipuer, & Loehlin, 1990; Ridley, 2003).

Given the established importance of both genetic and environmental factors, the question you might now be asking yourself is: What aspects of personality are affected by what types of biological and environmental influences? This is a big question whose answers are considered throughout this textbook. For now, though, we will provide a quick preview of some of the factors highlighted by contemporary findings in personality psychology.

Genetic Determinants

Genetic factors contribute strongly to personality and individual differences (Caspi, 2000; Plomin & Caspi, 1999; Rowe, 1999). Scientific advances are beginning to enable the personality psychologist to go beyond this rather general statement and to pinpoint specific paths of influence. One way to accomplish this is to identify a specific quality of personality that is thought to have a biological basis. Such qualities are often referred to as aspects of **temperament**, a term that refers to biologically based emotional and behavioral tendencies that are evident in early childhood (Strelau, 1998). A temperament characteristic that has been studied in this manner is fearfulness and inhibited behavior in reaction to novel circumstances, such as circumstances involving strangers (Fox, Henderson, Marshall, Nichols, & Ghera, 2005). Findings suggest that people differ in the functioning of brain systems in the frontal cortex and limbic system that are involved in fear response, and that these biological differences contribute to psychological differences in people's tendencies to experience fearful, inhibited behavior (Schmidt & Fox, 2002). Since genetic factors contribute to the development of the brain, this type of analysis enables the personality psychologist to understand links from genes to biological systems to behavior in a relatively precise manner. An interesting feature of this work is that it also shows that there is a role for the environment in the development of shy versus non-shy behavior. There is some evidence that temperamentally shy children who experience day care, where they encounter large numbers of other children every day, are less likely to remain shy than are children who are raised entirely at home (Schmidt & Fox, 2002).

Another advance in the field integrates work in personality psychology with findings in the field of molecular genetics. Rather than referring merely to the influence of an organism's overall set of genetic material, or the genome, researchers are beginning to identify specific elements of the genome that are involved in the development of elements of the nervous systems that affect people's behavior (Plomin & Caspi, 1998). A major focus of investigation is the link from genes to neurotransmitter systems (Grigorenko, 2002), that is, chemicals in the brain through which neurons communicate with one another. The functioning of neurotransmitters influences brain activity that in turn affects people's moods and reactions to stimuli in the environment. By linking variations in the genome to variations in these biochemicals, researchers can then begin to specify exactly how genetic mechanisms influence specific aspects of personality.

Genetic bases of personality also are explored by evolutionary psychologists, that is, psychologists who study the evolutionary basis of psychological characteristics (Buss, 1991, 1995, 1999, 2000; Buss & Kenrick, 1998; see

Determinants of Personality: Genetic differences and different life experiences, both within and outside the family, contribute to personality differences among siblings.

Chapter 9). Evolutionary psychologists propose that contemporary humans possess psychological tendencies that are a product of our evolutionary past. People are predisposed to engage in certain types of behavior because those behaviors contributed to survival and reproductive success over the course of human evolution. An evolutionary analysis of genetic influences differs fundamentally from the analyses reviewed in the two preceding paragraphs. In an evolutionary analysis, investigators are not interested in genetic bases of individual *differences*. Instead, they are searching for the genetic basis of human *universals*, that is, psychological features that all people have in common. Most of our genes are shared. Even so-called racial differences involve merely superficial differences in features such as skin tone; the basic structure of the human brain is universal (Cavalli-Sforza & Cavalli-Sforza, 1995). The evolutionary psychologist suggests, then, that we all inherit psychological mechanisms that predispose us to respond to the environment in ways that proved successful over the course of evolution. Such responses might come into play when we attract members of the opposite sex, take care of children, act in an altruistic manner toward members of our social group, or respond emotionally to objects and events. Much evidence suggests that a number of basic emotions (e.g., anger, sadness, joy, disgust, fear) are experienced in the same way across cultures (Ekman, 1992, 1993, 1994; Elfenbein & Ambady, 2002; Izard, 1991, 1994), as would be expected if these emotions were part of our evolutionary heritage.

Environmental Determinants

Even the most biologically oriented of psychologists recognizes that the environment plays a critical role in the development of our personalities. If we did not grow up in a society with other people, we would not even be persons in the way in which that term commonly is understood. Our concept of self,

THE EVOLUTION OF MIND AND PERSONALITY

Since the beginning of scientific psychology, writers have recognized that the human brain, like the rest of human anatomy, is a product of evolution. William James's (1890) *Principles of Psychology*, one of the first great textbooks in the field, concluded with a chapter that explained how Charles Darwin's theory of evolution was relevant to the understanding of mental structures.

The central idea in relating biological principles of evolution to psychological analyses of mind and personality is that, at birth, the human mind is *not* a blank slate. It is *not* the case that the mind, at birth, lacks any mental contents or inherent tendencies. Instead, thanks to processes of natural selection over the course of evolution, people are born with inherent tendencies and abilities. Neural mechanisms that produce psychological tendencies that proved adaptive over the course of evolution have become an inherited part of our mental makeup.

In the contemporary field, no personality scientists doubt that our personalities are, in part, a product of evolution. Yet major questions remain. How big a part of mental life is explained by evolutionary ancestry (as opposed to experiences that we have after we are born)? Has evolution given us a fixed set of tendencies that proved useful in the evolutionary past, or has it given us a brain that adapts flexibly to the demands of the present?

In recent years, these issues have been of interest not only to psychologists and other scientists, but to the public at large. In part, this is due to the writings of Steven Pinker, a psychologist at the Massachusetts Institute of Technology. In his book *The Blank Slate* (Pinker, 2002), Pinker suggests that society has been too slow to accept the notion that people are a product of their species' evolutionary past. People find it pleasant to think that psychological qualities can be changed through new experiences. We hope, for example, that improved parenting, better education, and more enlightened social policies can create a kinder and gentler world—a world with less prejudice and aggression and more tolerance and peace. But, Pinker points out, there might be features of human psychology that are enormously difficult to change because they are the products of evolution. Those psychological features that proved adaptive over the course of our evolutionary history may be fixed, "hardwired" features of the current human mind. Recognizing the influence of evolutionary factors on the shaping of the mind is then key to understanding the basic character of human nature. Such an understanding, in turn, may be critical to devising humane, effective social policies, and to recognizing when social policies will not work.

Pinker's analyses currently are a point of controversy in the field of psychology and beyond. Some feel that Pinker's evolutionary framework explains only very limited aspects of the human experience. For example, in reviewing Pinker's book in the magazine *The New Yorker*, the scholar Louis Menand notes that much of human activity seems completely disconnected from the actions and events of the evolutionary past. Many people devote effort to creating works of art, playing or listening to music, or studying systems of religious or philosophical thought. It is difficult to see how people's propensity to create and appreciate these novel, imaginative intellectual products can be explained in terms of evolutionary forces, since during much of evolution people devoted most of their time to activities directly related to survival and reproduction.

It might be possible for an evolutionary psychologist such as Pinker to explain, in retrospect, how evolutionary forces might have supported these complex, creative human capacities. But that raises a second concern. Writers fault evolutionary psychology for being based more on speculation than established fact. A biologist has judged that the evidence on which the arguments of evolutionary psychology are based is "surprisingly unrigorous. Too often, data are skimpy, alternative hypotheses are neglected, and the entire enterprise threatens to skip into undisciplined storytelling" (Orr, 2003, p. 18). A recent comprehensive review concludes that, in speculating on the environment of the distant past, evolutionary psychologists have overlooked the impact of the here-and-now environment of the present (Buller, 2005). Evidence indicates that the wiring of our brains is not entirely predetermined by evolved genetic factors. Instead, "the brain adapts to its local environment" (Buller, 2005, p. 199). As individuals develop, the exact wiring of one's brain is influenced by developmental experiences. Our personalities, then, reflect a biological brain that is shaped not only by universal forces of evolution, but by individual experiences during personal development.

Few if any personality scientists think that the mind, at birth, is a blank slate. Yet many question whether evolutionary psychology is an adequate framework for explaining the psychological functioning of persons. This remains a current question of interest and debate in the field.

SOURCE: Buller (2005); James (1980); Menand (2002); Orr (2003); Pinker (2002); Smith (2002).

our goals in life, and the values that guide us develop in a social world. Some environmental determinants make people similar to one another, whereas others contribute to individual differences and individual uniqueness. The environmental determinants that have proven to be important in the study of personality development include culture, social class, family, and peers.

Culture   Significant among the environmental determinants of personality are experiences individuals have as a result of membership in a particular culture. Each culture has its own institutionalized and sanctioned patterns of learned behaviors, rituals, and beliefs. These cultural practices, which in turn often reflect long-standing religious and philosophical beliefs, provide people with answers to significant questions about the nature of the self, one's role in one's community, and the values and principles that are most important in life. As a result, members of a culture may share personality characteristics. Interestingly, people often may be unaware of shared cultural tendencies because they take them for granted. For example, if you live in North America or Western Europe you may not appreciate the extent to which your conception of yourself and your goals in life are shaped by living in a culture that strongly values individual rights and in which individuals compete with one another in an economic marketplace to improve their financial and social status. Since everyone in these regions of the world experiences these cultural features, we take them for granted and may assume that they are universal. Yet much evidence indicates that people in other regions of the world experience different cultural features. Asian cultures appear to place a greater value on a person's contribution to his or her community, rather than on individualism and personal gain (Nisbett et al., 2001). In fact, even within the Western world, cultural beliefs about the individual's role in society have changed from one historical period to another. The idea that individuals compete against one another in an economic marketplace in order to improve their position in life is a feature of contemporary Western societies, but it was not evident in these same societies in the Middle Ages (Heilbroner, 1986).

Culture, then, may exert an influence on personality that is subtle yet pervasive. The culture we live in defines our needs and our means of satisfying them, our experiences of different emotions and how we express what we are feeling, our relationships with others and with ourselves, what we think is funny or sad, how we cope with life and death, and what we view as healthy or sick (Cross & Markus, 1999; Fiske et al., 1998; Markus & Kitayama, 1991).

Social Class   Although certain patterns of behavior develop as a result of membership in a culture, others may develop as a result of membership in a particular social class within a given culture. Many aspects of an individual's personality can only be understood by reference to the group to which that person belongs. One's social group—whether lower class or upper class, working class or professional—is of particular importance. Social class factors help determine the status of individuals, the roles they perform, the duties they are bound by, and the privileges they enjoy. These factors influence how individuals see themselves and how they perceive members of other social classes, as well as how they earn and spend money. Research indicates that socioeconomic status influences the cognitive and emotional development of the individual (Bradley & Corwyn, 2002). Like cultural factors, then, social class factors influence people's capacities and tendencies, and shape the ways people define situations and respond to them.

Family   Beyond the similarities determined by environmental factors such as membership in the same culture or social class, environmental factors lead to considerable variation in the personality functioning of members of a single culture or class. One of the most important environmental factors is the influence of the family (Park, 2004). Parents may be warm and loving or hostile and rejecting, overprotective and possessive or aware of their children's need for freedom and autonomy. Each pattern of parental behavior affects the personality development of the child. Parents influence their children's behavior in at least three important ways:

1. Through their own behavior, parents present situations that elicit certain behavior in children (e.g., frustration leads to aggression).
2. Parents serve as role models for identification.
3. Parents selectively reward behaviors.

At first, we may think of family practices as an influence that makes family members similar to one another. Yet family practices also can create differences within a family. Consider differences between male and female family members. Historically, in many societies, male children have received family privileges and opportunities that were unavailable to female children. These differences in how families have treated boys and girls surely did not make boys and girls similar to one another; they contributed to differences in male and female development. In addition to gender, other family practices that may produce differences between family members involve birth order. Parents sometimes express subtle preferences toward firstborn children (Keller & Zach, 2002), who tend to be more achievement-oriented and conscientious than later-born siblings (Paulhus, Trapnel, & Chen, 1999).

Peers   What environmental features outside of family life are important to personality development? The child's experiences with members of his or her peer group are one feature. Indeed, some psychologists view peer influences as more important to personality development than family experiences (Harris, 1995). Perhaps "the answer to the question 'Why are children from the same family so different from one another?' (Plomin & Daniels, 1987) is, because they have different experiences outside the home and because their experiences inside the home do not make them more alike" (Harris, 1995, p. 481). Peer groups socialize the individual into acceptance of new rules of behavior. These experiences may affect personality in an enduring manner. For example, children who experience low-quality friendships that involve a lot of arguing and conflict tend to develop disagreeable, antagonistic styles of behavior (Berndt, 2002).

PSYCHOPATHOLOGY AND BEHAVIOR CHANGE

Constructing a personality theory may strike you as an ivory tower activity, that is, an abstract intellectual exercise that fails to relate to the important concerns of everyday life. Yet personality theories are potentially of great practical importance. People often face complicated psychological problems: they are depressed and lonely, a close friend is addicted to drugs, they are anxious about sexual relations, frequent arguments threaten the stability of a romantic relationship. To solve such problems, one requires some sort of conceptual framework that specifies causes of the problem and factors that might bring about change. In other words, one needs a personality theory.

Historically, the practical problems that have been most important to the development of personality theories have involved psychopathology. Many of the theorists discussed in this book were also therapists. They began their careers by trying to solve practical problems they faced when trying to help their clients. Their theories were, in part, an attempt to systematize the lessons about human nature that they learned by working on practical problems in therapy.

Although not all personality theories had clinical origins, for any theory a crucial bottom line for evaluating the theoretical approach is to ask whether its ideas are of practical benefit to individuals and to society at large.

IMPORTANT ISSUES IN PERSONALITY THEORY   We have just reviewed four topic areas in the study of personality: (1) personality structure, (2) personality processes, (3) personality development, and (4) psychopathology and behavior change. Next, we will consider a series of conceptual issues that are central to the field. By "conceptual issues," we mean a set of questions about personality that are so fundamental that they may arise no matter what topic one is addressing, and that one must address no matter what one's theoretical perspective.

PHILOSOPHICAL VIEW OF THE PERSON

Personality theorists do not confine themselves to narrow questions about human behavior. Instead, they boldly tackle the big, broad question: What is the basic nature of human nature? Personality theorists, in other words, provide philosophical views about the basic nature of human beings. One critical consideration when evaluating a theory, then, is the overall view of the person that it provides.

Personality theories embrace strikingly different views of the essential qualities of human nature. Some incorporate a view in which people seem like rational actors. People reason about the world, weigh the costs and benefits of alternative courses of action, and behave based on these rational calculations. In this view, individual differences primarily reflect differences in the thought processes that go into these calculations.

Other perspectives recognize that humans are animals. The human organism, in this view, is primarily driven by irrational, animalistic forces. Rational thought processes are seen as relatively weak components of personality, compared to powerful animalistic drives.

During the latter decades of the 20th century, a popular metaphor for understanding persons was the computer metaphor. People were seen as information processors who stored and manipulated symbolic representations, much as a computer processes and stores information. Since people move around in the world, some argued that robots, rather than computers, provide a closer analogy to human nature (Carver & Scheier, 1998).

One should recognize that different views of human nature have arisen in different sociohistorical circumstances. Proponents of different points of view have had different life experiences and have been influenced by different historical traditions. Thus, beyond scientific evidence and fact, theories of personality are influenced by personal factors, by the spirit of the time, and by philosophical assumptions characteristic of members of a given culture (Pervin, 2002).

INTERNAL AND EXTERNAL DETERMINANTS OF BEHAVIOR

Is human behavior determined by processes inside the person or by external causes? The issues here concern the relationship between, and the relative importance of, internal and external determinants. All theories of personality recognize that factors inside the organism and events in the surrounding environment are important in determining behavior. However, the theories differ in the level of importance given to internal and external determinants.

Consider the differences in view of two of the most influential psychologists of the 20th century: Sigmund Freud and B. F. Skinner. According to Freud, we are controlled by internal forces that reside primarily in our unconscious minds. According to Skinner, environmental forces are paramount: "A person does not act upon the world, the world acts upon him" (1971, p. 211). In the Freudian view, then, the internal dynamics of the mind are causally responsible for overt patterns of behavior. To Skinner, the person is a passive victim of events in the environment.

Freud and Skinner represent views that most psychologists now would see as extreme. Virtually all personality psychologists today acknowledge that it is necessary to consider both external and internal determinants of human action.

Nonetheless, contemporary theories continue to differ markedly in the degree to which they emphasize one versus the other factor. These differences become apparent when one examines the basic variables—or, as we called them earlier, the basic units of analysis—of a given theory. Consider two perspectives you will read about in later chapters. In trait theories of personality, the basic units of analysis refer to structures in the person that purportedly are inherited and produce highly generalized patterns of behavior (McCrae & Costa, 1999). In social-cognitive theories of personality, the basic units of analysis are knowledge structures and thinking processes that are acquired through interaction with the social and cultural environment (Bandura, 1999; Mischel & Shoda, 1995). As you can infer from their basic units, these theories differentially emphasize internal and external determinants of personality.

CONSISTENCY ACROSS SITUATIONS AND OVER TIME

How consistent is personality from situation to situation? To what extent are you "the same person" when with friends as you are with your parents? Or when you are at a party versus a classroom discussion? And how consistent is personality across time? How similar is your personality now to what it was when you were a child? And how similar will it be 20 years from now?

Answering these questions is more difficult than it may appear. In part, this is because one has to decide on what counts as an example of personality consistency versus inconsistency. Consider a simple example. Suppose you have two supervisors at a job, one male and one female, and that you tend to act in an agreeable manner toward one supervisor and disagreeably toward the other. Are you being inconsistent in your personality? If one thinks that a basic feature of personality is agreeableness, then the answer is yes. But suppose this situation were analyzed by a psychologist who adheres to psychoanalytic theory, which suggests that (1) people you encounter in your adult life may symbolically represent parental figures, and that (2) a basic personality dynamic involves attraction toward one's opposite-sex parent and rivalry toward the same-sex parent—something called an "Oedipal complex." From this view, you may be acting in a very *consistent* manner. The different job supervisors may symbolically represent different parental figures, and you may be consistently reenacting Oedipal motives that cause you to act in a different manner toward one versus the other person.

Even if people agree on what counts as consistency, they may disagree about the factors that cause personality to be consistent. Consider consistency over time. It unquestionably is the case that individual differences are stable, to a significant degree, over long periods of time (Fraley, 2002; Roberts & Del Vecchio, 2000). If you are more extraverted than your friends today, you are quite likely to be more extraverted than these same people 20 years from now. But why? One possibility is that the core structures of personality are inherited and that they change little across the course of life. Another possibility, however, is that the environment plays a critical role in fostering consistency. Exposure to the same family members, friends, educational systems, and social circumstances over long periods of time may contribute to personality consistency over time (Lewis, 2002).

No personality theorist thinks that you will fall asleep an introvert and wake up the next morning an extravert. Yet the field's theoretical frameworks do provide different views on the nature of personality consistency and change,

Research on personality suggests that many personal qualities are highly stable over time. Qualities evident, for example, in adolescence may be apparent in the personality of the adult—as suggested by these portraits of former U.S. President Bill Clinton.

and on people's capacity to vary their personality functioning across time and place. To some theorists, variation in behavior is a sign of inconsistency in personality. To others, it may reflect a consistent personal capacity to adapt one's behavior to the different requirements of different social situations (Mischel, 2004).

THE UNITY OF EXPERIENCE AND ACTION AND THE CONCEPT OF SELF

Our psychological experiences generally have an integrated, or coherent, quality to them (Cervone & Shoda, 1999b). Our actions are patterned and organized, rather than random and chaotic. As we move from place to place, we retain a stable sense of ourselves, our past, and our goals for the future. There is a unity to our experiences and action.

Although we take it for granted that our experiences are unified, in some sense this fact is quite surprising. The brain contains a large number of information-processing systems, many of which function at the same time, in partial isolation from one another (Pinker, 1997). If we examine the contents of our own conscious experiences, we will find that most of our thoughts are fleeting. It is hard to keep any one idea in mind for long periods. Seemingly random ideas pop into our heads. Nonetheless, we rarely experience the world as chaotic or our lives as disjointed. Why?

There are two types of answers to this question. One is that the multiple components of the mind function as a complex system. The parts are interconnected, and the patterns of interconnection enable the multi-part system to function in a smooth, coherent manner. Computer simulations of personality functioning (Nowak, Vallacher, & Zochowski, 2002), as well as neuroscientific investigations of the reciprocal links among brain regions (Tononi & Edelman, 1998), are beginning to shed light on how the mind manages to produce coherence in experience and action.

The Concept of Self: Personality psychologists are interested in how the concept of self develops and helps to organize experience.

The second type of answer involves the concept of the self. Although we may experience a potentially bewildering diversity of life events, we do experience them from a consistent perspective, that of ourselves (Harré, 1998). People construct coherent autobiographical memories, which contribute to coherence in our understanding of who we are (Conway & Pleydell-Pearce, 2000). The concept of the self, then, has proven valuable in accounting for the unity of experience (Baumeister, 1999; Kehl & Koole, 2004; Robins, Norem, & Cheek, 1999).

VARYING STATES OF AWARENESS AND THE CONCEPT OF THE UNCONSCIOUS

Are we aware of the contents of our mental life? Or do most mental activities occur outside of awareness, or unconsciously?

On the one hand, much of the brain's activities unquestionably occur outside of awareness. Consider what is happening as you read this book. Your brain is engaging in large numbers of functions ranging from the monitoring of your internal physiological states to the deciphering of the marks of ink that constitute the words on this page. All this occurs without your conscious attention. You do not consciously have to think to yourself "I wonder if these squiggles of ink form words?" or "Maybe I should check to see if sufficient amounts of oxygen are getting to my bodily organs?" These functions are executed automatically. But these functions are not the ones of main interest to the personality psychologist.

Personality scientists ask whether significant aspects of personality functioning—motivation, emotions—occur outside of awareness. If there is evidence that they do, the personality scientist tries to conceptualize the mental systems that give rise to conscious and unconscious processes (Kihlstrom, 1990, 1999; Pervin, 1999, 2003). The fact that *some* brain functions occur outside of awareness does not imply that the most significant personality processes occur without our awareness. People engage in much self-reflection. They are particularly likely to reflect on themselves when they face life circumstances of great importance, where the decisions that are made (e.g., whether and where to attend college, whether to marry a certain person, whether to have children, what profession to pursue) have major long-term consequences. In these critical circumstances, conscious processes are influential. Thus, many personality psychologists study conscious self-reflection, even while recognizing that numerous aspects of mental life occur outside of awareness.

THE INFLUENCE OF THE PAST, PRESENT, AND FUTURE ON BEHAVIOR

Are we prisoners of our past? Or is our personality shaped by present events and personal aspirations for future? Theorists agree that behavior can be influenced only by factors operating in the present; a basic principle of causality is that presently active processes are the causes of events. In this sense, only the present is important in understanding behavior. But the present can be influenced by experiences in the remote past or in the recent past. Similarly, what one is thinking about in the present can be influenced by thoughts about the immediate future or the distant future. People vary in the extent to which they worry about the past and the future. And personality theorists differ in their concern with the past and the future as determinants of behavior in the present.

As you will see in the chapters ahead, some theorists suggest that we are primarily prisoners of our past. Psychoanalytic theory posits that personality structures are formed via experiences in childhood, and that the personality dynamics established then persist throughout the life course. Others are harshly critical of this psychoanalytic conclusion. Personality construct theory (Chapter 11) and social-cognitive theory (Chapters 12–13) suggest that people have the capacity to change their own personal capabilities and tendencies, and explore the social and psychological systems that give people this life-long capacity for personal agency (Bandura, 2006).

CAN WE HAVE A SCIENCE OF PERSONALITY? WHAT KIND OF A SCIENCE CAN IT BE?

A final issue of importance concerns the type of theory of personality that one reasonably can pursue. We have taken it for granted thus far that one can craft a science of personality, in other words, that the methods of science can inform the nature of persons. This assumption seems like a safe one. People are objects in a physical universe. They consist of biological systems comprised of physical and chemical parts. Science thus should be able to tell us something about them.

Nonetheless, one can reasonably question the forms of scientific analysis that can be applied to the understanding of persons. Much of the progress of science has involved analyses that are reductionistic. A system is understood by reducing a complex whole to its simpler parts, and showing how the parts give rise to the functioning of the whole.

Such analyses work wonderfully when applied to physical systems. A biological system, for example, can be understood in terms of the biochemistry of its parts. The chemistry, in turn, can be understood in terms of the underlying physics of the chemical components. But personality is not merely a physical system. People construct, and respond to, meaning. We strive to understand

The Effects of Early Experience. *Psychologists recognize that early life experiences can be important to personality development. Yet they disagree on another question: Are the personality characteristics that result from early experiences fixed throughout one's life? Or is personality malleable, with substantial change occurring later in the life course?*

ourselves and what events that we witness mean for us. There is no guarantee that the traditional scientific procedures of breaking a system into constituent parts will be sufficient to understand these processes of meaning construction. Indeed, numerous scholars have suggested that they may not, and have warned psychologists against importing the methods of the physical sciences into the study of human meaning systems (Geertz, 2000; Polkinghorne, 1988; Taylor, 1989). To such commentators, the idea that people have "parts" is "at best a metaphor" (Harré, 1998, p. 15). The risk of adopting this metaphor is that, to use a cliché, "the whole may be greater than the sum of the parts." By analogy, consider an analysis of a great work of art, such as da Vinci's *Mona Lisa*. In principle, one could analyze its parts: There's paint of one color over here, paint of some other color there, and so on. But this sort of analysis will not enable one to understand the greatness of the painting. This requires viewing the work as a whole and understanding the historical context in which it was made. By analogy, a listing of the psychological parts of an actual person may, in principle, fail to portray the whole individual and the developmental processes that contributed to his or her uniqueness. A question to ask yourself when reading this textbook, then, is whether the personality theorists are as successful as was da Vinci at providing holistic psychological portraits of complex individuals.

WHAT IS A PERSONALITY THEORY SUPPOSED TO DO?

As we have noted, a unique feature of the scientific field of personality psychology is that it contains more than one guiding theory. Multiple theories of personality inform us about human nature and individual differences. A natural question, then, is how to evaluate the theories, one versus the other.

How can one judge the strengths and limitations of the various theories? What are the criteria that should be used to evaluate them?

To evaluate something, one generally asks what it is supposed to do. One then can judge how well it is doing it. A more formal way to say this is that one asks about the *functions* that the entity is supposed to serve. One then can evaluate the degree to which it is carrying out those functions.

What, then, are the functions of a personality theory? What is a personality theory supposed to do? Like all scientific theories, theories of personality can serve three key functions: they can (1) organize existing information, (2) generate new knowledge about important issues, and (3) identify entirely new issues that are deserving of study.

The first of these functions is obvious. Research provides an array of facts about personality, personality development, and individual differences. Rather than merely listing these facts in an unordered manner, it would be useful to organize them systematically. A logical, systematic ordering of facts would enable one to keep track of what scientists know about personality. This can make it easier to put that knowledge to use.

The second function is somewhat less obvious. In any field of study, there are issues—involving both basic science questions and applications of scientific knowledge—that everyone in the field recognizes as important. A good theory fosters new knowledge about these issues. It is generative. The theory helps people to generate new knowledge about the topics they recognize as important to their field. In biology, Darwin's theory of natural selection was useful not only because it organized known facts about the world's flora and fauna. Its additional value is that it opened new pathways of knowledge about biology. In geology, the theory of plate tectonics is important not only because it systematizes questions about the spatial relations among land masses. It also may foster new knowledge about seismic events. In personality psychology, some theories have proven to be highly generative. They have prompted researchers who are familiar with the theory to use its ideas to generate new knowledge about personality.

The third function is of particular interest to both the personality scientist and the public at large. A personality theory may identity entirely new areas of study—areas that people might never have known about were it not for the theory. Psychodynamic theory opened the door to psychological issues that were utterly novel to most people: the possibility that our most important thoughts and emotions are unconscious, the possibility that events early in childhood determine our adult personality characteristics. Other theories also have this quality. Evolutionary psychology (reviewed in Chapter 9) makes the novel suggestion that contemporary patterns of thought and behavior are not learned in contemporary society but, instead, are inherited from our ancestral past. Behaviorism (Chapter 10) raises the possibility that actions that we attribute to our free choice, or free will, are ultimately caused by the environment. These theories' fascinating and sometimes radical hypotheses about human nature have prompted much valuable new investigation into human nature.

In sum, you can evaluate the theories you will learn about in this text by gauging their success in (1) organizing information, (2) generating knowledge, and (3) identifying important issues to study.

THE PERSONALITY THEORIES: AN INTRODUCTION

We have now reviewed a series of points: topics that must be addressed by a personality theory, important issues that arise as one confronts these topics, and criteria that can be used to evaluate a theory of personality. Now, in the final section of this chapter, we turn to the theories themselves.

THE CHALLENGE OF CONSTRUCTING A PERSONALITY THEORY

By this point in our chapter, it is clear that constructing a comprehensive theory of personality is extremely difficult. Theorists must pursue a challenging set of scientific goals that go beyond one's intuitive thinking about personality. They must address a broad set of *What*, *how*, and *why* questions about personality structure, processes, development, and change. They must consider determinants of personality ranging from the molecular to the sociocultural, and conceptual issues ranging from the philosophical view of persons that is embedded in their theory to the question of whether one can have a scientific theory of persons in the first place.

Does any one person do this ideally? Is there a single theory that is so comprehensive in its scope, so consistent with scientific evidence, and so uniquely able to foster new knowledge that it is accepted universally? The answer, quite simply, is no. There exist different theoretical frameworks. Each has its strengths, and each its limitations. More importantly, each has its unique virtues; in other words, each of a variety of theories provides some unique insights into human nature. It is for this reason that this textbook is organized around personality theories—plural.

THE PERSONALITY THEORIES: A PRELIMINARY SKETCH

What theoretical frameworks have had the biggest impact on the field? This book will introduce you to six theoretical approaches. We provide a brief sketch of these approaches here, so that you can get a sense of the terrain ahead.

We begin with psychodynamic theory (Chapters 3 and 4), the approach pioneered by Freud. Psychodynamic theory views the mind as an energy system; the basic biological energies of the body reside, in part, in the mind. Mental energies, then, are directed to the service of basic bodily needs. However, people generally cannot gratify sexual and other bodily desires whenever they wish. Instead, the drive to gratify bodily needs often conflicts with the dictates of society. Behavior, then, reflects a conflict between biological desires on the one hand and social constraints on the other. In psychoanalysis, the mind is said to contain different systems that serve different functions: satisfying bodily needs, representing social norms and rules, and striking a strategic balancing between biological drives and social constraints. An additional defining feature of psychodynamic theory is that much of this mental activity is said to occur outside of one's conscious awareness. We are not aware of the drives that underlie our emotions and behavior; they are unconscious.

Phenomenological theories, reviewed next (Chapters 5 and 6), contrast starkly with the psychodynamic view. Phenomenological theories are less concerned with unconscious process and more concerned with people's conscious experience of the world around them—that is, their phenomenological experience. Phenomenological theorists recognize that people have biologically based motives, yet they believe that people also possess "higher" motives involving personal growth and self-fulfillment, and that these motives are more important to personal well-being than are the animalistic drives highlighted by Freud. Finally, compared to psychodynamic approaches, phenomenological theory places much greater emphasis on the self. The development of a stable and coherent understanding of oneself is seen as key to psychological health.

Trait approaches to personality, reviewed in Chapters 7 and 8, differ strikingly from both of the previous formulations. The differences reflect not only different views about the nature of personality, but different scientific beliefs about the best way of building a personality theory. Most trait theorists believe that, to construct a theory of personality, one must begin by solving two scientific problems: (1) developing a reliable measure of individual differences, and (2) determining which individual differences are most important to measure. Once these problems are solved, one would be able to measure the most important individual differences in personality, and these measurements could serve as a basis for constructing a comprehensive theory of persons. A main development in the late–20th-century history of the field is that many personality psychologists came to conclude that these problems had, in fact, been solved. Much consensus has been achieved on the question of what individual differences are most important and on how they can be measured.

Chapter 9 addresses one of the most exciting aspects of contemporary personality science, namely, research on the biological foundations of personality. This includes findings regarding the genetic bases of personality traits, as well as work revealing the brain systems that underlie individual differences. In this chapter, we devote coverage not only to trait theories but to evolutionary psychology. Evolutionary psychologists explain contemporary patterns of social behavior in terms of mental mechanisms that are a product of our evolutionary past.

Chapter 10 introduces the ideas of behaviorism, which represent a learning approach to personality. In behavioral theories, behavior is seen as an adaptation to rewards and punishments experienced in the environment. Since different people experience different patterns of reward in different settings, they naturally developed different styles of behavior. Basic learning processes, then, are said to account for the stylistic variations in behavior that we call "personality." Behaviorism presents a profound challenge to the theories presented previously. To the behaviorist, the units of analysis of the previous theories—the psychodynamic theorist's "unconscious forces," the "self" of phenomenological theories, personality "traits"—are not causes of behavior. They merely are descriptions of patterns of thinking, emotion, and behavior that ultimately are caused by the environment that, according to the behaviorist, shapes our behavior.

Chapter 11 introduces a markedly different theoretical approach, that of personal construct theory. Personal construct theory addresses people's capacity to interpret the world. Unlike the behaviorist, who is most concerned with how the environment determines our experiences, the personal construct theorist studies the subjective ideas, or constructs, that people use to interpret the environment. One person may view the college environment as challenging, another as boring; one person may view dating circumstances as romantic, another as sexually threatening. Personal construct theorists explore the possibility that most individual differences in personality functioning stem from the different constructs that people use to interpret their world.

The final theoretical perspective is that of social-cognitive theory (Chapters 12 and 13). In some respect, social-cognitive theory is similar to the personal construct approach; social-cognitive theorists study personality by analyzing the thinking processes that come into play as people interpret their world. However, the social-cognitive perspective expands upon personal construct theory in at least two important ways. First, as suggested by its name, social-cognitive theory explores in detail the social settings in which people acquire knowledge, skills, and beliefs. Personality develops through back-and-forth influences, or *reciprocal interactions*, between people and the settings (i.e., the family, interpersonal, social, and cultural settings) of their lives. Second, social-cognitive theory devotes much attention to questions of *self-regulation*, which refers to the psychological processes through which people set goals for themselves, control their emotional impulses, and execute courses of action.

Chapter 14 considers personality in context. We explore contemporary research that illustrates the critical point that you often can learn much about people's personalities by studying the life contexts—the social situations, cultural settings, interpersonal relationships, etc.—that make up their life. This research heavily capitalizes on the social-cognitive perspective discussed in Chapters 12 and 13, while providing a broad portrait of contemporary psychological research on social settings and the individual. We end, in Chapter 15, by critically evaluating the field of personality psychology as a whole.

ON THE EXISTENCE OF MULTIPLE THEORIES: THEORIES AS TOOLKITS

The fact that this book presents these multiple theories at first might seem odd. Courses in most other scientific disciplines—e.g., chemistry, physics—are not organized around a series of different theories. Knowledge is organized by one commonly accepted conceptual framework. In part, this reflects the maturity of these other fields, which have been around longer than the science of psychology. Yet even the "mature sciences" may harbor different views of the same phenomenon. Suppose you were to ask a physicist about the nature of light. You might learn that physics has a theory that says that light is a wave. And you might learn that physics also has a theory that says that light is composed of individual particles. If you were to ask, "Which theory is right?" you would be told, "Neither." Light acts as a wave and as a particle. Both a wave theory and a particle theory capture important information about the nature of light.

The same is true for the personality theories. Each captures important information about human nature. As you read about them, you should not be asking yourself "Which theory was right, and which ones are wrong?" Instead, it is better to evaluate them by asking how useful they are in advancing basic knowledge and applications. Even a theory that gets some things wrong may have much value (Proctor & Capaldi, 2001).

As we were preparing this edition of this text, a colleague suggested to us a useful metaphor for thinking about personality theories. It is useful because it moves one away from simplistic right/wrong evaluations and toward a more sophisticated view. She suggested that theories are like toolkits. Each theory contains a set of "tools." Some of these tools are theoretical concepts. Others are research methods. Some are techniques for assessing personality. Yet others are methods for doing therapy. Each element of the theory is a tool in that each serves one or more functions; each, in other words, enables one to carry out one or more jobs. The jobs are things like describing individual differences, identifying basic human motivations, explaining the development of self-concept, identifying the causes of emotional reactions, predicting performance in work settings, or reducing psychological distress via therapy. These are jobs the psychologist wants to do. Each theory provides conceptual tools for doing them.

The toolkit metaphor has two benefits: it leads one (1) to ask good questions about personality theories and (2) to avoid asking bad ones. To see these benefits, imagine that you are evaluating actual physical toolkits. If you see a plumber, an electrician, and an auto mechanic each carrying a toolkit of their profession, you would not go up to any of them and say, "Your toolkit is wrong." The idea that a toolkit could be wrong hardly makes sense. A toolkit may be less good than another for doing a particular job. It may be less useful for a range of jobs than some other toolkit that contains more tools. It may be more practical than some other toolkit that contains more tools because the larger toolkit is unwieldy. You would evaluate toolkits by asking about what you can do with them and how they might be improved by adding, or sometimes removing, tools. You would not evaluate them by asking "Which one is correct?"

Similarly, when evaluating the different personality theories we present, we encourage you to ask questions such as "What can one do with the conceptual tools of this theory?" "What advantages do its conceptual tools have in relation to other theories?" or "What tools could be added to (or subtracted from) the theory to make it better?" These questions are better than asking "Which theory is right?"

The toolkit metaphor has a final implication. It suggests that the existence of multiple theories in contemporary personality psychology might not be such a bad thing. In the world of actual physical tools, when people have different toolkits they might learn new things from one another. They might add a tool from someone else's kit or be inspired to attempt someone else's job with the tools they have. In the long run, the diversity among toolkits may improve everyone's work. The same may be true in the world of theoretical tools. When there exist multiple theories, investigators are more likely to face research findings and theoretical arguments that challenge their favored view. The challenges may prompt them to refine, extend, and ultimately improve their own thinking. Theoretical diversity thus can accelerate the overall progress of a discipline. As one wise observer has put it, in commenting on the progress of the social and psychological sciences, the "deployment of distinct inquiries... [that] force deep-going reconsiderations upon one another" is what "drive[s] the enterprise erratically onward" (Geertz, 2000, p. 199).

We hope you enjoy your tour through the erratic, but progressing, enterprise of personality theory and research.

MAJOR CONCEPTS

Hierarchy   A relation between entities in which one of them is an example of, or serves the purpose of, the other. In any given personality theory, different variables often are related hierarchically.

Personality   Those characteristics of the person that account for consistent patterns of experience and action.

Process   In personality theory, the concept that refers to the motivational aspects of personality.

Structure   In personality theory, the concept that refers to the more enduring and stable aspects of personality.

System   A collection of highly interconnected parts that function together; in the study of personality, distinct psychological mechanisms may function together as a system that produces the psychological phenomena of personality.

Temperament   Biologically based emotional and behavioral tendencies that are evident in early childhood.

Trait   An enduring psychological characteristic of an individual; or a type of psychological construct (a "trait construct") that refers to such characteristics.

Type   A cluster of personality traits that may constitute a qualitatively distinct category of persons (i.e., a personality type).

Units of analysis   A concept that refers to the basic variables of a theory; different personality theories invoke different types of variables, or different basic units of analysis, in conceptualizing personality structure.

REVIEW

1. We all think about personality in our day-to-day lives. The work of personality theorists differs from this everyday thinking in that personality theories pursue five goals that are uncommon in everyday thinking about persons. They engage in (1) *scientific observations* that underlie theories that are (2) internally coherent and *systematic*, (3) *testable*, and (4) *comprehensive*, and that foster (5) useful *applications*.

2. Personality theories address *what*, *how*, and *why* questions about personality by developing theories that address four distinct topics: (1) personality structure, (2) personality processes, (3) personality development, and (4) personality change (including via psychotherapy).

3. Personality theorists have confronted a range of issues throughout the history of the field. In developing theories that encompass these issues, the theorist hopes to develop a framework that serves three scientific functions: (1) organizing existing knowledge about personality, (2) fostering new knowledge on important issues, and (3) identifying new issues for study.

4. The existence of multiple theories in the field can be understood by thinking of theories as toolkits, each of which provides unique conceptual tools for doing the jobs of the personality psychologist.

THE SCIENTIFIC STUDY OF PEOPLE

2

Three students in a course on personality work together on a research project. They have been instructed to develop a research method for studying the effects of achievement motivation on academic performance. At their first meeting, they realize that they have drastically differing opinions about how to proceed. Alex is convinced that the best approach is to follow one student over the course of the semester, carefully recording all relevant information (grades, changes in motivation, feelings about courses, etc.) to obtain a complete and in-depth picture of a particular case. Sarah, however, thinks little of Alex's idea because his conclusions would apply only to that one person. She suggests that the group develop a set of motivation questions and give the questions to as many students as possible. She then would examine the correlation between questionnaire responses and performance in school. Yolanda thinks that neither of these approaches is good enough. She thinks that the best way to understand things scientifically is to run experiments. She suggests an experimental manipulation that causes some people to feel motivated and others to feel unmotivated, followed by a measure of test performance.

The students' views illustrate the three major methods in personality research: *case studies, correlational studies* using questionnaires, and *laboratory experiments*. This chapter introduces you to these three research methods. First, however, we review the different types of information, or data sources, that might go into any study, as well as the general goals that investigators have when they conduct research on personality.

QUESTIONS TO BE ADDRESSED IN THIS CHAPTER

1. What kind of information is it important to obtain when studying personality?
2. What does it mean to say that scientific observations must be "reliable" and "valid"?
3. How should we go about studying people? Should we conduct research in the laboratory or in the natural environment? Through the use of self-reports or reports of others? Through studying many subjects or a single individual?
4. How much difference does it make to study people with one or another type of data? Or through one versus another approach to research? In other words, to what extent will the person "look the same" when studied from different vantage points or perspectives?

In Chapter 1, we suggested that, at an intuitive level, all people are personality psychologists. Both you and the professional personality scientist develop complex and insightful thoughts about people. The job of the personality scientist, however, differs from yours. The personality scientist must formulate his or her ideas very explicitly, so that they can be tested by objective scientific evidence.

Just as we all are intuitive personality theorists, we are also intuitive personality researchers. We observe differences among people, as well as consistent patterns of behavior within individuals. However, the "research" of the ordinary person differs from that of the personality scientist. Scientists follow established procedures to ensure that they obtain information that is as objective and accurate as possible. They check these procedures to ensure that their observations are reliable and stable, rather than occurring by chance or error. They report the procedures in publications, so that other investigators can replicate their procedures and verify their findings. Rarely in our daily lives do we do any of this in a systematic way.

This chapter is devoted to the research procedures of the personality psychologist. Our subsequent chapters explore personality theories. You should bear in mind, however, that questions about theory and research are not as separate as this division of chapters might suggest. It might seem as if psychologists first should conduct a large amount of "theory-free" research and then develop a theory to explain their findings. But this is impossible because there is no such thing as "theory-free" research. Research involves the systematic study of relationships among events. Generally, we need a theory to identify the events that are most important to study. We also need a theory to tell us how to study them. Suppose, for example, that you wanted to test the idea that people who are anxious about dating relationships do not perform as well as they should on exams in college courses because their anxiety interferes with their learning. To test this, you would have to begin by measuring people's level of anxiety. But how? It is impossible to proceed without making some theoretical assumptions. One option would be to ask people directly, "Are you anxious about dating?" But this option makes two risky assumptions: (1) that people are aware of their level of anxiety, and thus are capable of reporting it, and (2) that people will tell you, honestly and accurately, about their anxiety if you ask. These assumptions could be wrong, and a personality theory might specify exactly how they are wrong. For example, psychodynamic theories suggest that some people are so anxious that they are not even aware of their anxiety. They repress it. This theory suggests that you need a different research method. Other potential research procedures, such as measuring physiological arousal or brain functioning to index levels of anxiety, similarly rest on theoretical ideas about what anxiety is, what its underlying causes are, and how it is expressed. Thus, theory and research are closely linked. Theory without research can be mere speculation. Research without theory is an impossibility.

There is more than one way to get scientific information, or data, about persons. Consider the options. You could ask a person to tell you what she is like. Alternatively, you could observe her in her day-to-day activities to see for yourself. Or, since this would be rather time-consuming, you could ask other people who know this person well to report on her personality. A fourth possibility would be one that does not rely on anyone's subjective observations or judgments, but instead looks at objective facts about the person's life (school records, job performance, etc.).

THE DATA OF PERSONALITY PSYCHOLOGY

LOTS OF DATA

Personality psychologists have recognized these options and have defined four categories of data that one might use in research (Block, 1993). They also have created a handy acronym to make it easy to remember them. The four types of data are: (1) life record data (L-data), (2) observer data (O-data), (3) test data (T-data), and (4) self-report data (S-data)—or, LOTS of data. Personality psychologists consider four data types because each one, individually, has unique strengths and limitations (Ozer, 1999).

L-data consist of information that can be obtained from a person's life history or life record. For example, if one is interested in the relation between intelligence and school performance, one can make use of official school records of intelligence test scores and grades. If interested in the relation between personality and criminality, one does not have to ask people, "Have you committed any crimes?" and rely on the truthfulness of their answers. Instead, court records of arrests and convictions supply an objective measure of criminality. For many personality characteristics, however, such objective records are not available, so other data sources must be considered.

O-data consist of information provided by knowledgeable observers such as parents, friends, or teachers. Generally such persons are provided with a questionnaire or other rating form with which they rate the target individual's personality characteristics. For example, friends might complete a questionnaire in which they rate an individual's level of friendliness, extraversion, or conscientiousness. Sometimes observers are trained to observe individuals in their daily lives and to make personality ratings based on these observations. As one example, camp counselors have been trained to observe systematically the behavior of children at camp, in order to relate specific forms of behavior (e.g., verbal aggression, physical aggression, compliance) to features of the camp setting or to general personality characteristics (e.g., self-confidence, emotional health, social skills) (Shoda, Mischel, & Wright, 1994; Sroufe, Carlson, & Shulman, 1993). As is clear from these examples, O-data can consist of observations of very specific pieces of behavior or of more general ratings based on observations of behavior. In addition, data on any individual can be obtained from one observer or from multiple observers (e.g., one friend or many friends, one teacher or many teachers). In the latter case, one can check for agreement or reliability among observers.

T-data consist of information obtained from experimental procedures or standardized tests. For example, ability to tolerate delay of gratification might be measured by determining how long a child will work at a task to obtain a larger reward rather than a smaller reward that is immediately available (Mischel, 1990, 1999b). Performance on a standardized test such as an intelligence test would also be illustrative of T-data.

Finally, **S-data** consist of information provided by the subject himself or herself. Typically such data are in the form of responses to questionnaires. In these cases the person is taking the role of observer and making ratings relevant to the self (e.g., "I am a conscientious person"). Personality questionnaires can be relevant to single personality characteristics (e.g., optimism) or can attempt to cover the entire domain of personality. Self-reports clearly have limitations. People may be unaware of some of their own psychological characteristics. They may be motivated to present themselves in a positive manner to the psychologist administering the test. However, self-report measures are convenient, in that they are relatively easy to obtain. Also, they sometimes are the only valid way to assess a psychological characteristic of interest (e.g., subjective perceptions of oneself or a stimulus). Thus, self-reports are the most commonly used source of data in personality psychology.

The LOTS categories are a useful system for keeping track of the alternative sources of data the personality psychologist may employ. You will see many examples of these different types of evidence about personality throughout the chapters of this book. However, two points must be kept in mind. First, researchers do not need to choose only one source of data for their research. Quite commonly, they combine data sources. This combination can add to one's confidence in research findings. For example, researchers who try to identify the most important dimensions of individual differences find that analyses of different data sources (S and O data) yield the same dimensions; the same five personality factors are found whether one analyzes people's reports about themselves or other people's reports about them (McCrae & Costa, 1987). Such a finding bolsters confidence in the conclusion that these dimensions are, indeed, of basic importance.

The second point is that some forms of data do not easily fit into this four-category LOTS scheme. As the field of personality psychology has progressed, new types of measurement have been developed. Thus, additional categories may be necessary to capture the diversity of data that the contemporary psychologist uses to assess personality characteristics (Cervone & Caprara, 2001). For example, some researchers employ *implicit* individual-difference measures, that is, measures designed to tap beliefs or self-evaluations of which people may not be consciously (i.e., explicitly) aware (Fazio & Olson, 2003). One popular implicit measure involves reaction-time methodology, in which researchers measure how long it takes for people to answer a question. An implicit test of self-esteem, for example, might measure how long it takes people to respond to stimuli involving the self when those stimuli are associated with positive versus negative terms (Greenwald & Banaji, 1995; Greenwald et al., 2002). Other researchers employ diary methods, which are techniques in which people are asked to report about their psychological experiences soon after their occurrence, rather than completing a questionnaire that inquires about things that have happened in the distant past (Bolger, Davis, & Rafaeli, 2003). Diary methods have a major advantage. People may forget important details of experiences that they had a week, a month, or a year previously. By asking people to report on their current experiences one or more times every day, diary methods avoid the problem of forgetting, as well as eliminate biases that may occur when people try to remember emotionally significant events that occurred far in the past.

HOW DO DATA FROM DIFFERENT SOURCES RELATE TO ONE ANOTHER?

Having introduced four categories of data, a question to ask is whether measures obtained from the different types of data agree with one another (Pervin, 1999). If a person rates herself as high on conscientiousness, will others (e.g., friends, teachers) rate her similarly? If an individual scores high on a questionnaire measuring depression, will ratings given by a professional interviewer lead to a similar score? If an individual rates himself as high on extraversion, will he score high on that trait in a laboratory-designed situation to measure that trait (e.g., participation in a group discussion)?

The seemingly simple question of whether different data sources relate to one another is more complicated than it sounds. Numerous factors influence the degree to which data sources are related. One is the question of which data sources one is talking about. Personality psychologists frequently have found that self-reports (S-data) are often discrepant from scores obtained from laboratory procedures (T-data). Self-report questionnaires tend to involve broad judgments that relate to a wide variety of situations (e.g., "I generally am pretty even-tempered") whereas experimental procedures measure personality characteristics in a very specific context. This difference often is critical, resulting in discrepancies between the two types of data.

Self-reports (S-data) and observer reports (O-data) tend to be related more closely. Personality psychologists commonly find significant levels of agreement when comparing self-ratings to observer ratings (e.g., Funder, Kolar, & Blackman, 1995; McCrae & Costa, 1987). Yet here, too, different types of research procedures can lead to different conclusions (Coyne, 1994; John & Robins, 1994a; Kenny et al., 1994; McCrae & Costa, 1990; Pervin, 1996, 1999). When the personality characteristic being rated is highly evaluative (e.g., stupid, warmhearted), self-perception biases enter the rating process, lowering agreement between self and observer ratings (John & Robins, 1993, 1994a; Robins & John, 1997). Moreover, some personality characteristics are more observable and easier to judge than others (e.g., sociability versus neuroticism), leading to greater agreement between self and observer ratings as well as to greater agreement among ratings obtained from different observers of the same person (Funder, 1989, 1993, 1995; John & Robins, 1993). Furthermore, some individuals appear to be easier to read or more "judgable" than others (Colvin, 1993). In sum, a variety of factors—including the degree to which a personality characteristic is evaluative and observable, and the degree to which the person being rated is "judgable"—affect the correspondence between data sources.

In general, the different sources of data about personality should be recognized as having their own advantages and disadvantages. Self-report questionnaires have a clear advantage: People know a lot about themselves, so if a psychologist wants to know people, maybe the best thing to do is to ask them about themselves (Allport, 1961; Kelly, 1955). Yet, self-report methods have limits. People's descriptions of themselves on questionnaires can be influenced by irrelevant factors such as the phrasing of test items and the order in which items appear on a test (Schwarz, 1999). People also may lie or may unconsciously distort their questionnaire responses (Paulhus, Fridhandler, & Hayes, 1997), perhaps in an attempt to present themselves in a positive light. For such reasons, some researchers feel that the best measure of an individual's personality is questionnaire ratings by *others* who know the person. Yet here, too, problems may arise; different raters may sometimes rate the same person in quite different ways (Hofstee, 1994; John & Robins, 1994a; Kenny et al., 1994). As a result, some psychologists contend that the field should not rely so heavily on questionnaires—whether those questionnaires are self-reports or are reports by other people who are familiar with a given individual. Instead, objective measures of behavior and of biological systems underlying that behavior may be a more reliable source of evidence for building a science of personality (Kagan, 2003). Yet the personality psychologist is often interested in aspects of personal experience that do not have any simple behavioral or biological markers. If one wants to know about people's conscious perceptions of themselves and their beliefs about the world around them, then we're back where we started: the best thing to do is to ask them.

FIXED VERSUS FLEXIBLE MEASURES

Another way in which sources of data about personality can differ involves the question of whether measures are fixed or flexible. By "fixed," we are referring to procedures in which exactly the same measures (e.g., exactly the same test items) are administered to all the people in a psychological study, and scores for all the people are computed in exactly the same way. Such "fixed" procedures are, by far, the most commonly employed method in personality psychology. If psychologists want to know about people's characteristics, they generally give large groups of people precisely the same test items, and compute scores for everyone in a common manner. Doing so has obvious advantages. It yields a testing procedure that is objective and simple.

There are, however, two potential limitations to this fixed method of assessment. One is that some of the test items that the psychologist asks may be irrelevant to some of the individuals who are taking the test. If you have ever taken a personality questionnaire, you may have felt that some of the questions were good ones, in that they tapped into an important feature of your personality, whereas others were not good ones, in that they asked about things that are irrelevant to you. A fixed testing procedure does not differentiate between the two types of items; it simply adds up all of your responses and computes for you a total score on a test. The second limitation is that there may be features of your personality that are not on the test. You may possess some idiosyncratic psychological quality—an important past experience, a unique skill, a guiding religious or moral value, a long-term goal in life—that is not mentioned anywhere on the psychologist's test.

These limitations can, in principle, be overcome by adopting testing procedures that are more flexible, in other words, procedures that do something other than merely give all people a common set of questions. Various options are available (Cervone, Shadel, & Jencius, 2001; Cervone & Shadel, 2003). For example, one option is to give people a fixed set of test items, but to allow them to indicate which items are more or less relevant to them (Markus, 1977). Another is to give people unstructured personality tests, that is, tests in which the items allow people to describe themselves in their own words, rather than forcing them to respond to descriptions worded entirely by the experimenter. A question such as "True or false: I like going to large parties" would be a structured item, whereas the question "What activities do you enjoy on the weekends?" would be unstructured. Unstructured methods have proven to be quite valuable in assessing self-concept. These methods include asking people to list words or phrases that describe important aspects of their personality (Higgins, King, & Mavin, 1982), or to tell stories that relate their memories of important life experiences that they have had (Woike & Polo, 2001).

Personality psychologists have a technical vocabulary to describe these fixed versus flexible measures. Fixed measures that are applied in the same manner to all persons are referred to as **nomothetic**. The term comes from the Greek for "law," *nomos*, and refers here to the search for scientific laws that apply, in a fixed manner, to everyone. Flexible assessment techniques that are tailored to the particular individual being studied are referred to as **idiographic**. This term comes from the Greek *idios*, referring to personal, private, and distinct characteristics (as in the word "idiosyncratic"). In general, then, nomothetic techniques are ones that describe a population of persons in terms of a fixed set of personality variables, using a fixed set of items to measure them. Idiographic techniques, in contrast, have the primary goal of obtaining a portrait of the potentially unique, idiosyncratic individual. As you will see in later chapters, the personality theories differ in the degree to which they rely on fixed versus flexible, and nomothetic versus idiographic, testing procedures.

PERSONALITY THEORY AND ASSESSMENT

With the options of four different sources of data, and idiographic versus nomothetic testing procedures, how is one to choose? How does one select among the options available for getting information about persons? Inevitably, choices are shaped by theoretical considerations. One's theoretical views about personality determine what one thinks about different measurement procedures. Measuring personality is not like measuring the mass of a rock. Everyone agrees that the mass of a rock can be measured in terms of pounds (or something arithmetically equivalent, like kilograms). But since different personality theories use different units of analysis, as we discussed in Chapter 1, there is no uniform agreement among personality psychologists regarding exactly what personality variables should be measured and how to measure them.

To some personality psychologists, the important thing to measure is people's typical patterns of behavior. To others, who emphasize people's skills, capabilities, and plans for the future, it may be more important to measure people's life goals—which may or may not be reflected in a person's current behavior. (You may have the goal of becoming a parent, and this goal may be important in understanding your personality, but if you are not yet a parent then this feature of your personality may not be reflected in your current day-to-day behavior.) Many personality psychologists employ nomothetic assessment procedures, because they believe that there exists a small number of psychological characteristics that we each possess in greater or lesser amounts. Other theories try to capture the idiosyncrasy of the individual, and believe that nomothetic procedures provide only a superficial depiction of the depth of an individual's character.

The relations between theory and choice of measurement will be illustrated again and again as you read the subsequent chapters of this book. For now, note that the relation between theory and research procedures underscores a theme from our first chapter. It is impossible to study personality by first collecting a lot of data, and then creating a theory. This is because one needs a theory to decide what type of data it is most valuable to collect and how to interpret the data that one gets.

GOALS OF RESEARCH: RELIABILITY, VALIDITY, ETHICAL BEHAVIOR

No matter what question one is studying, and no matter what method one chooses, a research project cannot succeed unless its procedures possess two qualities. One's observations of personality (1) must be replicable (if the study is run twice it should turn out the same way both times), and (2) the measure must relate to the theoretical concept of interest in a given study. In the language of research, measures must be reliable and valid (West & Finch, 1997).

RELIABILITY

The concept of **reliability** refers to the extent to which observations can be replicated. The question is whether measures are dependable, or stable. If we give people a personality measure, and then give it to them again a short time later, we expect that the measure will reveal similar personality characteristics at the two time points. If it does not, it is said to be unreliable.

Various factors may affect the reliability of a psychological test. Some involve the psychological state of the people who are being observed. People's responses may be affected by transient factors such as what their mood happens to be at the time that they are observed. For example, if a person is taking the same personality test on two different days, and responses on one day are altered by a chance event that day that puts them in a good or bad mood, then scores on the test over the two days will differ. This resulting lack of reliability is a problem if the test is assumed to measure stable personality characteristics that are relatively uninfluenced by temporary states or moods. Other factors involve the test itself. Variations in instructions to subjects or ambiguities in test items can lower reliability. Carelessness in scoring a test or ambiguous rules for interpreting scores can also lead to a lack of agreement, or lack of reliability, among testers.

The notion of reliability commonly is measured in two different ways, with the different techniques providing answers to different questions about a test (West & Finch, 1997). One reliability question involves internal consistency: Do the different items on the test correlate with one another, as one would expect if each item is a reflection of a common psychological construct? The second question is one previously noted, namely, test-retest reliability: If people take the test at two different points in time, do their scores correlate with one another? The differences between the types of reliability are made plain by a simple example. Suppose one added a few intelligence test items to a test of extraversion. The test-retest reliability of measure would remain high (since people would probably have similar performance on the intelligence test items at different points in time). But the internal consistency of the test would be lowered (since responses on extraversion and intelligence test items probably would not be correlated).

VALIDITY

In addition to being reliable, observations must be valid. The concept of **validity** refers to the extent to which observations actually reflect the phenomena of interest in a given study. The concept of validity is best illustrated by an example in which a measure is not valid: One could assess people's intelligence by measuring the size of their head, and the measure could be perfectly reliable, but it would not be valid because head size is not actually an indicator of the mental capabilities that we call "intelligence" (Gould, 1981).

If there is no evidence that a given measure is valid, then it is of little use. Suppose, for example, that we have a reliable test for the personality traits of neuroticism or extraversion, but no evidence that the tests measure what they purport to measure. Of what use are they? To constitute a useful measure, we need evidence that the test is indicative of the psychological construct of interest. The test, in other words, must have construct validity (Cronbach & Meehl, 1955; Ozer, 1999).

To establish that a test possesses construct validity, personality psychologists generally try to show that the test relates systematically to some external criterion, that is, to some measure that is independent of (i.e., external to) the test itself. Theoretical considerations guide the choice of an external criterion. For example, if one were to develop a test of the tendency to experience anxiety and wanted to establish its construct validity, one would use theoretical ideas about anxiety to choose external criteria (e.g., physiological indices of anxious arousal) that the test should predict. One generally would establish validity by showing that the test correlates with the external criterion. However, in addition to correlational data, tests of validity might involve comparisons of two groups of people who are theoretically relevant to the test. A group of people who have been diagnosed by clinical psychologists as suffering from an anxiety disorder, for example, should get higher scores on the purported anxiety test than people who have not been so diagnosed; otherwise one obviously would not have a valid test of anxiety.

There are other aspects to "validity," as the term commonly is used (Ozer, 1999; West & Finch, 1997). For example, if one is proposing a new personality test, then one should be able to demonstrate that the test has "discriminant validity": it should be distinct, empirically, from other tests that already exist. If, hypothetically, one proposes a new test of "worrying tendencies" and finds that it correlates with existing tests of neuroticism, then the new test is of little value because it lacks discriminant validity.

In sum, reliability concerns the questions of whether a test provides a stable, replicable measure, and validity concerns the questions of whether a measure actually taps into the psychological construct it is supposed to be measuring. Reliability is necessary for validity. If a test is unreliable, that means that test scores are being affected by extraneous factors, which in turn implies that the scores are reflecting something other than the psychological construct of interest.

Note that questions of reliability and validity involve not only statistical issues in the analysis of tests, but theoretical issues in the test's interpretation. For example, for some psychological constructs, one might not expect measures of the construct to have high degrees of test-retest reliability. Suppose one wants to measure people's current emotional state, or mood. Since people's moods may fluctuate from day to day, it is natural that a mood measure may show low test-retest reliability. Similarly, questions of validity strongly involve conceptual considerations. Validity concerns the interpretation of a test (West & Finch, 1997). Questions that ask people about their tendencies to enjoy contemporary art, listen to classical music, and read books of philosophy may be only moderately valid if interpreted as indicators of intelligence, but may have high validity if interpreted as measures of intellectual tendencies or openness to experience (McCrae & Costa, 1999).

THE ETHICS OF RESEARCH AND PUBLIC POLICY

As a human enterprise, research involves ethical issues. Ethical questions arise in both the conduct of research and the reporting of research results. These questions are of enduring concern to psychology's scientific community (Smith, 2003). In part, this concern reflects the impact of a number of studies in past years that brought into sharp focus some of the issues involved. For example, in one research effort that won a prize from the American Association for the Advancement of Science, subjects were told to teach other subjects ("learners") a list of paired associate words and to punish them with an electric shock when an error was made (Milgram, 1965). The issue investigated was obedience to authority. Although actual shock was not used, the subjects believed that it was being used and often administered high levels despite pleas from the learners that it was painful. In another research effort in which a prison environment was simulated, subjects adopted the roles of guards and prisoners (Zimbardo, 1973). Subject "guards" were found to be verbally and physically aggressive to subject "prisoners," who allowed themselves to be treated in a dehumanized way.

Such programs are dramatic in terms of the issues they raise, but the underlying question concerning ethical principles of research is fundamental. Do experimenters have the right to require participation? To deceive subjects? What are the ethical responsibilities of researchers to subjects and to psychology as a science? The former has been an issue of concern to the American Psychological Association, which has adopted a list of relevant ethical principles (Ethical Principles of Psychologists, 1981). The essence of these principles is that "the psychologist carries out the investigation with respect and concern for the dignity and welfare of the people who participate." This includes evaluating the ethical acceptability of the research, determining whether subjects in the study will be at risk in any way, and establishing a clear and fair agreement with research participants concerning the obligations and responsibilities of each. Although the use of concealment or deception is recognized as necessary in some cases, strict guidelines are presented. It is the investigator's responsibility to protect participants from physical and mental discomfort, harm, and danger.

The ethical responsibility of psychologists includes the interpretation and presentation of results as well as the conduct of the research. Of late there has been serious concern in science generally with "the spreading stain of fraud" (*APA Monitor*, 1982). Some concern with this issue began many years ago with charges that Sir Cyril Burt, a once prominent British psychologist, intentionally misrepresented data in his research on the inheritance of intelligence. Unfortunately, this problem is not entirely a thing of the past; questions about the validity of data occasionally arise in the contemporary field (Ruggiero & Marx, 2001). The issue of fraud is one that scientists do not like to recognize or talk about because it goes against the essence of the scientific enterprise. Although fraudulent data and falsified conclusions are rare, psychologists are beginning to face up to their existence and to take constructive steps to solve the problem. Aside from professional integrity, the greatest safeguard against scientific fraud is the requirement that it be possible for other investigators to replicate all findings.

Much more subtle than fraud, and undoubtedly of much broader significance, is the issue of the effects of personal and social bias on the ways in which issues are developed and the kinds of data that are accepted as evidence in support for a given enterprise (Pervin, 2003). In considering sex differences, for example, to what extent are research projects developed in a way that is free from bias? To what extent is evidence for or against the existence of sex differences equally likely to be accepted? To what extent do our own social and political values influence not only what is studied but how it is studied and the kinds of conclusions we are prepared to reach (Bramel & Friend, 1981)? As noted, although scientists make every effort to be objective and remove all possible sources of error and bias from their research, this remains a human enterprise with the potential for personal, social, cultural, and political influence.

Finally, we may note the role of research in personnel decisions and the formulation of public policy. Though still in an early stage of development as a science, psychology does relate to fundamental human concerns, and psychologists often are called on to administer tests relevant to employment or admissions decisions and to suggest the relevance of research for public policy. Personality tests often are used as part of employment, promotion, or admission to graduate programs; research findings have influenced government policy in regard to immigration policy, early enrichment programs such as Head Start, and television violence. This being the case, psychologists have a responsibility to be careful in the presentation of their findings and to inform others of the limits of their findings in regard to personnel and policy decisions.

THREE GENERAL APPROACHES TO RESEARCH

Although all personality researchers hold the goals of reliability, validity, and theory development in common, they differ in strategy concerning the best routes to these goals. In some cases, the differences in research strategies are minor, limited to the choice of one experimental procedure or test over another. In other cases, however, the differences are major and express a more fundamental difference in approach. Research in personality has tended to follow one of three directions, and we now turn to a description of these approaches, including examples of each approach taken from the contemporary scientific literature in personality psychology.

CASE STUDIES AND CLINICAL RESEARCH

One way to learn about personality is to study individual persons in great detail. Many psychologists feel that in-depth analyses of individual cases, or **case studies**, are the only way to capture the complexities of human personality. In a case study, a psychologist has extensive contact with the individual who is the target of the study, and tries to develop an understanding of the psychological structures and processes that are most important to that individual's personality. Using a term introduced earlier, case studies inherently are *idiographic* methods, in that the goal is to obtain a psychological portrait of the particular individual under study.

Case studies may be conducted purely for purposes of research. Historically, however, case studies have commonly been conducted as part of clinical treatment. Clinical psychologists, of course, must gain an understanding of the unique qualities of their clients in order to craft an intervention, so the clinical setting inherently provides case studies of personality. Case studies by clinicians have played an important role in the development of some major theories of personality. In fact, many of the theorists we will discuss in this book were trained as clinical psychologists, counseling psychologists, or psychiatrists. They initially tried to solve the problems of their patients, and then used the insights obtained in this clinical setting to develop their theories of personality.

Tactics of Research: Case studies represent one approach to personality research.

Case Studies: An Example

To illustrate the insights that can be gained by a systematic case study, we will consider work by the Dutch personality psychologist Hubert Hermans (2001). Hermans is interested in the fact that people's thoughts about themselves—or their self-concept—are generally multifaceted. People think of themselves as having a variety of psychological characteristics. These concepts about the self develop as individuals interact with other people. Since we each have interactions with many different people, different aspects of our self-concept might often be relevant to different situations that feature different individuals. You might see yourself as being serious and articulate when interacting with professors, fun-loving and confident when hanging out with friends, and romantic yet anxious when on a date. To understand someone's personality, then, it might be necessary to study how different aspects of the self come into play as people think about their life from different viewpoints that involve individuals who play different roles in their life. Hermans (2001) refers to these different viewpoints as different "positions" one can take in viewing oneself.

The challenges of social life vary so greatly that we may adapt to them by being "different selves" in different settings.

This view of the self-concept raises a major challenge for most forms of research. Correlational and experimental studies generally provide a small amount of information about each of a large number of persons. But to understand the complexity of self-concept as Hermans describes it requires a large amount of information about a person and the individuals and social circumstances that make up that person's life. When this level of detail about the individual is required, personality psychologists turn to the technique of case studies.

Hermans (2001) reports a case study that reveals the complexity of personality in our modern day and age, in which people from different cultures come in contact with one another much more frequently than in the past, due to the migration of individuals from one part of the world to another for purposes of education or employment. The case he reports is that of a 45-year-old man from Algeria named Ali. Although this man grew up in northern Africa, for more than 20 years Ali had been living in northern Europe; he worked for a Dutch company and married a woman from the Netherlands.

As part of this case study, Hermans employed a systematic research method that can be used in the study of a single individual. The method is one in which an individual is asked to list characteristics that describe his or her own attributes, as well as listing people and situations that are important to him or her. The individual is then asked to indicate the degree to which each personal characteristic is important, or prominent, in each of the situations. Using these ratings, Hermans provides a graphic depiction of the organization of the individual's beliefs. In the graphs, an inner circle represents personal characteristics and an outer circle represents other people and situations.

Figure 2.1 represents these psychological characteristics in the case of Ali. The graph reveals an interesting fact about Ali. He views his life as having distinct components, and he exhibits different personality characteristics in these different life settings. One component of his self-concept involved family members, on both his own side of the family and his wife's. These people tended to be very accepting of him. When he was with these people, Ali was happy and outgoing, and was willing to make sacrifices for other individuals. Yet, Ali's view of himself and his social world contained a second component. As is readily understandable for someone who has moved to a new culture that may not always be accepting of immigrants, Ali recognized that some people discriminated against him or held political views with which he disagreed. With these people, he felt vulnerable and disillusioned. Interestingly, he also felt this way with his sister, whom both he and his wife viewed as "the witch of the family" (Hermans, 2001, p. 359). The detailed information provided by this case study, then, provides insight into the textures of this individual's life that is generally unavailable through other research methods.

Case Studies: Limitations

The benefits of case studies such as this one are clear. They can capture much of the complexity of an individual's personality, as it manifests itself in the unique circumstances of the person's life. However, case studies have two significant drawbacks.

The first is that, after one obtains a case study portrait of an individual, there is no way of knowing if the things one has learned about that individual apply to individuals in general. One cannot determine if the case study findings are

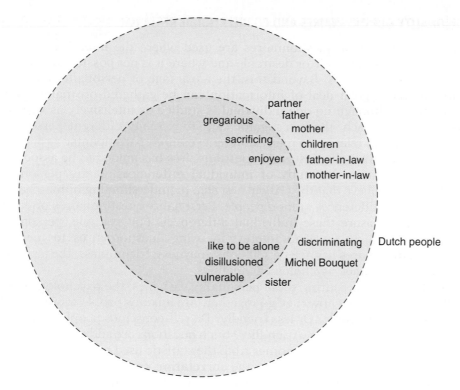

Figure 2.1   *Self-Concepts. Results from a case study of an Algerian man living in the Netherlands, married to a Dutch woman. From Hermans (2001).*

representative of the population at large. For example, although Ali seemed to have different experiences with people who did accept him in the new culture versus those who did not, the findings of this case study do not enable one to determine how common such experiences are among people in general.

The second limitation involves the task of identifying causes. In personality science, as in any science, researchers hope to identify the causes of the phenomena they study. They wish not only to describe a person, but to explain how an individual's personality develops and how personality characteristics and life events causally influence one another. A case study may provide a wonderful description, but it generally cannot provide a definite causal explanation. For example, imagine a clinical case study that describes changes in an individual's psychological well-being that occur over the course of a yearlong clinical treatment. The case study may describe the changes with great accuracy. But it cannot enable one to conclude, definitively, that the treatment caused the changes. Other events in the person's life may have had causal influence. The person may have improved simply as a result of personal maturity that was gained over the course of a year's time; the person may have improved, then, even if there had been no treatment.

The desire to study larger samples of persons and to establish the causal influence among variables motivates researchers to pursue the following two approaches to research: personality questionnaires and correlational research.

PERSONALITY QUESTIONNAIRES AND CORRELATIONAL RESEARCH

Personality tests and questionnaires are used where the intensive study of individuals is not possible or desirable and where it is not possible to conduct laboratory experiments. Beyond this, the advantage of personality question- naires is that a great deal of information can be gathered on many people at one time. Although no one individual is studied as intensively as with the case study approach, the investigator can study many different personality characteristics in relation to many different research participants.

The use of personality tests and questionnaires has tended to be associated with an interest in the study of individual differences. Many personality psychologists believe that the critical first step in understanding human nature is to chart the differences among people. Personality questionnaires often are designed to measure these individual differences. For example, personality psychologists might have an interest in using questionnaires to measure individual differences in anxiety, self-consciousness, friendliness, the tendency to take risks, or other psychological qualities.

In addition to measuring these personality variables, the psychologist gen- erally wishes to know how they go together. Are anxious people more friendly than less anxious people? Or less friendly? Do self-conscious people take fewer risks? Are risk-taking people friendlier? Such questions are addressed in **corre- lational research**. This term comes from the statistic used to gauge the degree to which two variables go together: the **correlation coefficient**. A correlation coefficient is a number that reflects the degree to which two measures are linearly related. If people who have higher scores on one variable tend also to have higher scores on the other one, then the variables are said to be *positively* correlated. (Anxiety and self-consciousness would tend to be correlated in this

Tactics of Research: Personality questionnaires are used to obtain a great deal of information about many subjects.

way.) If people who have higher scores on one variable tend to have *lower* scores on the other one, then the variables are said to be *negatively* correlated. (Anxiety and self-confidence might be correlated this way, since people who express low self-confidence are likely to report being relatively more anxious.) Finally, if two variables do not go together in any systematic linear manner, they are said to be uncorrelated. (Anxiety and friendliness may be uncorrelated, since both anxious and non-anxious people may be either friendly or unfriendly.) The correlation coefficient is computed in such a way that a perfect positive correlation—this is, a correlation in which the point falls exactly on a single line—is a correlation of 1.0. A perfect negative correlation is one of −1.0. A correlation of zero indicates that there is no linear relation between two measures.

Note that the term "correlational research" refers to a research *strategy*, not merely to a particular statistical measure (the correlation). The strategy is one in which researchers examine the relation among variables in a large population of people, where none of the variables is experimentally manipulated. In some circumstances, researchers may not compute a simple correlation coefficient to examine the relation between two variables; they may, for instance, use more complex statistical procedures that determine whether two variables are related, even after controlling for the influence of some other variables. (For example, one might ask whether intelligence test scores are related to personal income after controlling for other variables, such as the income level of one's parents.) Even if such alternative approaches to analyzing data are used, one would still have a correlational research strategy if one is looking at the relation among variables without manipulating these variables experimentally.

Correlational Research: An Example

A compelling example of the power of correlational research to answer questions that cannot be answered through any other technique is found in a study relating personality characteristics to longevity (Danner, Snowdon, & Friesen, 2001). The question being asked in this research is whether the tendency to experience positive emotions is related to how long people live. Prior work had established that people's emotional life can influence their physical well-being. For example, emotions are associated with activation of the autonomic nervous system (ANS); ANS activity, in turn, influences the cardiovascular system (Krantz & Manuck, 1984), which is critical to health. The implication of this prior work is that if one could identify people who differ in their tendencies to experience positive and negative emotions, and could follow these people for a long enough period of time, one might find that people who tended to experience high degrees of positive emotion will live longer. Note that this is a question that can *only* be answered through correlational research. A case study is not convincing because, even if one does identify a case in which someone experiences a lot of positive emotions and lives for many years, it is impossible to know if the single case is typical of people in general. An experimental study is impossible, both because one cannot easily manipulate people's general tendency to experience emotional states and because it would be unethical to manipulate a variable that might lower people's length of life.

Correlational research on this topic could be conducted thanks to a project known as the "nun study" (Danner et al., 2001). This is a study of a large

Research indicates that individuals who experience a relatively high level of positive emotions tend to live longer.

number of Catholic nuns living in the United States. The nuns in the study were all born before the year 1917. In 1930, they had been asked by an administrative official of the Catholic church to write an autobiography. The researchers, with the permission of the nuns, read these autobiographies and coded them according to the amount of positive emotions expressed in the writing. Some autobiographies contained relatively little positive emotional content (e.g., "I intend to do the best for our order, for the spread of religion and for my personal sanctification"), whereas others indicated that the writer experienced high degrees of positive emotion ("the past year ... has been a very happy one. Now I look forward with eager joy ..."; Danner et al., 2001, p. 806).

During the 1990s and the year 2000, approximately 40% of the nuns, who at the time ranged in age from 75 to 95 years, died. The researchers could relate the experience of positive emotions, as indicated in the biographies of 1930, to length of life at the end of the century.

This study revealed a strikingly large relation between emotional experience and length of life. Nuns who experienced more positive emotions in the 1930s lived longer. The relation between emotional experience and longevity can be represented by counting the number of positive emotion words that were used in the autobiographies and dividing the population into quartiles (i.e., four groupings, each representing approximately one-fourth of the population) ranging from low to high amounts of emotion words (Table 2.1). Of the nuns who had expressed a high amount of positive emotions, only about one-fifth died during the observation period. Of the nuns who expressed low amounts of positive emotion, more than half died! This is true even though the high and low groups were of the same age at the beginning of the observation period.

Table 2.1   Relation between Expression of Positive Emotions in Writing as Measured Early in Life and Longevity

Positive Emotion Words	Age	Died (%)
Quartile I (low)	79.9	55
Quartile II	81.1	59
Quartile III	79.7	33
Quartile IV (high)	79.0	21

SOURCE: Danner, D. D., Snowdon, D. A., & Friesen, W. V. (2001). Positive emotions in early life and longevity: Findings from the nun study. *Journal of Personality & Social Psychology*, 80, 804–813.

Correlational Research: Limitations

Correlational studies have been enormously popular among personality psychologists. Yet it is important to be aware of two limitations of this research strategy. The first limitation is one that differentiates correlational studies from case studies. Case studies provide richly detailed information about an individual. In contrast, correlational studies provide relatively superficial information about individual persons. A correlational study will provide information about an individual's scores on the various personality tests that happen to have been used in the research. But if there are some other variables that are important to an individual person, a correlational study generally will not reveal them.

The second limitation is one that case studies and correlational studies share. As in a case study, in a correlational study it is difficult to draw firm conclusions about causality. The fact that two variables are correlated does not mean that one variable necessarily caused the other. There could be a "third variable" that influenced both of the variables in one's study and that caused those variables to be correlated. For example, in the nun study, it is possible that some psychological, biological, or environmental factor that was not measured in the study caused some nuns to experience fewer positive emotions *and* to live less long. As a hypothetical example, if one conducted a study akin to the nun study with college students, one might find that positive emotionality would predict longevity. But that would not necessarily mean that the tendency to experience positive emotions during college caused people to live longer. For example, levels of academic success could function as a third variable. Students who are doing extremely well in college might experience more positive emotions as a result of their academic success. They also might obtain more lucrative jobs after graduation, again as a result of their academic success. Their high-paying jobs might enable them to pay for superior health care, which in turn could lengthen their life whether or not they continue to experience frequent position emotions. In this hypothetical example, emotions and length of life would be correlated, but not because of any direct causal connection between the two. The difficulty of drawing conclusions about causality from either case studies or correlational studies leads investigators to pursue a third approach to research, namely, laboratory experiments.

LABORATORY STUDIES AND EXPERIMENTAL RESEARCH

One of the great achievements of science is not a research finding but a research method: the controlled experiment. The key feature of a controlled

CURRENT APPLICATIONS

PERSONALITY AND HEALTH

As is evident from the "nun study" reviewed in the text, a major area of application for contemporary personality psychology is that of health. Investigators try to discover individual differences in personality qualities that are systematically related to health outcomes.

A particularly informative example of this research trend comes from recent work by a research team from Finland and the United States (Räikkönon, Matthews, & Salomon, 2003). The health outcome of interest to them was cardiovascular disease. As these authors review, the biological factors that put people at risk for cardiovascular problems are already well known. A cluster of factors including obesity, high blood pressure, abnormal levels of lipids (blood fats) in the bloodstream, and insulin resistance (a reduced sensitivity to the action of insulin) puts people at risk for heart problems. Also, it is known that the presence of this cluster of health problems—referred to as "metabolic syndrome"—tends to persist from childhood to adulthood; people who suffer from obesity and insulin resistance as children are likely to suffer from these same problems when they are adults.

It is important, then, to determine the causes of metabolic syndrome. The question the researchers asked is whether personality factors in childhood might predict the development of these biological risk factors.

The personality factor that they chose to study was hostility. This decision was based on prior research. Earlier work had demonstrated a relation, among adults, between cardiovascular problems and tendencies to react to life events with hostility and anger. The authors thus predicted that individual differences in hostility in children would predict the development of aspects of metabolic syndrome.

Note that this is a difficult prediction to test. The idea is not merely that hostility and cardiovascular risk factors will go together, or be correlated. The specific hypothesis is that hostility will *predict* the development of risk factors. Children who experience high amounts of hostility at one point in time are predicted to experience relatively *higher* levels of risk factors at a later point in time. Testing this idea requires a longitudinal research design, that is, a research project in which the relevant variables are assessed at different time points.

The authors executed such a research project. They studied a large group of African-American and European-American children and adolescents. Assessments were conducted twice, at time points separated by an average of more than three years. At both time points, the researchers examined children with high versus low amounts of the cardiovascular risk factors, and asked whether these children differed in their levels of hostility.

At time 1 (i.e., the first assessment session), some children did, and others did not, have the cardiovascular risk factors. The children who did not have those factors at time 1 were of particular interest; the researchers, specifically, were interested in whether these children would develop the biological risk factors by time 2, and whether the personality factor of hostility would predict who did, versus did not, develop the biological risks. Would children who were more hostile at time 1 develop the health problems that put people at risk for heart disease by time 2?

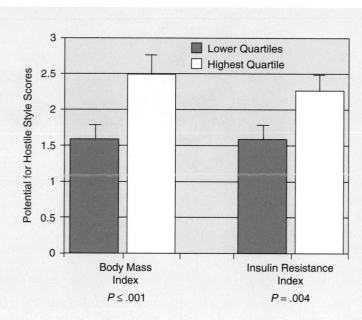

Figure 2.2   *The figure relates individual differences in hostility to the presence of biological factors that are known to put people at risk for cardiovascular problems. People with higher levels of two risk factors, involving body mass (left) and insulin resistance (right), were found to exhibit higher levels of hostility. From Räikkönon, Matthews, & Salomon (2003).*

The researchers found that, as they had expected, hostility predicted the development of cardiovascular risk factors. The graph (Figure 2.2) displays the results for two factors: obesity (measured by body mass index) and insulin resistance. The vertical axis plots levels of hostility, which were assessed by means of an interview; a trained interviewer asked the research participants a series of questions designed to reveal individual differences in their potential to react to situations with a hostile, competitive style of response. Children who developed the two features of the metabolic syndrome by time 2 were found to have differed in hostility at time 1. More hostile children, then, were more likely to develop the cardiovascular risk factors.

Further research is required to determine exactly what explains the link from hostility to health problems. As the authors explain, one possibility is that the development and maturation of biological systems (e.g., growth hormones) is responsible for both hostility and health problems. However, another possibility is that more hostile children are more likely to engage in behaviors that, in turn, create health risks. Hostility may be related to unhealthy lifestyles (smoking, alcohol use, reduced physical activity), and these lifestyles may contribute to the development of health problems. This latter possibility is particularly interesting because it raises the possibility that psychological interventions might have long-term health benefits. Interventions that teach children to control their tendencies to react to the world in a hostile manner may promote better lifestyles and superior health.

SOURCE: RÄIKKÖNEN, MATTHEWS, & SALOMON (2003).

experiment is that participants are assigned at *random* to an experimental condition. The overall experiment contains a number of different conditions that manipulate one or more variables of interest. If people in one condition respond differently than people in another, then one can conclude that the variable that was manipulated causally influenced their responses. This

One technique for learning about personality is laboratory research. Participants take part in activities in controlled laboratory settings that are designed to identify the ways that specific personality processes contribute to emotion, thinking processes, and performance.

conclusion is valid precisely because people are assigned to conditions randomly. Random assignment assures that there is no systematic relationship between the experimental conditions and people's pre-experimental psychological tendencies. If people in different conditions act differently after the experimental manipulation, despite being the same before it occurred, then the manipulation was the cause of the differences in response. This research strategy, in which variables are manipulated through the random assignment of persons to different conditions, is the hallmark of **experimental research**.

Experimental Research: An Example

A powerful example of experimental research comes from work by Claude Steele (1997) and colleagues, who have investigated a phenomenon known as "stereotype threat." Work on stereotype threat explores circumstances in which people are trying to perform well in front of others (e.g., they are taking an exam and other people, such as the course instructor, will know how well they have performed). In such situations, there sometimes exist negative stereotypes concerning the performance of particular social groups. For example, according to some stereotypes, women may not be as good at math as men, or people of different ethnic backgrounds might be thought to be more or less intelligent. If an individual is a member of a group for which there is a stereotype, and if the individual thinks of the stereotype, then a psychological threat arises. There is a threat in the individual's mind that he or she might confirm the stereotype. In many circumstances, this stereotype threat may interfere with one's performance. For example, if you are taking a difficult exam and become distracted by thoughts that you might confirm a stereotype associated with a group of which you are a member, then this distraction might, like any distraction, cause you to perform less well.

In principle, one could study stereotype threat processes through case studies or correlational studies. However, as we have noted, these approaches would not provide convincing evidence that stereotype threat causally influences performance. To explore this potential causal influence, Steele and colleagues have studied stereotype threat experimentally (Steele, 1997). For

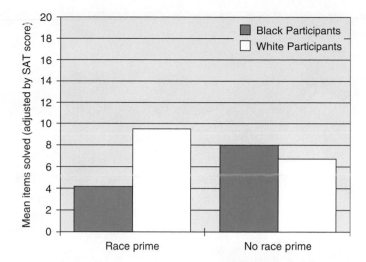

Figure 2.3   *Mean performance on a difficult verbal test, by Black and White research participants, in each of two experimental conditions. The condition varied in whether participants were (Race prime condition) or were not (No race prime condition) asked to indicate their race prior to taking the test. From Steele, 1997.*

example, they have examined the performance of African-American and European-American college students on verbal test items of the sort that might be included on an intelligence test; a negative stereotype about intelligence is one of various stereotypes about African Americans that persist in U.S. culture. The experiment featured two conditions. In one, all participants first completed a demographic questionnaire in which they were asked to indicate their race. In the other, the demographic questionnaire was omitted. Black and white students were assigned at random to one or the other condition. The results of the study revealed that completing the demographic questionnaire lowered the subsequent test performance of black students (Figure 2.3)—stereotype threat processes caused them to perform less well than whites. Although we review this study for the purpose of illustrating the experimental method, one, of course, should also note its social implications. By asking about racial background on demographic questionnaires, one may inadvertently produce differences in intelligence test scores. Thus, if a group of black students were to obtain lower intelligence test scores than white students, this would not necessarily mean that they possess less intelligence; instead, they could be suffering from stereotype-threat processes that cause the test scores to underestimate their actual intellectual capabilities.

Stereotype-threat processes can occur in other settings and with members of other groups. For example, women may be subject to negative stereotypes with regard to performance in mathematics. The threat of confirming these stereotypes may contribute to male-female differences in mathematics test performance. Consistent with this idea, gender differences in which men outperform women in mathematics have been shown to be eliminated when stereotype threat is reduced (Spencer, Steele, & Quinn, 1999). Experimental

Research indicates that if there exists a negative social stereotype about a group, then individual members of that group may perform less well on a test because of stereotype threat processes that interfere with their performance. This can occur even when the individuals are of high intelligence and ability.

research on stereotype threat thus illuminates a general psychological process that contributes to important life outcomes.

EVALUATING ALTERNATIVE RESEARCH APPROACHES

Having now reviewed the three major research strategies, we are in a position to evaluate them in detail. As we already have noted, each has strengths and limitations (Table 2.2).

Case Studies and Clinical Research: Strengths and Limitations

A major advantage of case studies, particularly as they are conducted in clinical settings, is that they overcome the potential superficiality and artificiality of correlational and experimental methods. In a case study, the investigator learns about deeply important aspects of an individual's life, which may not occur in a brief experiment or a survey questionnaire. Clinicians conducting case studies directly observe how the client thinks and feels about events. One examines the behavior of interest directly and does not have to extrapolate from a somewhat artificial setting to the real world.

A further advantage is that clinical research may be the only feasible way of studying some phenomena. When one needs to study the full complexity of personality processes, individual-environment relationships, and the within-person organization of personality, in-depth case studies may be the only option.

In-depth study of a few individuals has two main features that stand in contrast with research on groups (Pervin, 1983). First, relationships established for a group as a whole may not reflect the way any individual behaves or

Table 2.2 Summary of Potential Strengths and Limitations of Alternative Research Methods

Potential Strengths	*Potential Limitations*
CASE STUDIES AND CLINICAL RESEARCH	
1. Avoid the artificiality of laboratory.	1. Lead to unsystematic observation.
2. Study the full complexity of person–environment relationships.	2. Encourage subjective interpretation of data.
3. Lead to in-depth study of individuals.	3. Create entangled relationships among variables.
LABORATORY STUDIES AND EXPERIMENTAL RESEARCH	
1. Manipulate specific variables.	1. Exclude phenomena that cannot be studied in the laboratory.
2. Record data objectively.	2. Create an artificial setting that limits the generality of findings.
3. Establish cause–effect relationships.	3. Foster demand characteristics and experimenter expectancy effects.
QUESTIONNAIRES AND CORRELATION RESEARCH	
1. Study a wide range of variables.	1. Establish relationships that are associational rather than causal.
2. Study relationships among many variables.	2. Problems of reliability and validity of self-report questionnaires.
3. Large samples easily obtained.	3. Individuals not studied in depth.

the way some subgroups of individuals behave. An average learning curve, for example, may not reflect the way any one individual learns. Second, by considering only group data, one may miss some valuable insights into processes going on in particular individuals. Some time ago, Henry Murray argued for the use of individual as well as group studies as follows: "In lay words, the subjects who gave the majority response may have done so for different reasons. Furthermore, a statistical answer leaves unexplained the uncommon (exhibited- by-the-minority) response. One can only ignore it as an unhappy exception to the rule. Averages obliterate the 'individual characters of individual organisms' and so fail to reveal the complex interaction of forces which determine each concrete event" (1938, p. viii). At the same time, such research may involve subjective impressions on the part of researchers, resulting in different observations by each investigator. Insofar as researchers make observations on a subjective basis, they accumulate data that decline considerably in reliability and validity.

Regarding limitations of the case study method, we already have noted two: findings of one case study may not generalize to other people, and the case study method does not provide firm evidence that one psychological process causally influences another. There is a third limitation. Case studies often rely on the subjective impressions of researchers. Rather than relying exclusively on objective measurement procedures, one often must rely on impressionistic reports—for example, impressions of a client's progress written by his or her clinician. The problem is that these reports may reflect not only the qualities of the person being studied, but the qualities of the person who prepares the report. In a typical case study, there is no guarantee that a different researcher examining the same case would come to the same conclusions. This subjective element can lower the reliability and validity of case-study evidence.

Correlational Research and Questionnaires: Strengths and Limitations

As previously noted, a main advantage of correlational studies using questionnaires is that it is possible to study large numbers of people. This has always been an advantage of the correlational strategy; however, in the era of the Internet, it is an even bigger advantage since psychologists can put questionnaires on the Internet and thereby gather information from populations that are dramatically larger and more diverse than was typically previously available.

Another advantage of the correlational approach concerns reliability. Many questionnaires provide extremely reliable indices of the psychological constructs they are designed to measure (Epstein, 1979). This is important in that the reliability of the tests is necessary to detect important features of personality that might be overlooked if one employed measures lacking reliability. For example, researchers find that individual differences in personality traits are highly stable over time; people who differ in extraversion or conscientiousness in young adulthood will probably differ in middle- and later-adulthood as well (e.g., Costa & McCrae, 2002). One could not detect this fact unless the measures of the personality traits were highly reliable.

Regarding limitations, we have noted that correlational studies provide weaker evidence of causal relationship than do experimental studies and that they provide more superficial information about individuals than one generally acquires from a case study. A third limitation concerns the widespread reliance on self-report questionnaires. When describing themselves on a questionnaire, people may be biased to answer items in a way that has nothing to do with the exact content of the items or the psychological construct that the psychologist is trying to assess. These biases are called **response styles**. Two illustrative response-style problems can be considered. The first is called acquiescence. It involves the tendency to agree consistently (or disagree consistently) with items regardless of their content. For example, a test taker may prefer to say "yes" or " I agree" when asked questions, rather than saying " no" or "I disagree." The second response style is called social desirability. Instead of responding to the intended psychological meaning of a test item, a subject may respond to the fact that different types of responses are more or less desirable. If, hypothetically, a test item asks "Have you ever stolen anything from a store?", the answer "no" is clearly a more socially desirable response than "yes." If people are biased to answer questions in a socially desirable manner, then their test scores may not accurately reflect their true psychological characteristics.

A research report that highlights the problem of distortion of questionnaire responses, while also emphasizing the potential value of clinical judgment, is that of Shedler, Mayman, & Manis (1993). In this research, conducted by psychologists with a psychoanalytic orientation who were skeptical of accepting self-report data at face value, individuals who "looked good" on mental health questionnaire scales were evaluated by a psychodynamically oriented clinician. On the basis of his clinical judgments, two subgroups were distinguished: one defined as being genuinely psychologically healthy in agreement with the questionnaire scales and a second defined as consisting of individuals who were psychologically distressed but who maintained an illusion of mental health through defensive denial of their difficulties. Individuals in the two groups were found to differ significantly in their responses to stress. Subjects in the illusory mental health group were found to show much higher levels of coronary reactivity to stress than subjects in the genuinely healthy group. Indeed, the former subjects were found to show even greater levels of coronary reactivity to stress than subjects who reported their distress on the mental health questionnaire scales. The differences in reactivity to stress between the genuinely healthy subjects and the "illusory" healthy subjects were considered not only to be statistically significant but medically significant as well. Thus, it was concluded that "for some people, mental health scales appear to be legitimate measures of mental health. For other people, these scales appear to measure defensive denial. There seems to be no way to know from the test score alone what is being measured in any given respondent" (Shedler et al., 1993, p. 1128).

Those who defend the use of questionnaires note that such problems often can be eliminated through careful test construction and interpretation. Psychologists can reduce or eliminate the effects of acquiescence by varying the wording of items on a test so that consistent "yes" responses do not give one a higher overall test score. They can employ questionnaires that are specifically designed to measure the degree to which a given person tends to endorse socially desirable responses. Comprehensive personality questionnaires commonly include test items or scales to measure whether subjects are faking or trying to present themselves in a particularly favorable or socially desirable way. Including such scales in a research project, however, often is inconvenient or costly, and thus, such scales often are lacking in particular studies.

Laboratory, Experimental Research: Strengths and Limitations

In many ways, our ideal image of scientific investigation is laboratory research. Ask people for their description of a scientist, and they are likely to conjure up an image of someone in a sterile lab. As we have already seen, this image is too limited; personality psychologists employ a range of scientific methods, and laboratory research is but one of them. Yet it is an important one. The experimental approach, as we have noted, has the unique ability to manipulate variables of interest and thereby to establish cause-effect relationships. In the experiment that is properly designed and carried out, every step is carefully planned to limit effects to the variables of interest. Few variables are studied, so that the problem of disentangling complex relationships does not exist. Systematic relationships between changes in some variables and consequences for other variables are established so that the experimenter can say: "If X, then Y." Full details of the experimental procedure are reported so that the results can be replicated by investigators in other laboratories.

Psychologists who are critical of laboratory research suggest that too often such research is artificial and limited in relevance to other contexts. The suggestion is that what works in the laboratory may not work elsewhere. Furthermore, although relationships between isolated variables may be established, such relationships may not hold when the complexity of actual human behavior is considered. Also, since laboratory research tends to involve relatively brief exposures to stimuli, such research may miss important processes that occur over time. As you read about personality research in the subsequent chapters of this book, a question to ask yourself is how successful the different theories are in establishing experimental findings that generalize to real-world situations.

As a human enterprise, experimental research with humans lends itself to influences that are part of everyday interpersonal behavior. The investigation of such influences might be called the social psychology of research. Let us consider two important illustrations. First, there may be factors influencing the behavior of human subjects that are not part of the experimental design. Among such factors may be cues implicit in the experimental setting that suggest to the subject that the experimenter has a certain hypothesis and, "in the interest of science," the subject behaves in a way that will confirm it. Such effects are known as **demand characteristics** and suggest that the psycho-logical experiment is a form of social interaction in which subjects give purpose and meaning to things (Orne, 1962; Weber & Cook, 1972). The purpose and meaning given to the research may vary from subject to subject in ways that are not part of the experimental design and thereby serve to reduce both reliability and validity.

Complementing these sources of error or bias in the subject are unintended sources of influence or error in the experimenter. Without realizing it, experimenters may either make errors in recording and analyzing data or emit cues to the subjects and thus influence their behavior in a particular way. Such unintended **experimenter expectancy effects** may lead subjects to behave in accordance with the hypothesis (Rosenthal, 1994; Rosenthal & Rubin, 1978). For example, consider the classic case of Clever Hans (Pfungst, 1911). Hans was a horse that by tapping his foot could add, subtract, multiply, and divide. A mathematical problem would be presented to the horse and, incredibly, he was able to come up with the answer. In attempting to discover the secret of Hans's talents, a variety of situational factors were manipulated. If Hans could not see the questioner or if the questioner did not know the answer, Hans was unable to provide the correct answer. On the other hand, if the questioner knew the answer and was visible, Hans could tap out the answer with his foot. Apparently the questioner unknowingly signaled Hans when to start and stop tapping his hoof: The tapping would start when the questioner inclined his head forward, increase in speed when the questioner bent forward more, and stop when the questioner straightened up. As can be seen, experimenter expectancy effects can be quite subtle and neither the researcher nor subject may be aware of their existence.

It should be noted that demand characteristics and expectancy effects can occur as sources of error in all three forms of research. However, they have been considered and studied most often in relation to experimental research. In addition, as noted, experimental research often is seen as most closely approximating the scientific ideal. Therefore, such sources of error are all the more noteworthy in relation to this form of research.

Many of the criticisms of experimental research have been attacked by experimental psychologists. In defending laboratory experiments, the following statements are made: (1) Such research is the proper basis for testing causal hypotheses. The generality of the established relationship is then a subject for further investigation. (2) Some phenomena would never be discovered outside of the laboratory. (3) Some phenomena can be studied in the laboratory that would be difficult to study elsewhere (e.g., subjects are given permission to be aggressive in contrast with the often quite strong restraints in natural social settings). (4) There is little empirical support for the contention that subjects typically try to confirm the experimenter's hypothesis or for the significance of experimental artifacts more generally. Indeed, many subjects are more negativistic than conforming (Berkowitz & Donnerstein, 1982).

Even if one accepts these four points, there remains one criticism of laboratory research that is difficult, if not impossible, to overcome. It is that some phenomena simply cannot be produced in the laboratory. A personality theory may make predictions about people's emotional reactions to extreme levels of stress or their thoughts about highly personal matters. For such questions, laboratory methods may not work. It would be unethical to create extremely high levels of stress in the lab. In a brief laboratory encounter, people are unlikely to reveal any thoughts about matters that are highly personal. The personality scientist sometimes is not afforded the luxury of the simple laboratory study.

SUMMARY OF STRENGTHS AND LIMITATIONS

In assessing these alternative approaches to research we must recognize that we are considering potential, rather than necessary, strengths and limitations (Table 2.2). In fact, findings from one approach generally coincide with those from another approach (Anderson, Lindsay, & Bushman, 1999). What it comes down to is that each research effort must be evaluated on its own merits and for its own potential in advancing understanding rather than on some preconceived basis. Alternative research procedures can be used in conjunction with one another in any research enterprise. In addition, data from alternative research procedures can be integrated in the pursuit of a more comprehensive theory.

THE USE OF VERBAL REPORTS

All three forms of research—case studies, correlational studies, and laboratory experiments—commonly make use of verbal reports, that is, things people say about their psychological states. Research does not necessarily have to use verbal reports. For example, if one wants to know people's emotional reactions, one could code their facial expressions or physiological responses rather than asking them to report, verbally, the emotions they are feeling. Nonetheless, a very large percentage of research on personality relies on verbal report data.

In making use of verbal reports, we are confronted with special problems associated with such data. Treating what people say as accurate reflections of what has actually occurred or is actually going on has come under attack from two very different groups. First, psychoanalysts and dynamically oriented psychologists (Chapters 3 and 4) argue that people often distort things for unconscious reasons: "Children perceive inaccurately, are very little conscious of their inner states and retain fallacious recollections of occurrences. Many adults are hardly better" (Murray, 1938, p. 15). Second, many experimental psychologists argue that people do not have access to their internal processes and respond to interviewer questions in terms of some inferences they make about what must have been going on rather than accurately reporting what actually occurred (Nisbett & Wilson, 1977; Wilson, Hull, & Johnson, 1981). For example, despite experimenter evidence that subjects make decisions in accord with certain experimental manipulations, the subjects themselves may report having behaved in a particular way for very different reasons. Or, to take another example, when consumers are asked about why they purchased a product in a supermarket they may give a reason that is very different from what can experimentally be demonstrated to have been the case. In a sense, people give subjective reasons for behaving as they do, but may not give the actual causes. In sum, the argument is that whether for defensive reasons or because of "normal" problems people have in keeping track of their internal processes, verbal self-reports are questionable sources of reliable and valid data (West & Finch, 1997; Wilson, 1994).

Other psychologists argue that verbal reports should be accepted for what they are—data (Ericsson & Simon, 1993). The argument is made that there is no intrinsic reason to treat verbal reports as any less useful data than an overt motor response such as pressing a lever. Indeed, it is possible to analyze the verbal responses of people in as objective, systematic, and quantitative a fashion as their other behavioral responses. If verbal responses are not automatically discounted, then the question becomes, Which kinds of verbal responses are most useful and trustworthy? Here the argument is made that subjects can only report about things they are attending to or have attended to. If the experimenter asks the subject to remember or explain things that were never attended to in the first place, the subject will either make an inference or state a hypothesis about what occurred (White, 1980). Thus, if you later ask persons why they purchased one product over another in the supermarket when they were not attending to this decision at the time, they will give you an inference or a hypothesis rather than an account of what occurred.

Those who argue in favor of the use of verbal reports suggest that when they are elicited with care and the circumstances involved are appreciated, they can be a useful source of information. Although the term *introspection* (i.e., verbal descriptions of a process going on inside a person) was discredited long ago by experimental psychologists, there is now increased interest in the potential use of such data. In accepting the potential use of verbal reports, we may expand the universe of potential data for rich and meaningful observation. At the same time, we must keep in mind the goals and requirements of reliability and validity. Thus, we must insist on evidence that the same observations and interpretations can be made by other investigators and that the data do reflect the concepts they are presumed to measure. In appreciating the merits and vast potential of verbal reports, we must also be aware of the potential for misuse and naive interpretation. In sum, verbal reports as data should receive the same scrutiny as other research observations.

In Chapter 1, we considered the nature of personality theory: psychologists' efforts to systematize what is known about personality and to point research in directions that yield new knowledge. In this chapter, we have considered the nature of personality research: psychologists' efforts to bring objective scientific evidence to bear on their theories. We reviewed the kinds of data obtained by personality psychologists, and then the strengths and limits of three traditional types of personality research (case studies, correlational research, and laboratory experiments).

PERSONALITY THEORY AND PERSONALITY RESEARCH

As we already have noted, personality theory and personality research are not two separate, unrelated enterprises. They are inherently intertwined. Theory and research are related for two reasons, one of which we already have noted: Theoretical conceptions suggest avenues for exploration and specify the types of data that qualify as "evidence" about personality. Personality researchers are interested in a person's physiological reactions and are uninterested in their astrological signs because personality theories contain ideas that relate physiology to psychological functioning, while leaving no room for the influence of astrological forces.

Theory and research tend to be related in another way. Theorists have preferences and biases concerning how research should be conducted. The father of American behaviorism, John B. Watson, emphasized the use of animals in research in part because of his discomfort in working with humans. Sigmund Freud, founder of psychoanalytic theory, was a therapist who did not believe that important psychoanalytic phenomena could be studied in any manner other than in therapy. Hans Eysenck and Raymond Cattell, two trait theorists of historic importance, were trained, early in their careers, in sophisticated statistical methods involving correlation, and these methods fundamentally shaped their theoretical ideas. Historically, personality researchers have tended to fall on one or the other side of three issues associated with the three approaches to research: (1) "making things happen" in research (experimental) versus "studying what has occurred" (correlational), (2) all persons (experimental) versus the single individual (clinical), and (3) one aspect or few aspects of the person versus the total individual. In other words, there are preferences or biases toward clinical, experimental, and correlational research. Despite the objectivity of science, research is a human enterprise and such preferences are part of research as a human enterprise. All researchers attempt to be as objective as possible in the conduct of their research and generally they give "objective" reasons for following a particular approach to research. That is, the particular strengths of the research approach followed are emphasized relative to the strengths and limitations of alternative approaches. Beyond this, however, a personal element enters in. Just as psychologists feel more comfortable with one or another kind of data, they feel more comfortable with one or another approach to research.

Further, different theories of personality are linked with different research strategies and thereby with different kinds of data. In other words, the links among theory, data, and research are such that the observations associated with one theory of personality often are of a fundamentally different type than those associated with another theory. The phenomena of interest to one theory of personality are not as easily studied by the research procedures useful in the study of phenomena emphasized by another theory of personality. One personality theory leads us to obtain one kind of data and follow one approach to research whereas another theory leads us to collect different kinds of data and follow another approach to research. It is not that one or another is better but rather that they are different, and these differences must be appreciated in considering each approach to theory and research. This has been true historically, and remains true in the current scientific discipline (Cervone, 1991). Since the remaining chapters in this text are organized around the major theoretical approaches to personality, it is important to keep such linkages and differences in mind in comparing one theory with another.

PERSONALITY ASSESSMENT AND THE CASE OF JIM

As we have seen, personality research involves the effort to measure individuals on a personality characteristic assumed to be of theoretical importance. The term *assessment* generally is used to refer to efforts to measure personality aspects of individuals in order to make an applied or practical decision: Will this person be a good candidate for this job? Will this person profit from one or another kind of treatment? Is this person a good candidate for this training program? In addition, the term *assessment* often is used to refer to the effort to arrive at a comprehensive understanding of individuals by obtaining a wide variety of information about them. In this sense, assessment of a person involves administering a variety of personality tests or measures in the pursuit of a comprehensive understanding of his or her personality. As noted, such an effort also provides for a comparison of results from different sources of information. This book assumes that each technique of assessment gives a glimpse of human behavior, and that no one test gives, or can hope to give, a picture of the total personality of an individual. People are complex, and our efforts to assess personality must reflect this complexity. In the chapters that follow, we will consider a number of theories of personality and approaches to personality assessment. In addition, we will consider the assessment of an individual, Jim, from the standpoint of each theory and approach to assessment. Through this approach we will be able to see the relation between theory and assessment, and also to consider the extent to which different approaches result in similar pictures of the person.

Before we describe Jim, some details concerning the assessment project will be presented. Jim was a college student when, in the late 1960s, he volunteered to serve as a subject for a project involving the intensive study of college students. He participated in the project mainly because of his interest in psychology, but also because he hoped to gain a better understanding of himself. At the time, a variety of tests were administered to him. These tests represented a sampling of the tests then available. Obviously, theories of personality and associated tests that had not been developed at the time could not be administered. However, Jim agreed to report on his life experiences and to take some additional tests 5, 20, and 25 years later. At those times, an effort was made to administer tests developed in association with emerging theories of personality.

Thus, we do not have the opportunity to consider all the tests at the same point in time. However, we are able to consider the personality of an individual over an extended period of time, and thereby examine how the theories—and the tests—relate to what occurred earlier in life and what followed later. Let us begin with a brief sketch derived from Jim's autobiography and follow him throughout the text as we consider the various approaches to personality.

AUTOBIOGRAPHICAL SKETCH OF JIM

In his autobiography Jim reported that he was born in New York City after the end of World War II and received considerable attention and affection as a child. His father is a college graduate who owns an automobile sales business; his mother is a housewife who also does volunteer reading for the blind. Jim described himself as having a good relationship with his father and described his mother as having "great feelings for other people—she is a totally 'loving' woman." He is the oldest of four children, with a sister four years younger and two brothers, one five years younger and one seven years younger. The main themes in his autobiography concern his inability to become involved with women in a satisfying way, his need for success and his relative failure since high school, and his uncertainty about whether to go on to graduate school in business administration or in clinical psychology. Overall he felt that people had a high estimate of him because they used superficial criteria, but that inwardly he was troubled.

We have here the bare outline of a person. The details will be filled in as he is considered from the standpoint of different personality theories. Hopefully, by the end of the book, a complete picture of Jim will emerge.

MAJOR CONCEPTS

Case studies An approach to research in which one studies an individual person in great detail. This strategy commonly is associated with clinical research, that is, research conducted by a therapist in the course of in-depth experiences with a client.

Correlational coefficient A numerical index that summarizes the degree to which two variables are related linearly.

Correlational research An approach to research in which existing individual differences are measured and related to one another, rather than being manipulated as in experimental research.

Demand characteristics Cues that are implicit (hidden) in the experimental setting and influence the subject's behavior.

Experimental research An approach to research in which the experimenter manipulates a variable of interest, usually by assigning different research participants, at random, to different experimental conditions.

Experimenter expectancy effects Unintended experimenter effects involving behaviors that lead subjects to respond in accordance with the experimenter's hypothesis.

Idiographic (strategies) Strategies of assessment and research in which the primary goal is to obtain a portrait of the potentially unique, idiosyncratic individual.

L-data Life record data or information concerning the person that can be obtained from the person's life history or life record.

Nomothetic (strategies) Strategies of assessment and research in which the primary goal is to identify a common set of principles or laws that apply to all members of a population of persons.

O-data Observer data or information provided by knowledgeable observers such as parents, friends, or teachers.

Reliability   The extent to which observations are stable, dependable, and can be replicated.

Response style   The tendency of some subjects to respond to test items in a consistent, patterned way that has to do with the form of the questions or answers rather than with their content.

S-data   Self-report data or information provided by the subject.

T-data   Test data or information obtained from experimental procedures or standardized tests.

Validity   The extent to which observations reflect the phenomena or constructs of interest to us (also "construct validity").

REVIEW

1. Research involves the systematic study of relationships among phenomena or events. Four types of data are obtained in personality research: L-data, O-data, T-data, and S-data (LOTS). Three approaches to personality research are clinical research, laboratory experimentation, and correlational research using questionnaires.

2. All research shares the goals of reliability and validity—of obtaining observations that can be replicated and for which there is evidence of a relation to the concepts of interest. As a human enterprise, research involves ethical questions concerning the treatment of subjects and the reporting of data.

3. Clinical research involves the intensive study of individuals. This research method was illustrated by a case study involving the self-concept of an individual as he confronted the different social situations of his life.

4. In correlational research the investigator measures two or more variables and determines the degree to which they are associated with each other. Questionnaire measures are particularly important in correlational research. This research method was illustrated with research in which personality factors were found to predict longevity.

5. Experimental research involves the manipulation of one or more variables to determine their causal impact on outcomes of interest. This approach to research was illustrated by the manipulation of variables related to the phenomenon of stereotype threat.

6. Theories of personality differ in their preferences for types of data and approaches to research. In other words, there tend to be linkages among theory, type of data, and method of research. It is important to keep such linkages in mind as the major theories of personality are considered in the chapters that follow. A single case studied from the standpoint of each theoretical perspective also will be presented for illustrative and comparative purposes.

A PSYCHODYNAMIC THEORY: FREUD'S PSYCHOANALYTIC THEORY OF PERSONALITY

3

Chapter Focus

The number one player on the tennis team is getting ready to play for the state title. She has never met her opponent before, so she decides to introduce herself before the match. She strolls out onto the court where her opponent is warming up and says. "Hi, I'm Amy. Glad to beat you." You can imagine how embarrassed Amy was! Flustered, she corrected her innocent mistake and walked over to her side of the court to warm up. "Wow," Amy thought, "where did that come from?"

Was Amy's verbal slip so innocent? Freud wouldn't have thought so. In his view, Amy's silly mistake was actually a very revealing display of unconscious aggressive drives. Freud's psychoanalytic theory is illustrative of a psychodynamic and clinical approach to personality. Behavior is interpreted as a result of the dynamic interplay among motives, drives, needs, and conflicts. The research consists mainly of clinical investigations as shown in an emphasis on the individual, in the attention given to individual differences, and in attempts to assess and understand the total individual. Contemporary researchers, however, devote much attention to the challenge of studying psychodynamic processes in the experimental laboratory.

QUESTIONS TO BE ADDRESSED IN THIS CHAPTER

1. How did Freud develop his theory and how did historical and personal events shape this development?

2. What are the key features of Freud's theoretical model of the human mind?

3. How do people protect themselves against experiences of anxiety, and in what ways (according to Freud) are these anxiety-reduction strategies a centerpiece of personality dynamics?

4. How important is early childhood experience for later personality development?

SIGMUND FREUD (1856–1939): A VIEW OF THE THEORIST

Sigmund Freud was born in Moravia (in what is now the city of Fribor of the Czech Republic) in 1856. His family soon moved to Vienna, where he spent most of his life. Freud was the first child of his parents, but his father, 20 years older than his mother, had two sons by a previous marriage. His parents then had seven more children after his birth. Within this large group of family members, the intellectually precocious Sigmund was his mother's favorite—and he knew it. Later in life, Freud famously commented, from experience, that a man who has been the indisputable favorite of his mother "keeps for life the feeling of a conqueror, that confidence of success that often induces real success" (Freud, 1900, p. 26).

As a boy, Freud dreamed of becoming a great general or government official. But concern about anti-Semitism in these fields led Freud, who was Jewish, to contemplate a medical career instead. He enrolled in medical school at the University of Vienna, where he received training that profoundly shaped the

Sigmund Freud

personality theory he developed later in life. A key figure in Freud's intellectual development was a professor of physiology named Ernst Brücke. Brücke was part of an intellectual movement of the time known as **mechanism**. The mechanist movement argued that the principles of natural science could explain not only the behavior of physical objects, but human thought and behavior as well (Gay, 1998). People could be understood in terms of basic physical and chemical mechanisms. This way of thinking opened the door for a complete natural science of persons. Nowadays most scientists take this idea for granted. But in Freud's time, mechanism was a major point of debate. The counter-argument, an idea known as vitalism, was that a non-physical spiritual force is responsible for life. Brücke rejected vitalism, teaching instead that humans are dynamic physiological systems whose functioning adheres entirely to basic physical and chemical principles, such as the principle of conservation of energy. This teaching was a foundation for the dynamic view of personality Freud developed later in life (Sulloway, 1979).

After earning his medical degree, Freud worked in the field of neurology. Some of his early research involved a comparison of adult and fetal brains. He concluded that the earliest structures persist throughout life—a view that was a precursor to his later views of personality development. However, for financial reasons, including the need to support a family, Freud abandoned this research career and became a practicing physician.

In 1897, the year following his father's death, Freud was plagued by periods of depression and anxiety. To understand his problems, Freud began an activity that proved utterly fundamental to the development of psychoanalysis: a *self*-analysis. Freud analyzed the contents of his own experiences, concentrating in particular on the meaning of his dreams, which he thought would reveal unconscious thoughts and desires. He continued this self-analysis throughout his life, devoting the last half-hour of each workday to it.

In his therapeutic work, Freud tried a variety of techniques in an effort to uncover the underlying psychological causes of his patient's problems. For a while, he relied on the technique of hypnosis, which he learned about from the renowned French psychiatrist Jean Charcot. But, finding that not all patients could be hypnotized, he explored other methods, eventually hitting upon one that became crucial to his efforts: **free association**. In the free-association technique, the person being analyzed allows all of his or her thoughts to come forth without inhibition or falsification of any kind. The idea is to let one's thoughts flow freely, to discover potentially hidden associations among ideas. For Freud, the free-association technique was not only a treatment method but a scientific method. It provided the primary evidence for his theory of personality.

In 1900, Freud published his most significant work, *The Interpretation of Dreams*. In this book, Freud no longer was concerned merely with treating patients. He also was developing a theory of mind, that is, a theory of the basic structures and working principles of the human psyche.

Despite his brilliance, things did not go smoothly for Freud. In its first eight years of publication, *The Interpretation of Dreams* sold only 600 copies. Freud's views about the psychology of childhood, including his belief in infantile sexuality and its relation to perversions and neuroses, were ridiculed. Medical institutions that taught Freud's views were boycotted. An early follower, Ernest Jones, was forced to resign a neurological appointment for inquiring into the sexual life of his patients. At a personal level, during World War I Freud lost his financial savings and feared for the lives of two sons in the war. In 1920, a daughter, age 26, died. This historical context may have partly contributed to Freud's development, at age 64, of a theory of the death instinct—a wish to die, in opposition to the life instinct or a wish for survival.

Yet Freud persevered and gradually achieved recognition to match his intellectual achievements. Lectures in the United States in 1909 greatly enhanced Freud's profile outside of Europe. An International Psychoanalytic Association was founded in 1910. During these and subsequent years, Freud published prolifically, had a waiting list of patients, and achieved increasing fame. Thanks to his efforts and those of his followers, by the time of his death in London on September 23, 1939 (he had fled Vienna a year earlier to escape the Nazis), he was an international celebrity. Today, Freud's ideas and his psychoanalytic terminology are known even to people who never have read a word of his writing or never have taken a psychology course. Among 20th-century figures, Freud's contributions to Western intellectual life are exceeded perhaps only by those of Einstein.

Freud, the man, has been glorified by many as a compassionate, courageous genius. Others, noting his many battles and breaks with colleagues, see him as rigid, authoritarian, and intolerant of the opinions of others (Fromm, 1959). Whatever the interpretation of Freud's personality, he unquestionably pursued his work with great courage. When publishing his self-analyses, he bravely presented personal details of his own life. He courageously withstood the criticism of colleagues and the scorn of society at large. He did this, as he wrote to an associate, "in the service" of "a dominating passion... a tyrant [that] has come my way... it is psychology" (Gay, 1998, p. 74).

FREUD'S VIEW OF THE PERSON

Throughout this book, when we introduce a theory of personality we first will review the life of the theorist (as in the review of Freud's life above). Then, prior to detailing the given theory's treatment of personality structures and processes, we will present its overall view of the person. Each major theory of personality contains a broad conception of human nature, or a view of the person. We will present these overarching conceptions of human nature prior to moving to the other theoretical details. We do this for two reasons. First, these sections give you an immediate foundation for understanding. You quickly will gain knowledge of the most important ideas of a given theory—knowledge you can build upon when reading subsequent material.

FREUD'S VIEW OF THE PERSON

Second, these sections answer a question you might ask yourself: "Why should I bother to learn about these personality theories?" The answer is that the theories address big ideas: the nature of mind, of human nature, of society, and of the relation between the individual and social world. These "big picture" ideas will be summarized in the *View of the Person* sections of the text.

THE MIND AS AN ENERGY SYSTEM

Freud's theory of personality is fundamentally a theory of mind—a scientific model of the overall architecture of mental structures and processes. In formulating a model of mind, Freud explicitly "[considers] mental life from a *biological* point of view"(Freud, 1915/1970, p. 328). He recognizes the mind as part of the body, asks what the body is like, and derives principles of mental functioning from overall principles of physiological functioning.

As we noted above, to Freud the body is a mechanistic **energy system**. It follows, then, that the mind, being part of the body, also is a mechanistic energy system. The mind gets mental energies from the overall physical energies of the body.

An energy-system view of mind contrasts with alternative perspectives one could adopt. For example, one instead could view the mind as an information system. In an information system, material is merely stored somewhere and drawn upon when needed. Information on the hard drive of your computer, or information written into a book on the shelf of a library, is like this—it merely sits there inertly, in storage, to be accessed as needed. In Freud's energy model, however, mental contents do not merely sit in storage inertly. Mental contents *do* things. The mind contains instinctual drives that are "piece[s] of activity" that exert "pressure. . . [an] amount of force" (Freud, 1915/1970, p. 328) on the overall psychic apparatus. The overall mind, then, is a system that contains and directs these energetic forces.

If one takes this view, then the major scientific problem is to explain what happens to mental energy: how it flows, gets sidetracked, or becomes dammed up. Freud's view of mental energy includes three core ideas. One is that there is a limited amount of energy. If much energy is used in one way, less is available for other purposes. Energy used for cultural purposes, for example, is no longer available for sexual purposes, and vice versa. A second idea is that energy can be blocked from one channel of expression and, if it is blocked, the energy does not "just go away." Instead, it gets expressed in some other manner, along a path of least resistance. Finally, fundamental to Freud's energy model is that the mind functions to achieve a state of quiescence (Greenberg & Mitchell, 1983). Bodily needs create a state of tension, and the person is driven to reduce that tension to return to a quiet internal state. A simple example is that if you are lacking food, you experience the state of tension we call hunger, and this drives you to seek some object in the environment that satisfies your hunger, eliminating the tension and returning you to a state of quiescence. (Freud of course explores examples of dramatically greater complexity than this one, as you will see.) The goal of all behavior, then, is the pleasure that results from the reduction of tension or the release of energy. The personality theory of Freud that you will learn about in this chapter is basically a detailed model of the personality structures and processes that are responsible for this dynamic flow of mental energy.

Why the assumption that the mind is an energy system? It derives from developments in physics in Freud's time. The 19th-century physicist Helmholtz had presented the principle of conservation of energy: matter and energy can be transformed but not destroyed. Not only physicists but also members of other disciplines were studying the laws of energy changes in systems. Freud's medical training included the idea that human physiology could be understood in terms of physical forces that adhere to the principle of conservation of energy. The age of energy and dynamics provided scientists with a new conception of humans: "that man is an energy system and that he obeys the same physical laws which regulate the soap bubble and the movement of the planets" (Hall, 1954, pp. 12–13). Freud developed this general view into a well-specified theory of personality.

In psychoanalysis, then, ideas have mental energy associated with them and that energy remains stored in the mind (i.e., the energy is conserved). However, under special circumstances the energy associated with an idea can be released. The question of how this occurs is utterly central to psychoanalytic theory. Interestingly, the answer to this question did not at first come from Freud. Instead it was taught to him by a professional associate, the Viennese physician Joseph Breuer. In the summer of 1882, in an event of incalculably great importance to the development of psychoanalytic thought, Breuer told Freud about a patient of his named Anna O. (see Jones, 1961). Anna O. suffered from a bizarre collection of symptoms whose biological causes could not be determined: partial paralysis, blurred vision, persistent cough, and (perhaps most oddly) difficulty conversing in her native language, German, despite being able to speak fluently in her second language, English. These biologically inexplicable symptoms were known as hysterical symptoms, that is, symptoms of the disorder *hysteria*. (The term *hysteria* has been used since the days of ancient Greek medicine to refer to emotional disorders that manifest themselves in physical symptoms. In the contemporary psychiatric literature, this problem is known as somatization disorder.) Anna O. herself stumbled upon a treatment for her symptoms. She found that she would experience relief from a symptom if she could trace it to an event in her past. If she managed to become aware of a long-forgotten event that was the original cause of the symptom, and if she relived the original emotional trauma associated with that event, the symptom would then either be reduced in severity or completely go away.

Breuer, and then Freud, referred to this psychological experience as a **catharsis**. Catharsis refers to a release and freeing of emotions by talking about one's problems. (In colloquial terms, we might say that in catharsis the person gets an experience "off his chest" or gets it "out of his system.") By re-experiencing a traumatic event that she had stored away in her memory, Anna O. experienced a cathartic release of the pent-up mental energy that was causing her symptoms. Freud applied the cathartic method of treating hysterical symptoms to his own patients and reported great success.

The notion of catharsis has two implications for understanding the human mind. One is that, to Freud, it further confirms his view that the mind is an energy system. It is the release of the energy associated with long-forgotten memories that allows for the patient's improvement. The second implication is the following. Before a cathartic experience, Freud's patients appeared totally unaware that their symptoms were caused by the contents of their mind.

The traumatic events that originally caused their symptoms seemingly were completely forgotten. Yet the symptoms continued. This means that mental contents *of which people were unaware* were continuously active within their own minds. The mind, then, appears to have more than one part. It not only has a region of ideas of which people are consciously aware, but also a more mysterious, hidden region of ideas that lie outside of awareness. Freud refers to these ideas as *unconscious*. Freud's notion (which we review in detail below) that our day-to-day psychological life is governed by ideas that are unconscious revolutionized people's understanding of human nature.

When mental energy cannot be released, it does not merely disappear. It is conserved (as suggested by the physics principle of conservation of energy). Energy that would otherwise be released in the pursuit of sexual pleasure, but that is inhibited, may be channeled into other activities. A wide range of activities—indeed, Freud believed the whole range of cultural productivity—were expressions of sexual and aggressive energy that were prevented from expression in a more direct way.

THE INDIVIDUAL IN SOCIETY

A second major aspect of Freud's view of the person concerns the relation between the individual and society. Freud's conception is particularly powerful because it contrasts with an alternative view that had been central to Western culture. The alternative is that people are essentially good, but society corrupts them. People are born innocent but experience a world of temptations and fall from grace. This is the story of the Old Testament: Adam and Eve, created in God's image, are born with inherent innocence and goodness, but are corrupted through the temptation of Satan. This view also is prominent is Western philosophy. The great French philosopher Rousseau argued that, prior to the development of contemporary civilization, people were relatively content and experienced primarily feelings of compassion toward others. Civilization, he thought, changed things for the worse by creating competition for resources that, in turn, fostered feelings of jealousy and suspicion.

Freud turned this conception on its head. In psychoanalysis, sexual and aggressive drives are an inborn part of human nature. Individuals, functioning according to a *pleasure principle*, seek the pleasurable gratification of those drives. The role of society is to curb these biologically natural tendencies. A major function of "civilization [is] to restrict sexual life" (Freud, 1930/1949, p. 51). Society teaches the child that biologically naturally drives are socially unacceptable and maintains social norms and taboos that drive this lesson home. Civilized society, then, does not cause innocent children to "fall from grace." Children are far from grace when born; they possess erotic desires and aggressive drives that society takes steps to restrict. The response of civilization to these sexual drives of the individual is akin to the response of a politically dominant segment of society trying to maintain its power against a suppressed underclass: "fear of a revolt by the suppressed elements drives it to stricter precautionary measures" (Freud, 1930/1949, p. 51).

Freud's overall theory, then, includes not only a radical view of the mind but also this equally radical rethinking of the relation between the individual and society.

FREUD'S VIEW OF THE SCIENCE OF PERSONALITY

Freud's training in medical sciences gave him a deep appreciation of the relationship between theory and research and the need for sharp definitions of theoretical concepts. He wanted to establish a theory of persons that was as scientifically rigorous as theories in the physical and biological sciences. However, Freud recognized that, especially in the early stages of a science, speculative theorizing might be necessary. Thus, he boldly plunged ahead in theorizing, creating a conceptual framework of enormous breadth. Freud looked forward to future work, in his lifetime and beyond, that might confirm his core insights into human nature.

A unique aspect of Freud's approach to personality science was the type of data that he did, and did not, use to construct his theory. Unlike all the other personality theorists you will learn about in this book, Freud neither ran experiments in a laboratory nor created or used standard psychological tests. He had faith in only one of the three forms of evidence you learned about in Chapter 2: case study evidence. Freud based his theory entirely on clinical case studies, analyzed via the method of free association. He felt that this form of evidence was the only one that provided enough detail about the mind of the individual to yield valid conclusions about personality. Freud and others trained in his methods provided an incredible wealth of information about individual clients; probably no other method in psychology even approximates the information about the individual that is yielded in a psychoanalytic case study.

To the contemporary scientist, Freud's lack of interest in laboratory research is a subject of criticism. "Instead of training scientists," one scholar writes, "Freud ended up training practitioners in a relatively fixed system of ideas" (Sulloway, 1991, p. 275). Only after Freud's lifetime did large numbers of research psychologists investigate the questions of unconscious mental life that was addressed by Freud. One of our goals in this chapter and the next is to introduce you to contemporary research findings on psychoanalytical ideas.

FREUD'S PSYCHOANALYTIC THEORY OF PERSONALITY

You learned in Chapter 1 that theories of personality address a distinct set of topics that includes personality structures, processes, and development. The distinctions are particularly clear in the work of Freud. His psychoanalytic theory addresses each of these topics in much detail, as we will now see.

STRUCTURE

Freud's goal in analyzing personality structure was to provide a conceptual model for understanding the human mind. He asked, "What are the basic structures of the mind, and what do they do?" The highly original answers he provided are complex. Freud provided not one, but two conceptual models of the mind; the models complemented one another. One model addressed levels of consciousness: Are the contents of mind something that we are aware of (conscious) or not (unconscious)? The other concerns functional systems in the mind: What does a given mental system do? We review these models in turn.

CURRENT QUESTIONS ——————————————————————————————

WHAT PRICE THE SUPPRESSION OF EXCITING THOUGHTS?

Freud suggested that the price of progress in civilization is increased inhibition of the pleasure principle and a heightened sense of guilt. Does civilization require such an inhibition? What are the costs to the individual of efforts to suppress wishes and inhibit "unbridled gratification" of desires?

Research by Daniel Wegner and his associates suggests that the suppression of exciting thoughts may be involved in the production of negative emotional responses and the development of psychological symptoms such as phobias (irrational fears) and obsessions (preoccupation with uncontrollable thoughts). In this research, subjects were told not to think about sex. Trying not to think about sex produced emotional arousal, just as it did in subjects given permission to think about sex. Although arousal decreased after a few minutes in both groups, what followed differed for subjects in the two groups. In the first group, the effort to suppress exciting thoughts led to the intrusion of these thoughts into consciousness and the reintroduction of surges of emotion. This was not found when subjects were given the opportunity to think about sex.

The researchers suggest that the suppression of exciting thoughts can promote excitement; that is, the very act of suppression may make these thoughts even more stimulating than when we purposefully dwell on them. In sum, such efforts at suppression may not serve us well either emotionally or psychologically.

SOURCE: PETRIE, BOOTH, & PENNEBAKER, 1998; WEGNER, 1992; 1994; WEGNER et al., 1990.

Levels of Consciousness and the Concept of the Unconscious

What's going on in your mind? What thoughts are in your head? We generally answer this question by paying attention to our flow of thinking; for example, right now you may be thinking about the material in this chapter or about things you would prefer to be doing if you didn't have to read this chapter for class. This flow of thoughts—the mental contents that you are aware of just by paying attention to your own thinking—are called "conscious" thoughts. One of Freud's great insights is that the flow of conscious thoughts is *not* a complete answer to the question, What's going on in your mind? Far from it. To Freud, conscious thoughts are just a fragment of mental contents—a tip of the iceberg.

According to psychoanalytic theory, there are substantial variations in the degree to which we are aware of mental phenomena. Freud proposed three levels of awareness. The **conscious** level, as noted above, includes thoughts of which we are aware at any given moment. A **preconscious** level contains mental contents of which we easily could become aware if we attended to them. For example, before reading the present sentence, you probably were not thinking about your phone number; it was not part of your consciousness. But you easily could think of your phone number (indeed, you may be doing so right now!); it is a simple matter to attend to information that is in the preconscious and to bring it to consciousness. The third level is the **unconscious**. Unconscious mental contents are parts of the mind of which we are unaware and *cannot become aware* except under special circumstances. Why not? According to Freud, it is because they are anxiety provoking. We possess thoughts and desires that are so traumatic or socially unacceptable that consciously thinking about them provokes anxiety. "The reason why such ideas cannot become conscious is that a certain force opposes them" (Freud, 1923, p. 4). Our desire to protect ourselves from the anxiety these thoughts elicit forces them to reside outside of conscious awareness, in the unconscious.

Freud was not the first person to recognize that parts of mental life are unconscious. He was, however, the first to explore qualities of unconscious life in scientific detail and to explain a range of everyday behavior in terms of unconscious mental forces. How did he do this? Freud attempted to understand the properties of the unconscious by analyzing a variety of psychological phenomena: slips of the tongue, neuroses, psychoses, works of art, rituals. Of particular importance was his analysis of dreams.

Dreams   The content of dreams vividly reveals that the mind contains unconscious contents that differ dramatically from conscious thinking. In psychoanalytic theory, dreams have two levels of content: a manifest content, which is the storyline of a dream, and a latent content, which consists of the unconscious ideas, emotions, and drives that are manifested in the dream's storyline. What Freud found in analyzing dreams is that unconscious life can be utterly bizarre. The unconscious is alogical (opposites can stand for the same thing). It disregards time (events of different periods may coexist). It disregards space (size and distance relationships are neglected so that large things fit into small things and distant places are brought together). It deals in a world of symbols, where many ideas may be telescoped into a single word and where a part of any object may stand for many things. Through processes of symbolization, a penis can be represented by a snake or nose, a woman by a church, chapel, or boat, and an octopus engulfing a mother. An everyday action such as writing may symbolize a sexual act: The pen is the male organ and the paper is the woman who receives the ink (the semen) that flows out in the quick up-and-down movements of the pen (Groddeck, 1923). In *The Book of the It*, Groddeck gives many fascinating examples of the workings of the unconscious and offers the following as an example of the functioning of the unconscious in his own life.

I cannot recall her [my nurse's] appearance. I know nothing more than her name, Bertha, the shining one. But I have a clear recollection of the day she went away. As a parting present she gave me a copper three-pfennig piece. A Dreier... Since that day I have been pursued by the number three. Words like trinity, triangle, triple alliance, convey some thing disreputable to me, and not merely the words but the ideas attached to them, yes, and the whole complex of ideas built up around them by the capricious brain of a child. For this reason, the Holy Ghost, as the Third Person of the Trinity, was already suspect to me in early childhood; trigonometry was a plague in my school days... Yes, three is a sort of fatal number for me.

SOURCE: GRODDECK, *1923, p. 9.*

Freud's theory of dreams had a second component. In addition to positing two levels of dreams—their manifest and latent content—Freud proposed a particular relation between the two levels. The latent content consists of unconscious wishes. The manifest content is a wish fulfillment; the storyline of the dream (the manifest content) symbolically represents the fulfillment of unconscious wishes that it may be impossible to fulfill in everyday waking life. In the dream, the person can satisfy a hostile or sexual wish in a disguised and therefore safe way. A vengeful unconscious desire to kill someone, for example, may be expressed in a dream of a battle in which a particular figure is killed. In *The Interpretation of Dreams*, Freud analyzes a large number of dreams in the style of a detective, with each element of the dream treated as a clue to the underlying wish that the dream represents, but in disguised form.

The Motivated Unconscious   Although Freud believed the unconscious to be a region of mind that stores mental contents, it is critical to recognize that the nature of the storage is very different than, for example, the storage of books in a library. In a library, books are assigned their place based on logical grounds (a library classification system). Once on the shelf, the books just sit there doing nothing (until someone takes one off the shelf). The unconscious is nothing like this. It is not purely logical. And the material does not "just sit there." The unconscious is highly motivated.

Motivational principles come into play in two respects. First, mental contents enter the unconscious for motivated reasons. The unconscious stores ideas that are so traumatic that, if they were to remain in conscious awareness, they would cause psychological pain. These thoughts might include, for example, memories of traumatic life experiences; feelings of envy, hostility, or sexual desire directed toward a forbidden person; or a desire to harm a loved one. In keeping with our basic desire to pursue pleasure and avoid pain, we are motivated to banish such thoughts from awareness. Second, thoughts in the unconscious influence ongoing conscious experience. Indeed, that statement may be the best one-line summary of Freud's fundamental message to the world. Our ongoing psychological experiences—our conscious thoughts, feelings, and actions—are, according to Freud, fundamentally determined by mental contents of which we are unaware, the contents of the unconscious. Why did we have a strange slip of the tongue? A dream that seems to make no sense? A sudden experience of anxiety when nothing anxiety-provoking seemed to be happening? Strong feelings of attraction toward, or repulsion from, someone we just met? Feelings of guilt that seem irrational because we can't figure out anything that we did wrong? All such cases, to Freud, are motivated by unconscious mental forces.

Relevant Psychoanalytic Research   The unconscious is never observed directly. What evidence, then, supports the idea of an unconscious part of the mind? Let us review the range of evidence that might be considered supportive of the concept of the unconscious, beginning with Freud's clinical observations. Freud realized the importance of the unconscious after observing hypnotic phenomena. As is well known, people under hypnosis can recall things they previously could not. Furthermore, they perform things under posthypnotic suggestion without consciously knowing that they are behaving in accordance with that suggestion; that is, they fully believe that what they are doing

While some slips of the tongue may represent merely a confusion among choice of words, others seem to illustrate Freud's suggestion that slips express hidden wishes. (Illustration by Patrick McDonnell, 1987 Psychology Today Magazine, Sussex Publishers, Inc.)

is voluntary and independent of any suggestion by another person. When Freud discarded the technique of hypnosis and continued with his therapeutic work, he found that often patients became aware of memories and wishes previously buried. Frequently, such discoveries were associated with painful emotion. It is indeed a powerful clinical observation to see a patient suddenly experience tremendous anxiety, sob hysterically, or break into a rage as he or she recalls a forgotten event or gets in touch with a forbidden feeling. Thus, it was clinical observations such as these that suggested to Freud that the unconscious includes memories and wishes that not only are not currently part of our consciousness but are "deliberately buried" in our unconscious.

What of experimental evidence? In the 1960s and 1970s experimental research focused on unconscious perception or what was called **perception without awareness**. Can the person "know" something without knowing that he or she knows it? For example, can the person hear or perceive stimuli, and be influenced by these perceptions, without being aware of these perceptions? Currently this is known as *subliminal perception*, or the registration of stimuli at a level below that required for awareness. For example, in some early research one group of subjects was shown a picture with a duck image shaped by the branches of a tree. Another was shown a similar picture but without the duck image. For both groups the picture was presented at a rapid speed so that it was barely visible. This was done using a tachistoscope, an apparatus that allows the experimenter to show stimuli to subjects at very fast speeds, so that they cannot be consciously perceived. The subjects then were asked to close their eyes, imagine a nature scene, draw the scene, and label the parts. Would the two groups differ, that is, would subjects in the group "seeing" the picture with the duck image draw different pictures than subjects in the other group? And, if so, would such a difference be associated with differential recall as to what was perceived? What was found was that more of the subjects viewing the duck picture had significantly more duck-related images (e.g., "duck," "water," "birds," "feathers") in their drawings than did subjects in the other group. However, these subjects did not report seeing the duck during the experiment, and the majority even had trouble finding it when they were asked to look for it. In other words, the stimuli that were not consciously perceived still influenced the imagery and thoughts of the subjects (Eagle, Wolitzky, & Klein, 1966).

The mere fact that people can perceive and be influenced by stimuli of which they are unaware does not suggest that psychodynamic or motivational forces are involved. Is there evidence that such is or can be the case? Two relevant lines of research can be noted. The first, called **perceptual defense**, involves a process by which the individual defends against the anxiety that accompanies actual recognition of a threatening stimulus. In a relevant early experiment, subjects were shown two types of words in a tachistoscope: neutral words such as apple, dance, and child and emotionally toned words such as rape, whore, and penis. The words were shown first at very fast speeds and then at progressively slower speeds. A record was made of the point at which the subjects were able to identify each of the words and their sweat gland activity (a measure of tension) in response to each word. These records indicated that subjects took longer to recognize the emotionally toned words than the neutral words and showed signs of emotional response to the emotionally toned words before they were verbally identified (McGinnies, 1949). Despite criticism of such research (e.g., did subjects identify the emotionally toned words earlier but were reluctant to verbalize them to the experimenter?), there appears to be considerable evidence that people can, outside of awareness, selectively respond to and reject specific emotional stimuli (Erdelyi, 1984).

Another line of research has examined a phenomenon called **subliminal psychodynamic activation** (Silverman, 1976, 1982; Weinberger, 1992). In this work, researchers attempt to stimulate unconscious wishes without making them conscious. This generally is done by presenting material that is related to either threatening or anxiety-alleviating unconscious wishes and then observing participants' subsequent reactions. The material is shown for extremely brief periods of time, in theory, long enough to activate the unconscious wish but short enough so that it is not recognized consciously. In the case of threatening wishes, the material is expected to stir up unconscious conflict and thus to increase psychological disturbance. In the case of an anxiety-alleviating wish, the material is expected to diminish unconscious conflict and thus to decrease psychological disturbance. For example, the content "I Am Losing Mommy" might be upsetting to some subjects, whereas the content "Mommy and I Are One" might be reassuring.

In a series of studies, Silverman and colleagues produced such subliminal psychodynamic activation effects. In one study this method was used to present conflict-intensifying material ("Loving Daddy Is Wrong") and conflict-reducing material ("Loving Daddy Is OK") to female undergraduates. For subjects prone to conflict over sexual urges, the conflict-intensifying material, presented outside of awareness, was found to disrupt memory for passages presented after the subliminal activation of the conflict. This was not true for the conflict-reducing material or for subjects not prone to conflict over sexual urges (Geisler, 1986). What is key here is that the content that is upsetting or relieving to various groups of subjects is predicted beforehand on the basis of psychoanalytic theory and that the effects occur only when the stimuli are perceived subliminally or unconsciously.

Another interesting use of the subliminal psychodynamic activation model involves the study of eating disorders. In the first study in this area, healthy college-age women and women with signs of eating disorders were compared in terms of how many crackers they would eat following subliminal presentation of three messages: "Mama Is Leaving Me," "Mama Is Loaning It," "Mona Is Loaning It" (Patton, 1992). Based on psychoanalytic theory, the hypothesis tested was that subjects with an eating disorder struggle with feelings of loss and abandonment in relation to nurturance and therefore would seek substitute gratification in the form of eating the crackers once the conflict was activated subliminally through the message "Mama Is Leaving Me." Indeed, the eating disorder subjects who received the abandonment stimulus ("Mama Is Leaving Me") below threshold showed significantly more cracker eating than subjects without an eating disorder or subjects with an eating disorder exposed to the abandonment stimulus above threshold. This study was replicated with the additional use of pictorial stimuli—a picture of a sobbing baby and a woman walking away along with the "Mommy Is Leaving Me" message and a picture of a woman walking along with the neutral stimulus, in this case "Mommy Is Walking." Once more, significantly more crackers were eaten by the women with eating disorders subliminally exposed to the abandonment phrase and picture than by the women with eating disorders exposed to these stimuli above threshold or by the women without an eating disorder exposed to the stimuli above or below threshold (Gerard, Kupper, & Nguyen, 1993). Some view the research on perceptual defense and subliminal psychodynamic activation as conclusive experimental evidence of the importance of psychodynamic, motivational factors in determining what is "deposited into" and "kept in" the unconscious (Weinberger, 1992). However, the experiments have frequently been criticized on methodological grounds, and at times some of the effects have been difficult to replicate or reproduce in other laboratories (Balay & Shevrin, 1988, 1989; Holender, 1986).

Current Status of the Concept of the Unconscious   The concept of a motivated unconscious is central to psychoanalytic theory. But how is this idea viewed more generally by psychologists in the field? At this point almost all psychologists, whether psychoanalytic or otherwise, would agree that many mental events occur outside of conscious awareness and that unconscious processes influence what we attend to and how we feel. For example, consider the view of a leading contemporary researcher who is now a follower of psychoanalytic theory: "Our conclusion, perhaps discomforting for the layperson, is that unconscious influences are ubiquitous. It is clear that people sometimes consciously plan and act. More often than not, however, behavior is influenced by unconscious processes; that is, we act and then, if questioned, make our excuses" (Jacoby et al., 1992, p. 82).

Striking contemporary evidence of unconscious influences on everyday behavior comes from work by the social psychologist John Bargh and his colleagues (Bargh, 1997). For example, in one experiment research participants worked on a task with another individual. Unbeknownst to the participant, the other individual was part of the study—an experimental confederate. This confederate exhibited very poor abilities on the task. In this setting, then, the participant faced two conflicting goals. On the one hand, there is the goal of achieving: One is supposed to perform as well as possible. On the other hand, there is a personal or affiliation goal: Performing well might make the other person, who is doing poorly, feel bad, so one might achieve the goal of affiliating with the individual by lowering one's own performance. Bargh and colleagues (Bargh & Barndollar, 1996) manipulated the goals in a manner that did not call participants' conscious attention to them. Prior to the study, participants were asked to complete a word puzzle. In different experimental conditions, the words in the puzzle were related either to achievement or to affiliation. The idea is that the words would activate one versus the other goal, even if participants were unaware that this activation of goal contents was occurring. As predicted, compared to affiliation goals, activating achievement goals in the word puzzle caused participants to solve more problems when working on the task with the other individual. Importantly, participants in the study did not report being aware of the influence of the word puzzle task. Thus, their actions were caused by a goal of which they were not consciously aware.

The Psychoanalytic Unconscious and the Cognitive Unconscious There is an important point to consider about the previously discussed study (Bargh & Barndollar, 1996) and many others like it. On the one hand, the study demonstrates nonconscious influences on behavior, as Freud would have predicted. On the other hand, the content of the unconscious material in the study had little, if anything, to do with the material studied by Freud. Bargh and colleagues did not manipulate thoughts of sex or aggression. They did not study people's emotional reactions to material of deep psychological significance. Instead, they manipulated everyday social goals on a mundane laboratory task. Their findings, then, indicate the existence of unconscious influences, but these are unconscious influences that may have little to do with the psychological experiences discussed by Freud. This distinction—between the traumatic sexual and aggressive unconscious content of interest to Freud, and the relatively mundane unconscious content studied by many contemporary researchers in personality and social psychology—suggests that one should distinguish between the psychoanalytic unconscious and what has been called the cognitive unconscious (Kihlstrom, 1990, 1999; Pervin, 2003).

As we have seen, the psychoanalytic view of the unconscious emphasizes the irrational, illogical nature of unconscious functioning. In addition, the contents of the unconscious are presumed by analysts mainly to involve sexual and aggressive thoughts, feelings, and motives. Finally, analysts emphasize that what is in the unconscious is there for motivated reasons and these contents exert a motivational influence on daily behavior. In contrast to this, according to the cognitive view of the unconscious there is no fundamental difference in quality between unconscious and conscious processes. According to this view, unconscious processes can be as intelligent, logical, and rational as conscious processes. Second, the cognitive view of the unconscious

Table 3.1   Comparison of Two Views of the Unconscious: Psychoanalytic and Cognitive

Psychoanalytic View

1. Emphasis on illogical, irrational unconscious processes.
2. Content emphasis on motives and wishes.
3. Emphasis on motivated aspects of unconscious functioning.

Cognitive View

1. Absence of fundamental difference between conscious and unconscious processes.
2. Content emphasis on thoughts.
3. Focus on nonmotivated aspects of unconscious functioning.

emphasizes the variety of contents that may be unconscious, with no special significance associated with sexual and aggressive contents. Third, related to this, the cognitive view of the unconscious does not emphasize motivational factors. According to the cognitive view, cognitions are unconscious because they cannot be processed at the conscious level, because they never reached consciousness, or because they have become overly routinized and automatic. For example, tying one's shoe is so automatic that we no longer are aware of just how we do it. We act similarly with typing and where letters are on the keyboard. Many of our cultural beliefs were learned in such subtle ways that we cannot even spell them out as beliefs. As noted in Chapter 1, we are not even aware of them until we meet members of a different culture. However, such unconscious contents are not kept there for motivated reasons. Nor do they necessarily exert a motivational influence on our behavior. Finally, there is evidence that subliminal stimuli can affect our thoughts and feelings, but these stimuli need not be of special psychodynamic significance such as a threatening wish (Klinger & Greenwald, 1995; Nash, 1999) (Table 3.1).

Many of these contrasting views are captured in the following statement by Kihlstrom, a leading proponent of the cognitive view of the unconscious:

> The psychological unconscious documented by latter-day psychology is quite different from what Sigmund Freud and his psychoanalytic colleagues had in mind in Vienna. Their unconscious was hot and wet; it seethed with lust and anger; it was hallucinatory, primitive, and irrational. The unconscious of contemporary psychology is kinder and gentler than that and more readily bound and rational, even if it is not entirely cold and dry.
>
> SOURCE: KIHLSTROM, BARNHARDT, & TATARYN, 1992, p. 788.

Although efforts have been made to integrate the psychoanalytic and cognitive views of the unconscious (Bornstein & Masling, 1998; Epstein, 1994; Westen & Gabbard, 1999), differences remain. In sum, although the importance of unconscious phenomena is recognized, and the investigation of such phenomena has become a major area of research, the uniquely psychoanalytic view of the unconscious remains questionable for many, perhaps most, nonpsychoanalytic investigators.

Id, Ego, and Superego

In 1923, Freud significantly augmented his theorizing by presenting a second model of mind. He did not abandon his prior distinctions among conscious, preconscious, and unconscious regions of mind, yet he judged that "these distinctions have proved to be inadequate" (Freud, 1923, p. 7). The inadequacy was the following. There seemed to Freud to exist a psychological agency (the ego, see below) that had two important qualities. On the one hand, it was unitary in its functioning. It did a single type of thing in a coherent, consistent manner. Yet on the other hand it *varied* in its degree of consciousness. Sometimes its functioning involved conscious processes, but sometimes it functioned unconsciously. This clearly was a problem for psychoanalytic theory. Freud needed to capture the unitary quality of this psychological agency, and the distinction among levels of consciousness did not do it. Freud needed another conceptual tool. The one he forged proved to be among the most enduringly important features of psychoanalytic theory: the distinction among the id, the ego, and the superego. Each is a distinct mental system that carries out a particular type of psychological function.

The **id** is the original source of all drive energy—the "great reservoir" (Freud, 1923, p. 20) of mental energies. The psychological functions toward which the id directs these energies are very simple. The id seeks the release of excitation or tension. It carries out a mental function described earlier: the reduction of tension in order to return to a quiet internal state.

In carrying out this function, the id operates according to the **pleasure principle**, which is particularly simple to define: the id pursues pleasure and avoids pain. The point is that the id does not do anything else. It does not devise plans and strategies for obtaining pleasure or wait patiently for a particularly pleasing object to appear. It does not concern itself with social norms and rules; "it is totally non-moral" (Freud, 1923, p. 40). The id seeks immediate tension release, no matter what. The id cannot tolerate frustration. It is free of inhibitions. It has qualities of a spoiled child: It wants what it wants when it wants it.

The id seeks satisfaction in either of two ways: through action or merely by imagining that it has gotten what it wants. To the id, the fantasy of gratification is as good as the actual gratification.

In terms of the regions of mind outlined previously by Freud, the id functions entirely outside of conscious awareness. It is "unknown and unconscious" (Freud, 1923, p. 14).

In marked contrast to the id is the **superego**. The functions of the superego involve the moral aspects of social behavior. The superego contains ideals for which we strive, as well as ethical standards that will cause us to feel guilt if we violate them. The superego, then, is an internal representation of the moral rules of the external, social world. It functions to control behavior in accord with these rules, offering rewards (pride, self-love) for "good" behavior and punishments (guilt, feelings of inferiority) for "bad" behavior. The superego may function on a very primitive level, being relatively incapable of reality testing—that is, of modifying its action depending on circumstances. In such cases, the person is unable to distinguish between thought and action, feeling guilty for thinking something even if it did not lead to action. Furthermore, the individual is bound by black-white, all-none judgments and by the pursuit of perfection. Excessive use of words such as good, bad, judgment, and trial express a strict superego. But the superego can also be understanding and flexible. For example, people may be able to forgive themselves or someone else if it is clear that something was an accident or done under severe stress. In the course of development, children learn to make such important distinctions and to see things not only in all-or-none, right-or-wrong, black-or-white terms.

The third psychoanalytic structure is the **ego**. Whereas the id seeks pleasure and the superego seeks perfection, the ego seeks reality. The ego's function is to express and satisfy the desires of the id in accordance with two things: opportunities and constraints that exist in the real world, and the demands of the superego.

Whereas the id operates according to the pleasure principle, the ego operates according to the **reality principle**: gratification of the instincts is delayed until a time at which something in reality enables one to obtain maximum pleasure with the least pain or negative consequences. As a simple example, sexual drives in the id may impel you to make a sexual advance toward someone you find attractive. But the ego may stop you from acting impulsively; the ego would monitor reality, judging whether there is any chance that you might actually succeed and delaying action until it develops a strategy that might bring success. According to the reality principle, the energy of the id may be blocked, diverted, or released gradually, all in accordance with the demands of reality and the superego. Such an operation does not contradict the pleasure principle, but rather represents a temporary suspension of it.

"Double Scotches for me and my super-ego, and a glass of water for my id, which is driving."

Psychoanalytic Theory: Freud emphasized the concepts of id, ego, and superego as structures of personality. (Drawing by Handelsman; © 1972 The New Yorker Magazine, Inc.)

The ego has capabilities that the id does not. The ego can distinguish fantasy from reality. It can tolerate tension and create compromises through rational thought. Unlike the id, it changes over time, with more complex ego functions developing over the course of childhood.

Although the ego may sound like the decision-making "chief executive" of personality, Freud thought that the ego was weaker than the metaphor of an "executive" implies. The ego instead is "like a man on horseback, who has to hold in check the superior strength of the horse" (Freud, 1923, p. 15). It is the horse (the id) who provides all the energy. The rider tries to direct it, but, ultimately, the more powerful beast may end up going wherever it wants.

In sum, Freud's ego is logical, rational, and tolerant of tension. In its actions, it must conform to the dictates of three masters: the id, the superego, and the world of reality.

The concepts of conscious, unconscious, id, ego, and superego are highly abstract. Freud knew this. He did not intend to imply that there are three gremlin-like beings running around in your head. Instead, he judged that mental life involves the execution of three distinct psychological functions, and posited an abstract mental system that executes each of the functions. The nature of these structures becomes clearer and less abstract when one also considers the psychological processes through which their distinction functions are carried out. We turn to these processes now.

PROCESS

The process aspects of personality theory are, as we have noted, concerned with motivational dynamics. Within the energy model of mind embraced by Freud's psychoanalytic theory of personality, these dynamics involve mental energy: what it is, what it does, and how it is transformed such that it can motivate the diverse range of human behavior.

Freud's view of mental energy is thoroughly biological. In psychoanalytic theory, the source of all psychic energy lies in states of excitation within the body. These states seek expression and tension reduction. These states are called *instincts*, or *drives*. Though both words have been used when Freud's writing has been translated into English, the term *drive* captures Freud's idea better than does the term *instinct*. The word *instinct* commonly is used to describe a fixed pattern of action (e.g., a bird instinctually builds a nest). In contrast, a drive is a source of energy that can motivate any of a variety of specific actions depending upon the opportunities and constraints that are presented in a given environment. This idea, of drives, is what Freud had in mind when discussing personality processes.

Within this framework, two questions naturally arise: (1) How many basic human instinctual drives are there, and what are they? (2) What happens to the energy associated with these drives? In other words, how is it expressed in everyday experience and action? Freud answers the first question by presenting a theory of life and death instincts. He answers the second by analyzing the dynamics of functioning and mechanisms of defense.

Life and Death Instincts

Daily life consists of a wide array of activities: work, time with friends, education, time with romantic partners, sports, arts, music, and so forth.

Since most people engage in each of these activities, one might suppose that there is a basic human instinct for each one (an instinct to work, to have friends, to become educated, etc.). But this sort of "multi-instinct model" is *not* the sort of theory that Freud pursued. Instead, throughout his career, Freud tried to explain the diversity of human activity in terms of a very small number of instincts. He tried to achieve theoretical parsimony (as we discussed in Chapter 1), with the diverse complexities of human behavior being understood through a relatively simple theoretical formulation.

Freud's thoughts about the exact nature of mental drives changed during his career. In an earlier view, he proposed ego instincts, relating to tendencies toward self-preservation, and sexual instincts, relating to tendencies toward preservation of the species. In a later view—which stands as the final, classic psychoanalytic model—there were still two instincts, but they were the **life** and **death instincts**.

The life instinct includes drives associated previously with both the earlier ego and sexual instincts; in other words, the life instinct impels people toward the preservation and reproduction of the organism. Freud gave a name to the energy of the life instinct: **libido**. The death instinct is the very opposite of the life instinct. It involves the aim of the organism to die or return to an inorganic state. At an intuitive level, it may immediately strike you that the notion of a "death instinct" is unusual if not implausible. Why would people have an instinct to die? Such intuitions would match those of many psychologists, including many psychoanalysts; the death instinct remains one of the most controversial and least accepted parts of psychoanalytic theory. Yet the idea of a death instinct was consistent with some ideas of 19th-century biology with which Freud was familiar (Sulloway, 1979); it reflected Freud's idea, noted above, that a basic tendency of the organism is to seek a state of calmness. It also is consistent with observations of the human condition. Sadly, many people escape psychological problems through suicide, which can be understood as a manifestation of a drive to die. Furthermore, Freud felt that the death instinct was often turned away from oneself and directed toward others in acts of aggression. This occurs so commonly that some analysts refer to the instinct as an aggressive instinct.

This model of motivation processes is highly integrated with Freud's model of psychoanalytic structures. The sexual and death/aggressive drives are parts of one of the psychoanalytic structures, namely, the id. The id, as you will recall, is the first of the personality structures, that is, the one with which we are born. An implication, then, is that sexual and aggressive drives are part of the basic human nature that we are born with. We do not have to learn to have sexual and death/aggressive drives. We are born with them. To Freud, our psychological lives are essentially powered by these two basic drives.

The Dynamics of Functioning

If one posits only two instinctual drives, one faces an intellectual puzzle: How can one account for the diversity of motivated human activities, many of which do not seem obviously related to sex or aggression? Freud's creative solution to this problem was to posit that a given instinctual drive could be expressed in a wide variety of ways. The mechanisms of the mind can redirect the energy to diverse activities.

In the dynamics of functioning, what exactly can happen to one's instincts? They can, at least temporarily, be blocked from expression, expressed in a modified way, or expressed without modification. For example, affection may be a modified expression of the sexual instinct, and sarcasm a modified expression of the aggressive instinct. It is also possible for the object of gratification of the instinct to be changed or displaced from the original object to another object. Thus, the love of one's mother may be displaced to the wife, children, or dog. Each instinct may be transformed or modified, and the instincts can combine with one another. Football, for example, can gratify both sexual and aggressive instincts; in surgery there can be the fusion of love and destruction. It should already be clear how psychoanalytic theory is able to account for so much behavior on the basis of only two instincts. It is the fluid, mobile, changing qualities of the instincts and their many alternative kinds of gratification that allow such variability in behavior. In essence, the same instinct can be gratified in a number of ways and the same behavior can have different causes in different people.

Virtually every process in psychoanalytic theory can be described in terms of the expenditure of energy in an object or in terms of a force inhibiting the expenditure of energy, that is, inhibiting gratification of an instinct. Because it involves an expenditure of energy, people who direct much of their efforts toward inhibition end up feeling tired and bored. The interplay between expression and inhibition of instincts forms the foundation of the dynamic aspects of psychoanalytic theory. The key to this is the concept of **anxiety**. In psychoanalytic theory, anxiety is a painful emotional experience representing a threat or danger to the person. In a state of "free-floating" anxiety, individuals are unable to relate their state of tension to an external object; in contrast, in a state of fear, the source of tension is known. Freud had two theories of anxiety. In the first theory, anxiety was viewed as a result of undischarged sexual impulses—dammed-up libido. In the second theory, anxiety represented a painful emotion that acted as a signal of impending danger to the ego. Here, anxiety, an ego function, alerts the ego to danger so that it can act.

The psychoanalytic theory of anxiety states that at some point the person experiences a trauma, an incident of harm or injury. Anxiety represents a repetition of the earlier traumatic experience, but in miniature form. Anxiety in the present, then, is related to an earlier danger. For example, a child may be severely punished for some sexual or aggressive act. Later in life, this person may experience anxiety in association with the inclination to perform the same sexual or aggressive act. The earlier punishment (trauma) may or may not be remembered. In structural terms, what is suggested is that anxiety develops out of a conflict between the push of the id instincts and the threat of punishment by the superego. That is, it is as if the id says, "I want it," the superego says, "How terrible," and the ego says, "I'm afraid."

Anxiety, Mechanisms of Defense, and Contemporary Research on Defensive Processes

Anxiety is such a painful state that we are incapable of tolerating it for very long. How are we to deal with such a state? If, as Freud suggests, our minds harbor sexual and aggressive instincts that are socially unacceptable, then how do we manage not to be anxious all the time? Freud's answer to this question constitutes one of the most enduring aspects of his theory of personality. He proposed that we mentally defend ourselves against anxiety-provoking thoughts. People develop **defense mechanisms** against anxiety. We develop ways to distort reality and exclude feelings from awareness so that we do not feel anxious. These defense mechanisms are functions carried out by the ego; they are a strategic effort by the ego to cope with the socially unacceptable impulses of the id.

Some things are too terrible to be true.

SOURCE: BOB DYLAN

Denial   Freud distinguished among a number of distinct defense mechanisms. Some of them are relatively simple, or psychologically primitive, whereas others are more complex. A particularly simple defense mechanism is **denial**. People may, in their conscious thoughts, deny the existence of a traumatic or otherwise socially unacceptable fact; the fact is so "terrible" that they deny that it is "true," as Dylan's lyric above suggests. People may begin using the defense mechanism of denial in childhood. There may be denial of reality, as in a girl who denies she lacks a penis or in the boy, who, in fantasy, denies a lack of power, or denial of an internal impulse, as when an irate person protests, "I do not feel angry." The saying that someone "doth protest too much" specifically references this defense. Denial of reality is commonly seen where people attempt to avoid recognizing the extent of a threat. The expression "Oh, no!" upon hearing of the death of a close friend represents the reflex action of denial. Children have been known to deny the death of a loved animal and long afterward to behave as if it were still alive. When Edwin Meese, former attorney general in the Reagan administration, was asked how much he owed in legal bills, he replied, "I really don't know. It scares me to look at it, so I haven't looked at it." The mother of former U.S. President Bill Clinton was quoted as saying, "When bad things happen, I brainwash myself to put them out of my mind. Inside my head, I construct an airtight box. I keep inside it what I want to think about and everything else stays behind the walls. Inside is white, outside is black. The only gray I trust is the streak in my hair." A friend of the author's organizes her mail into three "in boxes" on her desk that are labeled "Unimportant Stuff," "Important Stuff," and "Stuff I'm Afraid to Look At." Initially, such avoidance may be conscious, but later it becomes automatic and unconscious, so that the person is not even aware of "not looking."

Denial of reality is also evident when people say or assume that "it can't happen to me" in spite of clear evidence of impending doom. This defense was seen in Jews who were victims of the Nazis. A book (Steiner, 1966) about the Nazi concentration camp Treblinka describes how the population acted as if death did not exist, in spite of clear evidence to the contrary. The extermination of a whole people was so unimaginable that individuals could not accept it. They preferred to accept lies rather than to bear the terrible trauma of the truth.

Is denial necessarily a bad thing? Should we always avoid self-deception? Psychoanalysts generally assume that although the mechanisms of defense can be useful in reducing anxiety, they also are maladaptive by turning the person away from reality. Thus, psychoanalysts view "reality orientation" as fundamental to emotional health and doubt that distortions about oneself and others can have value for adaptive functions (Colvin & Block, 1994; Robins

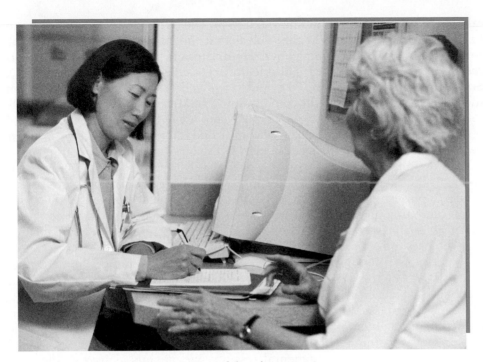

Denial: How much information is useful to the patient?

& John, 1996). Yet, some psychologists suggest that positive illusions and self-deceptions can be adaptive. Positive illusions about one's self, about one's ability to control events, and about the future can be good, perhaps essential, for mental health (Taylor & Armor, 1996; Taylor & Brown, 1988, 1994; Taylor et al., 2000). The answer to these differing views appears to depend on the extent of distortion, how pervasive it is, and the circumstances under which it occurs. For example, it may be helpful to have positive illusions about oneself as long as they are not too extreme. And denial and self-deception may provide temporary relief from emotional trauma and help the person avoid becoming overwhelmed by anxiety or depression. Denial may be adaptive where action is impossible, as when a person is in a situation that cannot be altered (e.g., a fatal illness), but is maladaptive when it prevents one from taking constructive action to alter a situation that can be changed.

Projection Another relatively primitive defense mechanism is **projection**. In projection, what is internal and unacceptable is projected out and seen as external. People defend against the recognition of their own negative qualities by projecting them on to others. For example, rather than recognize hostility in the self, an individual sees others as being hostile. Much laboratory research has been devoted to the study of projection. At first, researchers found it difficult to demonstrate the phenomenon in the lab (Halpern, 1977; Holmes, 1981). However, in more recent years investigators have documented that, in fact, people tend to project their undesired psychological qualities onto others.

Newman and colleagues have studied projection by analyzing specific thinking processes that might lead people to project their undesired qualities onto others (Newman, Duff, & Baumeister, 1997). The basic idea is that people tend to dwell on those features of themselves that they do not like. Whenever one dwells on a topic, the topic comes to mind easily—in the language of this research, the topic becomes "chronically accessible" (Higgins & King, 1981). So if you think that you are lazy, and you dwell on this feature of self, then the concept of laziness might come to mind relatively quickly and frequently for you. This reasoning puts one just one step away from the phenomenon of projection. This final step is that, whenever one interprets the actions of other people, one does so by using concepts in one's own mind. If one interprets others' actions using ideas that also are negative features of one's own self-concept, then one ends up projecting these negative features onto others. To return to our example, if "laziness" comes to mind quickly for you, and you see a person sitting on a beach in the middle of a workday, you might conclude that this is a lazy person. Someone else, in contrast, might merely conclude that the person is relaxing, rather than being lazy.

Experimental findings support this interpretation of projection (Newman et al., 1997). In this research, participants were exposed to bogus negative feedback on two personality attributes. They then were asked to try to suppress thoughts about one of the two attributes while they discussed the other one; such thought-suppression instructions often backfire, causing people subsequently to think about the personal quality that they were trying to suppress. Later in the experimental session, participants viewed a videotape that depicted a somewhat anxious-looking individual. Participants were asked to rate this person on a series of personality trait dimensions. Findings revealed that participants projected their suppressed negative quality onto others. In other words, they judged that the *other* person possessed the negative personality attribute that they themselves had been trying not to think about earlier in the experiment.

The work of Newman et al. (1997) highlights a theme that we have seen earlier in this chapter. On the one hand, their findings confirm an intuition of Freud's: People sometimes defend against their own negative qualities by projecting these qualities onto others. On the other hand, their work does not directly confirm the exact account of defensive processing provided by Freud. Unlike expectations based on Freudian theory, the findings of Newman et al. (1997) indicate that projection occurs with respect to relatively mundane psychological qualities (e.g., "laziness") that are not in any obvious way connected to the psychosexual instincts of the id. Furthermore, in explaining their findings, Newman et al. (1997) rely on explanatory principles that are based on principles of social cognitive psychology (discussed in Chapters 12 and 13) rather than on principles of psychoanalysis.

Isolation, Reaction Formation, and Sublimation   In addition to denial and projection, another way to deal with anxiety and threat is to isolate events in memory or to isolate emotion from the content of a memory or impulse. In **isolation**, the impulse, thought, or act is not denied access to consciousness, but it is denied the normal accompanying emotion. For example, a woman may experience the thought or fantasy of strangling her child without any associated feelings of anger. The result of using the mechanism of isolation is intellectualization, an emphasis on thought over emotion and feeling, and the development of logic-tight compartments. In such cases, the feelings that do exist may be split, as in the case where a man separates women into two categories, one with whom there is love but no sex and the other with whom there is sex but no love (Madonna-whore complex).

People who use the defense mechanism of isolation also often use the mechanism of **undoing**. Here the individual magically undoes one act or wish with another. "It is a kind of negative magic in which the individual's second act abrogates or nullifies the first, in such a manner that it is as though neither had taken place, whereas in reality both have done so" (A. Freud, 1936, p. 33). This mechanism is seen in compulsions in which the person has an irresistible impulse to perform some act (e.g., the person undoes a suicide or homicide fantasy by compulsively turning off the gas jets at home), in religious rituals, and in children's sayings such as "Don't step on the crack or you'll break your mother's back."

In **reaction formation**, the individual defends against expression of an unacceptable impulse by only recognizing and expressing its opposite. This defense is evident in socially desirable behavior that is rigid, exaggerated, and inappropriate. The person who uses reaction formation cannot admit to other feelings, such as overprotective mothers who cannot allow any conscious hostility toward their children. Reaction formation is most clearly observable when the defense breaks down, as when the model boy shoots his parents or when the man who "wouldn't hurt a fly" goes on a killing rampage. Of similar interest here are the occasional reports of judges who commit crimes or of pious religious figures who engage in inappropriate sexual conduct.

A defense mechanism that you may recognize in yourself is **rationalization**. Rationalization is a more complex, mature defense mechanism than a process such as denial in that in rationalization people do not simply deny that a thought or action occurred. In rationalization people recognize the existence of an action, but distort its underlying motive. Behavior is reinterpreted so that it appears reasonable and acceptable; the ego, in other words, constructs a rational motive to explain an unacceptable action that is actually caused by the irrational impulses of the id. Particularly interesting is that with rationalization the individual can express the dangerous impulse, seemingly without disapproval by the superego. Some of the greatest atrocities of humankind have been committed in the name of love. Through the defense of rationalization, we can be hostile while professing love, immoral in the pursuit of morality.

Another device used to express an impulse of the id in a manner that is free of anxiety is **sublimation**. In this relatively complex defense mechanism, the original object of gratification is replaced by a higher cultural goal that is far removed from a direct expression of the instinct. Whereas the other defense mechanisms meet the instincts head on and, by and large, prevent discharge, in sublimation the instinct is turned into a new and useful channel. In contrast to the other defense mechanisms, here the ego does not have to maintain a constant energy output to prevent discharge. Freud interpreted da Vinci's Madonna as a sublimation of his longing for his mother. Becoming a surgeon, butcher, or boxer can represent sublimations, to a greater or lesser degree, of aggressive impulses. Being a psychiatrist can represent a sublimation of "Peeping Tom" tendencies. In all, as noted, Freud felt that the essence of civilization is contained in a person's ability to sublimate sexual and aggressive energies.

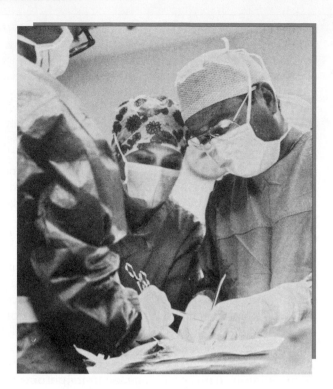

Sublimation: In performing surgery, aggressive impulses can be turned toward useful, constructive ends.

Every man has reminiscences which he would not tell to everyone but only to his friends. He has other matters in his mind which he would not reveal even to his friend, but only to himself, and that in secret. But there are other things which a man is afraid to tell even to himself, and every decent man has a number of such things stored away in his mind.

SOURCE: DOSTOYEVSKY'S *Notes from the Underground*

Repression   Finally, we come to the major defense mechanism of psychoanalytic theory: **repression**. In repression, a thought, idea, or wish is dismissed from consciousness. It is so traumatic and threatening to the self that it is buried in the unconscious, stored away in the depths of the mind. Repression is viewed as playing a part in all the other defense mechanisms and, like these other defenses, requires a constant expenditure of energy to keep that which is dangerous outside of consciousness.

Freud first recognized the defense mechanism of repression in his therapeutic work. After many weeks or months of therapy, patients would remember traumatic events from their past (and experience a catharsis, as we discussed earlier). Prior to recalling the event, the idea of the event, of course, was in the person's mind. But it was outside of the person's conscious awareness. Freud reasoned that the person first experienced the event consciously, but that the experience was so traumatic that the individual repressed it.

To Freud, these therapeutic experiences were sufficient evidence to establish the reality of repression. However, other investigators over the years have studied repression experimentally, in the lab. An early study was done by Rosenzweig (1941). He varied the level of personal involvement in a task, and then studied research participants' (in this case, college undergraduates)

recall of their success or failure on the activity. When participants were personally involved with the experiment, they recalled a larger proportion of tasks
that they had been able to complete successfully than tasks they had been
unable to complete; they presumably repressed the experiences of failure.
When the students did not feel threatened, they remembered more of the
uncompleted tasks. In similar research conducted years later, women high in
sex guilt and women low in sex guilt were exposed to an erotic videotape and
asked to report their level of sexual arousal. At the same time, their level of
physiological response was recorded. Women high in sex guilt were found to
report less arousal than those low in sex guilt but to show greater physiological
arousal. Presumably the guilt associated with sexual arousal led to repression
or blocking of awareness of the physiological arousal (Morokoff, 1985).

Particularly compelling evidence of the fact that people sometimes repress
psychological experiences comes from extensive research on *repressive coping
style*. The idea behind this line of research is that some people are particularly
prone to repress unacceptable experiences. You may know such people. If you
ask them how they are doing, they say, "fine, I'm OK," even if it is obvious
to you that they are experiencing a lot of stress and anxiety. Weinberger,
Schwartz, and Davidson (1979) conducted a seminal study in this area. These
investigators solved two problems confronted by anyone who wishes to do
research on this topic: (1) How does one identify people who are particularly
likely to repress events (i.e., "repressors")? The challenge, of course, is that
people who repress their own negative qualities are not likely to tell you that
they do so; they may not be consciously aware that they are repressors. (2) How
does one demonstrate that the repressors actually are experiencing stressful
emotions that they do not admit having? Weinberger and colleagues solved the
first problem by using a technique we discussed in Chapter 2, namely, a social
desirability scale. They administered a social desirability scale plus a self-
report measure of anxiety to a large group of undergraduates, and reasoned
that people who (a) report extremely low levels of anxiety, but also (b) score
high on social desirability (i.e., they give a wide variety of responses that seem
designed to hide undesirable personal qualities) are not actually people with
low levels of anxiety but, rather, highly anxious people who are repressing their
anxieties. Those with low anxiety levels, high anxiety levels, and repressors
were then invited to participate in a laboratory study in which they were asked
to complete word phrases, some of which contained material with sexual
or aggressive content. Physiological measures of anxious arousal were taken
while participants performed this task. The findings (Figure 3.1) revealed that
the repressors—who had described themselves, in their conscious self-reports,
as low in anxiety—were actually high in anxiety. The physiological measures
indicated that they experienced a level of anxious arousal that exceeded
not only the low anxious persons, but even the people who had described
themselves as high in anxiety.

In another fascinating study of repression, subjects were asked to think
back to their childhood and recall any experience or situation that came
to mind. They also were asked to recall childhood experiences associated
with each of five emotions (happiness, sadness, anger, fear, and wonder) and
to indicate the earliest experience recalled for each emotion. Subjects were
divided into repressors and two types of nonrepressors (high anxious and low
anxious nonrepressors) on the basis of their response to questionnaires. Did

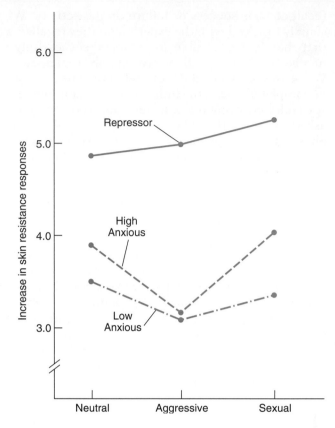

Figure 3.1 *Spontaneous skin resistance (a physiological index of anxiety) among three types of research participants (repressors, high anxious, and low anxious persons) as they responded to phrases containing neutral, aggressive, and sexual content. From Weinberger et al. (1979).*

the subjects differ in recall, as would be suggested by the psychoanalytic theory of repression? It was found that repressors recalled fewer negative emotions and were significantly older at the time of the earliest negative memory recalled (Figure 3.2). The authors concluded: "The pattern of findings is consistent with the hypothesis that repression involves an inaccessibility to negative emotional memories and indicates further that repression is associated in some way with the suppression or inhibition of emotional experiences in general. The concept of repression as a process involving limited access to negative affective memories appears to be valid" (Davis & Schwartz, 1987, p. 155).

Research along these lines supports the view that some individuals may be characterized as having a repressive style (Weinberger, 1990). They rarely report that they experience anxiety or other negative emotions; outwardly, they appear calm. However, their calmness appears to be bought at a price. Repressors react more to stress than do nonrepressors, and are more prone to develop a variety of illnesses (Contrada, Czarnecki, & Pan, 1997; Derakshan & Eysenck, 1997; Weinberger & Davidson, 1994). The cheerfulness of repressors sometimes masks high blood pressure and high pulse rates, which puts people at risk for illnesses such as heart disease and cancer (*APA Monitor*, 1990, p. 14). This fits with other evidence suggesting that a lack of emotional expressiveness is associated with increased risk of illness (Cox & MacKay, 1982; Levy, 1991; Temoshok, 1985, 1991).

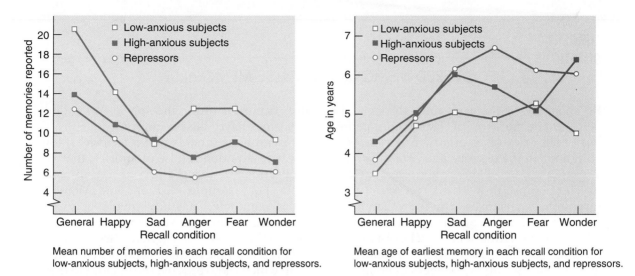

Mean number of memories in each recall condition for low-anxious subjects, high-anxious subjects, and repressors.

Mean age of earliest memory in each recall condition for low-anxious subjects, high-anxious subjects, and repressors.

Figure 3.2 *Repression and Affective Memories (Davis & Schwartz, 1987). (Copyright © 1987 by the American Psychological Association. Reprinted by permission.)*

In sum, contemporary research has firmly established that people are sometimes motivated to banish from their conscious experience thoughts that are threatening or painful. As Freud would have expected, some people who consciously report that they are free from psychological distress in reality harbor anxiety-related thought and emotions of which they appear not to be aware. On the other hand, it is not clear that contemporary experimental research supports the exact conception of repression put forth by Freud. Consider the research on repressive coping style. It documents repression among a *select subset* of people (repressors), whereas Freud's theory postulated that all persons repress emotionally traumatic material. Furthermore, this research documents repression using relatively simple laboratory stimuli that surely do not evoke the deep-seated and utterly traumatic experiences that Freud studied in his patients.

GROWTH AND DEVELOPMENT

In Chapter 1, we noted that the study of personality development encompasses two distinct challenges: identifying (1) general patterns that characterize the development of most or all people, and (2) factors that contribute to the development of differences among people. In his psychoanalytic theory, Freud combined these two concerns in a manner that was extraordinarily original. He proposed that all persons develop through a series of stages. He then proposed that events that occur at these stages are responsible for personality styles, and differences among individuals in personality styles, that are evident throughout life. Early-life experiences, and the particular stage at which these experiences occur, are said to have a permanent effect on personality; indeed, a strong psychoanalytic position would suggest that the most significant aspects of later personality are entirely determined by the end of the first five years of life.

CURRENT QUESTIONS

RECOVERED MEMORIES OR FALSE MEMORIES?

Psychoanalysts suggest that through the defense mechanism of repression people bury memories of traumatic experiences of childhood in the unconscious. They also suggest that under some conditions, such as psychotherapy, individuals can recall their forgotten experiences. On the other hand, others question the accuracy of adult recall of childhood experiences. The issue has reached headline proportions as individuals report recalling experiences of childhood sexual abuse and initiate lawsuits against individuals now recalled to be the perpetrators of the abuse. Although some professionals are convinced of the authenticity of these memories of sexual abuse, and suggest that a disservice is done to the person when we do not treat them as real, others question their authenticity and refer to them as part of a "false memory syndrome." While some view the recovery of these memories as beneficial to those who previously repressed the trauma of abuse, others suggest that the "memories" are induced by the probing questions of therapists convinced that such abuse has taken place.

An article in a professional psychological journal asks: "What scientific basis is there for the authenticity of memories of sexual abuse that were 'repressed' but then 'remembered' with the help of a therapist? How are scientists, jurists, and distressed individuals themselves to distinguish true memories from false ones?" Answering these questions is difficult. On the one hand, we know that people can forget events that subsequently are remembered. This is obvious from one's own experiences in remembering events from one's past. Yet there is an alternative possibility that is intriguing—indeed, somewhat disturbing. It is that we might sometimes "recall" events that

never occurred in the first place. We might sometimes have "false memories."

Research documents that it is possible for people to experience false memories, that is, recollections of events that did not, in fact, occur. For example, Mazzoni and Memon (2003) conducted a study involving three experimental sessions that each were separated in time by one week. In the first session, adult research participants completed a survey in which they reported the likelihood that they had experienced each of a large series of life events in their childhood. In session two, the experimenters conducted an experimental manipulation involving two of the events from the survey. The two events were minor medical procedures: a tooth extraction and the removal of a skin sample from one's small finger. For one of the events, participants merely were exposed to a paragraph of information about the type of event. For the other event, participants were asked to imagine the event occurring. In the third session, participants completed the survey again and reported any memories they had of the two target events. The hypothesis was that imagining the events—i.e., forming a mental imagine of the event occurring in one's life years earlier—could cause people to believe that the event, in fact, had occurred. This is what happened (see Figure 3.3). Whether they had imagined the tooth extraction or the removal of a skin sample, participants were more likely to believe that the event had occurred and to imagine some aspects of the event if they merely had been asked to imagine it a week earlier. A critical aspect of this particular study is that one of the events, the skin sample removal, surely had never occurred to the participants; medical records in the area that the study was conducted indicated that physicians never employed the

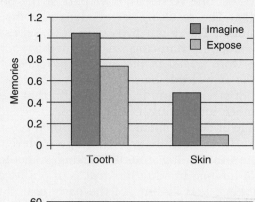

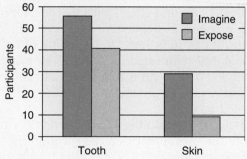

Figure 3.3 *The graphs display amount of memories recalled (top) and percentage of participants who experienced significant memory of events (bottom) as a result of either imagining the event occurring or merely being exposed to information about the event.*

procedure. Thus, the findings showed that participants ended up remembering information (e.g., aspects of the physical setting, the medical personnel involved) about an event that never had occurred.

This sort of study does not resolve the question of whether the memories of a particular client in therapy are accurate or false. In individual cases, this issue surely will remain controversial. Psychologists have no reliable method of distinguishing between "recovered memories" and "false memories" in each individual case. However, the research does demonstrate that it is at least possible for people to "remember" events that demonstrably had not occurred.

SOURCE: American Psychological Society Observer, 1992; Loftus, 1993, *New York Times*, April 8, 1994, p. A1; Mazzoni & Memon, 2003; Williams, 1994.

The Development of the Instincts and Stages of Development

By now, you should be able to figure out the primary question that Freud would ask in studying development. If one embraces an energy model of mind in which behavior is in the service of instinctual drives, then major questions involve the development of instincts: What is the nature of the instincts that the individual experiences, and must cope with, during the course of development?

Once again, Freud's answer is thoroughly biological. He theorized, first, that instinctual drives tend to center on particular regions of the body, which he called **erogenous zones**. He then suggested that the particular erogenous zone that is most important to biological gratification at a given point in time changes systematically across the course of development. At different points in development, in other words, one versus another part of the body is the primary focus of gratification. The resulting set of ideas is a theory of *psychosexual stages* of development. Development occurs in a series of distinct steps, or stages. And each stage is characterized by a bodily source of gratification. Freud's use of the word *sexual* in the phrase "psychosexual stages" corresponds more closely to our word *sensual*; each stage, then, is characterized by a distinct region of sensual gratification. Within that basic framework, the question is the number, and nature, of the stages.

Freud proposed that the first stage of development is one in which sensual gratification centers on the mouth. He called this the **oral stage** of development. Early oral gratification occurs in feeding, thumb sucking, and other mouth movements characteristic of infants. In adult life, traces of orality are seen in chewing gum, eating, smoking, and kissing. In the early oral stage the child is passive and receptive. In the late oral stage, with the development of teeth, there can be a fusion of sexual and aggressive pleasures. In children, such a fusion of instinctual gratification is seen in the eating of animal crackers. In later life, we see traces of orality in various spheres. For example, academic pursuits can have oral associations within the unconscious: one is given "food for thought," asked to "incorporate" material in reading, and told to "regurgitate" what has been learned on exams.

In the second stage of development, the **anal stage** (ages two and three), there is excitation in the anus and in the movement of feces through the anal passageway. The expulsion of the feces is believed to bring relief from tension and pleasure in the stimulation of the mucous membranes in that region. The pleasure related to this erogenous zone involves the organism in conflict. There is conflict between elimination and retention, between the pleasure in release and the pleasure in retention, and between the wish for pleasure in evacuation and the demands of the external world for delay. This latter conflict represents the first crucial conflict between the individual and society. Here the environment requires the child to violate the pleasure principle or be punished. The child may retaliate against such demands by intentional soiling. Psychologically, the child may associate having bowel movements with losing something important, which leads to depression, or may associate bowel movements with giving a prize or gift to others, which may create feelings of power and control.

In the **phallic stage** (ages four and five), excitation and tension is focused on the genitals. The biological differentiation between the sexes leads to psychological differentiation. The male child develops erections, and the new excitations in this area lead to increased interest in the genitals and the realization that the female lacks the penis. This leads to the fear that he may lose his penis—**castration anxiety**. The father becomes a rival for the affections of the mother, as suggested in the song "I Want a Girl Just Like the Girl That Married Dear Old Dad." The boy's hostility toward the father is projected onto the father, with the consequent fear of retaliation. This leads to what is known as the **Oedipus complex**. According to the Oedipus complex, every boy is fated to kill his father in fantasy and marry his mother. The complex can be heightened by actual seductiveness on the part of the mother. Castration anxiety can be heightened by actual threats from the father to cut off the penis. These threats occur in a surprising number of cases.

An interesting experimental illustration of the Oedipus complex is found in the subliminal psychodynamic activation studies we reviewed previously. As you read, in this research stimuli are presented to subjects subliminally in a tachistoscope. Particular stimuli presumably activate unconscious conflicts. In one study, researchers included stimuli designed to activate Oedipal conflicts. They then examined the effects of Oedipal activation on males' performance in a competitive situation (Silverman et al., 1978). The stimuli chosen to intensify versus reduce Oedipal conflict were "Beating Dad Is Wrong" and "Beating Dad Is OK." In addition, neutral stimuli (e.g., "People Are Walking") were presented. These stimuli were presented tachistoscopically after participants engaged in a dart-throwing competition. Participants were tested again for dart-throwing performance following subliminal exposure to each type of stimulus. As expected, the two Oedipal stimuli had clear-cut effects, and in different directions: the "Beating Dad Is OK" stimulus produced higher scores than the neutral stimulus, whereas the "Beating Dad Is Wrong" stimulus produced lower scores (Table 3.2). These results were not obtained when the stimuli were presented above threshold. Since these subliminal effects are not always found in psychological research, it is noteworthy that the authors emphasized that the experimental stimuli used and the responses measured must be relevant to the motivational state of the research participants. To assure this in their work, participants were first primed with picture and story material containing Oedipal content.

Developmental processes during the phallic stage differ for females versus males. According to Freud, females realize they lack a penis and blame the mother, the original love object. In developing **penis envy**, the female child chooses the father as the love object and imagines that the lost organ will be restored by having a child by the father.[1] Whereas the Oedipus complex is abandoned in the boy because of castration anxiety, in the female it is started because of penis envy. As with the male, conflict during this period is in some cases accentuated by seductiveness on the part of the father toward the female child. And, as with the male, the female child resolves the conflict by keeping the father as a love object, but gaining him through identification with the mother.

Table 3.2 Oedipal Conflict and Competitive Performance

Dart Score	"Beating Dad Is Wrong"	"Beating Dad Is OK"	"People Are Walking"
TACHISTOSCOPIC PRESENTATION OF THREE STIMULI			
Mean, Prestimulus	443.7	444.3	439.0
Mean, Poststimulus	349.0	533.3	442.3
Difference	−94.7	+90.0	+3.3

SOURCE: Partial results adapted from Silverman et al., 1978, p. 346. Copyright by the American Psychological Association. Reprinted by permission.

---

[1] Psychoanalytic theory has been criticized by feminists on a variety of grounds. Perhaps more than any other concept, the concept of penis envy is seen as expressing a chauvinistic, hostile view toward women. This issue will be addressed in Chapter 4 in the "Critical Evaluation" section.

Oedipus Complex, Competition, and Identification: For the male child to become competitive, there must not be too much anxiety about rivalry with the father. Photo depicts Albert Pujols of the St. Louis Cardinals and his son, Albert Jr.

Do children actually display Oedipal behaviors or are these all distorted memories of adults, in particular patients in psychoanalytic treatment? A study investigated this question through the use of parents' reports of parent-child interactions, as well as through the analysis of children's responses to stories involving parent-child interaction. It was found that at around age four, children show increased preference for the parent of the opposite sex and an increased antagonism toward the parent of the same sex. These behaviors diminish at around the age of five or six. What is interesting in this study is that although the researchers came from a differing theoretical orientation, they concluded that the reported Oedipal behaviors coincided with the psychoanalytic view of Oedipal relations between mothers and sons and between fathers and daughters (Watson & Getz, 1990). As part of the resolution of the Oedipus complex, the child identifies with the parent of the same sex. The child now gains the parent of the opposite sex through **identification** with, rather than defeat of, the parent of the same sex. The development of an identification with the parent of the same sex is a critical issue during the phallic stage and, more generally, is a critical concept in developmental psychology. In identification, individuals take on themselves the qualities of another person and integrate them into their functioning. In identifying with their parents, children assume many of the same values and morals. It is in this sense that the superego has been called the heir to the resolution of the Oedipus complex.

According to Freud, all major aspects of our personality character develop during the oral, anal, and phallic stages of development. After the phallic stage, the child enters a **latency stage** during which, according to Freud, the child experiences a decrease in sexual urges and interest. The onset of puberty, with the reawakening of the sexual urges and Oedipal feelings, marks the beginning of the **genital stage**. Dependency feelings and Oedipal strivings that were not fully resolved during the pregenital stages of development now come back to rear their ugly heads. The turmoil of adolescence is partly attributable to these factors. According to Freud, successful progression through the stages of development leads to the psychologically healthy person—one who can love and work.

Erikson's Psychosocial Stages of Development

Freud devoted little attention to development after the early years of life. All "the action" in personality development, Freud thought, occurred by the end of the phallic stage. Other psychologists who were deeply sympathetic to Freud's overall model of personality thought he had underestimated the importance of personality development later in life. They tried, then, to understand later-life development within a psychodynamic perspective. The most important of these theorists was Erik Erikson (1902–1994).

Erikson believed that development was not merely psychosexual, but also psycho*social*. Stages of development include social concerns (Table 3.3). To Erikson, the first stage of personality development is significant not just because of the localization of pleasure in the mouth, but because in the feeding situation a relationship of trust or mistrust is developed between the infant and the mother. Similarly, the anal stage is significant not only for the change in the nature of the major erogenous zone, but also because toilet training is a significant social situation in which the child may develop a sense

Erik H. Erikson

Table 3.3   Erikson's Eight Psychosocial Stages of Development and Their Implications for Personality

Psychosocial Stage	Age	Positive Outcomes	Negative Outcomes
Basic Trust vs. Mistrust	1 year	Feelings of inner goodness, trust in oneself and others, optimism	Sense of badness, mistrust of self and others, pessimism
Autonomy vs. Shame and Doubt	2–3 years	Exercise of will, self-control, able to make choices	Rigid, excessive conscience, doubtful, self-conscious shame
Initiative vs. Guilt	4–5 years	Pleasure in accomplishments, activity, direction and purpose	Guilt over goals contemplated and achievements initiated
Industry vs. Inferiority	Latency	Able to be absorbed in productive work, pride in completed product	Sense of inadequacy and inferiority, unable to complete work
Identity vs. Role Diffusion	Adolescence	Confidence of inner sameness and continuity, promise of a career	Ill at ease in roles, no set standards, sense of artificiality
Intimacy vs. Isolation	Early Adulthood	Mutuality, sharing of thoughts, work, feelings	Avoidance of intimacy, superficial relations
Generativity vs. Stagnation	Adulthood	Ability to lose oneself in work and relationships	Loss of interest in work, impoverished relations
Integrity vs. Despair	Later Years	Sense of order and meaning, content with self and one's accomplishments	Fear of death, bitter about life and what one got from it or what did not happen

of autonomy or succumb to shame and self-doubt. In the phallic stage the child must struggle with the issue of taking pleasure in, as opposed to feeling guilty about, being assertive, competitive, and successful.

For Erikson (1950), the latency and genital stages are periods when the individual develops a sense of industry and success or a sense of inferiority, and perhaps most important of all, a sense of identity or a sense of role diffusion. The crucial task of adolescence, according to Erikson, is the establishment of a sense of ego identity, an accrued confidence that the way one views oneself has a continuity with one's past and is matched by the perceptions of others. In contrast to people who develop a sense of identity, people with role diffusion experience the feeling of not really knowing who they are, of not knowing whether what they think they are matches what others think of them, and of not knowing how they have developed in this way or where they are heading in the future. During late adolescence and the college years, this struggle with a sense of identity may lead to joining a variety of groups and to considerable anguish about the choice of a career. If these issues are not resolved during this time, the individual is, in later life, filled with a sense of despair; life is too short, and it is too late to start all over again.

In his research on the process of identity formation, Marcia (1994) has identified four statuses individuals can have in relation to this process. In Identity Achievement, the individual has established a sense of identity following exploration. Such individuals function at a high psychological level, being capable of independent thought, intimacy in interpersonal relations, complex moral reasoning, and resistance to group demands for conformity or group manipulation of their sense of self-esteem. In Identity Moratorium, the individual is in the midst of an identity crisis. Such individuals are capable of high levels of psychological functioning, as indicated in complex thought and moral reasoning, and also value intimacy. However, they are still struggling with just who they are and what they are about, and are less prepared than the identity achievers to make commitments. In Identity Foreclosure, the individual is committed to an identity without having gone through a process of exploration. Such individuals tend to be rigid, highly responsive to group demands for conformity, and sensitive to manipulation of their self-esteem. They tend to be highly conventional and rejecting of deviation from perceived standards of right and wrong. Finally, in Identity Diffusion, the individual lacks any strong sense of identity or commitment. Such individuals are very vulnerable to blows to their self-esteem, often are disorganized in their thinking, and have problems with intimacy. In sum, Marcia suggests that individuals differ in how they go about handling the process of identity formation, with such differences being reflected in their sense of self, thought processes, and interpersonal relations. Although not necessarily establishing fixed patterns for later life, how the process of identity formation is handled is seen as having important implications for later personality development.

Continuing with his description of the later stages of life and the accompanying psychological issues, Erikson suggests that some people develop a sense of intimacy, an acceptance of life's successes and disappointments, and a sense of continuity throughout the life cycle, whereas other people remain isolated from family and friends, appear to survive on a fixed daily routine, and focus on both past disappointments and future death. Although the ways in which people do and do not resolve these critical issues of adulthood may have their roots in childhood conflict, Erikson suggests that this is not always the case and that they have a significance of their own (Erikson, 1982). In sum, Erikson's contributions are noteworthy in three ways: (1) he has emphasized the psychosocial as well as the instinctual basis for personality development, (2) he has extended the stages of development to include the entire life cycle and has articulated the major psychological issues to be faced in these later stages, and (3) he has recognized that people look to the future as well as to the past, and that how they construe their future may be as significant a part of their personality as how they construe their past.

Identity vs. Role Diffusion: In adolescence, a sense of ego identity is developed partly by having one's sense of self confirmed by the perceptions of friends.

The Importance of Early Experience   Psychoanalytic theory emphasizes the role of early life events for later personality development. Much of adult life is a repetition of themes established during the early developmental stages. Many contemporary researchers, however, suggest a much greater potential for development and change in personality across the entire life span. Although the issue is complex, with no uniform consensus (Caspi & Bem, 1990), many scholars highlight the fact that, to a degree not fully appreciated by Freud, changes in an individual's environment that occur later in life can bring about changes in personality (Kagan, 1998; Lewis, 2002). Indeed, in contrast to the themes established by Freud, a major trend in contemporary psychology is the study of personality dynamics across the entire course of life, from childhood to older adulthood (Baltes, Staudinger, & Lindenberger, 1999).

The complexities of the issue can be illustrated with two studies. The first, conducted by a psychoanalyst (Gaensbauer, 1982), involved the study of affect development in infancy. The infant, Jenny, was first studied systematically when she was almost four months old. Prior to this time, at the age of three months, she had been physically abused by her father. At that time she was brought to the hospital with a broken arm and a skull fracture. She was described by hospital personnel as being a "lovable baby"—happy, cute, sociable, but also as not cuddling when held and as being "jittery" when approached by a male. Following this history of abuse, Jenny was placed in a foster home, where she received adequate physical care but minimal social interaction. This was very much in contrast with her earlier experience with her natural mother, who spent considerable time with her and breast-fed her "at the drop of a hat." The first systematic observation occurred almost a month after placement in the foster home. At this time Jenny's behavior was judged to be completely consistent with a diagnosis of depression—lethargic, apathetic, disinterested, collapsed posture. A systematic analysis of her facial expressions indicated five discrete affects, each meaningfully related to her unique history. Sadness was noted when she was with her natural mother. Fearfulness and anger were noted when she was approached by a male stranger but not when approached by a female stranger. Joy was noted as a transient affect during brief play sequences. Finally, interest-curiosity was noted when she interacted with female strangers.

After she was visited in her foster home, Jenny was placed in a different foster home where she received warm attention. Following two weeks in this environment, she was again brought to the hospital for further evaluation, this time by her second foster mother. This time she generally appeared to be a normally responsive infant. She showed no evidence of distress and even smiled at a male stranger. After an additional month at this foster home, she was brought to the hospital by her natural mother for a third evaluation. Generally, she was animated and happy. However, when the mother left the room, she cried intensely. This continued following the mother's return despite repeated attempts to soothe her. Apparently separation from her natural mother continued to lead to a serious distress response. In addition, sadness and anger were frequently noted. At eight months old, Jenny was returned to her natural mother, who left her husband and received counseling. At the age of 20 months, she was described as appearing to be normal and having an excellent relationship with her mother. However, there continued to be the problem of anger and distress associated with separation from her mother.

From these observations, we can conclude that there was evidence of both continuity and discontinuity between Jenny's early emotional experiences and her later emotional reactions. In general, she was doing well and her emotional responses were within the normal range for infants of her age. At the same time, the anger reactions in response to separations and frustration appeared to be a link to the past. The psychoanalyst conducting the study suggested that perhaps isolated traumatic events are less important than the repeated experiences of a less dramatic but more persistent nature. In other words, the early years are important, but more in terms of patterns of interpersonal relationships than in terms of isolated events.

The second study, conducted by a group of developmental psychologists, assessed the relationship between early emotional relationships with the mother and later psychopathology (Lewis, et al., 1984). In this study, the attachment behavior toward their mothers of boys and girls one year of age was observed. The observation involved a standardized procedure consisting of a period of play with the mother in an unstructured situation, followed by the departure of the mother and a period when the child was alone in the playroom, and then by the return of the mother and a second free play period. The behavior of the children was scored systematically and assigned to one of three attachment categories: avoidant, secure, or ambivalent. The avoidant and ambivalent categories suggested difficulties in this area. Then at six years of age, the competence of these children was assessed through the completion by the mothers of a Child Behavior Profile. The ratings of the mothers were also checked against teacher ratings. On the basis of the Child Behavior Profile the children were classified into a normal group, an at-risk group, and a clinically disturbed group.

What was the relationship between early attachment behavior and later pathology? Two aspects of the results are particularly noteworthy. First, the relationships were quite different for boys than for girls. For boys, attachment classification at one year of age was significantly related to later pathology. Insecurely attached boys showed more pathology at age six than did securely attached boys. On the other hand, no relationship between attachment and later pathology was observed for girls. Second, the authors noted a difference between trying to predict pathology from the early data (prospective) as opposed to trying to understand later pathology in terms of earlier attachment difficulties (retrospective). If one starts with the boys who at age six were identified as being at risk or clinically disturbed, 80 percent would be found to have been assigned to the avoidant- or ambivalent-attachment category at age one. In other words, a very strong statistical relationship exists. On the other hand, if one took all boys classified as insecurely attached (avoidant or ambivalent) at age one and predicted them to be at risk or clinically disturbed at age six, one would be right in only 40 percent of the cases. The reason for this is that far more of the boys were classified as insecurely attached than were later diagnosed as at risk or disturbed. Thus, the clinician viewing later pathology would have a clear basis for suggesting a strong relationship between pathology and early attachment difficulties. On the other hand, focusing on the data in terms of prediction would suggest a much more tenuous relationship and the importance of other variables. As Freud himself recognized, when we observe later pathology, it is all too easy to understand how it developed. On the other hand, when we look at these phenomena prospectively, we are made aware of the varied paths that development can follow.

The Development of Thinking Processes

The most prominent aspect of Freud's work on development is his theory of psychosexual stages (reviewed above). In addition to the development of instinctual drives, however, Freud also addressed the development of thinking processes. Here, his work rests on a theoretical distinction between two different modes, or processes, of thinking; he called them primary and secondary process thought.

Before defining these terms, we note that Freud, with this distinction, addressed an issue of enormously broad significance. It is, in essence, the question of how the mind works—the processes through which the mind deals with information. We might think that the human mind, like a computer, processes information in one basic way. Your personal computer processes information the same way whether the computer is new or old, and whether the information being processed is emotionally exciting or boring. No matter what, information is processed digitally in the machine's central processing unit. Maybe the human mind is like this too. Then again, maybe it isn't—and Freud suggested it isn't. He concluded that the mind processes information in two distinctly different ways.

In psychoanalytic theory, **primary process** thinking is the language of the unconscious. Primary process thought is illogical and irrational. In primary process thinking, reality and fantasy are indistinguishable. These features of primary process thought—an absence of logic, a confusion of appearance and reality—may seem so odd at first that you may reject this aspect of Freudian theory. Yet consider some examples. As you grew up, you only gradually developed the capacity for logical, rational thought. Very young children do not have the capacity to formulate logical arguments. Yet they clearly are thinking! This means that they must be thinking in a manner that lacks adult rationality and logic. To Freud, they are thinking via primary process thought. Consider dreams. Sometimes you wake up when having a nightmare. Your heart may be racing and you may be in a cold sweat. If so, this means that your body was reacting to the contents of the dream, preparing its physiological systems to respond. But, of course, there is nothing to respond to: It's just a dream. This means that you were reacting to a fantasy as if it were real; in the dream, fantasy and reality are confused.

Secondary process thinking is the language of consciousness, reality testing, and logic. It develops only after the child first has the capacity for primary process thought, and thus is secondary. The development of this capacity parallels the development of the ego and superego. With the development of the ego, the individual becomes more differentiated, as a self, from the rest of the world and there is a decrease in self-preoccupation.

Contemporary psychologists have recognized, as did Freud, that the mind works according to more than one thinking process. Epstein (1994) has distinguished between experiential thinking and rational thinking. Experiential thinking, analogous to primary process thinking, is viewed as occurring earlier in evolutionary development and is characterized by being holistic, concrete, and heavily influenced by emotion. Often it is used in interpersonal situations to be empathic or intuitive. Rational thinking, analogous to secondary process thinking, is viewed as occurring later in evolutionary development and is characterized by being more abstract, analytical, and following the rules of logic and evidence. For example, rational thinking would be used in solving mathematical problems. The potential conflict between the two systems of thought can be seen in an experiment in which subjects were asked to choose between drawing a winning red jelly bean from a bowl that contained 1 out of 10 red jelly beans, and a bowl that contained 8 out of 100 red jelly beans (Denes-Raj & Epstein, 1994). Having been told the proportion of red jelly beans in the two bowls, subjects knew that the rational thing to do was to select the bowl with the higher proportion—1 out of 10. Yet, despite this, many subjects felt that their chances were better with the bowl that contained more red jelly beans, despite the poorer odds. This conflict between what they felt and what they knew expressed the conflict between the experiential and rational thought systems. According to Epstein (1994), the two systems are parallel and can act in conjunction with one another as well as in conflict with one another. Other psychologists have suggested other, related, two-part distinctions. Thinking processes have been described as analytic versus holistic (Bolte, Goschke, & Kuhl, 2003), as involving "hot" emotional processes versus relatively "cool" logical cognition (Metcalfe & Mischel, 1999), and as involving feeling states describable as "empathizing" versus rational thought processes that involve "systemizing" (Baron-Cohen, 2002). Many contemporary psychologists, then, feel that Freud was fundamentally correct in positing more than one form of thought; they tend to differ from Freud in the details, that is, in their specific beliefs about the nature of the two aspects of thinking. The study of primary versus secondary process thought, then, is one in which Freud's ideas remarkably anticipated future developments in the field.

This chapter has considered Freud's approach to three of the four topics addressed in a personality theory: structure, processes, and development. In our next chapter, we consider the fourth: clinical applications designed to improve people's lives. We also review alternative psychodynamic models developed throughout the 20th century in reaction to Freud's original theorizing.

MAJOR CONCEPTS

Anal stage   Freud's concept for that period of life during which the major center of bodily excitation or tension is the anus.

Anxiety   In psychoanalytic theory, a painful emotional experience that signals or alerts the ego to danger.

Castration anxiety   Freud's concept of the boy's fear, experienced during the phallic stage, that the father will cut off the son's penis because of their sexual rivalry for the mother.

Catharsis   The release and freeing of emotion through talking about one's problems.

Conscious   Those thoughts, experiences, and feelings of which we are aware.

Death instinct   Freud's concept for drives or sources of energy directed toward death or a return to an inorganic state.

Defense mechanisms   Freud's concept for those mental strategies used by the person to reduce anxiety. They function to exclude from awareness some thought, wish, or feeling.

Denial   The defense mechanism in which a painful internal or external reality is denied.

Ego   Freud's structural concept for the part of personality that attempts to satisfy drives (instincts) in accordance with reality and the person's moral values.

Energy system   Freud's view of personality as involving the interplay among various forces (e.g., drives, instincts) or sources of energy.

Erogenous zones   According to Freud, those parts of the body that are the sources of tension or excitation.

Free association   In psychoanalysis, the patient's reporting to the analyst of every thought that comes to mind.

Genital stage   In psychoanalytic theory, the stage of development associated with the onset of puberty.

Id   Freud's structural concept for the source of the instincts or all of the drive energy in people.

Identification   The acquisition, as characteristics of the self, of personality characteristics perceived to be part of others (e.g., parents).

Isolation   The defense mechanism in which emotion is isolated from the content of a painful impulse or memory.

Latency stage   In psychoanalytic theory, the stage following the phallic stage in which there is a decrease in sexual urges and interest.

Libido   The psychoanalytic term for the energy associated first with the sexual instincts and later with the life instincts.

Life instinct   Freud's concept for drives or sources of energy (libido) directed toward the preservation of life and sexual gratification.

Mechanism   An intellectual movement of the 19th century which argued that basic principles of natural science could explain not only the behavior of physical objects, but human thought and action.

Oedipus complex   Freud's concept expressing the boy's sexual attraction to the mother and fear of castration by the father, who is seen as a rival.

Oral stage   Freud's concept for that period of life during which the major center of bodily excitation or tension is the mouth.

Penis envy   In psychoanalytic theory, the female's envy of the male's possession of a penis.

Perception without awareness   Unconscious perception or perception of a stimulus without conscious awareness of such perception.

Perceptual defense   The process by which an individual defends (unconsciously) against awareness of a threatening stimulus.

Phallic stage   Freud's concept for that period of life during which excitation or tension begins to be centered in the genitals and during which there is an attraction to the parent of the opposite sex.

Pleasure principle According to Freud, psychological functioning based on the pursuit of pleasure and the avoidance of pain.

Preconscious Freud's concept for those thoughts, experiences, and feelings of which we are momentarily unaware but can readily bring into awareness.

Primary process In psychoanalytic theory, a form of thinking that is not governed by logic or reality testing and that is seen in dreams and other expressions of the unconscious.

Projection The defense mechanism in which one attributes to (projects onto) others one's own unacceptable instincts or wishes.

Rationalization The defense mechanism in which an acceptable reason is given for an unacceptable motive or act.

Reaction formation The defense mechanism in which the opposite of an unacceptable impulse is expressed.

Reality principle According to Freud, psychological functioning based on reality in which pleasure is delayed until an optimum time.

Repression The primary defense mechanism in which a thought, idea, or wish is dismissed from consciousness.

Secondary process In psychoanalytic theory, a form of thinking that is governed by reality and associated with the development of the ego.

Sublimation The defense mechanism in which the original expression of the instinct is replaced by a higher cultural goal.

Subliminal psychodynamic activation The research procedure associated with psychoanalytic theory in which stimuli are presented below the perceptual threshold (subliminally) to stimulate unconscious wishes and fears.

Superego Freud's structural concept for the part of personality that expresses our ideals and moral values.

Unconscious Those thoughts, experiences, and feelings of which we are unaware. According to Freud, this unawareness is the result of repression.

Undoing The defense mechanism in which one magically undoes an act or wish associated with anxiety.

REVIEW

1. Freud posited a mechanistic, deterministic, energy-based model of the mind. This model directly reflected the 19th-century scientific and medical training Freud received.

2. Freud built his theory on case-study evidence. In his view, the in-depth analysis of clinical cases was the only valid method for uncovering the dynamics of the conscious and unconscious mind.

3. The core of Freud's theory is an integrated analysis of both personality structures and personality processes. The structures are three mental systems, the id, ego, and superego, which function according to different operating principles that inherently conflict with one another. The processes involve mental energy whose origin is in the id, but whose expression is blocked or distorted by the actions of the ego, working within constraints represented in the superego.

4. Personality dynamics in psychoanalytic theory involve conflict. Impulsive drives in the id seek immediate expression, which conflicts with both the ego's desire to delay impulses to meet the constraints of reality and the superego's desire for actions that adhere to moral standards. Any given action, then, is a compromise among these competing desires of the different psychic agencies. Defense mechanisms are strategies employed by the ego to defend against the anxiety aroused by the unacceptable drives and desires of the id.

5. In the psychoanalytic theory of personality development, the individual progresses through a series of developmental stages. Each stage involves a distinct region of the body that serves as a primary focus of sensual gratification. These stages of development occur early in life, in childhood. To a greater extent than any other theory, Freud's psychoanalytic theory suggests that the experiences of early childhood have an enduring, immutable influence on the personality characteristics of the individual.

FREUD'S PSYCHOANALYTIC THEORY: APPLICATIONS, RELATED THEORETICAL CONCEPTIONS, AND CONTEMPORARY RESEARCH

4

Chapter Focus

When you were a kid, did you ever play the cloud game? It had to be a day when there were big white fluffy clouds against the blue background of the sky. You would lie on your back in the grass with a friend and stare at the clouds until you "saw" something. If you tried long and hard enough you could find all kinds of interesting things: animals, dragons, the face of an old man. Quite often, pointing out your discoveries to your friend was impossible. Exactly what you saw could only be seen by you. Why did you see the things you saw? It must have been something about you that you "projected" onto the cloud in the sky.

This is the basic idea behind projective tests such as the Rorschach Inkblot Test and the Thematic Apperception Test (TAT). In this chapter, we focus on these tests because they are techniques of personality assessment associated with psychodynamic theory. Projective tests use ambiguous stimuli to elicit highly individualistic responses which can then be interpreted by the clinician. This chapter also considers Freud's attempts to understand and explain the symptoms presented by his patients and his efforts to develop a systematic method of treatment. After considering more recent developments in psychoanalytic theory, including challenges to Freud's ideas from other psychodynamic theorists, we turn to a critical evaluation and summary.

QUESTIONS TO BE ADDRESSED IN THIS CHAPTER

1. How can one assess personality from a psychodynamic perspective?
2. What, according to psychoanalysis, are the causes of psychopathology and the best methods for treating psychologically distressed persons?
3. Why did some of Freud's early followers break with his approach, and what novel theoretical ideas did they advance?
4. What recent developments in personality psychology are inspired by Freud's work, and what does contemporary scientific evidence say about Freud's original psychoanalytical enterprise?

In the previous chapter, you learned the ideas that define Freud's psychoanalytic theory of personality. In this chapter, you will see what one can do with these ideas. The chapter discusses how the theoretical ideas of psychoanalysis can be applied to practical questions of personality assessment and psychological change in therapy.

We will also see "what one can do with" Freud's ideas in a second sense of this phrase. Throughout the 20th century, a series of psychologists judged that, rather than apply Freud's ideas, it would be better to change them. These theorists retained some key features of Freud's thinking—especially the study of internal mental dynamics, or "psychodynamics"—but significantly modified and extended other aspects of his original theory. A second goal of this chapter is to review these post-Freudian psychodynamic theories.

Finally, a third goal of this chapter concerns contemporary research. More than was the case in Chapter 3, we here examine contemporary research on psychodynamic processes. At the end of the chapter, we evaluate Freud's psychoanalytic perspective from the perspective of current research findings.

We begin with a challenge that is central to both personality theory and clinical practice, namely, the challenge of psychological assessment. This challenge, specifically, is to develop methods that shed light on the nature of an individual's personality, including causes of any psychological distress the individual is experiencing. Ideally, these methods would have two features. The first is obvious: They should be accurate, or valid (recall our discussion of validity in Chapter 2). The second is a bit more subtle. Assessment procedures should be quick and efficient. The clinician may need quickly to gain some insight into a client's personality, to make preliminary treatment decisions.

Consider for a moment how hard this challenge is from a psychoanalytic perspective. If you want to assess someone's personality, what would you do? You obviously could not "just ask" someone about psychoanalytic content. Direct questions—e.g., "How often do you think about killing one of your parents so you can have sex with the other one?"—are absurd for at least two reasons: The person being tested (1) *can't* answer the question (the relevant material is unconscious and its mere mention activates defense mechanisms that protect the material from reaching consciousness) and (2) even if the person could answer them they probably wouldn't want to; that is, most people would not want to reveal such aspects of their personality to others.

Freud addressed this challenge by using, as his tool of assessment, the free association technique. However, even if one were to assume its validity—a big "if"—the free association method clearly does not meet the goal of efficiency. It may take weeks or months to develop a client–therapist relationship that is sufficiently strong that the client will reveal deep-seated conflicts in free associations. Recognizing this, investigators inspired by Freud's theory sought new assessment methods. The most influential of these are a set of procedures known as **projective tests**.

PSYCHODYNAMIC PERSONALITY ASSESSMENT: PROJECTIVE TESTS

THE LOGIC OF PROJECTIVE TESTS

The defining feature of projective tests is that the test items are ambiguous. The person being assessed is asked to respond to each of a series of ambiguous test items. In order to respond to the item, the person must interpret it; that is, he or she must figure out what the test item looks like or means. The fundamental logic behind the projective tests is that the person's interpretations will be revealing of his or her personality. It is thought, in other words, that the individual will "project" aspects of his or her own personality onto the test item when interpreting it (hence the name "projective tests").

This use of ambiguous test items is utterly unlike other, more typical psychological questionnaires or surveys. When writing test items for a questionnaire, psychologists usually strive for clarity. A questionnaire item such as "Do you like things?" would usually be seen as a terrible test item because it is so ambiguous; "What things are you talking about?" the test taker might ask. But in projective assessment, this ambiguity is the very point of the test. The psychologist is interested in how the test taker constructs meaning out of the vague stimulus.

The psychologist of course is not interested in responses to test items per se. Responses to the test items are interesting only because they might be revealing of the individual's *typical* style of thinking, which in turn is interesting because it may be revealing of underlying, unconscious psychodynamics. A key assumption in the use of projective tests, then, is that the individual's interpretation of test items during a testing session with the psychologist will be indicative of how the person interprets typically ambiguous circumstances in his or her daily life.

Two projective tests have received particularly widespread use: the Rorschach Inkblot Test and the Thematic Apperception Test (TAT). Although these tests were not developed by Freud, they are related closely to psychoanalytic theory in three ways:

1. Psychoanalytic theory emphasizes the complex organization of personality functioning. The theory views personality as a dynamic system through which the individual organizes and structures external stimuli. Projective testing procedures allow people to respond in complex ways as they interpret test stimuli. People don't just say "yes or no" in response to test items. Instead, they formulate their own responses. The assessor thus can observe complex patterns of thinking, as required from a psychodynamic perspective.

2. Psychoanalytic theory emphasizes the importance of the unconscious and defense mechanisms. In projective tests, the purpose of the test and the way it will be interpreted are hidden from the subject. The test thus may get behind the defenses of the test taker.

3. Psychoanalytic theory emphasizes a holistic understanding of personality. The theorist is interested in the relations among parts of the person. Projective tests facilitate a holistic interpretation of the individual. The test is scored according to an overall patterning and organization of test responses rather than by interpreting any single response as an index of a particular personality characteristic.

THE RORSCHACH INKBLOT TEST

Although inkblots had been used earlier, Hermann Rorschach, a Swiss psychiatrist, first fully grasped their potential for personality assessment. He put ink

Hermann Rorschach

Rorschach Inkblot Test: The Rorschach interpreter assumes that the subject's personality is projected onto unstructured stimuli such as inkblots. (Drawing by Ross; © 1974 The New Yorker Magazine, Inc.)

on paper and folded the paper so that symmetrical but ill-defined forms were produced. He then showed these images to hospitalized patients. Through a process of trial and error, he identified inkblots that elicited different responses from different psychiatric groups. Rorschach settled on 10 such cards; the test, then, consists of 10 cards containing these inkblots.

When conducting the Rorschach test, the assessor only presents enough information to enable the person to complete the task. The test is presented as "just one of many ways used nowadays to try to understand people." People are asked to look at each card and tell the assessor what they see represented on the card. They are free to focus on the whole image or any part of the inkblot. After interpretations of the stimuli are provided, the assessor asks people to explain why they felt that a given test item represented what they said it did. All responses are recorded.

In interpreting these responses, one is interested in how the response, or percept, is formed, the reasons for the response, and its content. Percepts that match the structure of the inkblot suggest a good level of psychological functioning that is well oriented toward reality. On the other hand, poorly formed responses that do not fit the structure of the inkblot suggest unrealistic fantasies or bizarre behavior. The content of subjects' responses (whether they see mostly animate or inanimate objects, humans or animals, and content expressing affection or hostility) makes a great deal of difference in the interpretation of the subjects' personalities. For example, the assessor would make different interpretations of two sets of responses, one where animals are

Response: *"Two bears with their paws touching one another playing pattycake or could be they are fighting and the red is the blood from the fighting."*

Response: *"Two cannibals. Supposed to see something in this? African natives bending over a pot. Possibly cooking something—hope they're not man-eaters. I shouldn't make jokes—always liking humor. (Are they male or female?) Could be male or female. More female because of breasts here. But didn't impress me at first glance as being of either sex."*

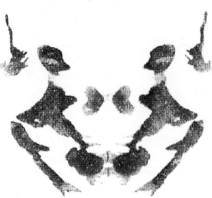

Figure 4.1   *Examples from the Rorschach Inkblot Test. The inkblot illustrations reproduced here are from the Rorschach location chart. The actual inkblot cards contain color. (Reprinted by permission of Hans Huber, Publishers.)*

seen repeatedly as fighting and a second where humans are seen as sharing and involved in cooperative efforts.

Content may be interpreted symbolically. An explosion may symbolize intense hostility; a pig, gluttonous tendencies; a fox, a tendency toward being crafty and aggressive; spiders, witches, and octopuses, negative images of a dominating mother; gorillas and giants, negative attitudes toward a dominating father; and an ostrich, an attempt to hide from conflicts (Schafer, 1954). Two illustrative stimuli and responses are presented in Figure 4.1.

When interpreting test responses, each response is used to suggest hypotheses or possible interpretations about the individual's personality, and the hypotheses are checked against other responses by the individual. The examiner also notes an unusual behavior and uses this as a source of data for further interpretation. For example, a subject who constantly asks for guidance may be interpreted as dependent. A subject who seems tense, asks questions in a subtle way, and looks at the back of the cards may be interpreted as suspicious and possibly paranoid.

Henry Murray

THE THEMATIC APPERCEPTION TEST (TAT)

A second widely used projective test is the Thematic Apperception Test (TAT), developed by Henry Murray and Christina Morgan. The TAT consists of cards with scenes on them. Most scenes depict one or two people, though some are more abstract. The assessor presents these ambiguous scenes one after the other and, for each, asks the person to make up a story based on the scene. The story includes what is going on, the thoughts and feelings of the people in the scene, what led up to the scene, and the outcome.

Since the scenes are ambiguous, the individual's personality may be projected onto the stimulus as he interprets it and may be revealed in the stories he tells. "The test is based on the well-recognized fact that when a person interprets an ambiguous social situation he is apt to expose his own personality as much as the phenomenon to which he is attending" (Murray, 1938, p. 530). The assumption is that people are not aware they are talking about themselves when weaving stories about the pictures. Their defenses thus can be bypassed. TAT responses can be scored systematically according to a scheme developed by Murray, or on a more impressionistic basis (Cramer, 1996; Cramer & Block, 1998).

Some TAT cards are shown to both male and female subjects, others to members of one sex only. An illustrative card and responses given to it by two different individuals are shown in Figure 4.2. Common themes given in response to this card are stories of disappointment with a parent, of parental pressure, and of sad thoughts about the past. In addition, some women appear to see the younger woman as having a vision of her evil self or of herself in old age (Holt, 1978).

The TAT has been used not only clinically but in experimental research, particularly in the area of human motivation. Research by the psychologist David McClelland and colleagues (McClelland, Koestner, & Weinberger, 1989) indicates that individual differences in motives, such as the motive to achieve, are uniquely revealed in the themes of stories created by research participants in response to TAT pictures.

Sample card from the Thematic Apperception Test

Illustration 1: *This is the picture of a woman who all of her life has been a very suspicious, conniving person. She's looking in the mirror and she sees reflected behind her an image of what she will be as an old woman—still a suspicious, conniving sort of person. She can't stand the thought that that's what her life will eventually lead her to and she smashes the mirror and runs out of the house screaming and goes out of her mind and lives in an institution for the rest of her life.*

Illustration 2: *This woman has always emphasized beauty in her life. As a little girl she was praised for being pretty and as a young woman was able to attract lots of men with her beauty. While secretly feeling anxious and unworthy much of the time, her outer beauty helped to disguise these feelings from the world and, sometimes, from herself. Now that she is getting on in years and her children are leaving home, she is worried about the future. She looks in the mirror and imagines herself as an old hag—the worst possible person she could become, ugly and nasty—and wonders what the future holds for her. It is a difficult and depressing time for her.*

Figure 4.2   *Illustrative TAT Card and Responses to It.*

PROJECTIVE TESTS: DO THEY WORK?

Projective tests have been widely used by personality and clinical psychologists during the past half-century. They have been administered to literally millions of persons (Lilienfeld, Wood, & Garb, 2000). Given their widespread use over the years, the natural question to ask is, "Do they work?"

By "work," in the context of psychological testing, one generally means "Do they predict important life outcomes?" In the terminology we introduced in Chapter 2, the question is whether the tests are valid. This question is more complicated than it sounds. There are at least two complications. The first is the possibility that projective tests predict some types of outcomes but not others. It might be impossible to give a simple yes or no answer to the question, "Do projective tests work?" because they might work, or be valid, for predicting only some types of outcomes. A second complication is that there are different ways of scoring projective tests. Over the years, different psychologists have developed different schemes for interpreting and classifying people's responses to projective test items (e.g., Cramer, 1991; Exner, 1986; Westen, 1990). It is possible, then, that some scoring systems might work well, whereas others might not.

These complications suggest that one cannot answer the question of whether projective tests work by considering only one or two isolated studies. Instead, what is required are comprehensive reviews of the various scoring schemes and the range of outcomes that the psychologist might wish to predict. A particularly extensive review of this sort was completed by Lilienfeld and colleagues (2000). These authors were attentive to the complexities involved in assessing the validity of projective tests. They reviewed research on a variety of projective methods, including the Rorschach and TAT, and on a variety of methods for scoring responses on these tests.

What did they find? On the one hand, their review indicated that some scoring methods are valid for some purposes. For example, when TAT stories are scored for the presence of themes related to achievement motivation, as suggested by psychologists such as David McClelland (McClelland, Koestner, & Weinberger, 1989), there is evidence that the TAT responses are correlated with measures of motivated behavior. TAT motive measures also predict the degree to which people remember daily events, with individuals showing greater memory for events that are linked to their motives (Woike, 1995; Woike, Gershkovich, Piorkowski, & Polo, 1999). However, such positive results proved to be exceptions. The review by Lilienfeld and colleagues (2000) indicated that projective tests commonly do not work. For example, although there may be a variety of ways to score Rorschach responses, the choice of scoring scheme seems not to make much difference; "the overwhelming majority of Rorschach indexes" (Lilienfeld et al., 2000, p. 54) were not consistently related to outcomes of interest. And although there may be some validity to methods for scoring achievement themes in TAT responses, "most TAT scoring systems" (p. 54), like the Rorschach systems, also lack validity.

These negative conclusions about the validity of projective tests are congruent with those of many other scholars (e.g., Dawes, 1994, Rorer, 1990) who have taken an objective look at research on projective tests and have found that they simply do not work well enough to be used in clinical practice. Indeed, the Lilienfeld group (2000) recommends that students of psychology no longer should obtain extensive training in the use of these tests, and notes that a committee of the American Psychological Association has concurred that projective tests should not be a component of 21st-century training in psychology.

Why don't projective tests work very well? That is, why is it that they rarely enable psychologists to predict life outcomes with high levels of accuracy? There are many possible reasons, but two stand out. The first concerns inter-judge reliability: If two psychologists (two "judges") score a person's responses to a projective test, will they agree with one another (will the judgments be reliable)? When using standard questionnaires, the reliability of scoring can be taken for granted; for example, if you take a multiple-choice test, a person or a machine-scoring system can score the test with perfect accuracy. But with projective tests, psychologists are not dealing with simple multiple-choice responses but rather with complex verbal statements that must be interpreted. The psychologist's interpretations may reflect not only the thoughts of the person taking the test, but those of the psychologist who does the scoring. The thoughts, feelings, and interpretive biases of the psychologist may influence the scoring of the test. If different psychologists have different interpretive biases, then inter-judge reliability will be low. Research indicates that projective tests often do suffer from this problem. The inter-judge reliability of scoring is not sufficiently high. Even when using the most well-developed of the Rorschach scoring systems, "only about half" of the Rorschach variables reach a "minimum acceptable threshold" of reliability (Lilienfeld et al., 2000, p. 33). If different psychologists do not even agree on how to score a person's test responses, then the scores that they compute are, of course, unlikely to yield accurate predictions of the person's behavior.

A second limitation is that the content of the projective test items commonly has nothing to do with the content of the test taker's day-to-day life. It might be that an individual exhibits a distinctive style of thinking when contemplating, for example, relations with members of the opposite sex to which he or she is attracted. A psychological test that contained stimuli representing members of the opposite sex might pick up on this thinking style. But there is no guarantee that the person's thinking style will manifest itself when he or she is confronted with abstract blotches of ink. The few projective tests that are successful tend to use "stimuli that are especially relevant to the construct being assessed" (Lilienfeld et al., 2000, p. 55). For example, researchers interested in people's thoughts about interpersonal relations might use TAT cards that feature interpersonal themes (Westen, 1991). But this commonly is not done; instead, context commonly has been disregarded, and a generic set of stimulus materials (e.g., the set of Rorschach cards) is used to predict an individual's thoughts and feelings in a wide variety of contexts. And here the predictions commonly fail. As you will see in subsequent chapters, other personality theories employ psychological testing procedures that are much more sensitive to these issues of social context than are the projective tests of psychodynamic theory.

What do the limitations of projective testing say about Freud's psychoanalytic theory of personality? Some might argue that they say very little. In evaluating Freud, it is important to recall that he himself did not develop or use projective tests. He relied entirely on the free association method in clinical interviews. So Freud's theory might be fine, even if the testing procedures developed by followers of Freud are flawed. However, one goal for a personality theorist is to provide guidelines that might inspire the construction of psychological testing procedures with high levels of reliability and validity. Whatever its other strengths, psychoanalysis generally has failed to achieve this goal. Although future developments may improve the validity of testing methods and thus respond to the criticisms that have been raised (Lilienfeld et al., 2000), psychological testing and prediction unquestionably is not a strength of the psychodynamic tradition.

PSYCHOPATHOLOGY Freud spent most of his professional time treating patients with neurotic disorders. He concluded that the psychological processes of his neurotic patients were basically similar to the psychological processes of people who were not suffering from neuroses and seeking therapy. Neuroses could be found, to one degree or another and in one form or another, in all people. Thus, Freud's analyses of pathology—its development, primary psychological dynamics, and treatment—are integral to his general theory of personality.

PERSONALITY TYPES

One aspect of Freud's analysis of pathology was developmental. Here, he addressed the question of why an individual would develop pathology, and why it would be a pathology of a particular type. This analysis is closely related to an idea you already have learned about, namely, Freud's theory of psychosexual stages of developmental (see Chapter 3). At any given developmental stage, the individual may experience a failure in the development of the instincts. Such failures are called **fixations**. If individuals receive so little gratification during a stage of development that they are afraid to go to the next stage, or if they receive so much gratification that there is no motivation to move on, a fixation will occur. If it does, later in life the individual will try to obtain the same type of satisfaction that was appropriate at the earlier stage (i.e., the one at which the fixation occurred). For example, an individual fixated at the oral stage may, as an adult, seek oral gratification in eating, smoking, or drinking.

A developmental phenomenon related to that of fixation is **regression**. In regression, the individual seeks to return to an earlier mode of satisfaction, an earlier point of fixation. Regression often occurs under conditions of stress, so that many people overeat, smoke, or drink too much alcohol only during periods of frustration and anxiety.

Since there are three distinct stages of early childhood development—oral, anal, and phallic—there are three personality styles that may result from fixations (Table 4.1).

The characteristics of the **oral personality** type, which results from fixation at the oral stage of development, involve themes of taking things into, towards, and for oneself. Oral personalities are narcissistic, that is, interested only in themselves. They do not have a clear recognition of others as separate and valuable entities. Other people are seen only in terms of what they can give (feed). Oral personalities are always asking for something, either in terms of a modest, pleading request or an aggressive demand.

The **anal personality**, which stems from fixation at the anal stage of development, reflects a transformation of gratifications of anal impulses in the childhood years. In general, the traits of the anal character relate to anal-stage processes that have not been completely relinquished. The important processes at that stage are bodily processes (accumulation and release of fecal material) and interpersonal relations (the struggle of wills over toilet training). Tying the two together, the anal person sees excretion as symbolic of enormous

Table 4.1   Personality Characteristics Associated with Psychoanalytic Personality Types

Personality Type	Personality Characteristics
Oral	Demanding, impatient, envious, covetous, jealous, rageful, depressed (feels empty), mistrustful, pessimistic
Anal	Rigid, striving for power and control, concerned with shoulds and oughts, pleasure and possessions, anxiety over waste and loss of control, concern with whether to submit or rebel
Phallic	*Male:* exhibitionistic, competitive, striving for success, emphasis on being masculine—macho—potent *Female:* naive, seductive, exhibitionistic, flirtatious

power. That such a view persists is shown in many everyday expressions such as the reference to the toilet as "the throne." The change from the oral to the anal character is one from "give me" to "do what I tell you," or from "I have to give you" to "I must obey you." The anal character is known by a triad of traits, called the anal triad: orderliness and cleanliness, parsimony and stinginess, and obstinacy. The emphasis on cleanliness is expressed in the saying "Cleanliness is next to godliness." The anal-compulsive personality has a need to keep everything clean and in order, representing a reaction formation against an interest in things that are disorderly and unclean. The second trait of the triad, parsimony/stinginess, relates to the anal-compulsive's interest in holding on to things, an interest dating back to a wish to retain the powerful and important feces. The third trait in the triad, obstinacy, relates to the anal character's infantile defiance against parting with stools, particularly on command by others. Dating back to toilet training and the struggle of wills, anal personalities often seek to be in control of things and have power or dominance over others.

Just as the oral and anal character types reflect partial fixations at the first two stages of development, the **phallic personality** character results from fixation at the phallic stage, during the Oedipus complex. Fixation here has different implications for men and women, and particular attention has been given to the results of partial fixation for males. Whereas success for the oral person means "I get," and success for the anal person means "I control," success for the phallic male means "I am a man." The phallic male must deny all possible suggestions that he has been castrated. For him, success means that he is "big" in the eyes of others. He must at all times assert his masculinity and potency, an attitude exemplified by Theodore Roosevelt's saying, "Speak softly but carry a big stick." The excessive, exhibitionist quality to the behavior of these people is expressive of the underlying anxiety concerning castration.

The female counterpart of the male phallic character is known as the hysterical personality. As a defense against Oedipal wishes, the little girl identifies to an excessive extent with her mother and femininity. She uses seductive and flirtatious behavior to maintain the interest of her father but denies its sexual intent. The pattern of behavior then is carried over into adulthood, where she may attract men with flirtatious behavior but deny sexual intent and generally appear to be somewhat naive. Hysterical women idealize life, their partners, and romantic love, often finding themselves surprised by life's uglier moments.

CONFLICT AND DEFENSE

Psychoanalytic theory proposes that psychopathology results from individuals' efforts to gratify instincts that were fixated at an earlier stage of development. The individual still seeks sexual and aggressive gratification in infantile forms. The problem for the person is that this potential gratification is associated with past trauma, such as the trauma of not having been able to express Oedipal desires. Expression of a wish thus may signal danger to the ego. This creates anxiety. There is, then, a conflict: A given desire and potential behavior is associated with both pleasure and pain. You may wish to indulge in sexual behavior but find that your desires are blocked by feelings of guilt or fear of punishment. You may wish to retaliate against powerful others

Table 4.2   Psychoanalytic Theory of Psychopathology

Illustrative Conflicts		Behavior Consequences of Defense Mechanisms
WISH	ANXIETY	DEFENSE
I would like to have sex with that person.	Such feelings are bad and will be punished.	Denial of all sexual behavior, obsessive preoccupation with the sexual behavior of others.
I would like to strike out at all those people who make me feel inferior.	If I am hostile they will retaliate and really hurt me.	Denial of wish or fear: "I never feel angry," "I'm never afraid of anyone or anything."
I would like to get close to people and have them feed me or take care of me.	If I do they will smother me or leave me.	Excessive independence and avoidance of getting close to people or fluctuations between approaching people and moving away from them; excessive need to take care of others.

(who symbolically represent the parents) but find your desire for revenge to be inhibited by anxieties about retaliation from powerful others (who again represent the parents). In all such cases, there is intra-psychic conflict between a wish and anxiety. The result often is that the individual can't "say no," can't be assertive, or otherwise feels blocked and unhappy (Table 4.2).

To reduce the painful experience of anxiety, defense mechanisms (see Chapter 3) are deployed. A person may, for example, deny sexual and aggressive feelings or project them onto others. If the defense is successful, the person no longer recognizes the feelings as their own and thus experiences less anxiety. If less successful, the energy associated with the unconscious sexual or aggressive drives may express itself in pathological **symptoms**. A symptom—such as a tic, psychological paralysis, or a compulsion—is a disguised expression of a repressed impulse. The meaning of the symptom, the nature of the dangerous instinct, and the nature of the defense all remain unconscious. A mother's obsession with the thought that something bad will happen to her child may, unknown to the mother, be caused by her own underlying rage at her child and anxiety about harm that she herself may do to it. A hand-washing compulsion may express both the wish to be dirty or do "dirty" things, and the defense against the wish is expressed in excessive cleanliness. Again, the person may be unaware of the wish or the defense and be troubled only by the symptom.

To summarize the psychoanalytic theory of psychopathology, in psychopathology there is a conflict between a drive or wish (instinct) and the ego's sense (anxiety) that danger will ensue if the wish is expressed (discharged). The wishes date back to childhood: Wishes and fears that were part of a specific time period in childhood are carried over into adolescence and adulthood. The person attempts to handle the painful anxiety that results from intra-psychic conflict via defense mechanisms. If the conflict is too great, the use of defense mechanisms can lead to neurotic symptoms or psychotic withdrawal from reality. Symptoms express the unconscious conflict between the wish or drive and anxiety. Each case of abnormal behavior, then, arises from an underlying conflict between a wish and a fear that dates back to an earlier period in childhood. Problems of adulthood, then, are a repetition of aspects of childhood. There continue to be childlike parts of us that, under stress and some other conditions, may become more active and troublesome.

PSYCHOLOGICAL CHANGE

How does psychological change come about? Once a person has established a way of thinking about and responding to situations, through what process does a change in personality take place? The psychoanalytic theory of growth suggests that there is a normal course of human personality development, one that occurs because of an optimum degree of frustration. Where there has been too little or too much frustration at a particular stage of growth, personality does not develop normally and a fixation takes place. When this occurs, the individual repeats patterns of behavior regardless of other changes in situations. Given the development of such a neurotic pattern, how is it possible to break the cycle and move forward?

INSIGHTS INTO THE UNCONSCIOUS: FREE ASSOCIATION AND DREAM INTERPRETATION

In therapy, the first challenge is to gain insight into the problematic psycho-dynamics of the patient. As you learned in Chapter 3, Freud's method for accomplishing this was the **free association** technique. The patient is asked to report to the analyst every thought that comes to mind, to delay reporting nothing, to withhold nothing, to bar nothing from coming to consciousness. Freud was interested in free associations to material that occurred not only in normal daily experiences, but in dreams. Dreams, as we discussed in the previous chapter, provide insight into unconscious desires. Through the free association method, the analyst and patient are able to go beyond the manifest content of the dream to the latent content, the hidden unconscious wish that the storyline of the dream expresses.

At first, Freud thought that making the unconscious conscious was sufficient to effect change and cure. This was in keeping with his original belief that repressed memories were a basis for pathology. However, Freud gradually realized that more than a simple recovery of memories was required. Patients needed to acquire emotional insight into their wishes and conflicts. The process of therapeutic change in psychoanalysis, then, involves coming to grips with emotions and wishes that were previously unconscious and struggling with these painful experiences in a relatively safe environment. If psychopathology involves fixation at an early stage of development, then in psychoanalysis individuals become free to resume their normal psychological development. If psychopathology involves damming up the instincts and using energy for defensive purposes, then psychoanalysis involves a redistribution of energy so that more energy is available for mature, guiltless, less rigid, and more gratifying activities. If psychopathology involves conflict and defense mechanisms, then psychoanalysis involves reducing conflict and freeing the patient from the limitations of the defensive processes. If psychopathology involves an individual dominated by the unconscious and the tyranny of the id, then psychoanalysis involves making conscious what was unconscious and putting under control of the ego what was formerly under the domination of the id or superego.

THE THERAPEUTIC PROCESS: TRANSFERENCE

In sum, then, psychoanalysis is viewed as a learning process in which the individual resumes and completes the growth process that was interrupted when the neurosis began. The principle involved is the re-exposure of a patient, under more favorable circumstances, to the emotional situations that could not be handled in the past. Such re-exposure is affected by the **transference** relationship and the development of a transference neurosis.

The term *transference* refers to a patient's development of attitudes toward the analyst based on attitudes held by that patient toward earlier parental figures. In the sense that transference relates to distortions of reality based on past experiences, transference occurs in everyone's daily life and in all forms of psychotherapy. For example, there is research evidence that individuals have mental images associated with emotions that are based on early interpersonal relationships. These emotionally laden mental representations influence the ways in which we view and respond to other individuals as well as feelings about ourselves. Often this occurs in an automatic, unconscious way (Andersen & Chen, 2002). In expressing transference attitudes toward the analyst, patients duplicate in therapy their interactions with people in their lives and their past interactions with significant figures. For example, if patients feel that the analyst's taking notes may lead to exploitation by the analyst, they are expressing attitudes they hold toward people they meet in their daily existence and earlier figures in their lives. In free associating, oral characters may be concerned about whether they are "feeding" the analyst and whether the analyst gives them enough in return; anal characters may be concerned about who is controlling the sessions; phallic characters may be concerned about who will win in competitive struggles. Such attitudes, often part of the unconscious daily existence of the patient, come to light in the course of analysis.

Although transference is a part of all relationships and of all forms of therapy, psychoanalysis is distinctive in using it as a dynamic force in behavior change. Many formal qualities of the analytic situation are structured to enhance the development of transference. The patient lying on the couch supports the development of a dependent relationship. The scheduling of frequent meetings (up to five or six times a week) strengthens the emotional importance of the analytic relationship to the patient's daily existence. Finally, the fact that patients become so tied to their analysts, while knowing so little about them as people, means that their responses are almost completely determined by their neurotic conflicts. The analyst remains a mirror or blank screen on which the individual projects wishes and anxieties.

Encouraging transference, or providing the circumstances that allow it to develop, leads to the development of the transference neurosis. It is here that patients play out, full-blown, their old conflicts. Patients now invest the major aspects of their relationship with the analyst with their wishes and anxieties from the past. The goal is no longer to get well, but to gain from the analyst what they had to do without in childhood. Rather than seeking a way out of competitive relationships, the patients may only seek to castrate the analyst; rather than seeking to become less dependent on others, they may seek to have the analyst gratify all their dependency needs. The fact that these attitudes have developed within the analysis allows patients and their analysts to look at and

Freud's consulting room.

understand the instinctual and defensive components of the original infantile conflict. Because the patient invests considerable emotion in the situation, the increased understanding is emotionally meaningful. Change occurs when insight has been gained, when patients realize, on both an intellectual and an emotional level, the nature of their conflicts and feel free, in terms of their new perceptions of themselves and the world, to gratify their instincts in a mature, conflict-free way.

Whereas guilt and anxiety prevented growth in the past, the analytic situation allows the individual to deal anew with the old conflicts. Why should the response be any different at this time? Basically, change occurs in analysis because of the three therapeutic factors. First, in analysis the conflict is less intense than it was in the original situation. Second, the analyst assumes an attitude that is different from that of the parents. Finally, patients in analysis are older and more mature; that is, they are able to use parts of their ego that have developed to deal with the parts of their functioning that have not developed. These three factors, creating as they do the opportunity for relearning, provide the basis for what Alexander and French (1946) call the "corrective emotional experience." Psychoanalytic theory suggests that through insight into old conflicts, through an understanding of the needs for infantile gratifications and recognition of the potential for mature gratification, and through an understanding of old anxieties and a recognition of their lack of relevance to current realities, patients may progress toward maximum instinctual gratification within the limits set by reality and their own moral convictions.

CURRENT APPLICATIONS

EMOTIONAL SUPPRESSION AND HEALTH

More than a century ago, psychoanalysts began to suggest that personality dynamics influence physical health. Some posited specific relations between particular types of conflicts and particular somatic difficulties; different disorders were thought to result from different emotional constellations. For example, peptic ulcers—described as the "Wall Street stomach"—were thought to result from an unconscious craving for love and dependence, which was defended against by an active, productive, aggressive lifestyle. Hypertension was thought to be associated with individuals who were gentle in outward manner but boiling with rage inside.

This line of reasoning eventually fell into disfavor. The relation between psychological factors and bodily illness seemed more complex than was originally suggested. Despite this, in historical retrospect the psychoanalytic thinking did open the door to phenomena of much importance. Today, personality psychologists document substantial links between personality and health (as we noted already in a "Current Applications" box in Chapter 2). A line of thinking that is closely related to psychodynamic ideas explores a particular type of personality dynamic: suppressing thoughts about emotionally traumatic materials, as opposed to discussing that material openly.

Evidence suggests that the suppression of emotion can be detrimental to one's health. For example, it may play a negative role in the course of cancer, ulcers, and heart disease. Alternatively, the expression, or non-suppression, of emotion may represent an active, adaptive style of coping that reduces the risk of illness and bodes well for the course of an illness.

Much work on this topic has been done by the psychologist James Pennebaker and his colleagues. They take a critical step in research that was not taken by Freud. Rather than reporting merely case studies in which an individual patient improves after talking about his or her problems, they run true experiments in which multiple people are assigned, at random, to conditions in which they either do or do not relate emotional experiences. This provides more convincing evidence of the link between emotional suppression and health. In these studies, people generally are asked to relate past experiences in writing; research participants write essays that describe thoughts and feelings during traumatic experiences. Compared to others, people who write about trauma routinely experience lower rates of physical illness (as indexed by objective measures such as number of visits to health care centers) in the months following their compositions of the essays. In addition, aspects of writing style predict health outcomes. Linguistic analyses indicate that improved health is experienced, in particular, by people whose writing style changes flexibly as they write. The flexibility in language use may indicate that the person, during the writing, is understanding their experiences in a complex way, from "multiple angles." This understanding of past trauma appears to benefit health.

SOURCE: CAMPBELL & PENNEBAKER, 2003; JENSEN, 1987; LEVY, 1984; PENNEBAKER, 1985, 1990; PETRIE, BOOTH, & PENNEBAKER, 1998; TEMOSHOK, 1985, 1991.

A Case Example: Little Hans

A deep appreciation of Freud's analysis of personality can be gained through his case studies. Freud reported in detail on a small number of cases. Although these case reports often were written early in his career and thus do not fully reflect his final structural model of personality, they nonetheless reveal his general approach to the complex conflicts and anxieties of the mind. We summarize one such case here, the case of Little Hans (published in 1909).

Little Hans was a five-year-old boy who suffered from an extreme fear, or a phobia. He feared that a horse would bite him, and therefore refused to leave the house. Freud's report of the case is unusual in that it did not involve a treatment by Freud himself; the boy was treated by his father. However, the father kept detailed notes on Hans's treatment and frequently discussed Hans's progress with Freud. Freud's interpretation of the case is highly illustrative of his psychoanalytic principles, particularly his theories of infantile sexuality, the Oedipus complex and castration anxiety, the dynamics of symptom formation, and the process of behavior change.

Events Leading up to Development of the Phobia

Our account of events in the life of Little Hans begins at age three. At this point he had a lively interest in his penis, which he called his "widdler." He derived much pleasure in touching his own penis and was preoccupied with "widdlers" in others. The interest in touching his penis, however, led to threats by his mother. "If you do that, I shall send you to Dr. A. to cut off your widdler. And then what will you widdle with?" Thus, there was a direct castration threat. Freud pinpointed this as the beginning of Hans's castration complex.

Hans's interest in widdlers extended to noting the large size of the widdlers of horses on the street and lions at the zoo, and analyzing the differences between animate and inanimate objects (animals have widdlers, unlike tables and chairs). Hans was curious about many things, but Freud related his general thirst for knowledge to sexual curiosity. Hans continued to be interested in whether his mother had a widdler and said to her, "I thought you were so big you'd have a widdler like a horse." When he was three and a half, a sister was born, who also became a focus for his widdler concerns. "But her widdler's still quite small. When she grows up, it'll get bigger all right." According to Freud, Hans could not admit what he really saw, namely, that there was no widdler there. To do so would mean that he would have to face his own castration anxieties. These anxieties occurred at a time when he was experiencing pleasure in the organ, as witnessed in his comments to his mother while she dried and powdered him after his bath.

HANS: Why don't you put your finger there?
MOTHER: Because that'd be piggish.
HANS: What's that? Piggish? Why? (laughing) But it's great fun.

Thus Hans, now more than four years old and preoccupied with his penis, began some seduction of his mother. It was at this point that his nervous disorders became apparent. The father, attributing the difficulties to sexual overexcitation due to his mother's tenderness, wrote Freud that Hans was "afraid that a horse will bite him in the street" and that this fear seemed somehow to be connected with his having been frightened by seeing a large penis. (Recall that Hans, at a very early age, noticed what large penises horses have and inferred that his large mother must "have a widdler like a horse. ") Hans was afraid of going into the street and was depressed in the evenings. He had bad dreams and was frequently taken into his mother's bed. While walking in the street with his nurse, he became extremely frightened and sought to return home to be with his mother. The fear that a horse would bite him became a fear that the horse would come into his room. He had developed a full-blown phobia, an irrational dread or fear of an object.

Interpretation of the Symptom

The father attempted to deal with his son's fear of horses by offering him an interpretation. Hans was told that the fear of horses was nonsense, that the truth was that he (Hans) was fond of his mother and that the fear of horses had to do with an interest in their "widdlers." On Freud's suggestion, the father explained to Hans that women do not have "widdlers." Apparently this provided some relief, but Hans continued to be bothered by an obsessive wish to look at horses, though he was then frightened by them. At this point, his tonsils were taken out and his phobia worsened. He was afraid that a white horse would bite him. He continued to be interested in "widdlers" in females. At the zoo, he was afraid of all the large animals and was entertained by the smaller ones. Among the birds, he was afraid of the pelican. In spite of his father's truthful explanation, Hans sought to reassure himself. "And everyone has a widdler. And my widdler will get bigger as I get bigger, because it does grow on me." According to Freud, Hans had been making comparisons among the sizes of widdlers and was dissatisfied with his own. Big animals reminded him of this defect and were disagreeable to him. The father's explanation heightened his castration anxiety, as expressed in the words "it does grow on me," as if it could be cut off. For this reason he resisted the information, and thus it had no therapeutic results. "Could it be that living beings really did exist which did not possess widdlers? If so, it would no longer be so incredible that they could take his own widdler away, and, as it were, make him into a woman."

At around this time, Hans reported the following dream. "In the night there was a big giraffe in the room and a crumpled one; and the big one called out because I took the crumpled one away from it. Then it stopped calling out; and then I sat down on top of the crumpled one." The father's interpretation was that he, the father, was the big giraffe, with the big penis, and the mother was the crumpled giraffe, missing the genital organ. The dream was a reproduction of a morning scene in which the mother took Hans into bed with her. The father warned her against this practice ("The big one called out because I'd taken the crumpled one away from it"), but the mother continued to encourage it. The mother encouraged and reinforced the Oedipal wishes. Hans stayed with her and, in the wish fulfillment of the dream, he took possession of her ("Then the big giraffe stopped calling out; and then I sat down on top of the crumpled one").

Freud's strategy in understanding Hans's phobia was to suspend judgment and to give his impartial attention to everything there was to observe. He learned that prior to the development of the phobia, Hans had been alone with his mother at a summer place. There, two significant events occurred. First, he heard the father of one of his friends tell her that a white horse there bit people and that she was not to hold her finger up to its mouth. Second, while pretending to be horses, a friend who rivaled Hans for the affection of the little girls fell down, hit his foot, and bled. In an interview with Hans, Freud learned that Hans was bothered by the blinders on horses and the black band around their mouths. The phobia became extended to include a fear that horses dragging a heavy van would fall down and kick their feet. It was then discovered that the exciting cause of his phobia—the event that capitalized on a psychological readiness for the formation of a phobia—was that Hans had witnessed a horse falling down. While walking outside with his mother one day, Hans had seen a horse pulling a van fall down and begin to kick its feet.

The central feature in this case was the phobia about the horse. What is fascinating in this regard is how often associations concerning a horse came up in relation to the father, the mother, and Hans himself. We have already noticed Hans's interest in his mother's "widdler" in relation to that of a horse. To his father, he said at one point: "Daddy, don't trot away from me." Could the father, who wore a mustache and eyeglasses, be the horse that Hans was afraid of, the horse that would come into his room at night and bite him? Or could Hans himself be the horse? Hans was known to play horse in his room, to trot about, fall down, kick about with his feet, and neigh. He repeatedly ran up to his father and bit him, just as he feared the horse would do to him. Hans was overfed. Could this relate to his concerns about large, fat horses? Finally, Hans was known to have called himself a young horse and to have a tendency to stamp his feet on the ground when angry, similar to what the horse did when it fell down. To return to the mother, could the heavily laden carts symbolize the pregnant mother and the horse falling down the birth or delivery of a child? Are such associations coincidental or can they play a significant role in our understanding of the phobia?

According to Freud, the major cause of Hans's phobia was his Oedipus conflict. Hans felt more affection for his mother than he could handle during the phallic stage of his development. Although he had deep affection for his father, he also considered him a rival for his mother's affections. When he and his mother stayed at the summer cottage and his father was away, he was able to get into bed with his mother and keep her for himself. This heightened his attraction for his mother and his hostility toward his father. For Freud, "Hans was really a little Oedipus who wanted to have his father 'out of the way,' to get rid of him, so that he might be alone with his handsome mother and sleep with her. This wish had originated during his summer holidays, when the alternating presence and absence of his father had drawn Hans's attention to the condition upon which depended the intimacy with his mother which he longed for." The fall and injury to his friend and rival during one of those holidays was significant in symbolizing the defeat for Hans of his rival.

The Solution to the Oedipal Conflict

When he returned home from the summer holidays, Hans's resentment toward his father increased. He tried to suppress the resentment with exaggerated affection. He arrived at an ingenious solution to the Oedipal conflict. He and his mother would be parents to children and the father could be the granddaddy. Thus, as Freud notes, "The little Oedipus had found a happier solution than that prescribed by destiny. Instead of putting his father out of the way, he had granted him the same happiness that he desired himself: He made him a grandfather and let him too marry his own mother." But such a fantasy could not be a satisfactory solution, and Hans was left with considerable hostility toward his father. The exciting cause of the phobia was the horse falling down. At that moment, Hans perceived a wish that his father might similarly fall down and die. The hostility toward his father was projected onto the father and was symbolized in the horse, because he himself nourished jealous and hostile wishes against him. He feared the horse would bite him because of his wish that his father would fall down, and fears that the horse would come into his room occurred at night when he was most tempted by Oedipal fantasies. In his own play as a horse and in his biting of his father, he expressed an identification with his father. The phobia expressed the wish and the anxiety and, in a secondary way, accomplished the objective of leaving Hans home to be with his mother.

In sum, both his fear that a horse would bite him and his fear that horses would fall down represented the father who was going to punish Hans for the evil wishes he was harboring against him. Hans was able to get over the phobia and, according to a later report by Freud, he appeared to be functioning well. What factors allowed the change? First, there was the sexual enlightenment by the father. Although Hans was reluctant to accept this and it at first heightened his castration anxiety, it did serve as a useful piece of reality to hold onto. Second, the analysis provided by his father and by Freud was useful in making conscious for Hans what had formerly been unconscious. Finally, the father's interest in and permissive attitude toward Hans's expression of his feelings allowed a resolution of the Oedipus conflict in favor of an identification with the father, diminishing both the wish to rival the father and the castration anxiety, and thereby decreasing the potential for symptom development.

To the contemporary personality scientist, the case of Little Hans is very limited if viewed as a scientific investigation. The father's interviewing was not systematic, his close adherence to Freud's thinking may have biased his observations and interpretations, and Freud was primarily dependent on secondhand reports. Though aware of these limitations, Freud nonetheless was impressed with the data on Hans. Whereas before he had based his theory on the childhood memories of adult patients, now, in the case of Little Hans, he began to observe the sexual life of children.

The case of Little Hans simultaneously gives us an appreciation of the wealth of information available to the analyst and the problems inherent in interpreting such data. This one case alone yields information relevant to multiple theoretical ideas: infantile sexuality, fantasies of children, functioning of the unconscious, the process of conflict development and conflict resolution, the process of symptom formation, symbolization, and the dream process. We see Freud's courage and boldness in trying to discover secrets of human functioning in spite of limitations in his observations. Yet we also see Freud interpreting data that most contemporary psychologists would reject; most 21st century psychological scientists would see the data this case provides as so unsystematic, and so potentially biased, that it could not serve as a foundation for scientific theorizing.

Rorschach and Thematic Apperception Test (TAT) Data **THE CASE OF JIM**

The Rorschach Inkblot Test and the thematic apperception test (TAT) were administered to Jim by a professional clinical psychologist. On the Rorschach, Jim gave relatively few responses—22 in all. This is surprising in view of other evidence of his intelligence and creative potential. It may be interesting to follow his responses to the first two cards and to consider the interpretations formulated by the psychologist, who also is a practicing psychoanalyst.

CARD 1

JIM: The first thing that comes to mind is a butterfly.

INTERPRETATION: Initially cautious and acts conventionally in a novel situation.

JIM: This reminds me of a frog. Not a whole frog, like a frog's eyes. Really just reminds me of a frog.

INTERPRETATION: He becomes more circumspect, almost picky, and yet tends to overgeneralize while feeling inadequate about it.

JIM: Could be a bat. More spooky than the butterfly because there is no color. Dark and ominous.

INTERPRETATION: Phobic, worried, depressed, and pessimistic.

CARD 2

JIM: Could be two headless people with their arms touching. Looks like they are wearing heavy dresses. Could be one touching her hand against a mirror. If they're women, their figures are not good. Look heavy.

INTERPRETATION: Alert to people. Concern or confusion about sexual role. Anal-compulsive features. Disparaging of women and hostile to them—headless and figures not good. Narcissism expressed in mirror image.

JIM: This looks like two faces facing each other. Masks, profiles—more masks than faces—not full, more of a façade, like one with a smile and one with a frown.

INTERPRETATION: He presents a façade, can smile or frown, but doesn't feel genuine. Despite façade of poise, feels tense with people. Repeated several times that he was not imaginative. Is he worried about his productivity and importance?

A number of interesting responses occurred on other cards. On the third card Jim perceived women trying to lift weights. Here again was a suggestion of conflict about his sexual role and about a passive as opposed to an active orientation. On the following card he commented that "somehow they all have an Alfred Hitchcock look of spooky animals," again suggesting a possible phobic quality to his behavior and a tendency to project dangers into the environment. His occasional references to symmetry and details suggested the use of compulsive defenses and intellectualization while experiencing threat. Disturbed and conflicted references to women come up in a number of places. On Card 7, he perceived two women from mythology who would be good if they were mythological but bad if they were fat. On the next to last card he perceived "some sort of a Count, Count Dracula. Eyes, ears, cape. Ready to grab, suck blood. Ready to go out and strangle some woman." The reference to sucking blood suggested tendencies toward oral sadism, something that also appeared in another percept of vampires that suck blood. Jim followed the percept of Count Dracula with one of pink cotton candy. The tester interpreted this response as suggesting a yearning for nurturance and contact behind the oral sadism; that is, the subject uses oral aggressive tendencies (e.g., sarcasm, verbal attacks) to defend against more passive oral wishes (e.g., to be fed, to be taken care of, and to be dependent).

The examiner concluded that the Rorschach suggested a neurotic structure in which intellectualization, compulsivity, and hysterical operations (irrational fears, preoccupation with his body) are used to defend against anxiety. However, it was suggested that Jim continues to feel anxious and uncomfortable with others, particularly authority figures. The report from the Rorschach concluded: "He is conflicted about his sexual role. While he yearns for nurturance and contact from the motherly female, he feels very guilty about the cravings and his intense hostility toward women. He assumes a passive orientation, a continual role playing and, behind a façade of tact, he continues his rage, sorrow, and ambition."

What kinds of stories did Jim tell on the TAT? Most striking about these stories were the sadness and hostility involved in all interpersonal relationships. In one story a boy is dominated by his mother, in another an insensitive gangster is capable of gross inhumanity, and in a third a husband is upset to learn that his wife is not a virgin. In particular, the relationships between men and women constantly involve one putting down the other. Consider this story.

> Looks like two older people. The woman is sincere, sensitive, and dependent on the man. There is something about the man's expression that bespeaks of insensitivity—the way he looks at her, as if he conquered her. There is not the same compassion and security in her presence that she feels in his. In the end, the woman gets very hurt and is left to fend for herself. Normally I would think that they were married but in this case I don't because two older people who are married would be happy with one another.

In this story we have a man being sadistic to a woman. We also see the use of the defensive mechanism of denial in Jim's suggestion that these two people cannot be married since older married people are always happy with one another. In the story that followed the aforementioned one, there is again the theme of hostile mistreatment of a woman. In this story there is a more open expression of the sexual theme, along with evidence of some sexual role confusion.

> This picture brings up a gross thought. I think of Candy. The same guy who took advantage of Candy. He's praying over her. Not the last rites, but he has convinced her that he is some powerful person and she's looking for him to bestow his good graces upon her. His knee is on the bed, he's unsuccessful, she's naive. He goes to bed with her for mystical purposes. [Blushes] She goes on being naive and continues to be susceptible to that kind of thing. She has a very, very sweet compassionate look. Could it possibly be that this is supposed to be a guy wearing a tie? I'll stick with the former.

The psychologist interpreting these stories observed that Jim appeared to be immature, naive, and characterized by a gross denial of all that is unpleasant or dirty, the latter for him including both sexuality and marital strife. The report continued: "He is vacillating between expressing sadistic urges and experiencing a sense of victimization. Probably he combines both, often in indirect expressions of hostility while feeling unjustly treated or accused. He is confused about what meaningful relationships two people can have. He is ambivalently idealistic and pessimistic about his own chances for a stable relationship.

Since he sees sex as dirty and as a mode for using or being used by his partner, he fears involvement. At the same time he craves attention, needs to be recognized, and is often preoccupied with sexual urges."

Across the Rorschach and TAT, a number of themes emerge. One involves a lack of warmth in interpersonal relationships, including a disparaging and at times sadistic orientation toward women. In relation to women, Jim has a conflict between sexual preoccupation and the feeling that sex is dirty and involves hostility. The second theme involves experiencing tension and anxiety behind a façade of poise. A third theme involves conflict and confusion about his sexual identity. Although there is evidence of intelligence and creative potential, there also is evidence of rigidity and inhibition in relation to the unstructured nature of the projective tests. Compulsive defenses, intellectualization, and denial are only partially successful in helping him deal with his anxieties.

Comments on the Data

This data about Jim highlights the most attractive feature of projective tests. Their disguise enables one to penetrate the façade of someone's personality (in psychoanalytic terms, his defenses) to view the person's underlying needs, motives, or drives. Information presented in his autobiography (Chapter 2) did not indicate the psychological themes evident in Jim's projective test responses.

As we not only examine psychoanalytic theory but also look forward to other theories to come, an interesting point arises. It is difficult to see how other theories of personality could make as much use of this data about Jim as psychoanalytic theory can. The assessment practices associated with other theories are unlikely to reveal this sort of information. It is only on the Rorschach that we obtain content such as "women trying to lift weights," "Count Dracula ready to grab, suck blood. Ready to go out and strangle some woman," and "pink cotton candy." The TAT is unique in revealing references to themes of sadness and hostility in interpersonal relationships. These responses allow for the psychodynamic interpretations. An important part of Jim's personality functioning appears to involve a defense against sadistic urges. The references to sucking blood and to cotton candy, together with the rest of his responses, allow for the interpretation that he is partially fixated at the oral stage. In relation to this, it is interesting to observe that Jim has an ulcer, which involves the digestive tract, and that he must drink milk to manage this condition.

RELATED THEORETICAL CONCEPTIONS AND RECENT DEVELOPMENTS

As Freud's fame grew, he attracted followers. As may be inevitable with any person of fame and the followers he or she attracts, some followed closely in his footsteps whereas others rejected one or more aspects of his thinking and embarked on new directions—directions they may never have considered were it not for Freud, yet that he himself would not have taken. In the remainder of this chapter, we review this post-Freudian psychodynamic tradition.

You might already be asking: Aren't all the theorists whose work is covered in *subsequent* chapters of this book also post-Freudian thinkers who rejected one or more aspects of Freud's thinking? The answer is yes; all subsequent theorists were quite familiar with Freud and found one or more aspects of his thinking to be wanting. Here, in this chapter, we are reviewing those theorists who retained a commitment to a psychodynamic perspective, in the overall Freudian tradition. These theorists, like Freud, grounded personality theory in the study of internal mental dynamics. They saw the mind as containing multiple systems, some of which function outside of conscious awareness. They used clinical experiences as a fundamental basis for their theorizing. In these and other ways, they were like Freud. Yet, as you'll now see, they also modified and expanded his work in highly significant ways.

TWO EARLY CHALLENGES TO FREUD: ADLER AND JUNG

Among the many early analysts who broke with Freud and developed their own schools of thought were Alfred Adler and Carl G. Jung. Both were early and important followers of Freud, Adler having been president of the Vienna Psychoanalytic Society and Jung president of the International Psychoanalytic Society. Both split with Freud over what they felt was an excessive emphasis on the sexual instincts.

Alfred Adler (1870–1937)

For approximately a decade, Alfred Adler was an active member of the Vienna Psychoanalytic Society. However, in 1911, when he presented his views to the other members of this group, the response was so hostile that he left it to form his own school of Individual Psychology. What ideas could have been considered so unacceptable to psychoanalysts?

Perhaps most significant in Adler's split from Freud was his greater emphasis on social urges and conscious thoughts than on instinctual sexual urges and unconscious processes. Early in his career Adler became interested in bodily inferiorities and how people compensate for them. A person with a weak bodily organ may attempt to compensate for this weakness by making special efforts to strengthen that organ or to develop other organs. Someone who stutters as a child may attempt to become a great speaker. A person with

Alfred Adler.

an auditory impairment may attempt to develop special listening or musical sensitivities. Adler gradually realized that there was a general principle here. People consciously experience feelings of inferiority and are motivated to compensate for these painful inferiorities. To Adler, "it is the feeling of inferiority, inadequacy, insecurity, which determines the goal of an individual's existence" (Adler, 1927, p. 72).

Adlerian thinking reformulates traditional Freudian interpretations. To take an historical example, U.S. president Theodore Roosevelt emphasized toughness by saying that one should carry a "big stick." To Freud, such statements are a defense against castration anxiety. An Adlerian might instead see this as expressing compensatory strivings against feelings of inferiority. As another example, Freudians might see an extremely aggressive woman as expressing penis envy, whereas Adlerians might see such persons as expressing a masculine protest or rejection of the stereotyped feminine role of weakness and inferiority. According to Adler, how a person attempts to cope with such feelings becomes a part of his or her style of life—a distinctive aspect of his or her personality functioning.

The principle of striving to compensate for inferiority does not apply merely to select individuals who suffer from a physical limitation. It applies to everyone. This is because everyone, in childhood, experiences inferiority. "One must remember that every child occupies an inferior position in life" (Adler, 1927, pp. 69–70). All young children see that they are less able to cope with objects and events than are adults or older children whom they encounter. Everyone, then, experiences the motivating force of inferiority feelings.

These Adlerian concepts are more socially oriented than are Freud's. To Adler, compensatory strivings reflect will to power, that is, the individual's efforts to be a powerful, effective social being by coping with inferiorities and feelings of helplessness. In neurotic form, strivings for superiority may be expressed in efforts to exert power and control over others. In healthier form, a person experiences an "upward drive" toward unity and perfection. In the healthy person the striving for superiority is expressed in social feeling and cooperation as well as in assertiveness and competition. From the beginning people have a social interest, that is, an innate interest in relating to people and an innate potential for cooperation.

Adler also emphasized people's feelings about the self, how they respond to goals that direct their behavior toward the future, and how the order of birth among siblings can influence their psychological development. In relation to birth order, many psychologists have noted the tendency for only sons or first-born sons to achieve more than later sons in a family. For example, 21 of the first 23 U.S. astronauts were first-born or only sons. Sulloway (1996) has placed the issue of birth order in an evolutionary context, suggesting that first-borns tend to be conscientious and conservative, preserving their first-place status in the family, whereas later-borns, seeking to establish alternative routes to status and success, are "born to rebel." Although this view remains controversial, support for Sulloway's account of "conservative first-borns" and "rebellious later-borns" comes from both his own research and that of others (Paulhus, Trapnell, & Chen, 1999). Many of Adler's ideas have found their way into the general public's thinking and are related to views later expressed by other theorists. Contemporary researchers, like Adler, have become interested in power as a fundamental determinant of human behavior (Keltner, Gruenfeld,

Adler's theory proposes that people are motivated to compensate for feelings of inferiority. These compensatory strivings can shape the development of a person's life. The motives explored by Adler sometimes are evident in the life stories of highly successful persons. The photo depicts Brain Wilson, founder of the Beach Boys, one of the most popular groups in the history of contemporary music. What was the origin of Wilson's success? His official website reports that "After years of abuse by his father, he was left nearly deaf in one ear, depressed and lacking self-esteem. 'I overcompensated,' he said. 'I felt inferior because I only had one good ear. I compensated for that inferiority, and made some superior music.' "

& Anderson, 2003). However, Adler's school of individual psychology itself has not had a major impact on personality theory and research.

Carl G. Jung (1875–1961)

Carl Jung's role in the history of psychodynamic theory is utterly unique. Early in his career as a physician, the Swiss scholar read the writings of Freud, was deeply impressed, and established a correspondence with the Vienna psychoanalyst. When Freud and Jung eventually met, they deeply impressed one another. They developed a relationship that was both professional and personal; their written correspondence suggests that they related as much in the style of father and son as professional colleagues. Freud came to view Jung as his "crown prince"—the person who would carry on Freud's psychoanalytic tradition after Freud's death. But this isn't what happened. Their relationship began to deteriorate beginning in 1909, due to a mixture of professional and personal conflicts (Gay, 1998). In 1914, Jung resigned his position as president of the International Psychoanalytic Association.

Why the split between Freud and Jung? From Jung's perspective, it was because he felt that Freud had over-emphasized sexuality. Jung viewed the libido not as a sexual instinct, but as a generalized life energy. Although sexuality is a part of this basic energy, the libido also includes strivings

Carl Jung

for pleasure and creativity. To Jung, this reinterpretation of the libido was the primary reason for his break with Freud. (Freud, in contrast, viewed their breakup in psychoanalytic terms, with Jung expressing Oedipal feelings toward his professional father, Freud.)

This reinterpretation of libidinal energy is just one feature that differentiates Jung's analytic psychology from Freud's psychoanalysis. Jung felt that Freud overemphasized the idea that our current behavior is a mere repetition of the past, with instinctual urges and psychological repressions of childhood being repeated in adult life. Instead, Jung believed that personality development also has a forward-moving directional tendency. People try to acquire a meaningful personal identity and a sense of meaning in self. Indeed, people are so forward-looking that they commonly devote efforts to religious practices that prepare them for a life after death.

A particularly distinguishing feature of Jung's psychology is his emphasis on the evolutionary foundations of the human mind. Jung accepted Freud's emphasis on the unconscious as a storehouse of repressed experiences from one's life. But he added to this idea the concept of the **collective unconscious**. According to Jung, people have stored within their collective unconscious the cumulative experiences of past generations. The collective unconscious, as opposed to the personal unconscious, is universal. It is shared by all humans as a result of their common ancestry. It is part of our human as well as our animal heritage, and thus is our link with the collective wisdom of millions of years of past experience: "This psychic life is the mind of our ancient ancestors, the way in which they thought and felt, the way in which they conceived of life and the world, of gods and human beings. The existence of these historical layers is presumably the source of belief in reincarnation and in memories of past lives" (Jung, 1939, p. 24).

The collective unconscious contains universal images or symbols, known as archetypes. Archetypes, such as the Mother archetype, are seen in fairy tales, dreams, myths, and some psychotic thoughts. Jung was struck with similar images that keep appearing, in slightly different forms, in different cultures that are distant from one another. For example, the Mother archetype might be expressed in different cultures in a variety of positive or negative forms: as life giver, as all giving and nurturant, as the witch or threatening punisher ("Don't fool with Mother Nature"), and as the seductive female. Archetypes may be represented in our images of persons, demons, animals, natural forces, or objects. The evidence in all cases for their being a part of our collective unconscious is their universality among members of different cultures from past and current time periods.

Another important aspect of Jung's theory is his emphasis on how people struggle with opposing forces within them. For example, there is the struggle between the face or mask we present to others, represented in the archetype of the persona, and the private or personal self. If people emphasize the persona too much, there may be a loss of sense of self and a doubting about who they are. On the other hand, the persona, as expressed in social roles and customs, is a necessary part of living in society. Similarly, there is the struggle between the masculine and feminine parts of ourselves. Every male has a feminine part (the archetype of the anima) and every female has a masculine part (the archetype of the animus) to their personality. If a man rejects his feminine part he may emphasize mastery and strength to an excessive degree, appearing cold and insensitive to the feelings of others. If a woman rejects her masculine part she may be excessively absorbed in motherhood. Psychologists currently interested in stereotyped sex roles would probably applaud Jung's emphasis on these dual aspects in everyone's personality, although they might question his characterizing some as specifically masculine and others as feminine. An interesting yet controversial feature of Jung's analysis is the contention that gender-role stereotypes are not a product of an individual's social experience, but of the experiences of one's ancestors over the course of evolution. A similar idea is found in contemporary evolutionary psychology (Chapter 9).

Jung emphasizes that all individuals face a fundamental personal task: finding unity in the self. The task is to bringing into harmony, or integrate, the various opposing forces of the psyche. The person is motivated and guided along the path to personal knowledge and integration by the most important of all Jungian archetypes: the self. In Jungian psychology "the self" does not refer to one's conscious beliefs about one's personal qualities. Instead, the self is an unconscious force, specifically, an aspect of the collective unconscious that functions as an "organizing center" (Jung and collaborators, 1964, p. 161) of the person's entire psychological system. Jung believed that the self often is represented symbolically in circular figures—the circle representing a sense of wholeness that can be achieved through self-knowledge. Mandalas, which are circular symbols that contain pathways toward a centerpoint, serve as vivid symbols of the struggle for knowledge of our true selves. Since the self is an archetype of the collective unconscious, and the collective unconscious is a universal aspect of human personality, according to Jungian theory one should expect to find similar symbolic representations of the self across diverse human cultures. And one does. Symbols found in human cultures separated widely in time and place often contain remarkably similar imagery that, according to Jung, represents the universal unconscious motive to grow in self-knowledge.

To Jung, the search for the self is a never-ending quest. "Personality as a complete realization of the fullness of our being is an unattainable ideal. But unattainability is no counter argument against an ideal, for ideals are only signposts, never goals" (Jung, 1939, p. 287). The struggle described here can become a particularly important aspect of life once people have passed the age of 40 and defined themselves to the outside world in a variety of ways.

The psychologist Carl Jung hypothesized that mandalas symbolize people's universal striving for a whole, complete sense of self. Since the archetype of the self is a universal feature of the human mind according to Jung, similar mandala symbols should be found across diverse cultures. And they are. These two mandalas, similar though they may be in overall design, come from very widely separated cultures; Tibet in central Asia (left) and a Native American society in the southwestern United States (right).

Another contrast in Jung's theory is that between introversion and extraversion. Everyone relates to the world primarily in one of two directions, though the other direction always remains a part of the person. In the case of introversion, the person's basic orientation is inward, toward the self. The introverted type is hesitant, reflective, and cautious. In the case of extraversion the person's basic orientation is outward, toward the outside world. The extraverted type is socially engaging, active, and adventuresome.

As with Adler, we have considered only some of the highlights of Jung's theory. Jung is considered by many to be one of the great creative thinkers of the 20th century. His theory has influenced intellectual trends in many fields outside of psychology. Jungian centers for clinical training continue to exist in many countries. Yet Jung's work has had little impact within scientific psychology. To a large degree, this reflects the fact Jung often did not state his ideas in a manner that could be tested according to standard scientific methods. His imaginative theorizing commonly was more speculative than that of other personality theorists—so speculative that elements of this theorizing are difficult, if not impossible, to support or to disprove through objective scientific methods.

THE CULTURAL AND INTERPERSONAL EMPHASIS: HORNEY AND SULLIVAN

Reinterpreting Motivational Forces

In the middle of the 20th century, a group of psychoanalytic theorists began a deep rethinking of basic psychoanalytic principles. These writers felt that, to a greater degree than Freud had appreciated, personality develops through interpersonal interactions. These interpersonal actions inherently occur within social and cultural contexts. Their work thus constitutes a cultural and interpersonal emphasis within the psychoanalytic tradition.

As the writers Greenberg and Mitchell (1983) have explained, there are two different ways of emphasizing interpersonal factors from a psychodynamic perspective. One adheres to traditional Freudian principles. In this classic psychoanalytic view, the motivational forces in the development of the individual are biological drives (the id's drives toward pleasure). The central features of personality development are the individual's efforts to manage these biologically based desires, which often conflict with social norms. Once personality structures are developed in this manner, they in turn influence social life. The instinctual drives, then, are primary: They are the initial forces driving development and are responsible for the formation of personality structure. Social relationships—e.g., with peers and friends—are of secondary importance. Social relationships do not determine personality structure in this traditional Freudian account. They are *determined by* personality structures whose development is an outgrow of the biologically-based desires of the id.

The ideas of interpersonal psychodynamic theorists such as Harry Stack Sullivan (reviewed below) differed strikingly from this Freudian tradition (Greenberg & Mitchell, 1983). The interpersonal view sees social relations as primary, not secondary. Personality structures are thought to develop through—i.e., as a result of—interactions with others. Other people display emotional styles that influence one's own emotional life. They provide evaluations that influence one's own self-concept. Acceptance by others becomes a basic motivational force.

Although many writers contributed to this interpersonal tradition, two figures of particular historical importance are Karen Horney and Harry Stack Sullivan.

Karen Horney (1885–1952)

Karen Horney was trained as a traditional analyst in Germany. She then came to the United States, in 1932. Shortly thereafter she split with traditional psychoanalytic thought and developed her own theoretical orientation and psychoanalytic training program.

A major difference between Horney's work and traditional psychoanalytic thinking involved the question of universal biological influences as opposed to cultural influences: "When we realize the great import of cultural conditions on neuroses, the biological and physiological conditions, which are considered by Freud to be their root, recede into the background" (1937, p. viii). Three considerations led her to this conclusion. The first was the role of culture in the development of gender identity. The influence of cultural factors on "ideas of what constitutes masculinity or femininity was obvious, and it became just as obvious to me that Freud had arrived at certain conclusions because he failed to take them into account" (1945, p. 11). Second was her association with another psychoanalyst, Erich Fromm, who drew her attention to social and cultural influences. Third, when moving from European culture to the United States, Horney judged that she observed differences in personality structure between European and U.S. patients.

Beyond this, these observations led her to conclude that interpersonal relationships are at the core of all healthy and disturbed personality functioning.

Karen Horney

Horney's emphasis in neurotic functioning is on how individuals attempt to cope with basic anxiety—the feeling a child has of being isolated and helpless in a potentially hostile world. According to her theory of neurosis, in the neurotic person there is conflict among three ways of responding to this basic anxiety. These three patterns, or neurotic trends, are known as moving toward, moving against, and moving away. All three are characterized by rigidity and the lack of fulfillment of individual potential, the essence of any neurosis. In moving toward, a person attempts to deal with anxiety by an excessive interest in being accepted, needed, and approved of. Such a person accepts a dependent role in relation to others and, except for the unlimited desire for affection, becomes unselfish, undemanding, and self-sacrificing. In moving against, a person assumes that everyone is hostile and that life is a struggle against all. All functioning is directed toward denying a need for others and toward appearing tough. In moving away, the third component of the conflict, the person shrinks away from others into neurotic detachment. Such people often look at themselves and others with emotional detachment, as a way of not getting emotionally involved with others. Although each neurotic person shows one or another trend as a special aspect of their personality, the problem is really that there is conflict among the three trends in the effort to deal with basic anxiety.

Before leaving Horney, we should consider her views concerning women. These views date back to her early work within traditional psychoanalytic thought and are reflected in a series of papers collected in *Feminine Psychology* (1973). As noted from the start, Horney had trouble accepting Freud's views of women. She felt that the concept of penis envy might be the result of a male bias in psychoanalysts who treat neurotic women in a particular social context: "Unfortunately, little or nothing is known of psychologically healthy women, or of women under different cultural conditions" (1973, p. 216). She suggested that women are not biologically disposed toward masochistic attitudes of being weak, dependent, submissive, and self-sacrificing. Instead, these attitudes indicated the powerful influence of social forces.

In sum, both in her views of women and in her general theoretical orientation, Horney rejected Freud's biological emphasis in favor of a social, interpersonal approach. Partly as a result of this difference, she held a much more optimistic view concerning people's capacity for change and self-fulfillment.

Harry Stack Sullivan (1892–1949)

Of the theorists considered in this section, Sullivan, an American, most emphasized the role of social, interpersonal forces in human development. His theory has been known as the Interpersonal Theory of Psychiatry (1953), and his followers created a Sullivan school of interpersonal relations.

In Sullivan's view, emotional experiences are not based in biological drives, as Freud posited, but in relations with others. This is true even in the early stages of life. For example, anxiety may be communicated by the mother in her earliest interaction with the infant; thus, from the start, anxiety is interpersonal in character rather than purely biological. The self, a critical concept in Sullivan's thinking, similarly is social in origin. The self develops out of feelings experienced while in contact with others and from reflected appraisals or perceptions by a child as to how he or she is valued or appraised by others. Experiences of anxiety as opposed to security in interpersonal relations contribute to the development of different pasts of the self. The "good me" is associated with pleasurable experiences; the "bad me" with pain and threats to security; and the "not me"—a part of the self that is rejected—is associated with intolerable anxiety.

Sullivan's emphasis on social influences is seen in his views on the development of the person. Like Erikson (Chapter 3), Sullivan judged that the developmental period beyond the time of the Oedipus complex contributed significantly to the overall development of the person. He particularly emphasized the juvenile era and preadolescence. During the juvenile stage—roughly the grammar school years—a child's experiences with friends and teachers begin to rival the influence of his or her parents. Social acceptance becomes important, and the child's reputation with others becomes an important source of self-esteem or anxiety. During preadolescence, a relationship with a close friend of the same sex becomes particularly important. This relationship of close friendship, of love, forms the basis for the development of a love relationship with a person of the opposite sex during adolescence. In later years, child psychologists highlighted the importance of early relationships with peers that were anticipated, years earlier, by Sullivan (Lewis et al., 1975).

Harry Stack Sullivan

Peers: Harry Stack Sullivan emphasized the importance of peers and a close friend of the same sex during preadolescence.

OBJECT RELATIONS, SELF PSYCHOLOGY, AND ATTACHMENT THEORY

Object Relations Theory

The interpersonal approach of Sullivan represented a significant break with the psychoanalytic tradition established by Freud. As you have just seen, the interpersonal approach of Sullivan placed greater emphasis on developmental experiences that occur after the Oedipal period (e.g., during preadolescence). We now consider schools of thought that moved in a different direction. A group of psychodynamic thinkers known as "object relations theorists" were, like Sullivan, interested in interpersonal relations. However, they presented ideas that "are essentially developmental theories that examine developmental processes and relationships *prior to* the Oedipal period" (St. Clair, 1986, p. 15).

You, the student, face an immediate potential obstacle in understanding object relations theory. It is the meaning of the word *object*. In psychodynamic theory, the word takes on a definition that differs from its typical use. We usually use the word *object* to refer to something that isn't human: a chair, a lamp, a box, and so forth. In object relations theory, however, the word *object* generally refers to a person. Psychoanalysts beginning with Freud posited that people have drives that are directed toward the thing that can satisfy the drive by reducing tension. This thing toward which the drive is directed is an object. Since the need to reduce tension generally is satisfied by a person (the hungry infant seeks the mother's breast, the adult is sexually attracted to another person), significant objects are persons.

In studying objects then, object relations theorists are interested in the world of interpersonal relations (Greenberg & Mitchell, 1983; Westen & Gabbard,

1999). They are concerned with how experiences with important people in the past are represented as parts or aspects of the self and then, in turn, affect one's relationships with others in the present. In some respects, this theorizing is close to Freud's original psychoanalytic model. Yet there is a difference. Object relations theorists do not explain all aspects of personality development, and later personality functioning, in terms of conflicts between biological drives and social constraints, as Freud did. Instead, they focus on mental representations of relationships with objects (i.e., others). Relationships experienced in early childhood determine the nature of the mental models, or mental representations, of others that one forms. Once formed, these mental representations remain in the mind. Later in life, the mental representations formed in childhood influence one's experiences in new relationships: "residues of past experiences ... shape [later] perceptions of individuals and relationships" (St. Clair, 1986).

Self Psychology and Narcissism

A theoretical development that is closely related to object relations theory is the set of ideas known, in psychodynamic theorizing, as self psychology. (Note that many psychologists who are *not* psychodynamic in their orientation also are interested in the self, and sometimes refer to their work as a "self psychology." In this section we specifically are addressing the self psychology that developed within the overall psychodynamic tradition.) The difference between object relations theory and self psychology is the following. Object relations theorists believe that the central events of early childhood involve mental representations of relations with other people; disturbances of development create negative representations of others. In self psychology, such as the theorizing of analysts Heinz Kohut or Otto Kernberg, it is thought that developmental experiences influence mental representations of oneself. If one experiences poor relations with others later in life, the self psychologist would attribute them to failures in the development of the self. For example, the person who fails to develop a distinct and positive sense of self in early childhood may, later in life, be particularly prone to seeking out relationships with other individuals who will affirm his or her worth; colloquially speaking, the person may seem psychologically needy, needing others to bolster his or her weak self-image.

A particular focus of self psychology is a phenomenon known as narcissism. Although the exact meaning of narcissism varies slightly from one psychodynamic theorist to another, the term generally refers to an investment of mental energy in the self. Theorists such as Kohut emphasized that directing energy narcissistically is part of everyone's personality development; all persons seek self development, control over the self, and a positive self image (St. Clair, 1986). In healthy, mature personality development, people can respond to their own needs while also being responsive to the needs of others. The narcissistic need to display features of the self may even display itself in socially positive ways, such as in creative products that display an artist's inner being (St. Clair, 1986). However, if developmental experiences result in less maturity, a person may display a narcissistic personality; that is, their narcissism may become a predominant feature of their personality, with negative implications for their relationships with others. In the narcissistic personality, the person has a grandiose sense of self-importance and is preoccupied

Murray's Narcissism Scale (1938, p. 181)
I often think about how I look and what impression I am making upon others.
My feelings are easily hurt by ridicule or by the slighting remarks of others.
I talk a good deal about myself, my experiences, my feelings, and my ideas.

Narcissism Personality Inventory (Raskin & Hall, 1979)
I really like to be the center of attention.
I think I am a special person.
I expect a great deal from other people.
I am envious of other people's good fortune.
I will never be satisfied until I get all that I deserve.

Figure 4.3   *Illustrative Items from Questionnaire Measures of Narcissism.*

with fantasies of unlimited success and power. Narcissists (i.e., individuals who develop a predominantly narcissistic personality) have an exaggerated feeling of being entitled to things from others, of deserving the admiration and love of others, and of being special or unique. Because so much mental energy is self-directed, narcissists lack empathy with the feelings and needs of others.

Although narcissists display positive self views, they also are vulnerable to blows to self-esteem. They need admiration from others. They at times idealize others around them yet at other times devalue others; in therapy it is not unusual for the narcissistic individual to idealize the therapist as extremely insightful at one moment and to berate the same therapist as stupid and incompetent at the next moment.

Narcissism has been the focus of much systematic research for many years. One goal in the study of narcissism is the development of assessment instruments that can distinguish narcissists from others. Henry Murray, who developed the TAT, also developed an early narcissism questionnaire (Figure 4.3). More recently, a Narcissistic Personality Inventory (NPI) (Raskin & Hall, 1979, 1981) has been developed (Emmons, 1987) (Figure 4.3). Individuals scoring high on the NPI have been found to use many more self-references (e.g., I, me, mine) than those scoring low (Raskin & Shaw, 1987). In another study a relationship was found between high scores on the NPI and being described by others as exhibitionistic, assertive, controlling, and critical-evaluative (Raskin & Terry, 1987). Individuals scoring high on narcissism have been found to evaluate their performance more positively than it is evaluated by peers or staff, demonstrating a significant self-enhancement bias relative to individuals scoring low on narcissism (John & Robins, 1994a; Robins & John, 1997). Moreover, whereas most people feel uncomfortable and self-conscious when they see themselves in a mirror or on videotape, this is not the case for narcissistic individuals. Just like the mythical Narcissus who admired his own reflection in a pond, narcissistic individuals spend more time looking at themselves in mirrors, prefer to watch themselves rather than another person on videotape, and indeed receive an "ego boost" from watching themselves on videotape (Robins & John, 1997).

Recently, researchers have focused on the thinking processes and interpersonal tendencies of narcissistic individuals (Morf & Rhodewalt, 2001; Rhodewalt & Sorrow, 2002). Narcissistic persons are found to have not only a self-aggrandizing attributional style but also fairly simple self-concepts and a cynical mistrust of others (Rhodewalt & Morf, 1995). These findings are consistent with the picture of the narcissist as a person preoccupied with the maintenance of his or her exaggerated self-esteem. In relation to this, it is not surprising that narcissistic individuals seek romantic partners who will be admiring of them, in contrast with non-narcissistic individuals who seek caring partners (Campbell, 1999).

Much of the research on narcissism has used correlational methods. Investigators commonly relate NPI scores to scores on other questionnaires or to observations of behavior (e.g., self-references, looking at self in the mirror). However, investigators increasingly have employed experimental methods. For example, building on clinical observations that narcissists respond to criticism or threat to self-esteem with feelings of rage, shame, or humiliation, Rhodewalt & Morf (1998) exposed individuals high and low on narcissism scores (NPI) to experiences of success and failure on two tests described as measures of intelligence. Since the items on the measures were moderately difficult, subjects would be uncertain about the accuracy of their responses and feedback concerning accuracy could be manipulated by the experimenters. To observe the effects of failure following success as opposed to preceding success, half the subjects received success feedback for the first test and failure feedback for the second test, and the other half the reverse order of feedback. Following each test, subjects were asked to respond to questions concerning their emotions and to indicate their attributions for their performance. As predicted, individuals high on narcissism (NPI) reacted to failure with greater anger than did individuals scoring low on narcissism, particularly when the failure followed success (Table 4.3). This result was consistent with the view that narcissistic anger is a response to perceived threats to the narcissist's grandiose self-image. In addition, individuals scoring high on narcissism were found to be particularly vulnerable to swings in self-esteem as a consequence of receiving positive and negative feedback about the self. Feelings of happiness were similarly greatly affected by such feedback (Table 4.3). Finally, narcissists were found to be more self-aggrandizing in attributing success to their own ability, and more blaming of others in accounting for failure, than were less narcissistic subjects. In sum, the experimental findings supported the clinical observations concerning the vulnerability of narcissists to blows to their self-esteem and their response to such blows with anger.

Attachment Theory

The last theoretical development we will discuss in this review of post-Freudian psychodynamic theories is attachment theory. Attachment theory is of particular relevance to the contemporary science of personality. Some writers believe that current research on attachment processes has resurrected psychodynamic theory within the scientific field (Shaver & Mikulincer, 2005), as Freud's theories had been severely criticized over the years.

Attachment theory originated in theoretical work by a British psychoanalyst, John Bowlby and was significantly advanced by the developmental psychologist Mary Ainsworth (Ainsworth & Bowlby, 1991; Bretherton, 1992; Rothbard & Shaver, 1994). Bowlby was interested in the effects of early separation from parents on personality development—a major problem in England during

Table 4.3   Self-Esteem, Anger, and Happiness Ratings of Subjects High and Low on Narcissism Following Success and then Failure (Left) and Following Failure and then Success (Right)

SOURCE: Adapted from Rhodewalt & Morf, 1998.

World War II when many children were sent to the countryside, far from their parents, to be safe from enemy bombing of the cities. In a traditional Freudian approach to this issue, one would inquire into how separation from the parents affected the development of instinctual drives (involving sex and aggression) during the Oedipal period. But here is where Bowlby's work differed from Freud. Based on his knowledge of ethology (a branch of biology focusing on the study of animals in their natural environment), Bowlby suggested that there exists a psychological system that is specifically dedicated to parent-child relationships. He called this the **attachment behavioral system (ABS)**.

According to Bowlby, the ABS is innate; that is, all persons have such a system as a result of their biological endowment. The ABS has motivational significance; it is a system that motives the infant to be close to—i.e., to seek physical proximity to—caregivers, especially when there is a threat in the environment. A young child clinging to adults for comfort and security, then, would be an example of a behavior motivated by the ABS. During development, as the infant gains a greater sense of security in its relations with adults, the proximity of adult attachment figures provides a "secure base" for explorations of the environment.

A key prediction of attachment theory is that the effects of developmental processes involving attachment are long lasting. There is a three-part rationale behind this prediction. First, child-parent relations are thought to create, in the child, symbolic mental representations involving the self and caregivers. The child, in other words, develops abstract beliefs and expectations about its relations to significant others. These mental representations are referred to as **internal working models**. Second, once formed, these mental representations endure; early relationships leave a kind of mental "residue" that persists. Note how this differs from classic psychoanalysis. In Freudian psychoanalysis, the enduring mental features involve mental energy associated with biological needs. In contrast, here in attachment theory the enduring features involve the self and social interactions—mental representations of social relationships that are formed through interactions with the parent (or other attachment figure). Third, Bowlby's attachment theory recognizes that there are individual differences in attachment. Different infants may experience different types of interactions with caregivers. Parents differ in how responsive they are to infants' needs, and these differences in parental responsiveness are posited to create different mental representations in the infant. These mental representations may result in different infants exhibiting different types of interactions with significant others, or different attachment styles.

These theoretical ideas received a major boost from research involving a novel methodology: the "Strange Situation" procedure developed by Mary Ainsworth (Ainsworth, Bleher, Waters, & Wall, 1978). This research procedure is designed to identify individual differences in attachment styles via direct observation of parent–child interactions. (A different, less convincing alternative might be merely to ask parents about their interactions with children. Direct behavioral observation is more convincing to the research psychologist because parents' reports might be inaccurate.) In the Strange Situation procedure, psychologists observe infants' responses to the departure (separation) and return (reuniting) of the mother or other caregiver in a structured laboratory setting. Based on these observations, Ainsworth and her colleagues classified infants into different attachment types. About 70 percent of infants were classified as being of a *Secure* attachment type; *secure* infants were those who were sensitive to the departure of the mother but greeted her upon being reunited, were readily comforted, and were then able to return to exploration and play. About 20 percent of infants displayed an attachment style that was labeled *Anxious-Avoidant*. This style was marked by little protest over separation from the mother and, upon her return, avoidance in terms of turning, looking, or moving away from the mother. Finally, about 10 percent of infants were classified as *Anxious-Ambivalent*; these infants had difficulty separating from the mother and reuniting with her upon her return. Their behavior mixed pleas to be picked up with squirming and insistence on being let down.

The great advantage of the Strange Situation paradigm is that it provides an objective procedure for inquiring into psychodynamic processes in child development. For example, if one wants to know whether attachment patterns are similar across cultures, one can employ the standardized Strange Situation paradigm in different cultural contexts (Van Ijzendoorn & Kroonenberg, 1988).

Attachment Styles in Adulthood   In more recent years, psychologists have used the attachment framework to understand not only parent-child relationships, but romantic relationships in adulthood. Individual differences in emotional bonds in infancy may be related to individual differences in the way emotional bonds are established later in life. To study this possibility, Hazan & Shaver (1987) had research participants complete a newspaper survey or "love quiz." As a measure of attachment style, the newspaper readers described themselves as fitting one of three categories in terms of their relationships with others. These three categories were descriptive of the three attachment styles (Figure 4.4). As a measure of their current style of romantic love, subjects were asked to respond to questions listed under a banner headline in the newspaper: "Tell Us About the Love of Your Life." Responses to the questions concerning the most important love relationship they ever had formed the basis for scores on 12 love experience scales (Figure 4.4). Additional questions were asked concerning each person's view of romantic love over time and recollections of childhood relationships with parents and between parents.

Did the different types of respondents (*secure, avoidant, anxious-ambivalent*) also differ in the way they experienced their most important love relationships? As the means for the three groups on the love scales indicate, this appears to be the case. Secure attachment styles were associated with experiences of happiness, friendship, and trust; avoidant styles with fears of closeness, emotional highs and lows, and jealousy; and anxious-ambivalent styles with obsessive preoccupation with the loved person, a desire for union, extreme sexual attraction, emotional extremes, and jealousy. In addition, the three groups differed in their views or mental models of romantic relationships: *Secure* lovers viewed romantic feelings as being somewhat stable but also waxing and waning, and discounted the kind of head-over-heels romantic love often depicted in novels and movies; *avoidant* lovers were skeptical of the lasting quality of romantic love and felt that it was rare to find a person one can really fall in love with; *anxious-ambivalent* lovers felt that it was easy to fall in love but rare to find true love. Finally, *secure* subjects, in comparison with subjects in the other two groups, reported warmer relationships with both parents, as well as between their two parents.

Subsequent research has extended these findings in two ways. First, it has been suggested that attachment style exerts a pervasive influence on people's relationships with others and on their self-esteem (Feeney & Noller, 1990). Second, attachment style appears to be related to orientation toward work: *Secure* subjects approach their work with confidence, are relatively unburdened by fears of failure, and do not allow work to interfere with personal relationships; *anxious-ambivalent* subjects are very much influenced by praise and fear of rejection at work and allow love concerns to interfere with work performance; *avoidant* subjects use work to avoid social interaction and, although they do well financially, are less satisfied with their jobs than secure subjects (Hazan & Shaver, 1990).

Although many of these studies of attachment style have relied on self-report measures, a clever study by Fraley and Shaver (1998) made use of naturalistic observation to examine the relation between attachment style and separation behavior in couples. In this study the behavior of couples temporarily separating from each other was observed in an airport. The research proceeded as follows: First a member of the research team approached couples waiting in the airport lobby and asked if they would be willing to fill out a questionnaire on "The Effects of Modern Travel on Close Relationships" that was

Adult Attachment Types
Which of the following best describes your feelings?

Secure (*N* = *319, 56%*): I find it relatively easy to get close to others and am comfortable depending on them and having them depend on me. I don't often worry about being abandoned or about someone getting too close to me.

Avoidant (*N* = *145, 25%*): I am somewhat uncomfortable being close to others; I find it difficult to trust them completely, difficult to allow myself to depend on them. I am nervous when anyone gets too close, and often love partners want me to be more intimate than I feel comfortable being.

Anxious/Ambivalent (*N* = *110, 19%*): I find that others are reluctant to get as close as I would like. I often worry that my partner doesn't really love me or won't want to stay with me. I want to merge completely with another person, and this desire sometimes scares people away.

Scale Name	*Sample Item*	*Attachment Types Means*		
		Avoidant	Anxious/ ambivalent	Secure
Happiness	My relationship with _____ (made/makes) me very happy.	3.19	3.31	3.51
Friendship	I (considered/consider) _____ one of my best friends.	3.18	3.19	3.50
Trust	I (felt/feel) complete trust in _____.	3.11	3.13	3.43
Fear of closeness	I sometimes (felt/feel) that getting too close to _____ could mean trouble.	2.30	2.15	1.88
Acceptance	I (was/am) well aware of _____'s imperfections but it (did/does) not lessen my love.	2.86	3.03	3.01
Emotional extremes	I (felt/feel) almost as much pain as joy in my relationship with _____.	2.75	3.05	2.36
Jealousy	I (loved/love) _____ so much that I often (felt/feel) jealous.	2.57	2.88	2.17
Obsessive preoccupation	Sometimes my thoughts (were/are) uncontrollably on _____.	3.01	3.29	3.01
Sexual attraction	I (was/am) very physically attracted to _____.	3.27	3.43	3.27
Desire for union	Sometimes I (wished/wish) that _____ and I were a single unit, a "we" without clear boundaries.	2.81	3.25	2.69
Desire for reciprocation	More than anything, I (wanted/want) _____ to return my feelings	3.24	3.55	3.22
Love at first sight	Once I noticed _____, I was hooked.	2.91	3.17	2.97

Figure 4.4 *Illustrative Items and Means for Three Attachment Types for 12 Love Experience Scales. (Hazan & Shaver, 1987. Copyright © 1987 by the American Psychological Association. Reprinted by permission.)*

to be used in a class project. Most (95 percent) couples agreed to participate. Each member of the couple filled out the questionnaire independently. Included in the questionnaire was a measure of attachment style. While the questionnaires were being completed, another member of the research team took a seat within viewing distance of the couple and then took notes on their interactions while they awaited flight departure. These behaviors were coded into attachment behavior categories such as *Contact Seeking* (e.g., kissing, watching from window after partner has boarded), *Contact Maintenance* (e.g., hugging, unwillingness to let go), *Avoidance* (e.g., looking elsewhere, breaking off contact), and *Resistance* (e.g., wanting to be held but also resisting contact, signs of anger or annoyance). The question addressed was whether individuals differing in attachment style would differ in their separation behavior. Such a relationship was found for women, although not for men. Compared to non-*avoidant* women, highly *avoidant* women were less likely to seek and maintain contact with their partners and to provide care and support to their partners, and were more likely to show withdrawal behavior such as pulling away and not making eye contact. Interestingly, the behavior of *avoidant* women was quite different when they were accompanying their partner in travel as opposed to separating from them. Whereas the above behaviors were true of *avoidant* women during separation, when they were to be flying with their partner (a setting that poses no threat of abandonment), they were more likely to seek care from and contact with their partners. In sum, at least for women, the attachment dynamics originally found in studies of children also applied in the context of adult romantic relationships.

Attachment Types or Dimensions?   As we noted, Ainsworth suggested that individual differences in attachment style could be understood in terms of three attachment types. In other words, she proposed what we called (back in Chapter 1) units of analysis involving type variables. The idea was that different attachment types are qualitatively distinct.

Although the idea that infants differ in attachment style makes sense, the specific notion that these differences involve qualitatively distinct categories of persons is less intuitive. It is rare that individual differences in observable psychological qualities differ categorically. Usually the psychological tendencies we observe—individual differences in anxiety, friendliness, and so forth—are each affected by a large number of factors. When any given outcome is affected by a large number of causes, the outcome usually varies dimensionally, not categorically. For example, a large number of factors affects people's scores on IQ tests: educational experiences, genetics, familiarity with the language and cultural assumptions of the test. As a result, IQ scores are distributed as a continuous dimension, not as distinct categories. A question for contemporary research on attachment styles, then, is, Do these styles really differ categorically?

Recent evidence suggests that the answer to this question is no. Fraley and Spieker (2003) examined data from a very large number of 15-month-old children who had participated in the Strange Situation paradigm. Rather than merely asking how many children fell into one versus another attachment category, they asked a logically prior question: Are there attachment categories in the first place? Or might the differences among children actually involve simple dimensions? This question can be addressed through somewhat complex,

Positive Other

Secure
(Comfortable with
intimacy and autonomy)

Preoccupied
(Preoccupied with
relationships)

Positive Self   **Negative Self**

Dismissing
(Dismissing of intimacy;
counter-dependent)

Fearful
(Fearful of intimacy;
socially avoidant)

Negative Other

Figure 4.5   *Bartholomew's Dimensions of Self and Other Internal Working Models and Associated Attachment Patterns. (Bartholomew & Horowitz, 1991; Griffin & Bartholomew, 1994. Copyright © 1994 by the American Psychological Association. Reprinted by permission.)*

yet highly informative, statistical procedures that ask whether different psychological characteristics go together so consistently that they form distinct categories (Meehl, 1992). The results indicated that, for attachment styles, this was not the case. Instead, variations in attachment involved continuous dimensions.

These findings raise the question of exactly what dimensions might best capture individual differences in attachment style. One possibility involves a theoretical model of individual differences in internal working models of the self and others (Bartholomew & Horowitz, 1991; Griffin & Bartholomew, 1994). Following Bowlby, according to this model attachment patterns can be defined in terms of two dimensions, reflecting the internal working model of the self and the internal working model of others (Figure 4.5). Each dimension involves a positive end and a negative end. Illustrative of the positive self end would be a sense of self-worth and expectations that others will respond positively. Illustrative of the positive other end would be expectations that others will be available and supportive, lending themselves to closeness. As can be seen in Figure 4.5, this model leads to the addition of a fourth attachment style, that of *Dismissing*. Individuals with this attachment pattern are not comfortable with close relationships and prefer not to depend on others, but still retain a positive self-image. Current research suggests some use for this four-pattern model, relative to the three-pattern model, but it is still an open question as to how many attachment patterns it is best to identify.

The research presented here just scratches the surface of what has become an important area of investigation. Attachment styles have been associated with partner selection and stability of love relationships (Kirkpatrick & Davis, 1994), with the development of adult depression and difficulties in interpersonal relationships (Bartholomew & Horowitz, 1991; Carnelley, Pietromonaco, & Jaffe, 1994; Roberts, Gotlib, & Kassel, 1996), with movement toward becoming more religious (Kirkpatrick, 1998), and with how individuals cope with crises (Mikulciner, Florian, & Weller, 1993). In addition, one study suggests that attachment style develops out of family experiences shared by siblings, rather than being strongly determined by genetic factors (Waller & Shaver,

1994). Thus, an impressive research record is beginning to develop (Cassidy & Shaver, 1999; Simpson & Rholes, 1998).

Yet it is important to note a number of points. First, despite suggestive evidence of continuity of attachment style, there also is evidence that these styles are not fixed in stone. At this point the amount of continuity over time of attachment style, and the reasons for greater or lesser continuity, remain issues of considerable debate (Fraley, 1999; Thompson, 1998). Second, these studies tend to look at attachment patterns as if each person had just one attachment style. Yet, there is evidence that the same individual can have multiple attachment patterns, perhaps one in relationships with males and another with females, or one for some contexts and another for different contexts (Baldwin, 1999; Sperling & Berman, 1994). Finally, it is important to recognize that much of this research involves the use of self-reports and the recall of experiences in childhood. In other words, we need more evidence about the actual behavior of individuals with different adult attachment patterns and research that follows individuals from infancy through adulthood. Some efforts, known as longitudinal research, currently are underway (Sroufe, Carlson, & Shulman, 1993). In sum, research to date supports Bowlby's view of the importance of early experience for the development of internal working models that have powerful effects on personal relationships. At the same time, further research is needed to define the experiences in childhood that determine these models, the relative stability of such models, and the limits of their influence in adulthood.

CRITICAL EVALUATION

Throughout our text, we not only will present theories of personality but also will evaluate them. We will do so by considering five criteria, each of which is a goal to be achieved in a formal scientific theory of personality. These criteria were presented in Chapter 1. As we discussed, the five criteria are the degree to which (1) the theory is based on good scientific observations, specifically, observations that are diverse in nature, are objective, and illuminate specific cognitive, affective, and biological systems of personality; whether the theory itself is (2) systematic, (3) testable, and (4) comprehensive; and whether the theory (5) yields valuable applications. After reviewing these five points, we will summarize the major contributions of the given theory.

SCIENTIFIC OBSERVATION: THE DATABASE

One of the most distinctive features of psychoanalysis is its database. Freud developed a novel form of scientific observation: the free association method. He based his theory almost entirely on the information yielded by this method.

Most contemporary personality scientists judge that Freud's exclusive reliance on the free association technique is a major drawback. Clinical observations of patients can provide a useful starting point for theorizing. But, for Freud, it was both a starting point and an ending point! He never pursued the sort of standardized, objective, replicable observations that are the hallmark of science. Instead, he relied on a free-association database that is limited in at least two respects. It is not at all diverse. Freud's clients were a relatively small number of fairly well-educated persons living in one particular city in central Europe. It is exceptionally risky to generalize from these observations to the psychological life of all persons. Secondly, there is no guarantee of objectivity in data collection. The person who is observing and interpreting the data—Freud—is the same person who developed the theory. One cannot know whether Freud's interpretation of his cases was biased by his own desire to find evidence that supported his theorizing.

Freud's clinical observations, then, are inadequate as a foundation for developing and testing a scientific theory, as many have noted (Edelson, 1984; Grunbaum, 1984, 1993). Rather than constituting unbiased observations of experiences and recollections by patients, many critics suggest that Freud often biased his observations through the use of suggestive procedures and by inferring that memories existed at the unconscious level (Crews, 1993; Esterson, 1993; Powell & Boer, 1994). Eysenck, a frequent and passionate critic of psychoanalysis, whose views we will consider later in this textbook, suggests that "we can no more test Freudian hypotheses on the couch than we can adjudicate between the rival hypotheses of Newton and Einstein by going to sleep under the apple tree" (1953, p. 229).

THEORY: SYSTEMATIC?

A second criterion for evaluating a personality theory is whether the theory is systematic. The theory should not be a disconnected set of statements about persons. Instead, its ideas should relate to one another in a logical, coherent manner.

On this score, Freud excels. The very different elements of the theory are interrelated in an exceptionally coherent manner. The process and structure aspects of the theory are related in a clear manner, with the id, ego, and superego (the psychological structures) playing different roles in the gratification of mental energy within the constraints of reality (the central personality processes, or dynamics). Freud's analyses of development in childhood, of psychological change in therapy, and of the role of society in civilizing the individual all follow logically from his analyses of personality structure and processes. Freud was an exceptional theorist, and his skill is clearly evident in the well-specified interrelations among the disparate elements of his theory.

THEORY: TESTABLE?

Although Freud systematically related the different elements of his theory to one another, this does not imply that the overall theory is testable in an unambiguous manner. A theory could be systematic yet still have features that make it difficult to test. Unfortunately, such is the case for psychoanalysis. It commonly is difficult to determine how, exactly, one could prove a theoretical prediction in psychoanalysis to be wrong.

The problem is that psychoanalysts can account for almost any outcome. Even opposite outcomes can be fit within the psychoanalytic explanatory system. Suppose a Freudian thinks that an instinctual drive will give rise to a certain form of behavior. If the behavior appears, the theory is confirmed. If the behavior does not appear, the psychoanalyst may conclude that the instinctual drive was so strong that defense mechanisms became active and prevented the behavior. Again the theory is confirmed. If some unanticipated form of behavior appears, the psychoanalyst could interpret it as a compromise between the instinct and a defense mechanism—again with no negative consequences for the theory as a whole.

Psychoanalysts are not unaware that their theoretical framework has this limitation. Some might even think that it is not a big problem; it is possible to construe psychoanalysis as a framework for interpreting events rather than as a scientific theory that makes specific testable predictions (Ricoeur, 1970). Most contemporary psychologists, however, feel that Freud's work should be assessed using the standard criteria for evaluating a scientific theory. These criteria include whether the theory is testable. A limitation of psychoanalysis, then, is that it is so flexible that—like a ruler made of pliable rubber that can be bent, twisted, pushed, and pulled to yield any of a variety of measurements of a given object—it fails to make hard-and-fast predictions that could be proven wrong. The "infinite pliability of defense mechanisms [is] the Freudian's insurance against ever encountering uninterpretable material" (Crews, 1998, p. xxv).

THEORY: COMPREHENSIVE?

Another question to ask about a personality theory is whether it is comprehensive. Does the theorist cover all aspects of personality, or merely concentrate on those that are most easily addressed by his or her theoretical system?

Both friend and foe of psychoanalysis must recognize that Freud's theory of personality is extraordinarily comprehensive. Freud addresses an exceptionally wide range of issues: the nature of mind, the relation between persons and society, dreams, sexuality, symbolism, the nature of human development, therapies for psychological change—the list goes on and on. Freud provides the most comprehensive of all the major personality theories. As you will see in subsequent chapters, many theories developed subsequent to Freud's say little or nothing about major aspects of the human experience that he addressed in depth.

APPLICATIONS

In many respects, applications are a strength of psychoanalytic theory. This should not be surprising. Psychoanalysis at first *was* an application; that is, Freud began his psychological work by addressing applied questions involving the treatment of hysteria. He only subsequently developed his work into a general theory of personality. Freud thus gave great effort to the challenge of applying psychological theory to the improvement of individual lives.

This effort was not in vain. A great many studies have evaluated the question of whether psychoanalytic therapy is effective in the decades since Freud first developed his therapy and theory. Since this is a textbook of personality theory and research, not of clinical applications, we will not review this work in detail. We merely raise two points. On the one hand, psychoanalysis unquestionably "works" (Galatzer-Levy, Bachrach, Skolnikoff, & Waldron, 2000). That is, if one asks whether people who enter into psychoanalytic therapy are better off than people who did not obtain therapy, and if one answers this question by reviewing the many therapy outcome studies that have been done over the years, one finds that psychoanalysis often benefits clients significantly. A second point, however, is that other therapies benefit clients, too. Other theories of personality have fostered alternative forms of treatment that often are of great benefit to clients, as you will see in the subsequent chapters of this book. These alternative treatments quite commonly do not feature the core elements of psychoanalysis (such as a search for conflictual unconscious contents that are the underlying cause of current problems), yet they still do work. Many psychologists see this as a major strike against psychoanalytic theory. Freud provided a specific theory of the origins of psychological distress and the steps needed for relieving it. To the extent that non-psychoanalytic therapies work, too, they raise questions about fundamental premises of Freud's theory.

MAJOR CONTRIBUTIONS AND SUMMARY

Even the harshest critic must recognize that Freud made major contributions to psychology. In closing our discussion of psychodynamic theories, we note contributions of two types.

By closely observing the working of the mind, Freud identified important phenomena that previously had been overlooked by psychologists. Even if one does not agree with Freud's *explanations* of all these phenomena, he must be created with identifying, as important targets of psychological study, phenomena of enormous significance: unconscious motivational and emotional processes; defensive strategies for coping with psychological threat; the sexually charged nature of childhood. If personality psychology had lacked Freud's insights into these phenomena, its history would have been much less rich.

A second contribution was his formulating a theory of sufficient complexity. By "sufficient" we mean that his ideas were complex enough to do justice to the complexities of human development and individuality. By obtaining richly detailed observations of persons and by willing to forge ahead with his theorizing, Freud provided a theory that accounts—rightly or wrongly—for almost all aspects of human behavior. No other theory of personality comes close to psychoanalysis in its comprehensiveness. Few others give comparable attention to the functioning of the individual as a whole. Even if one were to presume that multiple aspects of Freud's work were fundamentally wrong,

Table 4.4   Summary of Strengths and Limitations of Psychoanalytic Theory

Strengths	*Limitations*
1. Provides for the discovery and investigation of many interesting phenomena.	1. Fails to define all its concepts clearly and distinctly.
2. Develops techniques for research and therapy (free association, dream interpretation, transference analysis).	2. Makes empirical testing difficult, at times impossible.
3. Recognizes the complexity of human behavior.	3. Endorses the questionable view of the person as an energy system.
4. Encompasses a broad range of phenomena.	4. Tolerates resistance by parts of the profession to empirical research and change in the theory.

Freud at a Glance

Structure	Process	Growth and Development
Id, ego, superego; unconscious, preconscious, conscious	Sexual and aggressive instincts; anxiety and the mechanisms of defense	Erogenous zones; oral, anal, phallic stages of development; Oedipus complex

in its structure his psychoanalytic theory provides a model of what a truly comprehensive theory would look like.

Today, views concerning Freud's works and contributions range from the judgment that it is of little relevance to contemporary science to the view, emblazoned across the front of a major U.S. magazine on the occasion of the 150th anniversary of Freud's birth, that "Freud is *NOT* Dead" (*Newsweek*, March 27, 2006). Whereas some are critical of psychoanalytic errors made in the treatment of certain disorders (e.g., schizophrenia) (Dolnick, 1998) and of limited evidence supportive of psychoanalysis's major hypotheses, others are more supportive of its treatment methods and cite its enduring contributions to empirical research (Westen & Gabbard, 1999). We end by summarizing some of the strengths and limits of psychoanalytic theory (Table 4.4). Whatever the limits of his work, psychology has benefitted from the contributions of Freud, whose genius in observing human behavior has rarely been equaled.

MAJOR CONCEPTS

Anal personality   Freud's concept of a personality type that expresses a fixation at the anal stage of development and relates to the world in terms of the wish for control or power.

Attachment behavioral system (ABS)   Bowlby's concept emphasizing the early formation of a bond between infant and caregiver, generally the mother.

Collective unconscious   Carl Jung's term for inherited, universal, unconscious features of mental life that reflect the evolutionary experience of the human species.

Fixation   Freud's concept expressing a developmental arrest or stoppage at some point in the person's psychosexual development.

Free association   In psychoanalysis, the patient's reporting to the analyst of every thought that comes to mind.

Internal working model   Bowlby's concept for the mental representations (images) of the self and others that develop during the early years of development, in particular in interaction with the primary caretaker.

Oral personality   Freud's concept of a personality type that expresses a fixation at the oral stage of development and relates to the world in terms of the wish to be fed or to swallow.

Phallic personality   Freud's concept of a personality type that expresses a fixation at the phallic stage of development and strives for success in competition with others.

Projective test   A test that generally involves vague, ambiguous stimuli and allows subjects to reveal their personalities in terms of their distinctive responses (e.g., Rorschach Inkblot Test, Thematic Apperception Test).

Regression   Freud's concept expressing a person's return to ways of relating to the world and the self that were part of an earlier stage of development.

Pathology	Change	Illustrative Case
Infantile sexuality; fixation and regression; conflict; symptoms	Transference; conflict resolution; "Where id was, ego shall be"	Little Hans

Symptom In psychopathology, the expression of psychological conflict or disordered psychological functioning. For Freud, a disguised expression of a repressed impulse.

Transference In psychoanalysis, the patient's development toward the analyst of attitudes and feelings rooted in past experiences with parental figures.

REVIEW

1. Projective tests, such as the Rorschach Inkblot Test and Thematic Apperception Test (TAT), have been used by psychodynamically-oriented investigators to assess personality. They are valuable in that they provide disguised methods for tapping an individual's unique interpretations of the world, including the person's complex organization of individual perceptions. However, they also present problems of reliability and validity of interpretation.

2. The psychoanalytic theory of psychopathology emphasizes the importance of fixations, or failures in development, and regression, or the return to earlier modes of satisfaction. The oral, anal, and phallic character types express personality patterns resulting from partial fixations at earlier stages of development. Psychopathology is seen to involve conflict between instinctual wishes for gratification and the anxiety associated with these wishes. Defense mechanisms represent ways to reduce anxiety but can result in the development of symptoms. The case of Little Hans illustrates how a symptom, such as a phobia, can result from conflicts associated with the Oedipus complex.

3. Psychoanalysis is a therapeutic process in which the individual gains insight into and resolves conflicts dating back to childhood. The methods of free association and dream interpretation are used to gain insight into unconscious conflicts. Therapeutic use is also made of the transference situation, in which patients develop attitudes and feelings toward their therapist that relate to experiences with earlier parental figures.

4. A number of analysts broke with Freud and developed their own schools of thought. Alfred Adler emphasized social concepts more than biological concepts, and Carl Jung emphasized a generalized life energy and the collective unconscious. Analysts such as Karen Horney and Harry Stack Sullivan emphasized the importance of cultural factors and interpersonal relations, and were part of the group known as neo-Freudians.

5. Recent clinical developments in psychoanalysis have focused on problems of self-definition and self-esteem. Psychoanalysts in this group, known as object relations theorists, emphasize the importance of relationship seeking as opposed to the expression of sexual and aggressive instincts. The concepts of narcissism and the narcissistic personality have gained particular attention. Bowlby's attachment model and related research illustrate the importance of early experiences for later personal relationships, as well as other aspects of personality functioning.

6. An evaluation of psychoanalysis suggests its tremendous contribution in calling attention to many important phenomena and developing techniques for research and therapy. At the same time, the theory suffers from ambiguous, poorly defined concepts and problems in testing specific hypotheses.

A PHENOMENOLOGICAL THEORY: CARL ROGERS'S PERSON-CENTERED THEORY OF PERSONALITY

5

Chapter Focus

You are really nervous before a first date, so your mother gives you some advice: "Just be yourself. Your true self." But that advice doesn't seem too helpful. Well-intentioned though she may be, Mom raises two problems. First, you want to impress your date and get him or her to like you. What if your date does not like your "true self"? Even if you do like Mom's plan, there is a second problem: What exactly is your "true" self?

The nature of the self, and the tension between being yourself versus wanting to be liked by other people, are central concerns in the personality theory developed by Carl Rogers. Rogers first addressed these concerns in his work as a clinical psychologist. He combined his clinical insights with systematic empirical research to develop a theory of the totality of the individual that highlighted the person's efforts to develop a meaningful sense of self.

In addition to being a self theory, Rogers's work also can be categorized as a *phenomenological* theory. A phenomenological theory is one that emphasizes the individual's subjective experience of his or her world, in other words, his or her phenomenological experience. As a therapist, Rogers's overarching goal was to understand the client's phenomenological experience of the self and the world in order to assist the client in personal growth. As a theorist, his overarching goal was to develop a framework to explain the nature and development of the self as the core element of personality.

Rogers's phenomenological self theory can also be described by another term: *humanistic*. Rogers's work is part of a humanistic movement in psychology whose core feature was to emphasize people's inherent potential for growth.

This chapter, then, introduces you to the theory—the phenomenological, humanistic, self theory—that is the enduring legacy of one of the great American psychologists of the 20th century, Carl Rogers.

QUESTIONS TO BE ADDRESSED IN THIS CHAPTER

1. What is the self and why might one not act in a manner consistent with one's true self?

2. Freud viewed motivation in terms of tension-reducing, the pursuit of pleasure, and intra-psychic conflict. Is it possible to view human motivation, instead, in terms of personal growth, self-actualization, and feelings of congruence?

3. How important is it for us to have a stable self-concept? How important is it for our internal feelings to match our self-concept? What do we do when feelings are in conflict with our self-beliefs?

4. What are the childhood conditions that produce a positive sense of self-worth?

In the previous chapters, you learned about Freud's psychoanalytic theory of personality and related psychodynamic positions. We now introduce a second, entirely different perspective. It is that of the American psychologist Carl Rogers. His work exemplifies a phenomenological approach to the study of persons.

At the outset, you should consider how these conceptions, Freud's and Rogers's, are related. Rogers did not disagree with everything Freud said about persons. He recognized that Freud provided some insights about the workings of the mind that are of enduring value. Also, Rogers worked in a style that was similar in some ways to that of Freud. Rogers, like Freud, began his career as a therapist and based his general theory of personality primarily on his therapeutic experiences. However, these affinities are less important than are some deep differences. Rogers disagreed sharply with major emphases of Freudian theory: its depiction of humans as controlled by unconscious forces; its assertion that personality is determined, in a fixed manner, by experiences early in life; its associated belief that adult psychological experience is a repeating of the repressed conflicts of the past. To Rogers, these psychodynamic views did not adequately portray human existence or human potentials. Rogers thus provided a new theory of the person. It emphasized conscious *[handwritten: opposite of FREUD!]* perceptions of the present rather than merely unconscious residues of the past, interpersonal experiences encountered across the course of life rather than merely parental relations in childhood, and people's capacity to grow toward psychological maturity rather than merely their tendency to repeat childhood conflicts.

Rogers expands our conception of human nature, and in a very positive direction. To many contemporary psychologists, his positive conception of the person, developed during the mid-20th century, is of enduring importance. "Half a century on from when Rogers first developed his theory, it still has profound consequences for the person and their ability to maintain and enhance themselves" (McMillan, 2004, p. ix).

"I speak as a person, from a context of personal experience and personal learning." This is how Rogers describes himself, in a chapter entitled "This Is Me," in his 1961 book *On Becoming a Person*. The chapter is a personal, very moving account by Rogers of the development of his professional thinking and personal philosophy. Rogers states what he does and how he feels about it.

CARL R. ROGERS (1902–1987): A VIEW OF THE THEORIST

This book is about the suffering and the hope, the anxiety and the satisfaction, with which each therapist's counseling room is filled. It is about the uniqueness of the relationship each therapist forms with each client, and equally about the common elements which we discover in all these relationships. This book is about the highly personal experiences of each one of us. It is about a client in my office who sits there by the corner of the desk, struggling to be himself, yet deathly afraid of being himself. It is about me as I try to perceive his experience, and the meaning and the feeling and the taste and the flavor that it has for him. It is about me as I rejoice at the privilege of being a midwife to a new personality as I stand by with awe at the emergence of a self, a person, as I see a birth process in which I have had an important and facilitating part. The book is, I believe, about life, as life vividly reveals itself in the therapeutic process with its blind power and its tremendous capacity for destruction, but with its overbalancing thrust toward growth, if the opportunity for growth is provided.

SOURCE: ROGERS, 1961a, pp. 4–5.

✶✶

influence of childhood

Carl R. Rogers was born on January 8, 1902, in Oak Park, Illinois. He was reared in a strict and uncompromising religious and ethical atmosphere. His parents had the welfare of their children constantly in mind and inculcated in them a worship of hard work. Rogers's description of his early life reveals two main trends that are reflected in his later work. The first is the concern with moral and ethical matters. The second is the respect for the methods of science. The latter appears to have developed out of exposure to his father's efforts to operate their farm on a scientific basis and Rogers's own reading of books on scientific agriculture.

Rogers started his college education at the University of Wisconsin, majoring in agriculture, but after two years he changed his professional goals and decided to enter the ministry. During a trip to Asia in 1922, he had a chance to observe commitments to other religious doctrines as well as the bitter mutual hatreds of French and German people, who otherwise seemed to be likable individuals. Experiences like these influenced his decision to go to a liberal theological seminary, the Union Theological Seminary in New York. Although he was concerned about questions regarding the meaning of life for individuals, Rogers had doubts about specific religious doctrines. Therefore, he chose to leave the seminary, to work in the field of child guidance, and to think of himself as a clinical psychologist.

Rogers obtained his graduate training at Teachers College, Columbia University, receiving his Ph.D. in 1931. His education included exposure to both the dynamic views of Freud and the rigorous experimental methods then prevalent at Teachers College. Again, there were the pulls in different directions,

Carl R. Rogers

the development of two somewhat divergent trends. In his later life Rogers attempted to bring these trends into harmony. Indeed, these later years represent an effort to integrate the religious with the scientific, the intuitive with the objective, and the clinical with the statistical. Throughout his career, Rogers tried continually to apply the objective methods of science to what is most basically human.

[handwritten margin note: religious & scientific ① combine usually opposite ideas]

> Therapy is the experience in which I can let myself go subjectively. Research is the experience in which I can stand off and try to view this rich subjective experience with objectivity, applying all the elegant methods of science to determine whether I have been deceiving myself. The conviction grows in me that we shall discover laws of personality and behavior which are as significant for human progress or human relationship as the law of gravity or the laws of thermodynamics.
>
> SOURCE: ROGERS, 1961a, p. 14.

In 1968, Rogers and his more humanistically oriented colleagues formed the Center for the Studies of the Person. The development of the Center expressed a number of shifts in emphasis in the work of Rogers from work within a formal academic structure to work with a collection of individuals who shared a perspective, from work with disturbed individuals to work with normal individuals, from individual therapy to intensive group workshops, and from conventional empirical research to the phenomenological study of people. Rogers believed that most of psychology was sterile and generally felt alienated from the field. Yet the field continued to value his contributions. He was president of the American Psychological Association in 1946–1947, was one of the first three psychologists to receive the Distinguished Scientific Contribution Award (1956) from the profession, and in 1972 was the recipient of the Distinguished Professional Contribution Award.

With Rogers, the theory, the man, and the life are interwoven. In his chapter "This Is Me," Rogers lists 14 principles that he learned from thousands of hours of therapy and research. Here are some illustrations:

1. In my relationships with persons I have found that it does not help, in the long run, to act as though I were something that I am not.

2. I have found it of enormous value when I can permit myself to understand another person.

3. Experience is, for me, the highest authority . . . it is to experience that must return again and again, to discover a closer approximation to truth as it is in the process of becoming in me.

4. What is most personal and unique in each one of us is probably the very element which would, if it were shared or expressed, speak most deeply to others.

5. It has been my experience that persons have a basically positive direction.

6. Life, at its best, is a flowing, changing process in which nothing is fixed.

SOURCE: ROGERS, 1961a, pp. 16–17.

ROGERS'S VIEW OF THE PERSON

THE SUBJECTIVITY OF EXPERIENCE

Rogers's theory is built on a deeply significant insight into the human condition. In our daily living, we believe we experience an objective world of reality. When we see something occur, we believe it exists as we saw it. When we tell people about the events of our day, we believe we are telling them what really happened. We are so confident in our objective knowledge of an objective reality that we rarely question it. Yet we are wrong. Rogers instructs: "I do not react to some absolute reality, but to *my perception of* this reality" (Rogers, 1951/1977, p. 206, emphasis added). The "reality" we observe is really a "private world of experience... the phenomenal field" (Rogers, 1951/1977, p. 206).

This **phenomenal field**—the space of perceptions that makes up our experience—is a *subjective* construction. The individual constructs this inner world of experience, and the construction reflects not only the outer world of reality but the inner world of personal needs, goals, and beliefs. Inner psychological needs shape the subjective experiences that we interpret as objectively real.

Consider some simple examples. If a child sees an angry look from its mother, or you detect a disappointed look from a dating partner, these emotions—anger, disappointment—are the reality that is experienced. But this so-called reality could be wrong. Personal needs (to be accepted by the mother, to be attractive to the dating partner) may contribute to our perceiving the other as angry or disappointed. Yet people commonly fail to recognize this influence of inner needs on perceptions of the outer world. Failing to recognize this, the individual "perceives his *experience* as reality. His *experience* is his reality" (Rogers, 1959/1977, p. 207). We are sure things really exist as we saw them. Yet our seeing is not an objective recording of the world of reality, but a subjective construction that reflects our personal needs.

Rogers surely was not the first to have this intuition. Similar ideas can be traced back at least as far as the *Allegory of the Cave* by Plato, who depicted persons as perceiving mere shadows of reality, being unable to glimpse the objective world of existence. Rogers's uniqueness is his developing this insight into a theory of personality: a model of individual development and of the structures and dynamics of the mind, and methods for assessing personality and conducting therapy.

Feelings of Authenticity

Two additional aspects of Rogers's analysis of the subjectivity of experience define his core view of the person. The first is that people are prone to a distinctive form of psychological distress. It is a feeling of alienation or detachment—the feeling that one's experiences and daily activities do not stem from one's true, authentic self. Why do these feelings arise? Because we need the approval of others, we tell ourselves that *their* desires and values are our own. The child tries to convince itself that it really is bad to hit its baby sister, just as its parents say, even though it feels good to do so. The adult tries to convince herself or himself that it really is good to settle down into a traditional career and family lifestyle, as valued relatives instruct, even though he or she really feels like a life of independence. When this happens, the individual *thinks* but does not *feel* an attachment to its own values. "Primary sensory and visceral reactions are ignored" and "the individual begins on a pathway which he later describes as 'I really don't know myself'" (Rogers,

1951/1977, p. 213). Rogers relates the case of a client who described her experiences as follows: "I've always tried to be what the others thought I should be, but now I'm wondering whether I shouldn't just see that I am what I am" (Rogers, 1951/1977, p. 218).

Note how Rogers's conception of the deliberate/thoughtful and the instinctive/visceral aspects of the organism differs from Freud's. To Freud, visceral reactions were animalistic impulses that needed to be curbed by the civilized ego and superego. Distorting and denying these impulses was part of normal, healthy personality functioning. But to Rogers, these instinctive visceral reactions are a potential source of wisdom. Individuals who openly experience the full range of their emotions, who are "accepting and assimilating [of] all the sensory evidence experienced by the organism" (Rogers, 1951/1977, p. 219), are psychologically well adjusted.

Conflict between instinctive and rational elements of mind thus is not an immutable feature of the human condition in Rogers's view. Rather than conflict, persons can experience congruence. They can realize a state in which their conscious experiences and goals are consistent with their inner, viscerally-felt values.

The Positivity of Human Motivation

The final key aspect of Rogers's view of persons is his conception of human motivation. Rogers's clinical experiences convinced him that the core of our nature is essentially positive. Our most fundamental motivation is toward positive growth. Rogers recognized that some institutions may teach us otherwise. Some religions teach that we are basically sinful. The institution of psychoanalysis teaches that our basic instincts are sexual and aggressive. Rogers did recognize that people can, and often do, act in ways that are destructive and evil. But his basic contention is that, when we are functioning freely, we are able to move toward our potentials as positive, mature beings.

To those who called him a naive optimist, Rogers was quick to point out that his conclusions were based on decades of experience in psychotherapy:

> I do not have a Pollyanna view of human nature. I am quite aware that out of defensiveness and inner fear individuals can and do behave in ways which are incredibly cruel, horribly destructive, immature, regressive, antisocial, hurtful. Yet one of the most refreshing and invigorating parts of my experience is to work with such individuals and to discover the strongly positive directional tendencies which exist in them, as in all of us, at the deepest levels.
>
> SOURCE: ROGERS, 1961a, p. 27.

Here is a profound respect for people, a respect that is reflected in Rogers's theory of personality and his person-centered approach to psychotherapy.

A PHENOMENOLOGICAL PERSPECTIVE

Rogers takes a "phenomenological" approach to the study of persons. Here at the outset of our coverage of his work, then, we should explain what is meant by this lengthy term.

In psychology or other disciplines, such as philosophy, a phenomenological approach is one that investigates people's conscious experiences. The investigation, in other words, does not try to characterize the world of reality as it exists independent of the human observer. Instead, one is interested in the experiences of the observer: how the person experiences the world. One precursor to the contemporary psychologist's use of the term is the work of the 18th-century philosopher Kant, who distinguished the "noumenal world" (objects as they existed in and of themselves, independent of the observer) from the world of phenomena, that is, of conscious experiences.

A bit of reflection on the material of the previous two chapters should reveal why Rogers's position was so noteworthy within personality psychology. The psychodynamic tradition was *not* particularly interested in phenomenology. To Freud, conscious phenomenological experience is not the core of personality. Indeed, conscious experience may be related in only the most indirect ways to that core, which involves unconscious drives and defenses. As you will see in subsequent chapters, some other theories that initially were developed at around the same time as Rogers's—e.g., trait theory, behaviorism—devote relatively little attention to the textures and dynamics of everyday phenomenological experience. Rogers, then, was an important voice in promoting the psychological study of **phenomenology**.

Some readers—especially those of you with a background in the "hard" sciences—may object to the study of subjective conscious experience. It may seem less scientific than the study of the objective, real world. However, the greatest of scientists reminds us that, in the world of scientific investigation, conscious experience is the data that we have to work with: "The 'real' is in no way immediately given to us. Given to us is merely the data of our consciousness" (Einstein, quoted in Paranjpe, 1998, p. 44). The only way to make sense of the real world is, Einstein notes, the psychological act of "intellectual construction" (Paranjpe, 1998, p. 44). Rogers was directly concerned with these acts of psychological construction; in his theory of personality, he was particularly concerned with the acts of intellectual construction that fill people's thoughts about themselves.

ROGERS'S VIEW OF THE SCIENCE OF PERSONALITY

What does Rogers's concern with phenomenological experience have to do with his view of the science of personality? Are these two independent things: a phenomenological perspective on psychology on the one hand, and a viewpoint on science on the other? Or might one have an implication for the other?

A bit of reflection suggests that a marriage between a traditional conception of science and a concern with phenomenological experience may be a difficult one. Science, as we usually think of it, rests on clear-cut data. We use laboratory instruments to tell us about objective physical features (size, mass, electrical charge, etc.) of objects in the world. Rogers is telling us that our major interest in personality psychology is not external, measurable objects or behaviors. It is internal experience. These internal experiences have a subjective quality; their meaning rests on the interpretations of the person who is having the experience (the subject who is experiencing things) and cannot be determined by objective measures of physical response. A classic example of this point is the following. An external observer could, with objective scientific measures, determine whether a person quickly closed and opened her eye. But the objective measure would not reveal whether the person was (a) blinking due to a piece of dust falling in her eye, (b) winking at someone across the room, or was (c) feigning winking at someone across the room (i.e., was playacting the act of winking). To know this, we must know the meaning attached to the act by the person who is acting. The philosopher Charles Taylor (1985) has noted that this difference—the difference between physically measurable objects and internal psychological states with subjective meaning—signals a potentially deep division between traditional conceptions of science and the approach to personality of Carl Rogers. Rogers's phenomenological perspective, then, raises the question of whether one can have a science of personality that is modeled on the physical sciences.

HERMENEUTICS AND THE HUMAN SCIENCES

This question of the relation between and physical sciences and a science of persons is one that was asked long before Rogers. Beginning in the 19th century, particularly in the work of the German philosopher Wilhelm Dilthey, scholars expressed doubt that the principles of the natural sciences could be extended to the study of human psychology. They suggested, instead, that the psychology of persons requires a hermeneutical approach.

A hermeneutical approach is one in which the style of explanation resembles the style of thinking that we use when reading a novel. When we read about an action by a character in a novel or some other form of text, we interpret that action within the overall context provided in the text. We consider the character's personality, the character's recent past experiences, the character's relations to other characters in the book, the social setting in which the particular action is taking place, the overall cultural and historical setting in which the actors live, and so forth. Perhaps most importantly for illustrating a potential difference between the natural science and a science of persons, we ask whether the character's actions were good or bad; even the simplest of children's stories features good and bad characters whose actions respectively illustrate or violate some moral or ethical norm. Thus, in the case of our interpretations of characters in a work of fiction, there are three key steps: (1) we search for the meaning of a character's action, (2) meaning is deduced by examining the overall social and historical context in which the person is acting, and (3) we evaluate the ethical and moral goodness of actions. This much is obvious. The point of the hermeneutical argument, however, is that this is *not* the typical way of proceeding in the natural sciences. If we want to explain an event in the natural world—for example, we throw a rock into the air and want to explain why it moves in a parabolic curve on its way back to earth—we usually do not take any of the three steps outlined above. We do not (1) search for the meaning of the rock's behavior, (2) ask about the sociohistorical context in which it is moving, or (3) ask whether a parabola is a good path of movement for a rock. Instead, we appeal to universal laws of motion that explain the physical forces acting on the rock. We don't engage in a search for meaning, and the entire notion of goodness does not even apply; the laws of motion simply are what they are, and it does not make sense to ask if the rock is acting in a way that is ethically good. The hermeneutical argument, then, is that the understanding of humans—who act based on meaning that is constructed in a social world that contains moral and ethical standards—requires an approach that is closer to the understanding of texts than to the understanding of rocks.

Rogers's work can be understood as an attempt to draw on the best of both worlds. On the one hand, his concern with the subjective experiences of the individual led him to create an approach that was, to a significant degree, hermeneutic. In therapy, his main goal was not to classify his client within a scientific taxonomy or to identify some past causal factor that was a key determinant of his client's behavior. Instead, his goal was to gain a deep understanding of how his clients experienced their world. His efforts in this regard were similar to a reader's efforts to understanding the world as experienced by the narrator of a first-person novel or the author of an autobiography. On the other hand, Rogers had great respect for the scientific method and felt that psychology could eventually establish itself as a lawful science. He was particularly careful to subject his ideas about the effective forms of therapy to scientific test. Rogers made a valiant effort to wed the scientific and the human sides of personality science.

THE PERSONALITY THEORY OF CARL ROGERS

Having introduced Rogers, his overall view of human nature, and his conception of personality science, we now turn to the details: the specifics of Rogers's theory of personality.

STRUCTURE

The Self

In Chapter 1 we distinguished between structure and process aspects of personality theories. This distinction, useful in understanding the work of Freud, is useful again in understanding the theory of Carl Rogers. We first turn to the structure aspects of Rogerian theory, where the key structural concept is the self.

According to Rogers, the self is an aspect of phenomenological experience. It is one aspect of our experience of the world; that is, one of the things that fills our conscious experience is our experience of ourselves, or of "a self." Phrased more formally, according to Rogers the individual perceives external objects and experiences, and attaches meanings to them. The total system of perceptions and meanings make up the individual's phenomenal field. That subset of the phenomenal field that is recognized by the individual as "me," or "I" is the self. The **self**, or **self-concept**, represents an organized and consistent pattern of perceptions. Although the self changes, it always retains this patterned, integrated, organized quality. Because the organized quality endures over time and characterizes the individual, the self is a personality structure.

To Rogers, the self is not a little person inside of us. The self does not independently control behavior. Rather, the self is an organized set of perceptions that is possessed by the individual; it is the whole person who is responsible for his or her actions, not an independent "self." Second, the pattern of experiences and perceptions known as the self is, in general, available to awareness; that is, it includes conscious self-perceptions. Although individuals do have experiences of which they are unaware, the self-concept is primarily conscious. (Note that Rogers's use of the term *self* differs from that of Carl Jung, whose views were discussed in the previous chapter. Jung thought of the self as an unconscious archetypal force, whereas Rogers uses the term *self* to refer to our conscious self-concept.)

Rogers did recognize two different aspects to the self: an actual self and an **ideal self**. Rogers recognized that people naturally think about not only themselves in the present, but their potential selves in the future. They thus generate an organized pattern of perceptions not only of their current self, but of an ideal self that they would like to be. The ideal self, then, is the self-concept that an individual would most like to possess. It includes the perceptions and meanings that potentially are relevant to the self and that are valued highly by the individual. Rogers thus recognizes that our views of ourselves contain two distinct components: the self that we believe we are now, and the self that we ideally see ourselves becoming in the future.

Rogers maintained that he did not begin his theoretical work by deciding that it was important to study the self. In fact, he first thought that *self* was a vague, scientifically meaningless term. However, he listened carefully to his clients, who commonly expressed their psychological experience in terms of a self; clients would report that they "did not feel like themselves," "were disappointed in themselves," and so forth. It became clear to Rogers, then, that the self was a psychological structure through which people were interpreting their world.

Measuring Self-Concept

The Q-Sort Technique

Once he recognized the centrality of self-concept, Rogers knew that he needed an objective way to measure it. To this end, he primarily used the **Q-sort technique**, which had been developed by Stephenson (1953).

In the Q-sort, the psychologist administering the test gives the test taker a set of cards, each of which contains a statement describing a personality characteristic: "Makes friends easily," "Has trouble expressing anger," and so forth. Test takers sort these cards according to the degree to which each statement is seen as descriptive of themselves. This is done on a scale labeled *Most characteristic of me* on one end and *Least characteristic of me* on the other. People are asked to sort the cards according to a forced distribution, with most of the cards going in the middle and relatively few being sorted at either extreme end; this ensures that the individual carefully considers the content of each personality attribute in comparison to the others.

Two features of the Q-sort are particularly noteworthy. One is that it strikes an interesting balance between fixed and flexible measures (see Chapter 2). The same statements are given to all test takers; in this respect, the measure is fixed. But the tester does not merely give a person a score by adding up test responses in a fixed manner that is the same for all person. Instead, the test is flexible in that test takers indicate which subset of items is most characteristic of themselves, from their own point of view. Different subsets of items are characterized as most "like me" and "not like me" by different individuals. The test, then, yields a more flexible portrait of the individual than is obtained by other measures, whose content is entirely fixed (as you will see in subsequent chapters). Yet it is not entirely flexible. People must use statements provided by the experimenter, instead of their own self-descriptions, and must sort the

IS THE SENSE OF SELF UNIQUELY HUMAN?

Most dog owners have at some time experimented with placing a mirror in front of their dog. Is there self-recognition? Animal research suggests that most non-human species do not recognize themselves in mirrors, although some do. Chimpanzees display mirror self-recognition; if they have some exposure to mirrors, they will use the mirror to examine and groom themselves. Recent findings indicate that dolphins and elephants also recognize that the face in the mirror is their own. If one places a mark on an elephant's head and then a mirror in front of the elephant, the elephant will touch the mark on its head after seeing its reflection in a mirror.

Research on the development of self-directed mirror behavior in infants suggests that the development of self-recognition is a continuous process, starting as early as four months of age. At this point infants show some response to relationships between self-movements and changes in mirror images. And what of recognition of specific features of the self? If an infant looks at itself in the mirror, has rouge placed on its nose, and then looks in the mirror again, will the infant respond to the rouge mark in a way expressive of self-recognition? Such specific feature recognition, in terms of self-directed mirror behavior, appears to begin at about the age of one year.

The recognition of self, whether expressed through self-directed mirror behavior or otherwise, can be related to the development of consciousness and mind. Clearly it is a matter of considerable psychological significance. Not only does it mean that we can be aware of ourselves and have feelings about ourselves, but also that we can have knowledge of and empathy for the feelings of others. It would indeed be ironic if the very processes that allow us to feel worst about ourselves also provided us with the opportunity to feel most empathetic with others.

Mirror mirror on the wall, is that me after all? This appears to be a question that only members of a few species can address. In humans some maturation is required, but self-recognition begins to develop fairly early and remains a significant part of life thereafter.

SOURCE: LEWIS & BROOKS-GUNN, 1979; PLOTNIK, DE WAAL, & REISS, 2006; ROBINS, NOREM, & CHECK, 1999.

(Reprinted with special permission of King Features Syndicate.)

statements in a manner prescribed by the psychologist rather than according to a distribution that makes the most sense to them.

The second feature is that the Q-sort can be administered to individuals more than once in order to assess both the actual self and the ideal self. In the latter assessment, people are asked to categorize the statements according to the degree to which they describe the self that they ideally would like to be. By comparing the two Q-sorts, ideal and actual self, one can obtain a quantitative measure of the difference, or discrepancy, between the two aspects of self-concept. As you will see in Chapter 6, these discrepancies are important to psychopathology and therapeutic change.

The Semantic Differential   Another method that can be used for assessing self-concept is the semantic differential (Osgood, Suci, & Tannenbaum, 1957). Developed as a measure of attitudes and the meanings of concepts, rather than as a specific test of personality, the semantic differential nonetheless has value as a personality assessment technique. In filling out the semantic differential, the individual rates a concept on a number of seven-point scales defined by polar adjectives such as good-bad, strong-weak, or active-passive. Thus, a subject would rate a concept such as "My Self" or "My Ideal Self" on each of the polar adjective scales. A rating on any one scale would indicate whether the subject felt that one of the adjectives was very descriptive of the concept or somewhat descriptive, or whether neither adjective was applicable to the concept. The ratings are made in terms of the meaning of the concept for the individual.

Like the Q-sort, the semantic differential is a structured technique in that the subject must rate certain concepts and use the polar adjective scales provided by the experimenter. This structure provides for the gathering of data suitable for statistical analysis but, also like the Q-sort, it does not preclude flexibility as to the concepts and scales to be used. There is no single standardized semantic differential. A variety of scales can be used in relation to concepts such as father, mother, and doctor to determine the meanings of phenomena for the individual. For example, consider rating the concepts "My Self" and "My College" on scales such as liberal-conservative, scholarly–fun-loving, and formal-informal. To what extent do you see yourself and your college as similar? How does this relate to your satisfaction as a student at this college? In some research very similar to this, it was found that the more students viewed themselves as dissimilar to their college environment, the more dissatisfied they were and the more likely they were to drop out (Pervin, 1967a, b).

An illustration of the way in which the semantic differential can be used to assess personality is in a case of multiple personality. In the 1950s two psychiatrists, Corbett Thigpen and Harvey Cleckley, made famous the case of "the three faces of Eve." This was the case of a woman who possessed three personalities, each of which predominated for a period of time, with frequent shifts back and forth. The three personalities were called Eve White, Eve Black, and Jane. As part of a research endeavor, the psychiatrists were able to have each of the three personalities rate a variety of concepts on the semantic differential. The ratings were then analyzed both quantitatively and qualitatively by two psychologists (C. Osgood and Z. Luria) who did not

SELF IDEAL CONGRUENCE: GENDER DIFFERENCES OVER TIME?

Rogers's notion of the ideal self, and the Q-sort method he espoused, still influence contemporary research on the self-concept. One example is the work by Block and Robins (1993) who examined change in self-esteem from adolescence into young adulthood. Has your self-esteem changed from your early teens to your early twenties? According to Block and Robins, the answer to this question may depend on your gender: On average, self-esteem increases for males and decreases for females over these formative years of life.

Level of self-esteem was defined as the degree of similarity between the perceived self and the ideal self. Both of these constructs were measured by an adjective Q-sort, which includes such self-descriptive items as "competitive," "affectionate," "responsible," and "creative." Subjects whose perceived self was highly similar to their ideal self were high in self-esteem. In contrast, subjects whose perceived self was highly dissimilar to their ideal self were low in self-esteem.

Between the ages of 14 and 23 males became more self-confident and females became less self-confident. Whereas at age 14 they scored similar in self-esteem, by age 23 males were much higher. Apparently, males and females differ in how they experience the adolescent years and how they negotiate the transition into adulthood. For men, the news is good: This phase of life is associated with coming closer to one's ideal. Unfortunately, the opposite is true for women: They move further away from their ideal as they enter adulthood.

What are the personality attributes that characterize men and women with high self-esteem? Block and Robins used extensive interview data collected at age 23 and found that the high self-esteem women valued close relationships with others. High self-esteem men, in contrast, were more emotionally distant and controlled in their relationships with others. These sex differences in relationships reflect the very different expectations society holds for what it means to be a man or a woman. Not surprisingly, those young adults whose personalities fit these cultural expectations well are more likely to feel good about themselves and have a self-concept that is close to their ideal self.

Left unanswered by this study is a phenomenological question that would have been of interest to Rogers: What is the content of the ideal self? Do males and females differ in their perceptions of what constitutes the ideal? The ideal self seems particularly susceptible to external influence—what we perceive as valued in society. The content of the ideal self tells us something about the attributes a person values and thus uses to derive self-esteem. An interesting question for future research is how the content of the ideal self influences psychological adjustment. Does the person's ideal self capture characteristics of a self-actualized human being or society's definition of what constitutes the ideal man or woman?

Eve White   Perceives the world in an essentially normal fashion, is well socialized, but has an unsatisfactory attitude toward herself. The chief evidence of disturbance in the personality is the fact that ME (the self-concept) is considered a little bad, a little passive, and definitely weak.

Eve Black   Eve Black has achieved a violent kind of adjustment in which she perceives herself as literally perfect, but, to accomplish this break, her way of perceiving the world becomes completely disoriented from the norm. If Eve Black perceives herself as good, then she also has to accept HATRED and FRAUD as positive values.

Jane   Jane displays the most "healthy" meaning pattern, in which she accepts the usual evaluations of concepts by her society yet still maintains a satisfactory evaluation of herself. The self concept, ME, while not strong (but not weak, either) is nearer the good and active directions of the semantic space.

Figure 5.1   *Brief Personality Descriptions, Based on Semantic Differential Ratings, in a Case of Multiple Personality. (Osgood & Luria, 1954.)*

know the subject. Their analysis included both descriptive comments and interpretations of the personalities that went beyond the objective data. For example, Eve White was described as being in contact with social reality but under great emotional stress; Eve Black was described as out of contact with social reality but quite self-assured; and Jane was described as superficially very healthy but quite restricted and undiversified. A more detailed, although still incomplete description of the three personalities based on the semantic differential ratings is presented in Figure 5.1. The analysis on the basis of these ratings turned out to fit quite well with the descriptions offered by the two psychiatrists (Osgood & Luria, 1954).

PROCESS

As you have just seen, unlike Freud, Rogers did not present a highly elaborate model of personality structure, with personality divided into a number of parts. He instead presented a simple model that highlighted what he felt was the central structure in personality, namely, the self. A similar intellectual style is seen in his discussion of personality process. Rogers posited a single overarching motivational principle—one that, again, involves the self.

Self-Actualization

Rogers did not think that behavior was primarily determined by animalistic drive states, as did Freud. Rogers felt that, instead, the most fundamental personality process is a forward-looking tendency toward personality growth. He labeled this a tendency toward **self-actualization**. "The organism has one basic tendency and striving—to actualize, maintain, and enhance the experiencing organism" (Rogers, 1951, p. 487). In a poetic passage, Rogers described life as an active process, comparing it to the trunk of a tree on the shore of the ocean as it remains erect, tough, and resilient, maintaining and enhancing itself in the growth process: "Here in this palm-like seaweed was the tenacity of life, the forward thrust of life, the ability to push into an

It is always necessary that others approve of what I do. (F)

I am bothered by fears of being inadequate. (F)

I do not feel ashamed of any of my emotions. (T)

I believe that people are essentially good and can be trusted. (T)

Figure 5.2   *Illustrative Items from an Index of Self-Actualization. (Jones and Crandall, 1986.)*

incredibly hostile environment and not only to hold its own, but to adapt, develop, become itself" (Rogers, 1963, p. 2).

The concept of actualization refers to an organism's tendency to grow from a simple entity to a complex one, to move from dependence toward independence, from fixity and rigidity to a process of change and freedom of expression. The concept includes the tendency of each person to reduce needs or tension, but it emphasizes the pleasures and satisfactions that are derived from activities that enhance the organism.

Rogers himself never developed a measure of the self-actualizing motive. Over the years, however, others have done so. One such effort involves a 15-item scale that measures the ability to act independently, self-acceptance or self-esteem, acceptance of one's emotional life, and trust in interpersonal relations (Figure 5.2). Scores on this questionnaire measure of self-actualization have been found to be related to other questionnaire measures of self-esteem and health, as well as to independent ratings of individuals as self-actualizing persons (Jones & Crandall, 1986).

More recently, Ryff (1995; Ryff & Singer, 1998, 2000) has postulated a multifaceted conception of positive mental health, which includes self-acceptance, positive relations with others, autonomy, environmental mastery, purpose in life, and personal growth. The personal growth component is conceptually close to Rogers's view of the growth process and self-actualization. Her questionnaire, the Personal Growth Scale, defines someone high on personal growth as someone who has a feeling of continued development, has a sense of realizing their potential, is open to new experiences, and is changing in ways that reflect more self-knowledge and effectiveness. Additionally, there is evidence that people are happiest when pursuing goals congruent with the self (Little, 1999; McGregor & Little, 1998).

Self-Consistency and Congruence

The principle of self-actualization, by itself, clearly is not sufficient to account for the dynamics of personality functioning. Much of psychological life consists of conflicts, doubts, and psychological distress, rather than a continual march toward personal actualization. The theoretical challenge for Rogers, then, is to account for a more complete range of personality dynamics within his overall self-based theory of the person. One way Rogers accomplishes this is by positing that people seek self-consistency and a sense of congruence between their sense of self and their everyday experience. According to Rogers, the organism functions to maintain consistency (an absence of conflict) among self-perceptions and to achieve congruence between perceptions of the self and experiences: "Most of the ways of behaving which are adopted by the

*Self-Actualization: Rogers
emphasizes the basic tendency
of the organism toward
self-actualization.*

organism are those which are consistent with the concept of the self" (Rogers, 1951, p. 507).

The concept of **self-consistency** originally was developed by Lecky (1945). According to Lecky, the organism does not seek to gain pleasure and to avoid pain but, instead, seeks to maintain its own self-structure. The individual develops a value system, the center of which is the individual's valuation of the self. Individuals organize their values and functions to preserve the self-system. Individuals behave in ways that are consistent with their self-concept, even if this behavior is otherwise unrewarding to them. If you, for example, see yourself as a poor speller, you may try to behave in a manner consistent with this self-perception.

In addition to self-consistency, Rogers emphasized the importance to personality functioning of **congruence** between the self and experience. Rogers used the term *congruence* to refer to a family of phenomena that differ from one another (as he himself was aware), so defining the Rogerian term *congruence* is difficult. Rogers used the term *congruence* to refer to an "accurate matching" (Rogers, 1961, p. 339) between two psychological states. To use an example provided by Rogers, if you are at a party you find boring, but you tell the host that you're having a great time, there is a lack of congruence between your experience and your communication; this is an example of **incongruence**. In cases of congruence, there is an open, genuine match between two psychological qualities.

One important type of congruence, to Rogers, is the congruence between your sense of self and your awareness of your own actions and experiences. If you view yourself as a kind person who expresses empathy toward others, but you have an experience in which you think you were cold and unempathic, you confront an incongruence between your sense of self and your experience. If you think of yourself as a quiet person, but suddenly find yourself acting in a highly outgoing manner (e.g., at a party), you may experience a distressing sense of having acted in a way that is "not me." To Rogers, achieving a consistent sense of self is so important that people seek out experiences that are congruent with their existing self-perceptions.

States of Incongruence and Defensive Processes   Sometimes people do experience an incongruence between self and experience that suggests a basic inconsistency in the self. When this occurs, what happens? Rogers posits that anxiety is the result of a discrepancy between experience and the perception of the self. The person who, for example, believes that he or she never hates anyone, but who suddenly experiences hateful feelings, will be anxious after becoming aware of this incongruence. Once this happens, the person will be motivated to defend the self; he or she will engage in defensive processes. In this regard, Rogers's work is similar to Freud's. To Rogers, however, defensive processes are not centered on a defense against recognition of basic biological impulses in the id. They involve defense against a loss of a consistent, integrated sense of self.

To Rogers, then, when we perceive an experience as threatening because it conflicts with our self-concept, we may not allow the experience to be conscious. Through a process called **subception**, we can be aware of an experience that is discrepant with the self-concept before it reaches consciousness. The response to the threat presented by recognition of experiences that are in conflict with the self is that of defense. Thus, we react defensively and attempt to deny awareness to experiences that are dimly perceived to be incongruent with the self-structure.

Two defensive processes are **distortion** of the meaning of experience and **denial** of the existence of the experience. Denial serves to preserve the self-structure from threat by denying it conscious expression. Distortion, a more common phenomenon, allows the experience into awareness but in a form that makes it consistent with the self: "Thus, if the concept of self includes the characteristic 'I am a poor student,' the experience of receiving a high grade can be easily distorted to make it congruent with the self by perceiving in it such meanings as, 'That professor is a fool'; 'It was just luck'" (Rogers, 1956, p. 205). What is striking about this last example is the emphasis it places on self-consistency. What is otherwise likely to be a positive experience, receiving a high grade, now becomes a source of anxiety and a stimulus for defensive processes to be set in operation. In other words, it is the relation of the experience to the self-concept that is key.

Research on Self-Consistency and Congruence   An early study in this area was performed by Chodorkoff (1954), who found that subjects were slower to perceive words that were personally threatening than they were to perceive neutral words. This tendency was particularly characteristic of defensive, poorly adjusted

CURRENT QUESTIONS

CONSISTENT OR VARIABLE VIEW OF THE SELF: WHICH IS BETTER?

In everyday life, people play many different social roles. We are children, friends, lovers, students, workers, sometimes all of these within the same day. For each significant role that we play in life, we develop an image of ourselves within that role. How do you see yourself across the social roles that are important in your life? The following exercise is designed to let you explore this question for yourself.

Think about yourself in the roles of student, friend, and son or daughter. Then describe how you see yourself in that role by rating yourself on the five descriptive statements listed below using the following scale:

DISAGREE				AGREE
Strongly	A little	Neither/nor	A little	Strongly
1	2	3	4	5

How I see myself in each role:

	Son or Daughter	Friend	Student	Maximum discrepancy
Is assertive.	____	____	____	____
Tries to be helpful.	____	____	____	____
Is punctual.	____	____	____	____
Worries a lot.	____	____	____	____
Is clever, sharp-witted.	____	____	____	____

Once you have made your ratings, you are able to explore how consistent or variable your self-concept is across these roles. For each of the five statements, subtract the lowest from the highest of the three role ratings. Consider the first statement "Is assertive" as an example.

If you rated yourself a 5 in the Son/Daughter role, a 3 in the Friend role, and a 1 in the student role, then your maximum discrepancy score would be 5 minus 1 = 4. You might want to ask yourself what such a discrepancy means and how it may have developed. You can also calculate all five discrepancy scores and then add them together to create a total self-concept variability score. Your score should fall within the range of 0 to 20, with 0 representing a highly consistent view of self across these roles and 20 representing a highly variable self view. How variable is your self-concept in general?

As Donahue, Robins, Roberts, and John (1993) showed in two studies, some individuals see themselves as essentially the same person across their various social roles, whereas others see themselves quite differently. For example, one woman saw herself as fun-loving and easygoing across all her roles. In contrast, another woman saw herself as fun-loving and easygoing with her friends but as quite serious with her parents. Which of these two individuals is likely to be better adjusted—the first who has a more consistent self-concept across her roles or the second who has a more variable self-concept?

What would Rogers predict? Recall that Rogers theorized that the psychologically adjusted individual has a coherent and integrated self. Thus, Rogers's theory predicts that very high variability in the self-concept can be bad for mental health because it is indicative of fragmentation and a lack of an integrated "core" self. An alternative prediction is that variability is good because it provides specialized role identities that enable the individual to respond flexibly and adaptively to various role requirements (e.g., Gergen, 1971).

The results reported by Donahue and her colleagues clearly favored Rogers's position. Individuals with highly variable role identities were more likely to be anxious, depressed, and low in self-esteem. Their relationships with parents had been unusually difficult while growing up, and in early adulthood they were less satisfied with how they were doing in their relationships and in their careers. Not surprisingly, they also changed jobs and relationship partners more frequently than did individuals who had more coherent self-concepts.

These findings suggest that various forms of psychological problems and instability are related to inconsistencies in the self-concept across roles. In other words, the inconsistent self is fragmented, rather than specialized. When thinking about your own level of self-concept variability, however, do not assume that a high score is necessarily indicative of psychological problems. What is most important is that you feel comfortable with your particular style of negotiating your own self-image within your various social roles. If you don't feel comfortable, then you may want to consider ways in which you might strive for a more unified self-image across the social roles you act out in your daily life. A book by Harary and Donahue (1994) provides many useful exercises and detailed information about these issues.

SOURCE: DONAHUE, ROBINS, ROBERTS, & John, 1993; Harary & Donahue, 1994.

individuals. Poorly adjusted individuals, in particular, attempt to deny awareness to threatening stimuli.

Additional research by Cartwright (1956) involved the study of self-consistency as a factor affecting immediate recall. Following Rogers's theory, Cartwright hypothesized that individuals would show better recall for stimuli that are consistent with the self than for stimuli that are inconsistent. He hypothesized further that this tendency would be greater for maladjusted subjects than for adjusted subjects. In general, subjects were able to recall adjectives they felt were descriptive of themselves better than they were able to recall adjectives they felt were most unlike themselves. Also, there was considerable distortion in recall for the latter, inconsistent adjectives. For example, a subject who viewed himself as hopeful incorrectly recalled the word "hopeless" as being "hopeful," and a subject who viewed himself as friendly mistakenly recalled the word "hostile" as being "hospitable." As predicted, poorly adjusted subjects (those applying for therapy and those for whom psychotherapy had been judged to be unsuccessful) showed a greater difference in recall than did adjusted subjects (those who did not plan on treatment and those for whom psychotherapy had been judged to be successful). This difference in recall scores was due particularly to the poorer recall of the maladjusted subjects for inconsistent stimuli.

In a related study, an effort was made to determine the ability of subjects to recall adjectives used by others to describe them (Suinn, Osborne, & Winfree, 1962). Accuracy of recall was best for adjectives used by others that were consistent with the self-concept of subjects and was poorest for adjectives used by others that were inconsistent with the self-concept. In sum, the accuracy of recall of self-related stimuli appears to be a function of the degree to which the stimuli are consistent with the self-concept.

The studies just discussed relate to perception and recall. What of overt behavior? Aronson and Mettee (1968) found results that were consistent with Rogers's view that individuals behave in ways that are congruent with their self-concepts. In a study of dishonest behavior, they reasoned that if people are tempted to cheat, they will be more likely to do so if their self-esteem is low than if it is high; that is, whereas cheating is not inconsistent with generally low self-esteem, it is inconsistent with generally high self-esteem. The data gathered indeed suggested that whether or not an individual cheats is influenced by the nature of the self-concept. People who have a high opinion of themselves are likely to behave in ways they can respect, whereas people with a low opinion of themselves are likely to behave in ways that are consistent with that self-image.

More recent research supports the view that the self-concept influences behavior in varied ways (Markus, 1983). What is particularly noteworthy here is the suggestion that people often behave in ways that will lead others to confirm the perception they have of themselves—a self-fulfilling prophecy (Darley & Fazio, 1980; Swann, 1992). For example, people who believe they are likable may behave in ways that lead others to like them, whereas others who believe themselves to be unlikable may behave in ways that lead others to dislike them (Curtis & Miller, 1986). For better or for worse, your self-concept may be maintained by behaviors of others that were influenced in the first place by your own self-concept!

Another recent finding is that people with low self-esteem are so prone to maintain a consistent self-concept that they sometimes fail to take even simple actions that might put them in a better mood. They seem resigned to maintaining a poor self-image and the experience of negative emotions. Heimpel, Wood, Marshall, & Brown (2002) conducted a series of studies designed to test the hypothesis that people who report having low self-esteem are less motivated to change their negative moods, as compared to people with high self-esteem. In one study, people were put into a sad mood through a mood induction, that is, an experimental manipulation designed to create temporary positive or negative feelings. Research participants were then given the opportunity to select a videotape to watch. One of the videos from which people could select was a video of comedy routines—a topic that everyone thought would put them in a good mood. The selection of the comedy video when in a negative mood, then, would be a choice for inconsistency, specifically, a choice to take action to change one's mood from negative to positive, rather than maintaining a consistent negative mood. It might seem to you as if everyone would choose to put themselves in a better mood. But this is not what happened. Although the large majority of high self-esteem persons chose to watch the comedy video when in a negative mood, only a minority of low self-esteem persons chose to watch it (Heimpel et al., 2002). Most of the low self-esteem persons, in other words, failed to make a choice that would change their negative mood. Their choice produced consistency—a consistent negative mood even when they could have made themselves feel better. The tendency to maintain consistency in psychological experience, then, may sometimes override a simple hedonistic tendency to have emotionally positive experiences.

The Need for Positive Regard

We have seen, then, that individuals commonly try to act in accordance with their self-concept and that experiences inconsistent with the self-concept are often ignored or denied. But why? Why, in Rogerian theory, would the individual be distressed by a rift between experience and self and, therefore, be in need of defense? Why couldn't people accept all experiences, good and bad, as steps toward self-actualization?

Rogers answered this question by proposing that all persons possess a basic psychological need. It is a **need for positive regard**. The idea is that people need not only the obvious biological facts of life—food, water, shelter, and so on—but also something psychological. They need to be accepted and respected by others, that is, to receive others' positive regard.

Rogers sees the need for positive regard as a powerful force in the workings of personality. Indeed, it is so powerful that it can draw one's attention away from experiences of personal value. "The expression of positive regard by a significant social other can become [so] compelling" that a person becomes more attuned to "the *positive regard* of such others than toward *experiences* which are of positive value in *actualizing* the organism" (Rogers, 1959/1977, p. 225). People, then, can lose touch with their own true feelings and values in their pursuit of positive regard from others. This is how an individual can develop the feelings of detachment from their true self that we discussed at the outset of this chapter (see "Feelings of Authenticity," above). In pursuing positive regard from others, people may disregard or distort their experiences of their own inner feelings and desires.

Rogers's theory emphasizes the psychological need for positive regard.

This need for positive regard is particularly central to child development. The infant needs the parents' love, affection, and protection. The parents, throughout childhood, provide information on what is good, that is, what is regarded positively. A primary question is whether parents give the child positive regard unconditionally—that is, whether they show that they respect and prize the child no matter what. An alternative possibility is that the parents will show greater respect and love for the child only if the child adheres to some forms of behavior and not others. This alternative Rogers describes as **conditions of worth**; the child is made to feel like a worthy individual only if she has some thoughts and feelings, but not others.

If the child receives positive regard unconditionally, then there is no need to deny experiences. However, if children experience conditions of worth, then they need to balance their own natural tendencies with their need for positive regard from the parents. The child then may cope by denying an aspect of his or her own experience—essentially denying, or distorting, a feature of his or her true self. For example, suppose a male child shows interest in the arts but the parents discourage this, perhaps judging that their child should pursue activities that are more gender-stereotypical for males (e.g., sports). The child then may deny an interest in the arts, to attain the parents' regard. In so doing, the parents have created an interpersonal setting that causes the child to deny, and lose touch with, an aspect of his own self.

To summarize, Rogers did not feel a need to use the concepts of motives and drives to account for the activity and goal-directedness of the organism. For him, the person is basically active and self-actualizing. As part of the self-actualizing process, we seek to maintain a congruence between self and experience. However, because of past experiences with conditional positive regard, we may deny or distort experiences that threaten the self-system.

GROWTH AND DEVELOPMENT

Early in his career, prior to writing a formal theory of personality, Rogers spent much time working with children. In the city of Rochester, New York, he worked as a clinical psychologist in an office of the Society for the Prevention of Cruelty to Children and then as director of a guidance center that oversaw social agencies that served children in the local community (Kirschenbaum, 1979). Although Rogers did not do formal scientific research on personality development, he did gain much first-hand experience with the development of children and wrote extensively on the psychological treatment of children and youth. These early-career experiences are reflected in his later writings, which explore the development of personality from a phenomenological perspective.

To Rogers, development is not confined to the early years of life, as Freud suggested. People grow toward self-actualization throughout the life course, experiencing ever greater complexity, autonomy, socialization, and maturity. The self, after becoming a separate part of the phenomenal field early in life, continues to grow in complexity throughout life. Rogers's work suggested that developmental factors must be considered at two levels of analysis. At the level of parent–child interactions, the question is whether the parents provide an environment that is optimal for psychological growth; to Rogers, this would be an environment that provides unconditional positive regard. At the level of internal psychological structures, the question is whether individuals

Positive Regard: Healthy personality development is fostered through the communication of unconditional positive regard to the child.

experience congruence between self and daily experience or, conversely, distort aspects of their experience in order to attain others' regard and a consistent self-concept.

The major developmental concern for Rogers, then, is whether the child is free to grow, to be self-actualizing, or whether conditions of worth cause the child to become defensive and operate out of a state of incongruence. Healthy development of the self takes place in a climate in which the child can experience fully, can accept him- or herself, and can be accepted by the parents, even if they disapprove of particular types of behavior. This point is emphasized by most child psychiatrists and psychologists. It is the difference between a parent saying to a child, "I don't like what you are doing" and saying, "I don't like you." In saying "I don't like what you are doing," the parent is accepting the child while not approving of the behavior. This contrasts with situations in which a parent tells a child, verbally or in more subtle ways, that his or her behavior is bad and that he or she is bad. The child then feels that recognition of certain feelings would be inconsistent with the picture of him- or herself as loved or lovable, leading to denial and distortion of these feelings.

Research on Parent-Child Relationships

A variety of studies suggest that acceptant, democratic parental attitudes facilitate the most growth. Whereas children of parents with these attitudes show accelerated intellectual development, originality, emotional security, and control, the children of rejecting, authoritarian parents are unstable, rebellious, aggressive, and quarrelsome (Baldwin, 1949). What is most critical is children's

Fostering Creative Potential: Psychological conditions of safety and freedom help develop the creative potential of children.

perceptions of their parents' appraisals. If they feel that these appraisals are positive, they will find pleasure in their bodies and in their selves. If they feel that these appraisals are negative, they will develop insecurity and negative appraisals of their bodies (Jourard & Remy, 1955). Apparently, the kinds of appraisals that parents make of their children largely reflect the parents' own degree of self-acceptance. Mothers who are self-accepting also tend to accept their children (Medinnus & Curtis, 1963).

A classic study of the origins of self-esteem by Coopersmith (1967) further supported the importance of the dimensions suggested by Rogers. Coopersmith defined self-esteem as the evaluation an individual typically makes with regard to the self. Self-esteem, then, is an enduring personal judgment of worthiness, not a momentary good or bad feeling resulting from a particular situation. Children in the study completed a simple self-report measure of self-esteem, with most items coming from scales previously used by Rogers. Some findings involved the relation of self-esteem to other personality characteristics. For example, compared to children low in self-esteem, those high in self-esteem were found to be more assertive, independent, and creative in solving problems.

A more important aspect of Coopersmith's study is that it provided evidence on the critical question, What are the origins of self-esteem? Coopersmith obtained not only child self-esteem scores, but information about the children's perceptions of their parents and information about parental child-rearing attitudes, practices, and lifestyles (obtained via interviews with mothers).

Interestingly, indicators of social prestige that one might think would be influential—such as wealth, degree of education, job title—were *not* strongly related to children's self-esteem scores. Instead, children's self-esteem was related more strongly to interpersonal conditions in the home and the immediate environment. Children appeared to develop self-views through a process of reflected appraisal in which they used opinions of themselves that were expressed by others as a basis for their own self-judgments.

What specific parental attitudes and behaviors were important to the formation of self-esteem? Three were shown to be particularly influential. The first was the degree of acceptance, interest, affection, and warmth expressed by parents toward the child. Mothers who were more loving and developed closer relationships with their children had children with higher self-esteem. Children appeared to interpret the mother's interest as signifying that they were worthy persons deserving of others' attention and affection. The second important feature of parent-child interaction involved permissiveness and punishment. Parents of children with high self-esteem established, and firmly enforced, clear demands for appropriate behavior. They generally tried to affect behavior by using rewards. In contrast, the parents of low self-esteem children did not establish clear guidelines for behavior, were harsh and disrespectful toward children, tended to use punishment rather than reward, and stressed force and loss of love. The third feature was whether parent–child relations were democratic or dictatorial. Parents of children with high self-esteem had established and enforced extensive rules for conduct, yet, in so doing, they treated children fairly within these defined limits and recognized the rights and opinions of the child. Parents of children low in self-esteem set few and poorly defined limits, and were autocratic, dictatorial, rejecting, and uncompromising in their methods of control. Coopersmith summarized his findings as follows: "The most general statement about the origins of self-esteem can be given in terms of three conditions: total or nearly total acceptance of the children by their parents, clearly defined and enforced limits, and the respect and latitude for individual actions that exist within the defined limits" (1967, p. 236). Coopersmith further suggested that the important factor is the children's *perception of* the parents, not necessarily the specific actions the parents display. The total family climate influences the child's perception of the parents and their motives.

Another study further supports Rogers's contention that child-rearing conditions that provide children with psychological safety and psychological freedom will foster children's creative potential (Harrington, Block, & Block, 1987). Conditions of psychological safety are provided by parental expressions of unconditional positive regard for the child and empathic understanding. Psychological freedom is expressed in permission to engage in unrestrained expression of ideas. In a test of this view, child-rearing practices and parent-child interaction patterns were measured for children between the ages of three and five years (Figure 5.3). Remarkably, the researchers were able to obtain independent ratings (i.e., ratings not made by the parent) of creative potential in the children not during early childhood but years later, in adolescence. They found a significant positive association between childhood (preschool) environmental conditions of psychological safety and freedom and creative potential assessed both in preschool and, years later, in adolescence (Harrington, Block, & Block, 1987). The degree to which parent–child interactions

Creativity-fostering Environment

Parents respect the child's opinions and encourage expression of them.

Parents and child have warm, intimate time together.

Children are allowed to spend time with other children or families who have different ideas or values.

Parents are encouraging and supportive of the child.

Parents encourage the child to proceed independently.

The Creative Personality

Tends to be proud of accomplishments.

Is resourceful in initiating activities. Becomes strongly involved in activities.

Has a wide range of interests.

Is comfortable with uncertainties and complexities.

Perseveres in the face of adversity.

Figure 5.3 *Illustrative Characteristics of Creativity-fostering Environments and the Creative Personality. (Adapted from Harrington, Block, & Block, 1987.)*

were "Rogerian," then, appeared to be an important environmental factor contributing to personality development.

Despite such findings, some psychologists question whether the concept of self-esteem is sufficient for a science of personality. Critics generally think the term is too global. Most people have some aspects of their life in which they think well of themselves and others in which they are self-critical, and the self-esteem construct masks these cross-situational variations. Nonetheless, others feel that the concept of global self-esteem has merit, and that self-esteem has implications for many aspects of psychological functioning (Dutton & Brown, 1997). This present chapter of our text is devoted primarily to the presentation of Rogers's theory. In our next chapter, we turn in more detail to contemporary research that bears on these questions about self-esteem processes, and the utility of the construct of self-esteem for personality science.

Social Relations, Self-Actualization, and Well-Being Later in Life

According to Rogerian theory, the relation between social acceptance and positive self-regard is important not only to child development, but to personality functioning throughout life. Recent research bears on this hypothesis.

Roberts and Chapman (2000) analyzed data from a long-term longitudinal study of the psychological development of adult women. In this dataset, women were studied over a 30-year period extending from young adulthood into midlife. Although the study was not organized according to the personality theory of Carl Rogers, it did contain two measures that bear on Rogerian hypotheses. One was an index of psychological well-being; participants indicated their sense of well-being, including feelings of self-esteem, at four time points across the 30-year time period of the study. The second was an index of role quality, that is, whether people experienced supportive social relations in life roles including both marriage and work. Rogerian theory of course would predict that positive, supportive social relations would increase psychological well-being. The supportive relations should provide people with a sense of positive regard and make them less likely to engage in defensive processing that might contribute to psychological distress and a lower sense of self.

A key feature of this longitudinal research is that, by studying people at different points in their lives, the researchers could examine the impact of role quality on changes in well-being. These analyses generally were in accord with predictions that one would make from Rogerian theory. People who experienced a high degree of distress in their marriage and work roles experienced lower levels of well-being, whereas people who experienced more satisfying social roles showed positive changes in their well-being and personal maturity (Roberts & Chapman, 2000). Although it is difficult to establish causality in this type of research (that is, to determine whether social relations actually exerted a causal influence on well-being), the results are consistent with the Rogerian hypothesis that views of self and psychological well-being can change across the course of life and that the degree of positive regard one receives from significant individuals in one's life can contribute directly to these changes.

As you can see, Rogers's ideas continue to be of relevance to the contemporary field. In our next chapter, we look more closely at contemporary research that bears on Rogers's theorizing, while also considering clinical applications of his principles and alternative theoretical conceptions that relate strongly to Rogers's phenomenological perspective.

MAJOR CONCEPTS

Conditions of worth   Standards of evaluation that are not based on one's own true feelings, preferences, and inclinations, but instead that are based on others' judgments about what constitutes desirable forms of action.

Congruence   Rogers's concept expressing an absence of conflict between the perceived self and experience. Also one of three conditions suggested as essential for growth and therapeutic progress.

Denial   A defense mechanism, emphasized by both Freud and Rogers, in which threatening feelings are not allowed into awareness.

Distortion   According to Rogers, a defensive process in which experience is changed so as to be brought into awareness in a form that is consistent with the self.

Ideal self   The self-concept the individual would most like to possess. A key concept in Rogers's theory.

Incongruence   Rogers's concept of the existence of a discrepancy or conflict between the perceived self and experience.

Need for positive regard   In Rogerian theory, the fundamental human need to be accepted and respected by other persons.

Phenomenal field   The individual's way of perceiving and experiencing his or her world.

Phenomenology   The study of human experience; in personality psychology, an approach to personality theory that focuses on how the person perceives and experiences the self and the world.

Positive regard, need for   Rogers's concept expressing the need for warmth, liking, respect, and acceptance from others.

Q-sort technique   An assessment device in which the subject sorts statements into categories following a normal distribution. Used by Rogers as a measure of statements regarding the self and the ideal self.

Self-actualization   The fundamental tendency of the organism to actualize, maintain, enhance itself, and fulfill its potential. A concept emphasized by Rogers and other members of the human potential movement.

Self-concept (or the "Self")   The perceptions and meaning associated with the self, me, or I.

Self-consistency   Rogers's concept expressing an absence of conflict among perceptions of the self.

Subception   A process emphasized by Rogers in which a stimulus is experienced without being brought into awareness.

REVIEW

1. The phenomenological approach emphasizes an understanding of how people experience themselves and the world around them. The person-centered theory of Carl Rogers is illustrative of this approach.

2. Throughout his life Rogers attempted to integrate the intuitive with the objective, combining a sensitivity to the nuances of experience with an appreciation for the rigors of science.

3. Rogers emphasized the positive, self-actualizing qualities of the person. In his research he emphasized a disciplined effort to understand subjective experience, or the phenomenal field, of the person.

4. The key structural concept for Rogers was the self—the organization of perceptions and experiences associated with the "self," "me," or "I." Also important is the concept of the ideal self, or the self-concept the person would most like to possess. The Q-sort is one method used to study these concepts and the relation between them.

5. Rogers de-emphasized the tension-reducing aspects of behavior and, instead, emphasized self-actualization as the central human motive. Self-actualization involves continuous openness to experience and the ability to integrate experiences into an expanded, more differentiated sense of self.

6. Rogers also suggested that people function to perceive self-consistency and to maintain congruence between perceptions of the self and experience. However, experiences perceived as threatening to the self-concept may, through defensive processes such as distortion and denial, be prevented from reaching consciousness. A variety of studies support the view that people will behave in ways to maintain and confirm the perception they have of themselves.

7. People have a need for positive regard. Under conditions of unconditional positive regard, children and adults are able to grow within a state of congruence and be self-actualizing. On the other hand, where positive regard is conditional, people may screen experiences out of awareness and limit their potential for self-actualization.

8. Children are influenced in their self-judgments through the process of reflected appraisal. Parents of children with high self-esteem are warm and accepting but also are clear and consistent in their enforcement of demands and standards.

ROGERS'S PHENOMENOLOGICAL THEORY: APPLICATIONS, RELATED THEORETICAL CONCEPTIONS, AND CONTEMPORARY RESEARCH

6

Chapter Focus

A good friendship has qualities that are both wonderful and mysterious. If you're stressed out, if life is giving you too much to handle, talking to a friend—simply discussing your problems and having the person listen carefully—can make you feel better. It's hard to know why. Even if your friend doesn't have any specific advice, even if he or she doesn't offer any solutions to life's problems, the mere fact that the person is there for you, ready to listen, can make things feel better.

And what does your friend make you feel better about? School? Relationships? Maybe. But if you're lucky, your friend makes you feel better about that most important of things: you. By letting you explore and express your feelings, your friend somehow improves your sense of self. You end up accepting your limitations and appreciating your strengths.

Providing this type of relationship, and accomplishing this sort of change in self-concept, was Carl Rogers's goal in his client-centered therapy. His therapeutic approach, which was a foundation on which he built his theory of personality (Chapter 5), is one focus of this chapter. As you will learn, in therapy Rogers tried to discover how his clients denied and distorted aspects of their everyday experience. He then created a therapeutic relationship—a kind of trusting friendship in a therapeutic setting—within which clients could abandon these distortions, explore their true self, and thereby experience personal growth.

In addition to learning about this clinical application of Rogers's theory of personality, a second goal of this chapter is to review theoretical conceptions that are closely related to that of Rogers. We will consider three: (1) the human potential movement, including the contributions of the psychologist Abraham H. Maslow; (2) the positive psychology movement, a significant force in contemporary psychology; and (3) existentialism, a school of thought in philosophy that shows signs of increased influence in personality psychology.

Our third focus in this chapter is contemporary research on the self. Much current research in personality science bears on Rogers's ideas about self and personality. As you will see, some of the research confirms Rogers's original ideas, other research extends them in novel directions, and yet other research challenges Rogers's conclusions. For example, cross-cultural studies question whether the psychological dynamics studied by Rogers in the United States are a universal feature of human psychological experience. This third chapter focus, then, speaks to a primary goal of this book: enabling you, the student, to use contemporary research findings to evaluate critically the classic theoretical conceptions of human nature.

QUESTIONS TO BE ADDRESSED IN THIS CHAPTER

1. According to Rogers, how does psychological distress and pathology develop, and what factors are necessary to bring about psychological change in therapy?

2. How did writers in the human potential movement add to Rogers's understanding of human personality?

3. What does the contemporary positive psychology movement say about human personality and potentials?

4. What is existentialism, how do existentialist ideas relate to personality theory and research, and how do they relate, specifically, to the work of Rogers?

5. What are the implications of contemporary research—including cross-cultural research on self-concept, motivation, and personality—for Rogers's phenomenological theory?

We begin this chapter where Rogers began his own professional career: in the psychological clinic, facing the challenges of psychopathology and personality change. These clinical applications were integral to Rogers's development of his personality theory and remained a major focus of Rogers's work throughout his career. **CLINICAL APPLICATIONS**

Rogers's work in therapy involved more than just a set of techniques. It included a world view, that is, a broad perspective on the nature of the therapeutic setting. Rogers's thinking can be understood by contrasting it to Freud's. Freud, trained as a physician, treated his clients as patients. The client was a person with problems that had to be diagnosed and cured. The therapist was the person with diagnostic and curative expertise. Rogers, in contrast, emphasized the expertise and curative power of the client. In developing his therapeutic approach, "a person seeking help was not treated as a dependent patient but rather as a responsible client" (Rogers, 1977, p. 5). To Rogers, the client possesses an inherent drive toward psychological health. The therapist's task merely is to help the client to identify conditions that may interfere with personal growth, thereby allowing the person to overcome these obstacles and to move toward self-actualization.

PSYCHOPATHOLOGY

Self-Experience Discrepancy

Before we consider Rogers's approach to treating psychological distress, we should address a logically prior question: Where does psychological distress come from? If people have such a strong capacity for self-actualization, then why are they experiencing psychological distress in the first place? The core elements of Rogers's answer to this question were introduced in the previous chapter. They involve the self and whether the person experiences a congruence between self and experience.

To Rogers, healthy persons are individuals who can assimilate experiences into their self-structure. They are open to experiences rather than interpreting events in a defensive manner. It is such persons who experience a **congruence** between self and experience.

In contrast, the neurotic person's self-concept has become structured in ways that do not fit organismic experience. They deny awareness of significant sensory and emotional experiences. Experiences that are incongruent with the self-structure are subceived; that is, threatening events are detected below levels of conscious awareness and then are either denied or distorted. This distortion results in a discrepancy between actual psychological experiences and the self's awareness of experience, or a **self-experience discrepancy**. Such discrepancies involve a rigid defense of the self against experiences that might threaten the self-concept. Rogers (1961) gives the immediately recognizable example of "the intellectualizing person who talks about himself and his feelings in abstractions, leaving you wondering what is *actually* going on within him" (p. 64). Rogers's point, of course, is that you, the observer, are not the only person who is unaware of what is actually going on within him. By distorting his experiences, the person has lost an accurate sense of his true self.

Consistent with his rejection of a medical model, Rogers did not differentiate among types of pathology. He did not want a diagnostic scheme within which individual persons were classified and then treated merely as examples of one versus another type of psychological disorder. He did, however, differentiate among forms of defensive behaviors. For example, one such defensive behavior is rationalization. In rationalization, a person distorts behavior in such a way as to make it consistent with the self. If you view yourself as a person who never makes mistakes and then a mistake seems to occur, you may rationalize it by blaming the error on another person. Another defensive behavior is fantasy. A man who defensively believes himself to be an adequate person may fantasize that he is a prince and that all women adore him, and he may deny any experiences that are inconsistent with this image. A third example of defense behavior is projection. Here an individual expresses a need, but in such a form that the need is denied to awareness and the behavior is viewed as consistent with the self. People whose self-concept involves no "bad" sexual thoughts may feel that others are making them have these thoughts.

The descriptions of these defensive behaviors are quite similar to the ones given by Freud. For Rogers, however, the important aspect of these behaviors is their handling of an incongruence between self and experience by denial in awareness or distortion of perception: "It should be noted that perceptions are excluded because they are contradictory, not because they are derogatory" (Rogers, 1951, p. 506). Furthermore, the classification of the defenses is not as critical to Rogerian theory as it is to Freudian theory.

PSYCHOLOGICAL CHANGE

In our previous chapter you learned about Rogers's most important contribution to personality science: his theory of personality. Those ideas, however, were not Rogers's own highest priority. His main professional focus was the process of psychotherapy. Rogers committed himself to understanding how personality *change* can come about. The process of change, or of becoming, was his greatest concern. His most enduring contribution to understanding change was work in which he outlined necessary conditions of therapy; he described, in other words, types of circumstances and events that need to occur in the relationship between client and therapist in order for personality change to come about. This therapeutic approach, to many people, remains as vibrant and relevant today as it was when first formulated by Rogers a half-century ago (McMillan, 2004).

Therapeutic Conditions Necessary for Change

In his early work, Rogers emphasized the therapist's use of the technique of reflection of feeling. In this nondirective approach, therapists do not guide

CURRENT QUESTIONS

IDEAL SELF AND FEARED SELF — MOTIVATING FACETS OF THE SELF?

The day before a big test you find yourself visualizing what it would feel like to get an A. Then you imagine what it would be like to get an F. Both possibilities can feel very real. The A may seem so ideal, and the F so frightening, that you decide to study an extra hour.

What are your ideal and feared selves? Some research has emphasized the ideal self and the feared self and compared them with the current self as the individual perceives it (e.g., Harary & Donahue, 1994). Here is an exercise that you may find useful for thinking about your ideals and fears in relation to your current self-concept.

First think about how you see yourself in general and rate your current self-concept as you perceive it right now using the five descriptive statements listed below. Next, consider your ideal self—the way you wish your personality would be—and rate it using the same five statements. Finally, consider your feared self—the way you are afraid your personality might become—and rate it accordingly. For all three types of ratings,

use the following scale and enter your ratings in the appropriate column:

Disagree				Agree
		Neither/		
Strongly	*A little*	*nor*	*A little*	*Strongly*
1	2	3	4	5

Once you have completed your ratings, you can compute two discrepancy scores, one for the discrepancy between current and ideal self and another between current and feared self. For example, consider a person who is quite a partier (a current self rating of 5 on "outgoing") but feels that ideally she should be more reserved and spend more time on schoolwork (an ideal self rating of 3); the resulting current-ideal discrepancy (−2) indicates that she needs to cut back on social activities to get closer to the ideal self. Another person might feel he has overcome his shyness (a current self rating of 3 on "outgoing") but fears that he might drift back

How I see my various selves:

	Current Self	Ideal Self	Feared Self	Current minus Ideal	Current minus Feared
Outgoing, not reserved.	____	____	____	____	____
Forgiving, doesn't hold grudges.	____	____	____	____	____
Is lazy.	____	____	____	____	____
Is tense, easily stressed out.	____	____	____	____	____
Sophisticated in art, music, or literature.	____	____	____	____	____

into his lonely old self (a feared self-rating of 1). The resulting current-feared discrepancy (+2) is positive and indicates that for now he is successfully avoiding this feared self.

You might find it interesting to calculate the two discrepancy scores for each of the five rating dimensions and consider where your current self stands in relation to your ideal self and feared selves. Your current self might be further from your ideal self (and closer to your feared self!) on some dimensions more than others. Are these discrepant aspects of your personality ones that you would like to change? The key is to know what you want for yourself (your ideals), what you don't want (your fears), and what motivates you. Some people are inspired by visualizing their ideal self, and others are jump-started into action by the image of their feared self. Which one sounds more like you? If you want to change, a good way to start is to visualize the vast array of possibilities in your life.

the flow of events in therapy, but merely summarize, or reflect, back to the client an understanding of what the client says; such a technique can provide to the client a sense of feeling thoroughly and deeply understood by the therapist. Because some nondirective counselors were perceived as passive and uninterested, Rogers changed his focus to an emphasis on counselors being client-centered. In this **client-centered therapy**, the therapist not only uses the technique of reflection, but plays a more active role in understanding the experiences of the client.

Ultimately, Rogers believed that the critical variable in client-centered therapy is the nature of the interpersonal encounter that develops between the therapist and client, or what is referred to as the therapeutic climate (Rogers, 1966). Rogers described the ideal therapeutic climate in terms of a set of conditions, three of which are core conditions that he saw as necessary for therapeutic change to occur (McMillan, 2004). If therapists provide these conditions in a way that is phenomenologically meaningful to the clients, then therapeutic change should occur.

The three conditions hypothesized by Rogers to be critical to therapeutic movement are congruence or genuineness, unconditional positive regard, and empathic understanding.

The first of the three conditions is genuineness. Genuine therapists are themselves. They do not present a scientific or medical façade. Instead, the therapist is interpersonally open and transparent. The therapist experiences events in the therapeutic encounter in a natural manner and shares with the client his or her genuine feelings—even when feelings toward the client are negative. "Even with such negative attitudes, which seem so potentially damaging but which all therapists have from time to time, I am suggesting that it is preferable for the therapist to be real than to put on a false posture of interest, concern, and liking that the client is likely to sense as false" (Rogers, 1966, p. 188). The client thus experiences a real interpersonal relationship with the therapist, rather than the stilted, formal relationship that one might usually experience with a health care or mental health care provider.

Rogers's approach to therapy involves clients in direct, face-to-face interaction with the therapist, who tries to create a therapeutic climate that features genuineness, unconditional positive regard, and empathic understanding.

The second condition essential for therapeutic movement is **unconditional positive regard**. This means that the therapist communicates a deep and genuine caring for the client as a person. The client is prized in a total, unconditional way. The experience of respect and unconditional positive regard enables the client to explore their inner self with confidence.

Finally, the third therapeutic condition is **empathic understanding**. This refers to the therapist's ability to perceive the client's experiences as they are experienced by the client. The therapist strives to achieve empathy with the client during the moment-to-moment encounter of psychotherapy. The therapist, then, does not intellectually detach himself or herself from the encounter in order to provide a technical diagnosis of the client's problems. The client does not receive a reformulation of his or her life in technical psychological jargon. Instead, through active listening, the therapist strives to understand the meaning and subjective feeling of the events experienced by the client, and to make it clear to clients that they are, in fact, being understood empathically by their therapist.

In Rogers's view, these three therapeutic conditions are of fundamental importance, independent of the theoretical orientation of the therapist. The theory behind client-centered therapy thus has an "if-then" quality: If certain therapeutic conditions exist, then processes inherently will occur that lead to personality change.

Outcomes of Client-Centered Therapy

What the hell is wrong with me?
I'm not who I want to be.

SOURCE: The Clash

Having presented the core elements of Rogers's therapeutic approach, we now ask: Does it work? Does client-centered therapy benefit the client?

To determine whether a therapy works, one must first determine what it means, in principle, for a therapy to "work." What is the core aspect of psychological distress that should be relieved by therapy? Rogers's answer to this question is the one suggested—in more blunt terms than Rogers's—by the British punk rock band, The Clash. Deep psychological distress does not arise merely from objective events in the world. It results from an internal sense of personal inadequacy, from a sense that one is not "who I want to be"—or, in Rogerian terms, from a lack of congruence between one actual self and ideal self. For therapy to "work," then, the client should achieve greater actual–ideal self congruence.

Having said that, the research challenge is to devise scientifically objective and reliable methods of testing the hypothesis that one's therapy improves this core aspect of personality, the self-concept. Rogers contributed greatly to the development of research methods for meeting this challenge. He was part of a movement important to the profession of psychology, namely, the process of opening up the field of psychotherapy for systematic investigation. Rogers's main goal was to evaluate therapy through methods that were objective. He recognized that a big limitation in the methods of evaluating therapy provided by Freud and his followers was that their methods were too subjective. In psychoanalytic therapy, the only way for an outsider (i.e., someone other than the therapist and client) to evaluate the success of therapy was to read a case study written by the therapist. The problem here should be obvious to you. The case study may be biased. The therapist—the psychoanalyst whose professional success is supposed to be evaluated—is writing the case study that is the basis of the evaluation. In principle, the therapist might unwittingly overestimate the degree of beneficial therapeutic change that occurred when writing his or her case report. In his client-centered therapy, then, Rogers wanted a means of evaluating therapeutic success that was superior to the subjective reports of a therapist.

Rogers took a number of steps designed to allow the scientific community and the public at large to evaluate his therapeutic efforts. He allowed himself and his colleagues to be taped, and sometimes even filmed, while engaging in therapy. He and his colleagues employed objective measures of self-concept, such as the Q-sort (Chapter 5), so that therapy outcomes could be evaluated objectively. Such steps may seem obvious in retrospect—yet they were not taken by psychoanalysts.

A classic study that illustrates the efforts of Rogers and his students to meet the challenge of evaluating Rogerian therapy through objective procedures was conducted by Butler and Haigh (1954), two students of Rogers's. First consider their research hypothesis at a conceptual level: It was that Rogerian therapy would bring about, in clients, a greater congruence between the ideal and actual self. Now consider the challenge of moving from the abstract conceptual level to the concrete level of actually doing research. How would you test this idea about relations among different aspects of a person's self-concept? This is the hard part of personality psychology—moving smoothly and convincingly from the theoretical formulation to the research details. Butler and Haigh made this move by using the Q-sort. Specifically, they used it twice (at any given time of measurement). They asked research participants to complete one Q-sort procedure in which they rated their actual self (i.e., participants sorted items according to how they currently see themselves), and a second one in which participants rated their ideal self (i.e., they sorted items according to whether the attributes described features they ideally would like to possess). With two measures, it is possible to compute a correlation, for any given person, between the actual and ideal self Q-sortings. This correlation is, then, a numerical index of the degree of congruence between the actual and ideal self; a higher positive correlation indicates a greater congruence between the actual and ideal self.

With this index of actual–ideal self congruence in hand, then, Butler and Haigh (1954) looked at the effects of Rogerian therapy. They examined a group of people both before and after the individuals experienced an average of 31 sessions of Rogerian therapy. What did they find? Before therapy, the relation between people's actual and ideal self was quite low: the average correlation was zero. But after therapy, the congruence between these two aspects of self increased significantly. The average post-therapy correlation between the actual and ideal self Q-sorts was .34. Rogers's therapy worked, as evaluated by an objective measurement procedure, the Q-sort.

Having read that conclusion, there are at least two other questions you might ask yourself. First, were the effects of therapy long-lasting? Fortunately, Butler and Haigh (1954) tested for this by conducting a follow-up measurement 6 months after therapy ended. At the time of follow-up, the actual–ideal correlation remained about the same, .31. This suggests that therapeutic changes indeed do last. A second question is, Are psychologically distressed people who experience therapy as well off, after therapy, as people who were never distressed in the first place? This question does not have quite as happy an answer. Butler and Haigh (1954) also asked a group of persons who were not seeking counseling to complete the Q-sort measures, and in this group the ideal–actual self correlation was .58; this group, in other words, displayed considerably higher congruence between the actual and ideal self then did the therapy group after counseling. Nonetheless, Rogerian therapy was shown to produce significant gains.

In the years since the pioneering work of Butler and Haigh (1954), much work has evaluated the popularity and the effectiveness of Rogerian therapy. A recent appraisal of the status of client-centered therapy indicates that the approach flourished not only during Rogers's lifetime, but after his death. Therapeutic applications and scientific evaluations of the effectiveness of Rogerian therapy frequently were conducted in both the United States and Europe (Kirschenbaum & Jourdan, 2005). A clear majority of studies indicate that a combination of the three conditions identified by Rogers in fact do foster therapeutic change. Although it is difficult to evaluate the precise Rogerian prediction that each of the three conditions is necessary for change and that, in total, they are sufficient (Kirschenbaum & Jourdan, 2005), contemporary research, involving careful statistical summaries of the overall effectiveness of client-centered therapy, does support the more general contention that Rogers's interpersonal focus on the client is an effective therapeutic technique. Therapy changes included a decrease in defensiveness and an increase in openness to experience among clients, the development of a more positive and more congruent self, development of more positive feelings toward others, and a shift away from using the values of others to asserting their own evaluations. These results underscore the conclusion that Rogers's identification of conditions that foster success in psychotherapy is one of his most enduring contributions to psychology.

Presence

Rogers's view of the conditions necessary for therapeutic improvement changed relatively little over the years after he first formulated them. However, one addition is noteworthy. It is the notion of presence (see Bozarth, 1992; McMillan, 2004). Rogers gradually came to believe that "perhaps I have stressed too much the three basic conditions (congruence, unconditional positive regard, and empathic understanding)" (quoted in Bozarth, 1992) and that, in addition to these three relative objective features of the therapeutic setting, there was another feature that was more elusive, difficult to describe, almost mystical, yet of much importance. "When I am intensely focused on a client," Rogers came to believe, "just my presence seems to be healing" (quoted in Bozarth, 1992). Rogers became aware that, in particularly successful therapeutic encounters, he himself experienced his own core self in interaction with his clients, and responded to them in a deeply intuitive way that they sometimes were able to share with him. "I may behave in strange and impulsive ways in the relationship, ways which I cannot justify rationally... but these strange behaviors turn out to be *right*... my inner spirit has reached out and touched the inner spirit of the other" (Rogers, quoted in McMillan, 2004). To the client-centered therapist, these deeply intuitive, almost spiritual encounters can be highly transformative. Interpersonal experiences between client and therapist that seem "beyond words and logic" (McMillan, 2004, p. 65) are thought to foster deep psychological change.

CURRENT APPLICATIONS

DRINKING, SELF-AWARENESS, AND PAINFUL FEELINGS

Why do people abuse alcohol and drugs? Why, after treatment, do so many relapse? In Chapter 3 it was suggested that many alcoholics and drug addicts use the defense mechanism of denial to cope with painful feelings. However, evidence of this relationship was not presented, nor was there analysis of how the self is experienced by substance abusers. This would appear to be important since substance abusers commonly report that they use drugs to handle painful feelings, with alcoholics often reporting that they drink to create a blur that blots out the painful aspects of life. Though not conducted within the Rogerian framework, some recent research in this area is relevant to Rogers's views. The basic hypothesis of this research is that alcohol reduces self-consciousness and that alcoholics high in self-consciousness drink to reduce their awareness of negative life experiences. Individuals high in self-consciousness of inner experiences are those who would describe themselves in terms of statements such as the following: "I reflect about myself a lot;" "I'm generally attentive to my inner feelings;" "I'm alert to changes in my mood."

In laboratory research with social drinkers, it has been found that individuals high in self-consciousness consume more alcohol following failure experiences than do members of three other groups: those (1) high in self-consciousness following success experiences, and those low in self-consciousness after either (2) success or (3) failure experiences. Further, in a study of alcohol use in adolescents, it was found that increased alcohol use was associated with poor academic experience for students high in self-consciousness but not for those low in self-consciousness.

Defensive Behaviors: Alcohol can be used to reduce awareness of painful feelings.

But what of alcoholics? And what about relapse? The latter would appear to be particularly significant since one-half to three-quarters of all treated alcoholics relapse within six months of the end of treatment. In a study of relapse in alcohol abuse following treatment, results comparable to the above were found; relapse appeared to be a joint function of negative events and high self-consciousness. In many different populations and kinds of studies, a consistent relationship has been found between drinking, high self-consciousness, and experiences of personal failure. The research suggests that many individuals drink to reduce their level of awareness of painful negative experiences.

SOURCE: BAUMEISTER, 1991; HULL, YOUNG, & JOURILES, 1986; PERVIN, 1988.

The notion of presence, and its potential therapeutic benefits, has received little scientific attention. Yet the concept of presence, as used by Rogerians, is recognized in other intellectual circles and other cultures, which suggests that it may have a reality that is deserving of scientific study. For example, Tibetans refer to their social and political leader, the Dalai Lama, as *Kundun* which, in Tibetan, literally means "presence" (or "The Presence"). It is used to refer to the same psychological qualities recognized by Rogers: the powerful feeling of interpersonal connection created by the exceptional awareness and emotional openness of their spiritual leader.

A Case Example: Mrs. Oak

Statistical summaries of the overall effectiveness of Rogers's therapy, such as those cited above, are critical to evaluating the effectiveness of Rogers's therapy. Yet they fail to capture its spirit. The experience of a therapeutic encounter with Rogers is much better conveyed by a case study. Let us consider, then, a well-known case of Rogers's, that of Mrs. Oak. This case is available to us because, as part of his process of opening up clinical psychology for objective investigation, Rogers (with this client's permission, of course) taped therapy sessions and made transcripts available to the public.

As Rogers described in a 1954 book, Mrs. Oak was a housewife in her late 30s when she came to the University of Chicago Counseling Center. She reported having great difficulty in her relationships with her husband and her adolescent daughter. Mrs. Oak blamed herself for her daughter's psychosomatic illness. Mrs. Oak was described by her therapist as a sensitive person who was eager to be honest with herself and deal with her problems. She had little formal education but was intelligent and had read widely. Mrs. Oak was interviewed 40 times over a period of five-and-one-half months, at which point she terminated treatment.

In early interviews, Mrs. Oak spent much of her time talking about specific problems with her daughter and her husband. Gradually, though, the conversation shifted. She increasingly talked about her feelings:

[The] last time I was here I experienced a—an emotion I had never felt before—which surprised me and sort of shocked me a bit. And yet I thought, I think it has a sort of a—the only word I can find to describe it, the only verbalization is a kind of cleansing. I—I really felt terribly sorry for something, a kind of grief.

SOURCE: (p. 311)

The Dalai Lama, spiritual leader of Tibet. The Dalai Lama's consistently empathic focus in interpersonal interaction creates a powerful psychological climate that contributes to his being called Kundun, *which in Tibetan means "presence" (or "The Presence")—precisely the term that Rogers eventual came to use to capture the psychological effects of empathic focus that he observed occurring in his client-centered therapy.*

At first the therapist thought Mrs. Oak was a shy, almost nondescript person. He quickly sensed, however, that she was a sensitive and interesting person. His respect for her grew, and he described himself as experiencing a sense of respect for—and awe of—her capacity to struggle ahead through turmoil and pain. He did not try to direct or guide her; instead, he found satisfaction in trying to understand her, in trying to appreciate her world, in expressing the acceptance he felt toward her.

MRS. OAK: And yet the—the fact that I—I really like this, I don't know, call it a poignant feeling. I mean... I felt things that I've never felt before. I like that, too. Uh-uh... maybe that's the

THERAPIST: way to do it. I—I just don't know today.

THERAPIST: M-hm. Don't feel at all sure, but you know that you somehow have a real, a real fondness for this poem that is yourself. Whether it's the way to go about this or not, you don't know.

SOURCE: p. 314

Given this supportive therapeutic climate, Mrs. Oak began to become aware of feelings she had previously denied to awareness. In the 24th interview, she became aware of conflicts with her daughter that related to her own adolescent development. She felt a sense of shock at becoming aware of her own competitiveness. In a later interview, she became aware of the deep sense of hurt inside of her.

MRS. OAK: And then of course, I've come to… to see and to feel that over this… see, I've covered it up. (*Weeps*) But… and… I've covered it up with so much bitterness, which in turn I had to cover up. (*Weeps*) That's what I want to get rid of! I almost don't care if I hurt.

THERAPIST: (*Gently*) You feel that here at the basis of it, as you experienced it, is a feeling of real tears for yourself. But that you can't show, mustn't show, so that's been covered by bitterness that you don't like, that you'd like to be rid of. You almost feel you'd rather absorb the hurt than to… than to feel bitterness.
(*Pause*) And what you seem to be saying quite strongly is, "I do hurt, and I've tried to cover it up."

MRS. OAK: I didn't know it.
THERAPIST: M-hm. Like a new discovery really.
MRS. OAK: (*Speaking at the same time*) I never really did know. But it's… you know, it's almost a physical thing. It's… sort of as though I—I—I were looking within myself at all kinds of… nerve endings and—and bits of—of… things that have been sort of mashed. (*Weeping*)

SOURCE: p. 326

At first, this increased awareness led to a sense of disorganization. Mrs. Oak began to feel more troubled and neurotic, as if she were going to pieces. She also felt resentful that her therapist was not being very helpful and would not take responsibility for the sessions. During the course of therapy, she felt very strongly at times that the therapist didn't "add a damn thing." But in the course of therapy, she eventually developed exactly what Rogers was striving for in his client-centered approach: a sense of relationship with the therapist that, she came to recognize, was the basis of her therapeutic improvement. Although progress did not occur in all areas, by the end of therapy Mrs. Oak exhibited significant gains in many areas. She began to feel free to be herself, to listen to herself, and to make independent evaluations. She began to accept herself as a worthwhile human being. She decided that she could not continue in her marriage, arrived at a mutually agreeable divorce with her husband, and obtained and held a challenging job. Through the conditions created within the therapeutic environment, Mrs. Oak was able to break down defenses that had been maintaining a marked incongruence between her self and her experience. With this increase in self-awareness, she was able to make positive changes in her life and become a more self-actualized human being.

Throughout his career, Rogers consistently emphasized phenomenological experience, the self, and psychological change. Although this three-part focus was consistent, in other respects his interests shifted during his career. Early in his career, he combined clinical sensitivity with scientific rigor. Later, Rogers appeared to move increasingly toward sole reliance on personal, phenomenological studies: "To my way of thinking, this personal, phenomenological type of study—especially when one reads all of the responses—is far more valuable than the traditional 'hard-headed' empirical approach. This kind of study, often scorned by psychologists as being 'merely self-reports,' actually gives the deepest insight into what the experience has meant" (Rogers, 1970, p. 133). Rogers felt that the yield of orthodox scientific studies was minute compared to the insights obtained from clinical work.

A second shift of focus was from one-to-one therapy relationships to groups. In his book *On Encounter Groups* (Rogers, 1970), Rogers stated that small, intensive groups are more effective settings for psychological change. A group of particular interest to Rogers was the marital partnership group and alternatives to marriage (Rogers, 1972), where Rogers highlighted the importance of openness, honesty, sharing, and movement toward awareness of inner feelings in relationships. Rogers also extended his approach to administration, minority groups, interracial, intercultural, and international relationships. He expressed a revolutionary spirit in his belief that the person-centered approach could produce a change in the concepts, values, and procedures of our culture: "It is the evidence of the effectiveness of a person-centered approach that may turn a very small and quiet revolution into a far more significant change in the way humankind perceives the possible. I am much too close to the situation to know whether this will be a minor or a major event, but I believe it represents a radical change" (p. 286).

One drawback of these shifts in focus is that Rogers, in his later years, made relatively fewer contributions to our main topic of interest in this book: the study of the personality of the individual. Rather than reviewing Rogers's analyses of groups, then, we will return to the study of the individual via our book's case example, the case of Jim.

ROGERS'S SHIFT IN EMPHASIS: FROM INDIVIDUALS TO GROUPS AND SOCIETY

Semantic Differential: Phenomenological Theory

THE CASE OF JIM

Jim completed ratings of the concepts self, ideal self, father, and mother using the semantic differential (Chapter 5), a simple rating scale. Although the semantic differential is not the exact measure recommended by Rogers, its results can be related to Rogerian theory since its procedures have a phenomenological quality and assess perceptions of self and ideal self.

First, consider how Jim perceives his self. Based on the semantic differential, Jim sees himself as intelligent, friendly, sincere, kind, and basically good—as a wise person who is humane and interested in people. At the same time, other ratings suggest that he does not feel free to be expressive and uninhibited. Thus, he rates himself as reserved, introverted, inhibited, tense, moral, and conforming. There is a curious mixture of perceptions: being involved, deep, sensitive, and kind while also being competitive, selfish, and disapproving. There is also the interesting combination of perceiving himself as being good and masculine but simultaneously weak and insecure. One gets the impression of an individual who would like to believe that he is basically good and capable of genuine interpersonal relationships at the same time that he is bothered by serious inhibitions and high standards for himself and others.

This impression comes into sharper focus when we consider the self-ratings in relation to those for the ideal self. In general, Jim did not see an extremely large gap between his self and his ideal self. However, large gaps did occur on a number of specific scale items. For example, Jim rated his actual self as low on a weak-strong scale and his ideal self as high on the same scale; in other words, Jim would like to be much stronger than he feels he is. Assessing his ratings on the other scales in a similar way, we find that Jim would like to be more of each of the following than he currently perceives himself to be: warm, active, equalitarian, flexible, lustful, approving, industrious, relaxed, friendly, and bold. Basically two themes appear. One has to do with warmth. Jim is not as warm, relaxed, and friendly as he would like to be. The other theme has to do with strength. Jim is not as strong, active, and industrious as he would like to be.

Jim's ratings of his parents give some indication of where he sees them in relation to himself in general and to these qualities in particular. First, if we compare the way Jim perceives his self with his perception of his mother and father, he clearly perceives himself to be much more like his father than his mother. Also, he perceives his father to be closer to his ideal self than his mother, although he perceives himself to be closer to his ideal self than either his mother or his father. However, in the critical areas of warmth and strength, the parents tend to be closer to the ideal self than Jim is. Thus, his mother is perceived to be more warm, approving, relaxed, and friendly than Jim, while his father is perceived to be stronger, more industrious, and more active than Jim. The mother is perceived as having an interesting combination of personality characteristics. On the one hand, she is perceived as affectionate, friendly, spontaneous, sensitive, and good. On the other, she is perceived as authoritarian, superficial, selfish, unintelligent, intolerant, and uncreative.

Comments on the Data

Compared to the earlier data, involving the Rorschach (Chapter 4), we begin here to get another picture of Jim. We learn of his popularity and success through high school and of his good relationship with his father. We find support for the suggestions from the projective tests of anxiety and difficulties with women. Indeed, we learn of Jim's fears of ejaculating too quickly and not being able to satisfy women. However, we also find an individual who believes himself to be basically good and interested in doing humane things. We become aware of an individual who has a view of his self and a view of his ideal self, and of an individual who is frustrated because of the feelings that leave a gap between the two.

Given the opportunity to talk about himself and what he would like to be, Jim talks about his desire to be warmer, more relaxed, and stronger. We feel no need here to disguise our purposes, for we are interested in Jim's perceptions, meanings, and experiences as he reports them. We are interested in what is real for Jim—in how he interprets phenomena within his own frame of reference. We want to know all about Jim, but all about Jim as he perceives himself and the world about him. When using the data from the semantic differential, we are not tempted to focus on drives, and we do not need to come to grips with the world of the irrational. In Rogers's terms, we see an individual who is struggling to move toward self actualization, from dependence toward independence, from fixity and rigidity to freedom and spontaneity. We find an individual who has a gap between his intellectual and emotional estimates of himself. As Rogers would put it, we observe an individual who is without self-consistency, who lacks a sense of congruence between self and experience.

You now have seen the fundamentals of Rogers's phenomenological theory of personality. The remainder of this chapter presents two related topics. First, we consider theoretical conceptions that are related to Rogers's work. Specifically, we will consider three of them: (1) the human potential movement, (2) the positive psychology movement, and (3) existentialism. Next, we present contemporary research that bears on Rogerian theory. This research often is conducted by people who may not call themselves "Rogerians," yet their work addresses topics that are at the heart of Rogers's conception of human nature.

RELATED THEORETICAL CONCEPTIONS

THE HUMAN POTENTIAL MOVEMENT

Rogers is not the only theorist to have emphasized people's capacity for self-actualization. Others recognized that personality functioning involves more than a mere repetition of past motives and conflicts, as suggested by Freud. Instead people have potentialities; that is, a basic feature of personality functioning is that people have a capacity to move forward to realize their inherent potentials. This theme was developed in the middle of the 20th century by writers such as Murphy (1958), who placed the study of potentialities at the center of personality psychology, and Kurt Goldstein, who felt that, despite its merits, Freudian theory "fails to do justice to the positive aspect of life . . . to recognize that the basic phenomenon of life is an incessant process of coming to terms with the environment" (1939, p. 333). Such theoretical contributions to the **human potential movement** came to known as a "third force" in psychology (e.g., Goble, 1970), because they offered an alternative to psychoanalysis (Chapter 3) and to behaviorism (Chapter 10). We will consider one major theorist in the human potential movement, Abraham H. Maslow.

Abraham H. Maslow (1908–1970)

Abraham Maslow (1968, 1971), like Rogers, emphasized the positive aspects of human experience. He proposed that people are basically good or neutral rather than evil, with everyone possessing an impulse toward growth and the fulfillment of potentials. Psychopathology results from a twisting and

Abraham H. Maslow

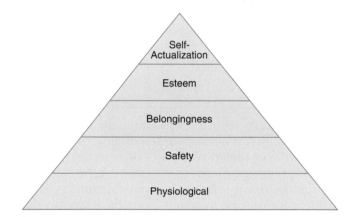

Figure 6.1 *Schematic Representation of Maslow's Hierarchy of Needs*

frustration of this essential nature of the human organism. To Maslow, social structures that restrict the individual from realizing his or her potential are a root cause of this frustration. Thanks in part to Maslow, the human potential movement became popular among individuals who felt excessively restricted and inhibited by their environment. Maslow speaks to these concerns and encourages the belief that things can be better if people are free to express themselves and be themselves.

In addition to this overall spirit, Maslow's views have been important in two ways. First, he suggested a view of human motivation that distinguishes between such biological needs as hunger, sleep, and thirst and such psychological needs as self-esteem, affection, and belonging. One cannot survive as a biological organism without food and water; likewise, one cannot develop fully as a psychological organism without the satisfaction of other needs as well. Thus, these needs can be arranged in a hierarchy from basic physiological needs to important psychological needs (Figure 6.1). Maslow suggested that, in their research and theorizing, psychologists have been overly concerned with basic biological needs, especially the organism's response to tension caused by biological deficits. While accepting that such motivation exists, Maslow highlighted higher-level motivational processes of the sort that are expressed when people are creative and are fulfilling their potential.

A second major contribution by Maslow (1954) was his intensive study of healthy, self-fulfilling, self-actualizing individuals. Maslow basically reasoned that, if one wants to learn about personality, there is no need to restrict one's study merely to either (1) everyday, normal personality functioning or (2) breakdowns in normal functioning that result in psychopathology. Instead, the psychologist should attend to the other end of the spectrum: people who are "abnormal" in that they are exceptionally positive, unusually highly-functioning, self-actualized individuals. Who are these people? Maslow considered individuals from history as well as from his own historical period (e.g., Abraham Lincoln, Albert Einstein, Eleanor Roosevelt; a more contemporary writer might consider figures such as Mother Theresa or Nelson Mandela). The point is that these exceptional figures possessed qualities that are informative to the personality psychologist because they tell us about human potentials. Maslow concluded that these people's features included the following characteristics: they accept themselves and others for what they are; they can be concerned with themselves but also are free to recognize the needs and desires of others; they are capable of responding to the uniqueness of people and situations rather than responding in mechanical or stereotyped ways; they can form intimate relationships with at least a few special people; they can be spontaneous and creative; and they can resist conformity and assert themselves while responding to the demands of reality. Maslow suggested that all of us have the potential to move increasingly in the direction of these qualities.

THE POSITIVE PSYCHOLOGY MOVEMENT

Maslow's focus on the positive aspects of human nature anticipated a contemporary movement in psychology. It is known as the positive psychology movement (Gable & Haidt, 2005; Seligman & Csikszentmihalyi, 2000) or sometimes called the human strengths movement (Aspinwall & Staudinger, 2002).

The writings of psychologists in the 21st century positive psychology movement echo themes sounded a half-century earlier by Rogers and writers in the human potential movement. Contemporary positive psychologists believe that, in the past, human frailty and psychopathology have been overemphasized (i.e., except in the words of people such as Rogers and Maslow). Psychologists have tended to examine individuals suffering from distress, to use those experiences as their foundation for theorizing about people in general, and as a result to end up with theories that emphasize the negative. Recall what you have learned about Freud. He was trying to build a model of personality that applied to all persons. Yet his database for the theory—the experiences on which he built his conception of the individual—almost entirely involved persons who were suffering from high levels of psychological distress.

What is the cost of focusing on distress and pathology? The positive psychologist argues that this focus causes the psychologist to overlook human strengths. One ends up with a distorted picture of personality that underemphasizes the positive. In an effort to rectify this, contemporary psychologists have tried to portray the nature of human strengths and virtues. The psychologist Martin Seligman, who has been key in promoting the positive psychology movement, has contributed much to this work (Seligman & Peterson, 2003).

Classifying Human Strengths

Seligman and colleagues (Seligman & Peterson, 2003) have tried to classify human strengths. In other words, to bring the positive side of human nature to the attention of psychological scientists and thereby to foster systematic research, they have tried to take an initial step that often is critical to scientific progress: the development of a comprehensive classification scheme. This effort has two parts. The first is to identify criteria that would cause a psychological characteristic to be called a strength. The second, then, is to use these criteria to identify a list of strengths.

Seligman and colleagues identified a set of criteria that are defining of human strengths. They include the following. For a characteristic to be a strength, it should be an enduring characteristic of the person that is beneficial in a variety of life domains. (Thus "creativity" would be classified as a strength, whereas a narrow-focused skill such as "good at poker" would not.) It should be something that both parents and the larger society try to foster in children, and that is celebrated by one's community when it is developed. (Qualities such as perseverance and honesty, and institutions that try to foster these qualities such as Girl Scouts and Boy Scouts illustrate what Seligman and colleagues have in mind.) Finally, a strength, these researchers suggest, is something that is valued in all or almost all cultures of the world. This set of features, then, are the criteria for calling something a human strength.

What, then, are the qualities that meet these criteria? Seligman and Peterson (2003) provide a preliminary list that groups strengths into six categories: wisdom, courage, love, justice, temperance (e.g., forgiveness), and transcendence (e.g., appreciation of beauty). These are qualities that we, today, immediately can recognize as positive features of the human personality. Importantly, they also are qualities that would be recognized as positive across cultures and across historical time periods. The point of listing these qualities—obvious as any such list may seem in retrospect—is that the process serves as a corrective to theories that emphasized the negative side of human experience. In psychoanalytic theory, many of these qualities would have been seen as secondary to human experience. They would be classified merely as products of the superego, which is ultimately weaker than the impulsive id. Positive psychology gives us a different view of the human condition. It suggests that these virtues are central to human experience, and can be enhanced by parenting and by social institutions.

The Virtues of Positive Emotions

In addition to its identification of human virtues, another notable quality of research associated with the positive psychology movement is its study of positive emotions. Psychologists commonly have studied emotions such as fear, anxiety, and anger. However, they have devoted less attention to the role of positive emotions—pride, love, happiness—in personality development and functioning.

A very positive step toward understanding these emotions has been taken by the psychologist Barbara Fredrickson, who has proposed a *broaden-and-build theory* of positive emotions (Fredrickson, 2001). This theory posits that positive emotions have a specific effect on thoughts and action. Positive emotions broaden thought and action tendencies. They widen the range of ideas that come to mind and the range of actions that individuals pursue. The positive emotion of interest, for example, leads people to pursue novel activities. The emotion of pride motivates one to continue the creative or achievement activities that caused one to feel proud of oneself. In this way, positive emotions contribute directly to the further building of human competencies and achievements.

Research has supported the predictions of Fredrickson's broaden-and-build theory. For example, in one study (Tugade & Fredrickson, 2004) research participants were presented with a stressful experience; they were told they were to give a public speech that would be videotaped. (If you picture yourself suddenly being asked to give a videotaped speech in front of strangers, you'll recognize that this is a stressor for most persons.) The investigators measured three qualities of interest: (1) how resilient people were, that is, individual differences in people's general tendency to recover from stress and deal effectively with novel situations; (2) physiological indications of stress, such as heart rate, as people prepared their speech; and (3) positive emotions, that is, the extent to which people reported feeling positive emotions during the experiment, despite the fact that it was stressful. As expected, people who scored high on resilience (i.e., people who generally tend to cope well with things) experienced lesser degrees of cardiovascular activity indicating stress. However, the key result of interest involved the third measure, positive emotions. People who experienced positive emotions during the study—people who were able to look on the bright side of things, remaining interested and amused during the experience of giving a speech—experienced less stress. Specifically, positive emotions mediated the relation between individual differences in resilience and cardiovascular reactions (Tugade & Fredrickson, 2004). This means that the primary reason that some people were resiliently calm is that they were able to experience positive emotions. As predicted by Fredrickson's theory, these people's positive emotions seemed to cancel out some of the effects of stress. They thus were able to remain more in control of their thoughts and actions and to feel less stressful arousal than others. People who experience more positive emotions, then, could be said to be more resilient. Positive emotions act as "coping resources that help buffer (psychologically and physiologically) against negative emotional life experiences" (Tugade & Fredrickson, 2004, p. 331).

Flow

A third notable area of investigation in positive psychology is Mihaly Csikszentmihalyi's work on the concept of *flow*. Flow describes a feature of conscious experiences. It refers specifically to positive states of consciousness with the following characteristics: a perceived match between personal skills and environmental challenge, a high level of focused attention, involvement in an activity such that time seems to fly by and irrelevant thoughts and distractions do not enter into consciousness, a sense of intrinsic enjoyment in the activity, and a temporary loss of self-consciousness such that the self is not aware of functioning or regulating activity.

Flow experiences can take place in activities as diverse as work, hobbies, sports, dancing, and social interactions. It is expressed in statements such as "When I am involved, everything just seems to come to me. I just float along, feeling both excited and calm, and want it to continue endlessly. It's not possible rewards that count but just the pleasure in the activity itself." Csikszentmihalyi's interest in the positive aspects of human functioning began with his observation during World War II that, although many people lost their decency, others expressed the best of what people can be. Subsequently he was influenced by the work of Carl Rogers and Abraham Maslow, leading to an emphasis on the study of strength and virtue as opposed to weakness and pathology.

These three areas of study—Seligman's classification of human values, Fredrickson's broad-and-build theory of positive emotions, and Csikszentmihalyi's work on flow—illustrate the promise and achievements of the positive psychology movement. Yet more work remains. A primary challenge is not only to show that some people have superior virtues and relatively positive emotional experiences. It is to show how these qualities can be developed in everybody. Commentators have noted that this remains a limitation of the field. Researchers have yet to identify social practices and community institutions that are best for building personal strengths (Gable & Haidt, 2005). We hope that some virtuous readers of this book will someday contribute to these research efforts.

EXISTENTIALISM

All ideas can be traced back to earlier ideas. All theorists—of personality or otherwise—build on foundations laid by earlier thinkers. In the case of Rogers, a critical foundation is the philosophical movement known as existentialism.

Although this is a textbook in psychology, not philosophy, existentialism is of relevance to us. This is because existentialism is a particularly "psychological" philosophy. Existentialists are not concerned with abstract questions about the structure of the universe or the limits of knowledge. Instead, they address the nature of the human experience. In doing so, they are not concerned with constructing grand, abstract theories. "Existentialism works at the level of personal meaning in contrast to general theory" (Marino, 2004, p. xii). Existentialists emphasize themes that became central to Carl Rogers: "freedom, choice, authenticity, alienation" (Marino, 2004, p. xiv),

Existentialist ideas and concerns have found expression in three domains of intellectual life: literature and related artistic products, philosophy, and psychology (Marino, 2004). In literature, the late-19th-century writing of Dostoevsky is a prime example of existentialist writing. The great Russian author explores, in exceptional depth, issues of freedom, determinism, responsibility, and the inner mental anguish that can arise as the individual reflects on these issues and, more generally, on his or her place in the world.

In philosophy, existentialism has its roots in the writings of the 19th-century Danish philosopher Søren Kierkegaard. Kierkegaard was critical of prior philosophical systems. Some such systems, he felt, spent too much time analyzing social and cultural systems rather than studying the individual person. Others that did examine the individual, he thought, placed too great an emphasis on human rationality. Kierkegaard felt that what was needed was a philosophy of the individual and his or her emotions, passions, and capacity for free will. These basic qualities of day-to-day human existence were so central to Kierkegaard's work that his body of thought became known as a philosophy of existence—that is, as **existentialism** (Solomon & Higgins, 1996).

Kierkegaard did not formulate research hypotheses or develop psychotherapy methods in the style of a psychologist. Yet his intellectual concerns greatly overlapped with a personality psychologist such as Rogers. Kierkegaard, like Rogers, was concerned with the sources of human psychological distress.

He judged that deep feelings of despair are an element of all human lives. Kierkegaard differentiated among different forms of despair, including the feelings that result from failing to be one's essential self (e.g., the feeling that you are a stranger to yourself), from concluding that one is not realizing one's potential (e.g., that one's life is a waste of time), and from questioning whether you really are an enduring "self" with a meaningful life and future—where those latter thoughts might be most likely to arise when individuals think about the fragility of life and inevitability of death. Thanks in part to Kierkegaard's influence, the ways in which people's realization of the inevitability of their own death influences their motivations and emotional experiences became a central focus of existentialist writing. (As a result, much existentialist writing in philosophy has a darker tone than does the writing of Rogers, with philosophers such as Kierkegaard devoting more attention to the phenomenology of despair and a sense of alienation from life and less attention than Rogers to human capacities for growth and self-actualization.)

In 20th-century psychology, existentialist themes are found in the writings of clinical psychologists who wrote about the human condition. A prominent example is Viktor Frankl (Frankl, 1955, 1958). Frankl's professional concern with people's struggle to find meaning in life was grounded in personal experience; he himself struggled to find meaning while imprisoned in a concentration camp during World War II. Frankl suggests that the will to find meaning is the most human phenomenon of all, since other animals never worry about the meaning of their existence. Existential frustration and existential neurosis involve frustration and lack of fulfillment of the will to find meaning. Such a neurosis does not involve the instincts or biological drives but rather is spiritually rooted in the person's escape from freedom and responsibility. In such cases the person blames destiny, childhood, the environment, or fate for what is. The treatment for such a condition, logotherapy, involves helping patients to become what they are capable of being, helping them to realize and accept the challenges of the opportunities that are open to them.

The Existentialism of Sartre: Consciousness, Nothingness, Freedom, and Responsibility

A twentieth-century existentialist philosopher who greatly advanced the intellectual tradition begun by Kierkegaard is the French writer Jean-Paul Sartre (1905–1980). Although Sartre was a philosopher, not a psychologist, his existentialist philosophy is of particular interest to personality psychology because it is grounded in theoretical analyses that are fundamentally psychological. Sartre was interested in people's mental capacities and their implications.

Sartre's concerns can best be introduced with an historical example. In the early 1940s, citizens of France faced a terrible crisis. Their country was occupied by the military forces of Nazi Germany. This national disaster confronted individuals with a hard personal choice. Should one accept that the Germans had occupied the land and collaborate with them (at least passively, by not resisting their rule)? Collaboration could enhance one's own personal safety. Alternatively, should one join the underground French resistance movement and fight the Nazi occupiers? This would bring great risk, but could help save the nation.

Existentialism is *not* directly concerned with the question: Which course of action should one choose? Instead, it addresses a more subtle question: What are the psychological capacities, and what is the nature of the psychological experience, of the individual facing such a choice? The fundamental issue is the question of free will. When facing a choice such as this, does the person have free will? Is it correct to say that persons basically are free to choose one versus another course of action? Or are the environmental forces (in this case, the powerful, threatening environment that was the Nazi occupation) so strong that the person does not really have choice? Maybe the environment fundamentally determines the person's behavior.

Consider how we think about free will versus determinism in cases that do not involve human beings. If we think of the behavior of, for example, a rock thrown into the air, we do not say that it chooses to fall back to earth. Its actions obviously are determined entirely by physical forces. Similarly, if we look at the behavior of an animal, we generally recognize that its behavior reflects instinctual behavior patterns that are triggered by environmental cues. So the question is: Is human behavior like this? Are our actions caused by the environment in the same sense that, for example, gravity causes a rock thrown into the air to fall back to earth?

Looking at human versus physical objects or animals, Sartre might say "vive la difference." To Sartre, the human case is entirely different. Humans, Sartre argues, are free to choose. Indeed, they are always free to choose; the individual cannot escape his or her capacities for free choice and the responsibilities that these capacities bring. To Sartre, when people do something they are not proud of and then say that they "had no choice," they simply are not being honest with themselves. They are escaping personal responsibility. Even extreme environments—even a Nazi occupation—does not eliminate the human capacity for free choice. A central feature of existentialism, then, is that people fundamentally are free, and therefore have responsibility for their personal choices and actions.

What is the basis of Sartre's claim? It is thoroughly psychological. Sartre believes that human freedom is based in people's distinctive mental abilities (Lavine, 1984). Unlike any other organisms, humans not only respond to the environment that is facing them, that is, to the things that are there. Humans also think about things that are *not* there, or what Sartre referred to as nothingness. People have the mental ability to think about alternative possibilities, how things might be different, future courses of action they could take, and so forth. These capacities, Sartre believes, give people freedom. The environment does not cause people to act in the same way that environmental forces cause objects to move about. Human beings are not like rocks, plants, or animals who lack humans' cognitive capacities. Because humans can raise questions and doubts about the world and can imagine future possibilities for themselves, they are free from the simple deterministic causality that controls the behavior of other objects in the world.

These cognitive capacities and the freedom they bring have one other implication. It concerns the question of whether there is such a thing as an essential human nature. Essentialism is a way of thinking that supposes that the most important thing about a person or thing is some inner core quality that it possesses. It essentially "is" that quality, even if one's experience of the thing does not suggest that quality at a particular time. To give an extremely simple example, if you cover a brown horse with white paint, it is not a white horse; it still possesses its essential quality of being a brown horse. If you put black stripes on the white paint, the horse does not become a zebra. Things have essential qualities. Sartre recognized this, but suggested that human beings are not like things. Humans are not born into the world with essential qualities. Instead, Sartre writes, "at first" a person "is nothing. Only afterward will he be something, and he himself will have made what he will be ... man is nothing else but what he makes of himself" (Sarte, 1957/2004, p. 345). To understand a person, Sartre argues, one must examine his or her current experience of the world, rather than search for some abstract, hidden, essential quality of the person. In Sartre's phrase, the person's existence precedes his or her essence. People, in their experiences, make something of themselves; you *make yourself into* a college student, or an athlete, or a parent, or a businessperson. Then that is what you become, and what you are to others. Your existence is primary. Your apparently essential features—your being a student, or a parent—follow.

To summarize, Sartre's existentialism has two core features. One is that people are free to choose and therefore have responsibility for their actions. The second is that existence precedes essence, that is, that individuals first experience the world and then, through their choice, make something of themselves.

Before we consider contemporary developments in existential psychology, it is important for you, the student, to ask yourself a question. We have just seen Sartre's classic existential statement on the human condition: that people have free choice. A person's defining feature, to Sartre, is the set of mental capacities that give us all free will. So this is what Sartre thought. The question to ask yourself is: What would other people think? What, according to other theorists, might be wrong with this argument? A moment's reflection on our previous chapters should cause you to realize that Freud would not agree with Sartre. Freud would say that Sartre underestimated the influence of unconscious mental forces that are uncontrollable. In Chapter 10, we will see that behavioral psychologists also disagreed with Sartre. They argued that the phenomenological experience of free will is an illusion that is caused by the environment (Skinner, 1971). Some contemporary research psychologists side with the behaviorists. They believe that most mental processes are automatic; that is, they occur spontaneously in response to environmental cues. Being automatic, these processes are not under people's control (Wegner, 2002). The existence of automatic processes, some conclude, significantly undermines the existentialists' arguments about freedom and self-control (Bargh, 2004). We will return to these issues in Chapter 10. For now, you should bear in mind that the question of environmental control versus personal control of one's own thought and behavior is one of the great issues that divides theorists of human nature.

Contemporary Experimental Existentialism

For many years, existentialist philosophy had very little impact on scientific psychology. It is easy to see why. Existentialists such as Sartre argued that people cannot be understood in terms of causal laws of the type pursued in the physical sciences. Research psychologists, in contrast, generally were trying to build a lawful science of human behavior. The research psychologists thus rejected the arguments of Sartre.

However, recent years have seen a surprising development. Some experimental psychologists have created a form of psychology that might previously "have been considered oxymoronic" (Pyszczynski, Greenberg, & Koole, 2004, p. 3). It is experimental existential psychology. As the name suggests, this work is an effort to bring together two ideas. On the one hand, investigators want to understand the issues raised by existentialists: questions involving the meaning of life, fears of death, and the nature of existence and personal responsibility. On the other hand, unlike Sartre, they have faith in experimental methods. They believe that experimental research can illuminate the topics studied by the existential philosophers.

A particularly compelling example of experimental existential research is work on people's awareness of death. As we noted above in our discussion of Kierkegaard, existentialists have long conjectured that thoughts of death are a central feature of human experience. Experimental existential psychologists have advanced beyond the earlier philosophical analyses by taking this general idea—people's awareness of, and fear of, death—and turning it into specific, testable hypotheses. A significant step forward in this regard is the terror management theory of Solomon, Greenberg, and Pyszczynski (e.g., 2004). Terror management theory (TMT) examines the consequences of the combination of two factors: people's desire to live (which people share with all other animals) and people's awareness of the inevitability of death (an awareness that is uniquely human). TMT posits that people's awareness of death makes them vulnerable to being completely overwhelmed by terrifying death anxiety. The question, then, is how people manage to avoid terror. How do people obtain meaning in life once they recognize that death is inevitable and (in principle) could occur at any time?

Terror management theorists suggest that part of the answer lies in social and cultural institutions. These institutions serve a psychological function: They protect against terror. The idea of TMT is that cultural institutions furnish meaning in life—even if one does dwell on the inevitability of death. How does this work? Well, the exact answer depends on where in the world you live; different cultures furnish different types of meaning systems. But a couple of examples makes the TMT point clear. In many cultures, religious institutions teach that there is an afterlife (e.g., a heaven and a hell). The belief in an afterlife buffers against the terror of death. Even if one starts to feel terrified at the prospect of the death of the body, one can find comfort in the belief in the afterlife of the soul. Other cultures emphasize that the individual is one component of a larger circle of persons: the family, the community, and so forth (see Chapter 14). Even though one may die as an individual, there is a sense in which one lives on in the life of one's offspring (see Chapter 14). The idea of TMT, then, is that these social practices are resources that help people to cope with the fear of death.

This idea has an interesting implication that has been tested in much experimental research. If one manipulates the *degree to which* people are thinking about death—in other words, if one manipulates the degree to which mortality is salient—there should be systematic variations in the degree to which people need their cultural worldviews. If cultural beliefs buffer against fear of death, and if people are induced to think about death, then they should display a stronger-than-usual need to possess, and to defend, their cultural beliefs. This mortality salience hypothesis has been tested in numerous studies. For example, Jonas and Greenberg (2004) conducted a relevant study in Germany. They asked participants to read and evaluate the quality of

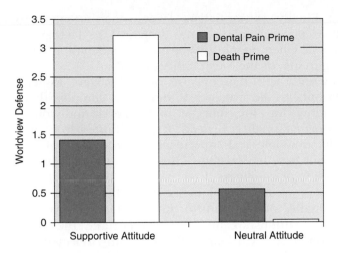

Figure 6.2 *Interaction between attitudes toward German reunification (supportive versus neutral) and mortality salience (priming of either death or, in a control condition, dental pain), in research by Jonas and Greenberg (2004).*

two essays about German reunification (i.e., the political reunification of the former East Germany and West Germany), one positive (i.e., emphasizing the good aspects of unification) and one negative. Participants also were asked to indicate their own personal attitudes toward reunification. The idea is that if a person was in favor of reunification, then his or her beliefs in the value of reunification should be strengthened by considerations of death, that is, by greater mortality salience. How to test this idea? Jonas and Greenberg did it through a simple strategy. Before reading the essays about reunification, participants were randomly assigned to one of two conditions in which they answered one of two types of questions. In a control condition, they were asked about experiences of dental pain. In a mortality salience condition, they were asked about experiences of death (e.g., "Jot down, as specifically as you can, what you think will happen to you as you physically die and once you are physically dead"; Jonas & Greenberg, 2004, p. 5).

Figure 6.2 displays the results of this study. As predicted by mortality salience theory, thoughts of death influenced the strength of people's cultural beliefs. Among people who were supportive of reunification (the two bars at the left of Figure 6.2), when participants were primed with thoughts of death, they more strongly defended their worldview. They were relatively more favorable in their evaluations of the positive unification essay and more critical of the negative one.

Summary: Existentialist Philosophy and Psychology

In summary, existentialism is a philosophical movement that is defined by its topics of primary interest. As we have seen, four features of existentialism stand out. First, existentialists are concerned with understanding existence—the person in the human condition. Second, existentialists are concerned with the individual. Rather than trying to understand human existence by searching for abstract theoretical principles, by studying broad political or social systems, or by engaging in metaphysical speculations about the universe and where it came from, the existentialist addresses the experiences of the individual person. Third, existentialists emphasize the human capacity for free choice, a capacity that comes from people's unique ability to reflect consciously on alternative possibilities. Finally, existentialists devote much attention to the phenomenological experiences of anguish and despair—the feelings of "existential crisis"—that result when people reflect on their alienation from the world, a loss of meaning in life, or the inevitability of death.

These concerns overlap greatly with the concerns of Carl Rogers. Rogers, like the existentialist philosophers, did not seek to develop a complex theoretical system that might allow him, for example, to categorize individuals as one versus another type or personality. Instead, Rogers wanted to understand the here-and-now phenomenological experience of the individual. We can appreciate the connections between existentialism and Rogers by considering Rogers's (1980) discussion of loneliness. In it, he emphasizes traditional existentialist themes. Rogers suggested that loneliness results from a number of factors: the impersonality of our culture, its transient quality and anomie, the fear of a close relationship, and, most important, the experience of trying to share one's self with another and being rejected: "A person is most lonely when he has dropped something of his outer shell or façade—the face with which he has been meeting the world—and feels sure that no one can understand, accept, or care for the part of his inner self that lies revealed" (quoted in Kirschenbaum, 1979, p. 351). Rogers's concern with the individual's sense of alienation from the world mirrored that of Kierkegaard. Indeed, a biography of Rogers (Kirschenbaum, 1979) notes Rogers's acknowledgment of his indebtedness to the writings of the Danish philosopher.

RECENT DEVELOPMENTS IN THEORY AND RESEARCH

DISCREPANCIES AMONG PARTS OF THE SELF

According to Rogers, then, psychological pathology results from discrepancies between self-concept and actual experience. Much contemporary research similarly focuses on the role of discrepancies in psychological distress. However, this work differs somewhat from that of Rogers. It tends to focus less on discrepancies between self and experience, and more on an internal psychological discrepancy: discrepancies between different parts of the self.

A particularly influential theory of discrepancies among parts of the self has been proposed by the psychologist Tory Higgins (1987, 1999). Higgins's work addresses the relation between aspects of self-concept and emotional experience. His work extends Rogers's thinking by differentiating between two aspects of one's future self. In addition to the ideal self, which was recognized by Rogers, Higgins suggests that everyone possesses an ought self, that is, an aspect of self-concept that is concerned with duties, responsibilities, and obligations. The ideal self, in contrast, centers on personal hopes, ambitions, and desires.

According to Higgins's theory, discrepancies between actual self and ideal self lead to dejection-related emotions. For example, if someone has an ideal self of being an A student but receives a C in a class, he or she would likely feel disappointed, sad, or even depressed. In contrast, discrepancies between self and ought self should lead to agitation-related emotions. For example, if someone has an ought self of being an A student but receives a C, he or she would likely feel fearful, threatened, or anxious. Thus, the distinction between ideal self and ought self is important because it helps separate two kinds of self-relevant emotions: those related to dejection (e.g., disappointment, sadness, depression) and those related to agitation (e.g., fear, threat, anxiety).

In research related to this theory, people are asked to describe how they actually are (their actual self) and how they ideally would like to be (their ideal self). Researchers determine the degree to which these different descriptions are discrepant. (For example, if you say, "I actually am lazy," and, "Ideally, I would be hardworking," that is coded as a self-discrepancy.) It is predicted that people with larger self-discrepancies will be more vulnerable to negative emotional experiences. In a key piece of research, Higgins, Bond, Klein, and Strauman (1986) found that people with large discrepancies between the actual self and ideal self were more likely to be depressed, whereas people with actual–ought discrepancies were more likely to be anxious. Because Higgins's theory and research methods are closely related to a personality theory you will learn about later in the text, social cognitive theory, we will return to his work in Chapter 13.

More recent findings by other investigators suggest that the relation between self-discrepancies and emotional experience is not fixed but, instead, can vary. An important factor is the degree to which people are aware of their self-discrepancies at any given time. If some feature of the social environment causes people to dwell on themselves, then discrepancies among aspects of the self-concept may influence emotional experience more strongly. Phillips and Silvia (2005) tested this idea using a simple experimental manipulation employed frequently in research on the self: a mirror. Looking at a mirror has the effect of drawing one's attention to oneself. In their research, some people completed measures of self-concept and of emotional experience while sitting at a table that faced a large mirror. Other people, in a different experimental condition, could not see themselves in a mirror. (The experimenters simply turned the mirror around so that its non-reflective back side faced the research participants.) The researchers found that self-discrepancies were linked more strongly to emotional experience in conditions of high self-awareness, that is, when people faced the mirror (Phillips & Silvia, 2005). The results indicate that, to understand the role of self-concept in psychological experience, one must consider situational factors with the power to draw attention to features of the self.

FLUCTUATIONS IN SELF-ESTEEM AND CONTINGENCIES OF WORTH

Rogers's ideas about the self implied that people possess a relatively stable sense of self-worth, or self-esteem. To bring about changes in people's sense of self, it appeared that systematic efforts, such as client-centered therapy, were required. In contrast to this view, some contemporary research suggests that self-esteem may fluctuate to a greater extent than Rogers had anticipated. Particularly informative work on this topic comes from Jennifer Crocker and colleagues (Crocker & Knight, 2005; Crocker & Wolfe, 2001).

Crocker and Wolfe (2001) are interested in "contingencies of self-worth." Their idea is that a person's self-esteem depends on—or is "contingent on"—positive and negative events. Self-esteem rises when we get an A+ in a class and falls when we get an F−. We feel better about ourselves when someone asks us out on a date, and worse when we ask someone out and they laugh at us and hang up the phone. It is these successes and failures that are the **contingencies of self-worth** on which self-esteem depends. Although a person's typical, average level of self-esteem may be relatively stable, one's day-to-day sense of self-worth may fluctuate considerably as one experiences these positive and negative contingent events.

In addition to the possibility of fluctuations in self-esteem, Crocker and Wolfe's theoretical framework highlights another point: People may differ in the degree to which any given event is, for them, a contingency of self-worth. One person might not care much about his or her grades in classes because he or she is basically interested in getting dates. Another might not be concerned with acceptance/rejection by dating partners, because his or her only big concern is academic grades. Such people should experience fluctuating self-esteem in different situations. "The impact of events" on one's self-esteem should depend "on the perceived relevance of those events to one's contingencies of self-worth" (Crocker & Wolfe, 2001, p. 594).

Crocker and colleagues have applied their theoretical ideas to a topic of particular relevance to those readers of this book who might be considering going to graduate school: fluctuations in self-esteem among college students as they receive acceptances and rejections from graduate programs (Crocker, Sommers, & Luhtanen, 2002). Participants in this study completed a measure of self-esteem, as well as measures of positive and negative affect, twice a week on a regular schedule, as well as on any days on which they received a notification of admission (or not) from a graduate program. This enabled the investigators to study fluctuations in self-esteem. At the outset of the study, the degree to which each participant's self-worth was contingent on academic success was measured; this was done by asking people to report the degree to which they get a self-esteem boost from events such as getting good grades. This procedure enabled the investigators to test the hypothesis that self-esteem would fluctuate as a result of acceptances/rejections, but only for students for whom academic success was an important contingency of self-worth. This hypothesis was confirmed (Figure 6.3). Among students who based their self-esteem on academic performance, self-esteem went up and down as a result of acceptances and rejections (respectively). However, among students for whom academic success was not a central element of self-worth, the same objective events—graduate school acceptances and rejections—had little impact on self-esteem.

The analyses of Crocker and colleagues are a valuable extension of Rogers's analyses of self-concept. They extend the work by identifying particular social contexts that contribute not only to typical, average levels of self-esteem, but to those day-to-day fluctuations in people's sense of self that are so much a part of everyday life.

INTERNALLY MOTIVATED GOALS AND AUTHENTICITY

In the middle of the 20th century, psychology experienced a decline of interest in the concept of the self. Many psychologists felt that it was difficult, if not impossible, to formulate a theory of self-concept that was scientifically sound. However, in the past 25 years, things have changed dramatically. Advances in psychological theory as well as in research methods ushered in what might be seen as an "era of self-concept." Research on the self probably became the

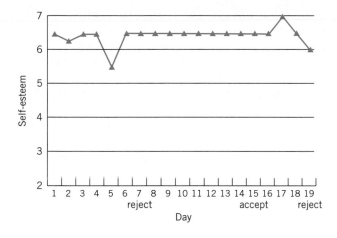

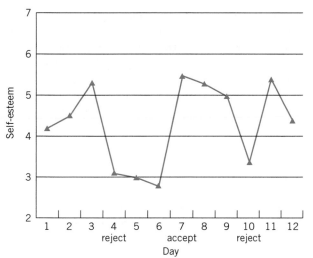

Figure 6.3 *Daily reports of self-esteem for two participants from Crocker, Sommers, and Luhtanen (2002). Participants in the top (bottom) panel did not (did) base their self-esteem on academic performance. For the student who did base self-esteem on academic performance, self-esteem varied as a result of graduate school acceptances and rejections.*

most frequently researched topic in personality and social psychology (Pervin, 1999, 2003; Robins, Norem, & Cheek, 1999; Leary & Tangney, 2002). However, relatively little of this research cites the work of Rogers. Much current interest in the self comes out of a cognitive orientation that differs from Rogers's theorizing. As we will discuss in more detail in Chapters 12 and 13, this cognitive orientation is more sensitive than was Rogers's to the possibility that people possess multiple views of self that vary from one context to another, rather than a global sense of self as Rogers discussed. Personality psychologists following this newer view would suggest that individuals may have multiple sources of self-esteem rather than a global self-esteem. For example, one recent study compared the specific view of self-esteem with the global view in terms of their ability to predict people's reactions to success and failure. What was found was that global self-esteem better predicted emotional reactions to performance outcomes than did specific self-esteem, suggesting that the effects of global self-esteem are not reducible to the way people think about their specific qualities. In agreement with Rogers, the investigators suggested that "high self-esteem is an unconditional feeling of affection for oneself that does not depend on the perception that one has any particular positive quality or qualities" (Dutton & Brown, 1997, p.146).

Another research trend that is in accord with Rogers's views is recent work on the concept of **authenticity**, defined as the extent to which a person behaves in accord with their self as opposed to behaving in terms of roles that foster false self-presentations (Ryan, 1993; Sheldon, Ryan, Rawsthorne, & Ilardi, 1997). A key idea in work on authenticity is that, to understand human experience, one cannot look merely at people's observable behaviors. One must explore inner feelings. Specifically, one must ask whether people feel that their activities are consistent with their true self—that is, are authentic—rather then being phony actions that express a false self. Certainly, we all are aware of times when we have felt we were being more "authentic" and other times when we felt we were being "inauthentic" or "phony." Is the degree to which an individual feels authentic in situations in daily life related to measures of satisfaction and well-being? Indeed, this has been found to be the case. That is, in accord with the prior theorizing of humanistic and phenomenologically oriented psychologists, authenticity was found to be associated with being a more fully functioning person. In addition to this overall relationship with psychological being, it was found that the more genuine and self-expressive people feel they are in a specific situation, the more extraverted, agreeable, conscientious, and open to experience they are likely to be in that situation (Sheldon et al., 1997). In other words, individuals may vary in their behavior from situation to situation, but the critical question is whether they feel they are being authentic and true to their self overall as well as in specific situations.

Related to the concept of authenticity is the question of the *kinds* of goals that individuals pursue. Is the individual pursuing goals that fit his or her enduring personal interests and values? Or are the individual's daily goals dictated by external sources or internal feelings of conflict, guilt, and anxiety (Deci and Ryan, 1991; Sheldon & Elliot, 1999)? Recall that in Chapter 5 there was discussion of intrinsic motivation, the motivation to engage in an activity because of interest in it rather than because of rewards associated with performance (i.e., extrinsic motivation). According to Deci and Ryan's (1985, 1991; Ryan & Deci, 2000) self-determination theory, people have an inherent psychological need to act in autonomous, self-determined ways and to engage in tasks that are intrinsically meaningful as opposed to action that is coerced, forced, or compelled, whether by internal forces or external forces. There are at least two critical elements to this difference. First, there is the question of whether action is autonomous, or self-initiated, as opposed to controlled by others, or externally regulated. In addition, there is the question of whether action is freely chosen as opposed to compelled. Action conducted out of feelings of guilt and anxiety would emanate from within the person but would have a compelled as opposed to freely chosen quality, and would not qualify as self-determined action. In sum, self-determined action is action that takes place because of its intrinsic interest to the person and its quality of being freely chosen.

Does it make a difference whether action is reflective of self-determined motivation? Recent research indeed suggests that people show greater effort and persistence in relation to autonomous goals than in relation to goals that are pursued only because of external pushes or internal sanctions such as anxiety or guilt (Koestner, Lekes, Powers, & Chicoine, 2002; Sheldon &

Elliot, 1999). In addition, there is evidence that the pursuit of self-determined, intrinsic, approach goals is associated with physical health and psychological well-being in contrast with the deleterious effects of the pursuit of forced, extrinsic, avoidance goals (Dykman, 1998; Elliot & Sheldon, 1998; Elliot, Sheldon, & Church, 1997; Kasser & Ryan, 1996). Thus, it is suggested that "to the extent that goal self-concepts do not represent or are not concordant with the true self, people may not be able to meet their psychological needs" (Sheldon & Elliot, 1999, p. 485). This conclusion is supported not only by individual experiments but by meta-analyses, that is, analyses of the results of *multiple* experiments in which one computes an overall index of the degree to which variables are related across a number of individual studies. Meta-analyses confirm the hypothesis that people make particularly good progress on personal goals when the goals are "self-concordant," that is, consistent with one's own personal values rather than being imposed by someone else (Koestner et al., 2002).

From a humanistic standpoint, these results make perfectly good sense. Yet, two caveats are worthy of note. First, it is important to keep in mind that it is not the goal per se that is important but why the goal is being pursued. For example, some research has argued that a goal such as financial success represents an extrinsic goal, implying external control, whereas a goal such as community involvement (e.g., making the world a better place) represents an intrinsic goal, implying autonomy, self-determination, and self-actualization (Kasser & Ryan, 1996). However, other research indicates that the same goal can be pursued for intrinsic or extrinsic reasons, suggesting that goals such as financial success and community involvement can express either motivation. On the basis of such reasoning, Carver & Baird (1998) predicted and found that endorsement of intrinsic reasons for a goal, whether financial success or community involvement, was associated with self-actualization in contrast with endorsement of extrinsic reasons for the same goals. In other words, in accord with self-determination theory, it was the motivation for the goal that was key. This is important in reminding us that we cannot assume that we know the motivation for a goal just from awareness of the content of the goal. The second caveat is the following: It is easy to assume that these principles of motivation apply to all people. However, recent research suggests that they may be culturally specific rather than universal features of human psychology. In this work, Anglo-American and Asian-American children were compared in terms of their relative intrinsic motivation when choices were (a) made for them versus (b) made by authority figures or peers. Anglo-American children showed more intrinsic motivation when they made their own choices. However, Asian-American children showed greater intrinsic motivation when their choices were made *for them* by trusted authority figures or peers (Iyengar & Lepper, 1999). Thus, the extent to which self-determination reflects a universal human need requires careful consideration and more research. More generally, the Rogerian emphasis on self-actualization may be most appropriate to understanding people who live in a Western culture in which Rogers formulated his theory.

CROSS-CULTURAL RESEARCH ON THE SELF

The research on intrinsic motivation among Asian-American and Anglo-American children that we have just reviewed raises a general question. Carl Rogers was an American psychologist. He developed his theory on the basis

CURRENT APPLICATIONS

DOES HIGH SELF-ESTEEM IMPROVE ONE'S LIFE?

Sometimes the ideas of personality theorists contribute to the ideas of a culture. Such is the case for Carl Rogers. As we have seen, his theory emphasizes the idea that people strive to maintain a positive sense of self. The influence of Rogers's thinking is one of a number of factors that has contributed to a widespread interest—among both psychologists and the public at large—in self-esteem. Everybody seems to know what self-esteem is, to view self-esteem as a good thing, and to want more of it. Educators commonly try to boost self-esteem in their students. People who craft social policy often try to enhance the esteem of members of society. The idea that high self-esteem is good and low self-esteem is bad is accepted so commonly that it seems nearly impossible that the idea might be limited—if not, in many applications, wrong. Yet that is the conclusion suggested by a recent scientific review.

Baumeister, Campbell, Krueger, & Vohs (2003) recently took on a large task: systematically reviewing the extensive scientific literature relating self-esteem to valued life outcomes such as higher levels of performance, interpersonal success, and health. If you subscribe to the belief that "self-esteem is good," their review might cause you to cancel your subscription. In one area of life after another, scientific results were found to yield little evidence that self-esteem contributes to positive life outcomes.

An important aspect of this review was that the authors focused on the relation between self-esteem and objective outcomes. Merely determining whether people who report having high self-esteem also say that "their life is great!" is not too valuable scientifically for an obvious reason: People who say that they have high self-esteem may be biased to report that their life "is great" even when things are not going well at all. The key question for the review, then, was whether self-reported self-esteem was related to important life outcomes measured through objective procedures—that is, procedures other than people's self-reports.

It is here that the scientific evidence was weak. The authors found that the existing scientific results "do not support the view that self-esteem has a strong effect on school achievement" (p. 13); "fail to confirm" the possibility that "people with high self-esteem [are] ... more popular and socially skilled than others" (p. 20); and yield "no strong evidence [that] ... high self-esteem leads to improved performance on the job" (p. 15). Data linking low "self-esteem to violence, aggression, and antisocial tendencies" was found to be "mixed at best" (p. 24).

Why are the links between self-esteem and positive life outcomes so weak? Baumeister and colleagues suggest that, in part, it is because high self-esteem may sometimes have negative effects. For example, people with highly inflated self-views may be narcissistic, acting in a self-centered way that alienates others (e.g., Colvin, Block, & Funder, 1995).

The authors suggest that these scientific findings have significant implications for social policy. Since the links between self-esteem and positive life outcomes often are surprisingly weak, it may make little sense for society to invest in educational programs and related initiatives that are designed merely to enhance people's views of themselves. With regard to the construct of self-esteem itself, they suggest the potential value of "splitting" the construct into "subcategories" (p. 38); the notion of self-esteem, in other words, may incorporate a number of personality processes that actually are distinct (narcissism, confidence in performance, beliefs about one's personality attributes, emotional tendencies). Some aspects of self-esteem may enhance performance even if others do not.

SOURCE: BAUMEISTER et al., 2003.

of clinical experiences with Americans. Most of the psychological research on self-processes conducted during Rogers's lifetime was conducted with citizens of the United States, Canada, or Western Europe. The question that arises, then, is as follows: Does Rogers's work provide us with a general view of human nature, or with a view that pertains primarily to people in the industrialized Western world? This is a deep and important question that has relevance far beyond the personality theory of Carl Rogers. All theoretical conceptions of human nature inevitably are constructed by people who live in a certain geographical location, in a certain culture, at a certain point in history. The question, then, is whether the theorist possibly can circumvent the limits of his or her circumstances to provide a theoretical framework that applies to all persons, in all cultures and all historical contexts.

In other sciences, theorists commonly do achieve this goal. The biologist who discovers the basic functioning of, for example, the immune system is safe in the assumption that the discovery applies to all people across time and place. The difficult question is whether this sort of assumption holds with regard to the psychological systems that we call personality. We will take up this question with respect to a particular feature of the theory of Carl Rogers, namely, his belief in a universal need for positive self-regard.

Is Positive Self-Regard a Human Universal?

As we have reviewed, Rogers believed that all people have a need for positive self-regard. To Rogers, unconditional acceptance of the individual, whatever

Research suggests that people in Western and Eastern cultures differ, with Western cultures promoting the enhancement of self-esteem and Eastern cultures supporting psychological tendencies that involve a striving for self-improvement.

his or her faults may be, is the pathway to psychological health. Such unconditional regard builds the individual's sense that he or she is a valued, prized person. In the absence of such unconditional regard, the individual's need for a positive self-view may be unfulfilled, leading to psychological distress.

But is this how things work for all persons the world over? If psychological processes regarding the self are akin to biological processes, then the answer is yes. But psychological processes involving the self may not be like this. The very notion of self—of one's identity, one's role in family and society, one's goals, one's purpose in life—is acquired socially. People acquire a sense of self from interaction with the individuals who make up their family, community, and wider culture. It is possible, then, that some cultures in essence *teach* people to have a need for positive regard; a culture that values the individual and individual achievements may foster the belief that individuals should enhance their own well-being. In principle, other cultures may teach people a different way of life that does not involve a striving for positive self-regard.

Compelling evidence that there are, in fact, variations from culture to culture in the nature and functioning of self-esteem are found in the study of differences between Japanese and American culture. Heine, Lehman, Markus, & Kitayama (1999) review evidence that the basic patterns and functions of self-esteem seem to vary from one culture to another. In the United States, most people report having relatively high self-esteem; as Rogers might have predicted, people seem biased to maintain positive self-views. But in Japan there is no sign whatsoever of this bias (Figure 6.4); as many people report low self-esteem as high self-esteem. In psychological studies conducted in the United States, people seem inevitably to engage in psychological strategies to maintain high self-esteem; for example, they compare themselves to others who are not doing well, they blame others for personal failure, and they lower the perceived importance of activities on which they cannot perform competently (reviewed in Brown, 1998). But Heine and colleagues (1999, p. 780) "are unable to find clear and consistent evidence of any self-esteem maintenance strategies within the Japanese psychological literature."

Rather than being prone to an enhancement of self-esteem, Heine and colleagues (1999; also see Kitayama & Markus, 1999; Kitayama, Markus, Matsumoto, & Norasakkunkit, 1997) contend that Japanese culture makes one prone to self-criticism. In Japan, this self-criticism serves a valuable personal and social function. It motivates people toward self-improvement that can benefit the individual and his or her society. In Japan, then, self-criticism is not "bad." It is not a sign of being depressed or down on oneself. Instead, it is "good"—that is, it is a functional, valuable way for individuals to mesh with their surrounding culture. Consistent with this view, tendencies toward self-criticism and the experience of discrepancies between the actual and ideal self are predictive of depression in North America, but are less strongly related to depression in Japan (Heine et al., 1999).

In summary, it appears that the cultures of the United States and of Japan teach people different ways of evaluating the self. If you, the reader, are a citizen of North America, then you may be particularly prone to engage in psychological strategies that maintain a positive view of self. If your professor gives you a bad grade on a paper, you may conclude that there is something wrong with the professor. If a romantic partner dumps you, you may conclude that the relationship wasn't all that important anyway. If you didn't get into

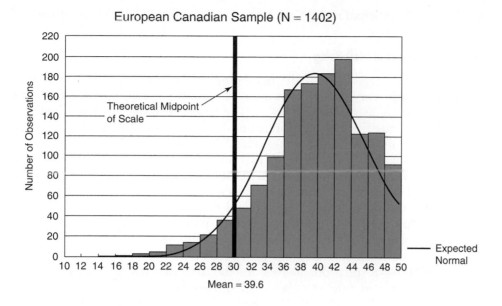

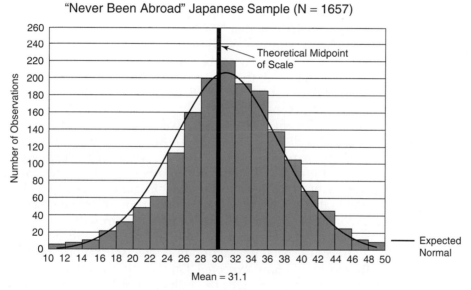

Figure 6.4 *Graphs display distributions of self-esteem scores among European Canadians and citizens of Japan. From Heine et al., 1999.*

the college of your choice, you may conclude that it was because you didn't take your application seriously enough. These conclusions are functional in the cultural system of the United States; they enable you to maintain a high sense of self-esteem in a culture that values high self-esteem. But if you are a citizen of Japan, you may be much more likely to draw other conclusions that are more self-critical; in so doing, you would be fitting in with a culture that values continual personal improvement. These variations in the nature and functioning of self-evaluation and self-esteem are understandable in light of contemporary research on culture and personality; however, these variations were not well anticipated by Carl Rogers when he formulated his theory of personality and self.

Regional Variations in Well-Being

Recent research suggests that the psychological dynamics of interest to Carl Rogers not only vary from one culture to another (e.g., American versus Japanese culture, as reviewed above). The research indicates that they also vary within culture from one region to another. Evidence comes from research conducted within the United States. Plaut, Markus, & Lachman (2002) analyzed data from a national survey of psychological well-being of Americans at midlife (the average participant was in his or her mid-40s). Plaut and associates reasoned that different geographic regions within the United States have societal patterns that are distinct enough, and relevant enough, to psychological well-being that they may produce different patterns of psychological experience. For example, the Rocky Mountain regions of the American West are typified by a particularly strong spirit of rugged individualism and of potentialities for growth—a spirit prevalent since the time that rugged, individualistic pioneers first moved into the area. In contrast, regions of the southeastern United States (the "Deep South") are typified by Southern grace and hospitality and a respect for the traditions of the past; the Plaut group (2002, p. 173) quotes William Faulkner as writing that "the past is alive in the South, in fact, it's not even past." Such sociocultural conditions, which look back to the past rather than ahead to the future, would not be expected to foster strong feelings of personal growth; combined with the fact that the most salient feature of the region's past is the South's defeat in the Civil War, these conditions might also foster a lower sense of self-acceptance.

As anticipated, these different social settings were associated with different patterns of psychological well-being (Figure 6.5). Americans in the southeastern United States reported experiencing relatively low levels of personal growth and self-acceptance as compared to Americans in other regions. Americans in the Mountain region, as well as those in the New England states (which are known for an individualism that dates back to the time of Puritan settlers) reported high levels of autonomy and a sense of personal growth.

To some degree, these results are consistent with the basic outlines of Rogerian theory. Patterns of social interaction predicted self-reported patterns of well-being, as Rogers would have expected. On the other hand, the analyses of Plaut and colleagues (2002) highlight the influence of broad sociocultural factors that received less attention from Rogers.

CRITICAL EVALUATION

We conclude our coverage of Rogers's theory by evaluating it critically. We do so in the same manner as we evaluated the psychodynamic approach, namely, by assessing its success in achieving five goals enumerated at the outset of our text, in Chapter 1. We then summarize the theory's major contributions.

SCIENTIFIC OBSERVATION: THE DATABASE

The first goal is to build a personality theory on a database of solid scientific observations. In many respects, the scientific observations on which Rogers based his theory are quite admirable. Far more than Freud, Rogers was

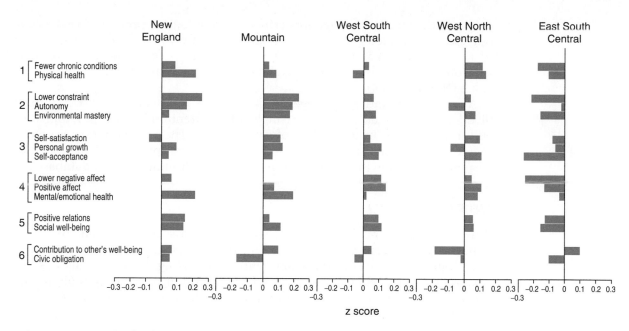

Figure 6.5   *Figure displays reports of psychological well-being among research participants living in different regions of the United States. From Plaut et al., 2002.*

sensitive to the fact that scientific observations must be objective. One must ensure that any personal biases are eliminated from the process of data collection. Rogers and his colleagues took a number of steps to achieve this objectivity. They used objective personality assessment techniques such as the Q-sort. They employed experimental methods to evaluate whether client-centered therapy is effective. Even when working with traditional clinical interview data, Rogers took a major step forward that was never taken by Freud. Rogers allowed (with his clients' permission) transcripts and recordings of his therapy sessions to be made public. Outside observers thus could verify Rogers's clinical reports.

Other features of Rogers's scientific observations seem limited in light of contemporary science. One limitation involves the type of personality assessment method he used. Rogers relied exclusively on measures that are explicit, that is, measures in which clients and research participants make statements about their personality that are formed through conscious self-reflection and are stated publicly. The limitation is that people may not be able—or willing—to put some aspects of their personality into words. There may exist personality qualities that people cannot articulate explicitly. Recognizing this, many contemporary researchers employ implicit measures of self-concept. Rather than relying on people's explicit, conscious self-reports, research employs subtle, indirect measures, such as indices of the speed with which people respond to certain words or ideas that are related to the self-concept (Asendorpf, Banse, & Mücke, 2002; Greenwald et al., 2002). These implicit measures often are correlated only modestly with explicit measures of self-concept. This, in turn, suggests that people possess implicit beliefs about the self that are not revealed by the explicitly self-reported methods Rogers relied upon. The general point is that the phenomenological approach may exclude from investigation critical psychological processes that occur outside of conscious experience. Rogers, a self-critical thinker, was aware of this problem. His response was that the phenomenological approach is a valuable, necessary one for psychology, but perhaps not the only one of value (Rogers, 1964).

A second limitation of Rogers's database is its relative lack of cultural diversity. Rogers devoted surprisingly little attention to the possibility of cultural variation in the nature of self-concept. The contemporary research reviewed above, in our discussion of culture and self processes, suggests that Rogers's theorizing may be compromised by this limitation in its database.

THEORY: SYSTEMATIC?

When one reads much of Rogers's work, it often seems surprisingly unsystematic. Rogers commonly wrote in an impressionistic style that lacked the strict logic structure of traditional scientific theorizing. However, this was not always the case. When Rogers turned his attention from writing about the process of therapy to writing a formal personality theory (Rogers, 1959), his work became far more systematic. He presents his theory of personality in a series of propositions that build systematically, one from the other. As a result, different elements of the theory are reasonably well integrated. One does not learn from Rogers merely that there are alternative types of parent-child interactions, alternative types of self-concept, and alternative types of psychological distress versus well-being. One also learns how these different phenomena are functionally interrelated. His theory specifies, for example, how childhood experiences influence the development of self-concept, which in turn influences emotional well-being.

The main limitation to Rogers's systematic theorizing is how little of it there is. Rogers devoted relatively little of his effort to the explication of systematic theory. A biographer notes that Rogers was "reluctant to begin theorizing in the first place" and that even when he began his theoretical work he was "still reluctant to place too great an emphasis on his own formulation" (Kischenbaum, 1979, p. 240). Even Rogers himself recognized the lack of development of his theoretical work. Reflecting back on the propositions of his own theory, Rogers (1959/1977, p. 232) laments its "immaturity ... only the most general description can be given of ... functional relationships" that, ideally, would be specified with mathematical rigor. In sum, Rogers provided a theory that was systematic, yet that was less systematic than that of some other theorists discussed in this text, if only because he composed less formal theoretical work than did others.

THEORY: TESTABLE?

If one asks whether Rogers provided a theory that is testable via standard scientific methods, the answer depends on which elements of his theory one is talking about. In some aspects of his work, Rogers defined constructs with great clarity and provided suggestions for personality assessments that could be used to measure those constructs. Rogers's work on the actual and ideal self stands out in this regard. He formulated these theoretical ideas with clarity. He indicated that the Q-sort is a viable method for assessing aspects of self-concept. As a result, he provided an overall theoretical conception of self-concept that was testable.

Other aspects of Rogers's work are far less testable. Consider his belief that there is a universal motive toward self-actualization. How would one test this idea? As we noted in Chapter 5, Rogers's writing about self-actualization sometimes is more poetic than scientific; Rogers does not provide the sort of clear definition of the construct that could guide research. He himself also provided no objective assessment tool for measuring a person's degree or level of self-actualization. Rogers also provided few conceptual tools for comparing his belief in a single self-actualizing motive to potential alternative beliefs, such as that there are a number of fundamentally distinct motives that each play a role in self-actualization (e.g., a motive to understand oneself, a motive to understand the spiritual world, a motive to be compassionate toward others, etc.). It is hard to know what kind of evidence Rogers would have accepted as evidence that there is not, in fact, a single overarching motive for self-actualization. This element of this theory, then, is not clearly testable.

THEORY: COMPREHENSIVE?

When introducing personality theories in Chapter 1, we explained that one task for the theorist is to develop a framework that is comprehensive. In psychology, theories abound. But the field houses few theories with the intellectual breadth to qualify as a theory of the whole person, or a theory of personality.

The first theory you learned about, Freud's, was extraordinarily comprehensive. It is difficult to formulate questions about personality, personality development, and individual differences that are not addressed, either directly or indirectly, in Freud's framework. The same cannot be said of the theory of Rogers. Consider some of the following questions. How does our evolutionary background contribute to the explanation of personality structure and functioning? How do emotional states influence thinking processes? If people are so self-actualizing, why are sexual and aggressive impulses so central to human experience? How does our genetic endowment interact with social influences in the course of development? Now consider the question "What does Rogers say about these issues?" A limitation of Rogers's work is that he simply does not say much at all about these issues. In this regard, and others, his work is not comprehensive.

If one were to ask why his work is relatively lacking in comprehensiveness, one simple answer is that he devoted much of his energies to developing individual and group therapies, rather than to basic theory and research on personality. A further answer, though, is that in Rogers's efforts—and the highly related efforts of other phenomenological, humanistic, and hermeneutic thinkers—to treat people as social beings, Rogers sometimes fails fully to treat people as biological beings. Sometimes we feel bad because of our views of ourselves. But sometimes we feel bad due to biochemical factors that influence our mood. Sometimes we are anxious because events are incongruent with self-perceptions. But sometimes we are anxious due to the activation of basic biological mechanisms that have nothing to do with self-perception (see Chapter 9). Integrating the biological and the social aspects of human nature is difficult. Rogers's failure to tackle this task head on makes his work

Rogers at a Glance

Structure	Process	Growth and Development
Self; ideal self	Self-actualization; congruence of self and experience; incongruence and defensive distortion and denial	Congruence and self-actualization versus incongruence and defensiveness

less comprehensive than some of the other personality theories we review in this text.

APPLICATIONS

Rogers's contributions to applied psychology are profoundly important. At least three aspects of his client-centered therapy are of enduring significance to the field. Rogers underscored the importance of the interpersonal relationship between client and therapist, while also providing techniques for building that relationship. He helped to establish objective methods for determining whether a given therapeutic approach actually benefited clients. Finally, and perhaps most importantly, he treated his clients as persons, not as patients. Rather than treating people as patients who harbored mental illnesses that needed to be diagnosed, he empowered clients by treating them as people who were capable, through the power of the self-actualizing motive, of improving their own lives. Few other figures in modern psychology can claim as strong a set of contributions to the field. Rogers's ability to generate not only abstract theory but useful applications is a great strength of his work.

MAJOR CONTRIBUTIONS AND SUMMARY

The contributions of Rogers to personality theory must be understood in historical context. Today, in early 21st century psychology, discussion of the role of the self is commonplace. Almost all personality psychologists recognize that cognitive and affective processes involving the self are central to personality structure and functioning. This, however, was not the case in Rogers's day. When he began his work in the mid-20th century, neither of the guiding theoretical models in the field, psychoanalysis and behaviorism, attended carefully to the role of self-processes. Rogers and his colleagues in the phenomenological and humanistic traditions contributed importantly to a historical re-direction of attention to aspects of human psychology that had been neglected.

We conclude by summarizing the strengths and limitations of Rogers's contributions (Table 6.1). We encourage you, the reader, to weigh these strengths and limitations against those of other theories you learn about in this text. We end by applauding Rogers for something he did uniquely. More than any

Pathology	Change	Illustrative Case
Defensive maintenance of self; incongruence	Therapeutic atmosphere: congruence, unconditional positive regard, empathic understanding	Mrs. Oak

Table 6.1   Summary of Strengths and Limitations of Rogers's Theory and Phenomenology

Strengths	*Limitations*
1. Focuses on important aspects of human existence that are neglected in many other theories, including self-concept and the human potential for personal growth.	1. Less comprehensive than some other theories, with little attention devoted to the biological bases of human nature.
2. Provides concrete therapeutic strategies that have proven useful in bringing about psychological change in therapy.	2. May exclude from research and clinical concern phenomena that lie outside of conscious experience.
3. Brings scientific objectivity and rigor to difficult-to-study processes involving both interpersonal relations and phenomenal experience.	3. Devotes little attention to the possibility of cultural variation or situation-to-situation variation in psychological structures and processes involving the self, and thus provides few tools for explaining those variations that exist.

other personality theorist, Rogers attempted to be objective about what is otherwise left to the artist:

> Slowly the thinker went on his way and asked himself: What is it that you wanted to learn from teachings and teachers, and although they taught you much, what was it they could not teach you? And he thought: It was the Self, the character and nature of which I wished to learn. I wanted to rid myself of the Self, to conquer it, but I could not conquer it, I could only deceive it, could only fly from it, could only hide from it. Truly, nothing in the world has occupied my thoughts as much as the Self, this riddle, that I live, that I am one and am separate and different from everybody else, that I am Siddartha; and about nothing in the world do I know less than about myself, about Siddartha.
>
> Source: Hesse, 1951, p. 40

MAJOR CONCEPTS

Authenticity   The extent to which the person behaves in accord with his or her self as opposed to behaving in terms of roles that foster false self-presentations.

Client-centered therapy   Rogers's term for his earlier approach to therapy in which the counselor's attitude is one of interest in the ways in which the client experiences the self and the world.

Congruence   Rogers's concept expressing an absence of conflict between the perceived self and experience. Also one of three therapist conditions suggested as essential for growth and therapeutic progress.

Contingencies of self-worth   The positive and negative events on which one's feelings of self-esteem depend.

Empathic understanding   Rogers's term for the ability to perceive experiences and feelings and their meanings from the standpoint of another person. One of three therapist conditions essential for therapeutic progress.

Existentialism   An approach to understanding people and conducting therapy, associated with the human potential movement, that emphasizes phenomenology and concerns inherent in existing as a person. Derived from a more general movement in philosophy.

Human potential movement   A group of psychologists, represented by Rogers and Maslow, who emphasize the actualization or fulfillment of individual potential, including an openness to experience.

Self-experience discrepancy   Rogers's emphasis on the potential for conflict between the concept of self and experience—the basis for psychopathology.

Unconditional positive regard   Rogers's term for the acceptance of a person in a total, unconditional way. One of three therapist conditions suggested as essential for growth and therapeutic progress.

REVIEW

1. For Rogers, the neurotic person is one who is in a state of incongruence between self and experience. Experiences that are incongruent with the self structure are subceived as threatening and may be either denied or distorted.

2. Research in the area of psychopathology has focused on the discrepancy between the self and ideal self, and the extent to which individuals disown or are vague about their feelings.

3. Rogers's focus was on the therapeutic process. The critical variable in therapy was seen as the therapeutic climate. Conditions of congruence (genuineness), unconditional positive regard, and empathic understanding were seen as essential to therapeutic change.

4. The case of Mrs. Oak, an early case published by Rogers, illustrates his publication of recorded therapy sessions for research purposes.

5. Rogers's views are part of the human potential movement, which emphasizes self-actualization and the fulfillment of each individual's potential. Kurt Goldstein, Abraham H. Maslow, and existentialists like Viktor Frankl are also representatives of this movement.

6. Contemporary work on existentialist concerns including feelings of authenticity, and on regional and cultural variations in the perceptions of self, extend Rogers's theorizing while also raising some questions about the universality of some psychological motives posited by Rogers.

TRAIT THEORIES OF PERSONALITY: ALLPORT, EYSENCK, AND CATTELL

7

Chris has just graduated from college and started a job in a new city. He feels lonely and wants to meet some new people. After some hesitation, he decides to place a personals ad. He stares at his blank computer screen—what should he write? What kinds of personality characteristics would you choose to describe yourself? He chooses "Unconventional, sensitive, fun-loving, happy, humorous, kind, slender graduate, 22, seeks similar qualities in sane soulmate." Somebody who can be described this way may indeed be a desirable date!

The personality characteristics that Chris has described are what are known as personality *traits*. Personality traits are psychological characteristics that are stable over time and across situations; it's a good bet that somebody who is sensitive and kind today will also be sensitive and kind a month from now. This chapter is about traits, defined as broad dispositions to behave in particular ways.

Specifically, in this chapter you will learn about three personality trait theories and their associated research programs. Two of these theories—those of Hans Eysenck and of Raymond Cattell—attempt to identify the basic *dimensions* of personality traits, that is, basic characteristics that everyone shares to a greater or lesser degree. The two associated research programs rely on a particular statistical procedure, *factor analysis*; this statistical procedure is used to identify the most basic individual differences in personality traits.

Historically, the trait approach has been popular in American and British psychology and, in the field's recent era, in personality psychology in Europe as well. Part of this popularity reflects the methodological sophistication of factor-analytic research methods and the relatively consistent research results that they yield. Part of this popularity also is rooted in the common-sense nature of trait theory; the scientific theories of personality traits have an intuitive appeal because their basic units of analysis, personality traits, are similar to simple nonscientific, "folk" understandings of personality.

QUESTIONS TO BE ADDRESSED IN THIS CHAPTER

1. What are the main ways in which individuals differ from one another in their feelings, thoughts, and behavior? How many different traits are needed to adequately describe these personality differences?

2. Does every person have a unique set of personality traits, or is it possible to identify a set of traits that is universal and that can serve as a taxonomy of individual differences?

3. If individuals can be described in terms of their characteristic traits, how are we to explain variability in behavior across time and situations?

We now introduce a third main perspective on personality, that of the trait theories. The trait theories differ strikingly from the Freudian and Rogerian perspectives you learned about in previous chapters. As you will see, the differences involve not only the substantive claims of the theories but the scientific database on which the theories rest.

Trait theorists emphasize that a central feature of the sciences is measurement. In the history of the physical sciences, scientific advances often could occur only after the development of tools for measuring physical phenomena precisely. If Galileo and Newton did not have relatively precise measures of time, mass, and other physical properties, they could not have verified that the motion of physical objects was lawful. If contemporary physicists did not have precise instruments for detecting the presence of subatomic particles, their science would be relatively speculative. Scientific progress often rests on precise measurement.

Contrast this emphasis with the approach of Freud and Rogers. Freud's work was virtually devoid of objective scientific measurement. He inferred the presence of mental structures of varying strength while providing no tools for measuring them. Freud relied merely on case study reports, which are more interpretative and thus subjective than traditional scientific measurement. Rogers was more attentive to measurement principles. Yet some of his central theoretical constructs (e.g., the self-actualization motive) were not accompanied by measurement principles (Rogers never provided a measure of individual differences, or intra-individual variations, in self-actualizing tendencies). Surveying this scene, the trait theorist asked: Could these prior thinkers be said to have made truly scientific progress? Their answer: no. The work of "Jung and Freud ... amounted scientifically almost to a disaster," concluded the trait theorist Raymond Cattell (1965, pp. 16–17). Trait theorists called for a new approach to the study of personality, one whose measures of psychological attributes were as objective and reliable as those found in the physical sciences. This chapter and the next review the progress they made.

A VIEW OF THE TRAIT THEORISTS

In our previous chapters, we introduced theoretical perspectives by reviewing the life of the primary theorist (Freud in Chapter 3, Rogers in Chapter 5). Our approach here, with the trait theories, is different. The difference reflects the nature of the theories and theorists. There simply is no single individual—no one dominant figure, no prime mover—in the trait theories of personality, in the way that there was in the psychodynamic and phenomenological traditions.

In the 20th century, the foundations for trait psychology were laid by three investigators whose work is of particular significance: Gordon Allport, Raymond Cattell, and Hans Eysenck. Their contributions are reviewed in the present chapter. In the contemporary 21st century field, much investigation centers around a theoretical perspective that endeavors to capitalize on the best aspects of the contributions of Allport, Cattell, and Eysenck. This approach, the five-factor model of personality, is reviewed in Chapter 8. Rather than providing biographical information for all these individuals right now, we include such information when introducing their respective contributions in the sections below.

Although the various trait theorists have made contributions that are distinct, their work features many common themes. There is a coherent "trait perspective" on personality. As you'll now see, it is a perspective that will seem immediately familiar. The trait theorist's main scientific constructs are quite similar to the words and ideas you use to discuss people in your everyday life.

TRAIT THEORY'S VIEW OF THE PERSON

People love to talk about personality. We can spend hours discussing people's characteristics: our boss is grumpy; our roommate, sloppy; our professor, quick-witted. (Well, we hope your professor is quick-witted rather than sloppy and grumpy.) We even discuss the loyalty of our dog and laziness of our cat. When talking about people we commonly use personality **trait** terms—words that describe people's typical styles of experience and action. Apparently, people think that traits are central to personality. Likewise, personality researchers associated with the trait approach consider traits to be the major units of personality. Obviously there is more to personality than traits, but traits have loomed large throughout the history of personality psychology.

THE TRAIT CONCEPT

What, then, is a trait? Personality traits refer to consistent patterns in the way individuals behave, feel, and think. If we describe an individual with the trait term *kind*, we mean that this individual tends to act kindly over time (weeks, months, maybe years) and across situations (with friends, family, strangers, etc.). In addition, if we use the word *kind* we usually mean that the person is at least as kind as the average person. If one believed that the person was less kind than average, he or she would not be described as "kind."

Trait terms, then, have two connotations: consistency and distinctiveness. By consistency, we mean that the trait describes a regularity in the person's behavior. The person seems predisposed to act in the way described by the trait term; indeed, traits often are referred to as "dispositions" or "dispositional constructs" (e.g., McCrae & Costa, 1999) to capture the idea that the person appears predisposed to act in a certain way. The idea of disposition highlights an important fact about trait terms as used by trait theorists of personality. If a trait theorist uses a trait term—e.g., *sociable*—to describe someone, she does not mean that the person *always* will act sociably, across all settings of life. As the Belgian trait psychologist De Raad (2005) recently emphasized, trait terms implicitly refer to behaviors in a type of social context. The sociable person would be expected, by the trait theorist, to be consistently sociable across settings that involve other people and in which sociable behavior is allowed by prevailing social norms. There is no expectation that the person would be sociable toward inanimate objects or act sociably when instructed by an authority figure to act otherwise. By the other connotation, distinctiveness, we mean simply that the trait theorist is concerned primarily with psychological characteristics in which people differ—features that therefore make one person distinct compared to others. In a sense of the word *trait* that *differs* from the way the word is used by trait theories of personality, one might say that traits of human beings include their capacity to reflect on themselves and to use language. These are traits that distinguish people from animals. However, these are *not* traits that distinguish different people from one another; *all* normally functioning adult humans can reflect on themselves, the future, and the past using language. Trait theorists of personality are interested in traits for which there are significant differences among people.

The decision to build a personality theory on trait constructs implies a certain view of the person. It implies that there is substantial consistency to individuals' lives. Contemporary social life presents many changes: People change schools and jobs, meet new friends, marry, unmarry, remarry, and move to different communities if not different countries. At any one point in time, life may present multiple roles: student, employee, son or daughter, parent, community member. The trait theorist's fundamental message is that, despite all these variations, there is a consistent personality "in there." People possess psychological qualities that endure, almost irrespective of time and place. Ⓧ

TRAIT THEORY'S VIEW OF THE SCIENCE OF PERSONALITY

The discussion that opened this chapter is revealing of the view of personality science implicit in most trait approaches. As you learned, a paramount interest of trait theorists is measurement. The ability to measure psychological traits reliably and validly is the utterly critical first step in building a science of personality in the trait-theoretical view.

This viewpoint displays a kind of conservatism that is valuable in the sciences. Both Freud and Rogers allowed themselves to create theories that went far beyond their available data; there were no direct, or indirect, measures of the strength of libidinal drives, of self-actualization motives, and so forth. Trait theorists of the mid-20th century rejected this sort of theorizing as too speculative. They felt that scientific measurement should constrain, and determine, theorizing. One should posit a personality structure if, and only if, the statistical analysis of carefully constructed measures suggests the existence of that structure.

Here in the early 21st century, this approach might appear *too* conservative. Science commonly advances through careful yet imaginative theoretical models that posit entities that cannot be observed (Harré, 2002). The physicist Niels Bohr posited what is now the standard model of the atom without being able to observe and measure relevant properties of subatomic particles. Quantum physics theorizes about features of the universe that, in principle, cannot be measured accurately, at least not without altering the entity being measured (Greene, 2004). Nonetheless, the careful, data-based measurements of the trait theorist may have enormous practical value in identifying and establishing a viable theory of personality traits.

SCIENTIFIC FUNCTIONS SERVED BY TRAIT CONSTRUCTS

A main question to ask about the trait theory's view of science is "Why posit trait constructs?" In other words, "What is it that trait constructs *do* in a science of personality?" Trait theorists use trait constructs to serve at least two, and sometimes three, scientific functions: description, prediction, and explanation.

Description

All personality trait theorists use trait constructs descriptively. Traits summarize a person's typical behavior, and thus describe what a person typically is like. Since description is a critical first step in any scientific endeavor, trait theories could be seen as providing basic descriptive facts that need to be explained by any theory of personality.

Most trait theorists seek not just to describe individual people, one at a time. They try to establish an overall descriptive scheme within which any and all persons can be described. They try, in other words, to establish a personality *taxonomy.* In any science, a taxonomy is a scientist's way of classifying the things being studied. Since trait constructs refer to consistent styles of experience and behavior, a trait taxonomy is a way of classifying people according to their characteristic, average types of experience and action.

Prediction

One question for a trait theorist is whether these classifications, within a taxonomy of personality traits, are of practical value. What can one do with knowledge of people's personality trait scores?

Throughout the history of the trait theories, a primary answer to this question is: You can predict things. People with different levels of a given personality trait may differ predictably in their everyday behavior. For example, if one knows college students' self-ratings on traits such as extraversion and conscientiousness, one can predict aspects of their personal environments, such as the decorations in, and degree of neatness of, personal office spaces and dorm rooms (Gosling, Mannarelli, & Morris, 2002). Often one can make predictions that have important practical value. Suppose you are running a business and want to hire employees who will turn out to be reliable, honest workers. You are faced with a job of prediction: How can you predict which applicants will be good employees? One way of making this prediction is by giving people tests that measure their characteristic personality traits; trait psychologists have been deeply involved in the practical task of predicting on-the-job performance (Roberts & Hogan, 2001).

Explanation

In addition to description and prediction, a third scientific task is explanation. If personality psychology aspires to be a science, then it must tackle the most important challenge for a scientific theory, namely, explanation. Note that prediction and explanation are very different things (Toulmin, 1961). For example, in ancient times Babylonians could describe and predict astronomical events such as lunar eclipses, but they appeared to have no scientific understanding whatsoever of why these events occurred as they did. In an opposite case, Darwin explained how organisms evolved through natural selection, but he did not literally predict the past evolutionary events (Toulmin, 1961).

Some trait theorists suggest that trait constructs can be used to explain a person's behavior. One might say that a student shows up on time for class and takes good lecture notes *because* the person is high on the trait of conscientiousness. However, not all trait psychologists use trait terms to accomplish this third scientific function, explanation. Some confine themselves to description and prediction. They view a trait taxonomy as being akin to a map. A map of the continents and oceans on earth does not explain why the continents and oceans have their particular location; for that explanation one needs additional scientific work (e.g., a theory of plate tectonics). Yet the map is still a crucial step in scientific progress.

As you will see in this chapter and again in Chapter 9, some psychologists try to move from description to explanation by identifying biological factors underlying a given trait. People who obtain high versus low scores on a personality trait test might differ systematically in a neural or biochemical system, which could be interpreted as the causal basis of the trait and trait-related behavior. This possibility, which many trait theorists pursue, raises another aspect of trait theory's view of the person. It is strongly biological. Most trait theorists believe that inherited biological factors are a primary determinant of individual differences in traits. We discuss this possibility, and the related scientific evidence, both in the present chapter and in Chapter 9.

In sum, trait theorists differ in their claims about the explanatory status of trait constructs. This raises an important point for you to keep in mind. There is no one trait theory. The trait theories are a family of interrelated, but not identical, perspectives. In the next section, we review features that most, if not all, trait theories share.

TRAIT THEORIES OF PERSONALITY: BASIC PERSPECTIVES SHARED BY TRAIT THEORISTS

A set of shared assumptions jointly define the trait approach. The most basic assumption is that people possess broad predispositions, called traits, to respond in particular ways. In other words, it is assumed that personality can be characterized in terms of an individual's consistent likelihood of behaving, feeling, or thinking in a particular way (e.g., their likelihood of acting in an outgoing and friendly manner, or of feeling nervous and worried, or of being reliable and conscientious). People who have a strong tendency to behave in these ways are described as being high on these traits, whereas people with a lesser tendency to behave in these ways are described as low on the traits. The person who frequently is outgoing would be called high on extraversion, whereas the unreliable, forgetful individual might be low on conscientiousness. All trait theorists agree that these generalized tendencies to act in one versus another manner are the fundamental building blocks of personality.

A related assumption is that there is a direct correspondence between the person's performance of trait-related actions and his or her possession of the corresponding trait. People who act (or report that they act) in a more extraverted or conscientious manner than others are thought, by the trait theorist, to possess more of (to be higher on) the corresponding traits of extraversion and conscientiousness. This point may seem so obvious that it isn't even worth stating. You may be thinking that "of course people who display more of the trait-related behavior have more of the trait." But note how this thinking contrasts with an earlier theory we covered, namely, psychoanalysis. To the psychoanalyst, someone who reports being more "calm and at ease" than other people may not, in reality, possess more of the psychological characteristic of calmness. Instead, such persons may be so anxious that they are repressing their anxieties and merely saying that they are calm. Psychoanalysis, as well as other personality theories we will cover later in the text, recognize that there may be highly indirect relations between overt behavior and underlying personality characteristics. In contrast, the research procedures of trait theory assume that overt behavior and underlying traits are linked in a more direct, one-to-one manner. If someone reports a low amount of trait-related behavior on a test of personality traits, then he or she is said to possess low amounts of the given trait.

Another shared assumption is that human behavior and personality can be organized into a hierarchy. A famous hierarchical analysis was provided

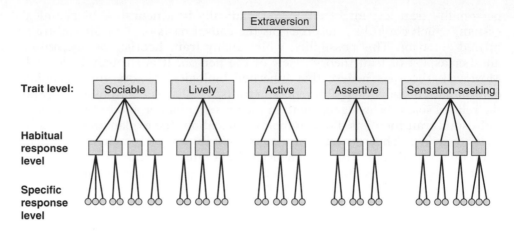

Figure 7.1   *Diagrammatic Representation of Hierarchical Organization of Personality: Extraversion-Introversion (E). (Note: Extraversion is one end of the E-I dimension. The other end, I, is not represented here.) (Adapted from Eysenck, 1970 and Eysenck, 1990)*

by Hans Eysenck (Figure 7.1), whose contributions are reviewed in more detail below. Eysenck suggested that, at its simplest level, behavior can be considered in terms of specific responses. However, some of these responses are linked together and form more general habits. Groups of habits that tend to occur together form traits. For example, people who prefer meeting people to reading also generally enjoy themselves at a lively party, suggesting that these two habits can be grouped together under the trait of sociability. Finally, at the highest level of organization, various traits may be linked together to form what Eysenck called secondary, higher-order factors or superfactors (which also are traits, but at the highest, most abstract level of generalization).

In sum, trait theories suggest that people display broad predispositions to respond in certain ways, that these dispositions are organized in a hierarchical manner, and that the trait concept can be a foundation for a scientific theory of personality.

THE TRAIT THEORY OF GORDON W. ALLPORT (1897–1967)

A figure of great historical importance to the development of trait theory, and personality psychology in general, was the Harvard University psychologist Gordon W. Allport. History remembers Allport as much for the issues he raised and the principles he emphasized than for a particular theory he created. Throughout his long and influential career, Allport highlighted the healthy and organized aspects of human behavior. This emphasis contrasted with other views of the time that emphasized the animalistic, neurotic, tension-reducing, and mechanistic aspects of behavior. Allport criticized psychoanalysis in this regard; he was particularly fond of telling the following story. While traveling through Europe at age 22, Allport decided it would be interesting to visit Freud. When he entered Freud's office, he was met with expectant silence as Freud waited to learn of Allport's mission. Finding himself unprepared for silence, Allport decided to start an informal conversation with the description of a four-year-old boy with a dirt phobia, whom he had met on the train. After he

Gordon W. Allport

completed his description of the boy and his compulsive mother, Freud asked, "And was that little boy you?" Allport describes his response as follows:

> Flabbergasted and feeling a bit guilty, I contrived to change the subject. While Freud's misunderstanding of my motivation was amusing, it also started a deep train of thought. I realized that he was accustomed to neurotic defenses and that my manifest motivation (a sort of rude curiosity and youthful ambition) escaped him. For therapeutic progress he would have to cut through my defenses, but it so happened that therapeutic progress was not here an issue. This experience taught me that depth psychology, for all its merits, may plunge too deep, and that psychologists would do well to give full recognition to manifest motives before probing the unconscious.
>
> SOURCE: ALLPORT, 1967, p. 8.

A particularly amusing aspect of this episode is that Allport personally was very meticulous, punctual, neat, and orderly—possessing many of the characteristics associated by Freud with the compulsive personality. Freud's question may not have been as far off as Allport suggested!

Allport's first publication, written with his older brother Floyd, centered on traits as an important aspect of personality theory (Allport & Allport, 1921). Allport believed that traits are the basic units of personality. According to him, traits actually exist and are based in the nervous system. They represent generalized personality dispositions that account for regularities in the functioning of a person across situations and over time. Traits can be defined by three properties—frequency, intensity, and range of situations. For example, a very submissive person would frequently be very submissive over a wide range of situations.

TRAITS: PERSONALITY STRUCTURE IN ALLPORT'S THEORY

In a now classic analysis of personality descriptors, Allport and Odbert (1936) differentiated personality traits from other important units of analysis in personality research. Allport and Odbert defined traits as "generalized and personalized determining tendencies—consistent and stable modes of an individual's adjustment to his environment" (1936, p. 26). Traits are thus different from

Table 7.1   Prototypical Examples of Traits, States, and Activities

Traits	States	Activities
Gentle	Infatuated	Carousing
Domineering	Pleased	Ranting
Trustful	Angry	Snooping
Timid	Invigorated	Leering
Cunning	Aroused	Reveling

Source: Chaplin et al., 1988.

states and activities which describe those aspects of personality that are temporary, brief, and caused by external circumstances. Chaplin, John, and Goldberg (1988) replicated Allport and Odbert's classifications of personality descriptors into three categories: traits, states, and activities. Table 7.1 lists examples of each of the three categories. For example, whereas a person may well be gentle throughout his or her lifetime, an infatuation (an internal state) typically does not last and even the most enjoyable carousing must come to an end.

Having distinguished traits from states and activities, the next question is whether there might exist different kinds of traits. Allport addressed this question by distinguishing among cardinal traits, central traits, and secondary dispositions. A **cardinal trait** expresses a disposition that is so pervasive and outstanding in a person's life that virtually every act is traceable to its influence. For example, we speak of the Machiavellian person, named after Niccolò Machiavelli's portrayal of the successful Renaissance ruler; of the sadistic person, named after the Marquis de Sade; and of the authoritarian personality who sees virtually everything in black and white, stereotyped ways. Generally people have few, if any, such cardinal traits. **Central traits** (e.g., honesty, kindness, assertiveness) express dispositions that cover a more limited range of situations than is true for cardinal traits. **Secondary dispositions** are traits that are the least conspicuous, generalized, and consistent. In other words, people possess traits with varying degrees of significance and generality.

Allport did not claim that a trait is expressed in all situations, regardless of the characteristics of the situation. He recognized the importance of the situation in explaining why a person does not behave the same way all the time. He wrote: "traits are often aroused in one situation and not in another" (Allport, 1937, p. 331). For example, even the most aggressive people can be expected to modify their behavior if the situation calls for nonaggressive behavior, and even the most introverted person may behave in an extraverted fashion in certain situations. A trait expresses what a person generally does over many situations, not what will be done in any one situation. According to Allport, both trait and situation concepts are necessary to understand behavior. The trait concept is necessary to explain the consistency of behavior, whereas recognition of the importance of the situation is necessary to explain the variability of behavior.

FUNCTIONAL AUTONOMY

Allport analyzed not only stable traits, but motivational processes. He emphasized the **functional autonomy** of human motives. This means that although the motives of an adult may have their roots in the tension-reducing motives of

Functional Autonomy: Sometimes a person may select an occupation for one reason, such as job security, and then remain in it for other motives, such as pleasure in the activity itself.

the child, as Freud suggested, the adult grows out of the early motives. In adult life, motives become independent of, or autonomous from, earlier tension-reducing drives. What originally began as an effort to reduce hunger or anxiety can become a source of pleasure and motivation in its own right. What began as an activity designed to earn a living can become pleasurable and an end in itself. Although hard work and the pursuit of excellence can be motivated originally by a desire for approval from parents and other adults, they can become valued ends in themselves—pursued independently of whether they are emphasized by others. Thus, "what was once extrinsic and instrumental becomes intrinsic and impelling. The activity once served a drive or some simple need; it now serves itself, or in a larger sense, serves the self-image (self-ideal) of the person. Childhood is no longer in the saddle; maturity is" (Allport, 1961, p. 229). This of course sets Allport's work apart from Freud's, since Freud explained adult behaviors in terms of early childhood drives whose basic motivational force endured throughout adulthood.

IDIOGRAPHIC RESEARCH

A final distinguishing feature of Allport's contributions is his emphasis on the uniqueness of the individual. Unlike the other trait theorists we will discuss, Allport primarily endorsed an idiographic approach to research. An idiographic strategy, as we explained in Chapter 2, focuses on the potentially unique individual. In-depth studies of individual persons are viewed as a path for learning about people generally. This approach contrasts with that of other trait theorists, who generally adopt nomothetic procedures in which large numbers of individuals are described in terms of a common, universal set of personality traits.

One illustration of Allport's idiographic procedures was analysis of his use of materials unique to the individual case. For example, Allport published 172 letters from a particular woman. The letters were the basis of a clinical characterization of her personality, as well as for quantitative analysis. This sort of idiographic research highlights the pattern and organization of multiple traits *within* a person rather than a person's standing, relative to others, on isolated trait variables.

COMMENT ON ALLPORT

To most personality psychologists, Allport is a revered figure. A recent biography (Nicholson, 2002) highlights his contributions not only to trait psychology, but to the overall emergence of the psychology of personality as a unique scientific discipline. Nonetheless, Allport's contributions were limited. He clarified the trait concept but did little research to establish the utility of specific trait concepts. He believed that many traits were hereditary, but did no research to substantiate this. He documented that people display unique and consistent patterns of trait-related behavior, but provided no detailed processing model to explain that behavior—in other words, no model of the exact psychological processes that motivate and guide the trait-related actions.

His emphasis of idiographic methods also backfired to some degree. Some felt it was anti-scientific, thinking that the study of individual idiosyncrasies conflicted with a scientific search for general laws. In retrospect, this was a poor reading of Allport's idiographic efforts. To build an adequate science of human beings, it may be utterly necessary to study individual persons in detail. Idiographic strategies may advance, rather than impair, a general understanding of persons. Allport, like Freud, recognized that detailed case studies may yield insight into general principles that are found across individual cases. Scientists in other human sciences recognize this similarly; for example, a famed anthropologist who studies, in detail, the meaning systems of particular cultures concludes that, as a general principle of scientific understanding, "the road to the general, to the revelatory simplicities of science, lies through a concern with the particular, the circumstantial, the concrete" (Geertz, 1973, p. 53).

This idiographic approach, however, is *not* the one pursued by most trait theorists other than Allport. Subsequent trait theorists put little stock in idiographic studies. Instead, contrary to Allport's suggestions, they studied populations of individuals and tried to identify the most important individual differences in the population at large.

Before presenting these theories, we will explain (1) the primary scientific problem faced by the trait theorists discussed in the remainder of this chapter, as well as Chapter 8, and (2) the statistical tool they used to solve it, namely, the statistical technique of factor analysis. We then turn to the trait theories of Raymond B. Cattell and Hans J. Eysenck.

IDENTIFYING PRIMARY TRAIT DIMENSIONS: FACTOR ANALYSIS

With the exception of Allport, trait psychologists generally have tried to identify a universal set of traits, that is, a set of traits that everyone has to a greater or lesser degree. Physically, everyone is more or less tall, heavy or thin, young or old, and so forth; height, weight, and age are universal dimensions that can be used to describe any and all persons. Psychologically, might there be a set of universal trait dimensions that can be used to describe the personality characteristics of any and all persons? If so, how can we identify those traits? Identifying a set of basic, universal traits is a scientific challenge that is fundamental to the history of trait theories of personality.

This challenge is made difficult by the fact that there seem to be so many traits. Some people are absentminded. Some people are agreeable. Some are aggressive. Some altruistic. Some antagonistic. Some argumentative. There are so many traits—and we're still in the *A*s! How can one possibly identify a simple yet comprehensive set of basic traits?

The key insight required to solve this problem is noticing that some traits go together; that is, they tend to co-occur. When talking about physical characteristics, no one is bewildered by the large number of physical features: long left arms, long right arms, long left legs, long right legs, long fingers, and so on. We recognize that these qualities co-occur and summarize their co-occurrence with a simple dimension: height (or size). Height, then, is a more basic physical trait than "length of left leg"; the lengths of individual body parts are just manifestations of the person's overall height.

Psychological traits also co-occur. Consider our list of traits two paragraphs above. More often than not, if one finds someone who is extremely argumentative and extremely aggressive, it is unlikely that he or she will be extremely altruistic and extremely agreeable. Intuition tells us that certain traits co-occur, which suggests that some traits may be manifestations of other more basic traits. The question, then, is: How can one identify the basic traits? Clearly one can't just rely on intuition. What is needed is a precise tool for identifying a basic structure of personality traits.

The tool that trait theorists have relied on is a statistical technique. The technique is called **factor analysis**. Factor analysis is a statistical tool for summarizing the ways in which a large number of variables go together, or co-occur. As you learned in Chapter 2, a correlation is a number that summarizes the degree to which *two* variables go together. If there were only two variables in which trait theorists were interested, then the technique of correlation would be sufficient for their purposes. However, the trait theorist is interested in a *lot* of variables. There seem to be hundreds of possible traits to measure. Once one measures them, there are hundreds and hundreds of correlations between one variable and another. Factor analysis is a statistical method for identifying patterns in this mass of correlations. Ideally, a factor analysis (i.e., a particular application of the general technique of factor analysis) will identify a small number of factors that summarize the intercorrelations among the large number of variables.

In a typical factor-analytic study, a large number of test items are administered to many subjects. Inevitably, some of these items are positively correlated with one another. People who answer a question (e.g., "Do you often go to loud and noisy parties?") in one way answer other questions (e.g., "Do you enjoy spending time with large groups of people?") in a similar manner. Some items are negatively correlated (e.g., responses to "Do you prefer to stay home at night rather than going out?" might be negatively correlated with answers to the two previous questions above). In principle, large clusters of items might be correlated in this manner. These clusters might reflect the influence of an underlying factor, that is, something that is responsible for the correlations among the items (in the way that height is responsible for the correlations among long leg, long arm, etc., in our example above). Factor analysis identifies these patterns, or clusters, or correlations. The technique of factor analysis, then, simplifies the information contained in a large table of correlations by identifying a small set of factors, where each factor represents one cluster of correlations.

The factors technically are merely mathematical. Factor analysis is a technique of mathematical statistics, not psychology. However, using their knowledge of personality, psychologists generally attach psychological labels to the factors. The labels are meant to identify the primary psychological content in the test items that correlate with one another. In our example above (the one with noisy parties, large groups of people, etc.), factor analysis would identify a mathematical factor that represents the correlations among the items, and the psychologist would give that factor a name such as "sociability."

Factor analysis is of the greatest importance to trait theories. It is the tool they use to identify the structures of personality. To most trait theorists, the factors that are identified in factor-analytic studies are the structures of personality. If a factor analysis identifies 6 mathematical factors that summarize correlations among personality test items, then the trait psychologist will usually refer to the resulting 6-dimensional mathematical structure as the "structure of personality."

The use of factor analysis to identify personality structures has some significant advantages as compared to the procedures used by previous theorists. Previously (e.g., in the work of Freud, Jung, or Rogers), theorists relied heavily on their intuition. They observed clinical cases and intuited that certain personality structures were responsible for their clients' behavior. But human intuition can be faulty (Nisbett & Ross, 1980). Rather than relying on intuition to identify personality structures, the trait theorist relies on an objective statistical procedure, factor analysis.

Note that the statistical procedure identifies patterns of covariation in test responses. It does not answer the question of why the responses covary. It is the researcher, using his or her knowledge of psychology and relying on his or her theoretical beliefs, who infers the existence of some common entity (the factor) and interprets it. Different psychologists may make different interpretations. For example, in the contemporary field, some researchers conclude that the core of extraversion is reward sensitivity, that is, that extraverts are highly motivated to attain positive, goal-related rewards (Lucas et al., 2000). Others, using similar correlational and factor-analytic methods, disagree, concluding instead that the core of extraversion is social attention; extraverts appear to enjoy being the object of attention (Ashton, Lee, & Paunonen, 2002).

Also, the exact nature of, and number of, factors one obtains hinges partly on subjective decisions about how exactly to conduct the analysis. Factor analysis is a complex set of techniques, not a simple arithmetic algorithm, and the researcher must choose exactly how to proceed. This is why, as you will now see, different investigators who each rely on factor analytic methods end up with somewhat different factors, and different numbers of factors, in their theories of personality.

Raymond B. Cattell was born in 1905 in Devonshire, England. He obtained a B.Sc. degree in chemistry from the University of London in 1924. Cattell then turned to psychology, obtaining a Ph.D. degree at the same university in 1929. Cattell did personality research and acquired clinical experience in Britain, and then moved to the United States in 1937. He spent much of his career as professor and director of the Laboratory of Personality Assessment at the University of Illinois. During his professional career, he was enormously prolific, publishing more than 200 articles and 15 books. Cattell stands as one of the most influential psychological scientists of the 20th century (Haggbloom et al., 2002).

THE FACTOR-ANALYTIC TRAIT THEORY OF RAYMOND B. CATTELL (1905–1998)

Early in his career, Cattell gained knowledge of the newly-developed (in his time) technique of factor analysis. He quickly exploited its potential. Specifically, with his background in chemistry Cattell recognized the importance to scientific advance of having a taxonomy of "basic elements," such as the periodic table of elements that is foundational to work in the physical sciences. Cattell judged that factor analysis could yield a set of basic psychological elements that would be foundational to personality psychology.

SURFACE AND SOURCE TRAITS: PERSONALITY STRUCTURE IN CATTELL'S THEORY

Cattell provided two conceptual distinctions that are both valuable for distinguishing among the multiplicity of personality traits. One distinction differentiates **surface traits** from **source traits**. Surface and source traits represent different levels of analysis; in this regard, Cattell relied on the idea, discussed above, that there are hierarchical relations among trait concepts. Surface traits represent behavioral tendencies that are literally superficial: They exist "on the surface" and can be observed. By examining patterns of intercorrelations among a large number of personality trait terms, Cattell was able to identify roughly 40 groups of trait terms that were highly intercorrelated. Each grouping, to Cattell, represented a surface trait.

The psychologist of course does not want merely to describe behavior "on the surface." The psychologist wants to identify psychological structures that underlie observable behavior tendencies. To this end, Cattell sought to identify source traits, that is, internal psychological structures that were the

Raymond B. Cattell

source, or underlying cause, of observed intercorrelations among surface traits. Note in this regard that the 40 source traits in Cattell's system are not statistically independent. The occurrence of some surface traits correlates with the occurrence of others. To understand this co-occurrence of traits, Cattell relied on the technique of factor analysis. He developed systematic measures of each of the 40 surface traits, administered these measures of surface traits to large numbers of people, and used factor analysis to identify patterns in the intercorrelations among the surface traits. The factors (i.e., the mathematical dimensions identified via factor analysis) that summarized the correlations among surface traits are, in Cattell's system, the source traits. These source traits that are revealed through factor analysis are the core personality structures in Cattell's theory of personality.

And what exactly are these source traits? Cattell identified 16 source traits. Rather than listing here the 16, we will rely on a handy conceptual tool Cattell himself provided. He grouped the 16 source traits into 3 categories: **ability traits**, **temperament traits**, and **dynamic traits**. Ability traits refer to skills and abilities that allow the individual to function effectively. Intelligence is an example of an ability trait. Temperament traits involve emotional life and the stylistic quality of behavior. The tendency to work quickly versus slowly, to be calm versus emotional, or to act impulsively or only after deliberation are all qualities of temperament. Finally, dynamic traits concern the striving, motivational life of the individual. Individuals who are more or less motivated differ in dynamic traits. Ability, temperament, and dynamic traits are seen as capturing the major stable elements of personality.

SOURCES OF EVIDENCE: L-DATA, Q-DATA, AND OT-DATA

How did Cattell identify these traits? What exactly was his scientific database? A great virtue of Cattell's work is that there was no *one* database. Cattell relied on three different types—or three different sources—of data about personality. His distinctions among three different types of data are enduringly valuable to personality science.

Cattell's distinctions, presented here, should seem familiar; they are a basis of the LOTS classification of data sources we presented in Chapter 2. Cattell distinguished among (1) life record data (**L-data**), (2) self-report questionnaire data (**Q-data**), and (3) objective-test data (**OT-data**).

The first, L-data, relates to behavior in actual, everyday situations such as school performance or interactions with peers. These may be actual counts of behaviors or ratings made on the basis of such observations. The second, Q-data, involves self-report data or responses to questionnaires, such as the Eysenck personality inventory discussed later in the chapter. The third, OT-data, involves behavioral miniature situations in which the subject is unaware of the relationship between the response and the personality characteristic being measured. Cattell himself developed a large number of these mini-situations; for example, a tendency to be assertive could be expressed in behaviors such as long exploratory distance on a finger maze test, fast tempo in arm-shoulder movement, and fast speed of letter comparisons. Ideally, the same factors or traits should be obtained from the three kinds of data.

Originally, Cattell began with the factor analyses of L-data and found 15 factors that appeared to account for most of an individual's personality. He

Table 7.2 Cattell's 16 Personality Factors Derived from Questionnaire Data

Reserved	Outgoing
Less intelligent	More intelligent
Stable, ego strength	Emotionality/neuroticism
Humble	Assertive
Sober	Happy-go-lucky
Expedient	Conscientious
Shy	Venturesome
Tough-minded	Tender-minded
Trusting	Suspicious
Practical	Imaginative
Forthright	Shrewd
Placid	Apprehensive
Conservative	Experimenting
Group-dependent	Self-sufficient
Undisciplined	Controlled
Relaxed	Tense

then set out to determine whether comparable factors could be found in Q-data. Thousands of questionnaire items were written and administered to large numbers of people. Factor analyses were run to see which items went together. The main result of this research is a questionnaire known as the Sixteen Personality Factor (16 P.F.) Questionnaire. Initially, Cattell made up neologisms, such as "surgency," to name his personality trait factors, hoping to avoid misinterpretations of them. Nonetheless, the terms given in Table 7.2 roughly capture the meanings of these trait factors. As can be seen, they cover a wide variety of aspects of personality, particularly in terms of temperament (e.g., emotionality) and attitudes (e.g., conservative). In general, the factors found with Q-data appeared to be similar to those found with L-data, but some were unique to each kind of data. Illustrative L-data ratings and Q-data items for one trait are presented in Figure 7.2.

Cattell was committed to the use of questionnaires, in particular, those derived from a factor-analytical perspective, such as the 16 P.F Questionnaire. On the other hand, he also expressed concern about the problems of motivated distortion and self-deception in relation to questionnaire responses. He also felt that the questionnaire is of particularly questionable utility with mental patients. Because of problems with L-data and Q-data, and because the original research strategy itself called for investigations with OT-data, Cattell's later efforts were concerned more with personality structure as derived from OT-data. It is the source traits as expressed in objective tests that are the "real coin" for personality research.

The results from L-data and Q-data research were important in guiding the development of miniature test situations; that is, the purpose was to develop objective tests that would measure the source traits already discovered. Thus, more than 500 tests were constructed to cover the hypothesized personality dimensions. These tests were administered to large groups of subjects, and repeated factoring of data from different research situations eventually led to the designation of 21 OT-data source traits.

As mentioned before, the source traits or factors found in L-data and Q-data could, for the most part, be matched to one another. How, then, do the

SOURCE TRAIT EGO STRENGTH VS. EMOTIONALITY/NEUROTICISM (L-DATA AND Q-DATA)

Behavior Ratings by Observer

Ego Strength		Emotionality/Neuroticism
Mature	vs.	Unable to tolerate frustration
Steady, persistent	vs.	Changeable
Emotionally calm	vs.	Impulsively emotional
Realistic about problems	vs.	Evasive, avoids necessary decisions
Absence of neurotic fatigue	vs.	Neurotically fatigued (with no real effort)

Questionnaire Responses*

Do you find it difficult to take no for an answer even when what you want to do is obviously impossible?
   (a) yes   (b) *no*

If you had your life to live over again, would you:
   (a) *want it to be essentially*   (b) plan it very differently?
the same?

Do you often have really disturbing dreams?
   (a) yes   (b) *no*

Do your moods sometimes make you seem unreasonable even to yourself?
   (a) yes   (b) *no*

Do you feel tired when you've done nothing to justify it?
   (a) *rarely*   (b) often

Can you change old habits, without relapse, when you decide to?
   (a) *yes*   (b) no

*Answer in italic type indicates high ego strength.

Figure 7.2 *Correspondence Between Data from Two Different Test Domains: L-data Ratings and Q-data Responses. (Cattell, 1965.)*

OT-data factors match those derived from L-data and Q-data? Despite the years of research effort, the results were disappointing: although some relations were found across all three data sources, no direct one-to-one mapping of factors was possible.

In summary, we have described four steps in Cattell's research. (1) He set out to define the structure of personality in three areas of observation, called L-data, Q-data, and OT-data. (2) He started his research with L-data and through the factor analysis of ratings came up with 15 source traits. (3) Based on research findings, he developed the 16 P.F. Questionnaire, which contains 12 traits that match traits found in the L-data research and four traits that appear to be unique to questionnaire methods. (4) Using these results to guide his research in the development of objective tests, Cattell found 21 source traits in OT-data that appear to have a complex and low-level relation to the traits found in the other data.

The source traits found in the three types of observations do not complete Cattell's formulation of the structure of personality. However, the traits presented in this section do describe the general nature of the structure of personality as formulated by Cattell. In other words, here we have the foundation for psychology's table of the elements—its classification scheme. But what is the evidence for the existence of these traits? Cattell (1979) cited the following: (1) the results of factor analyses of different kinds of data, (2) similar results across cultures, (3) similar results across age groups, (4) utility in the prediction of behavior in the natural environment, and (5) evidence of significant genetic contributions to many traits.

STABILITY AND VARIABILITY IN BEHAVIOR

Cattell did not view persons as static entities who behaved the same way in all situations. Social action depends not only on traits, but other factors as well. Cattell highlighted two other determinants: states and roles. **State** refers to emotion and mood at a particular, delimited point in time. One's psychological state is partly determined by the immediate situation one is in. Illustrative states are anxiety, depression, fatigue, arousal, and curiosity. To Cattell, the exact description of an individual at a given moment requires measurement of both traits and states: "Every practicing psychologist—indeed every intelligent observer of human nature and human history—realizes that the state of a person at a given moment determines his or her behavior as much as do his or her traits" (1979, p. 169).

Regarding the concept of **role**, Cattell noted that certain behaviors are more closely linked to social roles one must play than to personality traits one possesses. Social roles, not personality traits, explain why people shout at football games and not in churches (Cattell, 1979). Two people may act differently toward one another in different settings in which they play different roles. For example, a teacher may respond differently to a child's behavior in the classroom than when outside the classroom and no longer in the role of teacher.

In sum, although Cattell believed that traits foster stability in behavior across situations, he also recognized that a person's mood (state) and how they present themselves in a given situation (role) contribute to behavior: "How vigorously Smith attacks his meal depends not only on how hungry he happens to be, but also on his temperament and whether he is having dinner with his employer or is eating alone at home" (Nesselroade & Delhees, 1966, p. 583).

COMMENT ON CATTELL

One cannot help but be impressed with the scope of Cattell's efforts. His theorizing addressed all major aspects of personality theory, and his systematic research efforts laid a foundation for generations of trait-based researchers. One observer concluded that "Cattell's theory turns out to be a much more impressive achievement than has been generally recognized. ... Cattell's original blueprint for personality study has resulted in an extraordinarily rich theoretical structure" (Wiggins, 1984, pp. 177, 190). His primary personality assessment device, the 16 P.F Questionnaire continues to be used widely in applied settings that require the assessment of individual differences.

Despite this, if Cattell were here today he would be disappointed with the relative lack of impact his work exerts in contemporary personality science. This lack of impact may result, in part, from issues that are practical as much as they are scientific. Cattell provided a theoretical system with a lot of personality

"THE RIGHT STUFF": CHARACTERISTICS OF SUCCESSFUL BUSINESS EXECUTIVES

Some time ago Tom Wolfe wrote a book about the first U.S. team of astronauts. An all-male group, these were men who felt that they had the "right stuff"—the manly courage it took to make it as a test pilot and astronaut. Others had the necessary skill, but if they didn't have the right stuff they just didn't make it.

Most demanding occupations have their own kind of right stuff—the personality characteristics or traits that, in addition to skill, make for success. For example, what makes for a top business executive? According to some recent research, the difference between senior executives who make it to chief executive officer and those who

do not often is subtle. Members of both groups show considerable talent and have remarkable strengths, as well as a few significant weaknesses. Although no one trait discriminates between the two groups, those who fall short of their ultimate goal frequently are found to have the following characteristics: they are insensitive to others, untrustworthy, cold—aloof—arrogant, overly ambitious, moody, volatile under pressure, and defensive. In contrast, those who make it to the top are most characterized by the traits of integrity and understanding others.

Actually, there is a long history of efforts to define the abilities and personal qualities

Meg Whitman, President and CEO, eBay

of leaders. At one point, researchers began to give up on the hope of finding general leadership qualities. Leadership was seen as entirely situational in origin, with different skills and personal qualities being required in different situations. However, a recent review of the literature suggests that sounding the death knell of a trait approach to leadership probably was premature. Certain general qualities such as courage, fortitude, and conviction do stand out. In addition, the following traits seem to be generally characteristic of leaders: energetic, decisive, adaptive, assertive, sociable, achieving, and tolerant of stress.

Trait researchers, particularly those in industrial psychology, continue to try to define those personality characteristics that are essential for success in various fields. Thus, a variety of personality tests, including the 16 P.F., are used in many important aspects of personnel selection.

Source: *Psychology Today*, February 1983; Holland, 1985.

factors, 16. In practice, it is difficult for the basic or the applied psychologist to keep in mind this large number of factors when assessing the personality of individuals. Cattell would argue that this range of factors is necessary. Yet, in comparison to other theories, the approach is not parsimonious. As you will see in the remainder of this chapter and the next, other theorists tried to establish a simpler structure of personality traits.

There may be deeper problems behind this practical concern. Cattell was fundamentally interested in the problem of measurement. In most respects, that is a very good thing; inadequate measurement impairs a scientific program. However, in Cattell's work the measurement process was used not only for the purpose of measurement. It was used for a second purpose: theorizing. In other words, the basic structure of Cattell's theory (the number of, and content of, the source traits) was determined entirely by the results of the measurement process (factor analyses of measures of the surface traits). Basing theory on measurement is a risky strategy. The risk is that there may exist important qualities that one *should* be studying in a comprehensive theory, but that are not detected by one's measurement system. If this happens, the theory lacks coverage of the important topic. As one example, consider the fact that most people have a "life story" (McAdams, 2006). If you ask someone to tell you about themselves, they are likely to provide a narrative, or autobiographical story about themselves. It is not at all clear that the content of such stories can be captured by a numerical measurement of the sort employed by Cattell. If, in a literature class, you are asked to analyze the meaning of a story, we would *not* suggest that you do so by employing the statistical technique of factor analysis! To the extent that individuals possess psychological attributes, such as a life story, that are not reducible to a set of numbers, these attributes are overlooked by Cattell's measurement system and, thus, his theory. If Carl Rogers were here today, he surely would think that this was an enormous limitation for a personality theory.

THE THREE-FACTOR THEORY OF HANS J. EYSENCK (1916–1997)

In our concluding comments on Cattell, we noted that his 16-factor theory had a practical drawback: It is cumbersome in practical applications to track a large number of factors, 16. There may be a parallel scientific drawback. Sixteen factors may be too many on sheer scientific grounds. It might be that, hidden behind the 16 factors, there is a simpler and even more basic structure of personality traits. If one could identify this simpler trait structure, it might serve as the basis of a scientific model that is parsimonious, and also of applications that are simple and practical. This possibility was pursued with unique creativity and energy by one of the giants of 20th-century psychology, Hans Eysenck.

Hans J. Eysenck was born in Germany in 1916 and later fled to England to escape Nazi persecution. Like Cattell, his work was influenced by advances in statistical techniques, especially factor analysis. He also was influenced intellectually by the work of European psychologists who studied personality types (especially Jung and Kretschmer), by research on the heredity of psychological characteristics, and by the experimental work on classical conditioning by the Russian physiologist Pavlov (see Chapter 10).

Eysenck led a life characterized by enormous energy and productivity. His work included a broad sampling of both normal and pathological populations. He was an exceptionally prolific writer. In the scientific literature, he is one of the most influential and cited research psychologists of the 20th century (Haggbloom et al., 2002). In the 1980s, he founded and edited the journal *Personality and Individual Differences*, an international journal devoted primarily to research on personality traits, temperament, and the biological foundations of personality—all issues Eysenck cared deeply about. Eysenck died in 1997, after seeing through the re-publication of three of his early books and shortly after finishing his last book, *Intelligence: A New Look* (Eysenck, 1998).

Eysenck's role in the field was both constructive and critical. In addition to constructing a trait theory, he criticized other theories that he found flawed, particularly psychoanalysis. Eysenck, like Cattell, believed that the psychoanalysts' failure to provide precise, reliable measures of their psychological constructs was a serious shortcoming. In constructing a trait theory, Eysenck sought to avoid this problem through the use of reliable measures

Hans J. Eysenck

of individual differences. He felt that such measures also were necessary to identify the presumed biological foundations of each trait.

Eysenck's emphasis on biological foundations of personality traits is particularly noteworthy. He recognized that, without understanding the biology of traits, trait explanations could be circular—where circular explanations are those that go around in a conceptual circle, with a trait concept being used to explain the very behavior that served as the basis for inferring the existence of the trait in the first place. For example, think of a friend of yours who frequently talks in a friendly and outgoing manner to other people. How would you describe her behavior? You might say that she is "sociable." Now consider another question: How would you *explain* her behavior? You might say that she is acting sociable because she has the trait of sociability. But if you said this, you wouldn't be providing a very good explanation; indeed, your explanation would violate basic principles of scientific explanation (e.g., Nozick, 1981). The problem is that the only reason you know that your friend has the trait of sociability is because you saw her act in a sociable manner. Your explanation thus goes around in logical circles: it uses a word ("sociable") to describe a pattern of behavior, and then uses that same word to explain the existence of the pattern of behavior that was described. Eysenck recognized that trait theory can break out of such conceptual circles by going beyond the mere use of words and identifying biological systems that correspond to trait. We consider his degree of success in identifying such systems below.

"SUPERFACTORS": PERSONALITY STRUCTURE IN EYSENCK'S THEORY

To construct a personality theory Eysenck conducted factor analyses of participants' responses, as did Cattell. But he also took another step, specifically, a secondary application of the factor-analytic method. He conducted secondary factor analyses. A secondary factor analysis is a statistical analysis of an initial set of factors that are correlated with one another. In other words, when analyzing a broad spectrum of personality traits, an initial factor analysis might indicate the existence of a moderately large number of factors. In Cattell's case, in analyses of self-report data this number was 16. However, these factors are not statistically independent. When one obtains this number of factors, different factors are commonly correlated; people who obtain low (high) scores on one factor tend to obtain low (high) scores on another. (A glance back at Table 7.2 would suggest, on intuitive grounds, that this is true for some of Cattell's factors, such as "reserved" and "shy.") Since the factors are correlated, and factor analysis is a tool for identifying patterns in a set of correlations, the intercorrelations among the factors could be factor analyzed. This is what is called a secondary factor analysis.

This, then, is what Eysenck did. He used secondary factor analysis to identify a simple set of factors that were independent, that is, not correlated with each other. These secondary factors of course also are traits: They are consistent styles of emotion or behavior that distinguish people from one another, and the superfactors are continuous dimensions, with a high and a low end and with most people falling in the middle. But they are factor-analytic trait dimensions at the highest level of a hierarchy of traits, and thus Eysenck called them **superfactors** ("super" in the sense of "high").

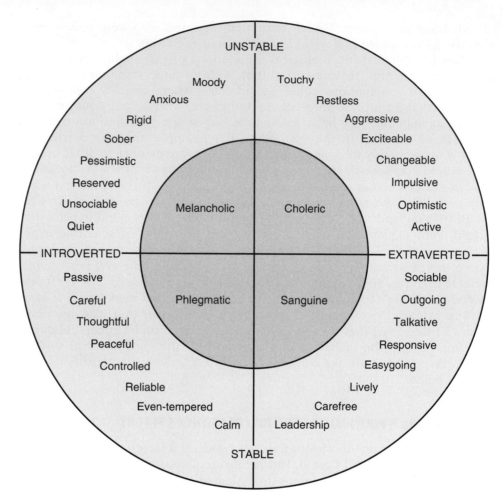

Figure 7.3 *The Relationship of Two Dimensions of Personality Derived from Factor Analysis to Four Greek Temperamental Types. (Eysenck, 1970). Reprinted by permission, Routledge & Kegan Paul Ltd., publishers.*

Eysenck at first identified two such superfactors, which he labeled (1) **introversion-extraversion** and (2) **neuroticism** (alternatively called emotional stability versus instability). Figure 7.3 shows how the superfactor serves as a high-level organizational scheme for lower-level traits. The superordinate concept of extraversion organizes lower-level traits such as sociability, activity, liveliness, and excitability. Neuroticism organizes traits such as anxious, depressed, shy, and moody (Figure 7.4). Figure 7.3 shows Eysenck's representation of the traits as two perpendicular lines that together define a psychological space of personality traits; it is the statistical fact that the traits are uncorrelated that allows Eysenck to represent them as two separate, independent, orthogonal (at a right angle) dimensions. In principle, any individual can be located within this two-dimensional space; in the Eysenck theoretical system, everyone has a greater or lesser amount of extraversion and neuroticism. Using a language we introduced earlier, this is a *nomothetic* system of personality traits.

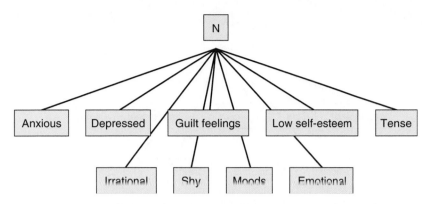

Figure 7.4   *The Hierarchical Structure of Neuroticism (N). (Eysenck, 1990). Reprinted by permission, Guilford Press.*

An interesting feature of Eysenck's system (also represented in Figure 7.3) is that it captures individual differences identified in ancient times. The Greek physicians Hippocrates (around 400 B.C.) and Galen (around 200 A.D.) proposed the existence of four basic personality types: melancholic, phlegmatic, choleric, and sanguine. Ancient Greek theorizing about the causes of personality types have since been repudiated. However, as Eysenck recognized, ancient scholars did validly identify important variations among people. People who the Greeks saw as being of a particular personality type (e.g., choleric) actually had a high amount of two associated personality traits (in the case of the choleric type, extraversion and emotional instability; see Figure 7.3). The fact that these variations in personality were evident in both the ancient world and contemporary society suggests that they might be fundamental features of human nature with a biological basis that transcends time and place.

Eysenck's initial work, then, identified two dimensions of normal variation in personality, that is, variations readily apparent in the personality qualities of people we know in our everyday life. We all recognize that our friends and family vary in the degree to which they are calm versus anxious, shy versus sociable, and Eysenck's model organizes these intuitions scientifically. After establishing these two dimensions, however, Eysenck added a third dimension. It organizes personality traits that, in the extreme, we might label as "abnormal": aggressiveness, a lack of empathy, interpersonal coldness, antisocial behavioral tendencies. This superfactor is called **psychoticism**. The hierarchical organization of characteristics associated with it appear in Figure 7.5. These resulting three factors, psychoticism, extraversion, and neuroticism, comprise Eysenck's complete model of personality structure. The factors are so well known in personality psychology that they commonly are referenced merely by their first letters: P, E, and N.

Measuring the Factors

With this model in hand, one then needs an assessment device to measure individual differences in P, E, and N. Eysenck provided this, too. He developed questionnaire measures (e.g., the Eysenck Personality Questionnaire) that contained simple self-report items designed to tap each of the factors (Figure 7.6). The typical extravert will answer "yes" to questions such as: Do

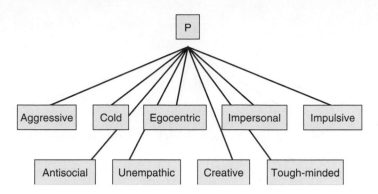

Figure 7.5   *The Hierarchical Structure of Psychoticism (P).*
(Eysenck, 1990). Reprinted by permission, Guilford Press.

other people think of you as very lively? Would you be unhappy if you could not see lots of people most of the time? Do you often long for excitement? The typical introvert will answer yes questions such as: Generally, do you prefer reading to meeting people? Are you mostly quiet when you are with people? Do you stop and think things over before doing anything? Note that Eysenck also included "lie scale" items to detect individuals who are faking responses in order to look good (Figure 7.6).

An important feature of Eysenck's work is that, like Cattell, he developed objective measures of traits, that is, measures that did not rely on subjective ratings in questionnaires. One such test, designed to differentiate extraverts from introverts, is Eysenck's "lemon drop test." A standard amount of lemon juice is placed on the subject's tongue. Introverts and extraverts (as identified by questionnaires) differ in the amount of saliva produced when this is done.

	Yes	No
1. Do you usually take the initiative in making new friends?	____	____
2. Do ideas run through your head so that you cannot sleep?	____	____
3. Are you inclined to keep in the background on social occasions?	____	____
4. Do you sometimes laugh at a dirty joke?	____	____
5. Are you inclined to be moody?	____	____
6. Do you very much like good food?	____	____
7. When you get annoyed, do you need someone friendly to talk about it?	____	____
8. As a child did you always do as you were told immediately and without grumbling?	____	____
9. Do you usually keep "yourself to yourself" except with very close friends?	____	____
10. Do you often make up your mind too late?	____	____

Note: The above items would be scored in the following way:
    Extraversion: 1 Yes, 3 No, 6 Yes, 9 No; *Neuroticism:* 2 Yes, 5 Yes, 7 Yes, 10 Yes; *Lie Scale:* 4 No, 8 Yes.

Figure 7.6   *Illustrative Items for Extraversion, Neuroticism, and Lie Scale from the Maudsley Personality Inventory and Eysenck Personality Inventory.*

Why might this be (we hope you are asking yourself)? The idea is that there may be a biological basis to the individual differences.

BIOLOGICAL BASES OF PERSONALITY TRAITS

Eysenck provided specific scientific models of the biological bases of individual differences. Note that, if you are Eysenck, you do need models (plural), not just one model. The traits (P, E, N) are statistically independent. One therefore needs a separate biological model for each of the three traits. The trait for which Eysenck's theorizing about underlying biology has proven most successful is extraversion.

Eysenck suggested that individual variations in introversion-extraversion reflect individual differences in the neurophysiological functioning of the brain's cortex. The idea is that introverts are more arousable; they experience more cortical arousal from events in the world. As a result, highly intense social stimuli (e.g., a loud party) make them *over*aroused—an aversive state that they avoid. The social behavior of introverts, then, is more inhibited because of the relatively greater arousal they experience. Conversely, extraverts experience less cortical arousal than introverts from a given stimulus and therefore seek out more intense social experiences. Research that directly measures the brain activity of introverts and extraverts provides some support for Eysenck's theorizing (Geen, 1997), as we review in Chapter 9, a chapter devoted to biological bases of personality. Eysenck himself generated much relevant evidence on the biology of this dimension, including evidence that introverts are more influenced by punishments in learning, whereas extraverts are more influenced by rewards.

Since the trait has a biological basis, individual differences in introversion-extraversion should be at least partly hereditary. (Note that the biological basis does not imply that a trait would be entirely hereditary, since one's experiences during child development influence one's biological makeup.) Studies of identical and fraternal twins commonly suggest that heredity does, in fact, play a major part in accounting for differences between individuals in E scores (Loehlin, 1992; Plomin, 1994; Plomin & Caspi, 1999). The following are other facts consistent with Eysenck's biological theorizing: the fact that the dimension of introversion-extraversion is found cross-culturally, that individual differences are stable over time, and that various indices of biological functioning (e.g., brain activity, heart rate, hormone level, sweat gland activity) correlate with E scores (Eysenck, 1990).

Regarding neuroticism, Eysenck hypothesized that the relevant biological system is not the brain's cortex (as in extraversion) but the autonomic nervous system. Individuals high on neuroticism may possess an autonomic nervous system that responds particularly quickly to stress and is slow to decrease this activity once danger disappears. The neurotic person thus seems "jumpy" and "stressed out." Unfortunately for Eysenckian theory, research has not consistently supported this physiological theory of neuroticism, as Eysenck himself fully recognized (Eysenck, 1990). Less is known about the biological basis for the psychoticism (P) dimension. However, here a genetic association is suggested, in particular an association linked with maleness; aggressiveness, a component of (P), is higher in men and may be affected by levels of testosterone (Eysenck, 1990).

EXTRAVERSION AND SOCIAL BEHAVIOR

Do people who differ in extraversion-introversion scores also differ in their everyday social behavior? A mountain of evidence speaks to this question; extraversion is probably the most extensively studied of all traits, in part because relevant behaviors are relatively easy to observe (Gosling et al., 1998). A review of the dimension presents an impressive array of findings (Watson & Clark, 1997). For example, introverts are more sensitive to pain than extraverts, they become fatigued more easily than extraverts, excitement interferes with their performance whereas it enhances performance for extraverts, and they tend to be more careful but slower than extraverts. The following additional differences have been found:

1. Introverts do better in school than extraverts, particularly in more advanced subjects. Also, students withdrawing from college for academic reasons tend to be extraverts, whereas those who withdraw for psychiatric reasons tend to be introverts.

2. Extraverts prefer vocations involving interactions with other people, whereas introverts tend to prefer more solitary vocations. Extraverts seek diversion from job routine, whereas introverts have less need for novelty.

3. Extraverts enjoy explicit sexual and aggressive humor, whereas introverts prefer more intellectual forms of humor such as puns and subtle jokes.

4. Extraverts are more active sexually, in terms of frequency and different partners, than introverts.

5. Extraverts are more suggestible than introverts.

This last finding is illustrated in a study of a hyperventilating epidemic in England (Moss & McEvedy, 1966). An initial report by some girls of fainting and dizziness was followed by an outbreak of similar complaints, with 85 girls needing to be taken to the hospital by ambulance—"they were going down like ninepins." A comparison of the girls who were affected with those who were not demonstrated that, as expected, the affected girls were higher in both neuroticism and extraversion. In other words, those individuals whose personalities were most predisposed to suggestion proved most susceptible to influence by suggestions of a real epidemic.

Finally, the results of an investigation of study habits among introverts and extraverts may be of particular interest to college students. The research examined whether such personality differences are associated with differing preferences for where to study and how to study, as would be predicted by Eysenck's theory. In accord with Eysenck's theory of individual differences, the following was found: (1) extraverts more often chose to study in library locations that provided external stimulation than did introverts, (2) extraverts took more study breaks than did introverts, (3) extraverts reported a preference for a higher level of noise and for more socializing opportunities while studying than did introverts (Campbell & Hawley, 1982). Extraverts and introverts differ in their physiological responses to the same noise level (introverts show a greater level of response), and each functions best at his or her preferred noise level (Geen, 1984). An important implication of such research is that different environmental designs for libraries and residence units might best fit the needs of introverts and extraverts.

PSYCHOPATHOLOGY AND BEHAVIOR CHANGE

Eysenck also developed a theory of abnormal psychology and behavior change. A core idea is that the type of symptoms or psychological difficulties a person experiences relate to basic personality traits and the nervous system functioning associated with the traits. A person develops neurotic symptoms because of the joint action of a biological system and environmental experiences that contribute to the learning of strong emotional reactions to fear-producing stimuli. Consistent with this suggestion of Eysenck's, the vast majority of neurotic patients tend to have high neuroticism and low extraversion scores (Eysenck, 1982, p. 25). In contrast, criminals and antisocial persons tend to have high neuroticism, high extraversion, and high psychoticism scores. Such individuals show weak learning of societal norms.

Despite the genetic component to personality traits and disorders, Eysenck was optimistic about treatment: "The fact that genetic factors play a large part in the initiation and maintenance of neurotic disorders and also of criminal activities, is very unwelcome to many people who believe that such a state of affairs must lead to therapeutic nihilism. If heredity is so important, they say, then clearly behavior modification of any kind must be impossible. This is a completely erroneous interpretation of the facts. What is genetically determined are predispositions for a person to act and behave in a certain manner, when put in certain situations" (1982, p. 29). It is possible for a person to avoid certain potentially traumatic situations, to unlearn fear responses, to learn appropriate social conduct, and thus to achieve a personality style that varies from his or her original predispositions. Eysenck thus was a major proponent of behavior therapy, which is the systematic applications of principles of learning and behavior change to therapy (see Chapter 10).

COMMENT ON EYSENCK

In many ways, Eysenck's contributions to personality science are exemplary. He upheld the highest standards of science while theorizing in a creative manner. He brought diverse forms of evidence to bear on questions of individual differences. His prolific writings delivered his messages about personality not only to fellow scientists, but to a wider intellectual public. If personality psychology had experienced 10 Eysencks instead of one, it would today be a much stronger field.

Historically, Eysenck was always prepared to swim against the tide. "I have usually been against the establishment and in favor of the rebels. Readers who wish to interpret this in terms of some inherited oppositional tendency, some acquired Freudian hatred of father substitutes, or in any other way are of course welcome" (1982, p. 298). Of course, this is Eysenck's own view of his own work. Many contemporary scholars would contend that the Eysenckian strategy of describing individual persons in terms of scores on a small number of universal personality dimensions is itself an establishment procedure against which the humanist might rebel.

One might ask why Eysenck has not been even more influential (see Buss, 1982; Loehlin, 1982). Many psychologists have moved away from Eysenck's views. (1) At least four factors have contributed to this. Alternative two- and three-dimensional models have been proposed that better fit the available data; for example, individual differences on the dimensions of impulsivity and anxiety, rather than E and N, often appear superior for describing biologically-based individual differences (Gray, 1990). (2) As Eysenck (1990) recognized, his theories of the biological bases of personality traits—particularly of neuroticism and psychoticism—lack consistent support. (3) On a point that involves the practice of science as a social activity, Eysenck's decision to found a new journal (see above) may partly have backfired. When a scientist starts a scientific journal, devotees of the scientist's position read it carefully, but others may not. Publications thus become isolated from the field's mainstream. The existence of a journal devoted strongly to research in the Eysenckian tradition may have contributed to isolating this tradition from the rest of psychology, thus lowering its impact outside of the United Kingdom, Eysenck's scientific home base. (4) Maybe more than two or three factors are needed to describe personality. It is not hard to think of personality characteristics—e.g., honesty, reliability, creativity—that cannot easily be fit into the Eysenckian system. Maybe trait theorists don't need as many as 16 basic traits. Yet they might need more than 2 or 3. This simple point is the foundation for the scientific investigations that we review in our next chapter.

MAJOR CONCEPTS

Ability, temperament, and dynamic traits   In Cattell's trait theory, these categories of traits capture the major aspects of personality.

Cardinal trait   Allport's concept for a disposition that is so pervasive and outstanding in a person's life that virtually every act is traceable to its influence.

Central trait   Allport's concept for a disposition to behave in a particular way in a range of situations.

Extraversion   In Eysenck's theory, one end of the introversion-extraversion dimension of personality characterized by a disposition to be sociable, friendly, impulsive, and risk taking.

Factor analysis   A statistical method for analyzing correlations among a set of personality tests or test items in order to determine those variables or test responses that increase or decrease together. Used in the development of personality tests and of some trait theories (e.g., Cattell, Eysenck).

Functional autonomy   Allport's concept that a motive may become independent of its origins; in particular, motives in adults may become independent of their earlier base in tension reduction.

Introversion   In Eysenck's theory, one end of the introversion-extraversion dimension of personality characterized by a disposition to be quiet, reserved, reflective, and risk avoiding.

L-data   In Cattell's theory, life-record data relating to behavior in everyday life situations or to ratings of such behavior.

Neuroticism   In Eysenck's theory, a dimension of personality defined by stability and low anxiety at one end and by instability and high anxiety at the other end.

OT-data   In Cattell's theory, objective test data or information about personality obtained from observing behavior in miniature situations.

Psychoticism   In Eysenck's theory, a dimension of personality defined by a tendency to be solitary and insensitive at one end and to accept social custom and care about others at the other end.

Q-data   In Cattell's theory, personality data obtained from questionnaires.

Role   Behavior considered to be appropriate for a person's place or status in society. Emphasized by Cattell as one of a number of variables that limit the influence of personality variables on behavior relative to situational variables.

Secondary disposition   Allport's concept for a disposition to behave in a particular way that is relevant to few situations.

Source trait   In Cattell's theory, behaviors that vary together to form an independent dimension of personality, which is discovered through the use of factor analysis.

———

State   Emotional and mood changes (e.g., anxiety, depression, fatigue) that Cattell suggested may influence the behavior of a person at a given time. The assessment of both traits and states is suggested to predict behavior.

Superfactor   A higher-order or secondary factor representing a higher level of organization of traits than the initial factors derived from factor analysis.

Surface trait   In Cattell's theory, behaviors that appear to be linked to one another but do not in fact increase and decrease together.

Trait   A disposition to behave in a particular way, as expressed in a person's behavior over a range of situations.

REVIEW

1. The trait concept represents people's broad dispositions to display a certain type of behavior or to have certain types of emotional experiences. Allport, one of the first trait theorists, differentiated among cardinal traits, central traits, and specific dispositions. He also suggested that some traits could only be identified through idiographic research strategies, that is, research strategies that are sensitive to potentially idiosyncratic qualities of particular individuals.

2. Many trait theorists use the statistical technique of factor analysis to develop a classification of traits. Through this technique a group of items or responses (factors) are formed, the items in one group (factor) being closely related to one another and distinct from those in another group (factor).

3. According to Eysenck the basic dimensions of personality are introversion-extraversion, neuroticism, and psychoticism. Questionnaires have been developed to assess people along these trait dimensions. Research has focused particularly on the introversion-extraversion trait dimension, where differences in activity level and activity preferences have been found. Eysenck suggests that individual differences in traits have a biological and genetic (inherited) basis.

4. Cattell distinguished among ability, temperament, and dynamic traits, as well as between surface and source traits.

TRAIT THEORY: THE FIVE-FACTOR MODEL; APPLICATIONS AND EVALUATION OF TRAIT APPROACHES TO PERSONALITY

8

Chapter Focus

You are applying to graduate school and Allport, Eysenck, and Cattell are writing you letters of recommendation. What would their three letters look like? Certainly they would differ. Eysenck would discuss your behavior and accomplishments in terms of his three broad superfactors, Cattell would consider twenty-some more specific traits, and Allport might weave a richly detailed idiographic portrayal, including many entirely unique trait configurations. While there might be some common themes in the letters, none of the theorists would ever give up his preferred theoretical position. That leads us to the question: How can we ever reach agreement about the basic traits if we cannot break this stalemate?

Suppose we proceed as follows. We ask a thousand people to write personality descriptions of a thousand others. Then we collect together all the trait-descriptive adjectives used in these descriptions. The result would be a list of personality descriptors that is not biased by any theoretical preconceptions. Certainly, with a thousand words, there would be considerable redundancy (e.g., perfect and flawless mean pretty much the same thing), permitting us to reduce the size of the list. If we then factor-analyze personality ratings on these traits, we should end up with the major dimensions of personality trait descriptions. The result may be a compromise that does not please everybody but at least it is arrived at through a fair set of procedures, and its practicality and usefulness will determine whether it is generally accepted in the field.

In this chapter we continue our discussion of trait theory and consider the efforts of trait researchers to reach a consensus using the procedures outlined above. We focus on the emerging consensus on the importance of five basic trait dimensions, and consider the evidence supporting this five-factor model as well as its application to the individual. The chapter concludes with an overall evaluation of the trait approach to personality.

QUESTIONS TO BE ADDRESSED IN THIS CHAPTER

1. Is it possible for trait researchers to reach a consensus on one model of the organization of personality traits?
2. How many and which trait dimensions are necessary for a basic description of personality?
3. Can a trait model derived from factor analysis be connected to the personality terms we use in everyday language? Would we expect such a model to be universal across cultures? Would we expect it to make sense in terms of our evolutionary heritage?
4. What are the implications of individual differences in traits for career choice, physical health, and psychological well-being?
5. How stable or variable are traits over time and across situations? That is, how much does one's personality change over time and from situation to situation?

268

In any area of study, one needs taxonomies. There must be an accepted way of classifying the objects of study. Is it a plant or an animal? An organic or an inorganic compound? A planned or a free market economy? An impressionist or an expressionist painting? Classification schemes—i.e., taxonomies—guide investigation and enable scholars to communicate findings to one another.

Personality psychology is no exception. The field can benefit from an agreed-upon taxonomy of individual differences in personality dispositions, or traits. With a trait taxonomy in hand, the researcher can study specified domains of traits, rather than examining separately the thousands of particular traits that make human beings individual and unique. Organizing the multiplicity of personality traits into a simple coherent taxonomy has been a major activity in personality psychology during the last quarter century. This chapter reviews the primary fruit of this effort: the five-factor model. Many researchers believe that individual differences can be usefully organized in terms of five broad, bipolar dimensions (John & Srivastava, 1999; McCrae & Costa, 2003), dimensions widely known in the professional field as the **Big Five**.

The five-factor model relates directly to ideas you learned about in Chapter 7. It is a trait approach, just like all the theories presented in the previous chapter. It is a *factor-analytic* trait approach, just like the theories of Eysenck and Cattell. (Its view of the person and view of personality science thus is the same as that presented at the beginning of Chapter 7.) So what's new about five-factor theory? In one word: evidence. A huge body of research evidence indicates that five factors—more than Eysenck's 3, less than Cattell's 16—are necessary and reasonably sufficient for a taxonomy of individual differences. In this chapter, we review this evidence.

So what is this evidence? The idea that five personality factors are the foundation of individual differences in personality rests on factor analyses of three types of data: (1) trait terms in the natural language, (2) cross-cultural research testing the universality of trait dimensions, and (3) the relation of trait questionnaires to other questionnaires and ratings. In this chapter, we consider each of these areas, as well as various applications of the model.

THE FIVE-FACTOR MODEL OF PERSONALITY: RESEARCH EVIDENCE

ANALYSIS OF TRAIT TERMS IN NATURAL LANGUAGE AND IN QUESTIONNAIRES

As you have learned from previous chapters, psychologists build personality theories on different types of variables—different units of analysis (Chapter 1). Most scientific theories, including most theories of personality, describe their main variables using a specialized scientific language; terms such as *superego*, *collective unconscious*, *actualization motive*, and so forth are introduced to describe a feature of human psychology. The five-factor model is not like this. Instead of creating a scientific language, five-factor theorists put faith in the natural language, that is, the regular, everyday language people use to describe personality. Specifically, they put faith in one aspect of the natural language: individual words (primarily adjectives) that describe persons.

The basic research procedure is to have individuals rate themselves or others on a wide variety of traits carefully sampled from the dictionary (John,

Lewis R. Goldberg

Angleitner, & Ostendorf, 1988). The ratings are then factor-analyzed (see Chapter 7 for a discussion of factor analysis) to see which traits go together. The questions to be answered are: (1) how many different factors are needed to understand the patterns of correlation in the data? and (2) what specifically are the factors?

Early work by Norman (1963), who drew upon research by Allport, Cattell, and others, indicated that five factors are necessary. Similar five-factor solutions were found repeatedly in studies that included a wide range of data sources, samples, and assessment instruments (John, 1990). All five factors were shown to possess considerable reliability and validity and to remain relatively stable throughout adulthood (McCrae & Costa, 1990, 1994, 2003). In 1981, Lewis Goldberg reviewed the existing research and, impressed with the consistency of its results, suggested that "any model for structuring individual differences will have to encompass at some level something like these 'Big Five' dimensions" (p. 159). "Big" was meant to refer to the finding that each factor subsumes a large number of more specific traits; the factors are almost as broad and abstract in the personality hierarchy as Eysenck's superfactors.

And what, exactly, are these factors? The terms Neuroticism (N), Extraversion (E), Openness (O), Agreeableness (A), and Conscientiousness (C) (Table 8.1) are used most commonly to label them. (They are made more memorable by the fact that their first letters spell the word **OCEAN**; John, 1990.) The meaning of the factors can best be seen by examining trait adjectives that describe individuals who score high and low on each (see Table 8.1). Neuroticism contrasts emotional stability with a broad range of negative feelings, including anxiety, sadness, irritability, and nervous tension. Openness to Experience describes the breadth, depth, and complexity of an individual's mental and experiential life. Extraversion and Agreeableness both summarize traits that are interpersonal; that is, they capture what people do with each other and to each other. Finally, Conscientiousness primarily describes task- and goal-directed behavior and socially required impulse control.

The factor definitions in Table 8.1 are based on the work by Costa and McCrae (1985, 1992). The definitions suggested by other researchers are quite

Table 8.1   The Big Five Trait Factors and Illustrative Scales

Characteristics of the High Scorer	Trait Scales	Characteristics of the Low Scorer
NEUROTICISM (N)		
Worrying, nervous, emotional, insecure, inadequate, hypochondriacal	Assesses adjustment vs. emotional instability. Identifies individuals prone to psychological distress, unrealistic ideas, excessive cravings or urges, and maladaptive coping responses.	Calm, relaxed, unemotional, hardy, secure, self-satisfied
EXTRAVERSION (E)		
Sociable, active, talkative, person-oriented, optimistic, fun-loving, affectionate	Assesses quantity and intensity of interpersonal interaction; activity level; need for stimulation; and capacity for joy.	Reserved, sober, unexuberant, aloof, task-oriented, retiring, quiet
OPENNESS (O)		
Curious, broad interests, creative, original, imaginative, untraditional	Assesses proactive seeking and appreciation of experience for its own sake; toleration for and exploration of the unfamiliar.	Conventional, down-to-earth, narrow interests, unartistic, unanalytical
AGREEABLENESS (A)		
Soft-hearted, good-natured, trusting, helpful, forgiving, gullible, straightforward	Assesses the quality of one's interpersonal orientation along a continuum from compassion to antagonism in thoughts, feelings, and actions.	Cynical, rude, suspicious, uncooperative, vengeful, ruthless, irritable, manipulative
CONSCIENTIOUSNESS (C)		
Organized, reliable, hard-working, self-disciplined, punctual, scrupulous, neat, ambitious, persevering	Assesses the individual's degree of organization, persistence, and motivation in goal-directed behavior. Contrasts dependable, fastidious people with those who are lackadaisical and sloppy.	Aimless, unreliable, lazy, careless, lax, negligent, weak-willed, hedonistic

SOURCE: Costa & McCrae, 1992, p. 2.

similar. For example, Goldberg (1992) has suggested an inventory of bipolar traits (e.g., silent-talkative) that individuals can use to rate their own standing on the Big Five dimensions. An abbreviated version of this inventory follows. Please consider the following instructions as you complete it:

Try to describe yourself as accurately as possible. Describe yourself as you see yourself at the present time, not as you wish to be in the future. Describe yourself as you are generally or typically, as compared with other persons you know of the same sex and of roughly your same age. For each of the trait scales listed, circle a number that best describes you on this dimension.

INTROVERSION VERSUS EXTRAVERSION

	Very	Moderately		Neither		Moderately		Very	
silent	1	2	3	4	5	6	7	8	9	talkative
unassertive	1	2	3	4	5	6	7	8	9	assertive
unadventurous	1	2	3	4	5	6	7	8	9	adventurous
unenergetic	1	2	3	4	5	6	7	8	9	energetic
timid	1	2	3	4	5	6	7	8	9	bold

ANTAGONISM VERSUS AGREEABLENESS

unkind	1	2	3	4	5	6	7	8	9	kind
uncooperative	1	2	3	4	5	6	7	8	9	cooperative
selfish	1	2	3	4	5	6	7	8	9	unselfish
distrustful	1	2	3	4	5	6	7	8	9	trustful
stingy	1	2	3	4	5	6	7	8	9	generous

LACK OF DIRECTION VERSUS CONSCIENTIOUSNESS

disorganized	1	2	3	4	5	6	7	8	9	organized
irresponsible	1	2	3	4	5	6	7	8	9	responsible
impractical	1	2	3	4	5	6	7	8	9	practical
careless	1	2	3	4	5	6	7	8	9	thorough
lazy	1	2	3	4	5	6	7	8	9	hardworking

EMOTIONAL STABILITY VERSUS NEUROTICISM

relaxed	1	2	3	4	5	6	7	8	9	tense
at ease	1	2	3	4	5	6	7	8	9	nervous
stable	1	2	3	4	5	6	7	8	9	unstable
contented	1	2	3	4	5	6	7	8	9	discontented
unemotional	1	2	3	4	5	6	7	8	9	emotional

CLOSEDNESS VERSUS OPENNESS TO NEW EXPERIENCE

unimaginative	1	2	3	4	5	6	7	8	9	imaginative
uncreative	1	2	3	4	5	6	7	8	9	creative
uninquisitive	1	2	3	4	5	6	7	8	9	curious
unreflective	1	2	3	4	5	6	7	8	9	reflective
unsophisticated	1	2	3	4	5	6	7	8	9	sophisticated

Very   Moderately   Neither   Moderately   Very

If you would like to know your Big Five scores, you can find out now. Simply add together all the five numbers you circled for E and divide that sum by 5. Then do the same for each of the other factors. How did you score? Did any one trait score much higher than another? Do you find your scores to be what you would have expected or surprising? How well do you think the scores capture your true personality? Do you think that your scores are a deep or merely a superficial description of your personality? Keep in mind that this inventory is not a formal, complete test of individual differences in the Big Five. However, it is fundamentally of the same structure as formal, "official" Big Five measures. The professional psychologists' tests commonly are longer. However, in recent years a number of Big Five researchers have shown that the five factors can be adequately measured with tests that are no longer, and in some cases actually are shorter (Gosling, Rentfrom, & Swann, 2003; Rammstedt & John, in press).

The Fundamental Lexical Hypothesis

The Big Five were designed to capture those personality traits that people consider most important to personality. Goldberg has spelled out the rationale for this approach in terms of the **fundamental lexical** (language) **hypothesis**: "the most important individual differences in human transactions will come to be encoded as single terms in some or all of the world's languages" (Goldberg, 1990, p. 1216). The hypothesis, then, is that over time humans have found some individual differences particularly important in their interactions and have developed terms for easy reference to them. These trait terms communicate information about individual differences that are important to our own well being or that of our group or clan. Thus, they are socially useful because they serve the purpose of prediction and control: They help us predict what others will do and thus control our life outcomes (Chaplin et al., 1988). They help answer questions about how an individual is likely to behave across a wide range of relevant situations.

There are some counter-examples to the lexical hypothesis. For example, some writers note that individuals differ in the degree to which they need variety in their lives, or the degree to which they can tolerate ambiguity when making decisions; contrary to the lexical hypothesis, there is no single term in the English language that corresponds to these qualities (McCrae & Costa, 1997). Nonetheless, the lexical hypothesis has been an important stimulant to research, and continues to guide much thinking in the field.

CROSS-CULTURAL RESEARCH: ARE THE BIG FIVE DIMENSIONS UNIVERSAL?

If there are universal questions concerning individual differences and human interaction, then one might expect the same basic trait dimensions to appear in many different languages; in other words, one might expect the Big Five factor structure to be universal. Fortunately, thanks to the efforts of international researchers conducting multinational studies, many research results begin to answer the question, are the big five dimensions universal?

Before considering these research results, we will consider the research methods. When asking whether the Big Five is found universally, across languages and cultures, methodological issues can make a big difference. One issue involves translation. Many researchers study the universality of personality traits by translating a personality questionnaire written in one language (e.g., English) into others (German, Japanese, etc.). Such translations can be tricky. Languages may lack one-to-one translations, and even words that translate the same (e.g., English *aggressive* and the German word meaning aggressive) do not necessarily mean the same (the German word for aggressive means hostile, rather than forceful-assertive). Thus, a word like *outgoing* (an extraversion trait) mistranslated from Japanese into English as *affectionate* (an agreeableness trait) might lead researchers to question whether they have found the same factor in the two languages. To illustrate such problems, Hofstee and colleagues (1997) identified 126 words that they could translate fairly directly across previous lexical studies in English, Dutch, and German and used them to compare the meanings of the factors in the three languages. Their findings showed considerable congruence across these three related languages, with one important exception: the Openness factor. The German and English were very similar, but the Dutch factor not only included the expected traits related to intellect and imagination (e.g., inventive, original, imaginative) but also emphasized traits related to unconventionality and rebelliousness. A similar variant of Openness was found in Italian and Hungarian trait studies (Caprara & Perugini, 1994).

It is important not to overstate evidence for universality. McCrae and Costa (1997) have taken a very strong position, suggesting that the Big Five personality structure is a human universal. The evidence for their conclusion involves translations of their Big Five instrument (the NEO-PI-R, to be considered shortly) into many languages. When researchers work with such translations, the same five factors result with great regularity. But you should note the potential limitation here. It is possible that the process of translating English-language questionnaires into another language forces the issue. The translation process may inadvertently impose certain psychological factors onto respondents in another culture, a culture where the factor may not arise spontaneously. For example, it might be that people in a given culture give relatively little thought to individual differences in Openness unless a psychologist asks them to think about this feature of personality.

This consideration highlights the importance of an alternative research strategy. Rather than imposing an English-language scale onto members of a different language group, one could study each language group's indigenous personality terms, that is, personality descriptors taken from the native language being studied. When this happens, findings become more complex (Saucier & Goldberg, 1996). Results often differ depending on whether the trait terms are imposed on members of a culture as opposed to being drawn from the language of that culture itself. As an example, consider research conducted by Di Blas & Forzi (1999), who explored the structure of personality terms in Italian. They did not do this by translating a scale from English into Italian; instead, they selected items directly from the indigenous language. They then asked people to rate themselves on these terms and used factor analysis to see if the Big Five structure, common in English, would replicate in Italian. It didn't; that is, not all five factors replicated consistently. Instead, Di Blas and Forzi (1999, p. 476) "found consistently that a three-factor solution was more stable across participants and observers"; extraversion, agreeableness, and conscientiousness, which generally are more replicable than the other two components of the Big Five model (Saucier, 1997), were the factors found consistently in Italian. The traditional trait factor of neuroticism was not found in the Italian language (Di Blas & Forzi, 1999), a null result similar to that of other investigators (Caprara & Perugini, 1994). The authors suggest that cultural variations in the perceptions of negative emotions in different interpersonal settings may explain the difference between Italian and English-language results (Di Blas & Forzi, 1999). Subsequently, De Raad and Peabody (2005) examined trait terms across 11 languages and concluded that "the Big Three—Extraversion, Agreeableness, and Conscientiousness—are cross lingually recurrent" whereas "the full Big Five Model is questionable" (De Raad & Peabody, 2005, p. 464).

Yet, sometimes seemingly large cultural variations seem not to make a big difference in the study of personality trait structures. For example, investigators have searched for the Big Five dimensions in the Turkish language and have found them, even when working with indigenous linguistic terms (Somer & Goldberg, 1999).

When scientific results vary from study to study, systematic reviews of the entire literature are of particular value. A recent review of attempts to recover the factor structure across multiple language groups concluded that the three factors identified in Italian and in the multi-language work of De Raad and Peabody—extraversion, agreeableness, and conscientiousness—could be found in most language groups; the other two factors (Neuroticism and Openness to Experience), then, are less cross-culturally reliable (Saucier, Hampson, & Goldberg, 2000).

The existence of variations in results from one country and language to another leads some to suggest that personality factors may exist that are unique to particular cultures. A potential example is a "Chinese tradition" factor (Cheung et al., 1996), which seems to capture values and attitudes considered important in traditional Chinese society. Such culture-specific factors are certainly possible, though further confirmation and replication is needed before we accept these factors as empirical fact. For example, it is possible that such factors do not reflect personality traits proper but other individual differences, such as attitudes and beliefs (e.g., conservative versus liberal).

In sum, there is growing evidence that people in diverse cultures, using very different languages, view individual differences in personality traits in ways similar to the Big Five. At least three of the factors are frequently found across cultures and language groups.

There is one caveat. Even if particular trait dimensions are identified cross-culturally, this does not necessarily mean that the various cultures all think about human nature in the same way. The results of trait-theoretical studies tell us what happens if researchers ask people within a culture to rate an individual's personality traits. But it is possible that, in some cultures, people do not typically think of others primarily in terms of personality traits, that is, in terms of a person's typical behavioral tendencies. Work in anthropology (Geertz, 1973) and cultural psychology (Heine et al., 1999; Markus & Kitayama, 1991) suggests that, in Asian cultures, people are relatively more attuned to an individual's relation to his or her family and social group, rather than to an individual's isolated psychological traits. For example, a detailed analysis of personality categories in Bali (Geertz, 1973) suggests that people commonly think of others in terms of their social status, public job title, and position within their family. These aspects of personhood are essential to defining the individual in that culture, even though they may be less central to selfhood in Western culture: although "we [focus] upon psychological traits as the heart of personal identity they [the Balinese], focusing on social position, say that their role is of the essence of their true selves" (Geertz, 1973, p. 386; also see Chapter 14). Studies of the cross-cultural replicability of the Big Five, then, inform us as to whether a given factor structure is replicated when people are asked to rate individuals' personality traits, but these findings do not inform us as to whether ideas other than personality traits are central to defining the individual in other cultures.

THE BIG FIVE IN PERSONALITY QUESTIONNAIRES

A variety of questionnaires have been developed to measure the Big Five. These include the abbreviated version of Goldberg's (1992) bipolar inventory

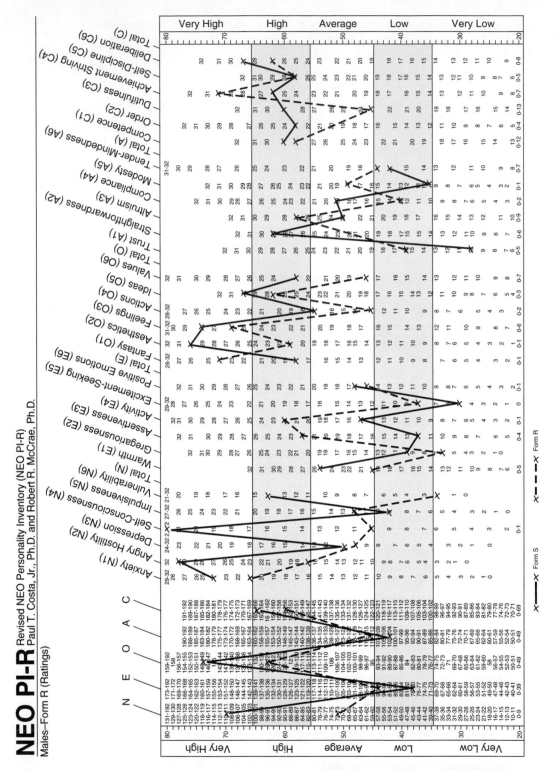

Figure 8.1   *Self-ratings and spouse-ratings on the NEO PI-R (Costa & McCrae, 1992, p.27). Adapted and reproduced by special permission from the publisher, Psychological Assessment Resources, Inc. Odessa, FL 33556, from the NEO PI-R, by Paul Costa and Robert McCrae. Copyright 1992 by PAT, Inc. Further reproduction is prohibited without permission of PAR, Inc.*

measuring the Big Five with trait adjectives described earlier in this chapter. A particularly well-developed questionnaire is called the NEO-Personality Inventory Revised (**NEO-PI-R**) (see Figure 8.1).

The NEO-PI-R and Its Hierarchical Structure: Facets

Costa and McCrae (1985, 1989, 1992) have developed a questionnaire, the NEO-PI-R, to measure the Big Five personality factors. Originally they had focused only on the three factors of Neuroticism, Extraversion, and Openness (thus the title NEO-Personality Inventory). Subsequently they added the factors of Agreeableness and Conscientiousness to conform to the five-factor model. In addition to measuring the five factors, they differentiated each factor into six narrower **facets**; facets are more specific components that make up each of the broad Big Five factors.

The six facets defining each Big Five factor are listed in Table 8.2, along with a famous individual or fictional character who exemplifies a prototypical high scorer for each factor. For example, in Costa and McCrae's NEO-PI-R, Extraversion is defined by these six facets: Activity Level, Assertiveness, Excitement Seeking, Positive Emotions, Gregariousness, and Warmth. Don't these six facets capture traits that would describe former president Bill Clinton? Each facet is measured by 8 items, so that the most recent NEO-PI-R consists of a total of 240 items (i.e., 5 factors × 6 facets × 8 items). For example, two items from the Activity facet scale are "My life is fast-paced" and "When I do things, I do them vigorously" (Costa & McCrae, 1992, p. 70). Indeed, most observers would agree that Clinton thrived on his fast-paced life in the White House, and he certainly did things vigorously, as the following newspaper report suggests:

> CLINTON PARTIES HEARTY. Between parties, golf and reading, he has little time to rest:
> Less than a week into the vacation on Martha's Vineyard, he's stayed out past 11 each night, played saxophone with a jazz band, briefly debated a bicycle courier and attended at least four fundraisers and several parties. That doesn't count his two rounds of golf and the dozen hefty books he brought along.
> Presidential vacations may say more about a chief
> executive's personality and inclinations than will a host of policy speeches. Ronald Reagan rode horses, cut brush, and made little fuss about summer reading lists. George Bush piloted loud powerboats. Richard Nixon walked the beach in black wing tips. Bill Clinton, renowned for his appetite for food, conversation, and ideas, apparently thinks vacations shouldn't be wasted on frivolities such as sleep but instead should be crammed with as much socializing, golfing, and reading as possible.
>
> SOURCE: SAN FRANCISCO Chronicle, August 25, 1999, p. A4.

When the NEO-PI-R is administered in research and clinical contexts, subjects indicate for each item the extent to which they agree or disagree, using a five-point rating scale. The resulting scales all have good reliability and show validity across different data sources, such as ratings by

Table 8.2   Each Big Five Factor Consists of Six Facets and Is Illustrated by an Individual or Fictional Character Who Exemplifies a Prototypical High Scorer

Extraversion	Gregariousness Activity Level Assertiveness Excitement Seeking Positive Emotions Warmth	Bill Clinton, U.S. President 1993–2001
Agreeableness	Straightforwardness Trust Altruism Modesty Tendermindedness Compliance	Radar, character from *M*A*S*H*
Conscientiousness	Self-discipline Dutifulness Competence Order Deliberation Achievement striving	Spock, character from *Star Trek*
Neuroticism	Anxiety Self-consciousness Depression Vulnerability Impulsiveness Angry hostility	Woody Allen, Movie Director
Openness to new experience	Fantasy Aesthetics Feelings Ideas Actions Values	Lewis Carroll, Author of *Alice in Wonderland*

peers or spouses. McCrae and Costa (1990, 2003) argue strongly for the use of structured questionnaires to assess personality and are critical of projective tests and clinical interviews, which they consider unsystematic and prone to biases. Evidence shows that their NEO-PI-R scales also agree well with other Big Five instruments, such as Goldberg's (1992) adjective inventories (John & Srivastava, 1999; Benet-Martinez & John, 1998). Nonetheless, it is important to point out that there are also some differences in which facets are emphasized on each instrument. For example, Costa and McCrae place the warmth facet on Extraversion, whereas other Big Five researchers find that warmth is more closely related to Agreeableness (John & Srivastava, 1999). Particular disagreement is found in the conceptualization of the fifth factor, Openness. Goldberg emphasizes intellectual and creative cognition, calling the factor Intellect or Imagination; McCrae (1996) criticizes this view as too narrow a definition of the Openness factor (see Table 8.2).

Integration of Eysenck's and Cattell's Factors Within the Big Five

Assuming that the NEO-PI-R is an adequate measure of the five-factor model of personality, one can ask a question that harkens back to our previous chapter: Can the personality factors of Cattell and Eysenck be understood within the five-factor system? Much evidence suggests that the answer is yes. Scores on the NEO-PI-R correlate as predicted with scores on other personality questionnaires, including Eysenck's inventories and Cattell's 16 personality factors (Costa & McCrae, 1992, 1994b).

These correlations are important theoretically. They allow one to integrate the older factor-analytic models with the Big Five and thus with each other. In particular, Eysenck's superfactors of Extraversion and Neuroticism are found to be virtually identical to the same-named dimensions in the Big Five, and Eysenck's Psychoticism superfactor corresponds to a combination of low Agreeableness and low Conscientiousness (Clark & Watson, 1999; Costa & McCrae, 1995; Goldberg & Rosolack, 1994). Cattell's 16 personality factors (Table 7.2) also map onto the broader Big Five dimensions (McCrae & Costa, 2003). For example, his scales Outgoing, Assertive, and Venturesome link with NEO-PI-R Extraversion; Trusting and Tender-minded link with Agreeableness; Conscientious, Controlled, and Sober with Conscientiousness; Emotional, Tense, and Apprehensive with Neuroticism; and Imaginative and Experimenting with Openness. Based on findings of this sort, proponents of the Big Five model suggest that it provides a comprehensive framework within which Eysenckian and Cattellian constructs can be integrated.

Moreover, the NEO-PI-R questionnaire relates meaningfully with other forms of measurement (e.g., Q-sort ratings) and with questionnaires derived from other theoretical orientations. Individual differences identified in Murray's motivational model of personality can be understood within the Big Five system or traits, which is important because it suggests a link between traits and motives (Pervin, 1999). Individual differences identified in biological research on temperament (see Chapter 9) can be described within the Big Five system (De Fruyt, Wiele, & Heeringen, 2000), which suggests that the factors might be reducible to underlying biological systems. Such findings support the boast that "no other system is as complete and yet as parsimonious" (McCrae & Costa, 1990, p. 51).

Another important strength of the NEO-PI-R is that forms are available for both self-report and ratings by others. In several studies, subjects' self-ratings have been compared with ratings by their peers and spouses. McCrae and Costa (1990) report substantial agreement of self-ratings with ratings by peers and with ratings by spouses on all five factors. Agreement between self and spouse is greater than that between self and peer, perhaps because spouses generally know each other better than do friends or because spouses talk a lot about each others' personalities (see Kenny, 1994). Two major findings have emerged from this research: (1) following the distinction between S-data and O-data sources we made in Chapter 2, the same five factors are found in both self-reports and observer ratings, and (2) observers agree reasonably well with each other about the standing of individuals on each Big Five dimension. These findings provide further evidence for the use of self-report measures and the five-factor model of personality.

PROPOSED THEORETICAL MODEL FOR THE BIG FIVE

Thus far, we have said little about a critical conceptual point. It is the question of the conceptual status of the trait constructs. In this regard, note that constructs for characterizing people come in different types. Some terms are merely descriptive labels. They label the way a person tends to act. Other terms refer to psychological properties that a person is said to possess; they refer to mental structures or processes that are causes of the person's behavior. An analogy outside of psychological characteristics makes the distinction between descriptive and causal constructs obvious. Consider physical characteristics and the term *attractive*. We often say that someone "is attractive" or is "more attractive than someone else." In doing so, we use the term *attractive* merely as a description. It describes, in a summary form, appealing characteristics involving physique, facial features, a cute smile, good hair, and so forth. We do not use the term *attractiveness* to refer to a separate biological system that causes the person to have the attractive physique, a cute smile, and so forth. Attractiveness does not cause someone to have good hair. Attractiveness is a descriptive label, not a biological structure that causally influences anything.

What about trait concepts such as the Big Five? Are they merely descriptions of psychological characteristics? Or might they also correspond to real psychological entities that individuals possess and that causally explain the individual's behavior? Many trait psychologists view the Big Five factors merely as descriptive. They view the constructs as a descriptive taxonomy of individual differences. However, in the 1990s a bolder theoretical view was put forth by McCrae & Costa (1996, 1999, 2003). They call their ideas **five-factor theory** (Figure 8.2). Five-factor theory claims that the five primary traits are

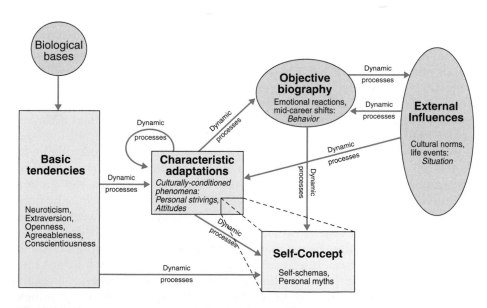

Figure 8.2   *A Representation of the Five-Factor Theory Personality System. (Core components are in rectangles; interfacing components are in ellipses.) (Costa & McCrae, 1999) Reprinted by permission, Guilford Press.*

Paul T. Costa, Jr.

Robert R. McCrae

more than mere descriptions of ways that people differ. The traits are treated as things that really exist; each is seen as a psychological structure that each and every person has in varying amounts (in the way that everyone has, for example, a certain degree of height in varying amounts). The traits are said to causally influence each individual's psychological development. Phrased more technically, in five-factor theory the idea is that the five factors are basic dispositional tendencies that are possessed universally, that is, by all individuals.

McCrae and Costa propose that the factors have a biological basis. Behavioral differences linked to the Big Five are said to be determined by genetic influences on neural structures, brain chemistry, and so on. Indeed, in proposing this model, McCrae and Costa felt that the biological basis of the factors was so strong that the basic five dispositional tendencies are not influenced directly by the environment; their contention was that "Personality traits, like temperaments, are endogenous dispositions that follow intrinsic paths of development essentially independent of environmental influences" (McCrae et al., 2000, p. 173). This position speaks to a a classic question in psychology: nature versus nurture (see Chapter 1). McCrae and Costa's theory is perhaps the strongest "nature" position possible—that is, the strongest possible claim that inherited biology (nature) determines personality and social experience (nurture) has little effect. As is evident from Figure 8.2, in five-factor theory traits are expressions of human biology. External influences are thought not to affect the traits (there are no arrows in the figure from external influences to trait variables). The claim that external influences have no influence on an individual's personality traits is a relatively unique claim of five-factor theory.

The second unique feature of the theory is the one we discussed above, namely, the claim that the traits are not merely descriptions of individual differences (akin to *attractiveness* in the earlier example) but also causal structure. Five-factor theory views traits as causal factors that influence the life course of each and every individual. The five traits are said to be the "universal raw material of personality" (McCrae & Costa, 1996, p. 66). In five-factor theory, then, a trait construct such as agreeableness serves two functions. It not only is (1) a "dimension of individual differences that applies to populations rather than people," but also is (2) "the underlying causal basis [of] consistent patterns of thoughts, feelings" where this causal analysis "applies directly to people" (McCrae & Costa, 2003).

What is one to think of five-factor theory? The model clearly has exceptional integrative potential. If it is basically correct, it would connect a biological view of traits and environmental influences to observable personality variables that are of such great concern to the other theoretical orientations represented in this book. Yet the model leaves open as many questions as it answers. Three issues seem particularly problematic for five-factor theory. Since these three issues are of broad, general importance to personality theory, we will consider them in some detail. The first problem is how to link personality structures to personality processes. Note the arrows specifying "Dynamic processes" in Figure 8.2. Trait theory has little to say about these processes; in McCrae and Costa's (1999) view, these are details to be filled in by other theoretical approaches to personality. This unquestionably is a significant theoretical limitation. A particular limitation is not merely that these dynamic processes are not filled in yet, but that it is not at all clear how, even in principle, they could be filled in. In general, personality theorists connect structures to processes by specifying the psychological mechanisms that make up the personality structure and then explaining how those mechanisms guide dynamic personality processing. For example, psychoanalysts posit that the basic mechanisms of the id involve unconscious, biologically based drives, and then explain how these unconscious forces influence observable behavior. But in five-factor theory, the biological and psychological mechanisms associated with the trait structures are unspecified. The traits are thought of merely as tendencies. Since the causal mechanisms associated with the traits are unknown, it is difficult even to begin building a model that links them to dynamic processes.

The other two problems concern the two unique features of five-factor theory noted earlier. One is the idea that traits are not affected by social factors. The problem is that research findings contradict this theoretical idea. Particularly interesting data comes from analyses of changes in personality trait scores that are observed across historical periods. Twenge (2002) reasoned that cultural changes across periods of the 20th century might have caused changes in personality. Consider changes in the United States in the middle versus latter decades of the century. Compared to the 1950s, in the 1990s people experienced a culture with higher divorce rates, higher crime rates, smaller family size, and less contact with one's extended family (due to greater job and educational mobility of the population). These sociocultural changes, Twenge finds, were associated with higher levels of anxiety. By examining mean-level scores on anxiety and neuroticism scales in research reports published in the 1950s through 1990s, Twenge was able to demonstrate that anxiety increased significantly during this period. She also found significant increases in extraversion across decades of the 20th century, perhaps reflecting American society's increasing concern with individualism and personal assertiveness (Twenge, 2002). As Twenge notes, these historical changes, which were found to be rather large in size, directly contradict the hypothesis that personality traits are unaffected by social factors.

The third concern regarding five-factor theory is conceptually subtle, yet deeply important. Five-factor theory claims that the five factors are possessed by all individuals. The claim, in other words, is that all individuals possess psychological structures corresponding to each of the factors, with individuals varying in their level on each trait. To five-factor theorists, the factors are analogous to bodily organs (Costa & McCrae, 1998), which might vary in size from one person to another. The problem is that this theoretical claim does not follow, in any direct or logically necessary way, from the available research evidence. The evidence that supports the five-factor model involves statistical analyses of populations of persons. When one examines populations, one finds that the five factors do a good job of summarizing individual differences in the population at large. But this finding does not demonstrate that each and every individual in the population possesses each of the five factors. Questions about populations and about individual persons involve different levels of analysis. A statement that may be true about a population of persons (e.g., "the native American population in the United States is shrinking") may not necessarily be true of any individual persons (no individual Native American "is shrinking"; cf. Rorer, 1990).

The question, then, is whether the factors identified when studying populations enable one to make any claims about psychological structures possessed by individual persons. Recently, this question has been taken up in detail by Borsboom, Mellenbergh, and van Heerden (2003). These writers emphasize that the analysis of populations and of individuals are entirely different things. The only way to claim validly that the five factors explain the personality functioning of individuals would be to conduct factor analyses of individuals one at a time and to find that, for each individual person, the five-factor model is recovered. As they write, "if one wants to know what happens in a person, one must study that person. This requires representing individual processes where they belong, namely at the level of the individual one cannot expect between-subjects analyses to miraculously yield information at this level" (Borsboom et al., 2003, p. 216).

At present, relatively few have even tried to find the five-factor structure at the level of the individual. Data that do exist suggest that the behavioral tendencies of individuals commonly differ from the tendencies described by the five-factor model (Borkenau & Ostendorf, 1998). To get an intuitive sense of how an individual's behavioral tendencies may differ from those described by the Big Five traits, think back to what you learned about psychoanalysis. According to the psychoanalytic notion of an Oedipal conflict, a person may display hostile behavior toward a same-sex parent and affectionate behavior toward an opposite-sex parent. In psychoanalysis, this varying, conflicting style of behavior is a basic behavioral tendency of the individual person. Yet nothing resembling Oedipal conflict is found as a single Big Five dimension. A factor analysis of between-person differences does not reveal this within-person style of behavior.

Theorists who are concerned with the difference between within-person and between-person analyses, then, argue that personality trait constructs identified in the study of differences among individuals in the population "abstract from the level of the individual [and] should, for this reason, not be conceptualized as explaining behavior at the level of the individual" (Borsboom et al., 2003, p. 215). In this view, the Big Five factors still provide enormously important information. The constructs valuably describe differences between individuals in the population at large. The point is that these constructs cannot be assumed also to describe factors in the head of each and every individual. Again, an analogy makes the point clear. Imagine you are in a used car lot filled with a hundred different cars. The terms you use to describe the cars—your "constructs" for discussing cars—might include reliability, sportiness, and luxury. These terms usefully describe differences between cars. But now imagine that you have bought a car, have driven it off the lot, but it breaks down and is towed to a mechanic who tries to fix it. When the mechanic opens the hood, he or she is not looking for "a reliableness" or "a sporty." The mechanic's constructs refer to qualities in the individual car: an electric system, a fuel injection system, and so on. Borsboom et al.'s (2003) point is simple. The terms that summarize differences between things (in the case of cars, reliability, sporty, etc.) cannot be assumed also to describe qualities in each of the things being described.

When this point is applied to five-factor theory, it suggests that there are no firm grounds for proposing that the five personality factors that describe differences between people also are qualities that exist in the head of each individual person being described. This is why there exist a variety of other personality theories despite the fact that the Big Five is so successful at describing individual differences. To most other personality theorists, the five factors do not solve the problem taken up by Freud, by Rogers, and by theorists discussed in subsequent chapters of this book: identifying personality structures *in the head of the individual* that explain his or her typical experiences and action.

AGE DIFFERENCES THROUGHOUT ADULTHOOD

Do people's scores on Big Five measures change systematically as they age? Or are levels of these personality traits stable throughout adulthood? The most direct way to answer this question is to study people over long periods of time, and to administer the same personality trait measures at the different time periods. Research employing this strategy yields consistent findings. There is much stability (Caspi & Roberts, 1999; McCrae & Costa, 1997; Roberts & Del Vecchio, 2000). Even over long periods of time, the correlations between measures from one time to another remain significant (Fraley & Roberts, 2005). This does not mean that there are no significant changes whatsoever in personality for people in general. It does not mean that no individual people (who might differ from a group average) change. However, it does mean that personality trait psychologists can be confident in concluding that the personality trait variables of their theories are capturing personal qualities that are substantially stable, over substantial periods of time, for substantial numbers of people.

Despite this stability, it is also the case that change is found. Older adults score significantly lower in Neuroticism, Extraversion, and Openness, and higher in Agreeableness and Conscientiousness than adolescents and young adults (Costa & McCrae, 1994b). On average, teenagers seem to be beset by more anxieties and concerns with acceptance and self-esteem (higher N), to spend more time on the phone and in social activities with their friends (higher E), are more open to all kinds of experience and experimentation (higher O), but also are more critical and demanding of specific others and society in general (lower A), and less conscientious and responsible than others (parents, teachers, police) expect them to be (lower C). Not surprisingly, we speak of "angry young men," not of "angry middle-aged men" or "angry grandfathers." The teenage years and early 20s are the times of greatest discontent, turbulence, and revolt.

However, these findings are ambiguous because, as noted above, the observed differences may reflect not age changes but cohort differences, that is, differences due to generation effects associated with growing up during different time periods. In other words, differences might be due to historical factors (e.g., growing up during the Depression as opposed to during World War II or during the tumultuous 1960s) rather than age factors. For example, today's college students might be less conscientious than their parents' generation when they were in college. Subsequent research by McCrae, Costa, and their collaborators (McCrae et al., 2000; McCrae & Costa, 2003) addressed this limitation by studying age differences in a wide range of cultures. To illustrate, Figure 8.3 shows the findings for Conscientiousness for five cultures. The means are shown for five age groups: 14–17, 18–21, 22–29, 30–49, and 50 and older; when Figure 8.3 shows no entry, then there were not enough subjects for that particular age group. Age trends were generally similar for men and women, and the predicted increase was observed in each culture: people became increasingly conscientious with age.

More generally, McCrae and colleagues (2000) were able to replicate the findings obtained earlier in the United States although they had to modify somewhat their strong earlier stance that there is no personality change after age 30—the new cross-cultural data suggest that some of these age trends

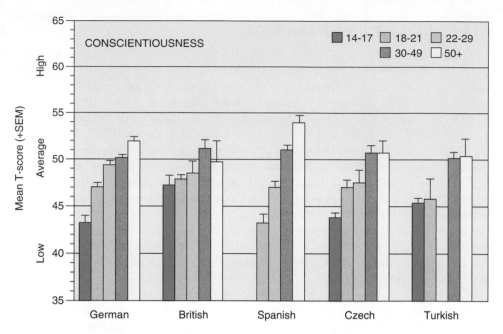

Figure 8.3   *Mean Levels of Conscientiousness in Five Cultures. T-scores are based on the mean and standard deviation of all respondents over age 21 within each culture. Error bars represent standard errors of the means. (McCrae et al., 2000) Copyright © 2000 American Psychological Association. Reprinted by permission.*

continue after age 30, though at a diminished rate. Note that the overall finding is quite astounding: the same pattern of personality trait change was observed across numerous diverse cultures, which differed considerably in their political, cultural, and economic conditions. These findings led McCrae and colleagues to argue that changes in personality trait levels are not closely linked to experiences across the life span; instead, as previously noted, they propose that age differences reflect intrinsic maturation, just like other biologically based systems (e.g., McCrae, 2002).

Yet other researchers provide evidence that suggests somewhat greater degrees of change and a bigger role for social factors. Ravenna Helson and colleagues (e.g., Helson & Kwan, 2000; Helson, Kwan, John, & Jones, 2002) have studied a group of women residing in northern California over a particularly long period of time. The women were first studied around 1960, when they were seniors in college. Subsequent measures were taken as late as 40 years later, when the women were 61 years old. Clear evidence of *changes* in personality across adulthood were found. For example, women changed in self-reports of norm orientation (the degree to which one controls emotional impulses in accord with social norms, a quality that correlated with Big Five Agreeableness and Conscientiousness; Helson & Kwan, 2000). On most norm-orientation measures, women's scores consistently increased with increasing age. Conversely, on measures of social vitality (a measure that correlates with extraversion), consistent changes were found in the opposite direction; women scored lower in social vitality with increasing age. A particularly interesting aspect of this study is evidence that changes in women's personality were

AGREEABLENESS INCREASES WITH AGE

At thirty-five, Cage was quick to point out that he had responsibilities. "I have people I have to take care of," Cage says. "Back then, I was living out my fantasies... I wanted to be unpredictable and frightening, and I guess I was. I can't really imagine myself getting that angry now. I haven't punched a wall in years."

SOURCE: *Rolling Stone*, 1999.

Nicolas Cage at age 35: No longer an angry man.

related to a sociocultural factor, namely, the women's movement, which began to usher in new ideas about gender and women's place in society during the 1960s and 1970s. Findings suggest that "women for whom the [women's] movement was important increased on Self-acceptance, Dominance, and Empathy scales, that is, they became more 'empowered' more confident, assertive, and involved in the affective understanding of others" (Helson & Kwan, 2000, p. 96). A recent review (Helson et al., 2002) indicates that such changes are found consistently across different studies and samples of research participants.

Further evidence of changes in personality trait scores during adulthood comes from work by Srivastava, John, Gosling, and Potter (2003). These researchers conducted an Internet survey. In the survey, a large sample of adults of varying ages from the United States and Canada completed a five-factor inventory. The analysis of survey responses revealed significant age-linked changes in most of the Big Five traits for both men and women. For example, self-ratings on the factor of Agreeableness increased significantly for both men and women between the ages of 31 and 50; as the authors note, these are years during which many adults are raising children and these nurturing experiences may alter agreeableness tendencies. The authors emphasize that these results "contradict the five-factor theory's brand of biologism" (Srivastava et al., 2003, p. 1051). In other words, they contradict the notion that personality trait levels are entirely inherited and are unaffected by social experiences (see Figure 8.2). Even though trait theories of personality devote less attention to social influences than do most of the other theoretical frameworks in the field, trait research increasingly provides evidence that personality develops across the course of life as a result of individuals' interactions with the social environment.

Other recent evidence of personality change comes from work that interestingly combines two theoretical approaches. Cramer (2003) explored the possibility that individual differences in the tendency to use alternative defense mechanisms (see Chapter 3) would predict changes in scores on Big Five traits. Her results indicated that the use of defense mechanisms in early adulthood predicted personality trait change in later adulthood; for example, people who tended to employ the relatively immature defense of denial and projection experienced higher levels of neuroticism in later years (Cramer, 2003). In summary, although trait scores are quite stable over time, there also is much indication that they can change in a meaningful, systematic manner.

INITIAL FINDINGS FROM CHILDHOOD AND ADOLESCENCE

The studies we just reviewed concern personality in adulthood. What about earlier periods of development? Much research has explored connections between infant temperament, childhood personality, and the Big Five in adulthood during the past decade (Halverson, Kohnstamm, & Martin, 1994). It is safe to suggest that earlier temperamental characteristics, such as sociability, activity, and emotionality (A. H. Buss & Plomin, 1984), develop and mature into dimensions we know as extraversion and neuroticism in adulthood. However, the exact linkages, and the processes by which this development takes place, have not yet been extensively studied.

One intriguing finding is that personality structure appears to be more complex and less integrated in childhood than in adulthood. Rather than the usual number of five factors, seven child factors were found in the United States (John, Caspi, Robins, Moffitt, & Stouthamer-Loeber, 1994). This finding was replicated in the Netherlands (van Lieshout & Haselager, 1994). Essentially, instead of one broad extraversion factor, the researchers found separate sociability and activity factors, and instead of one broad neuroticism factor, they found separate fearfulness and irritability factors. These findings suggest that the expression of personality may change over the course of development—during the course of adolescence, initially separate dimensions merge together to form the broader, more fully integrated personality dimensions we know in adulthood. The idea that the adult extraversion factor is foreshadowed by separate sociability and activity factors in childhood is consistent with the view that these two attributes are distinct, early emerging, and largely inherited temperament traits (A. H. Buss & Plomin, 1984) (see Chapter 9 for a discussion of temperament and heritability).

STABILITY AND CHANGE IN PERSONALITY

How stable are individuals in regard to their basic tendencies during the life course? To the extent that personality traits are like temperament, do they follow the biologically determined path of stable development suggested by Costa and McCrae? Is the rank ordering of individuals on the Big Five stable throughout life even if average levels change somewhat? We will have more to say about this issue in the next chapter but here we may note that differing points of view exist. For example, one view suggests that personality development is largely biologically determined and continuous, that "the child is father of the man" (Caspi, 2000, p. 158). Another view is that although there is evidence of trait consistency across the life course, it is not so high as to warrant the conclusion that change does not occur (Roberts & Del Vecchio, 2000). And a third view is that although general trait structure and levels remain fairly stable, there is evidence of change in individual trait levels (Asendorpf & van Aken, 1999). Of particular note here is evidence that parenting practices can impact personality development and that work experiences can impact personality development during young adulthood (Roberts, 1997; Suomi, 1999). At this point in time the data would appear to suggest the following: (1) Personality is more stable over short periods of time than over long periods of time. (2) Personality is more stable in adulthood than in childhood. (3) Although there is evidence of general trait stability, there are individual differences in stability during development. (4) Although there is evidence of general trait stability, the limits of environmental influence on change, during childhood and adulthood, remain to be determined.

MAYBE WE MISSED ONE? THE SIX-FACTOR MODEL

From the 1980s through the early years of the 20th century, the Big Five model was a consensus position among trait psychologists. The factors appear to be not only necessary, but reasonably sufficient to describe average differences among persons. Then something happened. Multiple data sets, compiled by an international team of researchers working with participants from a variety of nations, suggested that trait psychologists had "missed one." There appeared to be a 6th factor that was overlooked in prior analyses.

To get an intuitive sense of this factor, consider two hypothetical cases: (1) a smart, outgoing, hardworking, interpersonally agreeable and socially skilled chief executive of a corporation; (2) a smart, outgoing, hardworking, interpersonally agreeable and socially skilled chief executive of a corporation who engages in unfair business practices and lies about his company's finances. Clearly the people differ. But the differences seem not to be captured by the five-factor model. Both individuals may be similar in O, C, E, A, and N, but they differ in something else: honesty, or honesty/humility (Ashton et al., 2004, p. 363).

The question is whether this basic intuition—that people who are similar on Big Five traits might differ systematically on a 6th trait, the dimensions of honesty/humility—holds up not only at an intuitive level, but scientifically. If one analyzes self-ratings made using personality trait adjectives, and if one is careful to include in the pool of personality adjectives a wide range of attributes (so that no important global traits will be missed), does one actually find this sixth factor? Based on findings across seven different languages, the answer is yes (Ashton et al., 2004). In addition to the original five factors (some of which change subtly in their meaning when the sixth factor is identified), there is indeed a sixth factor of honesty-humility. Individual differences in the tendency to be truthful and sincere, as opposed to cunning and disloyal, are a reliable sixth factor (see Table 8.3).

The six-factor model—i.e., the five-factor model plus this additional factor of honesty—is a new development in trait psychology. It has not yet been incorporated fully into either basic theory or applied research. Thus, as we now turn to applications, we will return to the basic five-factor model. However, as you read the material ahead, you should recognize that individual

Mother Theresa, a Nobel Peace Prize winner who devoted her life to serving the poor, exemplified for millions around the world psychological traits including honesty and humility–the 6th trait factor in the six-factor model of personality.

Table 8.3   Adjectives defining the high and low poles of a 6th factor of individual differences identified across a range of languages

Language	*"Low" Pole of Factor*	*"High" Pole of Factor*
Dutch	sincere, loyal/faithful	cunning, smug
French	true/genuine, sincere	thoughtless, mean
German	honest, sincere	boastful, arrogant
Hungarian	veracious, just	pretending, haughty
Italian	honest, sincere	disloyal, megalomaniac
Korean	truthful, frank	flattering, pretentious
Polish	helpful, unselfish	egoistic, envious

SOURCE: Ashton et al., 2004.

differences in honesty and humility, versus dishonesty and/or egotism, may be under-represented in the five-dimensional model that has been so popular among trait psychologists. Furthermore, there may be additional factors that are under-represented. In a very recent study, De Raad (2006) noted that almost all research on the Big Five model has studied adjectives, but that the study of nouns and verbs might convey additional information about people. Factor analyses of a database including all three classes of words revealed *eight* factors, including factors (such as competence) not identified clearly in the Big Five or Big Six models (De Raad, 2006).

One of the great strengths of the Big Five model is that it provides psychologists with a comprehensive, widely accepted tool that can be used to solve applied problems. Employers, educators, clinical psychologists, and many others require a reliable means of assessing stable individual differences. Big five assessments are one such means, and thus have been applied widely, as we now review.

APPLICATIONS OF THE BIG FIVE MODEL

A possibility of interest to students of vocational (career) behavior is that variations in personality traits may predict the kinds of careers people choose and how they function in these occupations (De Fruyt & Salgado, 2003; Hogan & Ones, 1997; Roberts & Hogan, 2001). According to the five-factor model, individuals high in Extraversion should prefer and excel in social and enterprising occupations, relative to low-E individuals. People high on Openness to Experience should prefer and excel in artistic and investigative occupations (e.g., journalist, freelance writer) that require curiosity, creativity, and independent thinking—central features of high Openness. Much research indeed does suggest that the five-factor model is useful in predicting job performance (Hogan & Ones, 1997). A review of a large number of existing studies indicated that conscientiousness is related in a particularly consistent manner to performance across a variety of different types of jobs and a variety of different measures of job performance (Barrick & Mount, 1991). Nonetheless, some writers caution that personality characteristics beyond those in the Big Five model are important to predictions of workplace performance (Hough & Oswald, 2000; Matthews, 1997), and others find surprisingly weak results and caution that different measures of the same Big Five personality trait may fail to correspond with one another (Anderson & Ones, 2003, p. S62).

Another area of application is that of health. A long-term study indicates that more conscientious persons may live longer (Friedman et al., 1995a, 1995b). A large sample of children was followed for 70 years by several generations of researchers who kept track of which participants died and the causes of death. Adults who were conscientious as children (according to parent and teacher ratings at age 11) lived significantly longer and were about 30 percent less likely to die in any given year. Why do conscientious individuals live longer? That is, what are the causal mechanisms that lead to these differences in longevity? First, the researchers ruled out the possibility that environmental variables, such as parental divorce, explain the conscientiousness effects. Second, throughout their lives, conscientious individuals were less likely to die from violent deaths, whereas less conscientious individuals took risks that led to accidents and fights. Third, conscientious people were less likely to smoke

Personality trait research indicates that people who are high on the trait of conscientiousness take better care of themselves and live longer.

and drink heavily. The researchers suggest that conscientiousness is likely to influence a whole pattern of health-relevant behaviors. Thus, in addition to less likelihood of smoking and drinking heavily, they were more likely to do the following: engage in regular exercise, eat a balanced diet, have regular physicals and observe medication regimens, and avoid environmental toxins. Related findings recently have been presented by Hampson and colleagues. Children who differed in Big Five traits in childhood, as rated by teachers, were found to differ in self-reports of health-related behaviors when they were studied 40 years later (Hampson, Goldberg, Vogt, & Dubanoski, 2006). Traits were linked to health partly through their relation to daily activities and habits. For example, children who were rated as more extraverted were, in later years, more likely to engage in physical activities and also more likely to smoke; adult health status was predicted by physical activity (positively) and smoking (negatively; Hampson, Goldberg, Vogt, & Dubanoski, in press).

Five-factor theorists also believe that their model of personality traits can inform clinical diagnosis and treatment. They see many kinds of abnormal behavior as exaggerated versions of normal personality traits (Costa & Widiger, 2001; Widiger, Verhuel, & van den Brink, 1999). In other words, many forms of psychopathology are seen as falling on a continuum with normal personality rather than as representing a distinct departure from the normal (Widiger, 1993). For example, the compulsive personality might be seen as someone extremely high on both Conscientiousness and Neuroticism, and the antisocial personality as someone extremely low on both Agreeableness and Conscientiousness. Thus, it may be the pattern of scores on the five factors that may be most important. This suggests that the five-factor framework would prove valuable not only as a taxonomy of individual differences in everyday personality functioning, but also as a tool for clinical diagnosis.

There also has been interest in using the Big Five model in choosing and planning psychological treatments (Harkness & Lilienfeld, 1997). With an understanding of the individual's personality, the therapist may be in a better position to anticipate problems and plan the course of treatment (MacKenzie, 1994; Sanderson & Clarkin, 1994). Another potentially important contribution may be the guidance that can be given in selecting the optimal form of therapy (Costa & McCrae, 1992; Costa & Widiger, 1994; T. R. Miller, 1991). The principle here is that just as individuals with different personalities function better or worse in different vocations, so too they may profit more or less from different forms of psychological treatment. For example, individuals high in Openness may profit more from therapies that encourage exploration and fantasy than would individuals low on this factor. The latter may prefer and profit better from more directive forms of treatment, including the use of medication. One clinician writing about this notes that he has often heard a patient low on Openness say something like, "Some people need to lie on a couch and talk about their mother. My 'therapy' is working out at the gym" (T. R. Miller, 1991, p. 426). In contrast, the person high on Openness may prefer the exploration of dreams found in psychoanalysis or the emphasis on self-actualization found in the humanistic-existential approach.

In summary, the five-factor model has proven to have numerous valuable applications across diverse areas of psychology. Its greatest strengths have been in those settings in which investigators wish to predict individual differences in psychological and social outcomes. In these domains, numerous positive findings attest to the worth of the model. In other domains, the model is more limited. For example, it offers little unique insight into the causal dynamics underlying psychopathology, and thus to the clinician is more a way of merely describing disorders than explaining them (T. R. Miller, 1991). More generally, unlike the other theories covered in this book, the five-factor model has not generated unique therapeutic methods for helping people to change psychological qualities that are maladaptive for them.

Factor-Analytic Trait-Based Assessment

THE CASE OF JIM

Let us now return to the case of Jim and consider how his personality is depicted by personality trait questionnaires. We begin with Cattell's 16 P.F. The following brief description of Jim's personality was written by a psychologist who assessed the results of Jim's 16 P.F. but was unaware of any of the other data on him.

> Jim presents himself as a very bright and outgoing young man although he is insecure, easily upset, and somewhat dependent. Less assertive, conscientious, and venturesome than he may initially appear, Jim is confused and conflicted about who he is and where he is going, tends toward introspection, and is quite anxious. His profile suggests that he may experience periodic mood swings and may also have a history of psychosomatic complaints. Since the 16 P.F. has been administered to college students throughout the country, we can also compare Jim with the average college student. Compared to other students, Jim is

more outgoing, intelligent, and affected by feelings—easily
upset, hypersensitive, and often depressed and anxious.

The trait-based assessment classified Jim as extremely high on anxiety. This may relate to his dissatisfaction with his ability to meet the demands of life and to achieve what he desires. The high level of anxiety also suggests the possibility of physical disturbances and bodily symptoms. Also, Jim scored highly on what Cattell called tenderminded emotionality. This suggests that rather than being enterprising and decisive, Jim is troubled by emotionality and often becomes discouraged and frustrated. Although sensitive to the subtleties of life, this sensitivity sometimes leads to preoccupation and to too much thought before he takes action. On other traits, Jim's scores were nearer to the average rather than being extremely high or low.

The 16 P.F. revealed two features of Jim's personality with particular clarity. The first is the frequency of his mood swings. In reading the results on the 16 P.F., Jim stated that he has frequent and extreme mood swings, ranging from extreme happiness to extreme depression. During the latter periods, he tends to take his feelings out on others and becomes hostile to them in a sarcastic, "biting," or "cutting" way. Second, Jim expressed many psychosomatic complaints. Jim has had considerable difficulty with an ulcer and frequently must drink milk for the condition. Notice that although this is a serious condition that gives him considerable trouble, Jim did not mention it at all in his autobiography.

Despite its informativeness, one is left wondering whether 16 dimensions are adequate for the description of personality. The clinician also wonders whether a score in the middle of the scale means that the trait is not important for understanding Jim or simply that he is not extreme on that characteristic; the latter appeared to be the case. Yet, when one writes up a personality description based on the results of the 16 P.F., the major emphasis tends to fall on scales with extreme scores.

Perhaps most serious, however, is that the results of the 16 P.F. are descriptive, but not interpretive or dynamic. The test yields only a pattern of scores—not a whole individual. Although the Cattelian theory takes into consideration the dynamic interplay among motives, the results of the 16 P.F. appear unrelated to this portion of the theory. Jim is described as being anxious and frustrated, but anxious about what and frustrated for what reason? Why is Jim outgoing and shy? Why does he find it so hard to be decisive and enterprising? The results of the 16 P.F. tell us nothing about the nature of Jim's conflicts and how he tries to handle them. Note that the same problem would have arisen if Jim had been assessed in terms of five-factor scores; one still would have obtained a collection of test scores, but little understanding of how and why one score might relate to another.

Personality Stability: Jim 5 and 20 Years Later

The material on Jim presented so far was written at approximately the time of his graduation from college. Since then, much time has elapsed, and Jim agreed to be re-assessed. Five years after graduation, he was contacted and asked (1) to indicate whether there had been significant life experiences for him since graduation and, if so, how they affected him, and (2) to describe his personality and any ways it had changed since graduation. He responded:

> After leaving college, I entered business school. I only got into one graduate school in psychology; it was not particularly prestigious, whereas I got into a number of excellent business schools, and so on that basis I chose to go to business school. I did not really enjoy business school, though it was not terribly noxious either, but it was clear to me that my interest really was in the field of psychology, so I applied to a couple of schools during the academic year but did not get in. I had a job in a New York import-export firm over the summer, and disliked it intensely enough to once more write to graduate schools over the summer. I was accepted at two, and then went into a very difficult decision-making process. My parents explicitly wanted me to return to business school, but I eventually decided to try graduate school. My ability to make that decision in the face of parental opposition was very significant for me; it asserted my strength and independence as nothing else in my life ever had. Going through graduate school in the Midwest in clinical psychology was extremely significant for me. I have a keen professional identification as a clinician which is quite central to my self-concept. I have a system of thinking which is well-grounded and very central to the way I deal with my environment. I am entirely pleased with the decision I made, even though I still toy with the idea of returning to business school. Even if I do it, it would be to attain an adjunct degree; it would not change the fact that my primary identification is with psychology. I also fell in love during my first year in graduate school, for the first and only time in my life. The relationship did not work out, which was devastating to me, and I've not gotten completely over it yet. Despite the pain, however, it was a life-infusing experience.
> Last year I lived in a communal setting and it was a watershed experience for me. We worked a lot on ourselves and each other during the year, in our formal once-a-week groups and informally at any time, and it was a frequently painful, frequently joyful, and always a growth-producing experience. Toward the end of last year, I began a relationship which has now become primary for me. I am living with a woman, Kathy, who is in a master's program in social work. She has been married twice. It is a sober relationship with problems involved; basically, there are some things about her that I am not comfortable with. I do not feel "in love" at this point, but there are a great many things about her that I like and appreciate, and so I am remaining in the relationship to see what develops, and how I feel about continuing to be with her. I have no plans to get

married, nor much immediate interest in doing so. The relationship does not have the passionate feeling that my other significant relationship had, and I am presently trying to work through how much of my feeling at that time was idealization and how much real, and whether my more sober feelings for Kathy indicate that she's not the right woman for me or whether I need to come to grips with the fact that no woman is going to be "perfect" for me. In any event, my relationship with Kathy also feels like a wonderful growth-producing experience, and is the most significant life experience I am currently involved in. I do not think I've changed in very basic ways since leaving college. As a result of going into psychology, I think of myself as somewhat more self-aware these days, which I think is helpful. As I remember your interpretation of the tests I took back then, you saw me as primarily depressive. At this point, however, I think of myself as being primarily obsessive. I think I am prone to depression, but on balance see myself as happier these days—less frequently depressed. I see my obsessiveness as a deeply ingrained characterological pattern, and have been thinking for some time now about going into analysis to work on it (amongst other things, of course) . . .. I see myself as more similar to, than different from, the way I was five years ago. I think of myself as a witty, aware, interesting and fun-loving person. I continue to be quite moody, so sometimes none of these characteristics is in evidence at all. My sexual relationship with my girlfriend has put to rest my concern about my sexual adequacy (especially about premature ejaculation).

I still see myself as having an "authority" issue—i.e., being quite sensitive and vulnerable to the way in which those who have authority over me treat me. . .. I am extremely compulsive, I very efficiently get done what needs to be done, and experience considerable anxiety when I am not on top of things.

By the time he reached his 40s, Jim was practicing as a consulting psychologist in a medium-sized city on the West Coast. The most important subsequent events for him were marriage, the birth of a child, and the stabilization of a professional identity. He describes his wife as calm and peaceful, with a good sense of perspective on life. He feels that he has changed in a way that makes a lasting relationship possible: "I have a greater capacity for acceptance of the other and a clearer sense of boundaries between me and others—she is she and I am I. And, she accepts me, foibles and all."

Jim feels that he has made progress in what he calls "getting out of myself," but feels that his narcissism remains an important issue: "I'm selectively perfectionistic with myself, unforgiving of myself. If I lose money I punish myself. As a teenager I lost twenty dollars and went without lunches all summer long. I didn't need the money. My family has plenty of it. But what I did was unforgivable. Is it perfectionistic or compulsive? I push myself all the time. I must read the newspaper thoroughly seven days a week. I feel imprisoned by it a lot of the time.

Can I give up these rituals and self-indulgences with the birth of a child? I must."

Self-Ratings and Ratings by Wife on the NEO-PI

The NEO-PI was not available at the time of the original testing, but was administered, via both self-ratings and ratings of Jim by his wife, at later time periods. In terms of self-ratings, the most distinctive feature of Jim's personality is his very low standing on Agreeableness. The test classified him as antagonistic and tending to be brusque or even rude with others. Two other significant features of Jim's responses were his very high ratings on Extraversion and Neuroticism. On specific subscale scores, the test indicated that he sees himself as forceful and dominant, and prefers to be a group leader rather than a follower. In terms of Neuroticism, Jim's score is characteristic of individuals prone to have a high level of negative emotion and frequent episodes of psychological distress.

On the two remaining factors, Jim scored high on Conscientiousness and average on Openness. Additional personality correlates suggested in the report were that he likely uses ineffective coping responses in dealing with the stresses of everyday life and that he is overly sensitive to signs of physical problems and illnesses.

How similar a picture of Jim is given by his wife? On three of the five factors there is very close agreement. Both Jim and his wife saw him as very high on Extraversion, average on Openness, and very low on Agreeableness. There was a small difference in relation to Conscientiousness, with Jim rating himself slightly higher than his wife rated him. The big difference in ratings occurred in relation to Neuroticism, where Jim rated himself as very high and his wife rated him as low. Jim saw himself as much more anxious, hostile, and depressed than his wife rated him to be. In addition, whereas his responses suggest a person with ineffective devices for coping with stress and oversensitivity to physical problems, his wife's ratings portray an individual with effective coping devices and a tendency to discount physical and medical complaints.

How are we to evaluate such a level of agreement? In some ways, this is like asking whether a glass is half-filled or half-empty. The high level on some traits suggests that the self-ratings were basically accurate. Where there was disagreement, it is hard to know if Jim's wife was actually more accurate, or if Jim successfully hides some aspects of his personality—even from his spouse. His Rorschach report from about 20 years earlier suggested that Jim hides some negative emotions behind a façade of poise.

When we began our coverage of the trait approach in Chapter 7, we explained that traits refer to "consistency... regularity in the person's behavior." At the time we skipped over a question: How much consistency is there? Consider your own experiences. Are you consistently extraverted? Or conscientious? Or agreeable? Or are you sometimes extraverted and, at other times, shy and

THE PERSON-SITUATION CONTROVERSY

inhibited? Conscientious in some respects, but in others unreliable? Agreeable with some people some of the time, but sometimes in a disagreeable mood?

Since the 1960s, various writers have questioned whether there is enough consistency in social behavior even to support the idea of trait concepts as a centerpiece of personality theory. The most influential of these writers was Walter Mischel, whose book *Personality and Assessment* (1968) profoundly affected the field. Mischel's review of research evidence led him to conclude that people's behavior often varies, or is inconsistent from one situation to another. This inconsistency, he reasoned, reflects a basic human capability: the capability to discriminate between different situations and to vary one's actions in accord with the different opportunities, constraints, rules, and norms present in different circumstances. Mischel was not alone in his criticism; others similarly have noted the importance of situational factors in personality functioning, and explained that situational influences may contribute to the relative weakness of global personality traits in predicting behavior (e.g., Bandura, 1999; Pervin, 1994). In the 1970s and early 1980s, debate over these questions—what came to be known as the **person-situation controversy**—dominated much of the professional field.

In considering whether people are consistent in their personality traits, one must distinguish two aspects of such consistency: longitudinal stability and cross-situational consistency. The first, longitudinal stability, asks whether people high on a trait at one point in time are also high on that trait at another point in time. The second, cross-situational consistency, asks whether people high on that trait in some situations are also high on that trait in other situations. Trait theorists suggest that both are true, that is, that people are stable over time and across situations in their trait personality characteristics. The degree of cross-situational stability is what is questioned by critics of trait theory.

LONGITUDINAL STABILITY

There is good evidence of the longitudinal stability of traits, even over extended periods of time (Block, 1971; Caspi, 2000; Conley, 1985; Fraley & Roberts, 2005). Longitudinal consistency exists in at least three forms.

First, if one compares age groups, asking if 30-year-olds versus 50-year-olds differ on Big Five dimensions, one commonly finds rather small differences, a point that has been particularly emphasized by the five-factor theorists McCrae and Costa (1997, 2002). Second, if one asks about person-to-person longitudinal stability (i.e., if Person X is more extraverted than Person Y when they are both 30 years old, will Person X still be more extraverted than Person Y when they are 40 years old?) one again finds evidence of significant stability. Interestingly, these forms of stability are evident not only when people rate their own personality, but when other people rate their personality. "Husbands' and wives' views of their spouses' personalities confirm the essential stability of personality" (McCrae & Costa, 1990, p. 95). Third, there is evidence of longitudinal stability of specific trait-related behaviors. Suppose one picked a particular behavior that is an example of a broader trait. For example, if one is interested in the trait of honesty, one might study whether people cheat on tests (Hartshorne & May, 1929). If one is interested in conscientiousness, one might record whether students show up on time for a class or take clear lecture notes (Mischel & Peake, 1983). When researchers have studied such behaviors at different points in time—for example, examining whether students who show up for class and take good notes at the beginning of an academic semester continue to do so in the middle of the semester—they generally have found strong evidence of longitudinal stability (Hartshorne & May, 1928; Mischel & Peake, 1983).

Why might there be considerable longitudinal stability to personality traits? One obvious possibility is that genetically determined biological factors influence personality traits; since biological structures are relatively stable across time, the traits are too. But theorists of personality and development also have emphasized that environmental factors contribute to longitudinal stability (Lewis, 2002). People select and shape their environments so as to reinforce their traits. An extravert does not just wait for situations to happen but seeks out others and often encourages others to be extraverted as well. Finally, once perceived in a certain way, others behave toward a person in a way that perpetuates already existing characteristics. Thus, although personality can change, there are powerful forces operating to maintain stability over time.

Fraley and Roberts (2005) recently have brought sophisticated statistical analyses to the question of the degree to which individual differences are stable over time, despite the many experiences people have that may alter their psychological tendencies. These investigators do not ask merely, is there any continuity in individual differences over time? They instead ask a better question; they inquire about *patterns* of continuity. One possible pattern is that the differences between people are totally stable, with no changes ever occurring. Another is that the differences between people observed at one point in time shrink all the way to zero if one waits long enough, that is, if one extends one's scientific observations far enough into the future. Their results, however, reveal an interesting third possibility. If one examines individual differences at multiple points in time, over time the original individual differences become reduced but *not* all the way to zero. Even a large accumulation of environmental experiences may not eliminate the differences in Big Five trait scores one observes originally (Fraley & Roberts, 2005).

CROSS-SITUATIONAL STABILITY

The issue of cross-situational consistency is more complex than that of longitudinal consistency. One must consider a range of conceptual and methodological issues before one can make any sense of empirical results. One issue is how to decide that a person has acted, across situations, in a manner that we should call "consistent" or "inconsistent." It would not make sense for a person to behave the same way in all situations, nor would trait theorists expect this to happen. One would hardly expect evidence of aggressiveness in a religious ceremony or of agreeableness in a football game. The trait position that needs to be evaluated empirically is whether there is consistency across a range of situations where different behaviors are considered expressive of the same trait.

Another issue concerns research methodology. It is difficult to find consistency in specific behaviors performed in specific situations because single measures of behavior contain substantial error of measurement. To understand the notion of error of measurement, consider two different multiple-choice tests that you might take in the personality course in which you are enrolled. One test contains 50 questions written by your wise and thoughtful professor, who tries to ensure that all questions fairly represent the material in the course. The other test is written by the same wise and thoughtful professor, who continues to ensure that the questions are all fair, but on this second test there are only five questions instead of 50. The test with only five questions obviously is not as good of a test. It does not yield as accurate an estimate of your knowledge of the course material. To see why, suppose that you knew 100% of the answers to the questions but happened to make one stupid mistake in which you indicated "b" on a multiple-choice test item when you wanted to indicate "a." On the 50-item exam, you would still do great on the test: you'd have a 49/50, or 98%. But if the same thing happened on the shorter test, your one mistake would give you a 4/5, or only 80%. Psychologists use the notion of "error of measurement" to describe the fact that, as illustrated, shorter tests are more strongly affected by random factors that have nothing to do with one's true trait score.

Error of measurement is important in evaluating trait theory because, when asking about the consistency of personality traits, one must ensure that measures of the traits contain minimal error of measurement. As the psychologist Seymour Epstein (1983) has noted, research in personality psychology commonly has suffered from too much error of measurement. For example, a psychologist might construct a 50-item questionnaire to measure Conscientiousness, and then measure a single behavioral act of conscientious behavior to see if the trait predicts the behavior. But, in so doing, the psychologist may forget that the measure of behavior is, in essence, a one-item test. The research participant's conscientious behavior is only measured once. Since one-item tests have a high degree of error, the behavior measure may be so error-filled that it is impossible to predict. The solution to this problem is to sample a large number of behaviors and to average together, or aggregate, across multiple measures (Epstein, 1983). One reason trait psychologists like to use questionnaires is that they provide for the assessment of behavior in a wide range of situations that might be impossible to measure by other means.

So what happens if one takes these considerations into account and actually measures the consistency of trait-related behavior? One answer to this question comes from a study of the consistency of behaviors related to conscientiousness among college students, conducted by Mischel and Peake (1983). These investigators solved the problem of determining what counts as conscientiousness by asking students to nominate behaviors that represent the trait in a college environment (e.g., taking clear class notes). They solved the problem of error of measurement by measuring behaviors on multiple occasions and aggregating the measures together (Epstein, 1983). Their results yielded impressive evidence of longitudinal stability of trait-related behaviors (Table 8.4); people who were relatively high on conscientiousness at one point of the semester continued to act conscientiously later in the semester. However, levels of cross-situational consistency were relatively low (Table 8.4). It was commonly the case that students were conscientious in some settings (e.g., they took good lecture notes) but not conscientious in other settings (e.g., their dorm room was a mess). It is important to note that levels of cross-situational consistency were not zero; people did display some consistency in their trait-related behaviors. Furthermore, levels of cross-situational consistency are higher if one focuses

Table 8.4 Cross-situational Consistency and Temporal Stability of Conscientious Behavior

	Self-Perceived Consistency	
	High	*Low*
Cross-situational consistency	.15	.13
Temporal stability	.71	.47

NOTE: Cross-situational consistency and temporal stability examined among people who saw themselves as relatively consistent and inconsistent (High and Low Self-Perceived Consistency). Data are from behaviors judged as highly representative of the trait under study, conscientiousness.

SOURCE: Mischel & Peake, 1983

on a subset of the conscientious behaviors; for example, high consistency is found across a set of acts that relate specifically to classroom-related consistency (Jackson & Paunonen, 1985). Nonetheless, Mischel and Peake (1983) emphasize that a basic fact of social life is that people may vary their behavior from one situation to another. In so doing, they commonly may display behaviors that are inconsistent with respect to a broad personality trait. This result was consistent with findings from much earlier in the field's history; a classic study by Hartshorn and May (1928) similarly indicated that levels of longitudinal stability could be quite high, whereas the cross-situational consistency of behaviors related to a broad trait might be low.

Cross-Situational Variability in Trait-Related Behavior

A defining feature of the trait approach to personality is that individuals are characterized according to a statistical average: the average degree to which they possess, or display, a given personality trait. What was our instruction to you when you completed the Big Five inventory at the outset of this chapter? Following the logic of the trait approach, you were asked to "add together all the five numbers you circled for E and divide that sum by 5." You computed an average.

You readers who are thinking critically about the methods and assumptions of psychology (and we hope that's all of you!) may have asked yourself a question at this point in the chapter, something along the lines of "Why is one only interested in the average?" Even if we assume that people differ in their average display of trait-related behavior—and they clearly do, as findings reviewed previously indicate—it still might be that there is enormous variability *around* the average. An exciting recent advance in personality psychology is that researchers have developed methods for describing these variations around the average. In so doing, they have significantly expanded the field's understanding of personality and social behavior (e.g., Moskowitz & Hershberger, 2002; Moskowitz & Zuroff, 2005).

One important line of research is that of Fleeson (2001; Fleeson & Leicht, 2006). He asks research participants to record their current thoughts and feelings a few times a day, over a number of days. These ratings generally are done using Palm Pilots, that is, hand-hand computers. Rather than asking people merely to report their typical, overall level of a trait, Fleeson asks them to report on the degree to which they have exhibited a given type of trait-related behavior *during the past hour*. For example, a traditional extraversion item asks people whether they are talkative in general (e.g., "are you a talkative person?"). Instead of this, Fleeson asks, "During the previous hour, how well does 'talkative' describe you?" (Fleeson, 2001). By asking this question repeatedly, over a series of days, one obtains a large amount of information per person. With this information, one can determine not only average levels of behavior, but the degree to which people's behavior varies around the average.

There are, logically, two types of outcomes in research of this sort. On the one hand, maybe there won't be much variability. Maybe people are so consistent in their trait-related behavior that they will report the same level of the trait whenever they are asked. Alternatively, maybe there may be much variability. People might report high levels of a trait on some occasions, low levels of a trait on others. If so, the average level of the trait that they report simply would be a less interesting, less descriptive index of an individual's personality. (By analogy, suppose you wanted to describe the amount of sunlight received at the North Pole. Saying that "on average there is 12 hours of sunlight a day" is not very informative because the average fails to portray the fact that on some days there is no sunlight at all there, and on other days it's sunny round-the-clock—i.e., there is substantial variability.)

So how much variability in trait-related behavior is there? A lot! The results (see Figure 8.4) indicate that people show levels of variability that are "close to the maximum extreme possible" (Fleeson, 2001, p. 1016). Participants rated their behavior on a 7-point scale, with the values 1 and 7 being the low and high ends of the rating scale. As you can see from Figure 8.4, on the Big

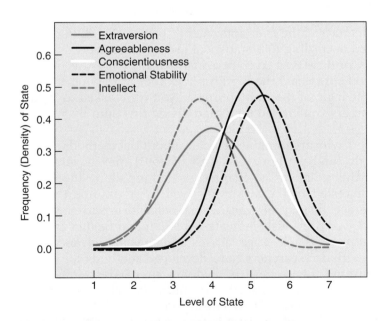

Figure 8.4   *Graph displays the average individual's distributions of psychological states that generally are construed as manifestations of each of the Big Five traits. The graph indicates that there is substantial within-person variability in trait-related behavior; that is, the average individual shows both high and low levels of the trait. (Fleeson, 2001). Reprinted with permission.*

Five traits of Extraversion ("Extra" in the figure), Conscientiousness ("Cons"), and Openness/Intellect ("Intellect"), the distribution of people's personality characteristics ranged all the way from the low to the high end of the scale. In other words, "the average individual routinely and regularly manifests all levels of" these traits and also "most levels of Agreeableness and Emotional Stability" (Fleeson, 2001, p. 1016). People do differ in their average level of behavior. But that's only a part of the story. As they adapt to the diverse challenges and opportunities of daily life, people vary their behavior substantially, and these variations simply are not described, or explained, by trait constructs.

What are we to conclude in light of this range of findings on personality consistency and variability? On the one hand, there surely is enough consistency across time, and across some situations, to reject the idea that people's behavior merely varies randomly or is determined entirely by the influences of environmental forces. People unquestionably display styles of emotion, thought, and action that are consistent across time and circumstances. So does this mean that all psychologists should embrace trait constructs as the basis of a personality theory? An alternative view is the following (see, e.g., Cervone & Shoda, 1999a; Mischel, 1968, 1999b). All psychologists, trait theorists or not, would agree that the cross-situational consistency of behaviors that are recognized as related to broad traits (such as the Big Five) is not particularly large. Whether one thinks that typical correlations are .2, .3, or .4, it remains that the majority of variation in day-to-day social behavior is not predictable from global trait measures. The alternative argument, then, is this: In building a theory of personality, why adopt constructs that one knows, for sure, only predict a minority of the variance in behavior? By analogy, if Isaac Newton had found that constructs such as "gravity" or "mass" enabled him to predict only a minority of variance in the behavior of physical objects (e.g., if his predictions correlated only .3 with observations of the physical world), would he have shouted "Eureka!" Or wouldn't he have sought better constructs that might yield better predictions? The second part of the argument involves a basic fact of social life: People strategically vary their behavior to meet their needs and goals. For example, even if you're low on conscientiousness, you might act conscientiously in class when there's a really important exam coming up, or you might be interpersonally conscientious when trying to make a good impression on a date. Such strategic variability in action is a natural part of life; the psychologist Brian Little (2005) uses the term *free traits* to refer to this capacity to display personality trait qualities that vary from one's more typical behavior. Many would argue that a science of personality must try to explain this variability. This requires additional types of personality variables, specifically, personality variables that do not merely describe typical forms of behavior, but that capture people's strategies for action, including strategies to vary their actions from one situation to another. Trait constructs, whatever their merits, do not describe or explain variations in action; they correspond to average behavioral consistencies (e.g., your typical level of conscientiousness) not to behavioral variability (the fact that you sometimes are and sometimes are not conscientious).

To many psychologists, these arguments imply that some other types of psychological constructs—something beyond merely personality trait variables (Cervone & Shoda, 1999a)—are required for a psychology of personality

All personality psychologists—including trait theorists—recognize that people's behavior changes as they confront different situations. But something that differentiates the theories we will discuss in subsequent chapters from the efforts of trait theorists is that subsequent theories do not merely recognize situation-to-situation variability in behavior. They also try explicitly to incorporate, into their theories, personality variables that explain this variability (as well as explaining consistencies in behavior). This perspective suggests a way of resolving the "person versus situation" debate. It can be resolved by dropping the word "versus" and recognizing that one may learn more about persons by examining systematically the ways in which they react and adapt to different situations (Cervone, Caldwell, & Orom, in press).

CRITICAL EVALUATION

We once again will evaluate a theoretical perspective by considering how well it achieves the five goals for a theory of personality that were reviewed back in Chapter 1. The evaluation of trait theory on these five criteria is a little more difficult than was the evaluation of psychodynamic and phenomenological theories (Chapter 4 and 6). This is because there is no one, single trait theory. Critical evaluations might vary depending on whether one is considering the trait theory of Allport, or Eysenck, or Cattell, or the lexical Big Five model, or the Five-Factor Theory of McCrae and Costa. In our evaluations, we will try to focus on main themes that are evident across the work of these different trait theorists.

SCIENTIFIC OBSERVATION: THE DATABASE

The first of these five criteria, as you will recall, is whether a theory is based on a sound body of careful scientific observations. On this point, the trait theories excel. Thanks in particular to the pioneering efforts of Cattell, the theoretical edifice of trait theory has, almost from its outset, been built on a strong foundation of objective scientific data. Rather than relying on subjective interpretations of clinical interviews, trait theorists have employed statistical analyses of objectively-scored personality tests. This objectivity is a major advantage.

The trait theorists' data not only is objective. It also is diverse. Large numbers of persons—of different ages, ethnicities, and sociocultural backgrounds—have taken part in the multinational enterprise that is personality trait testing.

A third advantage of the trait-theory database is that it includes more than self-reports. It is true that self-report measures have been central to the trait theorists' efforts. Yet many investigators have recognized that self-reports must be complemented by other forms of data: reports by observers, measures of objective life events, physiological indices of neural or biochemical systems that underlie a given trait (also see Chapter 9).

In many respects, then, the quality of the scientific database of trait theory is far superior to that of the psychodynamic or phenomenological theories. The one significant limitation to the database is that it so rarely employs the in-depth methods used by clinical theorists such as Rogers and Cattell. In trait-theoretic assessments, one learns about a few general qualities of persons—their overall trait levels—but not about the inner psychological dynamics of the individual. This limitation has led one commentator to conclude that a trait analysis, by itself, yields "a psychology of the stranger" (McAdams, 1994, p. 145), that is, a superficial analysis that is similar to the information one might know about a stranger one only meets casually, rather than the deeper information that can be yielded by a detailed case study.

THEORY: SYSTEMATIC?

Are the different elements of trait theory tied together systematically? Does the trait theorist provide a coherent, integrated account of personality structure, processes, and development?

For some theorists, the answer is yes. By analyzing not only traits, but states, roles, and motivational processes, Cattell did provide a statement about personality that was highly systematic. But Cattell's analyses of motivational processes has very little influence in contemporary psychology. By relating traits to biological mechanisms, Eysenck did provide a way of relating structures (enduring traits) to processes (of the nervous system). But except for work on the neurophysiology of extraversion, Eysenck's efforts to relate traits to biology were not entirely successful.

When one turns to more contemporary trait theories, one finds less in the way of systematic theory. As we noted earlier in this chapter, McCrae and Costa themselves readily admit that their five-factor theory does not actually specify the dynamic processes through which traits influence experience and behavior. Clearly any theory that fails to specify these processes is one that fails to provide an integrated account of personality structures, on the one hand, and personality dynamics on the other. If you are "grading" the personality theories, contemporary trait theory receives a relatively low grade on the task of providing a systematic account of diverse aspects of personality structure and dynamics.

THEORY: TESTABLE?

Trait theories deserve much higher marks on another task: developing a theory that is testable via objective evidence. Numerous aspects of trait theory can be tested objectively. Big Five theorists clearly make the prediction that factor analyses will yield five major dimensions of personality. Any other result—a six-factor solution, a three-factor solution, and so forth—clearly is a counter-example to the theoretical predictions. The fact that there can, in principle, be such clear-cut counter-examples means that trait theories have stated their ideas with admirable clarity.

Trait theorists make numerous other predictions that are open to unambiguous empirical tests. For example, they expect that individual differences on self-report personality traits will predict behavior, that genetically identical individuals will score similarly on such tests, and that trait scores will be relatively stable over time. In each case the trait theorist could, in principle, be proven wrong. Their ideas are open to objective empirical testing.

THEORY: COMPREHENSIVE?

In some respects, the trait theories are remarkably comprehensive. Trait theorists have been keenly aware that efforts to develop a taxonomy of personality traits would be of little value if important personality traits were left out of the taxonomy. They have tried to ensure, then, that all significant individual differences are incorporated into their factor-analytic studies of personality structure. They have gone to great efforts to ensure this, with lexical researchers combing the dictionary for all possible words that could be used to describe persons. In this way, their efforts are comprehensive.

Yet in other ways their efforts are lacking in comprehensiveness. This is evident if one thinks back to topics discussed in earlier chapters: the interplay of conscious and unconscious processes, the role of sexuality in personality development, the significance of dreams, the interpersonal relationship between a therapist and his or her client, the role of parents in fostering a sense of self-worth in children. What did trait theory say about these topics? Virtually nothing. These and many other topics of interest to other personality psychologists simply were not addressed by the primary trait theorists. Trait theorists have concentrated almost all their energies into the tasks of measuring individual differences, identifying the biological bases of those differences, identifying a comprehensive taxonomy of personality traits, and determining whether individual differences in trait predict individual differences in social behaviors. These are important tasks. But there are many other tasks that also are important to a comprehensive analysis of personality. Trait theories have relatively little to say about the conscious and unconscious mental dynamics of interest to Freud and the phenomenological experiences and interpersonal relations of interest to Rogers. In these ways, the trait theories are not as comprehensive as would be ideal.

There are two other ways in which trait theories lack comprehensiveness. One is the relative absence of analyses of personality processes. The theories tell us far more about the stable "building blocks" of personality—personality trait structures—than about dynamic personality processes. The other is a relative lack of attention to the individual. Except for Allport, trait theorists primarily focused on individual differences in the population rather than the inner mental life of the individual person. This is a significant limitation. By analogy, suppose one knew nothing about the workings of the human body, wanted to create a science of human biology, and began one's efforts with an individual-differences strategy: factor analyzing questionnaire reports of physical characteristics and tendencies among a large population of persons. In principle, one might identify factors such as attractiveness (a dimension of unattractive versus attractive), athleticism (unathletic versus athletic people), and healthiness (chronically sickly versus healthy persons). Such factors clearly would provide valid descriptions of individual differences; some people really are more attractive, athletic, and healthy than others. But for a science of biology one also would want to identify factors such as "circulatory system" and "nervous system." The individual-differences strategy may fail to identify these biological systems; since everyone possesses them, there may be no significant individual differences that would produce a statistical factor. The general point

Table 8.5   Summary of Strengths and Limitations of Trait Theory

Strengths	Limitations
1. Active research effort	1. The method: factor analysis
2. Interesting hypotheses	2. What does a trait include?
3. Potential ties to biology	3. What is left out or neglected?

is that one cannot confidently assume that the traits identified in factor analyses of individual differences are qualities that exist in the psyche of each and every individual. Big Five researchers recognize this; Saucier, Hampson, & Goldberg (2000, p. 28) write: "Clearly, the study of different lexicons [of personality description] can lead to a useful and highly generalizable classification system for personality traits, but this classification system should not be reified into an explanatory one. A model of descriptions does not provide a model of causes, and the study of personality lexicons should not be equated with a study of personality."

APPLICATIONS

It is easy to describe how trait theory has been applied, but trickier to evaluate the worth of these applications. This is because any such evaluations hinge on subjective judgments about the applied products that a personality theory should provide.

What trait theories do provide are tools for prediction. Trait theorists have identified a consensually accepted set of traits and developed reliable scales for measuring them. In so doing, they have provided a simple and valuable technology for predicting individual differences in psychological outcomes. The widespread use of these measures attests to their applied utility. Educational psychologists, clinical psychologists, industrial/organizational psychologists, and many other applied investigators have long employed measures of individual differences in global personality traits. If the provision of tools for the prediction of individual differences is the main applied product one wants from a personality theory, then trait theory applications can be judged a success.

However, other personality theorists want more. Every other personality theory discussed in this text provides not only a theory but a therapy. Freud and Rogers—and, as you will see in subsequent chapters, behaviorists, personal construct theorists, and social-cognitive theorists—each provide novel therapy techniques that are based on their theories. These therapies are the main applications of the given theory. But there is no "trait theory therapy." Trait theory (with the exception of some efforts by Eysenck) is the one body of theorizing that has not generated therapies for bringing about psychological change.

The trait theorist may say that developing therapies simply is not what their work is about. Trait theories are theories of stable individual differences and the bases of those individual differences. They are not theories of psychological

Trait Approaches at a Glance

	Structure	Process	Growth and Development
	Traits	Dynamic traits, motives associated with traits	Contributions of heredity and environment to traits

change. It thus may not be fair to evaluate trait theories negatively for their failure to produce novel forms of therapy.

MAJOR CONTRIBUTIONS AND SUMMARY

Psychologists working in the trait tradition rightly can claim to have made substantial gains (Table 8.5). This is most apparent by posing questions about personality that might be puzzling but that, thanks to the efforts of trait psychologists, have been answered convincingly: How many trait dimensions are needed to describe major individual differences in the population? Are people's standings in these dimensions consistent across time? Are there any relations between these individual differences and differences in social behavior? The answers "5 (or 6)," "yes," and "yes" can be provided with confidence, and enormous research backing, by the trait psychologist.

The ability to provide these answers is a major step forward. Outside of the halls of academia, people often desire a simple yet scientifically validated way of assessing individual differences in average psychological tendencies. There are so many potential individual differences that one might not even know how to get started on this task. But Cattell and Eysenck figured out a way to get started, and contemporary Big Five investigators provide a valuable and widely-accepted solution to the problem.

Another major strength of the trait approach is its capacity to move from a psychological to a biological level of analysis. Work in genetics and neurophysiology has begun to identify biological foundations of individual differences, as we review in the chapter ahead. Although all personality psychologists recognize that persons are biological beings, the trait model particularly lends itself to the integration of biological findings into a comprehensive model of personality. We continue to consider this wedding of psychology to biology in the chapter ahead.

MAJOR CONCEPTS

Big Five   In trait factor theory, the five major trait categories, including emotionality, activity, and sociability factors.

Facets   The more specific traits (or components) that make up each of the broad Big Five factors. For example, facets of extraversion are activity level, assertiveness, excitement seeking, positive emotions, gregariousness, and warmth.

Five-factor theory   An emerging consensus among trait theorists suggesting five basic factors to human personality: neuroticism, extraversion, openness, agreeableness, and conscientiousness.

Pathology	Change
Extreme scores on trait dimensions (e.g., neuroticism)	(No formal model)

Fundamental lexical hypothesis The hypothesis that over time the most important individual differences in human interaction have been encoded as single terms into language.

NEO-PI-R A personality questionnaire designed to measure people's standing on each of the factors of the five-factor model, as well as on facets of each factor.

OCEAN The acronym for the five basic traits: openness, conscientiousness, extraversion, agreeableness, and neuroticism.

Person-situation controversy A controversy between psychologists who emphasize the importance of personal (internal) variables in determining behavior and those who emphasize the importance of situational (external) influences.

REVIEW

1. In the later years of the 20th century, a consensus emerged among trait theorists around the Big Five, or five-factor, model of personality traits. Support for the model comes from the factor analysis of trait terms in language and the factor analysis of personality ratings and questionnaires.

2. The Big Five theorists' study of language rests on the fundamental lexical hypothesis, which is the hypothesis that the fundamental individual differences among people have been encoded into the natural language.

3. McCrae and Costa have proposed a theoretical model, the five-factor model, that emphasizes the biological basis of traits, which are construed in the model as basic tendencies. Substantial evidence of stability of overall trait structures and of individual differences in trait levels is consistent with this theoretical model. However, the model is questioned by evidence of change in personality trait levels, as well as evidence that at least one more trait factor, a sixth factor, is required to capture all major individual differences.

4. Research indicates that individual differences in five-factor scores significantly predict outcomes in domains of importance to applied psychologists, such as vocational guidance,

personality diagnosis, work behavior, and psychological treatment. A limitation of the five-factor trait model as an applied tool, however, is that it offers no specific recommendations concerning the process of personality change.

5. Although there is evidence for longitudinal stability in personality traits, much research also suggests that people show significant variability in trait-related behavior when they encounter different social contexts. To some, this variability in trait-related behavior suggests that trait constructs are inadequate as a basis for personality theory. Yet others judge that the stability in behavior across time and place that does exist is sufficient to support the utility of trait theories.

6. An overall evaluation of current trait theory suggests strengths in research, the formulation of interesting hypotheses, and the potential for ties to biology in relation to work on genetic contributions to personality and evolutionary developments. At the same time, questions can be raised concerning the method of factor analysis, the clarity of meaning of the trait concept, the neglect of such important areas of psychological functioning as the self, and a theory of personality change.

BIOLOGICAL FOUNDATIONS OF PERSONALITY

9

Chapter Focus

Why are some people generally happy and others sad, some energetic and others lethargic, some impulsive and others cautious, some excited and others calm, some optimistic and others pessimistic? Do we learn these styles of behavior? Or might they be part of our biological makeup? Often it is said that parents are believers in the importance of the environment, or nurture, when they have their first child, and believers in temperament differences, or nature, when they have their second child. Initial differences between children from the same family often are that great! Along similar lines, people looking into a nursery window generally are struck with the differences among the newly born—some active and others moving little, some spending a lot of time crying while others remain calm.

For centuries humans have tried to understand the relation between body and mind, between constitution and personality. And since the 1880s when Sir Francis Galton contrasted "nature" (heredity) with "nurture" (environment), psychologists have been concerned with the relation between the two. During the past few decades tremendous gains have been made in our understanding of biological processes. Are there biological processes that determine individual differences in temperament and personality? If so, which processes are key? The study of biological foundations of personality is a fast-moving field, and in this chapter we will try to capture both the insights that have been gained and the questions that remain.

QUESTIONS TO BE ADDRESSED IN THIS CHAPTER

1. Are infants born with differences in temperament? If so, what are the biological bases of these differences?

2. How can the study of human evolution inform our understanding of the personalities of contemporary humans?

3. What role do genes play in the formation of personality? How do they interact with the environment in the unfolding of personality?

4. What is the relation between brain processes and personality processes?

Sometimes scientists learn from accidents. The story about an apple falling on Newton's head—even if it is apocryphal—wisely instructs that insight into the systematic workings of nature can result from accidental occurrences.

Scientific understanding of biological bases of personality, the topic of this chapter, has benefited greatly from the accidental. The most famous accident was suffered by Phineas Gage, a construction foreman who in 1848 had the following "bad day on the job." Working on railroad construction, Gage was blasting a path through hard rock. Following procedures in which he was skilled, Gage drilled a hole in the ground, filled it with explosive powder, and inserted an iron rod. Next, a fuse was to be lit. Though Gage was an expert at this, on this occasion he was distracted and the charge blew up in his face. The explosion blew the iron rod through his left cheek, the base of his skull, and the front of his brain. It largely destroyed a part of Gage's frontal cortex. The rod then exited through the top of his head.

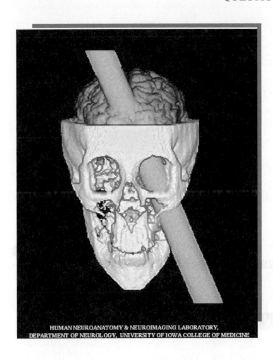

HUMAN NEUROANATOMY & NEUROIMAGING LABORATORY,
DEPARTMENT OF NEUROLOGY, UNIVERSITY OF IOWA COLLEGE OF MEDICINE

This illustration shows the location through which an iron rod blasted through the frontal cortex of Phineas Gage—who survived the accident, but experienced a profound change in his personality.

Gage was stunned but, miraculously, not killed. He was able to walk and speak. Indeed, he could describe what happened in full detail and communicate in a rational way. Yet Gage had changed deeply. As related by the eminent neurologist Antonio Damasio (1994), "Gage's disposition, his likes and dislikes, his dreams and aspirations are all to change. Gage's body may be alive and well, but there is a new spirit animating it. Gage was no longer Gage" (Damasio, 1994, p. 7). Once serious, industrious, energetic, and responsible, immediately after the accident Gage became irresponsible, thoughtless of others, lacking in planfulness, and indifferent to the consequences of his actions.

Gage's story suggests that there exist deep interconnections between brain functioning and personality functioning. Suppose the explosion had blown a hole in his leg instead of his brain. It still would have been a bad accident yet Gage likely would have been the same basic person as before. Gage simultaneously lost (1) frontal-brain material and (2) personality qualities. The fact that the two losses were simultaneous was—well, one might say it was no accident. Gage's case suggests that brain and personality are intimately, directly connected.

This chapter explores these connections between the biological brain and the psychological personality. We begin with a historical look at conceptions of temperament, which is considered by many to be a fundamental aspect of our personality and clearly was an aspect of Gage's personality that was changed when the iron rod pierced his brain. The rest of this chapter introduces you to contemporary scientific research on biological foundations of personality.

This chapter is a little different from the prior chapters of this book. Each of the chapters 3 through 8 has either introduced you to a theory (psychoanalysis, phenomenological theory, trait theory) or has reviewed applications and extensions of a given theory's core ideas. Here we focus more specifically on a set of scientific *findings*. These research results do not relate to only one particular theory. They instead constitute a body of knowledge that must be considered by all personality theorists. Many of the findings reviewed in this chapter relate particularly strongly to the trait theories you learned about in chapters 7 and 8. However, some address psychological phenomena discussed by Freud or Rogers, or by personality theorists you will learn about in subsequent chapters.

TEMPERAMENT: VIEWS OF MIND-BODY RELATIONSHIPS FROM THE PAST TO THE PRESENT

You have about as much choice in some aspects of your personality as you do in the shape of your nose or the size of your feet. Psychologists call this biological, inborn dimension of personality "temperament."

Source: Hamer & Copeland, 1998, p. 7.

What is temperament? Psychologists generally use the term to refer to individual differences in mood or quality of emotional response. As suggested by the quote above, these differences are viewed as primarily inherited and biologically based: "The concept of temperament refers to any moderately stable, differentiating emotional or behavioral quality whose appearance in childhood is influenced by inherited biology, including differences in brain neurochemistry" (Kagan, 1994, p. xvii). Many aspects of personality clearly do not have their basis in inherited biology. We acquire social skills, our self-concept, personal goals in life, and so forth through interaction with the social world. But other features of personality such as individuals' typical mood, their chronic level of activity, or their degree of emotional reaction in response to particular types of environmental stimuli may directly reflect individual differences in inherited biology. It is these individual differences in emotional quality that appear early, remain fairly stable, are inherited, and are based in biological processes that are referred to as temperament (Eisenberg, Fabes, Guthrie, & Reiser, 2000; Fox, Henderson, Marshall, Nichols, & Ghera, 2005; Rothbart, Ahadi, & Evans, 2000).

CONSTITUTION AND TEMPERAMENT: EARLY VIEWS

Scholars have long been interested in the possibility that psychological differences among people have a biological basis (reviewed in Kagan, 1994; Strelau, 1998). In ancient Greece, Hippocrates posited that variations in four basic psychological characteristics reflect variations in bodily fluids (see Chapter 7, Figure 7.3). The ancient Greeks' ideas about people reflected their beliefs about the universe in general. They thought that all of nature was composed of four elements: air, earth, fire, and water. Hippocrates and (centuries later) Galen suggested a similar fourfold analysis of bodily fluids and associated psychological characteristics. The four elements of nature were said to be represented in the human body by four humors (blood, black bile, yellow bile, phlegm), each corresponding to a temperament: sanguine, melancholic, choleric, phlegmatic. Individual differences in temperament corresponded to the predominance within the individual of one or another of the four humors. Similarly, diseases corresponded to excesses in one or another humor (e.g., too much black bile and depression). In other words, from these early times a classification of temperament types was proposed, one based on constitution or basic body chemistry.

CURRENT QUESTIONS

STRESS AND AGING: HOW DOES IT WORK?

Intuition tells us that one of the most important links between personality and biology involves the experience of stress. People who live calm, stress-free lives appear younger. Chronic psychological stress, in contrast, seems to speed aging. But are these intuitions correct? And if so, how does it work—how is psychological stress linked to biological aging?

A remarkable study of middle-aged women who experienced varying degrees of stress provides concrete answers to these questions (Epel et al., 2004). The key feature of this study was that it included a measure of a biological mechanism that is fundamental to cellular aging. One part of cells are telomeres, which are strands of DNA that form a kind of "cap" at the end of every chromosome. The telomere shortens slightly every time a cell replicates. With age, then, the telomere gets smaller. When the telomere

becomes too short, the cell no longer can divide. Telomere length thus is "a book-marker of a cell's biological (versus chronological) 'age'" (Epel et al., 2004, p. 17312).

What does this have to do with stress and personality functioning? The experience of stress affects the body's internal chemistry, including the cellular environment in which telomeres reside. People who are of the same chronological age but who experience different levels of daily stress, then, may have cells with telomeres of different lengths. The researchers (Epel et al., 2004) hypothesized that stress would have a negative affect on telomere length. It was predicted, in other words, that people who experience high amounts of stress would have shorter telomeres. At a cellular level, they would be biologically older.

How can one test this? One challenge is to identify how much stress people are

Photos depict former U.S. president Richard M. Nixon at the inauguration (left photo) and conclusion (right photo) of his presidency, which ended in his resignation from office after the Watergate scandal. At the time of his resignation, Nixon looked decades older than he had at the time of his inauguration, although the events actually were only about six years apart. Research suggests that the stresses of the office may have been responsible for Nixon's rapid biological aging.

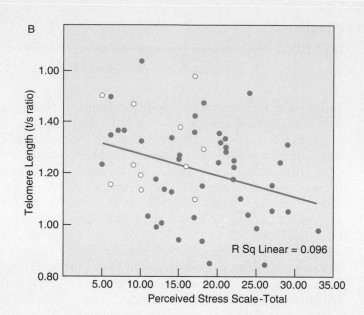

Figure 9.1 *The figure plots telomere length as a function of perceived stress for two groups: the low-stress (white) and high-stress (blue) mothers. Copyright © 2004 National Academy of Sciences, U.S.A.*

experiencing. The experimenters did this in two ways. First, they included a measure of perceived stress, that is, a self-report of how much stress one is experiencing. Second, they included in their study groups persons who differed on an objective life event that is stressful. Some of the women in the study were mothers of children with a chronic illness; day-to-day child care for these women thus was particularly stressful. A second, control group consisted of mothers of healthy children.

The other challenge is to measure telomere length. This was done through standard biological procedures. Blood samples were taken and analyzed to determine average telomere length for each participant.

The findings revealed a remarkably strong link between stress and telomere length

(Figure 9.1). The figure plots telomere length as a function of perceived stress for two groups: the low-stress and high-stress mothers. In both groups, higher stress predicted shorter-length telomeres. The highest levels of stress, and many of the shortest telomere lengths, were found in the group of mothers who were caring for a chronically ill child. When telomere lengths were translated into years (i.e., by relating telomere lengths found in the people in this study to data for the population at large), it was found that the effects of stress on aging are huge! High-stress persons showed a cellular age 9–17 years older than those who experienced low stress—a research result you might want to remember the next time a friend suggests that you "chill out."

The conceptions of the ancient Greeks were remarkably long-lasting. More than two millennia after Hippocrates, the great German philosopher Immanuel Kant turned his attention to questions of temperament. Kant, writing around 1800 A.D., thought some of the same things that Hippocrates thought in the 4th century B.C. Kant distinguished four types of temperament and felt that their basis was found in bodily fluids. He believed that variations in blood, rather than in the range of bodily fluids discussed by the Greeks, were the cause of variations in temperament. Yet the basic conceptualization remained curiously similar to that of the ancient Greeks. Needless to say, the details of these bodily fluid theories are completely rejected by all contemporary psychological scientists.

A very different but equally unsatisfactory theory of the biological bases of individual differences arose in the 19th century from the work of the German physician Franz Joseph Gall. Gall founded the field of **phrenology**, which tried to locate areas of the brain responsible for specific aspects of emotional and behavioral functioning (Figure 9.2). Gall did postmortem inspections of brains and attempted to relate differences in brain tissue to reports of the individual's capacities, dispositions, and traits before death. In particular, a possible relation between personality and bumps on the head was to be examined (the bumps purportedly being indicative of the development of underlying brain tissue). Phrenology gained great notoriety and popularity in the early 19th century. Gall's work was seen as a serious effort to locate aspects of personality functioning in specific parts of the brain. Subsequently, however, phrenology was utterly discredited. Contemporary research indicates that the brain simply does not work in the way that Gall assumed, with localized regions of brain being responsible for specific types of thought and social behavior. Instead, most complex actions and thought patterns are executed by the

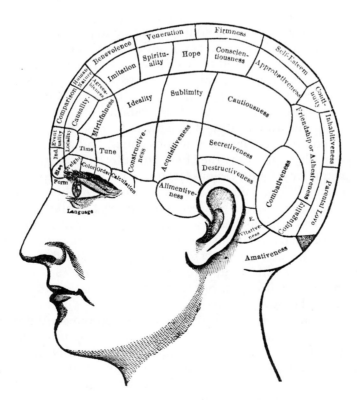

Figure 9.2 *Gall's Localization of Personality Functions of the Brain.*

synchronized action of multiple, interconnected regions of the brain (Bressler, 2002; Edelman & Tononi, 2000).

Efforts of enduring value to science finally were seen in the mid-19th century. Three publications were proved to be critical: Charles Darwin's *The Origin of Species* (1859) and *The Expression of Emotions in Man and Animals* (1872), and Gregor Mendel's *Experiments on Plant Hybrids* (1865). Darwin's *Origin*, of course, was foundational to the contemporary science of biology. His *Expression of Emotions* documented numerous close relations between emotional expression in humans and emotional expression in other complex mammals; in so doing, it contributed indirectly to the study of temperament and also foreshadowed the development of contemporary evolutionary psychology (discussed later in this chapter). Mendel's work reported eight years of research on the breeding of pea plant characteristics and served as the foundation for modern genetics.

Also of great historical note are the efforts of Francis Galton, who was a cousin of Darwin. Galton explored the potential inherited basis of individual differences in both personality and intelligence. In so doing, he sparked a "nature-nurture" controversy that has flared up repeatedly throughout the history of the field.

It also was during this time that the eminent psychiatrist Emil Kraepelin, born in the same year as Freud and a rival as the founder of modern psychiatry, attempted a classification of mental disorders that were believed to be largely hereditary. Noteworthy here is Kraepelin's emphasis on disorders of mood such as manic-depressive illness, now known as bipolar disorder (Barondes, 1998). In sum, during this period there was evidence of considerable interest in biological processes generally and their relation to personality in particular.

In the 20th century, investigators in both Europe and the United States became intrigued by the possibility of systematic links between psychological temperament and body types. The German psychiatrist Ernst Kretschmer tried to relate body type to personality early in the century (*Physique and Character*, 1925). Kretschmer devised a method of measuring body type, resulting in a classification of three fundamental types: pyknic (plump, round physique), athletic (muscular, vigorous physique), and asthenic (frail, linear physique). These physiques were then found to differ in incidence of psychiatric disorder, a pyknic physique being associated with manic-depressive disorder and an asthenic physique being associated with schizophrenia. Beyond this, Kretschmer assumed a relation between physique and normal personality (e.g., pyknic and extraversion, asthenic and introversion), although no evidence was presented for such a relationship. Kretschmer's work suffered from faulty methodology (e.g., he did not correct for the fact that manic-depressive disorder tends to occur later in life than schizophrenia and people tend to become heavier and rounded with age), but it laid the foundation for later work in constitutional psychology.

In the United States, a similar effort was carried out by William Sheldon (1940, 1942), who suggested that each person has an inherited basic biological structure (bodily physique, constitution) that determines his or her temperament. Sheldon defined three dimensions of physique that largely corresponded to those suggested by Kretschmer: endomorph (soft and round), mesomorphy (hard and rectangular, muscular), and ectomorphy (linear and fragile, thin, lightly muscled). Like Kretschmer, he suggested that physique was systematically related to temperament. Although his research appeared to yield systematic relations between body type and personality, his work, like Kretchmer's, proved to be plagued with methodological problems; subsequent work indicated that the relation between body type and personality was quite weak (Strelau, 1998).

An effort of the early 20th century that proved of more lasting value was the work of Pavlov, whose research we discuss in detail in Chapter 10. Much of Pavlov's work examined how the nervous system of organisms is modified by experience (see Chapter 10). Yet Pavlov also developed a theory of stable individual differences in nervous-system functioning that highlighted the possibility of variations in the "strength" of the nervous system, that is, in the degree to which normal nervous system functioning could be maintained in the face of high levels of stimuli or stress (Strelau, 1998).

CONSTITUTION AND TEMPERAMENT: LONGITUDINAL STUDIES

The historical efforts to study temperament that we have just reviewed were hampered not only by conceptual shortcomings, but by limitations in the scientific methods employed. A defining feature of those psychological characteristics called temperament is that they are present early in life and are relatively stable across the life course. Yet none of the aforementioned studies involved infants or longitudinal research (i.e., research that studies a group of persons over an extended period of time).

Beginning in the 1950s, things began to change. A pioneering scientific effort was the New York Longitudinal Study (NYLS) conducted by Alexander Thomas and Stella Chess (Thomas & Chess, 1977). These researchers followed over 100 children from birth to adolescence, using parental reports of infants' reactions to a variety of situations to define variations in infant temperament. On the basis of ratings of infant characteristics such as activity level, general mood, attention span, and persistence, they defined three infant temperament types: easy babies who were playful and adaptable, difficult babies who were negative and unadaptable, and slow-to-warm-up babies who were low in reactivity and mild in their responses. This study and subsequent studies found a link between such early differences in temperament and later personality characteristics (Rothbart & Bates, 1998; Shiner, 1998). For example, difficult babies were found to have the greatest difficulty in later adjustment, whereas easy babies were found to have the least likelihood of later difficulties. In addition, Thomas and Chess suggested that the parental environment best suited for babies of one temperament type might not be best for those of a different temperament type; that is, there is a goodness-of-fit between infant temperament and parental environment.

Following the NYLS research, Arnold Buss and Robert Plomin (1975, 1984) used parental ratings of behavior to define four dimensions of temperament: Emotionality (ease of arousal in upsetting situations, general distress), Activity (tempo and vigor of motor movements, on the go all the time, fidgety), Sociability (responsiveness to other persons, makes friends easily versus shy), and Impulsivity (ability to inhibit or control behavior, impulsive, easily bored), creating the acronym, EASI. The last of these dimensions (Impulsivity) was dropped because it was not found to be a clear dimension in subsequent factor analyses of questionnaires. However, research supported the view of Buss and

Plomin that temperament shows evidence of continuity over time and of being largely inherited, the latter based on evidence of greater similarity of mothers' ratings of monozygotic (identical) twins than dizygotic (fraternal) twins. Although noteworthy in the use of factor analysis to define dimensions of temperament and in the study of twins to determine inheritance of temperament, the research was problematic in the use of parental ratings rather than more objective measures of observation. Contemporary researchers recognized that parents may be systematically biased when rating the personality of their own children; for example, parents tend to overestimate the similarity of identical twins and to underestimate the similarity of fraternal twins (Saudino, 1997).

Many contemporary efforts to characterize the nature of psychological temperament resemble the research strategy of Buss and Plomin (1984). Researchers generally try to identify a small set of individual-difference dimensions that characterize major variations in temperament characteristics in the population at large (e.g., Goldsmith & Campos, 1982; Gray, 1991; Strelau, 1998). We do not dwell on the details of these efforts here because, in important respects, they are similar to the five-factor model we reviewed in detail in our previous chapter. Indeed, five-factor enthusiasts contend that the five personality traits measured in their questionnaires are an adequate framework for conceptualizing individual differences in temperament (Costa & McCrae, 2001). Instead, we now consider research in which investigators try to identify and assess specific biological systems that contribute to emotion and behavior. In other words, rather than relying on people's responses to questionnaires, the researchers directly measure behavior and examine the neural systems that contribute to that behavior.

BIOLOGY, TEMPERAMENT, AND PERSONALITY DEVELOPMENT: CONTEMPORARY RESEARCH

Inhibited and Uninhibited Children: Research of Kagan and Colleagues

A particularly noteworthy line of research on the biological bases of temperament has been spearheaded by the Harvard psychologist Jerome Kagan (1994, 2003). Kagan relates his contemporary ideas and research to an idea from ancient times that we noted above. It is Galen's suggestion, back in the second century, that each of us inherits a temperament that is based in our constitution or physiology. Kagan of course did not explore the specific suggestions of Galen involving bodily fluids. Instead, drawing on contemporary knowledge of neuroanatomy, he set out to identify the neural bases of individual differences in emotion and behavior.

A key to his research has been the use of objective laboratory measures of behavior. Rather than merely asking parents to report about the characteristics of their children, Kagan observed children directly, commonly in laboratory settings. Based on these observations, he became impressed with what appeared to be two clearly defined behavioral profiles in temperament: **inhibited** and **uninhibited temperament** profiles. Relative to the uninhibited child, the inhibited child reacts to unfamiliar persons or events with restraint,

The developmental psychologist Jerome Kagan has identified early differences in temperament, conceptualized as inhibited and uninhibited types.

avoidance, and distress, takes a longer time to relax in new situations, and has more unusual fears and phobias. Such a child behaves timidly and cautiously, the initial reaction to novelty being to become quiet, seek parental comfort, or run and hide. By contrast, the uninhibited child seems to enjoy these very same situations that seem so stressful to the inhibited child. Rather than being timid and fearful, the uninhibited child responds with spontaneity in novel situations, laughing and smiling easily.

Struck by such dramatic differences, Kagan set out to address the following questions: How early do such differences in temperament emerge? How stable are these differences in temperament over time? Can some biological bases for such differences in temperament be suggested? His central hypothesis was that infants inherit differences in biological functioning that lead them to be more or less reactive to novelty and that these inherited differences tend to be stable during development. According to the hypothesis, infants born highly reactive to novelty should become inhibited children whereas those born with low reactivity should develop into uninhibited children.

To test this hypothesis, Kagan brought four-month-old infants into the laboratory and videotaped their behavior while they were exposed to familiar and novel stimuli (e.g., mother's face, voice of a strange female, colorful mobiles moving back and forth, a balloon popping). The videotapes then were scored on measures of reactivity such as arching of the back, vigorous flexing of limbs, and crying. About 20 percent of the infants were designated as high-reactive, characterized by arching of the back, intense crying, and an unhappy facial expression in response to the novel stimuli. The behavioral profile suggested that they had been overaroused by the stimuli, particularly since the responses stopped when the stimuli were removed. In contrast, the low-reactive infants, about 40 percent of the group, appeared to be calm and laid-back in response to the novel stimuli. The remaining infants, about 40 percent, showed various mixtures of response.

To determine whether, as predicted, the high-reactive infants would become inhibited children and the low-reactive infants uninhibited children, Kagan again studied the children when they were 14 months old, 21 months old, and $4\frac{1}{2}$ years old. Again the children were brought to the laboratory and exposed to novel, unfamiliar situations (e.g., flashing lights, a toy clown striking a drum, a stranger in an unfamiliar costume, the noise of plastic balls rotating in a wheel

Research on temperament indicates that some children inherit a predisposition to become highly distressed in the presence of novel situations and people—even smiling, friendly ones!

at the first two ages, and meeting with an unfamiliar adult and unfamiliar children at the later age). In addition to behavioral observations, physiological measures such as heart rate and blood pressure in response to the unfamiliar situations were obtained.

Was consistency between early behavioral profiles of reactivity and later profiles expressive of inhibited and uninhibited types found? Kagan suggests that this indeed was the case. Thus, the high-reactive infants showed greater fearful behavior, heart acceleration, and increased blood pressure in response to the unfamiliar at 14 and 21 months of age than did the low-reactive infants. And such differences were maintained at the later testing at age $4\frac{1}{2}$ years of age. At this point it was found that the children who had been high-reactive infants smiled and talked less with the unfamiliar adult, and were more shy with unfamiliar peers than was the case for the children who had been low-reactive infants. Further testing in the eighth year of life indicated continuing consistency, with a majority of the children assigned to each group at age four months retaining membership in that group. In sum, there was considerable evidence of temperament stability and suggestions of a possible biological basis for these differences in temperament. As we will observe later in the chapter, additional evidence of differences in biological functioning was obtained subsequently.

Although there is consistency across time in temperament, there also is evidence of change (Fox et al., 2005). Many high-reactive infants did not become consistently fearful. Change in these children seemed particularly tied to having mothers who were not overly protective and placed reasonable demands on them (Kagan, Arcus, & Snidman, 1993). And, some of the low-reactive infants lost their relaxed style. Despite an initial temperamental bias, environment played a role in the unfolding personality. Thus, according to

Kagan, "any predisposition conferred by our genetic endowment is far from being a life sentence; there is no inevitable adult outcome of a particular infant temperament" (1999, p. 32). At the same time, Kagan points out that not one of the high-reactive infants became a consistently uninhibited child and it was very rare for a low-reactive infant to become a consistently inhibited child. Although change was possible, the temperamental bias did not vanish and it appeared to set some constraints on the direction of development. According to Kagan, "it is very difficult to change one's inherited predisposition completely" (1999, p. 41).

Another question explored in this line of research is whether temperament qualities vary dimensionally (e.g., like height) or categorically (e.g., like eye color or biological sex). Woodward, Lenzenweger, Kagan, Snidman, and Arcus (2000) employed statistical techniques that are designed to answer this question. These statistical methods are designed to identify categories or classes that may explain patterns of variation in data obtained from a large group of persons. To illustrate, suppose you did not know that some people are men and others are women. If you asked people a large number of questions about their personal habits, you might find out that there are distinct groups. A statistical analysis could indicate that some responses go together so strongly (e.g., people who say that they wear skirts also tend to say that they wear lipstick and own high-heel shoes) that they indicate a group of people that is a categorically distinct class (women). Woodward and colleagues (2000) found that the group of infants showing high reactivity (limb movements, crying) in response to novel situations is a distinct class. A distinct group of about 10 percent of a large population of children was found to be consistently more reactive than the population at large. This finding is important because it conflicts with an assumption that is commonly made by other researchers, namely, the assumption that individual differences in personality characteristics exclusively involve continuous dimensions rather than distinct categories.

Contemporary research also sheds light on the precise brain regions that contribute to inhibited and uninhibited tendencies (Schmidt & Fox, 2002). More than one region appears to be involved, with behavioral tendencies reflecting interactions among the different neural systems. One important region is the amygdala, a region of brain that, as we note below, is centrally involved in fear response. A second region is the frontal cortex, which is involved in regulating emotional response, in part by influencing the functioning of the amygdala. Interestingly, the functioning of these brain regions is not entirely determined by inherited factors; social experiences appear to modify brain functioning and thus influence children's emotional tendencies (Schmidt & Fox, 2002).

Research using neuro-imaging methods provides particularly clear evidence of the role of amygdala functioning in inhibited versus uninhibited temperament (Schwartz, Wright, Shin, Kagan, & Rauch, 2003). In this work, the researchers studied a group of young adults who had been categorized as being highly inhibited or uninhibited when they were only two years old. The adults participated in a laboratory study in which they viewed pictures of human faces. A key portion of the experiment involved participants' reactions to familiar faces (i.e., pictures of people that the participant had seen previously, in an earlier portion of the experiment) versus novel faces (people had not been seen previously); it was predicted that inhibited people respond more to the novel, unfamiliar faces. A particularly valuable feature of the research was the measurement technique used. A brain imaging technique, fMRI (described in more detail later in this chapter), was employed to determine the exact brain regions that became active as people viewed the familiar and novel faces. The fMRI measures provided clear support for the hypothesis that uninhibited versus inhibited persons differ in amygdala functioning (Figure 9.3). When they viewed the novel faces, adults who back when they were only two years old had been identified as inhibited children showed higher levels of amygdala activity. The results, then, provide striking evidence of a specific biological basis of this temperament characteristic, and show that these differences in biology can be stable over long periods of life.

Recent evidence is even beginning to identify a specific molecular basis for fear—at least in animals, whose neural systems of fear may resemble those of humans to a high enough degree that results could generalize to our species. In this work (Shumyatsky et al., 2005), researchers have identified a gene that contributes to levels of a protein, called stathmin, that influences the functioning of the amygdala. Mice with and without the stathmin gene differed in behavioral measures of fear, such as "freezing" in the presence of a potentially fear-provoking stimulus and exploring (or not) novel open spaces (Shumyatsky et al., 2005). A fascinating aspect of this work is that it was not only observational, but truly experimental (see Chapter 2). The research included genetic "knockout" techniques, in which genetic material is manipulated experimentally (Benson, 2004). Such techniques hold enormous promise for advancing scientific understanding of how genetic mechanisms influence the development of biological systems that contribute to psychological experience.

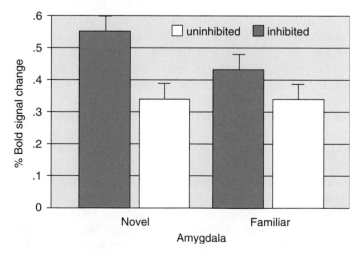

Figure 9.3   *fMRI measures of brain reactivity to novel and familiar faces among people who had been classified as uninhibited and inhibited. From Schwartz, Wright, Shin, Kagan, & Rauch (2003).*

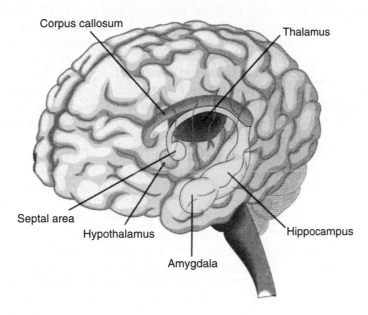

Figure 9.4 *The Limbic System. The limbic system, located within the cerebrum, consists of the septal area, amygdala, and hippocampus.*

Interpreting Data on Biology and Personality

In summary, there is clear evidence that genetically-based biological processes contribute to individual differences in the tendency to experience inhibition and fear in a particular type of context, namely, contexts involving novelty. Data indicate that the amygdala is involved in fear responses. The evidence for these conclusions is strong and clear. Nonetheless, it is important not to *over*interpret this evidence. There are four interpretations that may at first appear appealing, yet that would be overinterpretations, that is, conclusions that go beyond the actual data. We spell these out because these overinterpretations can occur whenever one asks questions about the biological bases of personality; in other words, they do not concern the biological bases merely of inhibited behavior.

First, one might conclude from this evidence that the main function of the amygdala is to produce fearful behavior. One might, in other words, conclude that the amygdala is a kind of fear-production machine. However, this would not be a safe conclusion because the amygdala can be involved in many psychological functions *other than* fear responses. The finding that a brain region is active during a particular type of response does not mean that it is specifically dedicated to that one type of response. By analogy, we use our hands for writing but hands are not a "writing machine"; we use them in a variety of other tasks.

Second, the data do *not* show that the amygdala is *the only* biological mechanism in fear responses. It is possible that many other systems are involved, too. In fact, it is possible that the amygdala is not even necessary for the experience of emotions such as fear, even if it usually is involved in the experiences. A fascinating study by Anderson and Phelps (2002) illustrates the point. They compared the daily emotional experiences of people with amygdala damage (lesions to and/or removal of portions of the amygdala, done surgically as a medical procedure to alleviate seizures these individuals had experienced) to people with normal, intact amygdalas. If the amygdala was necessary to the experience of emotions, these people's emotional lives should have differed dramatically. But it turns out that they did not differ at all! People with amygdala damage experienced the same range of emotions as did biologically normal persons. The authors conclude that "the complexity and richness of human emotional life do not appear to be supported by the amygdala alone" (Anderson & Phelps, 2002, p. 717).

Third, existing data do not show that fear, per se, is the primary psychological experience in which the amygdala is involved. Circumstances that evoke fear may contain *other features* (i.e., features other than the presence of a stimulus that is threatening), and the amygdala may primarily be involved in the processing of these other features. The primary possibility is novelty. Novelty of course is not the same thing as fear, yet it is related to fear closely. You rarely experience fear in response to familiar circumstances, even if those circumstances may, in principle, be harmful. For example, if you're standing on a sidewalk and cars are passing by, you do not recoil in fear every time you see a moving car. (At least we hope you don't!) This is true even though each car could, in principle, be harmful to you. You are used to seeing cars whiz by so you are not afraid of them, despite their potential for harm. People experience fear in response to potentially harmful events that are unusual, or novel. Kagan (2002) has reviewed evidence indicating that, in fact, "a state of surprise is a more reliable incentive for amygdalar activation than a state of fear" (p. 13).

Fourth, the fact that inherited differences in a biological system, the amygdala, play a role in fearful behavior may lead one to conclude that environmental experiences are unimportant to personality development, and a person's fearful tendencies cannot change. This conclusion, too, would be a mistake. Evidence of inheritance does not mean that the environment is unimportant. In fact, recent research (Fox et al., 2005) provides clear evidence that genetic factors interact with environmental factors in the prediction of behavioral inhibition in childhood. The environmental factor these researchers investigated was social support, specifically, the degree to which mothers provided nurturing, intimate social support when children were 4 years old. They also measured molecular genetic factors already known to be linked to inhibited behavioral tendencies. The genetic and the environmental factors were used together to predict inhibited behavior with peers when children were seven years of age. The main finding was that the link from genetics to behavior depended on the environmental factor, social support. Genetics were less strongly linked to behavior among children who received a high level of social support (Fox et al., 2005); high levels of social support, in other words, lessened the genetic differences that one would observe among children who experience less supportive environments. As the authors whom we quoted to open this section recognize, "Just because a person is born with a particular temperament, however, doesn't mean there is a simple set of instructions or blueprints. Nor does temperament mean that people are 'stuck' with their personalities from birth. On the contrary, one of the marvelous features of temperament is a built-in flexibility that allows us to adapt to life's hurdles and challenges. Everyone has the ability to grow and to change at every stage of life" (Haler & Copeland, 1998, p. 7).

Effortful Control and the Development of Conscience

Inhibitedness is not the only psychological quality of interest to students of temperament. Important advances also have been made in understanding the role of temperament in people's ability to exert influence over, or regulate, their own emotions and actions. The psychologist Mary Rothbart and her colleagues, for example, posit that a specific psychological quality is necessary to regulate one's emotions and actions. This is a quality they call **effortful control** (e.g., Rothbart, Ellis, Rueda, & Posner, 2003). People often need to stop doing one thing in order to do another. One might need to stop watching TV in order to start studying, to stop talking to a friend in order to pay attention to a teacher, to stop eating donuts in order to lose weight. Effortful control refers to this capacity; it is "the ability to suppress a dominant response in order to perform a subdominant response" (Rothbart et al., 2003, p. 1114).

A feature of research on effortful control that makes it of particular interest to personality theory is the potential relation between effortful control processes and the development of a psychological capacity that has been of great interest to personality theorists since the time of Freud. This capacity is moral conscience—or what Freud would have called superego functioning (see Chapter 3). It is the capacity to adhere to social norms by internalizing moral and ethical standards for behavior.

The basic question addressed in contemporary research is the one considered by Freud: What determines the development of a sense of conscience? Why do people differ in the degree to which they adhere to social norms and constraints? In trying to answer this question, Freud focused on the child's experience with the parents. An alternative focus would examine differences in inherited biology. A more interesting third possibility is that inherited biology and parental influence *both* influence the child's level of conscience. This third possibility has been explored in research by Grazyna Kochanska and her colleagues.

Kochanska and Knaack (2003) examined the relations among (1) effortful control, (2) the development of conscience, and (3) one particular aspect of parenting, namely, the degree to which mothers forcefully assert their authority in their interactions with children. Asserting parental authority may be important and beneficial in many settings. However, it also may carry a cost. When parents authoritatively control their children's action, the child may fail to develop his or her own internal controls. The child with authoritative parents may fail to internalize rules for proper social conduct. Kochanska and Knaack hypothesized that this may occur for reasons involving effortful control. Children who experience authoritative parenting may fail to fully

A child participating in the research program on effortful control by Kochanska and colleagues. The child is participating in a "Snack Delay" task in which children must try to wait with her hands on a table until an experimenter rings a bell before they can then have a snack. The research provides a behavioral measure of children's ability to control their behavior.

develop the self-control skills that enable them to regulate their behavior independently.

Testing these ideas is difficult, and Kochanska and Knaack's efforts in overcoming the difficulties are exemplary. Their work contains two critical features that also were evident in the work of Kagan and colleagues: (a) a *longitudinal* research design, that is, research in which the same people are studied over long periods of time, and (b) *behavioral* measures of the people studied, rather than merely measures involving the completion of questionnaires. When children were about 2–3 years of age, they were given behavioral tests of effortful control. These involved tasks such as slowing down one's walking, talking in a whisper, and delaying before eating a piece of candy. To learn about the mothers' behavior, the researchers also observed them directly. Mothers were observed while giving instructions to their children, and researchers coded the mothers' behavior to determine the degree to which their parenting style involved forceful assertiveness. Finally, much later in time, when children were almost 5 years old, they participated in lab activities designed to measure their sense of conscience. For example, children played a game in which they had the opportunity to cheat, and the experimenters observed them to determine whether they were cheating. They also were shown puppets, some of whom (in the storyline presented to children) always did what they were told whereas others did not; children indicated which of the puppets was more like them.

The developmental psychologist Grazyna Kochanska has explored the origins of children's capacity for self-control.

Research findings supported the predictions about the way authoritative parenting and effortful control contribute to the development of conscience (Kochanska and Knaack, 2003). The findings can be understood in a series of steps. First, the mothers' assertion of parental power was found to predict individual differences in the temperament quality of effortful control. To a highly significant degree, mothers who were more authoritative had children who were less able to succeed on the measures of effortful control. Second, effortful control predicted individual differences in conscience. Again, this was a very strong effect; to a highly significant degree, children who displayed greater capacity for effortful control also displayed, years later, a higher sense of conscience. Finally, the variations in effortful control accounted for the relation between parenting and the development of conscience (see Figure 9.5). Statistical analyses demonstrated that effortful control mediated the effects of parenting (Kochanska and Knaack, 2003).

Figure 9.5 *Conceptual representation of relations among mother's assertion of power, children's effortful control, and the development of conscience among children, based on data from Kochanska and Knaack (2003). The minus and plus signs indicate that higher levels of power assertion among mothers predicted lower levels of effortful control in children, and higher levels of effortful control predicted higher levels of conscience.*

This is natural selection: the non-random differential reproduction of genes. Natural selection has built us, and it is natural selection we must understand if we are to comprehend our own identities.

SOURCE: TRIVERS, 1976, p. v.

EVOLUTION, EVOLUTIONARY PSYCHOLOGY, AND PERSONALITY

When explaining the biological causes of a behavior, there are two types of causes that can be cited; they often are labeled "proximate" and "ultimate" causes. **Proximate causes** refer to biological processes operating in the organism at the time the behavior is observed. Suppose you take a break from reading this textbook to sit outside to get a tan. A proximate explanation of the tanning process would refer to the biological mechanisms in the skin that respond to sunlight, giving you a golden glow. (If, as a result of reading this example, you now are motived to work on your tan, we note that you could always take your textbook out in the sun with you.) Ultimate causes ask a different question: Why is a given biological mechanism a part of the organism, and why does it respond to the environment in a given way? An ultimate-cause explanation of the tanning process would ask why it is that humans possess skin that tans in response to intense, prolonged sunlight.

Ever since Darwin, ultimate-cause explanations have invoked principles of natural selection. Scientists try to understand how and why a given biological mechanism evolved. These understandings are grounded in the basic principle that some biological features are better than others, at least for organisms living in a given environment. The organisms that possess those features are more likely to survive, to reproduce, and thus to be the ancestors of future generations. Organisms lacking the adaptive biological feature are less likely to pass on their genes to the next generation. Across a number of generations, the population as a whole is increasingly populated by beings who possess the adaptive biological mechanism. The biological mechanism, then, evolves. This historical view, grounded in Darwinian principles of evolution via natural selection, provides an ultimate cause explanation.

In this section of the chapter, we introduce you to ultimate-cause, evolutionary-based interpretations of personality functioning. We do so by reviewing developments in the field of evolutionary psychology (Buss, 2005) and their applications to questions of personality and individual differences. Subsequent sections of this chapter review proximate-cause explanations of personality functioning that involve the actions of genes and neural systems.

EVOLUTIONARY PSYCHOLOGY

In recent years, many psychologists have tried to build evolutionary explanations of psychological functioning. As a review by Linnda Caporael (2001) explains, these efforts have been of more than one type. Although all contemporary psychologists recognize the importance of analyzing evolutionary forces, their analyses differ. As a result, there exist "evolutionary psychologies" (Caporael, 2001)—i.e., plural. Main points of difference involve the degree to which psychological tendency is seen as "hardwired" (i.e., as a biologically fixed, inevitable aspect of human nature) versus being a result of interactions between biology and culture. The latter perspective leaves open the possibility that different cultures will produce different psychological tendencies (e.g., Nisbett, 2003).

In the past 15 years, writers who highlight the evolutionarily "hardwired" aspects of human nature (Buss, 2005) have gained much prominence in personality psychology. Their work represents a startling challenge to many ways of thinking in the field. In this approach, contemporary human functioning is understood in relation to evolved solutions to adaptive problems faced by the species over millions of years (D. M. Buss, 1991, 1995, 1999). The idea is that basic psychological mechanisms are the result of evolution by selection, that is, they exist and have endured because they have been adaptive to survival and reproductive success. The fundamental components of human nature, then, can be understood in terms of **evolved psychological mechanisms** that have adaptive value in terms of survival and reproductive success. Such aspects of human nature, as our fundamental motives and emotions, can thereby be understood in terms of their adaptive value.

Four points about evolution and the human mind are highlighted in this approach to evolutionary psychology (Pinker, 1997; Tooby & Cosmides, 1992). First, the features of mind that evolved are ones that solve problems that are important to reproductive success. The critical feature in evolution is the passing on of genes. However, note that the reproduction-related problems do not merely involve acts of sexual reproduction. They include a wide range of problems relevant to the survival and reproduction of the organism. Consider the following simple example. Organisms need to see objects at a distance and to judge how near or far they are from those objects. An organism that could not make these judgments commonly would be at a disadvantage (e.g., when hunting or trying to protect itself from a predator). To solve this problem, our nervous systems have evolved a solution: a pair of eyes that enables us to see in depth. The psychological capacity, depth perception, reflects a specific neural system that has evolved because of its usefulness in solving a recurrent problem faced throughout evolution. The intriguing feature of contemporary evolutionary psychology is that it extends this type of analysis to include patterns of social behavior that solve significant social problems faced across the eons of evolutionary history.

A second point is that the evolved mental mechanisms are adaptive to the way of life of hundreds of centuries ago, when our ancestors were hunters and gatherers (Tooby & Cosmides, 1992). An implication is that we may have evolved psychological tendencies that no longer are good for us. For example, our taste preference for fat was "clearly adaptive in our evolutionary past because fat was a valuable source of calories but was very scarce. Now, however, with hamburger and pizza joints on every street corner, fat is no longer a scarce resource. Thus, our strong taste for fatty substances now causes us to over-consume fat. This leads to clogged arteries and heart attacks, and hinders our survival" (D. M. Buss, 1999, p. 38).

Third, evolved psychological mechanisms are domain-specific. According to evolutionary psychologists, we do not evolve a general tendency to survive. Instead, the body and mind consist of evolved mechanisms that solve specific problems that occur in specific types of settings, or domains. Fundamental aspects of human nature, such as specific motives and emotions, apply to specific problems and contexts. For example, evolution does not give us a general tendency to be afraid, but instead selects for psychological mechanisms that cause us to fear specific stimuli that have been threats to humans across the course of evolution. Similarly, evolution gives us specific emotions, such as jealousy, because these emotional reactions have proven adaptive in solving specific problems of social living. These domain-specific motives and emotions have remained as part of our human nature because they facilitated survival and reproductive success given the problems to be faced in our ancestral environment. Note that this makes evolutionary psychology quite different from the trait approaches we discussed in the previous two chapters. In trait theory, a context-free variable such as "agreeableness" might be seen as responsible for actions such as being agreeable on a date and being agreeable toward a young niece or nephew. In evolutionary psychology, these acts would be seen as merely superficially similar. Even though they might both be described as "agreeable" behaviors, they would be caused by different psychological mechanisms, since, throughout the course of evolution, attracting opposite-sex mates and caring for children were distinctly different problems of social life.

The fourth point concerns the components and overall structure of the mind, or what is commonly called the architecture of mental systems. One view of mental architecture is that the mind is like a computer. There is a central processing mechanism and all information, whatever its content, gets processed through this mechanism. If you are using your computer's word processor, the same processing mechanisms indeed will come into play whether you are writing a term paper or writing a love letter. Evolutionary psychologists reject this conception of mental architecture. Although they may view the mind as engaged in information processing, a core idea of evolutionary psychology is that the mind contains multiple information processing devices, each of which processes information from one specific domain of life (Pinker, 1997). Your computer may use the same mechanism to process a love letter and a term paper, but your brain does not. The task of attracting mates (through love letters or whatever other favored strategy you may have) is a distinct problem of great evolutionary significance. To solve it, we purportedly have evolved a mental system that comes into play when we face problems having to do with mate attraction. Since many different problems arise in different domains of life, the mind is said to consist of multiple domain-specific mental mechanisms. These mechanisms often are called mental "modules" (Fodor, 1983), a term that is meant to capture the fact that they are special-purpose mechanisms designed to carry out a domain-specific mental function.

Social Exchange and the Detection of Cheating

A key question then is: Which psychological mechanisms have evolved through selection and which adaptive problems did they evolve to solve? Seminal work on this question was conducted by the evolutionary psychologist Leda Cosmides (1989). She explored a particular type of social setting and associated problem that, she reasoned, has been of significance throughout the course of evolution. The social setting involves "social exchange," that is, the exchange of goods and services. Throughout evolution, part of people's social interaction has involved the mutual exchange of beneficial goods. For example, a person may agree to help another with child-care tasks one day if that other person agrees to do the same on another day. People in a village that grows a large amount of a particular crop may agree to exchange some of their food with people from another village that produces a desired manufactured product. In any such exchange, it is important to avoid being cheated. The ability to detect cheating has survival value. If you chronically fail to notice that a person who needs change has just asked you for "two tens for a five" instead of "two

Figure 9.6 *Schematic Illustration of Logical Problems Used in Cheating Detection Research. Each card has two sides. The research participant sees one side and must decide whether to turn over the card to see the other side in order to test a logical rule. In the top problem, the rule is "if P then Q," that is, "if there is a P on one side of the card then there should be a Q on the other side." In the bottom problem (constructed for the present illustration), the rule is "if Made $ then Paid Taxes" (i.e., if a person made a certain amount of money in a given year, then he or she paid taxes). When asked to test the "if P then Q" rule, research participants commonly fail to turn over the not-Q card. However, in problems having the structure of the "if Made $ then Paid Taxes" problem, participants commonly do correctly turn over the Not-Paid Taxes card to see if the person might have been cheating (i.e., if the person might not have paid taxes even though he or she made money).*

fives for a ten," then you gradually run out of resources that are required for social living, survival, and reproduction. You must be able to detect cheaters. Cosmides reasoned that cheating detection is of such great survival value that the mind contains distinct systems for the detection of cheaters.

She tested this in a clever manner that illustrates the evolutionary psychologists' overall approach to questions of mental architecture. Her work involved a particular type of logical reasoning task. In the task, people are asked to solve an "if then " problem, that is, to test a problem of logical relations in which one has to determine if a rule of the sort "if P then Q" is accurate (Figure 9.6). As you might guess from this description, such abstract logical problems generally are difficult. People in psychology experiments commonly fail to solve them. However, Cosmides herself reasoned that people would be good at solving the problem if its content related to the detection of cheating. Although people might be poor at solving the problem "if P then Q?" they might be quite good at solving a problem such as "if person made a lot of money, did he or she pay taxes?" If the problem concerns potential cheating, then the particular subsystem of mind that processes information about social contracts and cheating should come into play, and people should be better at solving the problem. This is precisely what Cosmides (1989) found. Although a minority of people correctly solve abstract "P then Q" problems, a large majority correctly solve the same problem if the content of the problem involves the detection of cheating.

More recent work suggests that the ability to solve cheating problems is a human universal, precisely as evolutionary psychologists would expect. Cheating detection abilities are found not only among U.S. college students, but among nonliterate research participants living in cultures that are isolated from the industrialized world (Sugiyama, Tooby, & Cosmides, 2002). Other evidence has begun to identify specific brain regions that are involved in reasoning about social exchange. This work involved study of a neuropsychological patient who, in a bicycle accident, had incurred a head injury that damaged portions of his brain's frontal cortex and amygdala. When tested on a variety of logical reasoning tasks, the patient performed normally (i.e., in a manner similar to persons without brain injury) when reasoning in domains other than social exchange, but showed impaired performance when trying to solve problems involving social contracts (Stone, Cosmides, Tooby, Kroll, & Knight, 2002). The findings suggest, then, that there exists a specific neural subsystem of the brain that has evolved to solve such problems.

Sex Differences: Evolutionary Origins?

Another domain to which evolutionary psychologists have turned their attention is sex differences. The evolutionary psychologist's reasoning is that, throughout evolution, male and female human beings have had different roles to play as a natural result of biological differences between the sexes. Differences, of course, are found in physical stature, as well as in child care (e.g., pregnancy, breast feeding). Since these differences have been consistent across the course of evolution, it is reasoned that the human mind has evolved sex-specific psychological tendencies. In other words, men and women, as a result of facing somewhat different problems across the course of evolution, are predicted to have somewhat different brains that predispose them to different patterns of thinking, feeling, and action.

Before considering this research, we alert the reader to the fact that drawing conclusions about psychological differences between men and women is a very tricky matter. Even if one finds such differences, it is hard to interpret them. True, men and women differ biologically. So one interpretation is that biology causes sex differences. But men and women also differ socially; specifically, they often develop within societies that do not treat men and women equally. Men commonly earn more money than women and hold more positions of power in society. It may be that, regardless of biological differences, any group within society that makes more money and holds more positions of power will differ, psychologically, from a group that earns less money and holds fewer positions of power. Sex differences, then, could be socially constructed, rather than being biologically caused. A core idea of evolutionary psychology, however, is that biology determines sex differences. Evolved psychological differences between men and women are seen as responsible for the gender differences we observe in society. This notion has been advanced most vigorously by the evolutionary psychologist David Buss (1989, 1999). He has considered sex differences in two aspects of male-female relationships: mate preferences and causes of jealousy.

Male-Female Mate Preferences

Do you like men who are rich and professionally successful? Do you like women who appear youthful and have "curvy" hips? If so, evolutionary psychologists think they know why. According to evolutionary theory, as introduced by Darwin, selection pressures across the course of human evolution have produced sex differences in preferences for mates. The particular features of men that are attractive to women, and the features of women that are attractive to men, are thought to be a product of evolution.

Two ideas underlie the contemporary evolutionary psychologist's analysis of sex differences. One is something called **parental investment theory** (Trivers,

1972). The theory is an analysis of the different costs, or investments, that men versus women have made in parenting throughout the ages. The core idea is that biological differences between the sexes cause women to invest more in parenting. Women can pass their genes on to fewer offspring than men potentially can. This is because of both the limited time periods during which they are fertile and, relative to men, the more limited age range during which they can produce offspring. In other words, parental investment is greater for females because of the greater "replacement costs" for them. Also, women of course carry the biological burden of pregnancy, which lasts for nine months. Men not only do not have to bear physical costs of pregnancy, but, unlike women, in principle can be involved in multiple pregnancies at the same time. It follows that females will have stronger preferences about mating partners than will males and that males and females will have different criteria for the selection of mates (Trivers, 1972). Women need men to help with the burdens of pregnancy and child care, and thus should seek men who have the potential for providing resources and protection. Men, in contrast, should be less interested in protection; instead, they are expected to focus on the reproductive potential of a partner (the person's youth and other biological markers of reproductive fitness). Although these preferences evolved ages ago, they still are present in the human mind. Thus, they should be evident in current social patterns. For example, since women are more interested than are men in a partner who can provide resources, the evolutionary psychologist would expect that, when on a dinner date, men would be more likely to pay for the dinner. Paying for dinner is viewed as an evolved strategy through which men display financial resources and thus add to their attractiveness to women.

In addition to parental investment theory, a second line of reasoning concerns parenthood. Since women carry their fertilized eggs, they can always be sure that they are the mothers of the offspring. On the other hand, males cannot be so sure that the offspring is their own, and therefore must take steps to ensure that their investment is directed toward their own offspring and not those of another male (D. Buss, 1989, p. 3). Thus follows the suggestion that males have greater concerns about sexual rivals and place greater value on chastity in a potential mate than do females.

The following are some of the specific hypotheses that have been derived from parental investment and parenthood probability theories (Buss, 1989; Buss, Larsen, Westen, & Semmelroth, 1992):

1. A woman's "mate value" for a man should be determined by her reproductive capacity as suggested by youth and physical attractiveness. Chastity should also be valued in terms of increased probability of paternity.

2. A man's "mate value" for a woman should be determined less by reproductive value and more by evidence of the resources he can supply, as evidenced by characteristics such as earning capacity, ambition, and industriousness.

3. Males and females should differ in the events that activate jealousy, males being more jealous about sexual infidelity and the threat to paternal probability, and females more concerned about emotional attachments and the threat of loss of resources.

Buss (1989) obtained questionnaire responses from 37 samples, representing over 10,000 individuals, from 33 countries located on 6 continents and 5 islands. There was tremendous diversity in geographic locale, culture, ethnicity, and religion. What was found? First, in each of the 37 samples males valued physical attractiveness and relative youth in potential mates more than did females, consistent with the hypothesis that males value mates with high reproductive capacity. The prediction that males would value chastity in potential mates more than would females was supported in 23 out of the 37 samples, providing moderate support for the hypothesis. Second, females were found to value the financial capacity of potential mates more than did males (36 of 37 samples) and the characteristics of ambition and industriousness in a potential mate to a greater extent than males (29 of 37 samples), consistent with the hypothesis that females value mates with high resource-providing capacity.

Causes of Jealousy

In subsequent research, three studies were conducted to test the hypothesis of sex differences in jealousy (Buss et al., 1992). In the first study, undergraduate students were asked whether they would experience greater distress in response to sexual infidelity or emotional infidelity. Whereas 60 percent of the male sample reported greater distress over a partner's sexual infidelity, 83 percent of the female sample reported greater distress over a partner's emotional attachment to a rival.

In the second study, physiological measures of distress were taken on undergraduates who imagined two scenarios, one in which their partner became sexually involved with someone else and one in which their partner became emotionally involved with someone else. Once more males and females were found to have contrasting results, with males showing greater physiological distress in relation to imagery of their partner's sexual involvement and women showing greater physiological distress in relation to imagery of their partner's emotional involvement.

The third study explored the hypothesis that males and females who had experienced committed sexual relationships would show the same results as in the previous study but to a greater extent than would males and females who had not been involved in such a relationship. In other words, actual experience in a committed relationship was important in bringing out the differential effect. This was found to be the case for males for whom sexual jealousy was found to be increasingly activated by experience with a committed sexual relationship. However, there was no significant difference in response to emotional infidelity between women who had and had not experienced a committed sexual relationship.

In sum, the authors interpreted the results as supportive of the hypothesis of sex differences in activators of jealousy. Although alternative explanations for the results were recognized, the authors suggested that only the evolutionary psychological framework led to the specific predictions.

Evolutionary Origins of Sex Differences: How Strong Are the Data?

Based on our coverage so far, evolutionary psychology appears to provide a quite convincing explanation of sex differences. Indeed, many contemporary psychologists find the theory convincing in this regard. However, in recent years new research findings have begun to raise questions about the validity of the theory as it applies to sex differences in social behavior. In evaluating evolutionary psychology, a major question is whether patterns of sex differences are found universally, that is, across all cultures of the world. Evolutionary psychology expects that sex differences will be universal. People share the same brain and physical anatomy. Humans share a common evolutionary past; throughout most of the evolutionary history of our species, all humans lived in the same region of the world, Africa. If evolved psychological mechanisms are the cause of sex differences in social behavior, then those sex differences should be similar in all regions of the world and all human cultures.

A contrasting idea is that sex differences are a product of features of the society in which people live. In societies that treat men and women very differently—for example, in which there are particularly large differences in the work opportunities available to men versus women and in the income that they earn—sex differences may be larger than in societies in which men and women share more equally in the goods of society. Such a result would contradict the predictions of evolutionary psychology.

Eagly and Wood (1999) have provided evidence on this question. They reanalyzed data from a multinational study of men's and women's preferences in mates. The evolutionary psychology prediction is that the same pattern of sex differences would be found in all cultures, with women preferring men who have the capacity to earn money and men preferring young women with domestic skills. On the one hand, some of Eagly and Wood's findings were consistent with evolutionary psychology. For example, when looking for a mate, men did tend to value the quality of being a good cook to a greater degree than did women. However, other findings contradicted evolutionary psychology by demonstrating the existence of variations in the nature of sex differences. Specifically, sex differences were found to be smaller within societies in which men and women have more similar roles within the overall social structure. In societies in which there was greater gender equality, women were less concerned with men's earning capacity, men were less concerned with women's housekeeping skills, and sex differences on these measures were smaller (Eagly & Wood, 1999). A subsequent review of anthropological research on sex differences similarly was "not very supportive of evolutionary psychology" (Wood & Eagly, 2002, p. 718). Instead of pointing to universal patterns of sex differences that result from biology alone, the data were consistent with a biosocial view of sex differences. In a biosocial perspective, sex differences reflect interactions between biological qualities of men and women and social factors, particularly those involving economic conditions and the division of labor within society (Wood & Eagly, 2002).

Additional data also are damaging to the initial conclusions that evolutionary psychologists drew regarding sex differences. Some of this work involves the re-analysis of data sets that originally were interpreted as being supportive of evolutionary psychology predictions. Miller, Putcha-Bhagavatula, & Pedersen (2002) note that initial studies of sex differences in mate preferences by Buss and colleagues sometimes failed to compare men and women on all relevant psychological variables. When re-analyzing these mate-preference data, the Miller group (2002) found that "across the data, what men desired most in a mate women desired most in a mate. [There were] extraordinarily

Sex differences in mate preferences have been shown to be smaller in societies in which women's earning capacity is similar to men's.

high correlations between men's and women's ratings for both short-term and long-term sexual partners" (p. 90).

The evolutionary psychologist's claim that men and women differ in the events that activate jealousy (Buss et al., 1992) is also contradicted by recent data (DeSteno, Bartlett, Braverman, & Salovey, 2002). These recent findings suggest that the original findings of evolutionary psychologists in this area may have resulted from a methodological artifact; an arbitrarily chosen feature of the research procedures may have artificially contributed to the results. Most of the original evolutionary psychological research on the topic involved a multiple-choice or "forced choice" method. Participants in research are asked if they would be more distressed if they found that their romantic partner (a) had sexual relations with another person or (b) formed a close emotional bond with another person. Note, first, that this is an odd question, particularly from an evolutionary psychological perspective. Over the course of human evolution, it cannot possibly be the case that people frequently were faced with learning simultaneously about a partner's sexual and emotional relations and then having to decide which is worse. Recognizing the oddity of this forced-choice procedure, DeSteno and colleagues (2002) also asked participants to consider the sexual and emotional scenarios one at a time and to indicate how upset they would be by each one. With this change in procedure, the sex differences in jealousy predicted by evolutionary psychology were no longer found. Instead, men and women were highly similar. Both were more distressed by sexual infidelity than by news of a partner's emotionally close nonsexual relationship.

Related findings come from the analysis of men's and women's physiological responses to imagining sexual versus emotional infidelity (Harris, 2000). If men and women possess different evolved modules of the sort suggested by parental investment theory, then they should respond differently to these two scenarios; men should react with stronger feelings of jealousy when imagining sexual infidelity and women should react more when envisioning emotional infidelity. In the careful research of Harris, women were not found to be more responsive to emotional (versus sexual) infidelity. Men did respond strongly to sexual infidelity but, as Harris points out, that may not have resulted from the infidelity but merely from the idea that sex occurred; men simply may respond relatively strongly to any scenario involving sexual content. On her physiological measures, Harris (2000) indeed found that men responded strongly to imagined sexual encounters whether or not infidelity was involved. Subsequent work similarly failed to find the sex differences predicted by evolutionary psychology when research participants were asked to contemplate actual instances of infidelity they had experienced, rather than the hypothetical instances of infidelity that some previous researchers had studied (Harris, 2002). The overall findings, then, contradict the evolutionary psychological account of sex differences in jealousy—an account that, as Harris (2000) noted, had previously been seen as a "showcase example of evolutionary psychology" (p. 1082).

In summary, then, data do not provide consistent support for evolutionary psychological hypotheses about sex differences in mate attraction and jealousy. The exact nature of gender differences that might exist, and the roles of evolutionary hardwiring versus social structure in bringing them about, thus remain to be defined.

Evolutionary Theory and the Big Five Personality Dimensions

How can one relate the evolutionary perspective to the trait-theory ideas discussed in our previous chapter? One answer to this question is the approach suggested by Goldberg (1981, 1990). According to his lexical hypothesis, trait terms emerged to help people categorize behaviors fundamental to the human condition. Big Five trait terms, then, may describe aspects of behavior that are important not only today, but that have been important throughout time, as language-using persons have evolved. Knowing whether a person is (1) active and dominant or passive and submissive, (2) agreeable or disagreeable, (3) can be counted on, (4) is unpredictable or emotionally stable, and (5) is smart would seem to be important in any complex community of interacting persons. If people have asked themselves these questions about persons throughout human history, then corresponding personality trait terms would enter the human lexicon.

Another possibility is that a given trait exists in the mind of humans because it has been important to human adaptation throughout evolution. We might need extraversion and conscientiousness, for example, to get along with others and to work on tasks that promote survival. However, when evaluating this possibility one must recall that the Big Five traits describe *differences between* people, not universal aspects of human psychology. Evolution commonly yields capacities that are universal, and for which differences between people are relatively unimportant to survival. For example, evolution yields a capacity among humans to use language, and all normally-functioning humans have this capacity. Tooby and Cosmides (2005) have explained how, in an evolutionary-psychological account, people may vary genetically in relatively superficial traits that were not critical to survival and reproduction throughout evolution.

In general, answers to the question of how the evolutionary view relates to the Big Five variables hinge on an issue we highlighted in the previous chapter, namely, whether one views the Big Five variables as (a) descriptions of people's psychological tendencies, or (b) structures that explain a person's behavior. The evolutionary view and the Big Five are quite compatible if one views the Big Five as descriptive. Evolutionary psychology potentially explains why these particular five individual differences are noticed and discussed when people observe and describe the psychological characteristics of others. However, it seems quite difficult to reconcile the perspective if one chooses to treat the Big Five as psychological structures that cause people's behavior, as is done in five-factor theory (McCrae & Costa, 1996). This is because the units of analysis in evolutionary psychology and in five-factor theory differ fundamentally. In evolutionary psychology, the basic units of analysis are domain-specific. Evolved psychological mechanisms solve domain-specific problems of living (attracting mates, detecting cheaters, etc.). In contrast, the units of analysis of five-factor theory are domain-general; a variable such as "extraversion" or "conscientiousness" does not make reference to any specific type of social domain in which the person is being extraverted or conscientious.

EVOLUTIONARY EXPLANATIONS: COMMENT

In earlier periods in the history of psychology, evolutionary explanations for human behavior either were ignored or fell into disfavor. Today, few psychologists question that an analysis of the evolution of our species can provide insight into the nature of the contemporary human mind. Investigators do differ greatly, however, in their beliefs about the degree to which evolutionary psychology can provide a basis for the analysis of personality.

On the one hand, some investigators are extremely enthusiastic. Buss, for example, suggests that an evolutionary framework offers virtually the only hope for bringing the field of psychology into some kind of theoretical order. He suggests that human behavior depends on psychological mechanisms and the only known cause of such mechanisms is evolution by natural selection. Thus, anyone interested in the social behavior of humans must take into account the evolutionary history of the behavior. According to this view, the biological roots of human nature, as expressed in the genes, are the link between evolution and behavior (Kenrick, 1994). Evolution is also seen to account for the social structures that other psychologists view as the causes of behavior; evolutionary psychologists suggest that culture itself is generated by evolved psychological mechanisms (Tooby & Cosmides, 1992).

At the same time, there are others who question how much evolutionary theory has to say about human functioning and who also caution about the implications that may be drawn from such a view. While not denying that we have an evolutionary history, these psychologists suggest humans have progressed to the point where they are much more free of genetically programmed responses. They caution us against interpreting social patterns as biologically based when they could reflect the influence of social forces. For example, Cantor (1990) suggests that in focusing on the problems of survival and reproduction, evolutionary psychologists have ignored much of

CURRENT QUESTIONS

EMOTIONS AND TRAITS: HOW SIMILAR ARE HUMANS AND OTHER ANIMALS?

Darwin's *The Origin of Species* suggested a continuity between humans and other species. In his book *The Expression of the Emotions in Man and Animals* he suggested a continuity of expressions of emotions in animals and people, that is, that many of the same basic emotions and accompanying facial expressions exist in both. There is evidence of a similarity of expression of what are called basic emotions (e.g., anger, sadness, fear, joy) in nonhuman primates and humans, in infants as well as adults, and across cultures (Ekman, 1993, 1998). Evolutionary psychologists suggest a continuity in traits between humans and other species, a view bolstered by the fact that humans and the great apes share over 98 percent of the same genes. Is there evidence of such a continuity of traits?

Gosling and John (1998, 1999) set out to consider the question of whether there are dimensions of personality common to a wide range of species, raising the question: "What are the major dimensions of animal personality?" In a review of the literature of descriptions of 12 species, ranging from octopuses, guppies, and rats to gorillas and chimpanzees, they found evidence that three of the human five-factor dimensions showed generality across species—E, N, and A: "The evidence indicates that chimpanzees, various other primates, dogs, cats, donkeys, and pigs, even guppies and octopuses all show individual differences that can be organized along dimensions akin to E, N, and (with the exception of guppies and octopuses) A" (1999, p. 70). However, a separate C factor was found only in chimps (King & Figueredo, 1997), our closest relatives. This may be because traits related to C, such as

following rules and norms, thinking before acting, and cognitively controlling impulses may be a relatively recent evolutionary development.

Are such similarities anthropomorphic projections on the part of humans or are they actual attributes of the animals? In a study of trait ratings of humans, dogs, and cats, Gosling and John again found evidence of three of the Big Five in dogs and cats as well as humans—E, N, and A, but no separate C factor. In a further study, they generated a list of "personality descriptors" of dogs, based on attributes human subjects most frequently used to describe dogs (e.g., affectionate, cuddly, energetic, happy, intelligent, nervous, lazy, loyal). One group of subjects then rated a human they knew on the "dog personality inventory" and another group of subjects rated a dog they knew on the same list of descriptors. Would the same factors emerge from the two groups of ratings, suggesting similar dimensions of personality for humans and dogs? Using the dog personality inventory for humans, they again found evidence of the Big Five: N, E, O, A, C. When the same rating items were applied to dogs, three factors similar to E, N, and A again emerged, with no separate C factor.

Overall, studies on animal personality suggested the following conclusions: (1) Animal personality can be assessed reliably. (2) The structure of personality traits in humans resembles that of chimps. (3) Non-primate mammals like dogs and cats seem to have a less differentiated personality structure, with three dimensions showing considerable, although not perfect, generality across many species. (4) Personality descriptions of other species are not mere anthropomorphic projections; that is, such descriptions are "all in the mind" of the human but instead reflect actual characteristics of the animal being rated. (5) Although only little research has been done, there is now some evidence for continuity of psychological qualities between humans and members of other species.

SOURCE: EKMAN, 1993, 1998; GOSLING & JOHN, 1998, 1999; KING & FIGUEREDO, 1997.

the diversity of social interaction and efforts to solve contemporary problems. In addition, Eagly and Wood (1999) suggest that the sex differences in human behavior emphasized by Buss and others can be accounted for by the different roles demanded of men and women as much as by evolved dispositions. Many feminists are concerned about Buss's interpretation of data about sex differences, claiming that such an interpretation ignores cultural factors, suggests that male-female differences are inevitable, and thus potentially provides members of society with an excuse for engaging in gender-biased behavior.

It is particularly noteworthy that critics of evolutionary psychology do not merely include psychologists who are interested in the impact of social forces. The critics also include biologists who are intimately familiar with evolutionary theory, but who feel that evolutionary psychologists have overstated the impact of evolutionary mechanisms on human thought and action. Biologists recognize that organisms develop in environmental and social settings. The settings the organism experiences shape its biological nature (Ehrlich, 2000; Lewontin, 2000). The nervous system develops in interaction with the social world, with neural connections being established and weakened as a function of people's experiences (Edelman & Tononi, 2000). Evolutionary psychologists commonly have supported their views by arguing against individuals who disregard the role of biology in psychological functioning. But, increasingly, these arguments are irrelevant. The greater challenge for evolutionary psychologists is to defend their views against the arguments of biologists who are intimately familiar with principles of natural selection and the workings of the human organism, but who conclude that evolutionary psychologists have erred by underestimating the importance of interactions between the biological person and the social environment (Lewontin, 2000).

A final consideration is that, even if one accepts the principles of evolutionary psychology, these principles fail to address some topics that are of central concern to personality psychology (Cervone, 2000). For example, almost all personality theorists recognize that personality reveals itself when people interpret ambiguous social situations. The interpretation of ambiguity, then, is a core concern of the field. It was the central issue in the projective testing favored by psychodynamic theorists (Chapter 4); the tests present ambiguous stimuli, and the personality psychologist is interested in individual differences in their interpretation. It is a central issue in the personal construct and social-cognitive theories discussed in subsequent chapters, which provide detailed analyses of how people assign meaning to ambiguous encounters (Chapters 12 and 13). In contrast, evolutionary psychology provides few if any tools for addressing this issue. Consider an example (Cervone, 2000).

Suppose you are playing cards with a group of friends, one of whom is a member of the opposite sex who you find attractive and who also seems to be winning most of the hands in the card game. What would the evolutionary psychologist predict about your behavior? Well, on the one hand, the prediction might be that your cheating-detection module will be activated. If so, you should engage in behavioral strategies to protect against cheating (e.g., staring at the person in a stern manner). On the other hand, the prediction might be that your mate-attraction module will be activated. If so, you should engage in strategies designed to make yourself attractive to the other person (flirting). The point of this example is that evolutionary psychology provides no tools for determining which of the two modules will be activated. The social situation is ambiguous. To some people, it may be a social exchange situation. To others, it may be an opportunity to attract a mate. It is obvious that people who interpret the situation one way versus another will subsequently engage in different behavioral strategies. The challenge for the personality psychologist is to explain why one person encodes the ambiguous situation as having to do with social exchange, whereas another person encodes it as an opportunity to attract a mate. This inherently requires an analysis of mental processes that come into play prior to domain-specific mental modules. The person has to figure out what the domain is in the first place. Evolutionary psychology does not tell us how people do this. It is difficult to see how a theory that says little about how people interpret ambiguous stimuli can serve as a general framework for the psychology of personality.

In sum, evolutionary psychology is a powerful theoretical framework of enormous importance to the psychology of personality. Yet it is difficult to determine whether, in the long run, evolutionary psychology will be an organizing framework for the field, or merely will supplement other frameworks by providing insight into the evolutionary foundations of psychological capacities that develop through interaction with the social world.

What makes us all human is our DNA.

SOURCE: HAMER, 1997, p. 111.

GENES AND PERSONALITY

Whatever we inherit that is common to us as humans, as well as what we inherit that makes us unique, exists through the action of genes. We inherit 23 pairs of chromosomes, one of each pair from each of our biological parents. The chromosomes contain thousands of genes. Genes are made up of a molecule called DNA and direct the synthesis of protein molecules. Genes may be thought of as sources of information, directing the synthesis of protein molecules along particular lines. It is the information contained in the genes that directs the biological development of the organism. It is this information that directs the biological development of the fertilized egg into a fetus, a fully formed neonate, an adolescent with secondary sex characteristics, and an elderly person with characteristics associated with the aged. The amount of information contained in the genes is truly remarkable.

In appreciating the relation of genes to behavior, it is important to understand that genes do not govern behavior directly. Thus, there is no "extraversion gene" or "introversion gene" and there is no "neuroticism gene." To the extent that genes influence the development of personality characteristics such as the Big Five, described in Chapter 8, they do so through the direction of the biological functioning of the body.

BEHAVIORAL GENETICS

The study of genetic contributions to behavior is called the field of **behavioral genetics**. Behavior geneticists employ a variety of techniques to estimate the degree to which variation in psychological characteristics is due to genetic factors. As we shall see, the methods of behavioral genetics also can, and do, provide evidence of environmental effects on personality. Behavioral geneticists employ three primary research methods: selective breeding studies, twin studies, and adoption studies.

Selective Breeding Studies

In **selective breeding** studies, animals with a desired trait for study are selected and mated. This selection and reproduction process is used with successive generations of offspring to produce a strain of animals that is consistent within itself for the desired characteristic. Selective breeding is not only a research technique, but it is used, for example, to breed race horses or breeds of dogs with desired characteristics.

Once one has created different strains of animals through selective breeding, one not only can study their typical behavioral tendencies, but it also is possible to subject the different strains to different experimentally controlled developmental experiences. Researchers then can sort out the effects of genetic differences and environmental differences on the observed behavior. For example, the roles of genetic and environmental factors in barking behavior or fearfulness can be studied by subjecting genetically different breeds of dogs to different environmental rearing conditions (Scott & Fuller, 1965).

Selective breeding research has enhanced our understanding of how genes contribute to problems that often are blamed solely on the individual. Consider work on alcoholism (Ponomarev & Crabbe, 1999). The researchers bred various strains of mice that proved to exhibit qualitatively different responses to alcohol. This work illustrated, then, that genes play a role in responsiveness to alcohol, addiction, and withdrawal. It contributed to a more complete understanding of the fact that genetic factors present some individuals with severe vulnerabilities to lifelong problems with alcohol (Hamer & Copeland, 1998).

Twin Studies

Even the most enthusiastic researcher realizes that selective breeding research cannot and should not be done with humans. Ethical factors force the researcher to consider alternatives. Fortunately for science, a ready alternative exists: human twins. Twins provide a naturally occurring experiment. What the scientist wants, ideally, is a circumstance in which there are known variations in degree of genetic similarity and/or environmental similarity. If two organisms are identical genetically, then any later observed differences can be attributed to differences in their environments. On the other hand,

These identical twins were reared apart and met only after reaching college age. Research has demonstrated that identical twins are surprisingly similar in their personalities even if they do not grow up together.

if two organisms are different genetically but experience the same environment, then any observed differences can be attributed to genetic factors. The existence of identical (monozygotic) twins and fraternal (dizygotic) twins offers a good approximation to this research ideal. Monozygotic (MZ) twins develop from the same fertilized egg and are genetically identical. Dizygotic (DZ) twins develop from two separately fertilized eggs and are as genetically similar as any pair of siblings, on the average sharing about 50 percent of their genes.

Researchers capitalize on these systematic differences between MZ and DZ twins by conducting **twin studies** to gauge the degree to which genetic factors explain person-to-person variations in psychological characteristics.

Two logical considerations underpin the twin method. The first is that, since MZ twins are genetically identical, any systematic difference between them must be due to environmental effects. Interestingly, then, the study of genetically identical persons is particularly valuable for revealing the effects of environmental experience. Second, it is the difference in similarity between MZ twin pairs and DZ twin pairs that is crucial to estimating the effects of genetics. Specifically, we know that MZ twins are more similar to one another genetically than DZ twins are similar to one another genetically. If genetics influence a given personality characteristic, then MZ twins, as a result of being more similar genetically, also should be more similar on the given personality characteristic than are DZ twins. If they are not, then there is no genetic effect. When studying both MZ and DZ twin pairs, then, the researcher can compare them (MZ similarity compared to DZ similarity on a trait of interest) to determine the magnitude of the influence of genetic factors. This genetic influence usually is expressed numerically in terms of a heritability coefficient (described below).

The twin strategy usually is conducted with twins who grow up in the same household. However, circumstances sometimes force parents to give up children for adoption early in life. As a result, MZ and DZ twins sometimes are reared apart. This creates a circumstance of remarkable interest to the psychological scientist and the public at large, namely, biologically identical people who are raised in different environments. What happens? Does biology win out, with genetically identical twins being psychologically identical despite their different experiences? Or do social experiences win out, with people differing substantially despite their identical genes? These questions can be answered thanks to an international data set that features large numbers of reared-apart twins who have completed various psychological measures (Bouchard, Lykken, McGue, Segal, & Tellegen, 1990). Results provide clear evidence that the effects of biology endure across different circumstances. On multiple personality trait measures, MZ twins raised apart were found to be similar to a significant degree; twin correlations indicating the degree of similarity between the twins were in the .45 to .50 range. Of particular interest is that MZ twins raised apart were about as similar to one another as were MZ twins raised together (Bouchard et al., 1990). Being raised in the same household did not make the twins more similar on broad personality trait measures. We return to this fascinating finding, and its interpretations and implications, after reviewing further research findings below.

Adoption Studies

Studies of children who grow up with caregivers other than their biological parents are called **adoption studies**. (Adoption studies sometimes involve identical twins, as in the research reviewed in the paragraph immediately above, but commonly may involve non-twin siblings.) Adoption studies offer another method for studying genetic and environmental effects. When adequate records are kept, it is possible to consider the similarity of adopted children to their natural (biological) parents, who have not influenced them environmentally, and compare this with the similarity to their adoptive parents, who share no genes in common with them. The extent of similarity to their biological parents is indicative of genetic factors while the extent of similarity to their adoptive parents is indicative of environmental factors.

Finally, such comparisons can be extended to families that include both biological and adoptive children. Take, for example, a family of four children; two of the children are the biological offspring of the parents and two of the children have been adopted. The two biological offspring share a genetic similarity with one another and with the biological parents that is not true for the two adopted children. Assuming the two adopted children are unrelated, they share no genes in common but share a genetic similarity with their parents and any siblings who might exist in other environments. Thus, it is possible to compare different parent-offspring and biological sibling-adoptive sibling combinations in terms of similarity on personality characteristics. For example, one can ask whether the biological siblings are more similar to one another than are the adoptive siblings, whether they are more similar to the parents than the adoptive siblings, and whether the adoptive siblings are more similar to their biological parents than to their adoptive parents. A yes answer to such questions would be suggestive of the importance of genetic factors in the development of the particular personality characteristic.

It should now be clear that in twin and adoption studies we have individuals of varying degrees of genetic similarity being exposed to varying degrees of

Table 9.1   Average Familial IQ Correlations (R)

As genetic similarity increases, so does the magnitude of the correlations for IQ, suggesting a strong genetic contribution to intelligence.

Relationship	Average R	Number of Pairs
REARED-TOGETHER BIOLOGICAL RELATIVES		
MZ twins	.86	4,672
DZ twins	.60	5,533
Siblings	.47	26,473
Parent–offspring	.42	8,433
Half-siblings	.35	200
Cousins	.15	1,176
REARED-APART BIOLOGICAL RELATIVES		
MZ twins	.72	65
Siblings	.24	203
Parent–offspring	.24	720
REARED-TOGETHER NONBIOLOGICAL RELATIVES		
Siblings	.32	714
Parent–offspring	.24	720

NOTE: MZ, monozygotic; DZ, dizygotic
SOURCE: Adapted from "Familial Studies of Intelligence: A Review," by T. J. Bouchard and M. McGue, 1981, *Science, 250,* p. 1056. © American Association for the Advancement of Science. Reprinted from McGue et al., 1993, p. 60.

environmental similarity. By measuring these individuals on the characteristics of interest, we can determine the extent to which their genetic similarity accounts for the similarity of scores on each characteristic. For example, we can compare the IQ scores of MZ and DZ twins reared together and apart, biological (nontwin) siblings reared together and apart, adoptive siblings and biological siblings with parents, and adoptive siblings with their biological and adoptive parents. Some representative correlations are presented in Table 9.1. The data clearly suggest a relationship between greater genetic similarity and greater similarity of IQ.

Heritability Coefficient

How, exactly, does the behavioral geneticist determine the degree to which genetic variations determine variations among people in a personality characteristic? This usually is done by computing what is called a **heritability coefficient**, or h^2 (it is h "squared" because numbers are squared when computing variations around an average score). The heritability coefficient represents the proportion of observed variance in scores that can be attributed to genetic factors. In a study involving both MZ and DZ twins, h^2 is based on the difference between the MZ and DZ correlations. If MZ twins (who share all their genes) are no more similar to one another than are DZ twins (who share half their genes), then there is no genetic effect: h^2 is zero. If MZ twins differ greatly from DZ twins, h^2 is large; its upper limit is 1.0, or 100% of the total variance. To the extent that h^2 is less than 1.0, there exists variance that is not accounted for by genetic factors; this remaining variance is explained by environmental variation.

Note that the heritability coefficient refers to variation in the population examined in a given study. There are two implications of this point. First, different heritability coefficients, for the same psychological trait, may be observed in different populations. For example, if one is studying a population in which many people have been subjected to environmental effects that exert a particular large influence on them (e.g., stress from disease or war), then the environmental effects in this group will be relatively large and h^2 will be relatively small (Grigorenko, 2002). Second, the heritability coefficient does not indicate the degree to which genetics accounts for the fact that a particular individual has a particular characteristic. It is a measure of variation in the population. For some attributes (e.g., a biological feature or psychological capacity possessed by all humans), there may be no person-to-person variation. The h^2 would be zero even if genetics explains why all people have the attribute. For other attributes (e.g., your ability to read), the attribute may be explained by an interaction of genetic and social factors, and it may make little sense to say that genetics versus the environment each accounted for X percent of the attribute. The h^2 is an estimate associated with a population and not a definitive measure of the action of genes.

Heritability of Personality: Findings

We now consider additional behavior genetic findings and the conclusions about personality to which they lead. An interesting feature of work in this area is that findings are often relatively consistent from study to study. This enables the behavior geneticist to summarize results with confidence. Here are two quotes featuring key summaries: "It is difficult to find psychological traits that reliably show no genetic influence" (Plomin & Neiderhiser, 1992) and "For almost every behavioral trait so far investigated, from reaction time to religiosity, an important fraction of the variation among people turns out to be associated with genetic variation. This fact need no longer be subject to debate" (Bouchard et al., 1990). These quotes reflect findings from numerous twin and adoption studies. These studies have been conducted on a wide variety of personality variables, often with large samples of research participants, and with the work extending over significant periods of time. The evidence of genetic influence is sometimes startling, as when identical twins reared apart and brought together as adults are found not only to look and sound alike but to have the same attitudes and share the same hobbies and preferences for pets (Lykken, Bouchard, McGue, & Tellegen, 1993). But beyond such almost eerie observations is a pattern of results strongly suggesting an important role for heredity in almost all aspects of personality functioning (Plomin & Caspi, 1999). Recent estimates of the overall heritability of personality traits converge on roughly 40 percent. Table 9.2 presents heritability estimates for a wide variety of characteristics. For comparative purposes, heritability estimates for height and weight are included, as well as a few other characteristics that may be of interest.

A criticism made of behavior-genetic research on personality is that most studies are based on self-report questionnaire methods. A recent study is important in this regard in that two independent peer reports as well as self-reports on the NEO Five-Factor Inventory were collected on a sample of 660 MZ twins and 304 DZ twins (200 same sex and 104 opposite sex). The investigators found good evidence of reliability of ratings in terms of peer-peer rating

Table 9.2 Heritability Estimates

The data indicate a strong genetic contribution to personality (overall estimate of 40% of the variance), a contribution not as large as that for height, weight, or IQ, but larger than that for attitudes and behaviors such as TV viewing.

Trait	h^2 estimate
Height	.80
Weight	.60
IQ	.50
Specific cognitive ability	.40
School achievement	.40
BIG FIVE	
Extraversion	.36
Neuroticism	.31
Conscientiousness	.28
Agreeableness	.28
Openness to Experience	.46
EASI TEMPERAMENT	
Emotionality	.40
Activity	.25
Sociability	.25
Impulsivity	.45
ATTITUDES	
Conservatism	.30
Religiosity	.16
Racial integration	.00
TV viewing	.20

NOTE: EASI = Four dimensions of temperament identified by Buss and Plomin (1984). E, emotionality; A, Activity; S, Sociability; I, Impulsivity.
SOURCES: Bouchard et al., 1990; Dunn & Plomin, 1990; Loehlin, 1992; McGue et al., 1993; Pedersen et al., 1998; Pedersen et al., 1992; Plomin, 1990; Plomin et al., 1990; Plomin & Rende, 1991; Tellegen et al., 1998; Tesser, 1993; Zuckerman, 1991.

agreement, good evidence of the accuracy of self-report in terms of self-peer rating agreement, and general support for earlier findings concerning genetic influence on all of the Big Five personality factors (Table 9.3) (Riemann, Angleitner, & Strelau, 1997).

Some Important Caveats

Before concluding this section, it is important to be aware of two inappropriate conclusions that can be drawn from the behavioral genetic data, conclusions that no behavioral geneticist would make. First, it is possible to draw the inappropriate conclusion that the heritability estimate indicates the extent to which a characteristic is determined by heredity. Even were one to accept the overall heritability estimate of 40 percent for personality, this would not mean that 40 percent of one's personality is inherited, or that 40 percent of some aspect of one's personality is inherited, or that 40 percent of the difference in personality between two individuals or groups of people is inherited. Similarly, a heritability estimate of 80 percent for IQ does not mean that 80 percent of intelligence is inherited, or that 80 percent of one's own intelligence

Table 9.3   Peer-Peer, Self-Peer, MZ and DZ (Self-Report), and MZ and DZ (Average Peer Report) Correlations on the NEO Five-Factor Inventory

	Peer-Peer	Self-Peer	Self-Report		Averaged Peer Report	
			MZ	DZ	MZ	DZ
N	.63	.55	.53	.13	.40	.01
E	.65	.60	.56	.28	.38	.22
O	.59	.57	.54	.34	.49	.30
A	.59	.49	.42	.19	.32	.21
C	.61	.54	.54	.18	.41	.17
Mean	.61	.55	.52	.23	.40	.18

NOTE: MZ, monozygotic; DZ, dizygotic
SOURCE: Adapted from Riemann, Angleitner, and Strelau, 1997, pp. 460, 461, 462.

is inherited, or that 80 percent of group differences in intelligence is due to heredity. Remember that the heritability estimate is a population statistic that varies with the characteristic measured, how the characteristic is measured, the age and other characteristics of the population investigated, and whether twin or adoption data are used. Again, the heritability index is an estimate of the proportion of the variance in a characteristic, measured in a particular way, in a specific population, that can be attributed to genetic variance.

A second inappropriate conclusion concerning heritability estimates would be the suggestion that because a characteristic has an inherited component, it cannot be changed. There is a very common assumption that if something is biological and inherited, it is fixed. Even sophisticated individuals, well aware of the flaw in this view, slip into making such a connection. Even if something is altogether determined by heredity, this does not mean that it cannot be altered by the environment. Dogs can be bred for specific characteristics but this does not mean that a particular environment cannot alter the characteristic. Similarly, as noted earlier, individuals may be born with certain temperaments but this does not mean that their temperaments are set for life (Kagan, 1999). Height is significantly determined by genes but can be influenced by the environment in terms of nutrition.

Molecular Genetic Paradigms

In recent years, researchers have begun to move beyond the traditional behavior-genetic paradigm. Instead of merely comparing different types of twins, they have turned to a direct examination of the underlying biology. This work employs molecular genetic techniques in an effort to identify specific genes that are linked with personality traits (Plomin & Caspi, 1999). By examining the genetic material of different individuals, researchers hope to show how genetic variations, or alleles, relate to individual differences in personality functioning. Ideally, one might be able to show how a genetic variation codes for alternative forms of a biological substance or system that, in turn, has psychological effects.

Initial research reported the discovery of a gene linked to the trait of novelty seeking, similar to Eysenck's P factor, and to low C on the Big Five (Benjamin et al., 1996; Ebstein et al., 1996). However, this finding has not been replicated uniformly in follow-up studies (Grigorenko, 2002). Perhaps more promising,

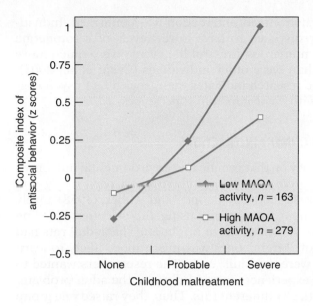

Figure 9.7 *Relations between antisocial behavior and both levels of childhood maltreatment and MAOA activity, which varies as a result of varying alleles of a particular gene. From Caspi et al., 2002.*

researchers recently have identified an interaction between a specific genetic mechanism and the social environment. This research studied the effects of maltreatment in childhood on the development of antisocial behavior later in life (Caspi et al., 2002). Despite such unfortunate maltreatment, some children have good developmental outcomes; they seem to be resilient in the face of early life stress. The question, then, was whether there might be a genetic basis to this resilience.

To answer this question, the researchers identified a subset of the study's population of participants who possessed a gene that has an important property: It codes for an enzyme that lowers the activity of certain neurotransmitters in the brain that are linked to aggressive behavior. Among those who had experienced maltreatment in childhood, people with this genetic variation were found to differ from others (Figure 9.7). Specifically, people who experienced severe maltreatment but who had the gene that produced high levels of the enzyme were less likely to display antisocial behavior in adulthood. The genetic variation, in other words, seemed to lower the negative impact of maltreatment. This exciting finding requires replication. However, it suggests a promising feature for molecular-genetic research on personality.

Subsequent work by this same research team has discovered molecular-genetic factors that make individuals more or less vulnerable to becoming depressed (Caspi et al., 2003). The genetic factor that was studied is one that influences levels of serotonin in the brain; specifically, the researchers studied a naturally-occurring genetic variation that involves two different versions of a gene that affects serotonergic activity. The researchers' expectation was not that possessing a particular genetic background would lead inevitably to the experience of depression. Instead, they again expected an interaction: Genes should predict the onset of depression only in people who have certain types of environmental experiences. The environmental experiences they investigated were those that involve high levels of stress. Adults were surveyed to determine the degree to which they recently had experienced stressful life events involving factors such as finances, health, employment, and interpersonal relationships.

The expectation of a gene-X-environment interaction was confirmed. Individuals who were genetically predisposed to have lower levels of serotonergic activity and who experienced numerous stressful life events were much more likely to become depressed than were other individuals (Caspi et al., 2003). Again, then, molecular-genetic research indicates that genes affect psychological outcomes in interaction with environmental experiences.

ENVIRONMENTS AND GENE-ENVIRONMENT INTERACTIONS

Genetic researchers realized early on that genetic and environmental influences are inextricably linked and interact in their influence on personality and behavior in adulthood. A classic study by Cooper and Zubek (1958) nicely illustrates such gene-environment interactions using the selective breeding research. In previous research, strains of maze-bright and maze-dull rats had been bred so that the strain of "bright" ones was much more likely to learn how to navigate a maze than were the "dull" ones. The researchers wanted to study how early environment experiences would influence the adult problem-solving capacity of these genetically different rats. Thus, they raised one group of each strain in an enriched, stimulating environment and another group of each strain in an impoverished environment. What happened? Compared to the normal lab environment, the enriched environment improved later learning ability in the dull rats but did not help the bright ones. Conversely, the impoverished environment markedly handicapped the bright rats but did not impair the dull group. Thus, even these rats were not prisoners of their genetic predispositions; the environment interacted with their genes in a crucial way, modifying the way these predispositions were expressed.

For human personality, if the behavioral genetic data indicate that roughly 40 to 50 percent of the variance for single personality characteristics and personality overall are determined by genetic factors, then the rest of the population variance is made up of some combination of environmental effects and measurement error. Indeed, one of the interesting aspects of recent developments in behavioral genetics has been the effort to use twin and adoption data to determine environmental effects on personality variables. Thus, although Plomin (1990) suggests that "genetic influence is so ubiquitous and pervasive in behavior that a shift in emphasis is warranted: ask not what is heritable; ask instead what is not heritable" (p. 112), at the same time he suggests that the "other message is that the same behavioral genetic data yield the strongest available evidence for the importance of environmental influence" (p. 115).

Shared and Nonshared Environment

In his book *Nature and Nurture*, Plomin (1990) suggests that behavioral genetics has two messages: nature and nurture. Behavioral genetics research leads to evidence concerning the importance of genes and of the environment. What behavioral geneticists are doing is not only estimating the proportion of the population variance of a characteristic that is due to heredity, but estimating the proportion that is due to different kinds of environments. A distinction is made between **shared environments** and **nonshared environments**. Shared environments consist of those environments shared by siblings as a result of growing up in the same family. Nonshared environments consist of those

Robert Plomin

environments that are not shared by siblings growing up in the same family. For example, siblings may be treated differently by parents because of sex differences, birth order differences, or life events unique to a particular child (e.g., illness in the child or financial difficulties during the youth of one child). In addition, each child typically grows up with a different peer group, an influence emphasized by some as of even greater importance for adult personality development than the family (Harris, 1998).

In behavioral genetics research, the issue of shared and nonshared environment effects is studied by assessing degree of resemblance in personality as a function of both degree of genetic similarity and degree of shared family environment. If shared environments are important, then biological siblings raised together will be much more similar than biological siblings raised apart. They also should be much more similar to their biological parents than are the siblings raised apart. In essence, biological siblings raised together should resemble one another, and their parents, beyond the degree that could be accounted for by common genes alone. In addition, if shared environments are important, then two adopted siblings raised together should be more similar than if they were raised apart. If nonshared environments are important, then these relationships should not hold. In essence, if nonshared environments are important, then biological siblings raised together will be no more similar than if they were raised apart.

Although we recognize sibling differences, and sometimes ask how two siblings raised in the same family can be so different, generally we say: "You know that they came from the same household." Yet, in one of the most striking findings from behavioral genetics, there is considerable evidence that shared environmental effects experiences shared as members of the same family are not nearly as important as nonshared environmental effects. Put differently, the unique experiences siblings have inside and outside the family appear to be far more important for personality development than the shared experiences resulting from being in the same family. In a groundbreaking paper in this area, the question asked was: "Why are children from the same family so different (Plomin & Daniels, 1987)?" The answer: nonshared environments! The suggestion made is that in addition to the 40 percent or so of personality that is due to genetic factors, approximately 35 percent is due to the effects of nonshared environments and only 5 percent due to shared environments, the rest being due to measurement error (Dunn & Plomin, 1990).

A study by Loehlin, McCrae, Costa, and John (1998) examined genetic and environmental effects in three different measures of the Big Five, with

Why Children from the Same Family Are So Different: Each sibling experiences a different, unique family environment.

results generally consistent with the above conclusions. Three findings stood out. First, all five of the Big Five dimensions showed substantial genetic influences of the same magnitude; that is, individual differences in A, C, and O were just as heritable as individual differences in E and N, which had been studied extensively in the context of Eysenck's model of these two superfactors (see Chapter 7). Second, these findings were independent of the effects of intellectual ability, which had also been measured and were controlled in the behavior-genetic analyses; that is, Openness was found to be a personality dimension independent of intelligence, with its own genetic basis. Third, from a methodological perspective, having available three measures for each Big Five factor made it possible to test generalizability across instruments and estimating error separately, rather than including it with the estimate of non-shared environment as in some previous research.

In an analysis of the data from the self-peer ratings of MZ and DZ twins on the NEO scale (Riemann, Angleitner, & Strelau, 1997), Plomin calculated the percentage of the variance due to genetic factors, shared environments, and nonshared environments (including measurement error) for both self and peer ratings on the Big Five. The resulting percentages closely approximate those reported earlier, although the percentages for genetic factors tend to be lower for peer ratings than self ratings (Figure 9.8) (Plomin & Caspi, 1999, p. 253).

Understanding Nonshared Environment Effects

These findings suggest that differences among families seem to matter less for the development of children than do differences within families. Recent research (Reiss, 1997; Reiss, Neiderhiser, Hetherington, & Plomin, 1999) has begun to focus on the particular processes linking genetic, family, and social influences on personality development during the important years of adolescence. This work focuses on the unique relationship between the parent

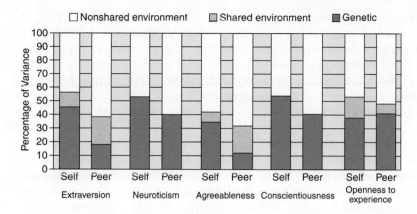

□ Nonshared environment   ▨ Shared environment   ■ Genetic

Figure 9.8 *Genetic (red), shared environment (gray), and nonshared environment (white) components of variance for self-report ratings and peer ratings for the Big Five personality traits. Nonshared environment effects include error of measurement. (Plomin & Caspi, 1999, p. 253.) Copyright © Guilford Press. Reprinted by permission.*

and each adolescent sibling in terms of conflict and negativity, warmth and support, and so forth. In other words, the research seeks to separate out the effects of parenting common to siblings in a family from the effects of parenting unique to each sibling. The evidence to date shows substantial differences in the way siblings are treated by their parents. What is striking, however, is that much of the parenting unique to each child seems to be due to the genetic characteristics of that child. That is, differences in the way parents treat each child seem to be due to different behaviors evoked in the parent by that child, in line with earlier suggestions that children from the same family grow up to be different in part because of genetic differences that lead them to be treated differently by the parents. Most students with siblings can readily testify to such differences in parental treatment!

Does the suggestion that children from the same family are different because of the effects of nonshared environments mean that family experiences are unimportant? Does this mean that early experiences are unimportant for personality development, in contrast with what psychoanalysts would have us believe? Although such conclusions have been drawn by some, this is not in fact what is suggested. Rather, the interpretation is that family influences are important, as are experiences outside the family, but it is the experiences unique to each child that are important rather than the experiences shared by children in the same family. Rather than the family unit being important for investigation, it is the unique experiences of each child in the family that are important.

Three Kinds of Nature-Nurture Interactions

Until now we have considered the effects of genes and environment on personality separately. However, nature and nurture always are interacting with one another: "The critical point to remember in all of this is that in the dance of life, genes and environment are absolutely inextricable partners" (Hyman, 1999, p. 27). Along with the continuous unfolding of the effects of genes and experience, three particular forms of gene-environment interactions have been distinguished (Plomin, 1990; Plomin & Neiderhiser, 1992). First, the same environmental experiences may have different effects on individuals with different genetic constitutions. For example, the same behavior on the part of an anxious parent may have different effects on an irritable, unresponsive child than on a calm, responsive child. Rather than a straightforward effect of parental anxiety that is the same for both kinds of children, there is an interaction between parental behavior and child characteristic. In this case the individual is a passive recipient of environmental events. Genetic factors are interacting with environmental factors but only in a passive, reactive sense.

In a second kind of nature-nurture interaction, individuals with different genetic constitutions may evoke different responses from the environment. For example, the irritable, withdrawn child may evoke a different response from the parent than will a calm, responsive child. Within the same family, siblings can evoke different parental behaviors that then set in motion two completely different patterns of parent-child interaction. Such differences were indicated in the research considered earlier on differential parental treatment of siblings associated with genetic differences in the children. Beyond this, differences in inherited characteristics lead to different responses from peers and others in the environment outside the family. Attractive children call forth different peer responses than do less attractive children. Athletic children call forth different responses than do unathletic children. In each case, a genetically determined characteristic evokes a differential response from the environment.

In the third form of gene-environment interaction, individuals with different constitutions select and create different environments. Once the individual is able to take an active form of interaction with the environment, which occurs at a fairly early age, genetic factors influence the selection and creation of environments. The extravert seeks out different environments than does the introvert, the athletic individual different environments than the unathletic individual, and the musically gifted individual different environments than the individual gifted in visual imagery. These effects increase over the course of time as individuals become increasingly able to select their own environments. By a certain point in time it is impossible to determine the extent to which the individual has been the recipient of an environmental effect as opposed to the creator of the environmental effect.

In sum, individuals can be relatively passive recipients of environments, they can play a role in environmental events through the responses they evoke, and they can play an active role in selecting and creating environments. In each case, there is a nature-nurture, gene-environment interaction. In considering the nature and nurture of personality, we must keep in mind that the development of personality is always a function of the interaction of genes with environments, that there is no nature without nurture and no nurture without nature. We can separate the two for purposes of discussion and analysis, but the two never operate independent of one another. Indeed, genetic factors and environmental experiences are so intertwined that the usual formulation "nature versus nurture" may not even make sense any more. Instead, it may be better to think of "nature via nurture" (Ridley, 2003). The basic nature of genetic material, in other words, is that it "creates new possibilities for the organism" (Ridley, 2003, p. 250) that are realized only if the organism encounters particular environments—that is, only if it is nurtured in a particular way.

CURRENT
APPLICATIONS

CAUSES OF INDIVIDUAL DIFFERENCES: GENES, SOCIAL EXPERIENCE — OR SOMETHING ELSE?

Psychology's most famous question—"Nature or nurture?"—suggests that there are two causes of behavior: (1) information encoded into the genes from the moment of conception and (2) information acquired via social experience after one is born. Much of psychology's inquiry into the determinants of individual differences rests on this dichotomy between biological/genetic/nature factors and social/learned/nurture factors.

However, there is something else to consider: the prenatal environment, that is, the environment experienced after conception but before birth. Startling findings document a role for prenatal factors in the determination of a psychological quality of great interest, namely, sexual orientation.

One correlate of sexual orientation among males is the number of older brothers one has. People who have more older brothers are, on average, somewhat more likely to have a homosexual rather than a heterosexual orientation. (Note that this statement only holds on average; that is, it is a probabilistic statement that describes a pattern of results found only when one studies large numbers of people.) A question, then, is, why this might be the case. What might link sexual orientation to the number of older brothers one has? One possibility is social experience. Maybe social interactions with large numbers of older males somehow influences sexual orientation. This, however, is *not* what recent findings suggest.

In a critical piece of research, the sexual orientation of males who were raised with varying numbers of older brothers living in their home was compared to the sexual orientation of a key comparison group: males who have the same numbers of older brothers, but whose brothers did *not* live in their household (e.g., people who were adopted or some of whose siblings were adopted). The findings revealed that sexual orientation was predicted by the number of older siblings one has *whether or not* those siblings grew up in one's own household! People with more older brothers were, probabilistically, more likely to have a homosexual orientation even in cases in which they were not raised with those older brothers.

How can this be? The investigator suggests that the key influence is in the prenatal environment. As women have more male children, they may develop an immune system response to male fetuses. This immune reaction could affect the biochemical environment of the subsequent male fetus, specifically influencing its brain development in such a way that the later child is less likely to develop a heterosexual orientation. Although these details are somewhat speculative and require further research, the existing findings do indicate a significant influence of prenatal factors on sexual orientation. In so doing, they expand the scope of factors that must be considered in analyses of personality development.

SOURCE: Bogaert, 2006.

As an approach to the question of biology and personality, work in both evolutionary psychology and in twin studies conducted by behavior geneticists has one frustrating feature: There isn't much biology. Evolutionary psychologists provide relatively little evidence regarding specific brain systems

NEUROSCIENCE AND PERSONALITY

underlying personality functioning. Twin studies tell us that genetic influences are relevant to personality, but they don't specify what exactly the biological influences are.

An alternative strategy, which avoids such frustration, is to directly explore brain and other bodily systems. Contemporary work on the neuroscience of personality seeks to understand how neural systems (specific parts of the brain as well as interconnected parts that work together), **neurotransmitters** (chemical substances that transmit information from one neuron to another), and hormones (chemical substances that travel through the bloodstream and affect the activity of bodily organs) contribute to psychological characteristics in behavior, and the interplay between psychological and bodily processes. Some of this work complements the trait theories of personality (Chapters 7 and 8) by discovering biological underpinnings of emotions that are central to personality traits. Other work is beginning to identify the neural foundations of higher-level psychological functions involving self-concept and reasoning about the social world.

LEFT AND RIGHT HEMISPHERIC DOMINANCE

Progress in understanding neural systems generally requires a combination of three things. One must (1) identify a psychological feature of interest, (2) possess enough knowledge of neuroanatomy and physiology that one can formulate a hypothesis about brain systems that might contribute to the psychological feature, and (3) possess a technology to measure relevant aspects of the brain system. These three features combine with great effectiveness in research on the brain and emotional experience.

The psychological feature of interest in this work is that people differ—one from another and, for any given person, from one time to another—in the degree to which their emotional experience is positive versus negative. People experience good versus bad moods. The aspect of neuroanatomy of interest is the anatomical feature that is most obvious if one looks at a brain: It has two halves, or two hemispheres. A possibility explored in research beginning with landmark studies by Richard Davidson (1994, 1995, 1998) is that the left versus right hemispheres are differentially involved in positive versus negative emotion. Relatively greater activation in the left frontal regions of the brain is hypothesized to correlate with approach-related emotions, which usually are emotionally positive. Relatively greater right-frontal activation was predicted to be associated with withdrawal-related emotions, which typically are negative.

The relative activation of one versus another hemisphere is referred to as hemispheric dominance. The prediction, then, is that right- (left-) hemispheric dominance will predict withdrawal/negative (approach/positive) emotion.

A technology for testing this possibility is available. It is the electroencephalograph, or EEG. EEG recordings detect electrical activity of the brain through a simple, painless procedure in which electrodes are placed on the scalp.

Research consistently has supported the idea that hemispheric dominance is linked to emotional experience. In one study, measures of hemispheric activity were taken before and during the showing of film clips designed to elicit positive or negative emotion. In addition, subjects rated their mood at baseline, prior to being shown the film clips, and their emotional experiences during each film clip. Individual differences in prefrontal asymmetry were found to be associated with baseline mood (left hemispheric dominance with positive affect and right hemispheric dominance with negative affect) and with emotional responses to the films, even after the contribution of baseline mood was statistically removed: "Those individuals with more left-sided prefrontal activation at baseline reported more positive affect to the positive film clips and those with more right-sided prefrontal activation reported more negative affect to the negative film clips. These findings support the idea that individual differences in electrophysiological measures of prefrontal activation asymmetry mark some aspect of vulnerability to positive and negative emotion elicitors" (Davidson, 1998, p. 316).

What about stable individual differences in the experience of positive and negative mood? Currently depressed and previously depressed individuals are found to have decreased left-anterior cortical activity relative to nondepressed individuals (Allen, Iacono, Depue, & Arbisi, 1993). Individuals with damage to the left-anterior brain region are likely to become depressed whereas those with damage to the right-anterior brain region are likely to become manic (Robinson & Downhill, 1995). Research on infants suggests a relation between individual differences in measures of prefrontal activation and affective reactivity, with infants who experience greater distress upon separation from their mothers showing greater right-sided prefrontal activation and lesser left-sided prefrontal activation than infants who showed little distress in this situation (Davidson & Fox, 1989). In line with this, Kagan (1994) reports evidence that inhibited children show more reactivity in their right hemisphere and uninhibited children dominance in the left hemisphere.

More recent work has shown that EEG measures can differentiate between two different aspects of emotional experience that are both negative: anxious arousal during a task and worrying prior to a task (Heller, Schmidtke, Nitschke, Koven, & Miller, 2002). Worrying is associated with stronger left-frontal brain activation than is anxious arousal (e.g., Hofmann et al., 2005). Worrying, then, is "a unique emotional state" (Hofmann et al., 2005, p. 472), not just a variation on the state of anxious arousal during a task. This finding from neuroscience has interesting implications for the personality trait theories. The five-factor trait of neuroticism combines different aspects of anxiety into one factor, whereas this neuroscientific evidence indicates the existence of different types of negative emotion that truly are distinct.

NEUROTRANSMITTERS AND TEMPERAMENT: DOPAMINE AND SEROTONIN

One of the areas in neuroscience receiving the greatest attention is that of neurotransmitter functioning, in particular the neurotransmitters dopamine and serotonin. We know that an excess in the neurotransmitter dopamine is implicated in schizophrenia while an underproduction of dopamine is implicated in Parkinson's disease. Dopamine also is associated with pleasure, being described as a "feel good" chemical (Hamer, 1997). Animals will perform responses that lead to administration of dopamine (Wise, 1996). Thus, dopamine appears to be central to the functioning of the reward system: "One way of characterizing the job of this dopamine circuit is that it's a reward system. It says, in effect, 'That was good, let's do it again, and let's remember exactly how we did it'" (Hyman, 1999, p. 25). Addictive drugs such as cocaine are viewed as "masquerading" as the neurotransmitter dopamine, leading to the experience of pleasure upon taking the drug but also to the experience of a low as the cocaine stops coming and the dopamine level drops.

The neurotransmitter serotonin also is involved in the regulation of mood. Modern drugs, known as SSRIs, selective serotonin reuptake inhibitors, are thought to alleviate depression through their prolongation of the action of serotonin at the synapses of neurons. SSRIs administered to normal individuals have been found both to reduce negative affective experience and to increase social, affiliative behavior (Knutson et al., 1998). Finally, we know that the hormone cortisol is associated with the stress response. Again returning to Kagan's (1994) research, inhibited children at the age of five were found to be high in reactivity to threat, as measured by cortisol response, although this was not as true at age seven.

The fact that neurotransmitters contribute to mood suggests that an analysis of brain chemistry can illuminate the topic with which we began this chapter: individual differences in temperament. Numerous investigators have explored the potential biochemical bases of temperament (Cloninger, Svrakic, & Przybeck, 1993; Depue, 1995, 1996, Depue & Collins, 1999; Eysenck, 1990; Gray, 1987; Pickering & Gray, 1999; Tellegen, 1985; Zuckerman, 1991, 1996). Although similarities appear among almost all of these models, and many are similar to the five-factor model described in Chapter 8, they do not always overlap in clear ways with one another. Thus, rather than exploring a number of such models, we will follow the lead of Lee Anna Clark and David Watson (1999; Watson, 2000) in their analysis of personality temperament.

Three Dimensions of Temperament: PE, NE, and DvC

According to Clark and Watson's (1999) model, individual differences in temperament can be summarized in terms of three big superfactors similar to those suggested by Eysenck and also corresponding, roughly, to three of the Big Five dimensions: NE (Negative Emotionality), PE (Positive Emotionality), and DvC (Disinhibition versus Constraint). Individuals high on the NE factor experience elevated levels of negative emotions and see the world as threatening, problematic, and distressing, whereas those low on the trait are calm, emotionally stable, and self-satisfied. The PE factor relates to the individual's willingness to engage the environment, with high scorers (like extraverts) enjoying the company of others and approaching life actively, with energy, cheerfulness, and enthusiasm, whereas low scorers (like introverts) are reserved, socially aloof, and low in energy and confidence. It is important to note that although NE and PE have opposite sounding qualities, they are independent of one another; that is, an individual can be high or low on each (Watson & Tellegen, 1999; Watson, Wiese, Vaidya, & Tellegen, 1999). This is because they are under the control of different internal biological systems. The third factor, DvC, does not involve affective tone, as was true for the first two factors, but rather relates to style of affective regulation, with high DvC scorers being impulsive, reckless, and oriented toward feelings and sensations of the moment whereas low scorers are careful, controlled by long-term implications of their behavior, and avoiding risk or danger.

The question, then, is whether one can identify biological correlates of the three factors. Building on work by Depue (1996, Depue & Collins, 1999), Clark and Watson suggest that PE is associated with the action of dopamine, the "feel good" chemical. In animal research, high dopamine levels are associated with approach behaviors, whereas deficits in this neurotransmitter are associated with deficits in incentive motivation. In all, Clark and Watson suggest that "individual differences in the sensitivity of this biological system to the signals of reward that activate incentive motivation and positive affect, and supportive cognitive processes, form the basis of the PE dimension of temperament" (1999, p. 414). Differences in hemispheric lateralization, with high PE scores being associated with left hemispheric dominance, may also be involved (Davidson, 1992, 1994, 1998).

Turning to DvC, Clark and Watson suggest that the biological basis of this factor is serotonin. According to them, humans low in this neurotransmitter tend to be aggressive and to show increased use of dopamine-activating drugs such as alcohol. Alcoholism also is associated with reduced serotonin functioning. Hamer (1997) also associates the neurotransmitter dopamine with thrill seeking, impulsivity, and disinhibition. There also is evidence that high levels of the hormone testosterone are associated with competitiveness and aggressiveness, both linked with high scores on DvC.

Clark and Watson suggest that less is known about the neurobiology underlying NE. However, there is a relation between low serotonin levels at the neuron synapses and depression, anxiety, and obsessive-compulsive symptoms. Hamer and Copeland (1998) relate low serotonin levels to a dark view of the world, analogous to Galen's melancholic temperament. Depue (1995) reports that animals low in serotonin are excessively irritable, and Hamer (1997) describes serotonin as the "feel bad" chemical. In addition, there is the evidence noted of a relation between right hemispheric lateralization and the tendency to experience negative emotions. Finally, there is evidence that excessive sensitivity of the amygdala likely plays a role in the tendency to experience high levels of anxiety and distress (LeDoux, 1995, 1999).

In assessing this work, one must recall that there is no one-to-one correspondence between biological processes and personality traits. Rather, each biological component appears to be associated with the expression of more than one trait and the expression of each trait is influenced by more than one biological factor: "Models of personality based on only one neurotransmitter are clearly too simplistic and will require the addition of other modifying factors" (Depue & Collins, 1999, p. 513). Thus, it is difficult to integrate all these neurobiological findings into the **three-dimensional temperament model** because we risk oversimplifying the neurobiology we know so far. The links between biology and temperament suggested in Table 9.4 are best described as initial hypotheses and as our best guesses of how things might hang together, to be tested further and revised as more data become available.

In addition, although brain localization of functions has advanced significantly, it is important to consider the brain as a total system. According to Damasio (1994), Gall was correct in suggesting that the brain consists of subsystem parts that are specialized in the function they play, as opposed to being one large, undifferentiated mass. However, not only was Gall not able to identify correctly the parts and functions, he was unaware of how the brain functions as a system. As Damasio puts it: "I am not falling into the phrenological trap. To put it simply: The mind results from the operation of each of the separate components, and from the concerted operation of the

Table 9.4   Suggested Links Between Biology and Personality

Amygdala Part of the primitive limbic system, the brain's emotional response center. Particularly important for aversive emotional learning.

Hemispheric Lateralization Dominance of the right frontal hemisphere associated with activation of negative emotions and personality traits of shyness and inhibition; dominance of the left frontal hemisphere associated with activation of positive emotions and personality traits of boldness and disinhibition.

Dopamine A neurotransmitter associated with reward, reinforcement, pleasure. High dopamine levels are associated with positive emotions, high energy, disinhibition, and impulsivity. Low dopamine levels are associated with lethargy, anxiety, and constriction. Animals and people will self-administer drugs that trigger the release of dopamine.

Serotonin A neurotransmitter involved in mood, irritability, and impulsivity. Low serotonin levels are associated with depression but also with violence and impulsivity. Drugs known as SSRIs (selective serotonin reuptake inhibitors) (e.g., Prozac, Zoloft, Paxil) are used to treat depression as well as phobias and obsessive-compulsive disorders. Exactly how they operate is not totally clear.

Cortisol A stress-related hormone secreted by the adrenal cortex that facilitates reactions to threat. Although adaptive in relation to short-term stress, responses to long-term, chronic stress can be associated with depression and memory loss.

Testosterone A hormone important in the development of secondary sex characteristics and also associated with dominance, competitiveness, and aggression.

Sources: Hamer & Copeland, 1998; Sapolsky, 1994; Zuckerman, 1995.

multiple systems constituted by those separate systems" (1994, p. 15). There is both differentiation-localization and organization-system. In sum, personality traits are linked with the functioning of the patterning of elements in the biological system rather than by single elements: "Psychobiology is not for seekers of simplicity" (Zuckerman, 1996, p. 128).

PLASTICITY: BIOLOGY AS BOTH CAUSE AND EFFECT

There is a tendency to think of biological processes as fixed and determining personality emotions and behaviors, as if the former is cause and the latter is effect. This way of thinking of course is not wrong. Yet it is not entirely right. Biology can change; it is, in a common metaphor, "plastic." It can be shaped and molded.

Recent findings provide much evidence of the **plasticity** of both neural systems and neurotransmitter systems (Gould, Reeves, Graziano, & Gross, 1999; Raleigh & McGuire, 1991). For example, although leadership in a monkey hierarchy is associated with high levels of serotonin, if the troop is reorganized so that leadership ranks are reversed, the new leaders develop higher levels of serotonin than when they were on the bottom (Raleigh & McGuire, 1991). Similarly, the relation between testosterone and aggression or competitiveness is bidirectional, with high testosterone facilitating greater aggression and competitiveness but competition and aggression also leading to higher testosterone levels (Dabbs, 2000). For example, not only does losing a competitive sports event result in lower testosterone levels but being a fan of a losing team does as well (McCaul, Gladue, & Joppe, 1992). In fact, just winning in a coin toss can result in an increase in testosterone level (Gladue, Boechler, & McCaul, 1989). These effects are so strong that Hamer and Copeland (1998)

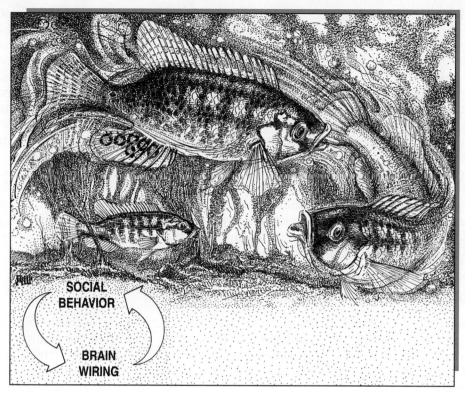

Brain Plasticity: Changes in brain structure are possible as a result of experience. In cichlid fish, dominant males have larger cells in the hypothalamus than do nondominant males. However, if defeated, the cells shrink along with changes in breeding behavior. (Illustration by Dimitry Schidlovsky.)

are led to conclude that "from song birds to squirrels, and mice to monkeys, an aggressive encounter changes testosterone levels. Winners get a blast of testosterone; losers get a drain. Humans are the same" (p. 112).

Recent research has shown that a specific type of early-life experience—maternal care—has long-term biological effects on organisms (Weaver, Meaney, & Szyf, 2006). This research is not done with people but with animals, specifically, laboratory rats. However, the similarity of basic biological systems from one mammalian species to another makes the findings relevant to the student of personality. Researchers find that rats who receive more maternal care in the first week of life, specifically, more licking and grooming from the mother are less fearful when they reach adulthood. (Fear is assessed by measuring how much time a rat spends exploring an unfamiliar area; higher levels of fear inhibit exploration.) Findings show not only that less good maternal care leads to higher levels of fear; the research also reveals the biological pathways through which maternal experience has this effect. Positive maternal experience creates a biochemical effect that influences gene expression in an area of the brain that is involved in reactions to stress, namely, the hippocampus. The effects on hippocampal functioning are long-lasting. Convincing evidence of this comes from research in which the detrimental effects of inadequate maternal care in the first week of life were *reversed* in adulthood. The investigators worked with a group of adult rats who displayed high fear, and injected into their brains a chemical that interferes with the hypothesized biochemical effects of detrimental maternal experience. These rats became less fearful (Weaver et al., 2006). The overall results in this line of research, then, show that genes do not affect behavior in a manner that is independent of the organism's experience with the world. Instead, "gene expression is significantly altered . . . [by] maternal care early in life" (Weaver et al., 2006, p. 3484).

Research on biological plasticity is of importance not only to psychologists in laboratories, but to society at large. Findings illustrate that biology is not a fixed feature of a person or group of persons. The biology of a group of people living in a particular environment may reflect not only inherent features of that group, but also the environment in which they happen to live. We consider here two recent examples of research on plasticity, the first of which involves a factor that, at first, might seem irrelevant to the biological bases of personality: the socioeconomic status of communities.

SOCIOECONOMIC STATUS OF COMMUNITIES AND SEROTONIN

As we have reviewed, a neurotransmitter that is important to emotional life is serotonin. People differ in levels of serotonergic activity in the brain, and these differences are linked to emotional experience, including the experience of depression. An important question, then, is where these differences come from.

Surely genetic factors play a role in the observed differences between people in serotonergic activity. Yet a recent research team (Manuck et al., 2005) looked at an entirely different factor. They speculated that differences in serotonin functioning could result from differences in socioeconomic status (SES). People in economically advantaged versus disadvantaged neighborhoods experience different factors in their daily lives (Gallo & Matthews, 2003). In neighborhoods that are economically poorer, people tend to experience higher levels of daily stress and may on average also experience lower levels of nutrition. Since the body responds to both nutrition and stress, these external environmental factors could affect internal biology, including serotonergic activity.

To test for this possibility, the researchers (Manuck et al., 2005) asked a large sample of adults to participate in a laboratory study. Participants were asked to ingest a substance that is, in the technical terminology, a serotonin agonist, where an agonist is a substance that mimics the action of another substance. In this case, since the researchers were interested in serotonin, they used a substance that is a serotonin agonist. After this was administered, the researchers took a blood sample and measured levels of a hormone, prolactin. Prolactin is of interest because serotonin stimulates the release of prolactin in the body. The great advantage of this research paradigm is that it allowed the investigators to examine, very directly, the possibility that people living in neighborhoods of different SES would have different biological functioning, specifically, that they would differ in peak prolactin levels, which are a direct indication of the body's responsivity to serotonin.

The findings provide remarkable evidence of sociocommunity variations in the functioning of a biological system with psychological importance. People

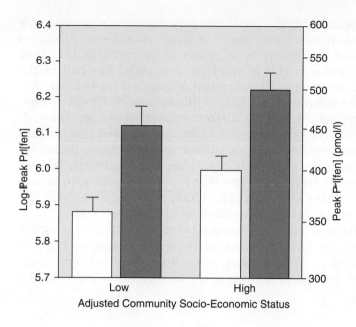

Figure 9.9 *Differences in biological functioning, specifically in peak prolactin levels, among men (white bars) and women (blue bars) living in communities of low and high socioeconomic status. Manuck et al., 2005.*

who lived in less economically advantaged neighborhoods displayed lower serotonergic responsivity, a finding that held similarly for both women and men (Figure 9.9). If you are thinking to yourself, "well, maybe the high-SES people differed on some personality traits from the low-SES people, and that explains the effect," then the news to report is that the researchers tested for this possibility, too. Measures of the five-factor traits, as well as a measure of IQ, were available. The differences between communities were *not* explained by any differences in five-factor traits or intelligence; the biological differences were observed even after statistically controlling for these factors (Manuck et al., 2005). Having ruled out these alternative possibilities, the authors conclude that "socio-economic inequalities among communities can, if perhaps modestly, affect even the neurobiology of their residents" which may help to explain "reported effects of low community SES on the prevalence of psychiatric disorders or behaviors associated with dysregulated central serotonergic function, such as depression, impulsive aggression, and suicide" (Manuck et al., 2005, p. 526).

ENVIRONMENTAL EXPERIENCE AND CHANGES IN BRAIN MATTER

One might think of the brain as a kind of computer. Just as we use the hardware of a computer to carry out tasks such as word processing and internet shopping, we use the "hardware" of our brain to carry out the tasks of daily life. This computer metaphor, however, has many drawbacks. One of the most important is that computers and brains differ in how they respond to experience. If you run a program over and over again on your computer, the computer's hardware does not change; it does not grow new hardware that does a better job of running the program. Evidence indicates, however, that the brain—very much unlike the hardware of a computer—does in fact change as a result of experience. This evidence provides a clear-cut illustration of the plasticity of neural systems.

Recent evidence (Draganski et al., 2004) involves experience on a simple task: juggling. The researchers used brain imaging techniques to obtain anatomical depictions of the brains of a group of research participants. They then divided the group in half at random, and asked one-half of the participants to learn how to juggle. They learned a simple three-ball juggling routine over a period of 3 months. At the end of this time period, both groups, jugglers and non-jugglers, returned to the lab for a second brain scan. The finding? Their brains differed! The brain imaging technique revealed that jugglers experienced a significant expansion of grey matter in the brain, in particular in a brain region involved in the perception of motion. The results, the authors note, "contradict the traditionally held view that the anatomical structure of the adult human brain does not alter, except for changes in morphology caused by ageing or pathological conditions" (Draganski et al., 2004, p. 311).

In sum, advances in neuroscience are providing exciting evidence of the two-way street that runs between biology and experience. Future years surely will expand our understanding of the biological bases of personality functioning, and of social and experiential contributions to the biology of the individual!

NEUROSCIENTIFIC INVESTIGATIONS OF "HIGHER-LEVEL" PSYCHOLOGICAL FUNCTIONS

Much of the work we have just reviewed primarily addressed emotional and motivational processes. Investigators related biological systems to psychological phenomena involving moods, basic impulses, and emotions such as fear. But what about the rest of personality functioning? Specifically, what about "higher level" psychological functions (e.g., self-concept, morality, etc.) that are at the heart of personality functioning and social behavior? Those psychological functions also require a biological brain. In principle, then, neuroscience can shed light on these complex psychological functions. We now turn to some recent research that attempts to do just that.

BRAIN AND SELF

A uniquely human capacity is the ability to reflect on the self: one's features, potentials, appearance to others, and so forth. A question of basic research interest concerns the nature of this capacity. Does it reflect people's overall cognitive capabilities? In other words, is the self just "one of those things we happen to think about?" Or is it unique? Might there be functionally distinct systems in the brain that come into play when we are thinking about ourselves as opposed to thinking about other people or things?

Recent work (Kelley et al., 2002) has investigated this question by using a brain imaging technique, **fMRI**. An fMRI (or functional magnetic resonance imaging) enables researchers to identify specific regions of the brain that are active when people perform a given task. This is done by analyzing changes in blood flow during task performance. If there is a particularly large change in blood flow in a given brain region during task performance, this provides evidence that the brain region is somehow involved in the performance of that task.

The task that participants performed in the research of Kelley and colleagues (2002) involved the rating of trait adjectives (dependable, polite, etc.). Participants made three types of ratings about the words. They judged (1) whether

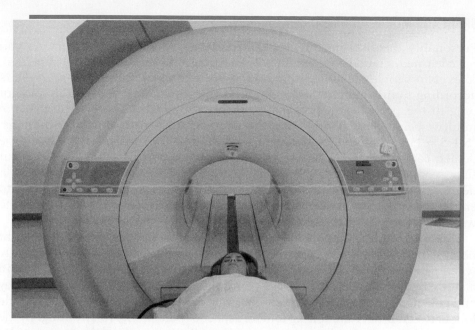

Participant taking part in magnetic resonance imaging (MRI) procedure. MRI techniques have greatly advanced science's understanding of brain systems involved in personality functioning.

the adjective (when presented to them) was presented in uppercase letters, (2) whether the adjective described George W. Bush, and (3) whether the adjective described themselves. The idea, then, is that there might be some brain regions that are uniquely active when people think about themselves ("Am I dependable?") as opposed to another person ("Is Bush dependable?") or cues unrelated to a person ("Is the word 'dependable' in uppercase type?"). An alternative possibility is that thinking about the self is no different than thinking about other people.

Kelley and colleagues (2002) found that, yes, there are regions of the brain that appear to be uniquely involved in judgments about the self. An area near the front of the brain—specifically, the medial prefrontal cortex, or MPFC—was "selectively engaged during self-referential judgments" (Kelley et al., 2002, p. 790). Compared to baseline recordings, fMRI recordings during task performance indicated that when participants were not performing the trait rating task, the MPFC was more involved in judgments about the self than judgments about Bush or about the typeface of the letters.

Such findings of course do not mean that this particular region of the frontal cortex is the biological "home of the self." Judging oneself with respect to trait adjectives is only one aspect of self-concept, and multiple brain regions surely come into play when people engage in any complex mental activity involving self-reflection. Yet, the findings provide intriguing initial evidence that neuroscientific research can inform complex questions about personality functioning. Future years are sure to see growing interest, and scientific evidence, on the question of the neural foundations of self-concept (see, e.g., Churchman, 2002).

BRAIN AND MORAL JUDGMENT

Personality theorists have long been interested in moral judgment. As you have learned, Freud proposed an entire structure of personality, the superego, to explain people's tendency to evaluate the actions of themselves and others according to moral and ethical standards. Moral judgments seem unique not only to the professional personality theorist, but probably also to you, the intuitive personality theorist. Suppose someone says the following two things: "$5 + 5 = 11$" and "poor people who need emergency medical care should be denied care unless they can pay for it." Both statements seem "wrong." But they seem wrong in different ways. The latter statement seems wrong in a deep, emotional way. Your sense that this opinion is morally wrong seems to engage emotional processes in a way that your knowledge that "11" was the wrong answer to "$5 + 5$" does not.

If moral judgments are, in fact, different from other judgments, then it might be possible to identify specific brain regions that come into play specifically when people engage in moral reasoning tasks. This possibility was pursued in a study by Greene, Somerville, Nostrum, Dailey, & Cohen (2001). Like Kelley and colleagues (2002), these researchers used fMRI to investigate the possible link between brain functioning and an aspect of personality functioning. In the work of Greene and colleagues, research participants were asked to consider a series of difficult choices, or dilemmas. Some of the choices were moral dilemmas; they involved issues such as the correctness of keeping money that one has found or harming someone if the harm resulted in a benefit to a large number of other people. Other choices were nonmoral; they involved decisions such as whether to take a bus versus a train to get to a given location. Participants were asked to judge whether or not a given course of action was appropriate as a response to each of the moral and nonmoral problems. The question, then, was whether different brain regions would be involved when people thought about the moral versus nonmoral tasks.

The researchers indeed did find that there was different involvement of brain regions in moral versus nonmoral reasoning. Of particular interest is that the brain regions involved in moral reasoning were those that, in previous research, had been shown to be involved also in the generation of emotional experiences (Greene et al., 2001). The fMRI data, in other words, confirmed the intuition stated above: The difference between moral and nonmoral reasoning is that moral reasoning is not "cold" factual thinking. Instead, it involves emotional responses that directly influence people's decision-making capabilities. These findings are part of a wide range of recent data demonstrating the role of the brain's emotional systems in psychological functions that previously had been thought of as purely cognitive in nature (Bechar, Damasio, & Damasio, 2000; Sanfrey et al., 2003). More generally, they demonstrate the power of neuroscientific research to inform questions about social thinking processes and personality that are a primary focus of theories that we will consider later in this text (Chapters 11 to 13).

In sum, we have reviewed here an array of findings that is potentially dizzying. They involve deep questions about personality and, simultaneously, complex techniques from the biological sciences. Yet some simple themes emerge from this complexity. On the one hand, contemporary research in personality psychology has succeeded in identifying specific neural and biochemical systems that contribute to personality functioning and to significant differences among persons. On the other hand, research on biology and personality has, to a surprising degree, highlighted the influence of the environment. Identical twins are not identical in their personalities. Similar people who encounter different social settings and experiences differ biologically. In the broad context of the theories of personality, the research results we have reviewed do confirm the intuitions of trait theorists that biology is fundamental to personality and individual differences. Yet they also support the intuitions of the theorists you will learn about in the chapters ahead, who commonly explore not only biology, but the environment, society, and culture, in their efforts to understand persons.

MAJOR CONCEPTS

Adoption studies An approach to establishing genetic-behavior relationships through the comparison of biological siblings reared together with biological siblings reared apart through adoption. Generally combined with twin studies.

Behavioral genetics The study of genetic contributions to behaviors of interest to psychologists, mainly through the comparison of degrees of similarity among individuals of varying degrees of biological-genetic similarity.

Effortful control A temperament quality involving the capacity to control one's actions by stopping one activity (a dominant response) in order to do another.

Evolved psychological mechanisms In evolutionary psychology, psychological mechanisms that are the result of evolution by selection; that is, they exist and have endured because they have been adaptive to survival and reproductive success.

fMRI (functional magnetic resonance imaging) A brain imaging technique that identifies specific regions of the brain that are involved in the processing of a given stimulus or the performance of a given task; the technique relies on recordings of changes in blood flow in the brain.

Heritability coefficient The proportion of observed variance in scores in a specific population that can be attributed to genetic factors.

Inhibited-uninhibited temperaments Relative to the uninhibited child, the inhibited child reacts to unfamiliar persons or events with restraint, avoidance, and distress, takes a longer time to relax in new situations, and has more unusual fears and phobias. The uninhibited child seems to enjoy these very same situations that seem so stressful to the inhibited child. The uninhibited child responds with spontaneity in novel situations, laughing and smiling easily.

Neurotransmitters Chemical substances that transmit information from one neuron to another (e.g., dopamine and serotonin).

Parental investment theory The view that women have a greater parental investment in offspring than do men because women pass their genes on to fewer offspring.

Phrenology The early 19th century attempt to locate areas of the brain responsible for various aspects of emotional and behavioral functioning. Developed by Gall, it was discredited as quackery and superstition.

Plasticity The ability of parts of the neurobiological system to change, temporarily and for extended periods of time, within limits set by genes, to meet current adaptive demands and as a result of experience.

Proximate causes Explanations for behavior associated with current biological processes in the organism.

Selective breeding An approach to establishing genetic-behavior relationships through the breeding of successive generations with a particular characteristic.

Shared and nonshared environments The comparison in behavioral genetics research of the effects of siblings growing up in the same or different environments. Particular attention is given to whether siblings reared in the same family share the same family environment.

Three-dimensional temperament model The three superfactors describing individual differences in temperament: Positive Emotionality (PE), Negative Emotionality (NE), and Disinhibition versus Constraint (DvC).

Twin studies An approach to establishing genetic-behavior relationships through the comparison of degree of similarity among identical twins, fraternal twins, and nontwin siblings. Generally combined with adoption studies.

REVIEW

1. Psychologists have long been interested in individual differences in temperament, relating such differences to constitutional factors. Advances in temperament research have come in the form of longitudinal studies and objective measures of behavior and constitutional-biological variables. Kagan's research on inhibited and uninhibited children is illustrative of such developments.

2. Evolutionary theory concerns ultimate causes of behavior, that is, why the behavior of interest evolved and the adaptive function it served. Work in the area of male-female mate preferences, emphasizing sex differences in parental investment and parenthood probability, and in male-female differences in causes of jealousy illustrate research associated with evolutionary interpretations of human behavioral characteristics.

3. Three methods used to establish genetic-behavior relationships are selective breeding, twin studies, and adoption studies. Twin and adoption studies lead to significant heritability estimates for intelligence and most personality characteristics. The overall heritability for personality has been estimated to be .4 to .5; that is, 40 to 50 percent of the variance in personality characteristics is due to genetic factors. However, there is evidence that heritability estimates are influenced by the population studied, personality characteristics studied, and measures used.

4. Associations between findings in neuroscience and personality have focused on the functioning of neurotransmitters such as dopamine and serotonin, on individual differences in hemispheric lateralization and emotional style, demonstrated in the work of Davidson, and on the functioning of parts of the brain such as the amygdala in relation to the processing of emotional stimuli and emotional memories. The three-dimensional temperament model proposed by Clark and Watson represents one attempt to systematize relations between the findings in neuroscience and personality. Many such links are suggested, although at this time a comprehensive model of biological processes and personality traits remains to be formulated.

5. In recent years, researchers in neuroscience have begun to identify specific brain regions that are involved in complex aspects of personality functioning such as judgments about the self and judgments of the morality of actions. This work generally relies on brain imaging techniques, particularly fMRI.

6. Although there is a tendency to think of biological processes as fixed, there is considerable evidence of plasticity or potential for change in neurobiological systems as a result of experience. Research on the biological foundations of personality, then, provides information not only about the role of genetics in personality, but also about the role of the environment.

BEHAVIORISM AND THE LEARNING APPROACHES TO PERSONALITY

10

Chapter Focus

Have you ever dated someone who did something that really annoyed you? A woman was particularly bothered by her boyfriend's constant moaning about how much schoolwork he had to do. She grew tired of constantly providing him with attention and sympathy—after all, she had just as much work! One day she was struck with a new idea: What if she simply ignored her boyfriend every time he complained? It worked! When she stopped pampering him, his complaining gradually disappeared; in the language of behaviorism, her attention to his problems had been serving as a positive reinforcement that had taught him to complain in the first place.

Without realizing it, this woman was using some of the basic principles of learning theory to change her boyfriend's behavior. This chapter considers approaches to personality that are based on theories of learning, and the overall approach to psychological science known as behaviorism. According to behaviorism, people gradually acquire their personality styles as a result of their experiences with the environment. Associated theories of learning specify the exact processes through which people are shaped by environmental experiences.

In this chapter, you will learn about theories of exceptional importance in the history of psychology: Pavlov's classical conditioning and Skinner's operant conditioning. These theories both share a commitment to the experimental testing of clearly defined hypotheses. Approaches to assessment and change are then considered, along with an overall critical evaluation of these approaches to personality.

QUESTIONS TO BE ADDRESSED IN THIS CHAPTER

1. Can principles of learning discovered in research on animals provide the basis for a theory of personality?

2. Is our behavior controlled by events (stimuli) in the environment?

3. If abnormal behavior is learned like all other behavior, can one base therapies on learning principles?

4. If our behavior is ultimately determined by the environment, as claimed by the behaviorists, do people have "free will"?

This chapter presents two theories of learning. They are not opposing views. Instead, they are complementary; they highlight different aspects of how people learn from environmental experiences. In combination, these two ideas—Pavlov's classical conditioning and Skinner's operant conditioning theories—provided the foundation for a view of psychology known as behaviorism.

During the middle of the 20th century, behaviorism was the predominant school of thought in scientific psychology. Behaviorism subsequently experienced a precipitous decline in influence, although the study of operant and classical condition remains a part of the contemporary field (Domjan, 2005; Staddon & Cerutti, 2003). Why—you may already be asking—should I learn about a school of thought that already has declined in influence? There is much to be learned from a review of behaviorism. Developing a comprehensive scientific theory of personality is no easy feat. It is instructive to see where past efforts have succeeded and failed. Furthermore, despite whatever limits it may have, the behaviorist school of thought gave rise to therapeutic methods of unquestioned value; we will consider some of them in this chapter. An additional point is that, in recent years, a number of researchers who would not label themselves "behaviorists" have nonetheless explored some of the themes that are defining of the behavioral approach. These include the ideas that much of our action is controlled directly by stimuli in the environment (Bargh & Ferguson, 2000; Bargh & Gollwitzer, 1994) and that our intuition that we are in conscious control of our behavior (rather than the environment being in control of us) is simply a "trick" (Wegner, 2003, p. 65) that our mind plays on us. Ideas that were originally highlighted by the behaviorists endure in the contemporary field.

We begin by considering behaviorism's view of the person. (Views of the main theorists, especially B. F. Skinner, appear later in the chapter.) Its viewpoint on psychology is best understood by way of analogy. Consider how we think about people's anatomy and physiology. It is reasonable to conceive of the body as a kind of "machine." Like any complex machine, the body is a collection of mechanisms (heart, lungs, sweat glands, and so forth) that perform various functions (respiration, regulation of temperature, etc.). Now return to our main topic: personality. Here the idea of a machine seems odd. Bodies seem machine-like, but personalities do not. People are spontaneous and fun-loving. They are conflicted and anxious. Brave and imaginative. Machines are not spontaneous, fun-loving, conflicted, anxious, brave, or imaginative. Intuitively, then, persons seem quite unlike machines.

Despite these intuitions, in the behaviorist view persons are machine-like. To B. F. Skinner, behaviorism's greatest spokesperson and most influential theorist, the interesting thing about machines is that people have "created the machine in [their] *own image*" (Skinner, 1953, p. 46, emphasis added). With advances in science during the past two centuries, Skinner writes, "we have discovered more about how the living organism works and are better able to see its machine-like properties" (1953, p. 47). When seeking to build a science of persons, the behaviorist assumes that persons can be viewed as collections of machine-like mechanisms. The behaviorist explores how these mechanisms learn, that is, how they change in reaction to environmental input.

Viewing persons as machine-like has a major implication. This implication is a second important feature of behaviorism's view of the person. The implication is a philosophical position known as **determinism.** Determinism is the belief that an event is caused by, or determined by, some prior event, with the cause being something that can be understood according to basic laws of science. When applied to questions of human behavior, determinism is the belief that people's behavior is caused in a lawful scientific manner. Determinism stands in opposition to a different belief, namely, the belief in "free will." As we explain in more detail below, behaviorists do not believe that people have free will, that is, they do not think it is correct to say that a person

BEHAVIORISM'S VIEW OF THE PERSON

freely chose to act in one way or another. Instead, they believe that people are part of a natural world, and that in the natural world events—including the behavior of persons—are causally determined. This belief is not new. It has been a part of the Western intellectual world for centuries. The great 17th-century philosopher Spinoza, for example, defended the belief that "In the mind there is no absolute or free will" (Spinoza, 1677/1952, p. 391). Contemporary behaviorists differed from Spinoza in their belief that, thanks to their research on classical and operant condition, there now is a firm scientific basis for believing in determinism. We will introduce you to this line of thought by reviewing behaviorism's view of the science of personality.

BEHAVIORISM'S VIEW OF THE SCIENCE OF PERSONALITY

As an approach to the science of personality, behaviorism differs enormously from the theories we discuss elsewhere in this book. The differences are revealed in the basic assumptions of the behavioral approach. There are two. The first is that behavior must be explained in terms of the causal influence of the environment on the person. Compare this to other theories. The other theories in this book primarily are theories about what's "in the head of" the person (psychodynamic structures, traits, etc.). They ask about how internal personality factors influence people's experiences and actions. Behaviorism, in contrast, is about what's in the environment. Behaviorists ask about how environmental factors causally determine people's behavior. The second assumption is that an understanding of people should be built entirely upon controlled laboratory research, where that research could involve either people or animals. Again, compare this to the other theories. One thing shared by the other personality theorists is that, in building theories of personality, the beings that were studied were persons. Behaviorists, in contrast, build a theory of persons in large part on a database involving animals. This may strike you as odd. Yet, as we review below, it exemplifies a strategy common in the sciences, a strategy of studying "simple systems."

ENVIRONMENTAL DETERMINISM AND ITS IMPLICATIONS FOR THE CONCEPT OF PERSONALITY

The most basic feature of behaviorism's view of the science of personality is that this science must study how environmental factors determine human behavior. They reason as follows. We human beings are physical objects in a physical universe. As such, we are subject to physical laws that can be understood through scientific analysis. Ever since the beginnings of modern physics hundreds of years ago, the behaviorists reason, scientists have recognized that the way to explain the behavior of any physical object is to identify the forces in the environment that act upon it, causing its behavior. Suppose we throw a rock into the air and observe its behavior: It travels in a curving, parabolic path back to earth. How do we explain this? We don't say that the rock "enjoys traveling in parabolic paths" or that it has "the trait of fallingness." Instead, we recognize that the behavior of a rock is fully determined by lawful environmental forces (the force and direction of our throw, plus gravity and perhaps air pressure). To the behaviorist, the behavior of people should be explained in exactly this same way. Just as environmental forces determine the trajectory of the rock, environmental forces determine the trajectories of our lives as we come into contact with, and are influenced by, one environmental factor after another. To the behaviorist, then, there is no more need to explain a person's behavior in terms of his or her attitudes, feelings, or personality traits than there is to explain the rock's behavior in terms of its attitudes, feelings, or rock traits. The rock doesn't fall to earth because it decided to fall, but because gravity caused it to fall. Similarly, people do not act as they do because they decided to act that way, but because environmental forces cause them to do so.

Behaviorists recognize that people have thoughts and feelings. But they view thoughts and feelings as behaviors that also are caused by the environment. If you say that "I took this personality psychology class because I thought it would be interesting" or "I broke up with my boyfriend because I felt our relationship wouldn't work out," a behaviorist would say that you were wrong. You didn't identify the right factor in your "because." To the behaviorist, the environment caused your behavior of taking the class. Furthermore, the environment caused your behavior of saying that you thought the class would be interesting! Similarly, features of the environment caused your feelings in the relationship and caused your decision to end it.

The most radical feature of the behaviorist worldview, then, is that it does not explain a person's actions in terms of their thoughts and feelings. Instead, it explains people's actions, thoughts, and feelings in terms of environmental forces that shape the individual. This, to the behaviorist, is the only way to build a scientifically credible study of behavior. Suppose, by analogy, that we were studying evolution and wanted to explain why primates who once walked on four legs later evolved into upright primates who walked on two legs. We would never explain this by saying that the four-legged walkers "got tired of walking on all fours" or "decided to stand straight up." Such explanations would be absurd. They would have no scientific utility. The evolutionary change from four- to two-legged walking was, we recognize, caused entirely by adaptive pressures in the evolutionary environment. To the behaviorist, saying that people act a certain way "because they decided to" has no more scientific value than saying that the primates evolved because they decided to do so. Instead of such nonscientific explanations, behaviorists urge us to identify the environmental factors that are the true cause of people's feelings, thoughts, and actions. The behaviorist B. F. Skinner states this thesis with the greatest clarity:

> We can follow the path taken by physics and biology by turning directly to the relation between behavior and the environment and neglecting supposed mediating states of mind. Physics did not advance by looking more closely at the jubilance of a falling body, or biology by looking at the nature of vital spirits, and we do not need to try to discover what personalities, states of mind, feelings, traits of character, plans, purposes, [or] intentions really are in order to get on with a scientific analysis of behavior.
>
> SOURCE: SKINNER (1971) *Beyond Freedom & Dignity*, p. 15.

What does all this have to do with the study of personality? Suppose, hypothetically, that the behaviorist could in fact explain all behavior in terms of general laws of learning. This, the behaviorist would claim, would completely *eliminate the need for* a distinct field of study called "personality theory" or "personality psychology." The variables in all the other theories of personality—psychoanalytic conflicts, personality traits, and so forth—would not, according to the behaviorist, be referring to real psychological entities in persons' heads. Instead, the variables of other theories would be seen merely as descriptive labels—descriptions of patterns of psychological experience that are, in reality, caused by the environment. If the environment causes a person to feel hostility toward a same-sex parent and attraction toward an opposite-sex parent, the psychoanalyst labels this an "Oedipal complex." If the environment causes a person to engage in energetic, outgoing, sociable behaviors, the trait theorist labels the person an "extravert." In these and infinite other cases, the personality term does not identify the cause of the person's behavior. The behaviorist views the term as merely a label for a pattern of action that is caused by the environment.

To the behaviorists, then, an understanding of the laws of learning promises to replace any and all personality theories. If behavior can be explained by the laws of learning, and if "personality" is just a label that describes the type of behavior a person has learned to do, then there is no need for a scientific theory of personality that is distinct from learning theory. Behaviorists were quite explicit about this. They looked forward to a day when theories of personality would be "regarded as historical curiosities" (Farber, 1964, p. 37).

The belief in environmental determinism has additional implications. One is that it highlights the potential **situational specificity** of behavior. Since environmental factors are the causes of behavior, people's behavioral style is expected to vary significantly from one environment to another. Note how this expectation differs from the approach of the trait theories (Chapters 7 and 8). Trait variables corresponded to consistent styles of behavior; these variables were meant to explain why a person acts in a consistent manner across diverse situations. In contrast, behaviorists expect that there will be substantial variability in action as people adapt to situations that present different rewards and punishments for different types of behavior.

Another implication involves the causes and treatment of psychopathology. Psychopathology is not understood as an internal problem—an illness in the person's mind. Instead, the behaviorist assumes that maladaptive, "abnormal" behavior is caused by maladaptive environments to which the person has been exposed. The implication of this assumption is profound. It is that the task of therapy is not to analyze underlying conflicts or to reorganize the individual's personality. Instead, the goal is to provide a new environment, that is, new learning experiences for the client. The new environment should cause the client to learn new and more adaptive patterns of behavior, as we discuss later in this chapter.

EXPERIMENTATION, OBSERVABLE VARIABLES, AND SIMPLE SYSTEMS

Another defining feature of the behavioral view of personality science is its research strategy. This strategy follows in a natural way from the belief in environmental determinism. If behavior is determined by the environment, then the way to do research is to manipulate environmental variables to learn how they influence behavior. Behaviorists base the study of human nature entirely on carefully-controlled laboratory experiments of this sort.

In designing research, behaviorists emphasize that one must study things that are observable. The researcher must be able to see the environmental and behavioral variables, so he or she can measure them with accuracy and systematically relate them to one another. This point may seem obvious. Yet this feature—being able to observe the psychological variables about which one is theorizing—is *not* a part of the other theories we have discussed. One cannot directly observe the id, an Oedipal conflict, an extraverted tendency, a motive to self-actualize, and so forth. The behaviorist argues that these other theories are too speculative, and thus not sufficiently scientific, because they contain variables that one cannot even observe. For this reason, behaviorists were harshly critical of virtually all other theories in psychology.

The attempt to study personality through experimental methods poses a severe challenge. It often may be impractical, as well as unethical, to manipulate environmental variables that may substantially affect people's everyday behaviors. Also, day-to-day human actions may be determined by such a large number of variables, and these variables may be so complexly related to one another, that it is difficult to sort out the potentially lawful relations between any one environmental factor and behavior. These difficulties lead the behaviorist to adopt the following research strategy. Rather than researching complex social actions, the behaviorist commonly studies simple responses. And rather than study complex human beings, the behaviorist studies simpler organisms, such as rats and pigeons. The original body of data upon which behavioral principles are based consists almost entirely of laboratory research on laboratory animals.

This research strategy may strike you as strange. "Why," you may be thinking, "would anyone think that they can learn about personality by studying animals?" This is a very good question. It is important, as one begins to learn about the behavioral approach, to recognize that the behaviorist's research strategy is not one that is unique to them. Instead, it is common in the sciences. It is the strategy of studying simple systems.

Suppose you were designing an airplane and were wondering if your craft would fly safely in windy weather. One strategy for answering this question would be to build an entire real plane, fill it with people, launch it into the sky, and see if it crashes when the wind kicks up. Of course, you would not do that. This strategy for learning about the flight characteristics of the plane is very costly and completely unethical. You would, instead, study something simpler than a real plane: perhaps a model plane in a wind tunnel, or a computer simulation of an airline and wind flows. You would recognize that this simpler system is not the same thing as a real plane. Yet you would reason that it contains important features that are the same as the features of the system in which you are really interested, that is, the real plane. A similar strategy might be adopted by biologists seeking to understand the side effects of a new drug. Although the researchers are interested in the effects of the drug on people, they would first study its effects on laboratory animals, under the assumption that there is enough similarity in the makeup of animals and people that the animal study will, at the very least, provide some valuable information about the effects of the drug on people. Even if we do not think about it explicitly, we all recognize the value of studying simple systems. None of us would get on a

Table 10.1 Basic Points of Emphasis of Learning Approaches to Personality

1. Empirical research is the cornerstone of theory and practice.
2. Personality theory and applied practice should be based on principles of learning.
3. Behavior is responsive to reinforcement variables in the environment and is more situation specific than suggested by other personality theories (e.g., trait, psychoanalytic).
4. Rejection of the medical symptom-disease view of psychopathology and emphasis instead on basic principles of learning and behavior change.

new plane if we learned that a model of the plane had repeatedly crashed in a wind tunnel, nor would we try a new headache medicine if we learned that it had killed a bunch of laboratory rats.

This, then, is the simple system strategy. It is a research strategy in which, for both practical and ethical reasons, one conducts scientific studies on a system that is simpler than the one in which the researcher fundamentally is interested. This is the strategy adopted by the behaviorist. Behaviorists are fundamentally interested in the complex social behavior of people. But, in order to run large numbers of ethical and logistically feasible laboratory experiments, they study relatively simple organisms and relatively simple responses that can easily be observed in the lab. In many ways, this strategy proved to be a great success. Research on learning processes generated some of the most robust and reliable findings in the history of experimental psychology. The question, of course, is whether the results of these experiments generalize from animals in the laboratory to humans in the social world.

Table 10.1 summarizes the basic points of emphasis in behaviorism that we have reviewed. With this background, we now begin our coverage of theories that were developed within this behavioral approach to psychological science. Specifically, we start where the approach itself began historically, with the ideas of John Watson and the associated research contributions of Ivan Pavlov.

WATSON, PAVLOV, AND CLASSICAL CONDITIONING

WATSON'S BEHAVIORISM

John B. Watson (1878–1958) was the founder of the approach to psychology known as **behaviorism**. He began his graduate study at the University of Chicago in philosophy and then switched to psychology. During these years he took courses in neurology and physiology and began to do biological research with animals. During the year before he received his doctorate, Watson had an emotional breakdown and had sleepless nights for many weeks. He described this period as causing him to become interested in the work of Freud (Watson, 1936, p. 274). He eventually completed his dissertation, which caused him to develop a particular attitude regarding the use of human subjects.

At Chicago, I first began a tentative formulation of my later point of view. I never wanted to use human subjects. I hated to serve as a subject.

John B. Watson

I didn't like the stuffy, artificial instructions given to subjects. I always
was uncomfortable and acted unnaturally. With animals I was at home.
I felt that, in studying them, I was keeping close to biology with my feet
on the ground. More and more the thought presented itself: Can't I find
out by watching their behavior everything that the other students are
finding by using O's (human subjects)?

SOURCE: WATSON, 1936, p. 276.

Watson left Chicago in 1908 to become a professor at Johns Hopkins University, where he served on the faculty until 1919. During his stay there, which was interrupted by a period of service during World War I, Watson developed his views on behaviorism as an approach to psychology. He first stated these views forcefully in a landmark paper published in psychology's leading journal, *Psychological Review*, in 1913. Public lectures and a book published in 1914 (*Watson's Behavior*) called further attention to a view of psychology that emphasized the study of observable behavior and rejected the use of introspection (observing one's own mental states) as a method of research. Watson's arguments were received enthusiastically by American psychologists. He was elected president of the American Psychological Association for 1915. He quickly expanded the theoretical base of his work by drawing on the findings of the Russian physiologist Pavlov (see below), incorporating them into his most significant book, *Psychology from the Standpoint of a Behaviorist* (1919). In 1920, he published a revolutionary study of the learning of emotional reactions with his student Rosalie Rayner (Watson & Rayner, 1920). At that time, he clearly was poised to be the dominant American psychologist of the 20th century.

This, however, is not how his career unfolded. In 1919, Watson divorced his wife and subsequently married his student, Rayner. This scandalous turn of events forced his resignation from Johns Hopkins and caused him to entirely abandon his research career. Instead, he entered the business world, spending his years in advertising studying potential sales markets. Watson appeared to take this turn of events in good spirit, reporting "that it can be just as thrilling to watch the growth of a sales curve of a new product as to watch the learning curve of animals or men" (Watson, 1936, p. 280). After 1920, Watson did write some popular articles and a book, *Behaviorism* (1924). But his career as a theorist and experimenter had ended.

Ivan Petrovich Pavlov

PAVLOV'S THEORY OF CLASSICAL CONDITIONING

Ivan Petrovich Pavlov (1849–1936) was a Russian physiologist who, in the course of his work on the digestive process, developed a procedure for studying behavior and a principle of learning that profoundly affected the field of psychology. Around the beginning of the 20th century, Pavlov was involved in the study of gastric secretions in dogs. As part of his research, he placed some food powder inside the mouth of a dog and measured the resulting amount of salivation. He noticed that after a number of such trials the dog began to salivate, even before the food was put in its mouth, to certain stimuli: the sight of the food dish, the approach of the person who brought the food, and so forth. Stimuli that previously did not elicit salivation (called neutral stimuli) could now elicit the salivation response because of their association with the food powder that automatically caused the dog to salivate. To animal owners this may not seem to be a startling observation. However, it led Pavlov to conduct significant research on the process known as classical conditioning.

Pavlov explored a broad range of scientific issues. In addition to his work on basic conditioning processes, he studied individual differences among his dogs, thereby stimulating a new field of temperament research (Strelau, 1997). He made important contributions to the understanding of abnormal behavior, using animal experiments to study disorganized behavior in dogs and human patients to study neuroses and psychoses, providing the foundation for forms of therapy based on principles of classical conditioning. In 1904 he was awarded the Nobel Prize for his work on digestive processes. His methods and concepts remain important today; they are among the most important in the history of psychology (Dewsbury, 1997).

Principles of Classical Conditioning

Classical conditioning is a process in which a stimulus that initially is neutral (i.e., that the organism initially does not respond to in any significant manner) eventually elicits a strong response. It elicits the response because the neutral stimulus becomes associated with some other stimulus that does produce a response. The process in which the organism learns to respond to the stimulus that originally was neutral is known as conditioning.

In the classic case studied in Pavlov's lab, a dog salivates the first time that food is presented. The response of salivation to food is *not* learned or conditioned; it is an automatic, built-in response of the organism. In the terminology of classical conditioning, food is an unconditioned stimulus (US) and the salivation in response to food is an unconditioned response (UR). "Unconditioned" here merely means that the connection between stimulus and response occurs without any learning, or conditioning. Pavlov then introduces a new stimulus, such as the sound of a bell. Initially, this sound is neutral; it does not elicit any strong response on the part of the dog in Pavlov's lab. Then the critical step in research is taken. Over a series of trials, the bell is sounded just before the presentation of food. After these learning trials, the bell is sounded without any food being presented. What happens? The dog now salivates merely upon hearing the ring of the bell. Conditioning has occurred. The previously neutral stimulus now elicits a strong response. At this point, the bell is called a conditioned stimulus (CS) and the salivation in response to the bell is a conditioned response (CR).

The point of this work of course does not concern merely dogs, bells, and food. The point is general. In theory, any emotion could be associated with any stimulus. The emotional responses that dogs—and people!—experience to events in the world could be determined largely by classical conditioning.

Through classical conditioning, one also can learn to avoid a stimulus that initially is neutral. This is called conditioned withdrawal. In early research on conditioned withdrawal, a dog was strapped in a harness and electrodes were attached to his paw. The delivery of an electric shock (US) to the paw led to the withdrawal of the paw (UR), which was a reflex response on the part of the animal. If a bell was repeatedly presented just before the shock, eventually the bell alone (CS) was able to elicit the withdrawal response (CR).

The experimental arrangement designed by Pavlov to study classical conditioning allowed him to investigate a number of important phenomena. For example, would the conditioned response become associated with the specific neutral stimulus alone or would it become associated with other similar stimuli? Pavlov found that the response that had become conditioned to a previously neutral stimulus would also become associated with similar stimuli, a process called **generalization.** In other words, the salivation response to the bell would generalize to other sounds. Similarly, the withdrawal response to the bell would generalize to sounds similar to the bell.

What are the limits of such generalization? If repeated trials indicate that only some stimuli are followed by the unconditioned stimulus, the animal recognizes differences among stimuli, a process called **discrimination.** For example, if only certain sounds but not others are followed by shock and reflexive paw withdrawal, the dog will learn to discriminate among sounds. Thus, whereas the process of generalization leads to consistency of response across similar stimuli, the process of discrimination leads to increased specificity of response. Finally, if the originally neutral stimulus is presented repeatedly without being followed at least occasionally by the unconditioned stimulus, there is an undoing or progressive weakening of the conditioning or association, a process known as **extinction.** Whereas the association of the neutral stimulus with the unconditioned stimulus leads to the conditioned response, the repeated presentation of the conditioned stimulus without the unconditioned stimulus leads to extinction. For example, for the dog to continue to salivate to the bell, there must be at least occasional presentations of the food powder with the bell.

DEATH BY HEROIN OVERDOSE: A CLASSICAL CONDITIONING EXPLANATION

Dwayne Goettel, 31, keyboardist and programmer for the influential industrial band Skinny Puppy, died from an apparent heroin overdose on August 23, 1995, in a bathroom at his parents' house. How could this have happened? As a bandmate told *Rolling Stone* magazine, Goettel had just returned to his parents' house to kick his habit.

Goettel is one of hundreds of heroin addicts who die each year of a reaction typically known as an "overdose." Yet, how these deaths happen still remains unclear. Why do some long-term heroin users die from a dose that would not be expected to be fatal for them? Research by Sheppard Siegel and his colleagues suggests that some instances of heroin overdose may result from a failure of tolerance. How does a heroin addict, who has spent years building up a tolerance to heavy doses of the drug, experience such a failure of tolerance? Pavlov's theory of classical conditioning provides the basis for an answer to this question.

Pavlov proposed that drug administration constitutes a conditioning trial. The unconditioned stimulus (US) is the bodily effect of the drug, and the unconditioned response (UR) is how the body compensates for those effects. Conditioning occurs when the US (the effect of the drug) becomes associated with a conditioned stimulus (CS)—such as environmental cues present when the drug is taken. In other words, as heroin users establish an addiction, they learn to associate the effects of the drug with the environment in which they usually take it. Soon, the environmental cues alone can bring about the compensatory effects even before the drug is taken. Thus, the environmental cues serve as a signal to the body that the effects of the

drug are about to take place. In preparation, the body reacts to the cues in a manner that helps compensate for the anticipated effects of the drug. This conditioned response (CR) builds tolerance to the drug by lessening the drug's effects.

This Pavlovian model of drug tolerance has an important implication: heroin addicts are at risk for overdose when they take the drug in an environment that has not previously been associated with the drug. If the environmental cues typically associated with the drug are absent, the conditioned response cannot occur, causing a failure of tolerance. The heroin user takes a heavy dose of the drug and the body is left unprepared for its effects.

Is there empirical evidence for this explanation? In an animal study, rats received daily injections of increasing dosages of heroin in one of two environments. In the final session of the experiment, all the rats were administered a dose of heroin; for this injection, half of the rats were in the same environment in which they had been administered heroin in the past (same-environment rats) and the other half were in an environment in which they had never been administered heroin before (different-environment rats). The different-environment rats were significantly more likely to die from the injection than the same-environment rats. Why? The different-environment rats had lower tolerance to heroin because they were in an environment not previously associated with the drug. Unlike the same-environment rats, they did not have the conditioned response stimulated by cues in the environment to prepare them for the effects of the drug.

The rat experiment supports the model, but does the same phenomenon occur in humans? For obvious reasons, the parallel experiment cannot be conducted on people, so we must rely on what heroin users who have survived an overdose tell us about their experience. This is exactly what Siegel did to complement the results of the rat experiment. He interviewed former heroin addicts who had been hospitalized for drug overdoses. The majority of the survivors reported that the setting in which the overdose episode occurred was atypical. For example, one person reported that he injected the drug in the bathroom of a car wash—for him, an unusual place to take the drug. These reports from human victims show that the Pavlovian model of drug tolerance is relevant and useful in understanding such tragic deaths as that of the musician Dwayne Goettel in his parents' bathroom.

SOURCE: *Rolling Stone*, Oct. 1995, p. 25; Siegel, 1984; Siegel et al., 1982.

Although the illustrations used relate to animals, the principles can apply to humans as well. For example, consider a child who is bitten or merely treated roughly by a dog. The child's fear of this dog may now be extended to all dogs—the process of generalization. Suppose, however, by getting help, the child begins to discriminate among dogs of various kinds and begins to be afraid only of certain dogs. We can see here the process of discrimination. Over time, the child may have repeated positive experiences with all dogs, leading to the extinction of the fear response altogether. Thus, the classical conditioning model may be potentially very helpful in understanding the development, maintenance, and disappearance of many of our emotional reactions.

PSYCHOPATHOLOGY AND CHANGE

Pavlov extended his analysis of condition to the study of phenomena of clinical interest. He developed explanations for phenomena such as psychological conflict and the development of neuroses. A classic example explored what came to be known as experimental neuroses in animals. In this research, a dog was conditioned to salivate to the image of a circle. Differentiation between a circle and a similar figure, an ellipse, was then conditioned; this was done by not reinforcing the response to the ellipse, while response to the circle continued to be reinforced. Then, gradually, the ellipse was changed in shape. Its shape was made to be closer and closer to a circle. At first, the dog could still discriminate between the circle and the ellipse. But then, as the figures became extremely similar, it no longer could tell them apart. What happened to the dog? Its behavior became disorganized; as Pavlov himself described:

After three weeks of work upon this discrimination not only did the discrimination fail to improve, but it became considerably worse, and finally disappeared altogether. The hitherto quiet dog began to squeal in its stand, kept wriggling about, tore off with its teeth the apparatus for mechanical stimulation of the skin, and bit through the tubes connecting the animal's room with the observer, a behavior which never happened before. On being taken into the experimental room the dog

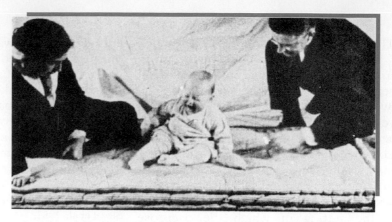

John Watson and Rosalie Raynor conducting research on the classic conditioning of emotional reactions with the 11-month-old Little Albert.

now barked violently, which was also contrary to its usual custom; in short, it presented all the symptoms of a condition of acute neurosis.

SOURCE: PAVLOV, 1927, p. 291.

Conditioned Emotional Reactions

Pavlov's work greatly influenced the thinking of John Watson. It inspired Watson to perform, with a person, the sort of conditioning research done by Pavlov with dogs. In 1920, Watson published one of the most famous, and infamous, studies in the history of psychology. It reported the conditioning of emotional reactions in an infant, an 11-month-old known as Little Albert.

In this research the experimenters, Watson and Rayner (1920), combined a stimulus that Little Albert was not afraid of—a small white laboratory rat—with an unconditioned stimulus that elicited fear—the noise produced by striking a hammer on a suspended steel bar. They then found that if the bar was struck immediately behind Albert's head just as he began to reach for a rat, he began to develop fear of the rat. After a few experimental trials, the instant the rat alone (without the noise) was shown to Albert, he began to cry. He had developed what is called a **conditioned emotional reaction.** Furthermore, Albert's fear generalized, just as dogs' responses had generalized in Pavlov's lab. Albert began to fear not only white rats, but other white and furry objects—including, Watson and Rayner report, the white beard of a Santa Claus mask! Despite some evidence that Albert's emotional reaction was not as strong or as general as expected (Harris, 1979), Watson and Rayner concluded that many fears are conditioned emotional reactions. On this basis they criticized the more complex psychoanalytic interpretations.

The Freudians twenty years from now, unless their hypotheses change, when they come to analyze Albert's fear of a seal skin coat will probably tease from him the recital of a dream upon which their analysis will show that Albert at three years of age attempted to play with the pubic hair of the mother and was scolded violently for it. If the analyst has sufficiently prepared Albert to accept such a dream when found as an explanation of his avoiding tendencies, and if the analyst has the authority and personality to put it over, Albert may be fully convinced that the dream was a true revealer of the factors which brought about the fear.

SOURCE: WATSON AND RAYNER, 1920, p. 14.

Systematic Desensitization

A major advance in the application of classical condition principles to questions of psychopathology was the development of a therapeutic technique known as systematic desensitization. The technique was developed by Joseph Wolpe, a psychiatrist from South Africa who became familiar with the writings of Pavlov.

Wolpe viewed persistent reactions of anxiety as a learned response that could be un-learned. He developed a therapy that was designed to provide this "un-learning." Phrased more technically, his therapy technique of **systematic desensitization** was designed to inhibit anxiety through **counterconditioning.** In counterconditioning, a person learns a new response that is physiologically incompatible with an existing response. If the existing response to a stimulus is fear or anxiety, then the goal might be to have the person learn a new response such as relaxation. Once the person learns, through new classical conditioning experiences, to experience relaxation in response to the previously feared stimulus, his or her fear should be eliminated.

In practice, systematic desensitization involves a number of phases (Wolpe, 1961). After determining whether the patient has a problem that can be treated by systematic desensitization, the therapist trains the patient to relax. This generally is done through deep muscle relaxation; the patient relaxes one part of the body after another. The next phase of treatment involves the construction of an anxiety hierarchy. This is a procedure in which the therapist tries to obtain from the patient a list of stimuli that arouse anxiety. These anxiety-arousing stimuli are grouped into themes such as fear of heights or fear of rejection. Within each group or theme, the anxiety-arousing stimuli are then arranged in order from most disturbing to least disturbing. For example, a theme of claustrophobia (fear of closed spaces) might involve placing the fear of being stuck in an elevator at the top of the list, an anxiety about being on a train in the middle of the list, and anxiety in response to reading of miners trapped underground at the bottom of the list. A theme of death might involve being at a burial as the most anxiety-arousing stimulus, the word "death" as somewhat anxiety-arousing, and driving past a cemetery as only slightly anxiety-arousing. Patients can have many or few themes and many or few items within each anxiety hierarchy.

With the construction of the anxiety hierarchies completed, the patient is ready for the desensitization procedure itself. The patient has learned to calm the self by relaxation, and the therapist has established the anxiety hierarchies. Now the therapist encourages the patient to achieve a deep state of relaxation and then to imagine the least anxiety-arousing stimulus in the anxiety hierarchy. If the patient can imagine the stimulus without anxiety, then he or she is encouraged to imagine the next stimulus in the hierarchy while remaining relaxed. Periods of pure relaxation are interspersed with periods of relaxation and imagination of anxiety-arousing stimuli. If the patient feels

CURRENT APPLICATIONS

WHAT MAKES SOME FOODS A TREAT AND OTHERS DISGUSTING?

Most people love some odors and food tastes and are disgusted by others. Often these responses date back to childhood and seem nearly impossible to change. Can classical conditioning help us to understand them and their power?

Consider some research on food tastes. What makes some foods so unpleasant—even disgusting—that we have emotional reactions to just the thought of them? Eating worms, or drinking milk that has a dead fly or dead cockroach in it are examples. The interesting thing about some of these reactions is that a food that evokes disgust in one culture can be considered a delicacy in another, and disgust might be evoked by a dead fly or cockroach in the milk even if one is told that the insect was sterilized before it was put in the milk. Having seen the dead insect in the milk, one might not even be prepared to drink a different glass of milk, the disgust reaction now having generalized to the milk itself.

According to the researchers of such reactions, a possible explanation lies in the strong emotional reaction that becomes associated with a previously neutral object. In classical conditioning terms, the disgust response becomes associated with, or conditioned to, a previously neutral object such as milk or another food: "We believe that Pavlovian conditioning is alive and well, in the flavor associations of billions of meals eaten each day, in the expression of affects of billions of eaters as they eat away, in the association of foods and offensive objects, and in the association of foods with some of their consequences."

If this is the case, then it suggests that many things that we like, perhaps even feel addicted to, are the result of classical conditioning. This being the case, it may be possible to change our emotional reactions to certain objects through the process of classical conditioning.

SOURCE: *Psychology Today*, July 1985; Rozin & Zellner, 1985. Copyright © 1985 American Psychological Association. Reprinted by permission from Psychology Today.

Conditioned food responses: Many strong and persisting emotional responses to foods, such as a disgust response to worms, are acquired through the process of classical conditioning. (Copyright © 1985 American Psychological Association. Reprinted by permission from Psychology Today.)

Behavior Therapy: One aspect of behavior therapy involves the extinction of learned fears or phobias. (Copyright © Sidney Harris.)

"Leave us alone! I am a behavior therapist! I am helping my patient overcome a fear of heights!"

anxious while imagining a stimulus, he or she is encouraged to relax and return to imagining a less anxiety-arousing stimulus. Ultimately the patient is able to relax while imagining all stimuli in the anxiety hierarchies. Relaxation in relation to the imagined stimuli generalizes to relaxation in relation to these stimuli in everyday life. "It has consistently been found that at every stage a stimulus that evokes no anxiety when imagined in a state of relaxation will also evoke no anxiety when encountered in reality" (Wolpe, 1961, p. 191).

A number of clinical and laboratory studies have indicated that systematic desensitization is, in fact, an effective treatment procedure. These successful results led Wolpe and others to question the psychoanalytic view that, as long as the underlying conflicts remain untouched, the patient is prone to develop a new symptom in place of the one removed (symptom substitution) (Lazarus, 1965). According to the behavior therapy point of view, no symptom is caused by unconscious conflicts. There is only a maladaptive learned response, and once this response has been eliminated, there is no reason to believe that another maladaptive response will be substituted for it.

A Reinterpretation of the Case of Little Hans

In this section the application of the learning theory approach will be observed in a case presented by Wolpe and Rachman (1960) that gives us an excellent opportunity to compare the behavioral approach with that of psychoanalysis. In fact, it is not a case in the same sense as other cases that have been presented. Rather, it is a critique and reformulation of Freud's case of Little Hans.

As we learned in Chapter 4, the case of Little Hans is a classic in psycho-analysis. In this case, Freud emphasized the importance of infantile sexuality and Oedipal conflicts in the development of a horse phobia, or fear. Wolpe and Rachman are extremely critical of Freud's approach to obtaining data and of his conclusions. They make the following points: (1) Nowhere is there evidence of Hans's wish to make love to his mother. (2) Hans never expressed fear or hatred of his father. (3) Hans consistently denied any relationship between the horse and his father. (4) Phobias can be induced in children by a simple conditioning process and need not be related to a theory of conflicts or anxiety and defense. The view that neuroses have a purpose is highly questionable. (5) There is no evidence that the phobia disappeared as a result of Hans's resolution of his Oedipal conflicts. Similarly, there is no evidence that insight occurred or that information was of therapeutic value.

Wolpe and Rachman feel handicapped in their own interpretation of the phobia because the data were gathered within a psychoanalytic framework. They do, however, attempt an explanation. A phobia is regarded as a conditioned anxiety reaction. As a child, Hans heard and saw a playmate being warned by her father that she should avoid a white horse lest it bite her: "Don't put your finger to the white horse." This incident sensitized Hans to a fear of horses. Also, there was the time when one of Hans's friends injured himself and bled while playing with horses. Finally, Hans was a sensitive child who felt uneasy about seeing merry-go-round horses being playfully beaten. These factors set the condition for the later development of the phobia. The phobia itself occurred as a consequence of the fright Hans experienced while watching a horse fall down. Whereas Freud suggested that this incident was an exciting cause that allowed the underlying conflicts to be expressed in terms of a phobia, Wolpe and Rachman suggest that this incident was the cause.

Wolpe and Rachman see a similarity here to Watson's conditioning of fear in Little Albert. Hans was frightened by the event with a horse and then generalized his fear to all things that were similar to or related to horses. The recovery from the phobia did not occur through the process of insight, but probably through a process of either extinction or counterconditioning. As Hans developed, he experienced other emotional responses that inhibited the fear response. Alternatively, it is suggested that perhaps the father's constant reference to the horse in a nonthreatening context helped to extinguish the fear response. Whatever the details, it appears that the phobia disappeared gradually, as would be expected by this kind of learning interpretation, instead of dramatically, as might be suggested by a psychoanalytic, insight interpretation. The evidence in support of Freud is not clear, and the data, as opposed to the interpretations, can be accounted for in a more straightforward way through the use of a learning theory interpretation.

RECENT DEVELOPMENTS

For some time interest in classical conditioning declined among personality psychologists. However, recently there has been increased recognition of the potential contributions of concepts and procedures associated with classical conditioning theory. One illustrative area of research is the use of classical conditioning procedures to demonstrate that people can unconsciously develop fears and attitudes toward others (Krosnick, Betz, Jussim, Lynn, & Kirschenbaum, 1992; Ohman & Soares, 1993). For example, a stimulus, such as a picture with positive or negative affective value, can be presented subliminally (i.e., below the threshold of awareness) in association with another stimulus, such as another photo. Thus, a person will come to dislike a photo unconsciously associated with negative emotion and come to like a photo unconsciously associated with positive emotion. One can speculate in this regard how many of our attitudes and preferences are classically conditioned on a subliminal or unconscious basis. Consider, for example, the following conclusion of a leading social psychologist: "The aversive prejudice, once created, may be difficult to consciously eliminate." People can have egalitarian beliefs and still act prejudicial in certain situations—their impulsive, automatic reaction when faced with a member of that minority group may be negative. This doesn't mean that people are lying about nonprejudicial attitudes. It's that these attitudes reside coincidentally with a conditioned aversive reaction learned early in childhood (Cacioppo, 1999, p. 10).

In a surprising turn of events, researchers recently have related classical conditioning principles to a topic that we previously associated with the phenomenological theory of Rogers, namely, self-esteem. Baccus, Baldwin, and Packer (2004) reasoned that expressions of high self-esteem are responses that could be altered through classical conditioning. Participants in their research took part in a conditioning task in which both words and pictures appeared on a computer screen. In an experimental condition, words that were self-relevant (i.e., words that the given participant said described himself or herself) appeared in combination with pictures of people who were smiling. This experimental condition was designed as a classical conditioning process in which positive emotions would be paired with the self. In another condition, a control condition, such words were paired with a mixture of pictures: some smiling, some frowning, some looking neutral. Afterwards, participants completed self-esteem measures. The researchers compared the effects of the experimental condition (i.e., the condition with the faces with were consistently smiling) to the control condition for the group of participants overall, and for subgroups of participants who, based on pre-experimental measures, had low versus high self-esteem in general. As the graph shows (see Figure 10.1), classical conditioning increased feelings of self-esteem. People who saw smiling faces paired with words that are defining of them displayed higher levels of self-esteem than control-group subjects.

The studies we have just reviewed primarily involve applications of conditioning principles to questions of human behavior. However, another major development concerns the study of basic neural and biochemical processes that mediate classical conditioning. Put simply, the question is, "What actually happens in the brain when an organism acquires a new response to a stimulus?" Although many contemporary scientists contribute to an understanding of this issue, an investigator of particular note is Eric Kandel of Columbia University in New York, who was awarded the Nobel Prize in medicine in 2000 for his research on the topic. Kandel's research is a classic example of the simple systems strategy we overviewed previously. In order to understand what happens in the brain when an organism learns a new response, Kandel studied an organism much simpler than the one studied by Pavlov (the dog). Kandel studied a type of sea slug called Aplysia. Aplysia have relatively few nerve cells, which makes it easier to study the role of specific individual cells in classical conditioning. Aplysia also exhibit a simple response, the gill-withdrawal reflex, that can be modified through conditioning. Kandel's findings reveal that the conditioning process, at the neural level, involves changes in the strength of connections among neurons (Kandel, 2000). The synapses of neurons that comprise the gill-withdrawal reflex become more strongly associated as a

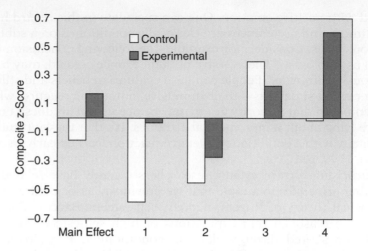

Figure 10.1 *Effects of conditioning ("experimental" group) on a measure of implicit self-esteem. The graph displays the overall effect of conditioning versus a control group in the two bars on the left ("main effect"), and then displays results for separate subgroups of participants, namely, people of (1) low implicit and explicit self-esteem, (2) low implicit and high explicit self-esteem, (3) high implicit and low explicit self-esteem, and (4) high implicit and explicit self-esteem.*

result of conditioning. Kandel's work is an exceptional example of how basic research in the neurosciences can inform the study of learning and, potentially, the understanding of human personality.

SKINNER'S THEORY OF OPERANT CONDITIONING

Although John Watson dropped out of the field of psychology, others picked up the banner of behaviorism during the middle of the 20th century. These included historically significant figures such as Clark Hull, who developed a highly systematic drive theory of learning, and John Dollard and Neal Miller, who attempted to show how Hull's theory could address phenomena involving drives and intrapsychic conflicts that were of interest to psychoanalysts. Even these important contributions, however, were eventually overshadowed by those of another researcher who became one of the most influential figures in all of 20th century psychology.

The most influential behavioral researcher, theorist, and spokesperson was the Harvard psychologist B. F. Skinner (1904–1990). Indeed, Skinner is probably the most well-known American psychologist of the last century; a recent quantitative analysis of the impact of individual psychologists on the field as a whole ranked Skinner as the singularly most eminent psychologist of the 20th century (Haggbloom et al., 2002). Skinner's eminence reflects his exceptional skill at articulating the broad implications of behavioral principles. In Skinner's hands, behaviorism was not just an approach to the psychology of learning. It was an all-encompassing philosophy that promised a comprehensive account of human behavior, as well as technologies for improving the human experience.

B. F. Skinner

A VIEW OF THE THEORIST

> The scientist, like any organism, is the product of a unique history. The practices which he finds most appropriate will depend in part upon his history.
>
> SOURCE: SKINNER, 1959, p. 379.

In this passage, Skinner takes the point of view that has been argued in each of the theory chapters in this book, that is, that psychologists' orientations and research strategies are, in part, consequences of their own life history and expressions of their own personalities.

B. F. Skinner was born in Pennsylvania, the son of a lawyer who was described by his son as having been desperately hungry for praise and a mother who had rigid standards of right and wrong. Still, Skinner (1967) described his home during his early years as a warm and stable environment. He reported a love for school and showed an early interest in building things. This desire to build things is particularly interesting in relation to the behavioral emphasis on laboratory equipment in the experimental setting, and because it contrasts with the absence of such an interest in the lives and research of the clinical personality theorists.

At about the time Skinner entered college, his younger brother died. Skinner commented that he was not much moved by his brother's death and that he probably felt guilty for not being moved. Skinner went to Hamilton College and majored in English literature. At that time, his goal was to become a writer, and at one point he sent three short stories to Robert Frost, from whom he received an encouraging reply. After college, Skinner spent a year trying to write, but concluded that at that point in his life he had nothing to say. He then spent six months living in Greenwich Village in New York City. During this time he read Pavlov's *Conditioned Reflexes* and came across a series of articles by Bertrand Russell on Watson's behaviorism. Russell thought that he had demolished Watson in these articles, but they aroused Skinner's interest in behaviorism.

Although Skinner had not taken any psychology courses in college, he had begun to develop an interest in the field and was accepted for graduate work in psychology at Harvard. He justified his change in goals as follows: "A writer might portray human behavior accurately, but he did not therefore understand it. I was to remain interested in human behavior, but the literary method had failed me; I would turn to the scientific" (Skinner, 1967, p. 395). Psychology appeared to be the relevant science. Besides, Skinner had long been interested in animal behavior (recalling his fascination with the complex behaviors of a troupe of performing pigeons). Furthermore, there would now be many opportunities to make use of his interest in building gadgets.

During his graduate school years at Harvard, Skinner developed his interest in animal behavior and in explaining this behavior without reference to the functioning of the nervous system. After reading Pavlov, he disagreed with Pavlov's contention that, in explaining behavior, one could go "from the salivary reflexes to the important business of the organism in everyday life." However, Skinner believed that Pavlov had given him the key to understanding behavior. "Control your conditions (the environment) and you shall see order!" During these and the following years, Skinner (1959) developed some of his principles of scientific methodology: (1) When you run into something interesting, drop everything else and study it. (2) Some ways of doing research are easier than others. A mechanical apparatus often makes doing research easier. (3) Some people are lucky. (4) A piece of apparatus breaks down. This presents problems, but it can also lead to (5) serendipity—the art of finding one thing while looking for something else.

After Harvard, Skinner moved first to Minnesota, then to Indiana, and then returned to Harvard in 1948. During this time he became, in a sense, a sophisticated animal trainer; he was able to make organisms engage in specific behaviors at specific times. He turned from work with rats to work with pigeons. Finding that the behavior of any single animal did not necessarily reflect the average picture of learning based on many animals, he became interested in the manipulation and control of individual animal behavior. Special theories of learning and circuitous explanations of behavior were not necessary if one could manipulate the environment so as to produce orderly change in the individual case. In the meantime, as Skinner notes, his own behavior was becoming controlled by the positive results being given to him by the animals "under his control" (Figure 10.2).

Figure 10.2   *"Boy, have I got this guy conditioned! Every time I press the bar down he drops a piece of food." (Skinner, 1956.)*

The basis of Skinner's **operant conditioning** procedure is the control of behavior through the manipulation of rewards and punishments in the environment, particularly the laboratory environment. However, his conviction concerning the importance of the laws of behavior and his interest in building things led Skinner to take his thinking and research far beyond the laboratory. He built a "baby box" to mechanize the care of a baby, teaching machines that used rewards in the teaching of school subjects, and a procedure whereby pigeons could be used militarily to land a missile on target. He wrote a novel, *Walden Two* (1948), in which he describes a utopia based on the control of human behavior through positive reinforcement (reward) rather than punishment. Skinner committed himself to the view that a science of human behavior and the technology to be derived from it must be developed in the service of humankind. In an interview published within his obituary notice in the *New York Times* (August 20, 1990), Skinner related that "all humans are controlled"—that is, it is inevitable that people's behavior is ultimately under the control of whatever environments they experience—"but the idea of behaviorism is to eliminate coercion, to apply controls by changing the environment in such a way as to reinforce the kind of behavior that benefits everyone" (pp. A1, A12).

Skinner was considered by many to be the greatest contemporary American psychologist. He received many awards, including the American Psychological Association's award for Distinguished Scientific Contribution (1958) and the National Medal of Science (1968). In 1990, shortly before his death, he became the first recipient of the American Psychological Association's Citation for Outstanding Lifetime Contribution to Psychology.

SKINNER'S THEORY OF PERSONALITY

Let's begin our discussion of Skinner's theory of personality by contrasting its general qualities with those of the theories you already have learned about in the previous chapters. Each of the previous theories (and, to give you a preview, each of the ones discussed subsequently in this book) emphasizes structural concepts. Freud used structural concepts such as id, ego, and superego; Rogers used concepts such as self and ideal self; and Allport, Eysenck, and Cattell used the concept of traits. Each theorist, then, inferred the existence of a psychological structure in the head of the individual that accounted for the person's consistent styles of emotion and behavior. In contrast, Skinner's behavioral approach greatly deemphasizes structure. This is for two reasons. First, behaviorists view behavior as an adaptation to situational forces. They thus expect situational specificity in behavior: If the situational forces change, so does the behavior. If behavior varies from one situation to another, then there is little need to propose structural concepts to explain the supposed consistency of personality. The second reason involves a general approach to constructing a theory. As we explained earlier, the behaviorists wanted to build a theory based on observable variables. They felt that only observable variables could be verified by basic research. Inferring the existence of invisible personality structures was seen by Skinner, then, as a way of thinking that was not properly scientific.

The fact that Skinner does not propose a series of personality structures makes his work entirely different from the other personality theories. In fact,

Skinner rejected the view that his ideas constituted a personality theory. He saw himself as replacing the personality theories with a new way of thinking about behavior.

Structure

The key structural unit for the behavioral approach in general, and Skinner's approach in particular, is the response. A response may range from a simple reflex response (e.g., salivation to food, startle to a loud noise) to a complex piece of behavior (e.g., solution to a math problem, subtle forms of aggression). What is critical to the definition of a response is that it represents an external, observable piece of behavior that can be related to environmental events. The learning process essentially involves the association or connection of responses to events in the environment.

In his approach to learning, Skinner distinguishes between responses elicited by known stimuli, such as an eyeblink reflex to a puff of air, and responses that cannot be associated with any stimuli. These responses are emitted by the organism and are called **operants**. Skinner's view is that stimuli in the environment do not force the organism to behave or incite it to act. The initial cause of behavior is in the organism itself. "There is no environmental eliciting stimulus for operant behavior; it simply occurs. In the terminology of operant conditioning, operants are emitted by the organism. The dog walks, runs, and romps; the bird flies; the monkey swings from tree to tree; the human infant babbles vocally. In each case, the behavior occurs without any specific eliciting stimulus. It is in the biological nature of organisms to emit operant behavior" (Reynolds, 1968, p. 8).

Process: Operant Conditioning

The most important concept in the Skinnerian analysis of psychological processes is **reinforcer**. A reinforcer is something that follows a response and increases the probability of the response occurring again in the future. Suppose a pigeon is pecking at a disk. If the pecking is followed by the provision of some food and the pigeon therefore pecks at the disk more frequently in the future, the food is a reinforcer. Suppose a baby in a crib is crying. If the crying draws the attention of adults who rush over to care for the infant and the infant therefore cries more frequently in the future, the attention from adults is reinforced. Learning by reinforcement is a process in which the probability of a given response is altered by the presentation of a reinforcer.

What counts as a reinforcer in any given situation, then, is defined according to the effects of the potential reinforcer on behavior. Often it is difficult to know ahead of time what will serve as a reinforcer. This may vary from individual to individual. Finding a reinforcer may turn out to be a trial-and-error operation. Stimuli that originally do not serve as reinforcers may come to do so through their association with other reinforcers. Some green rectangular pieces of paper (i.e., money) become **generalized reinforcers** because they are associated with many other reinforcing stimuli.

Skinner developed a specialized piece of laboratory apparatus to study the effects of reinforcers on behavior. It has become known as the "Skinner box." The exact details of a Skinner box vary a bit depending upon the organism for which it is designed. A Skinner box designed for research with a rat would have a lever that the rat may press and some mechanism for delivering a reinforcer such as a food pellet. One would present the reinforcer and determine whether it influenced the frequency with which the rat engaged in the behavior of pressing the lever. Skinner saw this simple environment as the best setting to observe the elementary laws of behavior.

These laws are discovered by varying the nature of the reinforcements and observing the effects on the behavior of the organism in the Skinner box. The variations are done according to different **schedules of reinforcement**. The term *schedules of reinforcement* refers to the relation between behavior and when a reinforcement occurs. The general idea is that reinforcements need not occur after every response. They may be given only some of the time. Different schedules are different patterns of occurrence of the reinforcers. One distinc-tion between schedules of reinforcement differentiates reinforcements that are based on the passage of time from those based on numbers of responses. In a time-based schedule, known as an interval schedule, the reinforcement appears after a certain time period (e.g., one minute) regardless of the number of responses. In contrast, in a response-based interval, reinforcements appear only after a certain *number* of responses (e.g., presses of a bar, pecks of a key) have been made, no matter how long it takes for the responses to occur. Another distinction is whether the reinforcement occurs the same way all the time or very randomly. As an everyday example, a person might have a job in which he is paid on an interval schedule (e.g., he receives a weekly salary) whereas another person may be paid according to the number of responses he or she performs, no matter how long it takes (e.g., being paid $X to mow someone's lawn). A second distinction differentiates reinforcement schedules that are **fixed** from those that are **variable**. In fixed schedules the relation of behaviors to reinforcers remains constant. In variable schedules this relation changes unpredictably. To illustrate: Imagine yourself standing in front of each of two machines. Both require you to put money in the machine and to press a button, whereupon you may get a reinforcement. If the machine is a soft-drink dispenser, the experience is routine and uninteresting. If no soft drink (the reinforcer) comes out the first time, you stop putting money into the machine. If the machine is a slot machine in a casino, the same event—putting money into a machine, pressing a button—is exciting! If no money (the reinforcer) comes out, you do not stop putting money in. Instead, many people put more and more money into the machine. The difference between the two settings is the different schedule of reinforcement. The slot machine features a random schedule, the soda machine a fixed schedule. In both the Skinner lab with rats, and the casino with people, the variable schedule produces higher rates of response.

The behaviorists were remarkably successful in identifying systematic rela-tions between the schedule of reinforcement for a given behavior and the frequency with which that behavior occurred. In research with animals in Skinner boxes, the results were so reliable that they could be replicated with virtually every individual animal put in the box (Ferster & Skinner, 1957). Response-based schedules repeatedly generated higher levels of response than interval schedules. The highest response rates occurred with response-based schedules that were variable (i.e., like a slot machine or other gambling device). These highly consistent operant conditioning results, combined with the equally consistent research results Pavlov and colleagues found when studying classical conditioning, gave behaviorists an exceptionally solid set

Why do people gamble, even after losing large amounts of money? Behaviorists explain that the cause is the schedule of reinforcement. Gambling devices feature variable ratio schedules of reinforcement that create high, persistent levels of behavior.

of findings on which to build their theorizing. These solid research findings contributed enormously to the appeal of behaviorism in the mid-20th century.

How do animals learn to do anything more complex than pressing a lever? According to Skinner, complex behavior results from a process known as **shaping** or (equivalently) **successive approximations.** Through a gradual, step-by-step process one reinforces increasingly complex behaviors that approximate, to a greater and greater degree, the final behavior that is desired. The behavior of the organism is "shaped" until it matches a desired response. For example, suppose you want a rat in a Skinner box to run around in circles. You can't just wait until it runs around in circles and then reinforce it, because it might never spontaneously run around in circles. Instead, you first reinforce a simple response such as running (whether in circles or not). You would then wait until the animal started to run in a curved path and reinforce it only then. Once this happened, you should wait until it ran in at least a half circle and reinforce it then. Eventually you can train the animal to run in circles. Much animal training (in circuses, zoos, and South Florida tourist attractions) is done in this manner. Skinner recognized that complex human learning also may occur in a step-by-step process of successive approximations.

In addition to the use of pleasant events as reinforcers, Skinnerians note that the removal or avoidance of an *un*pleasant stimulus also can be a reinforcing. For example, suppose you are feeling so anxious about going to a social event that you suddenly decide not to go, and that once you make this decision your anxiety goes away. The lessening of anxiety may reinforce the behavior of saying "I'm not going to social events." The reduction of the negative occurrence, the anxiety, is reinforcing.

Skinnerians also recognize that the presentation of aversive stimuli can influence behaviors. In the behavioral vocabulary, these stimuli are **punishments**. In punishment, an aversive stimulus follows a response, decreasing the probability of that response occurring again. Skinnerians generally are against the use of punishment, whose effects tend to be temporary and whose administration may lead people to rebel against their use. Throughout his career, Skinner emphasized the value of positive reinforcement in shaping behavior.

Growth and Development

Skinner did not posit any principles of development other than the operant conditioning principles reviewed above. To Skinner, as children develop, they learn more and more responses as a result of naturally-occurring reinforcement experiences. The process is no different, in terms of general principles, than the case of a rat who learns more and more responses as a result of systematic shaping experiences in a Skinner box.

This mechanistic view of development does have practical implications that may be beneficial. It suggests that parents should attend carefully to exactly how and when they are reinforcing the child's behavior. If one wants the child to behave in a certain way, the most effective procedure, according to Skinner, is not to lecture the child about proper forms of behavior or to punish the child for things it does wrong. The most effective procedure, according to Skinner, is to reinforce good behavior immediately after it occurs.

In its treatment of development, then, behaviorism differs from the other theories in this book. To Skinner, development does not occur in any particular sequences of stages. There are no conflicts that everyone necessarily experiences. No new structures spring up in the mind at one versus another point in development. Instead, the set of behaviors that a person can perform simply increases gradually, as they experience more reinforcements.

Psychopathology

The learning theory position on psychopathology may be stated as follows: The basic principles of learning provide a completely adequate interpretation of psychopathology. Explanations in terms of symptoms with underlying causes are not necessary. According to the behavioral point of view, behavioral pathology is not a disease. Instead, it is a response pattern learned according to the same principles of behavior as are all response patterns.

The Skinnerians argue against any concept of the unconscious or a "sick personality." Individuals are not sick; they merely do not respond appropriately to stimuli. Either they fail to learn a response or they learn a maladaptive response. In the former case, there is a behavioral deficit. For example, individuals who are socially inadequate may have had faulty reinforcement histories in which social skills were not developed. Having failed to be reinforced for social skills during socialization as children, as adults they have an inadequate response repertoire with which to respond to social situations.

Reinforcement is important not only for the learning of responses but also for the maintenance of behavior. Thus, one possible result of an absence of reinforcement in the environment is depression. According to this view, depression represents a lessening of behavior or a lowered response rate. The

*Superstitious Behavior:
Skinner suggested that
superstitious behavior is based
on an accidental relationship
between a response and
reinforcement.*

depressed person is not responsive because positive reinforcement has been withdrawn (Ferster, 1973).

When a person learns a **maladaptive response**, the problem is that a response has been learned that is not considered acceptable by society or by others in the person's environment. This may be because the response itself is considered unacceptable (e.g., hostile behavior) or because the response occurs under unacceptable circumstances (e.g., joking at a formal business meeting). Related to this situation is the development of superstitious behavior (Skinner, 1948). Superstitious behavior develops because of an accidental relationship between a response and reinforcement. Thus, Skinner found that if he gave pigeons small amounts of food at regular intervals regardless of what they were doing, many birds came to associate the response that was coincidentally rewarded with systematic reinforcement. For example, if a pigeon was coincidentally rewarded while walking around in a counterclockwise direction, this response might become conditioned even though it had no cause-effect relationship with the reinforcement. The continuous performance of the behavior would result in occasional, again coincidental, reinforcement. Thus, the behavior could be maintained over long periods of time.

In sum, people develop faulty behavior repertoires, what others call "sick" behavior or psychopathology, because of the following: They were not reinforced for adaptive behaviors, they were punished for behaviors that later would be considered adaptive, they were reinforced for maladaptive behaviors, or they were reinforced under inappropriate circumstances for what would otherwise be adaptive behavior. In all cases there is an emphasis on observable responses and schedules of reinforcement rather than on concepts such as drive, conflict, unconscious motives, or self-esteem.

Behavioral Assessment

How does one assess personality in a behavioral approach? Since the theory says that one must understand the relation between behavior and the environment, one does not assess the person in isolation. One assesses the person's responses to different environments. The behavioral approach to assessment, then, emphasizes three things: (1) identification of specific behaviors, often called **target behaviors or target responses**; (2) identification of specific environmental factors that elicit, cue, or reinforce the target behaviors; and (3) identification of specific environmental factors that can be manipulated to alter the behavior. A behavioral assessment of a child's temper tantrums, for example, would include a clear, objective definition of temper tantrum behavior in the child, a complete description of the situation that sets off the tantrum behavior, a complete description of the reactions of parents and others that may be reinforcing the behavior, and an analysis of the potential for eliciting and reinforcing other nontantrum behaviors (Kanfer & Saslow, 1965; O'Leary, 1972). This **functional analysis** of behavior, involving the effort to identify the environmental conditions that control behavior, sees behavior as a function of specific events in the environment. The approach has also been called the **ABC assessment**: one assesses the Antecedent conditions of the behavior, the Behavior itself, and the Consequences of the behavior.

Behavioral assessment generally is closely tied to treatment objectives. For example, consider the task of assisting a mother who came to a clinic because she felt helpless in dealing with her four-year-old son's temper tantrums and general disobedience (Hawkins, Peterson, Schweid, & Bijou, 1966). The psychologists involved in this case followed a fairly typical behavioral procedure to assessment and treatment. First, the mother and child were observed in the home to determine the nature of the undesirable behaviors, when they occurred, and which reinforcers seemed to maintain them. The following nine behaviors were determined to constitute the major portion of the boy's objectionable behavior: (1) biting his shirt or arm; (2) sticking out his tongue; (3) kicking or biting himself, others, or objects; (4) calling someone or something a derogatory name; (5) removing or threatening to remove his clothing; (6) saying "NO!" loudly and vigorously; (7) threatening to damage objects or persons; (8) throwing objects; and (9) pushing his sister. Observation of the mother-child interaction suggested that the objectionable behavior was being maintained by attention from the mother. For example, often she tried to distract him by offering him toys or food.

The treatment program began with a behavioral analysis of how frequently the boy expressed one of the objectionable behaviors during one-hour sessions conducted in the home two to three times a week. Two psychologists acted as observers to ensure that there was high reliability or good agreement concerning recording of the objectionable behavior. This first phase, known as a baseline period, lasted for 16 sessions. During this time, mother and child interacted in their usual way. Following this careful assessment of the objectionable behavior during the baseline period, the psychologists initiated their intervention, or treatment program. Now the mother was instructed to tell her son to stop or to put him in his room by himself without toys each time he emitted an objectionable behavior. In other words, there was a withdrawal of the positive reinforcer for objectionable behavior. At the same time, the mother was instructed to give her son attention and approval when he behaved in a desirable way. In other words, the positive reinforcers were made contingent on desirable behavior. During this time, known as the first experimental period, the frequency of objectionable behaviors was again counted. As can be seen in Figure 10.3, there was a marked decline in the frequency of objectionable behavior. In the pre-experimental baseline phase, dozens of objectionable behaviors commonly were observed during any given

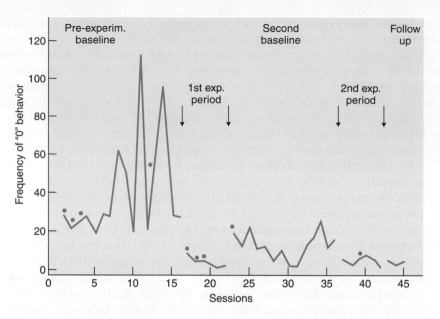

Figure 10.3   *Number of 10-second Intervals per 1-hour Session, in Which Objectionable Behavior Occurred. Dots indicate sessions in which reliability was tested. (Hawkins et al., 1966) Copyright © 1966 by Academic Press, Inc. Reprinted by permission.*

one-hour period. In contrast, during the first experimental period, only 1 to 8 such responses per session were observed.

Following the first experimental treatment period, the mother was instructed to return to her former behavior to determine whether it was the shift in her reinforcement behavior that was determining the change in her son's behavior. During this second baseline period, her son's objectionable behavior ranged between 2 and 24 per session (Figure 10.3). There was an increase in this behavior, though not a return to the former baseline level. However, the mother reported that she had trouble responding in her previous way because she now felt more "sure of herself." Thus, even during this period she gave her son more firm commands, gave in less after denying a request, and gave more affection in response to positive behaviors in her son than was previously the case. Following this there was a return to a full emphasis on the treatment program, resulting in a decline in objectionable behavior (second experimental period). The rate of objectionable behavior was found to remain low after a 24-day interval (follow-up period), and the mother reported a continuing positive change in the relationship.

The study we just reviewed illustrates an experimental method known as an **ABA research design** (Krasner, 1971). In this research design, one measures behavior at one point in time (the "A" time period), introduces a reinforcer and measures behavior again at a second time point (the "B" period), and then one *takes away* the reinforcer to see if the behavior returns to its original level (one returns to the "A" state of affairs). Instead of assigning groups of people to different experimental conditions, then, the Skinnerian studies a given individual at multiple time points in the presence or absence of a given reinforcer. Skinner believed that this was a more powerful method of research than are the typical experimental strategies used in psychology.

One last important point about behavioral assessment is that it illustrates the distinction between a **sign** and a **sample approach** to assessment (Mischel, 1968, 1971). In a sign approach, a given test response is seen as an indicator of (i.e., a "sign" of) some inner characteristic possessed by the individual. For example, if the person says, "I like parties!" a trait theorist implicitly embracing a sign approach might say that the response indicates that the person has a particular inner characteristic, such as the trait of extraversion. In a sign approach, then, the question one asks is, "What inner characteristic is the response a sign of?" This is *not* the question behaviorists ask. Behaviorists adopt a sample approach. When assessing a person who emits a certain response (does something, says something, etc.), the behaviorists view the response merely as a sample of behavior, that is, as one example of the sort of behavior the person engages in when faced with a particular stimulus. If the person says, "I like parties!" then the behaviorist will merely conclude that saying "I like parties!" is a behavior that, in the past, has been reinforced for this individual. There will be no additional inferences about unseen psychological structures in the head of the individual. This approach may seem superficial. Yet it has big advantages. It stops the psychologist from engaging in highly speculative inferences about inner mental life—inferences that may be little more than guesses. It also helps to identify reinforcers in the environment that, in principle, could be changed in a manner that helps a given individual.

Behavior Change

Behaviorists developed an applied technique for using reinforcement principles in real-world settings. This technique is known as a **token economy** (Ayllon & Azrin, 1965). A behavioral technician rewards, with tokens, behaviors that are considered desirable. The tokens, in turn, can be exchanged by the patient for desirable products, such as candy and cigarettes. For example, hospitalized psychiatric patients may receive reinforcing tokens for activities such as serving meals or cleaning floors. In a tightly controlled environment, such as a state hospital for long-term psychiatric patients, it is feasible to make almost anything that a patient wants contingent on the desired behaviors.

Research evidence supports the effectiveness of token economies. They are effective in increasing behaviors such as social interaction, self-care, and job performance in severely disturbed patients and mentally retarded individuals. They also have been used to decrease aggressive behavior in children and to decrease marital discord (Kazdin, 1977).

Token economy programs represent a very straightforward application of operant conditioning principles to the problem of behavior change. Target behaviors are selected and reinforcement is made contingent on performance of the desired responses. This is completely consistent with the behavioral emphasis on how the environment acts upon people, as opposed to how people act upon the environment. The behaviorist working on human behavior change is, in essence, a social engineer. The scientific technology developed in the behavioral laboratory is applied directly to real-world problems of behavior change. Watson suggested that through control of the environment he could train an infant to become any type of specialist he might select. Skinnerian social engineers take this principle one step further. As seen in the development of token economies, as well as in the development of communes based on Skinnerian principles, there is an interest in the design of environments that will control broad aspects of human behavior.

Free Will?

Skinner's operant behaviorism seems to have uplifting implications. By studying the influence of the environment on behavior, behaviorism gives rise to a technology of behavior change that can be usefully applied to the solution of human problems.

Yet Skinner's behaviorism also has an implication that is disturbing. It is one that Skinner was quite aware of, and that he explained in detail in a book titled *Beyond Freedom and Dignity* (Skinner, 1971). The implication is that people do not have free will. If the environment is the cause of our action, then we ourselves cannot be the cause of our behavior. And if we ourselves are not the cause of our behavior, then we do not truly have freedom to act. We do not make free choices. We do not have free will.

Skinner was quite aware that people believe that they have free will. But he concluded that this belief is an illusion. To illustrate how this could be, consider the following circumstances. Suppose that you are speeding down a highway in your red sports car; as you see a police car up ahead, you slow down to avoid a ticket. If a passenger asks you "Why did you slow down?" you are not likely to say, "Because I have free will and decided to." Instead, you will recognize that the environment caused your behavior. The presence of the police officer was an environmental cause of your slowing down. Now suppose a passenger asks, "Why did you buy a red sports car?" Here you are not likely to cite environmental causes. Instead, you are likely to say, "Because I decided to" or "Because I like red sports cars." You feel you had free will regarding your car purchase. But here is where Skinner says you are wrong. In Skinner's behaviorism, your behavior of slowing down and your behavior of buying a red sports car are both caused by the environment. But in the former case, the environment is simple, immediate, and obvious. You cannot miss the fact that the police officer is the cause of your slowing down. But in the latter case, the environmental causes are complex and extended over a long period of time. Dozens of previous experiences (previous reinforcements and punishments) might have contributed to your behavior of buying a red sports car. It is impossible for you to remember all of them and assess their effects on your decision. But that does not mean that they were not there. In these cases, in which the environmental causes of behavior are complex, people essentially lose track of the multifaceted environmental causes and erroneously conclude that their behavior was caused by a single factor: themselves. Skinner concluded that people live with an illusion of free will—a conclusion similar to that reached by some contemporary research psychologists (Wegner, 2003).

Skinner did not argue against the notion of free will merely to disturb people. Quite the opposite. He felt that the solution of personal and social problems required a systematic application of behavioristic technology. Furthermore, he felt that people would not accept this technology if they thought that it infringed on their free will. Skinner recognized that people do not like to think that their behavior is being controlled, and therefore that they would argue against an application of behavioral technology. But Skinner turned this argument on its head by contending that behavior is always controlled by the environment. Recognizing this fact, and rejecting traditional notions of free will would, Skinner argued, open the door to a humane application of behavioral technology.

Before leaving this topic, we caution that many scholars have rejected Skinner's arguments about free will. Phenomenological theorists felt that Skinner's view underestimated the human being's inherent capacities; indeed, Rogers (1956) debated Skinner on the topic. More recent personality theorists (see Chapters 12 and 13) similarly contend that Skinner underestimated people's capacity to exert free will by failing to consider people's ability to think in a creative manner about the environment they face and how that environment can be changed. Philosophers also have criticized Skinner. Dennett explains that Skinner provided an insufficient analysis of the concept of free will; even if one accepts Skinner's basic principles, people still have capacities that enable them to engage thoughts and actions that deserve to be called acts of free will (Dennett, 1984). The recognition that the brain is a bodily organ that evolved and functions according to deterministic scientific principles is not incompatible with the idea that people have a significant capacity for free will and thus have personal responsibility for their actions (Dennett, 2003).

Perhaps the most devastating critique of behaviorist principles comes from the famed linguist and political scientist Noam Chomsky (1987). Chomsky notes that there is a very large gap between the experimental evidence that Skinner has at his disposal and the arguments he is making. Skinner's arguments concern the environmental control of human social behavior. But his database consists of animals in boxes. Skinner's discussions of human behavior thus are not a simple application of scientific evidence. Instead, they are a substantial leap beyond the scientific evidence that actually is available. "Claims [of the sort Skinner makes] must be evaluated in terms of the evidence presented for them," Chomsky writes. "In the present instance [Skinner's **Beyond Freedom and Dignity**], this is a simple task. No evidence is presented" (Chomsky, 1987, p. 160). Chomsky's point is that Skinner did not in any way demonstrate, scientifically, that people do not have free will. Instead, he used an experimental database involving small animals, plus a philosophical position about the causes of behavior, to construct an argument against the notion of human free will. Cogent counter-arguments are available.

CRITICAL EVALUATION

The behavioral perspective we have just reviewed contrasts starkly with the personality theories in previous chapters. The contrast is seen most clearly by considering what the behaviorist would say about those theories. Psychoanalysis would be seen as utterly non-scientific, because it speculates about unseen internal variables that cannot be observed and measured. Phenomenological theory would be seen as a soft-headed view that falls into the trap of viewing people as the causes of their own behavior, rather than recognizing that the true cause is the environment. Trait theory would be just as bad in the behaviorist's eyes; it would be seen as dealing merely with superficial descriptions of behavior, rather than their causes. If behaviorism had been fully successful, all these other theories would have been swept aside.

But it was not successful. The theories reviewed in the previous chapters remain intellectually viable today. They fuel much basic and applied activity in contemporary personality science. Behaviorism, in contrast, has far fewer adherents today than in decades past. This is true despite the solid scientific contributions of Pavlov, Skinner, and their followers, and despite the successful applications to which this basic research gave rise. This overall state of affairs prompts one to evaluate the strengths and the limits of the behavioral approach.

SCIENTIFIC OBSERVATION: THE DATABASE

The behaviorists' commitment to basing theory on systematic research is a major strength of their work. Their respect for scientific methodology was beneficial on both scientific and administrative grounds. Scientifically, it contributed to an approach to persons that avoided the overly speculative qualities that were evident in previous perspectives. Administratively, the solid scientific database that behaviorists' established made psychology seem more credible in the eyes of other scientists, and thus contributed to the growth of the field in universities in the 20th century.

Yet in other ways the scientific observations that formed the basis of behaviorism are limited. The limitation is obvious; the original database consisted primarily of research with animals (dogs, rats, pigeons). We humans possess psychological abilities not shared by our furry friends: the ability to use language, the ability to reason about events of the past, the ability to contemplate alternative potential outcomes in the future. These capacities are not represented in a database consisting of research with animals and, as a result, are not well represented in the behaviorists' theorizing. This is a major cause of the downfall of behaviorism in the last third of the 20th century. The primary reason that behaviorism lost influence in psychology was that it overlooked phenomena that are fundamental to human life. Perhaps the main phenomenon is the one that was so central to the phenomenological approaches: meaning, that is, the question of how people assign subjective meaning to environmental events. In their research, the behaviorists skipped this question. Rats and pigeons in Skinner boxes simply do not engage in processes of meaning construction. They don't ask themselves questions such as "Hey, why is the guy in the lab coat over there giving me all this food just for pressing a lever?" But people ask themselves such questions all the time. Behavioristic theory and research simply provided little insight into the psychological processes involved in the construction of subjective meaning. Beginning in the 1960s, however, experimental psychologists working *outside of* the framework of behaviorism began making progress in the study of memory, language, emotions, belief systems—topics that informed the study of internal cognitive processes involved in the construction of meaning. Their progress caused interest in behaviorism to wane.

THEORY: SYSTEMATIC?

Whatever the limits of behaviorism, the behaviorists were very systematic theorists. Pavlov and Skinner constructed careful, logically coherent accounts of classical and operant conditioning. Different phenomena—the rate with which an organism performs a response in response to reinforcement, the initial learning of that response, the persistence of the response if reinforcement ceases—are all explained through a single, coherent conceptual system.

In some ways obtaining a theory whose parts are related systematically was easier for the behaviorists. This is because they have less theory; that is, theirs is an approach in which there is less theorizing about inner mental structures and processes than one finds in other theoretical accounts. The behaviorist thus does not face that task of relating numerous theoretical constructs to one another.

THEORY: TESTABLE?

Did the behaviorists provide a theory that is testable? If one asks about the behavior of animals in laboratory settings, the answer is yes. One can directly test predictions about the influence of classical and operant conditioning experiences on the emotional and behavioral responses of the organism in controlled laboratory settings. Within these settings, the behaviorists' ideas are as testable as are ideas one might find in the biological or physical sciences.

But what if one leaves the lab and enters the complex world of everyday human life? Here behavioristic analyses sometimes become ambiguous. Consider an example suggested by Chomsky (1959) in a deservedly famous critique of Skinner's behaviorism. Suppose you are in an art museum gazing at a complex artistic composition. Skinner would say that your reactions to the piece are determined by your past history of operant and classical conditioning when exposed to similar stimuli. If you say, "I like it," that is because, in the past, similar stimuli have been positively reinforcing; they have caused the feelings we call "liking" and reinforced the behavior of saying "I like it." How would you test this idea? A huge problem is that, in the practical case presented here, it is hard to know what "stimuli" the person was responding to when saying "I like it." The composition of the painting? Its color? The originality of the artist? The picture frame? In a Skinner box one can be confident in knowing the stimuli that control behavior because there are so few stimuli. But in the everyday world, it commonly is impossible to know what people are responding to in the first place. One might be able to find this out by asking the person after the fact; after they act, you could ask them what they were responding to. But if one has to ask people, after the fact, then there is no way to *predict* their behavior. One can only tell an after-the-fact behavioristic story. And if one only is providing after-the-fact stories, then one's theory is not testable.

THEORY: COMPREHENSIVE?

Thanks in large part to the brilliant creativity of Skinner's writing, behaviorism is highly comprehensive. In just one of his books (Skinner, 1953), Skinner manages to extend behavioral principles to an analysis not only of individual behavior, but of group behavior, the functioning of government and the rule of law, religion, psychotherapy, economics, education, and culture. In another volume (Skinner, 1974) he analyzes perception, language, emotion and motivation, and self-concept. Skinner and other behaviorists consider the full range of psychological and social phenomena that are to be addressed in a personality theory. Whatever the shortcomings of behaviorism, it does consider an exceptionally wide range of individual and social phenomena.

Learning Approaches at a Glance

Structure	Process	Growth and Development
Response	Classical conditioning; instrumental conditioning; operant conditioning	Schedules of reinforcement and successive approximations

APPLICATIONS

The behaviorists displayed a valuable pragmatic bent. They moved quickly from research in laboratories with animals to practical applications designed to help people. Maybe they moved too quickly; behaviorists did not raise, as carefully as might have been necessary, the question of how the psychology of people may differ from the psychology of animals in Skinner boxes and classical conditioning studies. Nonetheless, behaviorists succeeded in developing practical applications that remain of value to psychology today. Indeed, they developed more valuable applications than did most theorists whose work today is more influential in personality psychology. In particular, the growth of behavior therapy is an application of immense practical value.

MAJOR CONTRIBUTIONS AND SUMMARY

The contributions of behaviorism are enormous (Table 10.2). The behaviorists showed how a comprehensive psychology could be built on an objective database of highly replicable research. They developed numerous applications that continue to be of practical benefit. They applied sophisticated psychological analyses to questions of deep importance to understanding human nature (e.g., the question of free will). They also valuably drew psychologists' attention to the impact of situational factors on behavior. By studying patients in their offices or asking people to fill out questionnaires in laboratories, the

Table 10.2   Summary of Strengths and Limitations of Learning Approaches

Strengths	*Limitations*
1. Committed to systematic research and theory development.	1. Oversimplifies personality and neglects important phenomena.
2. Recognizes the role of situational and environmental variables in influencing behavior.	2. Lacks a single, unified theory; gap between theory and practice.
3. Takes a pragmatic approach to treatment which can lead to important new developments.	3. Requires further evidence to support claims of treatment effectiveness.

Pathology	Change	Illustrative Case
Maladaptive learned response patterns	Extinction; discrimination learning; counterconditioning; positive reinforcement; imitation; systematic desensitization; behavior modification	Reinterpretation of Little Hans

theorists whose work we covered previously removed individuals from the normal, everyday environments of their daily lives. The behaviorists explained that, to understand people's behavior, one must understand the environmental factors that are the behavior's cause.

A final contribution of behaviorism is indirect. The behaviorists provided clear and forceful statements about human nature that other, subsequent theorists thought were deeply wrong. The behaviorists, then, stimulated the thinking of most of the theorists discussed in the remaining chapters of this book. They each were intimately familiar with the claims of the behaviorists and were skeptical about those claims. This skepticism motivated them to provide alternative approaches to the study of personality, as you will see in the chapters ahead.

MAJOR CONCEPTS

ABA research design A Skinnerian variant of the experimental method consisting of exposing one subject to three experimental phases: (A) a baseline period, (B) introduction of reinforcers to change the frequency of specific behaviors, and (A) withdrawal of reinforcement and observation of whether the behaviors return to their earlier frequency (baseline period).

ABC assessment In behavioral assessment, an emphasis on the identification of antecedent (A) events and the consequences (C) of behavior, and (B) a functional analysis of behavior involving identification of the environmental conditions that regulate specific behaviors.

Behavioral assessment The emphasis in assessment on specific behaviors that are tied to defined situational characteristics (e.g., ABC approach).

Behaviorism An approach within psychology, developed by Watson, that restricts investigation to overt, observable behavior.

Classical conditioning A process, emphasized by Pavlov, in which a previously neutral stimulus becomes capable of eliciting a response because of its association with a stimulus that automatically produces the same or a similar response.

Conditioned emotional reaction Watson and Rayner's term for the development of an emotional reaction to a previously neutral stimulus, as in Little Albert's fear of rats.

Counterconditioning The learning (or conditioning) of a new response that is incompatible with an existing response to a stimulus.

Determinism The belief that people's behavior is caused in a lawful scientific manner; determinism opposes a belief in free will.

Discrimination In conditioning, the differential response to stimuli depending on whether they have been associated with pleasure, pain, or neutral events.

Extinction   In conditioning, the progressive weakening of the association between a stimulus and a response; in classical conditioning extinction occurs because the conditioned stimulus is no longer followed by the unconditioned stimulus, and in operant conditioning it occurs because the response is no longer followed by reinforcement.

Fixed (schedules of reinforcement)   Schedules of reinforcement in which the relation of behaviors to reinforcers remains constant.

Functional analysis   In behavioral approaches, particularly Skinnerian, the identification of the environmental stimuli that control behavior.

Generalization   In conditioning, the association of a response with stimuli similar to the stimulus to which the response was originally conditioned or attached.

Generalized reinforcer   In Skinner's operant conditioning theory, a reinforcer that provides access to many other reinforcers (e.g., money).

Maladaptive response   In the Skinnerian view of psychopathology, the learning of a response that is maladaptive or not considered acceptable by people in the environment.

Operant conditioning   Skinner's term for the process through which the characteristics of a response are determined by its consequences.

Operants   In Skinner's theory, behaviors that appear (are emitted) without being specifically associated with any prior (eliciting) stimuli and are studied in relation to the reinforcing events that follow them.

Punishment   An aversive stimulus that follows a response.

Reinforcer   An event (stimulus) that follows a response and increases the probability of its occurrence.

Sample approach   Mischel's description of assessment approaches in which there is an interest in the behavior itself and its relation to environmental

conditions, in contrast to sign approaches that infer personality from test behavior.

Schedule of reinforcement   In Skinner's operant conditioning theory, the rate and interval of reinforcement of responses (e.g., response ratio schedule and time intervals).

Shaping approximation   In Skinner's operant conditioning theory, the process through which organisms learn complex behavior through a step-by-step processes in which behavior increasingly approximates a final, target response.

Sign approach   Mischel's description of assessment approaches that infer personality from test behavior, in contrast with sample approaches to assessment.

Situational specificity   The emphasis on behavior as varying according to the situation, as opposed to the emphasis by trait theorists on consistency in behavior across situations.

Successive approximation   In Skinner's operant conditioning theory, the development of complex behaviors through the reinforcement of behaviors that increasingly resemble the final form of behavior to be produced.

Systematic desensitization   A technique in behavior therapy in which a competing response (relaxation) is conditioned to stimuli that previously aroused anxiety.

Target behaviors (target responses)   In behavioral assessment, the identification of specific behaviors to be observed and measured in relation to changes in environmental events.

Token economy   Following Skinner's operant conditioning theory, an environment in which individuals are rewarded with tokens for desirable behaviors.

Variable (schedules of reinforcement)   Schedules of reinforcement in which the relation of behaviors to reinforcers changes unpredictably.

REVIEW

1. The school of thought known as behaviorism promoted a learning approach to personality. The learning approach suggests that the patterns of social behavior that we see as indications of an individual's personality are learned through environmental experience.

2. Pavlov's work on classical conditioning, combined with Watson's extension of this work to humans in the case of Little Albert, provided the

first foundation for a behavioral approach to the study of persons.

3. B. F. Skinner provided a second foundation for behaviorism in his work on operant conditioning. Skinner and his colleagues developed a highly systematic database showing how reinforcements determine the behavior of animals in Skinner boxes.

4. Skinner explained how principles of learning were relevant to questions of profound importance, including the question of whether people have free will.

5. Behaviorists did not merely conduct laboratory research with animals. They developed many useful applications of the principles of learning. These include clinical applications, in which the goal of the clinician is to provide new environmental experiences through which the client can learn new, more adaptive forms of behavior. Systematic desensitization and token economy programs are two examples of the application of behavioral principles.

6. Behaviorism dominated psychology in the mid-20th century, but then its influence waned. This largely is because behaviorism failed to provide convincing research-based explanations for uniquely human phenomena, such as people's inherent tendency to assign subjective meaning to events. The growth of cognitive psychology, a foundation for theories discussed later in this book, caused the downfall of behaviorism.

A COGNITIVE THEORY: GEORGE A. KELLY'S PERSONAL CONSTRUCT THEORY OF PERSONALITY

11

You've just finished a novel that you thoroughly enjoyed. Excitedly, you call a friend to recommend the book, telling him about the exquisitely detailed descriptions of the characters and the settings. To your dismay, your friend informs you that he has already read the book—and hated it! "Thin plot, slow moving," he complains. How could this be? Your "environment" (the book) was the same, yet you had utterly different experiences. You had completely different thoughts about exactly the same environmental stimulus.

This is what George Kelly's personal construct theory is all about: how each individual uniquely perceives, interprets, and conceptualizes the world. Just as you and your friend differed in your reading of the book, people differ in the way they "read" the persons and events of social life. To Kelly, these differences are at the heart of personality functioning. Our thoughts, emotional reactions, moods, goals, behavioral tendencies—virtually everything of interest to the personality psychologist—are, to Kelly, a product of our interpretations of the world. Individual differences in emotion and action, then, derive from individual differences in these interpretations. These ideas were the foundation of a cognitive theory of personality, a method of personality assessment, and an approach to therapy that were developed by one of the most innovative and impactful figures in the history of personality psychology: George Kelly.

QUESTIONS TO BE ADDRESSED IN THIS CHAPTER

1. What is the goal of the personality scientist when he or she constructs a theory?

2. In what ways are your thoughts, in your daily life, similar to the mental activities of the psychological scientist? What did Kelly mean by suggesting that people are like scientists (his "person-as-scientist" metaphor)?

3. How can one learn about people's beliefs and individual differences in belief systems?

4. How can an analysis of personal constructs explain psychological distress and inform the practice of psychotherapy?

In earlier chapters, you learned about two theories of personality that originated in clinical work: Freud's psychoanalysis and Rogers's phenomenological theory. This chapter considers a third theory that developed primarily out of contact with clients in therapy. Work as a therapist naturally directs one's attention to the "whole person." In other words, rather than focusing on one psychological variable or another, the therapist must confront whole, complex, intact individuals who experience multiple goals and feelings that cohere in meaningful ways. Like the clinician/theorists Freud and Rogers, George Kelly aimed to understand the whole individual.

Although sharing these characteristics with Freud and Rogers, Kelly's overall theory differs from theirs. Freud emphasized animalistic forces in the unconscious. Kelly highlights the uniquely human capacity to reflect on oneself, the world, and the future. Regarding Rogers, Kelly's and Rogers's contributions are similar in some respects (see Epting & Eliot, 2006); both of them were concerned with creating a theory of the whole, coherent person. But Kelly, in his personal construct theory of personality, explored in much greater detail the specific cognitive processes through which people categorize people and things and construct meaning out of the events of their day.

Why is Kelly's work called a "personal construct" theory? Kelly used the word *construct* to refer to ideas or categories that people use to interpret their world. Some of these categories are universal. For example, if you and a friend both stare out the window during a boring moment in your professor's lectures and spot a 20-foot-tall green and brown leafy object, you probably will both categorize it as "a tree." We all have in our head the category "tree" and we all apply this category to 20-foot-tall green and brown leafy objects. But some categories vary from person to person. People differ in whether they possess the given category and in where they use it. Suppose your professor sees you and your friend staring out the window at the tree, stops the lecture, and asks you both to start paying attention to class. You may categorize the professor as an "attentive teacher" whereas your friend may see her as a "condescending intellectual." In the language of Kelly's personal construct theory, you two will have used different personal constructs ("attentive teacher," "condescending intellectual") to interpret your professor's behavior. The use of these constructs would have great implications for your subsequent thoughts and feelings. You may admire the professor for her attention, whereas your friend may feel insulted by her condescension. To Kelly, an individual's personality can be understood in terms of the collection of personal constructs or the personal construct system that he or she uses to interpret the world.

In this text we label Kelly's work a *"cognitive"* theory, a term that derives from the Latin verb that means "to know" and that, in contemporary psychology, generally refers to thinking processes. A cognitive theory of personality, then, is a theory that places the analysis of human thinking processes at the centerpoint of the analysis of personality and individual differences. Kelly himself did not use the term *cognitive* to describe his theory, thinking it was too restrictive and that it suggested an artificial division between cognition (thinking) and affect (feeling). However, "cognitive" remains the most popular classification of Kelly's theory, and for good reason (Neimeyer, 1992; Winter, 1992). The constructs that people possess comprise their knowledge of the world, and these constructs are used in the acquisition of new knowledge. People apply their constructs to the interpretation of daily events through mental procedures that generally are termed *cognitive processes*; these include categorizing people and things, attributing meaning to events, and predicting events.

Kelly's most important work in personality theory was published in 1955. At that historical point, Kelly's emphasis on complex human cognitive processes was ahead of its time. Behaviorism dominated academic psychology in the 1950s. Contemporary cognitive psychology had not yet developed. Kelly's work, then, anticipated subsequent developments in the field. Throughout the last quarter of the 20th century—that is, years after Kelly's death—psychologists increasingly interpreted human behavior in terms of cognitive processes through which people interpret and understand their world. A supporter of personal construct theory has noted that "Kelly's theory enjoys the irony of becoming increasingly contemporary with age" (Neimeyer, 1992, p. 995).

Kelly provided not only an academic theory but an approach to life. He challenged people—both the people he saw in therapy and the people who were his contemporaries in psychology—to think in new terms, to view the world in new ways, to try on new constructs. He similarly would invite and challenge you, the student, to "try on" the novel ideas of personal construct theory.

GEORGE A. KELLY (1905–1966): A VIEW OF THE THEORIST

The nature of George Kelly, the person, comes through in his writing. He appears to have been the kind of person he encouraged others to be—an adventuresome soul who is unafraid to think unorthodox thoughts and who dares to explore the unknown.

Kelly's philosophical and theoretical positions stem, in part, from the diversity of his experience (Sechrest, 1963). Kelly grew up in Kansas and obtained his undergraduate education there at Friends University and at Park College in Missouri. He pursued graduate studies at the University of Kansas, the University of Minnesota, and the University of Edinburgh, and received his Ph.D. from the State University of Iowa in 1931. He developed a traveling clinic in Kansas, was an aviation psychologist during World War II, and was a professor of psychology at Ohio State University and Brandeis University.

Kelly's early clinical experience was in the public schools of Kansas. He found that when teachers referred pupils to his traveling psychological clinic, their complaints appeared to say something about not only the pupils, but the teachers themselves. Kelly tried to understand the teacher's reports as an expression of the teacher's construction or interpretation of events. For example, if a teacher complained that a student was lazy, Kelly did not look at the pupil to see if the teacher was correct in the diagnosis; rather he tried to understand the behaviors of the child and the way the teacher perceived these behaviors, that is, the teacher's construction of them that led to the complaint of laziness. This was a significant reformulation of the problem. In practical terms, it led to an analysis of the teachers as well as the pupils, and to a wider range of solutions to the problems. Furthermore, it led Kelly to the

George A. Kelly

view that there is no objective, absolute truth—phenomena are meaningful only in relation to the ways in which they are construed or interpreted by the individual.

Kelly gradually came to reject "black or white" solutions to complex psychological problems. He instead preferred a more subtle and complex approach. His goal was to test interpretations of events, to reconstrue or reinterpret phenomena, and thereby to challenge traditional concepts of objective reality. He felt free to play in the world of make-believe, encouraging people to imagine alternative realities. He challenged the theorizing of others, yet viewed his own theory as only a tentative formulation that eventually would be replaced. Kelly accepted the frustration and challenge, the threat and joy, of exploring the unknown.

Like all persons, Kelly can be viewed as a product of his times and his culture. He lived in an early/mid-20th century Midwestern America that valued practical solutions to practical problems more than it valued esoteric theorizing about abstract metaphysical concerns. This was an America whose intellectual life was shaped by pragmatism, a philosophical school teaching that ideas should be evaluated on practical grounds, by asking how embracing the ideas would affect individuals and society in the long run (Menand, 2002a). Kelly viewed his own theory as a construction—a kind of tool that had value if it achieved a practical goal, namely, the goal of enabling people to improve their lives by thinking in new ways about their problems and themselves.

KELLY'S VIEW OF THE SCIENCE OF PERSONALITY

In previous chapters we introduced personality theories by reviewing, in order, the given theorist's (1) view of the person and (2) view of the science of personality. Here, when presenting the work of Kelly, we reverse that order. Why? To Kelly himself, questions about science come first. This is for two reasons: (1) To a greater extent than other theorists Kelly based his theory of persons on an explicit view of science and the nature of scientific inquiry. (2) Unlike other theorists, he used the contemporary notion of scientific inquiry as a metaphor for understanding the psychological activities of the everyday person (as we review in the "View of the Person" section below). To best understand Kelly's theory, then, it is best to learn about his view of science, and then his view of persons.

In developing a view of science, the fundamental question Kelly raised is, "What are scientists doing when they are constructing theories?" One view is that the scientist is searching for truth. Maybe there is a "true" theory out there and, armed with the methods of the sciences, the diligent scientist can find it. This conception implies that all theories can be evaluated as being true or false. A different view, adopted by Kelly (and many contemporary scientists and philosophers of science, e.g., Proctor & Capaldi, 2001) is that "true versus false" is not the right question to ask about a scientific theory. The problem is that any complex and well-formulated theory is likely to seem true in some respects but not others. An alternative question to ask, then, is whether and how a theory is useful. Does the theory enable one to do some useful things that one could not do without the theory? This question does raise another one:

How does one evaluate a theory's usefulness? Kelly reasoned that scientists often are interested in predicting events; they find it useful to be able to predict how events will turn out. This reasoning converts questions about utility into questions about prediction: What important events can one predict using a given theory?

The simple idea of evaluating a theory according to its usefulness for making predictions has a significant implication. Different theories may enable one to make different types of predictions. Thus, different theories each may be uniquely useful. This implies that one does not need to choose between theories, accepting one as right and seeing the others as wrong. Instead, it may be valuable to see the world through the lens of different theories, each of which may enable one to see something interesting. Kelly called this idea **constructive alternativism**: Alternative scientific constructs each may provide a useful view of the world. According to this position, scientific theorizing does not involve the pursuit of a singular theory that is objectively "correct." Instead, there are efforts by scientists to *construe* events—to interpret phenomena in order to make sense of them. Rather than there being a single correct theory, there are always alternative scientific constructions available from which to choose, each of which may be valuable for some purposes. (Kelly's argument should remind you of the toolkit metaphor introduced in Chapter 1.)

In Kelly's view, then, the enterprise of personality science is not concerned with the discovery of truth or, as Freud might have suggested, the uncovering of things in the mind previously hidden. Rather, it is an effort to develop scientific construct systems that are useful in predicting events. Different personality theories each may make unique and valid predictions about persons.

Kelly developed these ideas in part because he was concerned about the tendency toward dogma in psychology. He thought psychologists believed that constructs of inner states and traits actually existed rather than understanding them as "things" in a theoretician's head. If someone is described as an introvert, we tend to check to see whether he is an introvert, rather than checking the person who is responsible for the statement. Kelly's position against "truth" and dogma is of considerable significance. It allows one to establish an "invitational mood" in which one is free to invite many alternative interpretations of phenomena and to entertain propositions that initially may seem absurd. The invitational mood is a necessary part of the exploration of the world, for the professional scientist as well as for the patient in therapy.

According to Kelly, it is this invitational mood that allows one the freedom to develop creative hypotheses. A hypothesis should not be asserted as a fact, but instead should allow the scientist to pursue its implications as if it were true. Kelly viewed a theory as a tentative expression of what has been observed and of what is expected. A theory has a **range of convenience**, indicating the boundaries of phenomena the theory can cover, and a **focus of convenience**, indicating the points within the boundaries where the theory works best. Different theories have different ranges and different foci of convenience.

For Kelly, theories were modifiable and ultimately expendable. A theory is modified or discarded when it stops leading to new predictions or leads to incorrect predictions. Among scientists, as well as among people in general, how long one holds on to a theory in the face of contradictory information is partly a matter of taste and style.

1. Different theories provide different constructions of phenomena. Different theories also have different ranges of convenience and different foci of convenience.
2. An extreme emphasis on measurement can be limiting and lead to viewing concepts as "things" rather than as representations.
3. The clinical method is useful because it leads to new ideas and focuses attention on important questions.
4. A good theory of personality should help us to solve the problems of people and society. Theories should be evaluated pragmatically, by asking what practical advantages the theory yields in the prediction and solution of psychological problems.
5. Theories are designed to be modified and abandoned.

Figure 11.1 *Some Components of Kelly's View of Science.*

Kelly's view of science is not unique, yet its clarity of expression and points of emphasis remain important (Figure 11.1). In addition to highlighting the utility of a theory (rather than its truth versus falsity), Kelly also questioned other traditional assumptions. These include psychologists' extreme emphasis on measurement. In Kelly's time, and today, much work in personality psychology is devoted to the precise measure of individual differences in one versus another psychological construct. Kelly felt that this emphasis on measurement leads personality theorists erroneously to view theoretical concepts as if they are real things in people's heads. The psychologist inadvertently becomes a technician whose primary expertise is in statistics, rather than being a scientist whose primary expertise is in the study of the human mind. A third feature of Kelly's view of science is that it leaves room for clinical as opposed to purely experimental methods. He considered the clinical method useful because it speaks the language of hypothesis, because it leads to the emergence of new variables, and because it focuses on important questions. Here we have a fourth significant aspect of Kelly's view of science: It should focus on important issues. Kelly felt that psychologists often feared doing anything that might not be recognized as science. This fear caused them to avoid studying important aspects of human experience that are difficult to test scientifically. Kelly urged that psychologists stop trying to look scientific and get on with the job of understanding people. He believed that a good scientific theory should encourage the invention of new approaches to the solution of the problems of people and society.

KELLY'S VIEW OF THE PERSON

Kelly's view of science connects directly to his view of persons. Kelly felt that scientists and laypersons (i.e., nonscientists in their everyday life) are engaged in the same task. They both use constructs to predict events. The scientists' constructs surely may differ from those of the layperson; they may be stated in a more precise manner and (depending on the science) may involve mathematical concepts rather than words. Yet the scientists' and laypersons' tasks are fundamentally similar. Both try to develop ideas (i.e., constructs) that enable them to predict events. The personality scientist may have a formal theory that enables her to make some types of predictions (e.g., a trait theorist might be able to predict your scores on personality traits 5 years from now based on your scores today). But your wise grandmother may have an informal, nonscientific theory that enables her to make a different set of predictions (e.g., whether one versus another type of discussion will cheer you up if you're having a down day). In both cases, the person is using accumulated knowledge to make predictions.

This reasoning underlies a metaphor that is central to Kelly's view of persons. It is the **person-as-scientist** metaphor. To Kelly, the central features of everyday life involve our attempts to develop ideas that enable us to predict significant events in our daily life. We want to be able to predict whether we will, for example, pass an upcoming exam, succeed in getting a date, or get out of a state of depression. We also want to predict which types of experiences might help us to achieve these goals. In making these predictions, Kelly argues, we operate as scientists. Like scientists, we develop theories ("maybe I'm the sort of person who needs to work with friends when studying for exams"), we test hypotheses ("this time I'll try a different strategy of asking for a date and see what happens"), and we weigh evidence ("last time I tried to relieve my depression by eating a lot of desserts, but that didn't work").

The person-as-scientist view has two further consequences. First, it highlights the fact that people are essentially oriented toward the future. "It is the future which tantalizes man, not the past. Always he reaches out to the future through the window of the present" (Kelly, 1955, p. 49). Much of human thinking indeed is directed toward future events. Of the personality theories we have discussed so far, Kelly's is the one that most directly confronts this basic fact of mental life.

The second consequence is the following. If scientists can usefully adopt different theories to make different types of predictions, then so can laypersons. Just as there can be constructive alternativism in the domain of scientific constructs discussed previously, there can be constructive alternativism in the domain of personal constructs. People have the capacity to think constructively about the environment—to re-think their usual ways of construing the world. The individual can develop alternative theoretical formulations, can try on different constructs, and in so doing can devise novel strategies for dealing with the challenges and conflicts of life.

This view of people's capacity to think constructively about the world yields a new understanding of an issue discussed in the previous chapter of this book, namely, free will and determinism. To behaviorists such as Skinner, people merely responded to the environment. They thus were controlled by environmental forces and lacked free will. To Kelly, however, people do not respond passively to the environment. They think actively about it. Furthermore, they think actively about their own thinking processes. People can decide that they have not thought properly about something, and think about it differently. These thinking capacities make human beings both free and determined. "This personal construct system provides him [humankind] with both freedom of decision and limitations of action—freedom, because it permits him to deal with the meaning of events rather than forces him to be helplessly pushed about by them, and limitation, because he can never make choices outside the world of alternatives he has erected for himself" (Kelly, 1955, p. 58). Having "enslaved" ourselves with these constructions, we are able to win freedom again and again by reconstruing the environment and life. Thus, we are not victims of past history or of present circumstances unless we choose to construe ourselves in[1] that way.

These points are the general principles upon which Kelly built a theory of personality structures and processes. We now turn to the details of that theory.

STRUCTURE

The key structural variable in Kelly's theory of personality is the personal construct. A **construct** is an element of knowledge. It is a concept used to interpret, or construe, the world. People use constructs to categorize events. This is not something you necessarily do consciously; people do not say to themselves, "Um, I think I will use a construct now." It is something that happens automatically and inevitably. When experiencing events you try to make sense of them, and to make sense of them you have to use some element of knowledge that you already possess. In Kelly's language, you use a personal construct.

The core idea of Kelly's theory is that a person anticipates events by observing patterns and regularities. People notice that some events share characteristics that distinguish them from other events. Individuals distinguish similarities and contrasts. They observe that some people are tall and some are short, that some are men and some are women, that some things are hard and some are soft. It is this construing of a similarity and a contrast that leads to the formation of a construct. Without constructs, life would be chaotic; we wouldn't be able to organize our world, to describe and classify events, objects, and people.

According to Kelly, at least three elements are necessary to form a construct: two of the elements must be perceived as similar to each other, and the third element must be perceived as different from these two. The way in which two elements are construed to be similar forms the **similarity pole** of the construct; the way in which they are contrasted with the third element forms the **contrast pole** of the construct. For example, observing two people helping someone and a third hurting someone could lead to the construct kind/cruel, with kind forming the similarity pole and cruel the contrast pole. Kelly stressed the importance of recognizing that a construct is composed of a similarity/contrast comparison. This suggests that we do not understand the nature of a construct when it uses only the similarity pole or the contrast pole. We do not know what the construct respect means to a person until we know what events the person includes under this construct and what events are viewed as being opposed to it.

A construct is not dimensional in the sense of having many points between the similarity and contrast poles. Subtleties or refinements in construction of events are made through the use of other constructs, such as constructs of quantity and quality. For example, the construct black/white in combination

---

[1] Kelly's references to "man the scientist" and "man the biological organism" may strike students as sexist. It should be remembered that Kelly was writing in the 1950s, prior to efforts to remove sexism from language.

with a quantity construct leads to the four-scale value of black, slightly black, slightly white, and white (Sechrest, 1963).

As we already noted, Kelly recognizes that human thinking is future-oriented; we spend much of our time thinking about, and planning for, future events. This thinking also involves the use of personality constructs. People use constructs, then, not only to interpret events that have occurred to them, but to plan for future occurrences. As we explain in our coverage of the process aspects of Kelly's theory (discussed subsequently), the idea that people use constructs to anticipate events is the fundamental postulate of Kelly's theory.

Constructs and Their Interpersonal Consequences

It is fascinating to observe the diversity of constructs that individuals use. If you watch television and turn on a program with religious content, a speaker may describe people as moral versus immoral. If you turn on a political program, a speaker may describe people as liberal versus conservative. On a sports program, commentators may say that a person is a "clutch" player versus someone who "chokes." These bipolar ideas (moral–immoral, liberal–conservative, clutch–chokes) are examples of what Kelly called personal constructs.

Who are we learning about when we hear someone use constructs of this sort? Are we learning merely about the persons being described? Or are we learning also about the speakers—the people providing the descriptions? Kelly contends that people reveal aspects of their own personality in the constructs they use to describe others: "One cannot call another person a bastard without making bastardy a dimension of his own life also" (Kelly, 1955, p. 133). The different constructs are parts of the personalities of the people we are speaking.

Such differences in construct systems can have important interpersonal consequences. They often contribute to failures in communications between groups. You may find yourself in conversation with someone who uses constructs that conflict with yours. A friend of one of the authors once said: "Isn't there a winner and a loser in every relationship?" Well, maybe not; the friend seemed unaware that "winner/loser" is only a possible, not a necessary, construct. Another person might have used the construct compromising/uncompromising person or compassionate/uncompassionate person.

Difficulties in communication could also result when groups who see themselves as being in opposition to one another fail to recognize that they actually have many constructs in common. Becoming aware of the commonalities in construct systems could benefit communication. Simpson, Large, & O'Brien (2004) recently used ideas from Kelly's theory to show how communication between two such groups can be improved. They worked with two groups of professionals who, they report, often experience tensions and failures to communicate in a particular professional setting, namely, a hospital. The two groups were: (1) clinical health professionals who were responsible for patient care, and (2) hospital managers who were responsible for the hospital's business operations and whose background often was outside of health care. Within a workshop to improve communication between the groups, Simpson et al. asked the clinicians and managers to enumerate the characteristics that they say was ideal for a clinician and for a manager. The idea was to make explicit the personal constructs that people held regarding an ideal professional of both types (clinician and manager). The groups then observed each other's personal construct lists. "What was ... surprising to them," Simpson et al.

(2004, p. 55) report, "was the areas of commonality between the two groups." The previously opposed groups learned that they held many constructs in common. This facilitated subsequent discussions between them.

Types of Constructs and the Construct System

People often can express their personal constructs in words. Kelly refers to constructs that can be expressed in words as "verbal" constructs. Not all constructs have this quality. Kelly distinguished between two different types of constructs: **verbal** and **preverbal**. A verbal construct can be expressed in words, whereas a preverbal construct is one that is used even though the person has no words to express it. A preverbal construct is learned before the person develops the use of language. Kelly suggested that the verbal/preverbal distinction captures some phenomena that Freudians would call conscious versus unconscious.

Sometimes one end of a bipolar construct is not available for verbalization; it is characterized as being **submerged**. If a person insists that people do only good things, one assumes that the other end of the construct has been submerged since the person must have been aware of contrasting behaviors to have formed the "good" end of the construct. Thus, constructs may not be available for verbalization, and the individual may not be able to report all the elements that are in the construct. In spite of the recognized importance of preverbal and submerged constructs, ways of studying them have not been highly developed by personal construct psychologists.

In addition to distinguishing between types of constructs (verbal and preverbal), another important aspect of Kelly's theoretical system concerns people's overall collection of constructs. The constructs people use are believed to be organized as part of a system. In the personal construct system, constructs differ in terms of the circumstances to which they apply. Each construct within the system has a range of convenience and a focus of convenience. A construct's range of convenience comprises all those events for which the user would find application of the construct useful. A construct's focus of convenience comprises the particular events for which application of the construct would be maximally useful. For example, the construct caring/uncaring, which might apply to people in all situations where help is given (range of convenience), would be particularly applicable in situations where special sensitivity and effort are required (focus of convenience).

In addition, some constructs are more central to the person's construct system than are others. There are **core constructs** that are basic to a person's functioning and that can be changed only with great consequences for the rest of the construct system. In contrast, **peripheral constructs** are much less basic and can be altered without serious modification of the core structure. If you have strong beliefs about religion and weaker beliefs about art, your conception of "creative–uncreative" art may be a peripheral construct that easily can be changed, whereas your conception of "sinful–holy" acts may be a core personal construct that is virtually unchangeable.

A person's construct system is organized hierarchically. An example of a hierarchy in the animal kingdom is ANIMAL/Dog/golden retriever. In a hierarchy, the broadest and most inclusive constructs are the **superordinate constructs** at the top of the hierarchy (e.g., ANIMAL). These superordinate

CURRENT APPLICATIONS

HAVING WORDS FOR WHAT YOU SEE, TASTE, AND SMELL

"Why are we so inarticulate about these things?" said a student in referring to tastes, odors, and touch sensations. What would the implications be if we had a greater vocabulary for experience, that is, if we had more constructs for such phenomena? Can having more taste constructs develop one's sense of taste? More odor constructs one's sense of smell? Is the secret to becoming a food connoisseur the development of one's construct system?

At one time it was thought that language determines how we perceive and organize the world. In light of today's evidence, such a view seems too extreme. We are capable of sensing and recognizing many things for which we have no name or concept. However, having a concept or construct may facilitate experiencing and recalling some phenomena. For example, research on odor identification suggests that having the right words to describe an odor facilitates recognition of the odor: "People can improve their ability to identify odors through practice. More specifically, they can improve it through various cognitive interventions in which words are used to endow odors with perceptual or olfactory identity." A name for a smell helps to transform it from vague to clear. Not just any word will do, since some words seem to capture better the sensory experience than others do. The important fact, however, is that cognition does play an important role in virtually all aspects of sensory experience.

In sum, expanding one's sensory construct system alone may not provide for increased sensitivity to sensory experience but, together with practice, it can go a long way toward doing so. Want to become a food connoisseur? Practice, but also expand your construct system.

SOURCE: *Psychology Today*, July 1981.

Unity of Constructs: Having relevant constructs may facilitate sensitivity to tastes and odors.

Core Constructs: Marital difficulties can revolve around the use of core constructs such as guilty/innocent.

constructs include more narrow and specific constructs, such as dog, cat, and giraffe in our example. In turn, each of these middle-level constructs includes a large number of even more narrow **subordinate constructs** (e.g., golden retriever, German shepherd, poodle, etc.). Constructs, then, differ in their breadth and inclusiveness.

It is important to recognize that the constructs within the person's construct system are interrelated. Behavior, then, expresses the construct system rather than a single construct. Change in one construct can trigger changes in other parts of the system. Although constructs generally are consistent with one another, some constructs conflict with others, which produces strain and difficulties for a person in making choices (Landfield, 1982).

To summarize, according to Kelly's theory of personal constructs, an individual's personality is made up of his or her construct system. A person uses constructs to interpret the world and to anticipate events. The constructs a person uses thus define his or her world. People naturally differ from one another in the constructs they use and in the organization among constructs in their overall system of knowledge. If you want to understand a person, you must know something about the constructs that person uses, the events subsumed under these constructs, the way in which these constructs tend to function, and the way in which they are organized in relation to one another to form a system (Adams-Webber, 1998).

Assessment: The Role Construct Repertory (Rep) Test

How does the psychologist learn about a person's construct system? How, in other words, does one go about the task of personality assessment in personal construct theory?

Kelly's first step in answering this question is to express faith in the wisdom of the person who is being assessed. "If you don't know what is going on in a person's mind, ask him; he may tell you" (1958b, p. 330). Kelly placed great faith in people's ability to report on their own personality; in this way, he differed strikingly from Freud.

As part of his personal construct theory, Kelly developed his own assessment technique: the **Role Construct Repertory Test (Rep test)**. Kelly's assessment procedure is very closely tied to his theory; the Rep test is perhaps the singularly best example of an assessment instrument that is directly related to the core elements of a given personality theory.

The Rep test consists of two steps: (1) the development of a list of persons about whom personality ratings will be made; this is called the Role Title List and (2) the elicitation of constructs; that is, the test-taker is asked to engage in a task that will elicit his or her personal constructs. In the first step, people are asked to indicate the names of specific people who fill various roles in their life: mother, father, a teacher you liked, or a neighbor you find hard to understand, and so forth. Generally, people fitting 20 to 30 roles are identified. Next comes the critical novel step in Kelly's testing procedure. The examiner picks three specific figures from the list and asks the test-taker to indicate how two of these people are alike and are different from the third. For example, suppose a test-taker is given the names of persons identified in the roles Mother, Father, and Liked Teacher. They might say that Father and Liked Teacher are similar and are different from Mother. They might then say that Father and Liked Teacher are similar in that they are "outgoing," and different from Mother who is "shy." The point is *not* that one is learning about the mother, father, and teacher of the person taking the test! The point is that one is learning about *the person who is taking the test*; one learns that the person has, in his or her head, the construct "shy–outgoing." With each presentation of a new triad, the test-taker generates a construct. The construct given may be the same as a previous one or a new construct. Illustrative constructs given by one person are presented in Table 11.1.

Note how the structure of the Rep test follows directly from Kelly's theory. The theory says that constructs are used to evaluate how two entities are similar and different from others. The test directly taps this form of thinking. The theory says that people cannot be fit into any simple taxonomy of personality

Table 11.1   Role Construct Repertory Test: Illustrative Constructs

Similar Figures	Similarity Construct	Dissimilar Figure	Contrasting Construct
Self, Father	Emphasis on happiness	Mother	Emphasis on practicality
Teacher, Happy person	Calm	Sister	Anxious
Male friend, Female friend	Good listener	Past friend	Trouble expressing feelings
Disliked person, Employer	Uses people for own ends	Liked person	Considerate of others
Father, Successful person	Active in the community	Employer	Not active in the community
Disliked person, Employer	Cuts others down	Sister	Respectful of others
Mother, Male friend	Introvert	Past friend	Extravert
Self, Teacher	Self-sufficient	Person helped	Dependent
Self, Female friend	Artistic	Male friend	Uncreative
Employer, Female friend	Sophisticated	Brother	Unsophisticated

traits or types. The test is highly flexible; it allows people to express how they construe the world and makes no attempt to fit them into a pre-existing taxonomy of personality types.

Unique Information Revealed by Personal Construct Testing

As you can tell from the description above, the Rep test is rather complicated. Administering and scoring the test is a more complex, time-consuming procedure than, for example, merely giving people a small set of standard personality trait tests and computing Big Five scores (see Chapter 8). Is the effort worth it? Does one actually learn unique information about the individual being tested by following the procedures suggested by Kelly? Or might it be possible to get the same information by using simpler procedures based on trait theory?

This question has been examined systematically in research by Grice (2004). He administered two types of tests to a sample of research participants: (1) an idiographic grid procedure that was modeled closely after Kelly's Rep test for assessing personal constructs, and (2) a nomothetic grid technique in which people made personality ratings using a fixed set of Big Five markers, rather than using the potentially unique personality descriptors that are revealed by Kelly's procedure. The question, then, is the degree to which the idiographic personal construct procedure reveals information that is unique, that is, information that is not revealed by the nomothetic Big Five procedure.

This question was addressed by statistical analyses of these two forms of personality assessment. The findings revealed that the procedures overlapped only partly. Specifically, about half of the variation in personality ratings made in personal construct testing was predictable from Big Five scores, whereas the other half was unique (Grice, 2004). Kelly's personal construct method would, then, appear to be well worth the effort. Half of the information that is learned about individuals through Kelly's test would be lost if one employed merely Big Five testing methods. As Grice (2004, p. 227) explains, "when left to their own devices" in Kelly's idiographic procedure, people commonly go "beyond personality traits (viz. the Big Five) to describe themselves and other people."

Cognitive Complexity/Simplicity

As noted, people may differ not only in the content of individual constructs they possess, but in the overall structure and organization of their construct systems. How, exactly, might one person's system of personal constructs differ from another's? A possibility that has received much attention is that construct systems differ in their complexity; researchers have studied the **cognitive complexity versus simplicity** of construct systems.

Work on cognitive complexity began years ago, soon after Kelly first proposed his theory. An early effort of historical significance was that of Bieri (1955), who contributed substantially to conceptions of construct systems. To Bieri, a cognitively complex system is one that contains many constructs that do not merely overlap with each other. (If one of your constructs for thinking about people is "smart–dumb" and another is "intelligent–unintelligent," these two constructs will be said to overlap.) Bieri anticipated that a more complex cognitive system would enable a person to differentiate between people and events in their world in a fine-grained manner. This would have a practical

CURRENT APPLICATIONS

A REP TEST FOR CHILDREN: HOW DO THEY CONSTRUE PERSONALITY?

What kinds of constructs do you use to differentiate among people you know? For example, how are your mother and father similar to each other but different from yourself? Has the way you construe the similarities and differences between your parents and yourself changed since you were a child? A study by Donahue (1994) suggests that your construct system has changed both in content and in form. Donahue used a simplified version of Kelly's Rep test to elicit the constructs eleven-year-olds use to describe personality. The children nominated nine individuals: self, best friend, an opposite-sex peer "who sits near you at school," a disliked peer, mother (or mother figure), father (or father figure), a liked teacher, the ideal self, and a disliked adult. The individuals' names were written on cards, and presented in sets of three. For example, to elicit the first construct, the children had to consider the self, the best friend, and the liked teacher. They then generated a word or phrase to describe how two of the individuals were alike, and an opposite word to describe how the third person was different from the other two. In this way, each child generated nine constructs.

What kinds of constructs did the children use? In terms of content, Donahue categorized the constructs according to the "Big Five" dimensions of personality description—extraversion, agreeableness, conscientiousness, emotional stability, and openness to experience (see Chapter 8). Although the children used constructs from all Big Five domains, the vast majority of their constructs dealt with Agreeableness (e.g., "is nice" versus "gets into fights") and Extraversion ("wants to be in charge" versus "likes to play quiet"). In contrast to the personality descriptions of adults, the children used the other three Big Five dimensions much less frequently. Thus, most of their constructs were interpersonal in nature—reflecting the importance of getting along with their peers, parents, and teachers.

In terms of form, Donahue coded six distinct ways of structuring or expressing personal constructs: facts ("from Oklahoma"), habits ("eats lots of sweets"), skills ("is the marble champion"), preferences ("likes comic books"), behavioral trends ("always in trouble with the teacher"), and traits ("shy"). As expected, the children used fewer trait descriptors and many more facts than adults. These findings suggest that children's construct systems are more concrete and become more abstract and psychological as they mature into adults.

These findings show that the Rep test allows us to see how personal construct systems are defined across ages in terms of both content and form. Of course, many other interesting comparisons are possible. For example, how do you think the construct systems of women and men differ? What about those of different ethnic groups or cultures? The Rep test allows us to explore both what is unique and what is shared in the way we construe the world around us.

SOURCE: DONAHUE (1994).

implication. Cognitively complex persons, thanks to their fine-grained differentiation among persons, should be more able to predict the social behavior of individuals they know.

To evaluate his predictions, Bieri asked a group of students to participate in the following study. He first asked students to describe the personality of others in the class. He did this in the style of the Rep test, asking people to indicate a construct that made two other people similar and different from a third. He did this for a series of sets of three class members. Bieri then gauged the complexity of the construct systems that people displayed. If somebody in the study always used the same construct when evaluating others, they got a low complexity score. If they used a large number of different constructs, providing subtle and nuanced descriptions of different persons, they got a high score. Then, separately, Bieri asked people to complete a multiple-choice test. The test items asked students to try to predict the social behavior of other students in the class; specifically, participants were asked to try to predict others' responses to a variety of everyday social situations. (People also rated their own tendencies, and these self-ratings were taken as the "correct" test responses.) As predicted, individual differences in the complexity of construct systems were significantly related to individual differences in the ability to predict others' behavior. Cognitively complex students were more accurate in predicting the behavior of others than were cognitively simple subjects. Furthermore, cognitively complex subjects were more able to recognize differences between themselves and others; they were less likely to draw the mistaken conclusion that other people would respond in the same manner that they themselves would. Presumably it was the greater number of constructs available to complex participants that enabled them to predict behavior more accurately.

Subsequent work revealed more about cognitive complexity/simplicity. People high in complexity differ from those low in complexity in the way that they handle inconsistent information about a person. High-complex persons try to use the inconsistent information in forming an impression, whereas low-complex persons commonly form an impression that is consistent by rejecting all information inconsistent with that impression (Mayo & Crockett, 1964). More complex individuals are better able to understand and take on the role of others (Adams-Webber, 1979, 1982; Crockett, 1982). In terms of the Big Five dimensions described in Chapter 8, complexity is related most strongly to the fifth factor, openness to new experiences (Tetlock, Peterson, & Berry, 1993).

Contemporary researchers continue to study the complexity versus simplicity of cognitive construct systems. They are particularly interested in the complexity of beliefs about the self, or "self-complexity." Much of this interest was spurred by seminal research conducted by Patricia Linville (1985). Linville reasoned that people may differ significantly in their levels of self-complexity. Some people may possess a small number of central beliefs about the self that come into play repeatedly in one or two central circumstances in their lives. Other people may be involved in numerous life roles and may possess a rich array of different skills and personal tendencies, each of which comes into play in different settings. For example, you might have two friends, one of whom is a pre-med student who studies 60 hours a week and describes himself as being "smart" and "diligent," and the other of whom is a student, parent, church volunteer, part-time employee, and a weekend athlete, and who sees herself as having a distinct personal style in each of these different settings. The latter person would be seen as being higher in self-complexity.

Research by Linville (1985, 1987) indicated that higher levels of complexity serve as a buffer against stress. People with high self-complexity, in other words, seemed emotionally better off when things were particularly stressful in their lives. For example, if a student high in self-complexity were to fail a test, the existence of other life roles (parent, employee, etc.) seemed to serve as a useful cognitive distraction that helped them to avoid prolonged negative mood. A recent review indicates, however, that self-complexity is not consistently found to be a buffer against stress, and suggests that improvements in the measurement of self-complexity are needed (Rafaeli-Mor & Steinberg, 2002).

Finally, another promising area of contemporary study is "social identity complexity" (Roccas & Brewer, 2002). Social identity complexity refers to the complexity of people's mental representations of the social groups to which they belong. People who live in a multicultural society may recognize complex interrelations among multiple group identities.

In sum, then, the study of cognitive complexity versus simplicity stands as the most highly investigated aspect of individual differences in personal construct systems.

PROCESS

The process aspects of Kelly's personal construct theory radically departed from traditional theories of motivation available in his time. As already mentioned, the psychology of personal constructs does not interpret behavior in terms of motivation, drives, and needs. For personal construct theory, the term *motivation* is redundant. This term assumes that a person is inert and needs something to get started. But, if we assume that people are basically active, the controversy as to what prods an inert organism into action becomes a dead issue. "Instead, the organism is delivered fresh into the psychological world alive and struggling" (Kelly, 1955, p. 37). Kelly contrasted other theories of motivation with his own position in the following way:

> Motivational theories can be divided into two types, push theories and pull theories. Under push theories we find such terms as drive, motive, or even stimulus. Pull theories use such constructs as purpose, value, or need. In terms of a well-known metaphor, these are the pitchfork theories on the one hand and the carrot theories on the other. But our theory is neither of these. Since we prefer to look to the nature of the animal himself, ours is probably best called a jackass theory.
>
> SOURCE: KELLY, 1958a, p. 50.

Anticipating Events

A basic task for scientific psychology is to explain why humans are active and why they direct their actions toward one goal versus another. In Kelly's time, the traditional way to explain such human capacities was in terms of "motives." Different motives presumably powered different forms of behavior. Kelly, as we noted, rejected the concept of motive. How, then, did he explain the direction of activity?

CURRENT APPLICATIONS

COGNITIVE COMPLEXITY, LEADERSHIP, AND INTERNATIONAL CRISES

Studies in the field of political psychology have related cognitive complexity—simplicity (an aspect of personality important to personal construct theory) to the behavior of political and governmental leaders. Findings have fascinating implications for politics, leadership, and international relations.

For example, would one suspect that greater or lesser cognitive complexity would be advantageous for a revolutionary leader? A study of successful and unsuccessful leaders of four revolutions (American, Russian, Chinese, Cuban) found that low cognitive complexity was associated with success during the phase of revolutionary struggle but high complexity was associated with success in the post-struggle consolidation phase. A categorical, single-minded approach appears desirable at first, but

Many Americans view George W. Bush as a strong leader who is able to deal well with crises, despite the fact that—or maybe because—his approach to problems can be characterized as low cognitive complexity.

a more complex, integrative style succeeds during the later phase. This may help to explain why revolutionary leaders sometimes fare poorly as leaders of post-revolutionary democratic governments.

Studies of international relations suggests that complexity of communications predicts the likelihood of war. War is less likely when diplomatic communications are of greater cognitive complexity. The complexity of Israeli and Arab speeches delivered to the United Nations General Assembly was significantly reduced prior to each of the four wars in the Middle East (1948, 1956, 1967, 1973). Communications between the United States and the Soviet Union were much less complex prior to the outbreak of the Korean War than prior to crises resolved without war, such as the Berlin blockade and the Cuban missile crisis. Indeed, if one examines transcripts (May & Zelikow, 1997) of communications among U.S. governmental officials during the Cuban missile crisis, and between U.S. and Soviet leaders at the time, one finds that President Kennedy's success in averting nuclear holocaust rested on an exceptionally cognitively complex and subtle analysis of military and diplomatic manoeuvres.

Other work relates cognitive complexity to political conservatism versus liberalism. More liberal views often are embraced by people higher in "integrative complexity." Integrative complexity is a term that the psychologist Philip Tetlock uses to describe the degree to which people differentiate among, and then cognitively integrative, multiple perspectives on issues. Someone who thinks in a single-minded way, focusing on only one or two big issues, would be low in integrative complexity. Reviews of large numbers of studies, conducted in many countries, indicate that people lower in complexity tend to hold politically conservative views (Jost et al., 2003, p. 353). The following quotation from the politically conservative U.S. president George W. Bush may be illustrative: "Look, my job isn't to try to nuance."

SOURCE: JOST, GLASER, KRUGLANSKI, & SULLOWAY, 2003; SUEDFELD & TETLOCK, 1991.

Kelly addressed this issue in what he termed the **fundamental postulate** of personal construct theory. According to this postulate, people's psychological processes are channeled by the ways in which they anticipate events. Kelly felt that the entire range of psychological outcomes that are of interest to the personality psychologist are shaped by people's anticipations of the future. People use their personal construct system to anticipate what the future will bring. Thus, the fundamental postulate links the structure aspects of Kelly's theory (the personal construct system) to ongoing dynamic processes.

In experiencing events, an individual observes similarities and contrasts, thereby developing constructs. On the basis of these constructs, individuals, like true scientists, anticipate the future. As we see the same events repeated over and over, we modify our constructs so that they will lead to more accurate predictions. Constructs are tested in terms of their predictive efficiency. But what accounts for the direction of behavior? Again, like the scientist, people choose the course of behavior that they believe offers the greatest opportunity for anticipating future events. Scientists try to develop better theories, theories that lead to the efficient prediction of events, and individuals try to develop better construct systems. Thus, according to Kelly, a person chooses the alternative that promises the greatest further development of the construct system.

In making a choice of a particular construct, the individual, in a sense, makes a bet by anticipating a particular event or set of events. If there are inconsistencies in the construct system, the bets will not add up; they will cancel each other out. If the system is consistent, a prediction is made that can be tested. If the anticipated event does occur, the prediction has been upheld and the construct validated, at least for the time being. If the anticipated event does not occur, the construct has been invalidated. In the latter case, the individual must develop a new construct or must loosen or expand the old construct to include the prediction of the event that took place.

In essence, then, individuals make predictions and consider further changes in their construct systems on the basis of whether those changes have led to accurate predictions. Notice that individuals do not seek reinforcement or the avoidance of pain; instead, they seek validation and expansion of their construct systems. If a person expects something unpleasant and that event occurs, he or she experiences validation regardless of the fact that it was a negative, unpleasant event. Indeed, a painful event may even be preferred to a neutral or pleasant event if it confirms the predictive system (Pervin, 1964).

One should understand that Kelly is not suggesting that the individual seeks certainty, such as would be found in the repetitive ticking of a clock. The boredom people feel with repeated events and the fatalism that comes as a result of the inevitable are usually avoided wherever possible. Rather, individuals seek to anticipate events and to increase the range of convenience or boundaries of their construct systems. This point leads to a distinction between the views of Kelly and the views of Rogers. According to Kelly, individuals do not seek consistency for consistency's sake or even for self-consistency. Instead, individuals seek to anticipate events, and it is a consistent system that allows them to do this.

Anxiety, Fear, and Threat

Thus far, Kelly's system appears to be reasonably simple and straightforward. The process view becomes more complicated with the introduction of the concepts of anxiety, fear, and threat. Kelly defined anxiety in the following way: **Anxiety** is the recognition that the events with which one is confronted lie outside the range of convenience of one's construct system. One is anxious when one is without constructs, when one has "lost his structural grip on events," when one is "caught with his constructs down." People protect themselves from anxiety in various ways. Confronted by events they cannot construe—that is, that lie outside their range of convenience—individuals may broaden a construct and permit it to apply to a greater variety of events, or they may narrow their constructs and focus on minute details. For example, suppose an individual who has the construct caring person/selfish person and considers herself a caring person finds herself acting in a selfish way. How can she construe herself and events? She can broaden the construct caring person to include selfish behavior, or probably more easily in this case restrict the construct caring person to important people in her life, rather than people generally. In the latter case, the construct applies to a more limited set of people or events.

In contrast to anxiety, one experiences **fear** when a new construct appears to be about to enter the construct system. Of even greater significance is

Encountering people from different cultures is an experience that may expand one's construct system.

the experience of threat. **Threat** is defined as the awareness of imminent comprehensive change in one's core structure. A person feels threatened when a major shakeup in the construct system is about to occur. One feels threatened by death if it is perceived as imminent and if it involves a drastic change in one's core constructs. Death is not threatening when it does not seem imminent or when it is not construed as being fundamental to the meaning of one's life.

Threat, in particular, has a wide range of ramifications. Whenever people undertake some new activity, they expose themselves to confusion and threat. Individuals experience threat when they realize that their construct system is about to be drastically affected by what has been discovered. "This is the moment of threat. It is the threshold between confusion and certainty, between anxiety and boredom. It is precisely at this moment when we are most tempted to turn back" (Kelly, 1964, p. 141). The response to threat may be to give up the adventure to regress to old constructs to avoid panic. Threat occurs as we venture into human understanding and when we stand on the brink of a profound change in ourselves.

Threat, the awareness of imminent comprehensive change in one's core structure, can be experienced in relation to many things. Consider, for example, the experience of music majors who are going to perform before a music jury that will determine whether they pass for the semester. To what extent can they be expected to experience threat associated with the possibility of failure? Why should some music majors experience more performance anxiety than others? Following Kelly, two psychologists tested the hypothesis that students would feel threatened by the possibility of failure by a music jury to the extent that such failure implied reorganization of the self-construal component of their construct system. To test this hypothesis, at the beginning of the semester, music majors were administered a Threat Index consisting of 40 core constructs (e.g., competent/incompetent, productive/unproductive, bad/good) in relation to which they first rated the self and then the self-if-performed-poorly on the jury. The Threat Index score consisted of the number of core constructs on which the self and self-if-performed-poorly were rated on opposite poles. Anxiety was measured through the use of a questionnaire at the beginning of the semester and three days before the onset of the music juries. Consistent with personal construct theory, those students who reported that failure on the jury would result in the most comprehensive change in self-construal were also those who reported the greatest increase in anxiety as the date of the jury approached (Tobacyk & Downs, 1986).

Unfortunately, the investigators in this study used the concept of anxiety in a way that was not necessarily consistent with Kelly's views. Even more significant, what was not studied in this case was the experiences of students anticipating the possibility of performing much better before the jury than would be expected on the basis of their self-construal; that is, would comprehensive change as a result of unexpected exceptional performance also be associated with threat? This is important since in Kelly's view it is the awareness of imminent comprehensive change in the construct system that is threatening, not failure per se.

Some personal construct psychologists have focused their research attention on attitudes toward death, both in terms of the ways in which death is construed and the amount of threat associated with death (Moore & Neimeyer, 1991; Neimeyer, 1994). In terms of how death is construed, research suggests that people use constructs such as purposeful/purposeless, positive/negative, acceptance/rejection, anticipated/unanticipated, and final/afterlife. In terms of the amount of threat associated with death, research has involved measurement of the discrepancy between the ways in which individuals construe themselves and the ways in which they construe death. In other words, in personal construct theory terms, death threat is high when the person is unable to construe death as relevant to the self. As measured by the Threat Index, individuals rate themselves and their own death on constructs such as healthy/sick, strong/weak, predictable/random, and useful/useless. An individual's threat score represents the difference between the two sets of ratings. Presumably in the case of a large self/death discrepancy, interpretation of the death construct as relevant to the self would involve comprehensive change in one's construct system. Death threat, as defined in this way, has been found to be lower in hospice patients than general hospital patients, lower in individuals open to feelings as opposed to those who repress feelings, and lower in self-actualizing individuals as opposed to individuals less oriented toward growth and self-actualization.

What makes the concepts of anxiety, fear, and threat so significant is that they suggest a new dimension to Kelly's view of human functioning. The dynamics of functioning can now be seen to involve the interplay between the individual's wish to expand the construct system and the desire to avoid the threat of disruption of that system. Individuals always seek to maintain and enhance their predictive systems. However, in the face of anxiety and threat, individuals may rigidly adhere to a constricted system instead of venturing out into the risky realm of expansion of their construct systems.

To summarize the process aspects of personal construct theory, Kelly assumes an active organism, and he does not posit any motivational forces. For Kelly, people behave as scientists in construing events, in making predictions, and in seeking expansion of the construct system. Sometimes, not unlike the scientist, we are made so anxious by the unknowns and so threatened by the unfamiliar that we seek to hold on to absolute truths and become dogmatic. On the other hand, when we are behaving as good scientists, we are able to adopt

Development of the Construct System. Being exposed to many stimuli facilitates development of the construct system. Aware of this, some parents try to develop "superbabies."

the invitational mood and to expose our construct systems to the diversity of events that make up life.

GROWTH AND DEVELOPMENT

No personality theory is completely comprehensive. All have areas in which they are less fully developed than would be ideal. An area in which personal construct theory is not fully developed is its treatment of growth and development.

Kelly was never explicit about the origins of construct systems. He stated that constructs are derived from observing repeated patterns of events. But he did little to elaborate on the kinds of events that lead to differences like the ones between simple and complex construct systems. Kelly's comments relating to growth and development thus are limited. He emphasizes the development of preverbal constructs in infancy and the interpretation of culture as involving a process of learned expectations. People belong to the same cultural group in that they share certain ways of construing events and have the same kinds of expectations regarding behavior.

Developmental research associated with personal construct theory generally has emphasized two kinds of change. First, there has been exploration of increases in complexity of the construct system associated with age (Crockett, 1982; Hayden, 1982; Loevinger, 1993). Second, there has been exploration of qualitative changes in the nature of the constructs formed and in the ability of children to be more empathic or aware of the construct systems of others (Adams-Webber, 1982; Donahue, 1994; Morrison & Cometa, 1982; Sigel, 1981). In terms of construct system complexity, there is evidence that as children develop they increase the number of constructs available to them, make finer differentiations, and show more hierarchical organization or integration. In terms of empathy, there is evidence that as children develop they become increasingly aware that many events are not related to the self and increasingly able to appreciate the constructs of others (Sigel, 1981).

Two studies have been reported that are relevant to the question of the determinants of complex cognitive structures. In one study, the subjects' level of cognitive complexity was found to be related to the variety of cultural backgrounds to which they had been exposed in childhood (Sechrest & Jackson, 1961). In another study, parents of cognitively complex children were found to be more likely to grant autonomy and less likely to be authoritarian than were the parents of children low in cognitive complexity (Cross, 1966). Presumably, the opportunity to examine many different events and to have many different experiences is conducive to the development of a complex structure. One would also expect to find that children who experience a long-standing and severe threat from authoritarian parents would develop constricted and inflexible construct systems.

The question of factors determining the content of constructs and the complexity of construct systems is of critical importance. In particular, it is relevant to the field of education, since a part of education appears to be the development of complex, flexible, and adaptive construct systems. Unfortunately, Kelly himself made few statements in this area. Kelly's theory simply did not treat questions of development as thoroughly as would have been ideal. Relatively little contemporary research on personality development is directly guided by the postulates of personal construct theory.

PSYCHOPATHOLOGY

Although Kelly's analysis of development may have been insufficiently developed, the same cannot be said for his treatment of psychopathology. Kelly devoted volume 2 of his monumental 1955 volume to clinical applications of personal construct theory.

According to Kelly, psychopathology is a disordered response to anxiety. As in the theories of Freud and Rogers, the concepts of anxiety, fear, and threat play a major role in Kelly's theory of psychopathology. However, these concepts, although retained, were redefined in personal construct theory. For Kelly, psychopathology is defined in terms of disordered functioning of a construct system. The person-as-scientist metaphor remains relevant here. Only a poor scientist retains a theory and makes the same predictions despite repeated research failures. Similarly, only a poorly functioning person retains his or her construct system, unchanged, if it repeatedly yields incorrect predictions.

At the root of such rigid adherence to a construct system are feelings of anxiety, fear, and threat. Kelly stated that one could construe human behavior as being directed away from ultimate anxiety. Psychological disorders are disorders involving anxiety and faulty efforts to reestablish the sense of being able to anticipate events:

> There is a sense in which all disorders of communication are disorders
> involving anxiety. A "neurotic" person casts about frantically for new
> ways of construing the events of his world. Sometimes he works on
> "little" events, sometimes on "big" events, but he is always fighting off

anxiety. A "psychotic" person appears to have found some temporary solution for his anxiety. But it is a precarious solution, at best, and must be sustained in the face of evidence which, for most of us, would be invalidating.

SOURCE: KELLY, 1955, pp. 895–896.

Fundamental to Kelly's view of psychopathology, then, are people's efforts to avoid anxiety (the experience that one's construct system is not applicable to events) and to avoid threat (the awareness of imminent comprehensive change in the construct system). To protect against anxiety and threat, an individual employs protective devices. This view resembles that of Freud. Indeed, Kelly suggested that in the face of anxiety, individuals may act in ways that will make their constructs unavailable for verbalization, that is, not consciously available. Thus, for example, in the face of anxiety, individuals may submerge one end of a construct or suspend elements that do not fit well into a construct. These are responses to anxiety that seem very similar to the concept of repression.

CHANGE AND FIXED-ROLE THERAPY

In personal construct theory, the target of change is the client's personal construct system. Therapists try to foster the development of better construct systems. If the continued use of invalid constructs is pathological, then psychotherapy is the process of helping clients to improve their predictions by developing better constructs. One strives to make the client a better scientist. Psychotherapy is a process, then, of reconstructing the construct system. Some constructs are replaced, some new ones added, some are tightened, others loosened, some made more permeable, others less permeable.

How does one do this? Kelly developed a specific technique called **fixed-role therapy**. The goal of fixed-role therapy is to enable clients to think about themselves in new ways. The therapist wants clients to behave in new ways, to construe themselves in new ways, and thereby to become new people. One technique for accomplishing this goal is the use of a personality sketch. In therapy, after establishing a basic understanding of the client, a psychologist or team of psychologists writes a sketch of a new person, an alternative type of person that the client can "try out" as a way of expanding his or her construct system. After the personality sketch is drawn up, it is presented to the client. The client decides whether the sketch sounds like someone he would like to know, and whether he would feel comfortable with such a person. This is done to ensure that the new personality will not be excessively threatening to the client. In the next phase of fixed-role therapy, the therapist invites the client to act as if he were that person. For about two weeks, the client is asked to forget who he is and to be this other person. If the new person is called Tom Jones, then the client is told the following: "For two weeks, try to forget who you are or that you ever were. You are Tom Jones. You act like him. You think like him. You talk to your friends the way you think he would talk. You do the things you think he would do. You even have his interests and you enjoy the things he would enjoy." The client may resist, he may feel that this is playacting and that it is hypocritical, but he is encouraged, in an accepting manner, to try it and see how it works. The client is not told that this is what he should eventually be, but he is asked to assume the new personality. He is asked to give up being himself temporarily so that he can discover himself.

*Fixed-Role Therapy. In Kelly's fixed-role therapy clients are encouraged to behave
and represent themselves in new ways. Drawing by Lippman; Copyright © 1972 The
New Yorker Magazine, Inc.*

During the following weeks, the client eats, sleeps, and feels the role.
Periodically, he meets with the therapist to discuss problems in acting
the role. There may be some rehearsing of the personality sketch in the
therapy session so that the therapist and client will have a chance to
examine the functioning of the new construct system when it is actually
in use. The therapist must be prepared to act as if he or she were various
persons and to accept the invitational mood. The therapist must at every
moment "play in strong support of an actor the client who is continually
fumbling his lines and contaminating his role."

SOURCE: KELLY, 1955, p. 399

   Many characteristics in the sketch contrast sharply with the person's current
functioning; Kelly suggested that it might be easier for people to play up what
they believe to be the opposite of the way they generally behave than to behave
just a little bit differently. Behaving in accord with the sketch is thought to
set in motion processes that will have effects throughout the construct system.
Fixed-role therapy, then, does not aim at the readjustment of minor parts of
personality. Instead, it aims thoroughly to reconstruct a personality. It does so
by offering a new role, a new personality, that the client can try out in the safe
setting of therapy.

   Fixed-role therapy was not the only therapeutic technique discussed or used
by Kelly (Bieri, 1986). However, it is one that is particularly associated with
personal construct theory, and it does exemplify some of the principles of the
personal construct theory of change. The goal of therapeutic change is the
individual's reconstruction of the self. The individual drops some constructs,

creates new ones, does some tightening and loosening, and develops a construct system that leads to more accurate predictions. The therapist encourages the client to make believe, to experiment, to spell out alternatives, and to reconstrue the past in the light of new constructs. The process of therapy is complex. Different clients must be treated differently, and the resistance to change must be overcome. However, positive change is possible in a situation where a good director assists in the playing of the human drama or a good teacher assists in the development of a creative scientist.

THE CASE OF JIM   **Rep Test: Personal Construct Theory**

Jim took the group form of Kelly's Rep test separately from the other tests (Figure 11.2). Here we have a test that is structured in terms of the roles given to the subject and the task of formulating a similarity-contrast construct. However, the subject is given total freedom in the content of the construct formed. As noted previously in this chapter,

CONSTRUCT	CONTRAST
Self-satisfied	Self-doubting
Uninterested in communicating with students as people	Interested in communicating with students as people
Nice	Obnoxious
Sensitive to cues from other people	Insensitive to cues
Outgoing–gregarious	Introverted–retiring
Introspective–hung up	Self-satisfied
Intellectually dynamic	Mundane and predictable
Outstanding, successful	Mediocre
Obnoxious	Very likable
Satisfied with life	Unhappy
Shy, unsure of self	Self-confident
Worldly, openminded	Parochial, closeminded
Open, simple to understand	Complex, hard to get to know
Capable of giving great love	Somewhat self-oriented
Self-sufficient	Needs other people
Concerned with others	Oblivious to all but his own interests
So hung up that psychological health is questionable	Basically healthy and stable
Willing to hurt people in order to be "objective"	Unwilling to hurt people if he can help it
Closeminded, conservative	Openminded, liberal
Lacking in self-confidence	Self-confident
Sensitive	Insensitive, self-centered
Lacking social poise	Secure and socially poised
Bright, articulate	Average intelligence

Figure 11.2 *Rep Test Data—Case of Jim.*

the Rep test is derived logically from Kelly's theory of personal constructs. Two major themes appear in these constructs. The first theme is the quality of interpersonal relationships. Basically this involves whether people are warm and giving or cold and narcissistic. This theme is expressed in constructs such as gives love/is self-oriented, sensitive/insensitive, and communicates with others as people/is uninterested in others. A second major theme concerns security and is expressed in constructs such as hung up/healthy, unsure/self-confident, and satisfied with life/unhappy. The frequency with which constructs relevant to these two themes appear suggests that Jim has a relatively constricted view of the world—that is, much of Jim's understanding of events is in terms of the warm/cold and secure/insecure dimensions.

How do the constructs given relate to specific people? On the sorts that involved himself, Jim used constructs expressing insecurity. Thus, Jim views himself as being like his sister (so hung up that her psychological health is questionable), in contrast to his brother, who is basically healthy and stable. In two other sorts of constructs, he sees himself as lacking self-confidence and social poise. These ways of construing himself contrast with those involving his father. His father is construed as being introverted and retiring, but also as self-sufficient, open-minded, outstanding, and successful.

The constructs used in relation to Jim's mother are interesting and again suggest conflict. On the one hand, his mother is construed to be outgoing, gregarious, and loving; on the other, she is construed to be mundane, predictable, close-minded, and conservative. The close-minded, conservative construct is particularly interesting since, in that sort, Jim's mother is paired with the person with whom he feels most uncomfortable. Thus, the mother and the person with whom he feels most uncomfortable are contrasted with his father, who is construed to be open-minded and liberal. The combination of sorts for all persons suggests that Jim's ideal person is someone who is warm, sensitive, secure, intelligent, open-minded, and successful. The women in his life—his mother, sister, girlfriend, and previous girlfriend—are construed as having some of these characteristics but also as missing others.

Comments on the Data

The Rep test gives us valuable data about how Jim construes his environment. Jim's world tends to be perceived in terms of two major constructs: warm interpersonal/cold interpersonal relationships and secure, confident/insecure, unhappy people. Through the Rep test we gain an understanding of why Jim is so limited in his relationships to others and why he has so much difficulty in being creative. His restriction to only two constructs hardly leaves him free to relate to people as individuals and instead forces him to perceive people and problems in stereotyped or conventional ways. A world filled with so little perceived diversity can hardly be exciting, and the constant threat of insensitivity and rejection can be expected to fill Jim with a sense of gloom.

The data from the Rep test, like Kelly's theory, are tantalizing. What is there seems so clear and valuable, but one is left wondering about what is missing. There is a sense of the skeleton for the structure of personality, but one is left with only the bones. Jim's ways of construing himself and his environment are an important part of his personality. Assessing his constructs and his construct system helps us to understand how he interprets events and how he is led to predict the future. But where is the flesh on the bones—the sense of an individual who cannot be what he feels, the person struggling to be warm amid feelings of hostility and struggling to relate to women although confused about his feelings toward them?

RELATED POINTS OF VIEW AND RECENT DEVELOPMENTS

Psychology is different today than it was in Kelly's time. In his day, Kelly's emphasis on human cognitive processes was radical. Today, such an emphasis is mainstream. It is in this sense that Kelly anticipated future developments in the field. As we will see in the next chapter, contemporary social-cognitive approaches to personality embrace many of the same assumptions about human nature that are found in personal construct theory.

Although Kelly's theory attracted considerable attention when it was presented in 1955, it differed so greatly from the field's traditions that it spawned little research in the following decade. It was only in later years that many leads suggested by personal construct theory were explored (Neimeyer & Neimeyer, 1992). A major focus has been the Rep test and the structure of construct systems. Studies of the reliability of the Rep test suggest that the responses of individuals to the role title list and constructs used are reasonably stable over time (Landfield, 1971). Beyond this the Rep test has been used to study a variety of individuals with psychological problems, the construct systems of married couples, and people with varied interpersonal relationships (Duck, 1982). Modifications of the Rep test have been used to study the structural complexity of construct systems, the perception of situations, and, as noted, the use of nonverbal constructs. Almost every aspect of Kelly's theory has received at least some study (Mancuso & Adams-Webber, 1982). The organization of the construct system and changes in this organization associated with development are particularly noteworthy topics (Crockett, 1982). The developmental principles emphasized suggest many similarities in the developmental theories of Kelly and Piaget: (1) an emphasis on progression from a global, undifferentiated system to a differentiated, integrated one; (2) increasing use of abstract structures to handle more information more economically; (3) development in response to efforts to accommodate new elements in the cognitive system; and (4) development of the cognitive system as a system, as opposed to a simple addition of new parts or elements.

Other relevant research has roots in Kelly's personal construct theory, although it is conducted within the framework of more contemporary approaches to personality (Chapters 12 and 13). For example, the psychologist Tory Higgins (1999) has developed an approach to cognitive constructs and personality functioning that is highly compatible with Kelly's, and the social-cognitive theorist Walter Mischel has directly extended Kelly's analysis of encoding constructs as a core feature of personality (Chapter 12). Other investigators have recently considered a question to which Kelly devoted relatively little attention, namely, the possibility of cultural differences in the constructs used and how constructs are formed (Chapter 14). These contemporary developments relate to personal construct theory, but only in an indirect way.

The contemporary personality psychologist has, at his or her disposal, a battery of findings, theoretical concepts, and research methods in the study of human cognition that were unavailable to Kelly. Contemporary investigators commonly use these tools to analyze precisely the same phenomena that interested Kelly. Yet they rarely do so by using the precise terms and theoretical formulations of personal construct theory. Even though Kelly remains an extraordinarily respected figure, today the details of his theory often are viewed as expendable precisely as Kelly himself might have anticipated.

CONTEMPORARY ANALYSES OF PERSON-SITUATION BELIEFS

One illustration of this point is found in contemporary analyses of person-situation beliefs, where current research is highly compatible with the principles of personal construct theory, even though it is not directly guided by the precise ideas formulated by Kelly.

As you will recall from our coverage of the Rep test, Kelly was interested in capturing the ways in which people's beliefs come into play as they think about particular people who are significant to them. The idea is that it is not sufficient to study the person's beliefs in a manner that is isolated from life contexts. Personal constructs do not merely "sit in the head." They are used to make sense of the social world. Kelly explored the ways in which people use personal constructs to categorize the persons and relationships of their lives.

A similar emphasis is seen in contemporary research on relationship schemas. A *schema* is an elaborate body of knowledge about a person or thing. People use such knowledge to make judgments, quickly and efficiently, about ongoing events. For example, if you spend a lot of time listening to contemporary music, you may have an elaborate body of knowledge about musicians, bands, and musical styles—you have a "music schema." Using this schema, you can quickly make decisions about music (whether you like a particular band, a particular song, etc.). As studied in particular by Mark Baldwin (1999), a relationship schema, then, is a well-developed belief about interpersonal relationships. A relationship schema is an integration of different types of knowledge. People mentally integrate knowledge about themselves, knowledge about other people or types of people (parents, teachers, romantic partners, etc.), and knowledge about social settings (family get-togethers, classes, dates, etc.) into coherent bodies of knowledge. This integrated body of knowledge—the relationships schema—then guides people's anticipations of future events. Recent findings indicate that relationship schemas influence people's expectancies about interpersonal relationships, and that these expectancies influence people's thoughts and feelings in social encounters (Baldwin, 1999) precisely as Kelly would have predicted.

Other recent work has explored a particular feature of people's overall construct system, namely, the degree to which a person's knowledge is highly integrated versus compartmentalized. This line of research focuses on people's constructs about themselves and whether these constructs are evaluated as positive or negative (i.e., good or bad). Everybody recognizes that there are both positive and negative features to their personality. But, as analyzed by Carolin Showers (2002), people differ in the degree to which constructs representing these features are grouped together, or compartmentalized. As Showers illustrates (Table 11.2), some people group together their positive features, seeing them as

Table 11.2   Examples of Compartmentalized Organization ("Harry") and Integrative Organization ("Sally") for
Identical Items of Information about Self as Student

"Harry": Compartmentalized organization		"Sally": Integrative organization	
Renaissance scholar (+)	*Taking tests, grades (−)*	*Humanities classes (+/−)*	*Science classes (+/−)*
+ Curious	− Worrying	+ Creative	+ Disciplined
+ Disciplined	− Tense	− Insecure	+ Analytical
+ Motivated	− Distracted	+ Motivated	− Competitive
+ Creative	− Insecure	− Distracted	− Worrying
+ Analytical	− Competitive	+ Expressive	+ Curious
+ Expressive	− Moody	− Moody	− Tense

NOTE: A positive or negative valence is indicated for each category and each item. The symbol
+/− denotes a mixed-valence category.
SOURCE: Adapted from Showers (1992a). Copyright © 1992 by the American Psychological
Association. Adapted by permission.

separate from negative aspects of self. "Harry" (Table 11.2) associated positive
constructs with his "Renaissance scholar" self and negative constructs with his
self-as-test-taker. "Sally," in contrast, views herself in terms of a mix of positive
and negative constructs in different social settings. Research suggests that different types of compartmentalization have different implications for people's
emotional experiences. Importantly, the effects here are not simple ones. It is
not the case that people who show high versus low degrees of compartmentalization are, in general, significantly happier or sadder than others. Instead there
is an interaction between features of the personal construct system and features of the environment. When people encounter situations that bring to mind
positive features of the self, individuals who compartmentalize their constructs
experience more positive moods. It appears that, since positive features of self
are grouped together, thoughts about one positive aspect of self activate other
positive thoughts, lifting people's mood. However, when people encounter
situations that bring to mind negative features of self, then individuals who do
not compartmentalize have more positive (or perhaps less negative) emotional
experiences. In these negative situations, an integrated organization of positive
and negative constructs (as shown by "Sally," Table 11.2) is beneficial because
negative thoughts are associated with positive constructs that serve to protect
one against extremely negative emotional experiences (Showers, 2002).

   Research such as that of Baldwin (1999) and Showers (2002) explores the
psychological processes of interest to Kelly. The nature and organization
of people's personal constructs are found to explain significant features of
personality functioning. In this regard, the results can be seen as supporting
personal construct theory. Yet this contemporary research is not grounded in
personal construct theory. These contemporary scientists, in other words, do
not turn specifically to Kelly's theorizing as a basis for their research. (Indeed,
they do not find it necessary even to refer to Kelly's theory in the papers that
we have cited here.) Instead, reflecting developments in the contemporary
field, they ground their research in social-cognitive analyses of personality
functioning analyses to which we turn in our subsequent chapters.

SCIENTIFIC OBSERVATION: THE DATABASE

How does Kelly's theory fare on the five criteria with which we have been evaluating the theories of personality? On criterion #1, scientific observations, Kelly fares well. As a clinician, his observations included detailed, in-depth analyses of the sort one associated with theorists such as Freud and Rogers. Yet, as a person who developed a testing instrument, the Rep test, he succeeded in providing a reliable, objective means of assessing the personality attributes of the individual. The Rep test is particularly noteworthy in that it fit his theory ideally. By the standards of mid-20th century psychology, then, Kelly's database of scientific observations was quite admirable.

By contemporary standards, however, Kelly's database seems limited. His observations of personality did not thoroughly include cultural diversity; he did his work exclusively within a North American culture (the United States). He did not have at his disposal a diversity of methodological tools, such as the reaction-time techniques and priming techniques employed by social-cognitive psychologists who share Kelly's interest in construct systems and personality (Chapters 12–13). One can hardly blame Kelly for failing to invoke research procedures that developed only after his time. Nonetheless, by contemporary standards Kelly's scientific database is lacking in diversity.

THEORY: SYSTEMATIC?

Personal construct theory is highly systematic. Kelly was a careful theorist. He composed his theoretical writing in a logical, formal style. Personal construct theory features a well-specified series of theoretical postulates and associated corollaries. By constructing his theory in this formal style, Kelly was able coherently to relate each element of his theory to his overall conceptual framework.

Kelly did have one advantage compared to most other personality theorists. It is that he presented his entire theory at one point in time, in one place: his 1955 volume. It is easier to achieve systematic coherence in one's career contributions if all those contributions are made within one book, rather than being expressed in a series of books and papers written over a long period of time, during which one's theoretical views may shift.

THEORY: TESTABLE?

Kelly took two key steps that make his theory testable. He defined the terms of personal construct theory quite precisely. Second, he developed an objective assessment procedure that perfectly matched the theory: the Rep test. By combining theoretical precision with objective measurement, one can derive and test numerous theory-based predictions: that variations in cognitive complexity will correlate with the accuracy of social predictions, that anxiety will result when events fall outside one's construct system, that fixed-role therapy will foster the development of new constructs in clients, and so forth.

Nonetheless, Kelly's work also contains central features that are not open to test. Imagine that you went up to Kelly and said that "I don't think people are like scientists" or "I don't believe that psychological processes are channeled by the way people anticipate events" or "I don't believe in constructive alternativism as a general principle of human psychology." It is hard to imagine that Kelly would think that these disagreements, which involve bedrock features of personal construct theory, could be resolved by empirical test. These challenges do not involve testable predictions but, instead, theoretical *assumptions*. Kelly makes certain assumptions about personality, states them as basic premises and postulates, and then builds his theory logically from those premises. This, of course, is true of all theorists. For example, for Freud the idea that the mind is an energy system was an assumption, not a conclusion based on systematic data and not, in and of itself, a testable prediction. Kelly's theory, then, is not unique in resting on theoretical assumptions that are not open to direct test. However, in Kelly's case the number and range of such assumptions seem particularly significant. One can imagine reformulating psychoanalytic theory while dropping the assumption that the mind is an energy system (Erdelyi, 1985). But if one dropped the assumption that psychological processes are channeled by the way people anticipate events, or the assumption that people can engage in constructive alternativism, one would no longer have anything that resembled personal construct theory. The untestable assumptions are particularly significant in Kelly's work.

THEORY: COMPREHENSIVE?

If one accepts the fundamental postulate of Kelly's theory, that all psychological processes are channeled by the ways in which people anticipate events, then Kelly's theory is seen as comprehensive. In principle, the theory applies to all circumstances in which people use their personal constructs to anticipate events—and this, to Kelly, is essentially all the circumstances of interest to the personality psychologist.

However, if one questions the fundamental postulate rather than merely accepting it on faith, then personality construct theory appears to lack comprehensiveness. It provides a wonderful portrait of those circumstances in which people act "like scientists." But what about other circumstances, in which people act like members of a crazed mob, or like drunks, or like irrational love-struck Romeos and Juliets? An early reviewer of Kelly's work suggested that "I rather suspect that when some people get angry or inspired or in love, they couldn't care less about their [personal construct] systems as a whole! One gets the impression that the author is, in his personality theory, overreacting against a generation of irrationalism" (Bruner, 1956, p. 356).

There are additional ways in which Kelly's work is less comprehensive than some other theories presented in our text. The process aspects of the theory are not as well specified as would be ideal. For example, how does the individual know which construct will be the best predictor? How does one know which end of the construct (similarity or contrast) to use? There is less discussion of personality growth and development than would be optimal; in an ideal world, Kelly would have specified and tested ideas about how, through the course of child development, people acquire one versus another type of construct system. There is relatively little discussion of emotions by Kelly, though some subsequent personal construct theorists have addressed this shortcoming (McCoy, 1981). A particular limitation, with regard to emotions, is that Kelly primarily takes a unidirectional view of personal constructs and emotion;

his theory explains how personal constructs influence emotional experience but says little about how emotions influence the personal constructs that come to mind for the individual at a given point in time. Contemporary research documents the importance of this "other direction," in which emotional states influence cognitive contents and processes (Forgas, 1995).

Finally, there is a limitation we saw in the work of Rogers, whose theoretical approach is similar to that of Kelly in significant ways. Like Rogers, Kelly tells us more about humans as cognitive and social beings than as biological beings. Questions of evolution, genetics, and inherited individual differences in temperament receive far less attention than is required for a truly comprehensive theory of persons. Contemporary developments in the study of biology and mind, for example, would force significant expansions of, and probably alterations in, personal construct theory. For example, one recent development is the study of "embodied" cognition (Lakoff & Johnson, 1999; Niedenthal, Barsalou, Winkielman, Krauth-Gruber and Ric, 2005). The idea is that conceptual processes such as reasoning, categorization, and judgment (what Kelly called "construing") are not carried out by one single cognitive system (what Kelly called the personal construct system). Instead, a number of distinct systems are involved, especially those systems that also are involved in perception. A model that is referred to as a "perceptual symbols systems" approach (Barsalou, Simmons, Barbey, & Wilson, 2003) indicates how different mental structures, involving different modalities (auditory, motoric, visual), contribute to cognitive processing. The role of these perceptual systems is apparent from the perceptual metaphors that we use even when thinking about objects and events that do not literally have the perceptual qualities. Some of these metaphors involve the idea of perceiving objects in three-dimensional space. When we reason abstractly via metaphors such as "in" and "out" (e.g., "Bush is *in* the Republican party") or "in front" and "behind" ("Business leaders are *behind* Bush's efforts"), concepts about physical containers and about objects being in front of another from the perspective of our position in visual space are used to reason conceptually. Other common perceptual metaphors involve taste ("Bush's victory was a *bitter* blow to liberals"), smell ("Bush's foreign policy *stinks*"), or the whole body (e.g., "The Congressman's moral *slips* caused him to *fall* from power," where bodily falling is a metaphor for construing moral lapses). These embodied aspects of personal constructs seem central to human reasoning, but receive scant attention in personal construct theory.

APPLICATIONS

Applications are a strong point for personal construct theory. Like Freud and Rogers, Kelly was a clinical psychologist. He based his theorizing on clinical experience and accompanied his theory of personality with detailed principles for conducting theory. He developed an objective personality assessment method that, in principle, can be used whenever the applied psychologist wishes to predict individual differences in some psychological outcome. (We say "in principle" only because Kelly's Rep has been used in such applications much less frequently than have methods based on the trait theories of personality.)

As we noted above, the entire second volume of Kelly's (1955) main published work, *The Psychology of Personal Constructs,* is devoted to therapeutic applications of his theoretical system. Kelly, then, deserves high marks for

Kelly at a Glance

Structure	Process	Growth and Development
Constructs	Processes channelized by anticipation of events	Increased complexity and definition to construct system

translating theory to practice. Indeed, one's sense from reading Kelly's work is that his theoretical efforts were fundamentally motivated by, and thus in the service of, an applied goal: enabling people to improve their lives by reconstruing their circumstances.

MAJOR CONTRIBUTIONS AND SUMMARY

Kelly's structural model of personality was a significant contribution to personality theory. Soon after its publication, Bruner (1956) called personal construct theory the single greatest contribution of the decade between 1945 and 1955 to the theory of personality functioning. Kelly displayed exceptional imagination and boldness in forging a theory that was so *un*like the behavioristic and psychodynamic perspectives that dominated psychology in his day. For this, Kelly is to be applauded.

In the decades after Kelly presented the theory, however, his perspective did not develop and flourish to quite the degree one might have expected. Some suggested that progress was retarded by reverence to Kelly, insularity, and orthodoxy (Rosenberg, 1980; Schneider, 1982). As noted by a follower of Kelly, without new ideas no theory of personality can survive (Sechrest, 1977). By the late 1980s, a review concluded that, except among a group of enthusiasts, Kelly's ideas often were neglected (Jankowicz, 1987). This was less true in England, where Kelly's ideas are widely known and are part of the training of most clinicians. However, in the United States, the high respect accorded to Kelly's ideas by those who know them well is not matched by a high degree of overall attention and impact on the field (Winter, 1992). In the contemporary field, Kelly's biggest impact it indirect. His work significantly contributed to the thinking of social-cognitive theorists, whose contributions are discussed in the two chapters ahead.

In sum, personal construct theory has both strengths and limitations (Table 11.3). On the positive side, there is the following: (1) The theory makes a significant contribution by bringing to the forefront of personality the importance of cognition and construct systems. (2) It is an approach to personality that attempts to capture both the uniqueness of the individual and the lawfulness of people generally. (3) It has developed a new, interesting, and theoretically relevant assessment technique, the Rep test. On the negative side, there is the following: (1) The theory shows relative neglect of certain important areas, especially development. (2) It has remained outside of mainstream research relating work in cognitive psychology to personality. Many of these approaches give lip service to Kelly's contributions but proceed along independent lines.

Pathology	Change
Disordered functioning of the construct system	Psychological reconstruction of life; invitational mood; fixed-role therapy.

Table 11.3   Summary of Strengths and Limitations of Personal Construct Theory

Strengths	Limitations
1. Places emphasis on cognitive processes as a central aspect of personality.	1. Has not led to research that *extends* the theory.
2. Presents a model of personality that provides for both the lawfulness of general personality functioning and the uniqueness of individual construct systems.	2. Leaves out or makes minimal contributions to our understanding of some significant aspects of personality (growth and development, emotions).
3. Includes a theory-related technique for personality assessment and research (Rep test).	3. Is not as yet connected with more general research and theory in cognitive psychology.

MAJOR CONCEPTS

Anxiety   An emotion expressing a sense of impending threat or danger. In Kelly's personal construct theory, anxiety occurs when the person recognizes that his or her construct system does not apply to the events being perceived.

Cognitive complexity/simplicity   An aspect of a person's cognitive functioning that is defined at one end by the use of many constructs with many relationships to one another (complexity) and at the other end by the use of few constructs with limited relationships to one another (simplicity).

Construct   In Kelly's theory, a way of perceiving, construing, or interpreting events.

Constructive alternativism   Kelly's view that there is no objective reality or absolute truth, but only alternative ways of construing events.

Contrast pole   In Kelly's personal construct theory, the contrast pole of a construct is defined by the way in which a third element is perceived as different from two other elements that are used to form a similarity pole.

Core construct   In Kelly's personal construct theory, a construct that is basic to the person's construct system and cannot be altered without serious consequences for the rest of the system.

Fear   In Kelly's personal construct theory, fear occurs when a new construct is about to enter the person's construct system.

Fixed-role therapy   Kelly's therapeutic technique that makes use of scripts or roles for people to try out, thereby encouraging people to behave in new ways and to perceive themselves in new ways.

Focus of convenience   In Kelly's personal construct theory, those events or phenomena that are best covered by a construct or by the construct system.

Fundamental postulate   (of Kelly's personal construct theory) The postulate that all psychological processes of interest to the personality psychologist are shaped, or channeled, by the individual's anticipation of events.

Peripheral construct   In Kelly's personal construct theory, a construct that is not basic to the construct system and can be altered without serious consequences for the rest of the system.

Person-as-scientist Kelly's metaphor for conceptualizing persons; the metaphor emphasizes that a central feature of everyday personality functioning is analogous to a central feature of science, namely, using constructs to understand and predict events.

Preverbal construct In Kelly's personal construct theory, a construct that is used but cannot be expressed in words.

Range of convenience In Kelly's personal construct theory, those events or phenomena that are covered by a construct or by the construct system.

Role Construct Repertory Test (Rep test) Kelly's test to determine the constructs used by a person, the relationships among constructs, and how the constructs are applied to specific people.

Similarity pole In Kelly's personal construct theory, the similarity pole of a construct is defined by the way in which two elements are perceived to be similar.

Submerged construct In Kelly's personal construct theory, a construct that once could be expressed in words, but now either one or both poles of the construct cannot be verbalized.

Subordinate construct In Kelly's personal construct theory, a construct that is lower in the construct system and is thereby included in the context of another (superordinate) construct.

Superordinate construct In Kelly's personal construct theory, a construct that is higher in the construct system and thereby includes other constructs within its context.

Threat In Kelly's personal construct theory, threat occurs when the person is aware of an imminent, comprehensive change in his or her construct system.

Verbal construct In Kelly's personal construct theory, a construct that can be expressed in words.

REVIEW

1. The personal construct theory of George Kelly emphasizes the way in which the person construes or interprets events. Kelly viewed the person as a scientist—an observer of events who formulates concepts or constructs to organize phenomena and uses these constructs to predict the future. People always are free to reconstrue events.

2. Kelly viewed personality in terms of the person's construct system—the types of constructs the person formed and how they were organized. Constructs are formed on the basis of observations of similarities among events. Core constructs are basic to the system, whereas peripheral constructs are less important. Superordinate constructs are higher in the hierarchy and include other constructs under them, whereas subordinate constructs are lower in the hierarchy.

3. Kelly developed the Role Construct Repertory Test (Rep test) to assess the content and structure of the person's construct system. The Rep test has been used to study the extent to which the person can be described as cognitively complex or simple, indicating the extent to which the person can view the world in differentiated terms.

4. According to Kelly, the person experiences anxiety when aware that events lie outside the construct system, experiences fear when a new construct is about to emerge, and experiences threat when there is the danger of comprehensive change in the construct system. Disordered responses to anxiety can be seen in the way constructs are applied to new events (excessively permeable or impermeable), in the way constructs are used to make predictions (excessive tightening or loosening), and in the organization of the entire construct system (constriction or dilation). Psychotherapy is the process of reconstructing the construct system. In Kelly's fixed-role therapy, clients are encouraged to represent themselves in new ways, behave in new ways, and construe themselves in new ways.

5. Research on personal construct theory has focused mainly on the Rep test. Recent research has shown that Kelly's idiographic assessment procedures reveal much information about the individual that is not revealed by nomothetic tests based on trait theory. Other work has explored the complexity/simplicity of construct systems in a manner that is related to, yet not directly guided by, the postulates of personal construct theory.

SOCIAL-COGNITIVE THEORY: BANDURA AND MISCHEL

12

Chapter Focus

Do you remember your first day of high school? Perhaps you don't care to! What could be more unnerving than not knowing how to act, especially in an environment where "fitting in" is paramount? Although she was really anxious and unsure of what to expect, one young woman decided to approach the first day of high school as an opportunity to learn. Her plan was to model herself after the most successful seniors in the school. She paid close attention to what they talked about, what they wore, where they went, and when they went there. Soon, she was the coolest freshman in the class.

This young woman was very influenced by her new environment, but she was also an active agent in choosing how to respond to that influence. This idea, that behavior is the result of an interaction between the person and the environment, is a key concept in the social-cognitive theory of personality. This theory is distinctive in its emphasis on the social origins of behavior and the importance of cognition (thought processes) in human functioning. People are viewed as capable of actively directing their own lives and learning complex patterns of behavior in the absence of rewards. Social-cognitive theory has developed considerably during the past few decades and today is an important force in the science of personality.

QUESTIONS TO BE ADDRESSED IN THIS CHAPTER

1. What is the role of thinking, or "cognitive," processes in personality?
2. How do people learn complex social behaviors?
3. How can one scientifically analyze people's capacity for personal agency, that is, their ability to influence their actions and the course of their own development?
4. In what ways do variations—as opposed to consistencies—in a person's behavior reveal the nature of his or her personality?

Social-cognitive theory has its historical origins in the behavioral/learning tradition (Chapter 10). Beginning in the 1950s, some theorists tried to capitalize on the virtues of the learning approach while shifting learning theory's focus of attention away from the behavior of animals in boxes and toward the actions and experiences of human beings in the social world. Reflecting these origins, the social-cognitive approach originally was known as "social learning" theory. During the past quarter century, however, investigators have adopted the "social-cognitive" label. The change in terminology is significant. It calls attention to the two central features of contemporary theorizing: (1) that human thought processes, or "cognitive" processes, should be the centerpoint of analyses of personality; and (2) that cognition develops in social context; in other words, people acquire their thoughts about themselves and the world through social interaction. The theory thus is "social-cognitive."

Social-cognitive theory is the last personality theory we will review in this book. Since you now have learned a lot about the other theories, we will introduce it by relating it to the previous ones. Social-cognitive theorists have been critical of each of the theories presented previously (see Bandura, 1986, 1999; Mischel, 1999, 2001). A review of these criticisms provides a good initial orientation to the main ideas of the social-cognitive approach.

RELATING SOCIAL-COGNITIVE THEORY TO THE PREVIOUS THEORIES

To the social-cognitivist, psychoanalysts *over*emphasize unconscious forces and the influence of early childhood experience. Social-cognitive theorists recognize that much cognition is unconscious, but believe that people's conscious thinking processes are of exceptional importance to personality. They recognize that early childhood experiences are influential, but believe that people have the capacity to develop and grow across the course of life.

Social-cognitive theorists are highly critical of trait theory. They question its most basic premise: That personality can be understood in terms of people's overall, average tendencies (e.g., their average trait levels). Social-cognitivists believe that personality is revealed not only in average levels of behavior but in patterns of *variability* in action. Are you shy with some people but outgoing with others? Motivated on some tasks but lazy on others? Social-cognitive theory sees this variability from one situation to another as indicative of your underlying personality (Mischel & Shoda, 1995; Mischel, 1999; Shoda, 1999).

Social-cognitive theorists also view evolutionary psychology as an inadequate basis for a psychology of personality. An evolutionary perspective fails to explain the vast changes in human social life that are observed from one historical period to another (Bandura, 2006; Bussey & Bandura, 1999). A century ago, evolutionary psychologists might have explained why women, compared to men, are evolutionarily predisposed to stay at home rather than entering the workforce. Now that women have entered the workforce in massive numbers, such an explanation makes little sense.

Finally, social-cognitive theory rejects the basic tenets of behaviorism. Behaviorism depicts organisms as controlled by environmental rewards and punishments. Social-cognitive theorists, in contrast, argue that people are at least partly "in control." People's thinking abilities give them the capacity to motivate and direct their actions. Social-cognitive theory is fundamentally a theory of human agency, that is, a theory of the psychological systems that enable people to play an active role in the course of their own development (Bandura, 2006). Social-cognitive theory also contrasts with behaviorism by showing how people learn new patterns of behavior by observation, or "modeling," even in the absence of reinforcement (Table 12.1).

Table 12.1 Distinguishing Features of Social-Cognitive Theory

1. Emphasis on people as active agents.
2. Emphasis on social origins of behavior.
3. Emphasis on cognitive (thought) processes.
4. Emphasis on both average behavioral tendencies and variability in behavior.
5. Emphasis on the learning of complex patterns of behavior in the absence of rewards.

The two previous theories that are most similar to social-cognitive theory are phenomenological theory and personal construct theory. Social-cognitive theory shares their interest in how people construct personal meaning out of the events of their lives, and how beliefs about the self contribute to these processes of meaning construction. Although social-cognitivists spend a lot of their time in psychological laboratories running experiments, they also are humanists. They emphasize people's capacity to influence their destinies and try to develop methods to help people achieve their potentials (Bandura, 2006). Despite these similarities, social-cognitive theory differs from these two older theories. A big difference is that social-cognitivists provide a lot of critical details about specific cognitive processes in personality functioning that are missing in the phenomenological and personal construct approach. They are able to do this by drawing on contemporary research findings that were unavailable to earlier theorists.

Many contemporary personality psychologists contribute to social-cognitive theory (Cervone & Shoda, 1999b). However, two people have made extraordinarily seminal contributions that mark them as the primary social-cognitive personality theorists: Albert Bandura and Walter Mischel. Their work is complementary. Although they focus on somewhat different aspects of personality functioning, their contributions complement one another and contribute to a coherent body of social-cognitive theory and research.

A VIEW OF THE THEORISTS

ALBERT BANDURA (1925–)

Albert Bandura grew up in northern Alberta, Canada and went to college at the University of British Columbia. After graduation he chose to do graduate work in clinical psychology at the University of Iowa because it was known for its excellence in research on learning processes. Even then, Bandura was interested in the application of learning theory to clinical phenomena. In an interview, Bandura indicated that he "had a strong interest in conceptualizing clinical phenomena in ways that would make them amenable to experimental test, with the view that as practitioners we have a responsibility for assessing the efficacy of a procedure, so that people are not subjected to treatments before we know their effects" (quoted in Evans, 1976, p. 243). At Iowa he was influenced by Kenneth Spence, a follower of the behaviorist Clark Hull, and by the general emphasis on careful conceptual analysis and rigorous experimental investigation. During that time he was also influenced by the writings of Neal Miller and John Dollard, who had begun to apply behavioral principles to the study of personality and social behavior.

After obtaining his Ph.D. at Iowa in 1952, Bandura went to Stanford University, where he has spent his entire career. At Stanford, Bandura began to work on interactive processes in psychotherapy, as well as on family patterns that lead to aggressiveness in children. The work on familial causes of aggression, conducted in collaboration with Richard Walters—his first graduate student—identified the central role of modeling influences (learning through observation of others) in personality development. These findings and consequent laboratory investigations of modeling processes resulted in the books *Adolescent Aggression* (Bandura & Walters, 1959) and *Social Learning*

Albert Bandura

and Personality Development (Bandura & Walters, 1963); the latter volume, in particular, laid the foundations for the social-cognitive perspective on personality that developed throughout the latter third of the 20th century. In 1969, Bandura published the volume *Principles of Behavior Modification*, a book that reformulated the practice of behavior therapy by directing therapists' attention to the thinking processes of their clients, rather than to the environmental factors and conditioning processes emphasized by behaviorists (Chapter 10).

During the past quarter century, Bandura has devoted much of his attention to "self-processes," that is, to thinking processes involving personal goals, self-evaluation, and beliefs about one's own capabilities for performance (1977a, 1997). His central interest is in the ways in which these thinking processes give people the capacity for personal agency, that is, give them the capacity to contribute to their own experiences, actions, and personal development. This focus makes Bandura's social-cognitive theory an "agentic" conception of human nature (Bandura, 1999, 2001). In studying personal agency, Bandura does not analyze the individual in isolation. Instead, he addresses societal factors, such as social and economic conditions, that influence people's beliefs about their ability to influence events (Bandura, 2006).

Bandura describes his work as a multifaceted research program aimed at clarifying human capabilities that should be emphasized in a comprehensive theory of human behavior. His most significant effort to formulate such a theory is the monumental volume *Social Foundations of Thought and Action* (Bandura, 1986). This book organizes a vast body of psychological knowledge about personality processes and structures into a coherent conceptual framework, and stands as the definitive statement of Bandura's theoretical position.

Bandura has received numerous awards for distinguished scientific achievement. In 1974 he was elected president of the American Psychological Association (APA). In 1980 he received the Association's Distinguished Scientific Contribution Award "for masterful modeling as researcher, teacher, and theoretician." In 2004 he received APA's Award for Outstanding Lifetime Contribution to Psychology. He has received honorary degrees from universities throughout North American and Europe.

Walter Mischel

WALTER MISCHEL (1930–)

Walter Mischel was born in Vienna and lived his first nine years "in easy playing distance of Freud's house." He describes the possible influence of this period as follows:

> When I began to read psychology Freud fascinated me most. As a student at City College (in New York, where my family settled after the Hitler-caused forced exodus from Europe in 1939), psychoanalysis seemed to provide a comprehensive view of man. But my excitement fizzled when I tried to apply ideas as a social worker with "juvenile delinquents" in New York's Lower East Side: somehow trying to give those youngsters "insight" didn't help either them or me. The concepts did not fit what I saw, and I went looking for more useful ones.
>
> SOURCE: MISCHEL, 1978, personal communication.

Mischel did his graduate work at Ohio State University, where he studied with both the personal construct theorist George Kelly and the personality theorist Julian Rotter, who extended behavioral principles to the study of human behavior by exploring people's expectations about environmental reinforcements. Kelly's influence is seen in Mischel's interest in constructs through which people encode information. Rotter's influence is seen in Mischel's study of outcome expectancies and outcome values for determining action in a situation (Mischel, 1999). After earning his Ph.D., Mischel spent a number of years at Harvard University and then, like Bandura, joined the faculty of Stanford University. During this time (1965) he participated in a Peace Corps assessment project that had a profound influence on him. In this project it was found that global trait measures did a poor job of predicting performance; in fact, they did less well than self-report measures. This increased Mischel's skepticism concerning the utility of traditional personality theories, such as trait and psychoanalytic theory, that emphasize stable and broadly generalized personality characteristics (Mischel, 1990). The definitive statement of this skepticism was the 1968 book *Personality and Assessment*, mentioned in Chapter 8. This book is probably the single most influential volume in personality psychology in the last 40 years. It challenged the entire body of theoretical assumptions and methodological practices that were associated with both psychoanalysis and trait theory. Mischel's arguments became the cornerstone of the "person-situation controversy" that was central to the field in the 1970s and 1980s (Chapter 8). Mischel describes his skepticism concerning the utility of broadly generalized personality variables, such as global trait constructs, as follows:

> Characterizations of individuals on common trait dimensions (such as "Conscientiousness" or "Sociability") provided useful overall summaries of their average levels of behavior but missed, it seemed to me, the striking discriminativeness often visible within the same person if closely observed over time and across situations. Might the same person who is more caring, giving, and supportive than most people in relation to his family also be less caring and altruistic than most people in other contexts? Might these variations across situations be meaningful stable patterns that characterize the person enduringly rather than random fluctuations? If so, how could they be understood and what did they reflect? Might they be worth taking into account in personality assessment for the conceptualization of the stability and flexibility of human behavior and qualities? These questions began to gnaw at me and the effort to answer them became a fundamental goal for the rest of my life.
>
> SOURCE: MISCHEL, as quoted in Pervin, 1996, p. 76.

In addition to critiquing previous approaches, in 1973 Mischel provided an alternative: a set of cognitive-social personal variables (Mischel, 1973). More recently, Mischel and colleagues have broadened their theoretical perspective by explaining how these variables can be understood as a complex, inter-connected system of cognitive and affective processes that underlies human individuality (Mischel & Shoda, 1995).

In 1978 Mischel received the Distinguished Scientist Award from the Clinical Psychology Division of the American Psychological Association, and in 1983 was cited by the Association for his outstanding contributions to personality theory and assessment. Since 1984 he has been a professor of psychology at Columbia University. In 1999, he accepted a position as editor of the *Psychological Review*, the most important publication outlet for theoretical papers in the field of psychology. In 2002–2003 he served as president of the Association for Research in Personality. In 2004 he was elected as a member of the U.S. National Academy of Sciences. This is an exceptionally rare honor; Mischel is the only member of the National Academy of Sciences elected specifically on the basis of his or her contributions to personality theory and research.

IMPACT OF THE THEORISTS

In addition to these biographical details, it is noteworthy to consider the overall impact of Bandura's and Mischel's scientific contributions. A recent review (Haggbloom et al., 2002) assessed the scientific impact of the psychologists of the 20th century. This assessment included a systematic analysis of the frequency with which psychologists' work was cited in scientific journals and psychology textbooks. Through this measure, the authors were able to construct an objective ranking of the most impactful, eminent psychologists of the past century. Both Bandura and Mischel were ranked among the centuries' top 25 most impactful psychologists. Indeed, the work of only three psychologists was ranked as more influential than Bandura's: Skinner, Piaget, and Freud.

A different perspective on these rankings is to note that, at the time of the writing of this edition of this textbook, there are only four living individuals who were ranked among the 25 most eminent psychologists of the previous century. Two of them were the social-cognitive personality theorists Bandura and Mischel. Thus, Bandura and Mischel are not only among the most significant contributors to personality psychology; they are among the most significant contributors to the field of psychology at large.

SOCIAL-COGNITIVE THEORY'S VIEW OF THE PERSON

The simplest way to understand the social-cognitive theory view of the person is to ask, "What is a person?" What makes some beings "persons" and others "not persons"? Three psychological qualities are essential features of persons: (1) Persons are beings who can reason about the world using language. (2) Persons can reason about not only present circumstances, but events in their past and hypothetical events in the future. (3) This reasoning commonly involves reflection on the self—the being who is doing the reasoning. People, then, are beings who can use language to reason—in past, present, and future tense—about themselves and the world (Harré and Secord, 1972). The social-cognitive view is that these three qualities are overwhelmingly important aspects of personality.

This view of persons may seem so obvious that it did not even need to be stated. But note how it differs from some earlier theories. Psychoanalysts highlighted animalistic impulsive forces in the unconscious. Behaviorists treated people as machines and based a theory of persons on the study of animals. Trait theorists report that the Big Five personality traits are found in animals, too (Gosling & John, 1999). Yes, people and other complex mammals do share many neuroanatomical features and behavioral capacities. But social-cognitive theory severely questions whether these shared features can or should be the basis of the study of human personality. The study of personality is about persons, and persons' unique cognitive capacities are a main focus of social-cognitive theory.

Centering a personality theory on human cognitive capacities (Bandura, 1999) has a critical implication. It highlights people's capacity to overcome environmental influences and animalistic emotional impulses, and to gain control over the course of their lives. Mischel describes the emerging image of the human being as follows:

> The image is one of the human being as an active, aware problem-solver, capable of profiting from an enormous range of experiences and cognitive capacities, possessing great potential for good or ill, actively constructing his or her psychological world, and influencing the environment but also being influenced by it in lawful ways. . . . It is an image that has moved a long way from the instinctual drive-reduction models, the static global traits, and the automatic stimulus-response bonds of traditional personality theories. It is an image that highlights the short comings of all simplistic theories that view behavior as the

exclusive result of any narrow set of determinants, whether these are habits, traits, drives, reinforcers, constructs, instincts, or genes and whether they are exclusively inside or outside the person.

SOURCE: MISCHEL, 1976, p. 253.

Social-cognitive theory's view of the science of personality differs in a significant way from that of most prior theories. Prior theorists commonly developed a scientific theory of persons by working outside of the mainstream of psychological science. The personality theorist generally was a lone investigator, constructing theoretical structures whose assumptions and terminology often bore little resemblance to ideas found elsewhere in the field. Freud, Rogers, and Kelly are classic examples of this approach to theory development.

Social-cognitive theory takes a different approach. In developing a theory of personality, social-cognitive theorists try to capitalize on scientific advances throughout psychology, as well as advances in other sciences that study human nature and social behavior (Cervone & Mischel, 2002). They believe that personality psychology has an integrative task (Caprara & Cervone, 2000). The personality psychologist should integrate knowledge from diverse branches of psychology—developmental, social, cognitive, cultural, neuroscience—into a coherent portrait of human nature and the differences among persons.

Another important feature of the social-cognitive view of personality science is that it emphasizes the study of individual persons. Using a term introduced earlier (Chapter 7), social-cognitive theorists have employed not only "nomothetic" but also "idiographic" research methods. They have developed theories and research methods that speak to the idiosyncrasies of the unique individual.

Finally, Bandura and Mischel have been intensely interested in the practical applications of their theoretical ideas. They stress that a "bottom line" for evaluating a theory is whether it yields practical tools that benefit human welfare (e.g., Bandura, 1969).

SOCIAL-COGNITIVE THEORY'S VIEW OF THE SCIENCE OF PERSONALITY

The personality structures emphasized by social-cognitive theory mainly involve cognitive processes. Four structural concepts are particularly noteworthy: competencies and skills, expectancies and beliefs, behavioral standards, and personal goals.

SOCIAL-COGNITIVE THEORY OF PERSONALITY: STRUCTURE

COMPETENCIES AND SKILLS

The first type of personality structure in social-cognitive theory is skills, or **competencies**. The core insight of the theory is that differences between people whom we observe may not be caused only by differences in emotions or motivational impulses, as other theories have emphasized. Instead, the differences may reflect variations in people's skill in executing different types of action. Some people may, for example, act in an introverted manner because they lack the social skills that are required to execute socially effective extraverted acts. Others may be conscientious because they have acquired a large degree of cognitive skills that enable them to adhere to social norms.

Of particular interest to social-cognitive theorists, then, are cognitive competencies and skills in solving problems and coping with the challenges of life (Cantor, 1990; Mischel & Shoda, 1998, 1999). Competencies involve both ways of thinking about life problems and behavioral skills in executing solutions to them. They involve two types of knowledge: procedural and declarative knowledge (Cantor & Kihlstrom, 1987). Declarative knowledge is knowledge that we can state in words. Procedural knowledge refers to cognitive and behavioral capacities that a person may have without being able to articulate the exact nature of those capacities; the person can execute the behavioral "procedure" without being able to say how they did it. For example, you may be good at cheering up a friend who is feeling depressed, yet may not be able to say in words precisely what it is that you do that enables you to succeed at this task. Competencies, then, involve a combination of declarative and procedural knowledge.

A focus on competencies has two implications. The first involves **context specificity**. The term refers to the fact that psychological structures that are relevant to some social situations, or contexts, may be irrelevant to others. Context specificity is a natural feature of skills (Cantor & Kihlstrom, 1987). A person may have excellent study skills, but these are of little use when it comes to getting a date or resolving an argument. Different contexts present different challenges that require different competencies. A person who is competent in one context may not be competent in another. This emphasis on context specificity (also see Chapter 14) differentiates social-cognitive theory from trait approaches (Chapters 7 and 8), which feature context-free personality variables. Social-cognitive theory generally rejects context-free variables—particularly when discussing cognitive competencies. The last thing social-cognitivists would do is to assume that one person is "generally more competent" than another. Instead, they recognize that any person's competencies may vary considerably from one domain of life to another.

The second implication involves psychological change. Competencies are acquired through social interaction and observation of the social world (Bandura, 1986). A person who is lacking skills in a particular area of life can change. They can engage in new interactions and new observations of the world and thereby acquire new competencies. The ideas of social-cognitive theory therefore can be applied directly to clinical applications that are designed to boost people's life skills (Chapter 13).

BELIEFS AND EXPECTANCIES

The other three social-cognitive structures can be understood by considering three different ways that people may think about the world (Cervone, 2004). One set of thoughts involves beliefs about what the world *actually is like* and what things probably will be like in the future. These thoughts are called beliefs and—when the beliefs are directed to the future—**expectancies**. A second class of thinking involves thoughts about what things *should* be like. These thoughts are evaluative standards, that is, mental criteria (or standards) for evaluating the goodness or worth of events. A third class of thinking involves thoughts about what one *wants to achieve in the future*. These thoughts are called personal **goals**. In addition to competencies, then, the other three main social-cognitive personality structures are beliefs and expectancies, evaluative standards, and goals. We first will consider beliefs and expectancies, which we will refer to simply as "expectancies" here because social-cognitive theory so strongly emphasizes the role in personality functioning of people's beliefs about prospective future events.

Social-cognitive theory contends that a primary determinant of our actions and emotions is our expectations about the future. People have expectancies concerning topics such as the likely behavior of other people, the rewards or punishments that may follow a certain type of behavior, or their own ability to handle the stress and challenges. It is this system of thoughts about the future that constitutes the person's expectancies.

As was the case with skills and competencies, a person's expectations may vary considerably from one situation to another. Everyone expects that the same action might elicit different reactions in different situations (e.g., loud, jovial behavior at a party versus a church). People naturally discriminate between situations, expecting different opportunities, rewards, and constraints in different settings. Although researchers sometimes do study generalized expectations, most social-cognitive investigators study expectancies in a domain-linked manner. In other words, they assess people's expectancies with regard to specific areas, or domains, of their life. Social-cognitive theorists recognize that the capacity to vary expectations and behavior from one situation to another is basic to survival. No animal could survive if it failed to make such discriminations. Humans, because of their tremendous cognitive capacity, make an incredible variety of discriminations among situations.

A key point in the social-cognitive approach is that, when forming expectancies, people may group together situations in ways that are highly idiosyncratic. One person may group together situations involving school versus social life, and perhaps have high expectations in one domain and low expectations in the other. Another person may think of situations in terms of relaxing circumstances versus circumstances that make them anxious—where both relaxing and anxiety-provoking circumstances could occur both at school and in social life. Yet anther person may possess a cognitive category that involves "opportunities to get a date"—where those opportunities could be relaxing or anxiety-provoking, and could arise in social settings or at school. People naturally "slice up" the situations of their life in different ways, and thus, may display idiosyncratic patterns of expectancies and social behavior. According to social-cognitive theorists, the essence of personality lies in these differing ways in which unique individuals perceive situations, develop expectations about future circumstances, and display distinct behavior patterns as a result of these differing perceptions and expectations.

This focus on expectancies differentiates social-cognitive theory from behaviorism. In behaviorism, behavior was understood as being caused by reinforcements and punishments in the environment. In social-cognitive theory, in contrast, behavior is explained in terms of people's *expectations about* rewards and punishments in the environment (Bandura, 1969, 1986; Mischel, 1973). This is an important difference. The shift to studying expectations, as opposed to merely environmental events, enables the social-cognitive theorist to explain why two different people may react differently to the same environment. The two people may experience similar environmental events, yet develop different expectations about what is likely to happen in the future.

The Self and Self-Efficacy Beliefs

Although some of our expectations concern other people, expectations of particular importance to personality functioning involve the self. Bandura (1997, 2001) has been at the forefront in emphasizing that people's expectations about their own capabilities for performance are the key ingredient in human achievement and well-being. He refers to these expectations as perceptions of self-efficacy. **Perceived self-efficacy**, then, refers to people's perceptions of their own capabilities for action in future situations.

Why are self-efficacy perceptions so important? It is because self-efficacy perceptions influence a number of different types of behavior that, in turn, are necessary for human achievement. Consider some area of life in which you have achieved success. For example, if you are a reader of this textbook, you probably were quite successful in high school and thereby succeeded in gaining admission to college. What was required for this success? You had to: (1) decide to commit yourself to college admission, (2) persist in study in order to learn material in high school and achieve high grades, and when taking important exams you had to (3) remain calm and (4) think in a highly analytical manner. It is precisely these four behavioral mechanisms that are influenced by self-efficacy perceptions (Bandura, 1997). People with a higher sense of self-efficacy are more likely to decide to attempt difficult tasks, to persist in their efforts, to be calm rather than anxious during task performance, and to organize their thoughts in an analytical manner. In contrast, people who question their own capabilities for performance may fail even to attempt valuable activities, may give up when the going gets rough, tend to become anxious during task performance, and often become rattled and fail to think

Self-efficacy Beliefs: Self-efficacy beliefs are based in part on experiences with success and failure. Mark Wohlers was a successful pitcher until he lost control, to the extent that he bounced the ball to the plate or threw it over the batter's head. His confidence plummeted from what had been a very high level to near zero. Trying to regain his confidence, he said: "Confidence comes with success. The way I pitched the other day built a little more confidence .... It's just getting out there and having success." (New York Times, March 9, 1997, p. D7)

and act in a calm, analytical manner (colloquially speaking, one might say that a person with a low sense of self-efficacy tends to choke on difficult activities).

These influences of self-efficacy are spelled out further throughout this chapter and later in this book. For now, however, it is important to consider in a little more detail how Bandura conceptualizes perceived self-efficacy and how his strategy for assessing perceived self-efficacy follows from this conceptualization. Perceived self-efficacy differs from what may appear to be similar concepts. Perceived self-efficacy differs from self-esteem. Self-esteem refers to people's overall (or "global") evaluation of their personal worth. Perceived self-efficacy, in contrast, refers to people's appraisals of what they are capable of accomplishing in a given setting. Thus, perceived self-efficacy differs from self-esteem in two ways: (1) Perceived self-efficacy is not a global variable; instead, it is recognized that people commonly will have different self-efficacy perceptions in different situations. (2) Perceived self-efficacy is not an abstract sense of personal worth, but a judgment of what one can do. Imagine that you have a big math exam coming up. You may have a perfectly high sense of self-esteem. Yet, at the same time, you may have a low sense of self-efficacy for getting a high grade on the exam. Social-cognitive theory would predict that you would be anxious about the exam, even though you may have a high sense of overall self-esteem. These theoretical differences have proven to be quite significant in practice. Although the relations between self-esteem measures and performance are often quite weak (Baumeister, Campbell, Krueger, & Vohs, 2003), a large and diverse set of research findings indicates that the relation between measures of perceived self-efficacy and performance is strong (Bandura & Locke, 2003; Stajkovic & Luthans, 1998).

A second distinction of importance concerns the difference between self-efficacy expectations and outcome expectations (Bandura, 1977a). Outcome expectations are beliefs about the rewards and punishments that will occur if one performs a given type of behavior. Self-efficacy expectations are beliefs about whether one can perform the behavior in the first place. Suppose you are considering what major to choose in college. You might believe that there are high rewards (e.g., high financial income in the future) if you were to major in electrical engineering. You would, then, have high outcome expectations with respect to electrical engineering. But you might also think that you are not personally capable of executing the behaviors (e.g., passing all the math, physics, and engineering courses) required to major in electrical engineering. You would have low self-efficacy expectations with respect to electrical engineering. Social-cognitive theory contends that efficacy expectations generally are more important than are outcome expectations as a determinant of behavior. If people lack a sense of efficacy for accomplishing something, the rewards associated with accomplishing that goal are probably irrelevant to them. You are unlikely to select electrical engineering as your major, despite its financial attractions, if you have a low sense of self-efficacy for completing the required courses.

In terms of assessment, Bandura emphasizes what he calls a **microanalytic research** strategy. According to this strategy, detailed measures of perceived self-efficacy are taken before performance of behaviors in specific situations. Specifically, people are asked to indicate their degree of certainty in performing specific behaviors in designated contexts. A self-efficacy scale for athletic performance in, for example, the sport of basketball would *not* ask a vague question such as "Do you think you are a good basketball player?" (The question is vague because the word "good" is so ambiguous: Good compared to your teammates? Compared to a member of the NBA—a collegiate basketball player? Compared to your little brother?) Instead, test items would describe specific actions and accomplishments and ask people to indicate their confidence in attaining them: For example, "How confident are you that you can make at least 75% of your free throws during a basketball game?" or "How confident are you that you can dribble upcourt with a basketball even if you are covered by a skilled defensive player?" This assessment strategy follows directly from the theoretical considerations above. In terms of theory, Bandura recognizes that self-efficacy perceptions may vary, for any individual, from one situation to another. In terms of assessment methods, then, situation-specific measures are employed in order to capture this variability. Such measures are much better for capturing the psychological characteristics of the individual. Global self-concept measures are criticized because they "[do] not do justice to the complexity of self-efficacy perceptions, which vary across different activities, different levels of the same activity, and different situational circumstances" (Bandura, 1986, p. 41).

Self-Efficacy and Performance

A basic claim of social-cognitive theory is that self-efficacy perceptions causally influence behavior. If you think critically about such claims, you may already have a counter-argument: Maybe self-efficacy perceptions do not really play a causal role. Maybe some other factor is really the cause. One possible other factor is people's actual level of skill. Skill levels might influence both self-efficacy perceptions and behavior, and account for the relation between perceived self-efficacy and motivated action. For example, everyone has a high sense of self-efficacy for picking up a 5-pound weight (we're confident that we can do it) and a low sense of self-efficacy for picking up a 500-pound weight (we perceive ourselves as incapable of doing it). But there's no need to appeal to the notion of perceived self-efficacy to explain why we actually can lift the light weight and not the heavy one. Our behavior can be understood simply in terms of our inherent physical capacities. How, then, do we know that we ever need to appeal to the notion of perceived self-efficacy to explain behavior?

Social-cognitivists have addressed this question through experimental strategies. The idea is to experimentally manipulate perceived self-efficacy while holding other factors—such as people's actual skills—constant. Once self-efficacy perceptions are manipulated experimentally, one can see whether the variations in perceived self-efficacy causally influence behavior.

Of course, one needs a strategy for manipulating perceived self-efficacy. Ideally, the manipulation would be simple and subtle, to ensure that it influenced perceived self-efficacy but did not also influence people's actual skills on the task.

One research strategy has been to employ a technique known as "anchoring" manipulations. Anchoring refers to a thinking process that comes into play when people try to figure out the answer to a problem. What often happens is that the final answer that people reach is greatly influenced by whatever people happen to think of *first* when they try to solve the problem; their final answer is "anchored on" their initial guess. Surprisingly, this occurs even when the initial guess is determined by factors that are completely random and obviously irrelevant to the problem (Tversky & Kahneman, 1974). For example, imagine you are trying to guess a numerical quantity such as the population in millions of the nation of Russia. Suppose that just before you make your estimate someone pulls a random number out of a hat, reads it aloud: "639," and then asks "Do you think there are more or less than 639 million people living in Russia?" You would know that 639 is way too high, and you would know that it also is irrelevant to the real answer because it was chosen randomly. Nonetheless, if you respond like most research participants in anchoring studies, when you then guessed the actual population your guess would be much higher than if you never had been exposed to the random value. ("Hmm," you might think, "it can't be 639 million. Um ... maybe it's 400 million.") Your final guess would be "anchored" in the direction of the large number. Conversely, if you first were exposed to a *low* anchor value (e.g., in our population example, the value 20 million), your final guess would probably end up lower ("Hmm, 20 million, that can't be right. Maybe it's, um ... 70 million"). The presentation of random anchor values, then, is a way of experimentally manipulating people's judgments.

Cervone and Peake (1986) applied anchoring techniques to the question of self-efficacy judgment and behavior. Prior to performing a task that had a series of items, participants were asked to judge whether they could solve "more or less than X" of the items. In high and low anchor conditions, the "X" was a number that corresponded to a high versus low level of performance. This number appeared to be random, literally drawn out of a hat. People then judged exactly how many items they could solve (their level of self-efficacy on the task). Findings indicated that the anchoring manipulation affected perceived self-efficacy; participants exposed to high and low random numbers had high and low self-efficacy perceptions (Figure 12.1, left panel). This circumstance, then, is exactly what one needs to test the claim that self-efficacy causally influences behavior; thanks to the anchoring manipulation, people *differ* in perceived self-efficacy while being the *same* on other factors, such as actual skills on the task. To provide this test, the experimenters asked people to work on the task and measured their behavioral persistence (i.e., how long they tried working on the problems before giving up). Variations in self-efficacy were found to create corresponding variations in behavior (Figure 12.1, right panel). The groups that had high versus low self-efficacy perceptions differed in their subsequent behavior—even though the high versus low differences were created experimentally, and merely by presenting random anchor values.

Such findings provide strong evidence for a central aspect of social-cognitive theory, namely, that people's subjective perceptions of themselves have a unique causal influence on their own behavior. Even when a seemingly irrelevant situational factor causes people to have relatively high or low judgments of self-efficacy, these judgments can affect subsequent decisions and actions.

Note that this sort of finding provides strong evidence *against* a behavioral view of cognition and behavior. Recall that, in behaviorism (Chapter 10), behavior was explained in terms of environmental events rather than cognitive processes. When looking at Bandura's self-efficacy research, a behaviorist might argue that a person's actions *and* their self-efficacy perceptions are both

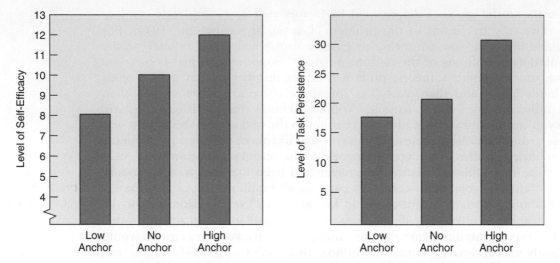

Figure 12.1   *Mean levels of perceived self-efficacy and behavior as a function of exposure to apparently random high versus low anchor values. From Cervone & Peake, 1986.*

caused by the environment. In this behaviorist view, self-efficacy perceptions would *not* be seen as a cause of behavior but merely as a thinking process that happens to be correlated with the environmental events that are the true causes of people's behaviors. By analogy, the behaviorist might point out that the hood of your car gets hot when you drive at high speed, yet the heating of the hood is not a cause of the car's high speed. It merely is an event that happens to be correlated with the true causes. The counter-argument, from social-cognitive theory, is that if you manipulate self-efficacy perceptions experimentally, then you find changes in subsequent behavior. This strongly suggests that self-efficacy perceptions do play a causal role, rather than merely being correlated with other factors that are the "true causes" of behavior. If you heat up the hood of your car, it doesn't suddenly go faster. But if you increase people's perceptions of self-efficacy, then changes in behavior do, in fact, result.

GOALS

The third type of personality structure in social-cognitive theory is goals. A goal is a mental representation of the aim of an action or course of actions. A basic belief of social-cognitive theory is that people's ability to envision the future enables them to set specific goals for action and thus, to motivate and direct their own behavior. Goals, then, contribute to the human capacity for self-control. Goals guide us in establishing priorities and in selecting among situations. They enable us to go beyond momentary influences and to organize our behavior over extended periods of time.

A person's goals are organized in a system. In a goal system, some goals are more central or important than others. Goal systems often are understood as having a hierarchical structure. Goals at a higher level in the hierarchy (e.g., get accepted into law school) organize lower-level goals (e.g., get good grades in college) which, in turn, organize lower-level aims (e.g., study for

CURRENT APPLICATIONS

SELF-EFFICACY AND CONDOM USE: HOW TO CHANGE BEHAVIOR

The AIDS epidemic has complicated sexual relations, particularly for young people. In effect, sex education has become a form of preventive medicine. Awareness is definitely a step in the right direction, and knowing the facts about HIV, AIDS, and risky behavior is certainly important. But is it enough to influence young people's behavior? One study suggests not. This research tested whether an intervention program based on social-cognitive theory could improve HIV prevention. More specifically, would it help to increase safe-sex self-efficacy?

Bandura (1992) had proposed a conceptual model linking social-cognitive theory and perceived self-efficacy to the control of sexual activities that would put individuals at risk for HIV infection and AIDS. Essentially, Bandura's model promotes the idea that how we perceive our ability to cope with a situation and to control its outcome is the key to influencing actual behavior.

A study by Basen-Engquist (1994) tested Bandura's model with a quasi-experimental field study involving college students. The subjects were divided into three groups. One group participated in a safe-sex efficacy workshop, another group heard a didactic lecture on HIV, and the third group was a control who heard a lecture about an unrelated topic. As expected, an immediate post-test showed that the first and second groups scored higher on safe-sex self-efficacy and were more likely to report the intention to use a condom than the control group. The follow-up two months later, however, revealed that the group in the safe-sex efficacy workshop was more likely than both other groups to have increased in actual condom use. In other words, it was the manipulation of safe-sex self-efficacy, not mere information about HIV, that produced the change in behavior.

This research demonstrates that HIV prevention efforts must consider the psychology of safe-sex behavior. So much attention has been placed on increasing awareness through education that the question of how information is actually used by young people has been obscured. The discrepancy between intended and actual condom use in the group who received the HIV lecture suggests that information does not get translated into actual behavior as readily as educators would hope. Social-cognitive theory, and perceived self-efficacy in particular, may provide the important psychological link between education and behavior change.

SOURCE: BASEN-ENGQUIST (1994).

exams). Goal systems, however, are not rigid or fixed. People may select among goals, depending on what seems most important to them at the time, what the opportunities in the environment appear to be, and their judgments of self-efficacy for goal attainment.

People's goals on a task may differ in a variety of ways (Locke & Latham, 1990, 2002). One obvious variation is in the level of challenge, or difficulty, of goals. For example, in a college class, some people may have the goal merely of passing the course, whereas others may adopt the challenging goal of getting an A in the class. Another variation involves the nearness, or proximity, of goals. One person may set a proximal goal, that is, a goal that involves an aim that is coming up soon. Others may set distal goals, that is, goals that specify achievements that are far in the future. For example, if one's goal is to lose weight, a proximal goal might be losing 1 pound each week, whereas a distal goal would be losing 12 pounds in the next 3 months. Research findings indicate that proximal goals often have a bigger influence on one's current behavior than do distal goals (Bandura & Schunk, 1981; Stock & Cervone, 1990). In part, this is because distal goals allow one to "slack off" in the present. For example, the person who wants to lose 12 pounds in 3 months might convince herself that she can go off her diet one week and still meet the long-term aim.

In addition, goals may differ in a manner that involves the subjective meaning of an activity. On any challenging task, some people may have the goal of developing more knowledge and skills on the task; the meaning of the task is that it is an opportunity to learn. Others, in contrast, may be more concerned with goals such as not embarrassing themselves in front of others. These differences between "learning" and "performance" goals (Dweck & Leggett, 1988) are discussed in Chapter 13.

Goals are related to the previous social-cognitive personality construct: expectancies. Expectancies influence the process of goal setting. When selecting goals, people generally reflect on their expectations about their performance. People with higher perceptions of self-efficacy often set higher goals and remain more committed to them (Locke & Latham, 2002). Conversely, goals may influence expectancies and may interact systematically with expectancies as people work on tasks and receive feedback on their performance (Grant & Dweck, 1999). For example, suppose you take an exam and learn that your score was identical to the average score in the class. If your goal was merely to learn something about the course material and to earn a passing grade, then you might be perfectly satisfied with your performance. However, if your goal was to perform exceptionally well in the course in order to impress your friends and your professor, then you might interpret the average grade very negatively and become discouraged, especially if your expectations are that you no longer can achieve your ultimate aims in the course.

EVALUATIVE STANDARDS

The fourth personality structure in social-cognitive theory is evaluative standards. A mental standard is a criterion for judging the goodness, or worth, of a person, thing, or event. The study of evaluative standards, then, addresses the ways in which people acquire criteria for evaluating events and how these evaluations influence their emotions and actions.

Of particular importance in social-cognitive theory are evaluative standards concerning one's self, or "personal standards." Personal standards are fundamental to human motivation and performance. Social-cognitive theory recognizes that people commonly evaluate their ongoing behavior in accordance with internalized personal standards. As an example, imagine that you are writing a term paper for a course. What are you thinking about? On the one hand, you have in mind the content of the material for the paper: the main facts you have to cover, the thesis you are trying to develop, and so forth. On the other hand, inevitably you will find yourself thinking of something else. You will be thinking about the quality of your own writing. You will evaluate whether the sentences you have written are good enough or have to be revised. In other words, you have in mind evaluative standards that you use to judge the goodness or worth of your own behavior. Much of the writing and revising process is one in which you try to alter your own behavior (i.e., your writing) to bring it in line with your own personal standards for writing.

Evaluative standards often trigger emotional reactions. We react with pride when we meet our standards for performance and we are dissatisfied with ourselves when we fail to meet our own standards. Bandura refers to such emotions as **self-evaluative reactions**; we evaluate our own actions and then respond in an emotionally satisfied or dissatisfied way toward ourselves as a result of this self-evaluation (Bandura, 1986).

Social-cognitive theory emphasizes that evaluative standards are central to behavior that we call "moral" versus "immoral." Some of the evaluative standards that we learn involve ethical and moral principles concerning the treatment of other people. Although everyone in a given society may be familiar with such principles, sometimes people do not use them to regulate their own behavior. For example, everyone knows that it is wrong to steal things from a store or to include plagiarized material in a term paper, yet some people still do these things; they selectively "disengage" their moral standards when it is to their personal advantage to do so (Bandura, Barbaranelli, Caprara, & Pastorelli, 1996). People who disengage their moral standards say things to themselves that temporarily enable them to disregard their own standards for behavior. For example, a student who is tempted to cheat on a test might say something like "everybody cheats on tests, so it must be ok." The disengagement of evaluative standards enables people to perform acts that they normally would not perform due to internalized moral sanctions. A recent study by Osofsky, Bandura, and Zimbardo (2005) provides a striking example of this point. The evaluative standard of relevance to their study was the moral sanction against killing a fellow human being. Everyone possesses moral standards indicating that killing is wrong. Yet some people in U.S. society kill people as part of their profession; they are executioners who carry out death penalties. How do they do it? How can people who, in general, believe that killing is bad execute prisoners? To answer this question, Osofsky et al. studied personnel who work at maximum-security prisons. Prison personnel differed in the degree to which they were involved in the execution process. Some personnel were relatively uninvolved in executions (e.g., they counseled the prisoner's family members) whereas others were highly involved (e.g., they administered lethal injections). Osofsky et al. asked all participants to complete a scale measuring the tendency to disengage from moral standards involving executions. They found that the degree to which people displayed moral disengagement varied as a function of their level of involvement in executions. Prison personnel who were directly involved in executions displayed much higher levels of moral disengagement than did others; they were more likely to endorse statements such as "An execution is merciful compared to a murder" and "Nowadays the death penalty is done in ways that minimize the suffering of the person being executed" (Osofsky et al., 2005). Such statements enable one temporarily to disregard, or "disengage," prohibitions against killing.

Large, excited crowds–such as crowds of fans celebrating a sports victory–are a setting in which people are more likely to disengage their usual evaluative standards and thereby more likely to engage in violent, antisocial behavior.

The study of evaluative standards is another point that differentiates social-cognitive theory from behaviorism. In a behavioristic experiment, evaluative standards are determined by the experimenter. The experimenter decides that a given number of lever presses by a rat, for example, are enough presses to receive a reinforcement. Social-cognitive theorists note that such experiments fail to address a basic fact of human life. In the human case, evaluative standards are not always set by an outside agent. They are determined by the individual. People have their own personal standards for evaluating their own behavior. There certainly are external influences on these internal standards. Personal standards have social foundations; people commonly acquire standards for performance by observing the performances of others (Bandura, 1986). But once they are acquired, standards and self-evaluative reactions serve as a kind of internal guidance system through which people direct their own actions. Ongoing behavior, then, is determined by this internal psychological system, not by forces in the environment, as the behaviorists had argued.

THE NATURE OF SOCIAL-COGNITIVE PERSONALITY STRUCTURES

In social-cognitive theory, the four personality structures we have reviewed—beliefs and expectancies, goals, evaluative standards, and competencies and skills—are not treated as four independent "objects" in one's head. Instead, these four personality structures should be understood as referring to distinct classes of thinking. Each of the four is a cognitive subsystem within the overall system of personality. The theoretical claim is that cognitions about what the world actually is like (beliefs), about one's aims for the future (goals), and about how things normatively should be (standards) play distinct roles in personality functioning and, thus, should be treated as distinct personality structures. Similarly, the declarative and procedural knowledge that gives people the capacity to act in an intelligent, skilled manner (competencies) is seen as being psychologically distinct from beliefs, goals, and evaluative standards, and thus, as constituting a distinct personality structure.

Given this view of cognition and personality, the social-cognitive theorist would never assign to a person a single score that is supposed to represent "how much" of each variable they have. Social-cognitive theorists believe that personality is far too complex to be reduced to any simple set of scores. Instead, each of these four personality structures refers to a complex system of social cognition. People have a large number of goals, a wide spectrum of beliefs, an array of evaluative standards, and a diversity of skills. Different personality structures come into play in different social situations. By studying this complex system of social-cognitive structures, and its interaction with the social world, the social-cognitive theorist tries to grapple with the true complexity of the individual.

SOCIAL-COGNITIVE THEORY OF PERSONALITY: PROCESS

Social-cognitive theory addresses the dynamics of personality processes in two different ways. The first involves general theoretical principles. Social-cognitive theorists have presented two theoretical principles that they think scientists should use when analyzing the dynamics of personality processes. One is an analysis of the causes of behavior that is called reciprocal determinism. The other is a framework for thinking about internal personality processes, which is called a cognitive-affective processing system (CAPS) framework.

After we review these two ideas—reciprocal determinism and the CAPS model—we will consider the second way in which social-cognitive theory addresses personality processes. By way of preview, this second way is by analyzing psychological functions that are of particular importance in a scientific analysis of personality and individual differences. Three types of psychological functions have received particular attention; these are (1) observational learning (or learning through "modeling"), (2) motivation, and (3) self-control.

RECIPROCAL DETERMINISM

Bandura (1986) has introduced a theoretical principle known as **reciprocal determinism**. This principle addresses the issue of cause-and-effect in the study of personality processes.

The problem Bandura is trying to solve is the following. When analyzing a person's behavior, there generally are three factors to consider: the person, his or her behavior, and the environmental setting in which the person acts. In this three-part system, how are we to analyze causes and effects? What causes what? Should one say that the person, with his or her personality attributes, is the cause of behavior (as implied in some trait theories of personality)? Should one say that the environment is the real cause of behavior (as argued by the behaviorists)? Bandura thinks we should not say either of these things because both statements are too simplistic. Instead, he argues that causality is a "two-way street." Stated more formally, causality is reciprocal. Each of the three factors under consideration—behavior, personality characteristics, and the environment—are causes of one another. The factors are reciprocal determinants. Bandura's principle of reciprocal determinism, then, contends that personality, behavior, and the environment must be understood as a system of forces that mutually influence one another across the course of time (Figure 12.2).

To understand this principle intuitively, imagine yourself in conversation with someone whom you find attractive. You might smile, look attentive, and try to alter the topics of conversation in a manner that makes a good impression on the other person. Now, from the perspective of a personality scientist, how are we to understand causality in this conversation? What causes what? On the one hand, one could say that the environment causes your behavior. The other person's physical and social attractiveness has caused you to act in a certain way. This is not incorrect; yet it is insufficient. The environment is something that you interpreted, and your particular interpretations are influenced by beliefs and feelings of yours—that is, your personality characteristics. Further, your ability to make a good impression depends on your social skills—another feature of your personality. In addition, your behavior alters the environment you experience. If you skillfully make a good impression, then the other person will be in a better mood, will like you more, will be smiling, will be attentive to you, and so on. In other words, through your own actions, you will have created a more positive social environment. Finally, if you are successful, your behavioral success may alter your mood and your sense of self; there will be an influence of your own behavior on your own personality. It is futile to isolate one factor as "the cause" and the other as "the effect" in such a system. Instead, personality, behavior, and the environment must be understood as factors that reciprocally determine one another.

Figure 12.2   *Schematic representation of Bandura's principle of reciprocal determinism, which posits that personality, behavior, and the environment must be understood as a system of forces that mutually influence one another. From Bandura (1997).*

The principle of reciprocal determinism constitutes a rejection of the views of other theories. Some theories explain behavior primarily in terms of inner forces: the inner conflicts of psychoanalysis, the motive for self-actualization of the phenomenological theories, the genetically-determined dispositions of the trait theories, and the evolved psychological modules of evolutionary psychology. Others explained behavior in terms of external forces—behaviorism being the paradigm case. Bandura rejects this entire discourse about "inner versus outer" or "internal versus external" forces as woefully inadequate because it fails to recognize that the person's internal psychology and the social environment influence one another reciprocally. People are influenced by environmental forces, but they also choose how to behave. The person is both responsive to situations and actively constructs and influences situations. People select situations as well as are shaped by them; the capacity to choose the type of situation that one will encounter is seen by social-cognitive theorists as a critical element of people's capacity to be active agents who influence the course of their own development.

PERSONALITY AS A COGNITIVE-AFFECTIVE PROCESSING SYSTEM (CAPS)

In recent years, social-cognitive theorists increasingly have emphasized that personality should be understood as a system. The term "system" generally refers to something that has a large number of parts that interact among each other. The behavior of the system reflects not only the isolated parts, but the ways in which the parts are interconnected. Systems with a very large number of highly integrated parts often exhibit highly complex and coherent forms of behavior, even if the parts are relatively simple. Dynamic interactions among the parts give rise to the system's complexity. An example of this is the brain. It performs remarkably complex actions despite the fact that its parts—neurons—are relatively simple. The complex interconnections among the parts give rise to the brain's complex capabilities (Damasio, 1994; Edelman & Tonini, 2000).

Social-cognitive theory views personality as a complex system. Social-cognitive variables do not operate in isolation from one another. Instead, the various cognitions and affects interact with one another in an organized fashion; as a result, there is an overall coherence to personality functioning (Cervone & Shoda, 1999b).

A systems view of structure has been articulated by Mischel and Shoda (1995). They present a **cognitive-affective processing system (CAPS)** model of personality (Figure 12.3). The CAPS model has three essential features. First, cognitive and emotional personality variables are seen as being complexly linked to one another. It is not merely the case that people have a goal (e.g., get more dates), a level of competency (e.g., low dating skills), a particular expectancy (e.g., low perceived self-efficacy for dating), and certain evaluative standards and self-evaluative reactions (e.g., feeling emotionally dissatisfied with oneself when it comes to dating). Instead, their personality system features these cognitions and affects *and* interrelations among them. Thoughts about one's goals may trigger thoughts about skills, which in turn trigger thoughts about self-efficacy, all of which may affect one's self-evaluations and emotions.

The second key feature of the CAPS model concerns the social environment. In this model, different aspects of social situations, or "situational features,"

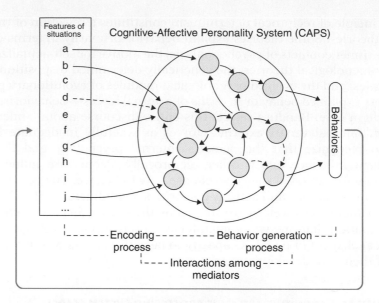

Figure 12.3   *Schematic representations of the cognitive-affective processing system (CAPS) theory of Mischel and Shoda. From Mischel and Shoda (1995).*

activate subsets of the overall personality system. For example, a situation in which you are in a conversation with someone about a date they had last weekend may activate the system of goals and expectancies involving dates outlined in the paragraph above. In contrast, a conversation about politics, sports, or classes at school may activate an entirely different set of cognitions and affects.

The third feature follows naturally from the second one. If different situational features activate different parts of the overall personality system, then people's behavior should *vary* from one situation to another. Suppose, hypothetically, that an individual's personality system contains negative thoughts and feelings about their dating skills but positive thoughts and feelings about their academic abilities. Situational features that activate one versus the other concern (dating versus academic performance) should produce, in the individual, entirely different patterns of emotion and action. Although the individual's personality system is stable, his or her experiences and action nonetheless should change from one situation to another as different subsets of the overall personality system become active. This is perhaps the most distinctive feature of the CAPS model (Mischel & Shoda, 1995). It contends that not only average levels of behavior but also *variations* in behavior are a defining aspect of personality.

Empirical research by Mischel and his associates illustrates the CAPS approach (Shoda, Mischel, & Wright, 1994). In this work, children were observed in various settings during a 6-week period at a summer camp; illustrative settings were woodworking, cabin meeting, classroom, mealtime, playground, and watching TV. Within these settings, situations were defined in terms of whether the interaction involved a peer or an adult counselor and whether the interaction was positive or negative in nature (e.g., the child was praised versus punished by a counselor or teased by a peer). For each child, observations were made regularly on the basis of the frequency with which each of five types of behavior occurred in each of the defined situations: verbal aggression (teased, provoked, or threatened); physical aggression (hit, pushed, physically harmed); whined or displayed babyish behavior; complied or gave in; talked prosocially. These observations were made on an hourly basis, 5 hours a day, 6 days a week, for 6 weeks—an average of 167 hours of observation per child. This yielded an unusually large amount of observation of each child in terms of behaviors expressed in a variety of situations over the course of time.

When analyzing these data, the investigators plotted *if . . . then . . . profiles.* In an *if . . . then . . .* profile analysis, one plots an individual person's behavior in each of a variety of different situations. One then determines if the individual's behavior varies systematically from one person to another. One might be able to determine that "if" the person encounters a particular type of situation, "then" that person tends to act in a certain manner. The "if's" and "then's" may vary from one person to another. The profile analysis thus captures idiosyncratic tendencies exhibited by unique individuals.

What, then, were the findings? Of course there was evidence of considerable differences in behaviors expressed in different situations. People do behave differently in different types of situations. In general, behavior is different on the playground than in the classroom, in a cabin meeting than in woodworking. And, of course there were individual differences in average expressions of each of the five observed types of behavior. As trait theorists suggest, there are individual differences in average expressions of behavior across situations. However, the more critical question for social-cognitive theory is whether individuals can be described in terms of their distinctive patterns of situation-behavior relationships. In other words, do individuals differ in their patterns of behavior even if their overall levels are the same? Can two individuals express the same average level of aggressive behavior, be the same on a trait such as aggressiveness, but differ in the kinds of situations in which they express their aggressiveness? Mischel and his associates indeed found clear evidence that individuals have distinctive, stable profiles of expressing particular behaviors in specific groups of situations. Consider, for example, the verbal aggression profiles of two individuals in relation to five types of psychological situations (Figure 12.4). Clearly the two differ in their profiles of expressing verbal aggression across the various situations. Each behaves reasonably consistently within specific groups of situations but differently between groups of situations. Averaging behavior across situations would mask such distinctive patterns of situation-behavior relationships.

Interestingly, laypersons—that is, people who are not trained professionally in psychology—appear naturally to recognize the importance of *if . . . then . . .* variability in action. This was demonstrated in recent studies by Kammrath, Mendoza-Denton, and Mischel (2005). In one study, laypersons were asked how they expected people with different personality characteristics to behave in different situations. Results indicated that laypersons did not anticipate that people would act in a uniform, consistent manner in different contexts. Instead, they anticipated *if . . . then . . .* variability; they expected that people's behavior would vary substantially from one situation to another. In a second study, participants were told about the actions of individuals whose behavior

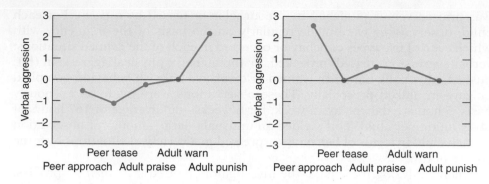

Figure 12.4 *Illustrative intraindividual profiles of verbal aggression for two individuals across five types of psychological situations. (Adapted from Shoda, Mischel, & Wright, 1994, p. 6.)*

varied distinctively across different situations. Research participants were not befuddled by these violations of trait-like consistency in behavior. Instead, they inferred that people possessed motives that explained their patterns of variability in conduct (Kammrath et al., 2005).

What can be concluded from this program of research? Mischel and his associates suggest that individuals have distinctive profiles of situation-behavior relationships, what are called **behavioral signatures**. "It is this type of intra-individual stability in the pattern and organization of behavior that seems especially central for a psychology of personality ultimately devoted to understanding and capturing the uniqueness of individual functioning" (Shoda, Mischel, & Wright, 1994, p. 683). Mischel and colleagues emphasized that these unique patterns of behavior would be completely overlooked if one merely asked about people's overall, average behavioral tendencies. Two people who, for example, display the same average level of anxiety may be fundamentally different people. An *if . . . then . . .* profile analysis might reveal that one person is anxious in achievement settings and the other is anxious when it comes to romantic relationships. The analysis would indicate that the different people have different personality dynamics—despite the fact that they might happen to get the same score on "global trait anxiety" if a researcher averages together their responses in the different situations of their life. The basic message Mischel and colleagues send to other psychologists, then, is: Don't average together the different situations of their life! Instead, look closely at individuals and the distinctive patterns of variability in action that they display in different circumstances.

OBSERVATIONAL LEARNING (MODELING)

So far, we have outlined four personality structures that are central to social-cognitive theory and have reviewed two theoretical principles that Bandura and Mischel use to understand the nature of personality and the causes of behavior. We now can see these theoretical ideas put into action. Social-cognitive theorists use these theoretical principles to understand two main psychological activities, or what we will call here two psychological functions: (1) acquiring new knowledge and skills, particularly through processes of

*Observational Learning: Aggressive behavior can be learned
from the observation of such behavior on television. (Etta
Hulme, reprinted by permission of NEA, Inc.)*

observational learning; and (2) exerting control over, or self-regulating, one's own actions and emotional experiences.

The first of these two psychological functions concerns the question of how people acquire knowledge and skills. How do we learn social skills? How do we acquire particular beliefs, goals, and standards for evaluating our behavior? Previous theories commonly have overlooked these questions. There is little explicit discussion of the acquisition of beliefs and social skills in most of the previous theories we have discussed. The theory that addressed the topic most explicitly was behaviorism. As you will recall, behaviorists claim that people learn things through a trial-and-error learning process called shaping, or successive approximation. Over a large series of learning trials, reinforcements gradually shape a complex pattern of behavior. Although there are lots of errors at first, through reinforcement processes behavior gradually approximates a desired pattern.

In a profoundly important development for psychology, Albert Bandura succeeded in explaining the shortcomings of this behavioral theory and in providing psychology with an alternative theoretical explanation. In retrospect, the shortcomings of the behavioral approach seem obvious. Sometimes learning simply cannot occur by a trial-and-error because the errors are too costly. As an example, consider the first time you ever drove a car. According to the behaviorists, reinforcements and punishments would gradually shape safe driving behavior on your part. On Day 1 of driving you might get into 9 or 10 traffic accidents, but due to reinforcement processes on Day 2 you might only have 5 or 6 accidents, and after a few more trials the errors would disappear and the environment would have shaped safe driving behavior. Is this what actually happened? We sure hope not! In reality, the first time you sat behind the wheel—before you ever had been reinforced or punished for specific driving behaviors—you already were able to drive a car fairly adequately. What needs to be explained is the human capacity to learn such skills in the absence of prior rewards and punishments.

Social-cognitive theory explains that people can learn merely by observing the behaviors of others. The person being observed is called a model, and this **observational learning** process is also known as **modeling**. People's cognitive capacities enable them to learn complex forms of behavior merely by observing a model performing these behaviors. As Bandura (1986) has detailed, people can form an internal mental representation of the behavior they have observed, and then can draw upon that mental representation at a later point in time. Learning by modeling is evident in innumerable domains of life. A child may learn language by observing parents and other people speaking. You may have learned some of the basic skills for driving (where to put your hands and feet, how to start the car, how to turn the wheel) merely by observing other drivers. People learn what types of behavior are acceptable and unacceptable in different social settings by observing the actions of others.

This modeling process can be much more complex than simple imitation or mimicry. The notion of "imitation" generally implies the exact replication of a narrow response pattern. In modeling, however, people may learn general rules of behavior by observing others. They then can use those rules to self-direct a variety of types of behavior in the future. Bandura's conceptualization of modeling also is narrower than the psychodynamic notion of identification. Identification implies an incorporation of broad patterns of behavior exhibited by a specific other individual. Modeling, in contrast, involves the acquisition of information through the observation of others, without implying that the observer internalizes entire styles of action exhibited by the other individual.

The individual who is observed in the process of observational learning (i.e., the model) need not be someone who is physically present. In contemporary society, much modeling occurs through the media. We may learn styles of thought and action from people whom we never meet, but whom we merely observe on television or other media sources. A social concern is that television often models antisocial behavior such as aggression; research indicates that exposure to high levels of aggression in the media when one is a child can cause people to learn aggressive patterns of behavior that are evident later in life. Huesmann and colleagues (Huesmann, Moise-Titus, Podolski, & Eron, 2003) performed a long-term longitudinal study on the question of whether exposure to violence in the media during childhood leads to higher levels of aggression later in life. Among both men and women, people who saw high levels of violence when they were 6 to 10 years old turned out to be more aggressive in early adulthood. The link between media violence in childhood and aggression in adulthood held up even when the researchers statistically controlled for factors other than media exposure (e.g., socioeconomic status) that might possibly be correlated with levels of aggression. Bandura's research on modeling clearly has important social implications.

Acquisition versus Performance

An important part of the theory of modeling is the distinction between **acquisition** and **performance**. A new, complex pattern of behavior can be learned or acquired regardless of reinforcers, but whether or not the behavior is performed will depend on rewards and punishments. Consider, for example, the classic study by Bandura and his associates to illustrate this distinction (Bandura, Ross, & Ross, 1963). In this study three groups of children observed a model expressing aggressive behavior toward a plastic Bobo doll. In the first group, the aggressive behavior by the model was not followed by any consequences (No Consequences). In the second group, the model's aggressive behavior was followed by rewards (Reward), and in the third group it was followed by punishment (Punishment). Following observation of the model's aggressive behavior, children from the three groups were presented with two conditions. In the first condition, the children were left alone in a room with many toys, including a Bobo doll. They were then observed through a one-way mirror to see if they would express the aggressive behaviors of the model (No Incentive condition). In the next condition, the children were given attractive incentives for reproducing the model's behavior (Positive Incentive condition).

Two relevant questions can be asked. First, did the children behave aggressively when they were given an incentive to do so as opposed to when they were not? Many more imitative aggressive behaviors were shown in the Incentive condition than in the No Incentive condition (Figure 12.5). In other words, the children had learned (acquired) many aggressive behaviors that were not performed under the No Incentive condition but were performed under the Incentive condition. This result demonstrated the use of the distinction between acquisition and performance. Second, did the consequences to the model affect the children's display of aggressive behavior? Observation of behavior in the No Incentive condition indicated clear differences; children who observed the model being punished performed far fewer imitative acts than did children in the Model Rewarded and No Consequences

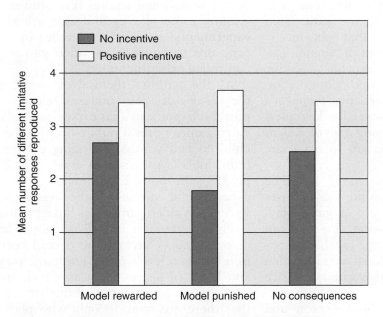

Figure 12.5 *Mean Number of Different Imitative Responses Reproduced by Children as a Function of Response Consequences to the Model and Positive Incentives. (Bandura, 1965) Copyright 1965 by the American Psychological Association. Reprinted by permission.*

DON'T BLAME ME; IT WAS THAT VIDEO GAME!

In November 2002, a teenager in the state of Wisconsin was arrested for auto theft. This was no minor case of theft; the teen was charged with stealing about 100 vehicles! What could cause such behavior? Hostile impulses buried deep in the teen's unconscious? A lifelong trait of criminality?

As reported by the Associated Press, the teenager himself had a much simpler explanation: "He had been inspired by the video game 'Grand Theft Auto.'" In the game, players control animated figures who violently battle law enforcement officials as they go on crime rampages, including the theft of autos. As the local police chief in Wisconsin reported, after playing this game for many hours the teenager felt that stealing real cars would be "challenging and fun." In the language of social-cognitive theory, the game provided psychological models of illegal behavior, including the anticipated benefits (fun, challenge) of that behavior.

This, of course, is just a single, isolated case. It does not provide scientific evidence that playing video games actually contributed to this particular teenager's behavior. Nor does it answer the key question: In general, does playing a lot of violent video games cause a person to act more violently in the real world?

This question can be answered. It can be done by evaluating a large number of cases in which one can measure both game playing and real-world aggression. One then can determine the overall degree to which exposure to violent and criminal acts in video games is related to real-world aggressive behavior.

The psychologists Craig Anderson and Brad Bushman have provided an analysis of this sort. They analyzed the results

obtained in 35 research reports examining the relation between violent video game playing and various measures of real-world aggression. Their sample included more than 4,000 participants who had taken part in both correlational studies (i.e., studies correlating game playing and aggression) and experimental studies (i.e., studies in which exposure to violence in video games was controlled experimentally).

As the authors themselves summarize, the results of their analyses "clearly support the hypothesis that exposure to violent video games poses a public-health threat to children and youths, including college-age individuals" (Anderson & Bushman, 2001, p. 358). In both experimental and non-experimental studies, higher exposure to violence in video games was linked to higher levels of aggression, as well as to lower levels of prosocial behavior. The overall correlation between levels of violent game playing and levels of aggression was a little under .2. Although a correlation of this size means that there are many people who play violent video games yet are not violent in other aspects of their life, it nonetheless is large enough to indicate unequivocally that violent game playing can have a detrimental effect on large numbers of people.

Subsequent research by the authors indicates one way in which game playing has its effects (Bushman & Anderson, 2002). Playing violent games produces a "hostile expectation bias." In this experimental research, people played either a nonviolent or a violent video game. They subsequently were asked whether various interpersonal conflicts depicted in stories (that were not part of the game) involved feelings of aggression and hostility on the part of the story characters. People who had played the violent game subsequently were biased to think that the story characters were feeling and acting aggressively and were having aggressive thoughts. This result implies that people who play violent video games may, in their day-to-day life, more frequently think that other people around them are having hostile, aggressive thoughts. This, of course, could contribute to hostile feelings and actions on their part.

It appears, then, that "fun" and "challenge" are not the only feelings created by violent video games.

SOURCES: ANDERSON & BUSHMAN, 2001; Associated Press, Nov. 14, 2002. Bushman & Anderson, 2002.

groups (Figure 12.5). This difference, however, was wiped out by offering the children attractive incentives for reproducing the model's behavior (Positive Incentive). In sum, the consequences to the model had an effect on the children's performance of the aggressive acts but not on the learning of them.

Vicarious Conditioning

A number of other studies have since demonstrated that the observation of consequences to a model affects performance but not acquisition. The difference between acquisition and performance suggests, however, that in some way the children were being affected by what happened to the model; that is, either on a cognitive basis, on an emotional basis, or both, the children were responding to the consequences to the model. The suggestion here is that the children learned certain emotional responses by sympathizing with the model, that is, vicariously by observing the model. Not only can behavior be learned through observation, but emotional reactions such as fear and joy can also be conditioned on a vicarious basis: "It is not uncommon for individuals to develop strong emotional reactions toward places, persons, and things without having had any personal contact with them" (Bandura, 1986, p. 185).

The process of learning emotional reactions through observing others, known as **vicarious conditioning**, has been demonstrated in both humans and animals. Thus, human subjects who observed a model expressing a conditioned fear response were found to develop a vicariously conditioned emotional response to a previously neutral stimulus (Bandura & Rosenthal, 1966; Berger, 1962). Similarly, in an experiment with animals it was found that an intense and persistent fear of snakes developed in younger monkeys who observed their parents behave fearfully in the presence of real or toy snakes. What was particularly striking about this research is that the period of observation of their parents' emotional reaction was sometimes very brief. Further, once the vicarious conditioning took place, the fear was found to be intense, long-lasting, and present in situations different from those in which the emotional reaction was first observed (Mineka, Davidson, Cook, & Kleir, 1984).

Although observational learning can be a powerful process, one should not think that it is automatic or that one is bound to follow in the footsteps of others. Children, for example, have multiple models and can learn from parents, siblings, teachers, peers, and television. In addition, they learn from their own direct experience. Beyond this, as children get older they may actively select which models they will observe and attempt to emulate.

SELF-REGULATION AND MOTIVATION

As we have just reviewed, one central personality process in social-cognitive theory is the acquisition of knowledge and skills, which is commonly accomplished through observational learning. A second process concerns putting that knowledge into action. In other words, it involves questions of human motivation.

Social-cognitive theory addresses human motivation primarily by examining the motivational impact of thoughts related to oneself, or self-referent thinking. The general idea is that people commonly guide and motivate their own actions through their thinking processes. Key thinking processes often involve the self. Consider your own motivational processes as they relate to this course in personality psychology. You may have enrolled in the course because you expected that you would find the material interesting. You may have calculated an expected grade you could earn in the course; in selecting this course, you may have avoided other course options in which you expected that you might earn a low grade. During the time you have been in the course, you may have set personal goals for performance in the class and may have guided your own studying by reminding yourself that "I've got to finish reading these chapters before the mid-term exam!" It is these personal expectations, personal goals, and talking-to-oneself that social-cognitive theory sees as being at the heart of human motivation.

The general term for personality processes that involve the self-directed motivation of behavior is **self-regulation**. The term is meant to imply that people have the capacity to motivate themselves: to set personal goals, to plan strategies, to evaluate and modify their ongoing behavior. Self-regulation involves not only getting started in goal attainment, but avoiding environmental distractions and emotional impulses that might interfere with one's progress.

The process of self-regulation inherently involves all of the social-cognitive personality structures that we have reviewed thus far. People regulate their behavior by setting personal goals and by evaluating their ongoing behavior according to evaluative standards for performance. Expectancies also are critical; in particular, high expectations of self-efficacy may be necessary if people are to persevere in their goals despite running into setbacks along the way.

In its study of self-regulation, social-cognitive theory emphasizes the human capacity for foresight—our ability to anticipate outcomes and make plans accordingly (Bandura, 1990). Thus, according to Bandura, "most human motivation is cognitively generated" (1992, p. 18). People vary in the standards they set for themselves. Some individuals set challenging goals, others easy goals; some individuals have very specific goals, others ambiguous goals; some emphasize short-term, proximal goals while others emphasize long-range, distal goals (Cervone & Williams, 1992). In all cases, however, it is the anticipation of satisfaction with desired accomplishments and dissatisfaction with insufficient accomplishments that provide the incentives for our efforts. In this analysis, people are seen as proactive rather than as merely reactive. People set their own standards and goals, rather than merely responding to demands from the environment. Through the development of cognitive mechanisms such as expectancies, standards, and self-evaluation we are able to establish goals for the future and gain control over our own destiny (Bandura, 1989a, b, 1999).

Self-Efficacy, Goals, and Self-Evaluative Reactions

Research in social-cognitive theory has examined how these multiple personality processes—self-efficacy perceptions, goals, and self-evaluation of one's ongoing behavior—combine to contribute to self-regulation. Bandura and Cervone (1983) studied the effects of goals and performance feedback on motivation. The hypothesis tested was that performance motivation reflects both the presence of goals and the awareness of how one is doing relative to standards: "Simply adopting goals, whether easy or personally challenging ones, without knowing how one is doing seems to have no appreciable motivational effects" (1983, p. 123). The assumption was that greater discrepancies between standards and performances would generally lead to greater self-dissatisfaction and efforts to improve performance. However, a critical ingredient of such efforts is self-efficacy judgments. Thus, the research tested the hypothesis that self-efficacy judgments, as well as self-evaluative judgments, mediate between goals and goal-directed effort.

In this research, subjects performed a strenuous activity under one of four conditions: goals with feedback on their performance, goals alone, feedback alone, and absence of goals and feedback. Following this activity, described as part of a project to plan and evaluate exercise programs for postcoronary rehabilitation, subjects rated how self-satisfied or self-dissatisfied they would be with the same level of performance in a following session. In addition, they recorded their perceived self-efficacy for various possible performance levels. Their effortful performance was then again measured. In accord with the hypothesis, the condition combining goals and performance feedback had a strong motivational impact, whereas neither goals alone nor feedback alone had comparable motivational significance (Figure 12.6). Also, subsequent effort was most intense when subjects were both dissatisfied with substandard performance and high on self-efficacy judgments for good attainment. Neither dissatisfaction alone nor positive self-efficacy judgments alone had a comparable effect. Often effort was reduced where there were both low dissatisfaction with performance and low perceived self-efficacy. There was, then, clear evidence that goals have motivating power through self-evaluative and self-efficacy judgments.

Performance feedback and self-efficacy judgments also are important to the development of intrinsic interest. Psychologists have been able to enhance students' interest in learning and performance by helping them to break down

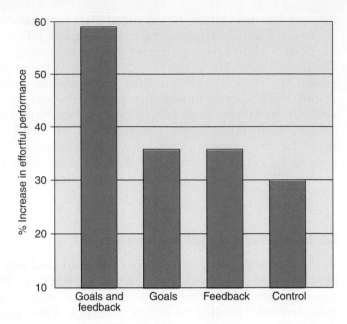

Figure 12.6 *Mean Percentage Increase in Effortful Performance under Conditions Varying in Goals and Performance Feedback. (Bandura & Cervone, 1983) Copyright © 1983 by the American Psychological Association. Reprinted by permission.*

tasks into subgoals, helping them to monitor their own performance, and providing them with feedback that increased their sense of self-efficacy (Bandura & Schunk, 1981; Morgan, 1985; Schunk & Cox, 1986). Intrinsic interest thus develops when the person has challenging standards that provide for positive self-evaluation when met, and the sense of self-efficacy in the potential for meeting those standards. It is such intrinsic interest that facilitates effort over extended periods of time in the absence of external rewards. Conversely, it is difficult to sustain motivation where one feels that the external or internal self-evaluative rewards are insufficient, or where one's sense of efficacy is so low that a positive outcome seems impossible. Self-perceived inefficacy can nullify the motivating potential of even the most desirable outcomes. For example, no matter how attractive it might seem to become a movie star, people will not be motivated in that direction unless they feel that they have the necessary skills. In the absence of such a sense of self-efficacy, becoming a movie star remains a fantasy rather than a goal that is pursued in action.

Self-efficacy beliefs also influence how people cope with disappointments and stress in the pursuit of life goals. Research generally suggests that human functioning is facilitated by a personal sense of control (Schwarzer, 1992). Self-efficacy beliefs represent one aspect of such a sense of control. A study of women coping with abortion demonstrated the importance of self-efficacy beliefs in coping with stressful life events (Cozzarelli, 1993). In this research, women about to obtain an abortion completed questionnaire measures of personality variables such as self-esteem and optimism, as well as a self-efficacy scale measuring expectations concerning successful post-abortion coping. For example, the scale included items asking about whether the women thought they would be able to spend time around children or babies comfortably and whether they would continue to have good sexual relations following abortion. Following abortion, and then, three weeks later, measures of mood and depression were obtained (e.g., the degree to which the women were feeling depressed, regretful, relieved, guilty, sad, good). The results clearly supported the hypothesis that self-efficacy was a key determinant of post-abortion adjustment. The contribution of personality variables such as self-esteem and optimism was also related to post-abortion adjustment. However, their effects appeared to occur through their contribution to feelings of self-efficacy.

In sum, perceptions of self-efficacy have been shown to have diverse effects on experience and action, in the following ways:

Selection Self-efficacy beliefs influence the goals individuals select (e.g., individuals with high self-efficacy beliefs select more difficult, challenging goals than do those who are low self-efficacy beliefs).

Effort, Persistence, and Performance Individuals with high self-efficacy beliefs show greater effort and persistence, and perform better relative to individuals with low self-efficacy beliefs (Stajkovic & Luthans, 1998).

Emotion Individuals with high self-efficacy beliefs approach tasks with better moods (i.e., less anxiety and depression) than individuals with low self-efficacy beliefs.

Coping Individuals with high self-efficacy beliefs are better able to cope with stress and disappointments than are individuals with low self-efficacy beliefs. Bandura summarizes the evidence concerning the effects of self-efficacy beliefs on motivation and performance as follows: "Human betterment has been advanced more by persisters than by pessimists. Self-belief does not necessarily ensure success, but self-disbelief assuredly spawns failure" (1997, p. 77).

To summarize the social-cognitive view of motivation, a person develops goals or standards that serve as the basis for action. People consider alternative courses of action and make decisions on the basis of the anticipated outcomes (external and internal) and the perceived self-efficacy for performing the necessary behaviors. Once action has been taken, the outcome is assessed in terms of the external rewards from others and one's own internal self-evaluations. Successful performance may lead to enhanced self-efficacy and either a relaxation of effort or the setting of higher standards for further effort. Unsuccessful performance or failure may lead to giving up or continued striving, depending on the value of the outcome to an individual and to his or her sense of self-efficacy in relation to further effort.

SELF-CONTROL AND DELAY OF GRATIFICATION

The research on motivational processes that we have just reviewed was concerned with the following type of situation. Sometimes you need to *do* something, but you can't get yourself to do it. For example, you might need to start working on a term paper that is due at the end of the semester, but for some reason you can't get yourself to start actually doing the writing. It is under these circumstances that clear goals and standards for performance, and a strong sense of self-efficacy, are beneficial.

Now we turn to a different type of psychological problem. Sometimes you need to *stop* doing something. There may be some behavior that you find quite enjoyable, but that is socially inappropriate and/or potentially harmful to yourself or others. Smoking, overeating, and driving your car down the highway at 100 mph are obvious examples. Here, the psychological challenge is the opposite of the one we analyzed above. You need to curtail the intrinsically enjoyable behavior. You need to control your impulsive reactions because, in the long run, it is better if you do not give in to them. When these cases of self-control involve putting off something good in the present in order to attain something better in the future (e.g., not having that extra piece of pie now so that, in the future, one will be in better health), the phenomenon is referred to as "delay of gratification."

Learning Delay of Gratification Skills

Research in social-cognitive theory suggests that people's capacity to delay gratification has a social basis. Modeling and observational learning are important to the development of performance standards for success and reward that serve as a basis for delay of gratification. Children exposed to models who set high standards of performance for self-reward tend to limit their own self-rewards to exceptional performance to a greater degree than do children who have been exposed to models who set lower standards or to no models at all (Bandura & Kupers, 1964). Children will model standards even if they result in self-denial of available rewards (Bandura, Grusec, & Menlove, 1967) and will also impose learned standards on other children (Mischel & Liebert, 1966). Children can be made to tolerate greater delays in receiving gratification if they are exposed to models exhibiting such delay behavior.

The effects of a model on delay behavior in children are well illustrated in research by Bandura and Mischel (1965). Children found to be high and low in delay of gratification were exposed to models of the opposite behavior. In a live-model condition, each child individually observed a testing situation in which an adult model was asked to choose between an immediate reward and a more valued object at a later date. The high-delay children observed a model who selected the immediately available reward and commented on its benefits, whereas the low-delay children observed a model who selected the delayed reward and commented on the virtues of delay. In a symbolic-model condition, children read verbal accounts of these behaviors, the verbal account again being the opposite of the child's pattern of response. Finally, in a no-model condition, children were just appraised of the choices given the adults. Following exposure to one of these three procedures, the children were again given a choice between an immediate reward and a more valuable reward. The results were that the high-delay children in all three conditions significantly altered their delay-of-reward behavior in favor of immediate gratification. The live-model condition produced the greatest effect (Figure 12.7). The low-delay children exposed to a delay model significantly altered their behavior in terms of greater delay, but there was no significant difference between the effects of live and symbolic models. Finally, for both groups of children, the effects were found to be stable when the tests were readministered four to five weeks later.

As mentioned previously, the performance of observed behaviors clearly is influenced by the observed consequences to the model. For example, children who watch a film in which a child is not punished for playing with toys that were prohibited by the mother are more likely to play with prohibited toys than are children who see no film or see a film in which the child is

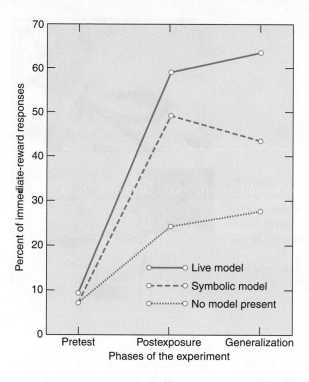

Figure 12.7 *Mean Percentage of Immediate-Reward Responses by High-Delay Children on Each of Three Test Periods for Each of Three Experimental Conditions. (Bandura & Mischel, 1965) Copyright © by the American Psychological Association. Reprinted by permission.*

punished (Walters & Parke, 1964). The old saying "Monkey see, monkey do" is not completely true. It would be more appropriate to say "Monkey sees reward or is not punished, monkey does." After all, the monkey is no fool.

Mischel's Delay of Gratification Paradigm

In addition to the issue of social influences such as modeling on delay of gratification, another question involves the exact cognitive processes that enable someone to control their impulses. What can you do if you want to control your impulses? What mental strategies enable people to delay gratification? Much insight into this question comes from an exceptionally informative line of research pioneered by Mischel (1974; Metcalfe & Mischel, 1999).

In Mischel's **delay of gratification** paradigm, an adult who is interacting with a young child (usually one of preschool age) informs the child that she needs to leave the child alone for a few minutes. Before leaving, the adult teaches the child a game. The game involves two different rewards. If the child can wait patiently until the adult comes back, she gets a large reward (e.g., a few marshmallows). If the child simply cannot wait for the adult to return, the child can ring a bell and the adult will return immediately; however, if this happens, the child earns only a smaller reward (e.g., one marshmallow). The child, then, can earn the larger reward only by delaying gratification. The dependent measure is how long children are able to wait before ringing the bell.

A critical experimental manipulation in this setting is whether children can see the reward—or, phrased more technically, whether the rewards are available for attention. In one experimental condition, children could see the rewards. In another, the rewards were not available for attention; they simply

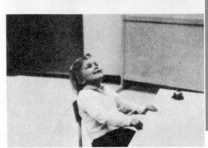

Photos depict a child in the delay of gratification research of Mischel and colleagues (see text). The child is shown a reward (a small pretzel is depicted) and can ring the bell if she cannot wait for the experimenter to return. As depicted in the lower photo, children generally are more successful at waiting if they look away from the rewards and distract themselves from the frustration of having to wait.

were covered up. This simple experimental manipulation proved to have a huge effect on children's delay abilities (Figure 12.8). When the rewards were covered up, most children were able to wait a relatively long time. But when the children were looking at the rewards, they had an enormously hard time controlling their impulses. It appears that looking at rewards that one is not supposed to have primarily is a frustrating experience that children have a hard time handling (Mischel, 1974). Being unable to look at the rewards, then, makes the situation easier to handle.

Subsequent work showed that the key factor in delay of gratification is what is going on in children's heads as they try to wait for the large reward. Children do well at the task if they employ cognitive strategies that distract them from the attractive qualities of the rewards. If children are taught to think about how marshmallows resemble some non-food object (e.g., clouds), or are asked to form mental images in which they think of the rewards as if they are merely photos rather than are real things, or are taught to sing songs to themselves or play other mentally distracting games during the delay period, then they are able to delay gratification even if the rewards are in sight (Mischel & Baker, 1975; Mischel & Moore, 1973; Moore, Mischel, & Zeiss, 1976). "Thus, what is in the children's heads—not what is physically in front of them—crucially affects their ability to purposefully sustain delay in order to achieve their preferred but delayed goals. . . . If the children imagine the real objects as present they cannot wait long for them. In contrast, if they imagine pictures of the objects, they can wait for long time periods" (Mischel, 1990, p. 123). Imagining a mere picture of the object is a "cool" encoding (Metcalfe & Mischel, 1999), that is, a way of thinking about the stimulus that does not activate "hot," impulsive emotional systems. People seem more capable of controlling their emotional reactions, then, when they focus their attention on less emotional features of a given situation; the impact of "hot" versus "cool" encoding for interpersonal behavior is reviewed in Chapter 14.

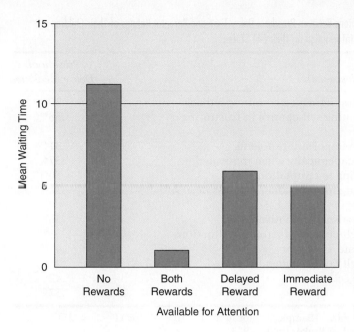

Figure 12.8 *Mean minutes of voluntary waiting time for the delayed reward in each attention condition. (From Mischel & Ebbesen, 1970).*

Mischel's delay of gratification findings vividly illustrate the human capacity for self-control. It is instructive to contrast his social-cognitive approach with behaviorism. The behaviorist looking at Mischel's paradigm might have argued that the main determinant of children's behavior would be the reward contingencies. The problem with that argument is that children in the different experimental conditions (Figure 12.8) all had *exactly the same* reward contingencies; they all got the same small and large rewards based on the same behavior. Mischel's research, then, illustrates the power of something that classic behaviorism never thought of, namely, *mental representations* of rewards.

Since this research involves children, one may wonder about the implication of the results for later personality development. Mischel investigated this question by relating the delay of gratification scores of preschool children to measures of their cognitive and social competence in adolescence, covering a time span of approximately 10 years. Adolescent competence scores were based on parental ratings of their children's cognitive and self-control skills. In addition, parents were asked to provide their children's SAT verbal and quantitative scores, information that was found to be reliable when checked against score information provided by the Educational Testing Service. The results indicated considerable continuity between preschool measures of delay in a laboratory situation and measures of cognitive and social competence obtained in adolescence (Table 12.2) (Shoda, Mischel, & Peake, 1990). Mischel concludes that the results "give a general picture of the child who delayed in preschool developing into an adolescent who is seen as attentive, able to concentrate, able to express ideas well, responsive to reason, competent, skillful, planful, able to think ahead, and able to cope and deal with stress maturely. . . . Perhaps most important, the attributes suggested by the adolescent ratings are consistent with the cognitive competencies essential for delay revealed by

Table 12.2   Illustrative Correlations Between Preschool Delay Time and Parental Ratings of Their Children's Competencies and Information on Their SAT Scores

Parental Responses to Questionnaire Items (Adolescence)	*Preschool Delay Measure*
1. Likelihood of being sidetracked by minor setbacks	−.30*
2. Likelihood of exhibiting self-control in frustrating situations	.58***
3. Ability to cope with important problems	.31*
4. Ability to do well academically when motivated	.37*
5. Likelihood of yielding to temptation	−.50***
6. Likelihood of settling for immediate but less desirable choice	−.32*
7. Ability to pursue goals when motivated	.38*
8. Ability to exhibit self-control in tempting situations	.36*
9. Ability to concentrate	.41**
10. Ability to exhibit self-control when frustrated	.40*
11. SAT Verbal	.42*
12. SAT Quantitative	.57

*$p < .05$ **$p. < .01$ ***$p. < .001$ (Sample size for items $1 - 10 = 43$, for $11 - 12 = 35$)
(Adapted from Shoda, Mischel, & Peake, 1990, p. 983).

the experimental research, namely the ability to divert and control attention strategically in the pursuit of one's goal" (1999, p. 484).

Social-Cognitive View of Growth and Development

In addition to the importance of direct experience, social-cognitive theory emphasizes the importance of models and observational learning in personality development. Individuals acquire emotional responses and behaviors through observing the behaviors and emotional responses of models (i.e., the processes of observational learning and vicarious conditioning). Whether acquired behaviors are performed similarly depends on directly experienced consequences and the observed consequences to models. Through the experiencing of **direct external consequences**, individuals learn to expect rewards and punishments for specific behaviors in specific contexts. Through **vicarious experiencing of consequences** to others, individuals acquire emotional reactions and learn expectancies without going through the often painful step of experiencing consequences directly. Thus, through direct experience and observation, through direct experiencing of rewards and punishments, and through vicarious conditioning, individuals acquire such important personality characteristics as competencies, expectancies, goals-standards, and self-efficacy beliefs. In addition, through such processes individuals acquire self-regulatory capacities. Thus, through the development of cognitive competencies and standards people are able to anticipate the future and reward or punish themselves for relative progress in meeting chosen goals. The latter **self-produced consequences** are of particular significance in maintaining behavior over extended periods of time in the absence of external reinforcers.

It is important to recognize that social-cognitive theory is opposed to views that emphasize fixed stages of development and broad personality types.

According to Bandura and Mischel, people develop skills and competencies in particular areas. Rather than developing consciences or healthy egos, they develop competencies and motivational guides for action that are attuned to specific contexts. Such a view emphasizes the ability of people to discriminate among situations and to regulate behavior flexibly according to internal goals and the demands of the situation.

SUMMARY

This chapter has reviewed the basic principles of the social-cognitive approach to personality. They include three main ideas.

Personality is conceptualized in terms of four types of variables: competencies, beliefs and expectancies, goals, and evaluative standards. These cognitive personality structures develop as a result of social experience, and thus are called "social-cognitive."

Personality is understood as a cognitive-affective processing system. The notion of *system* is critical; different social-cognitive structures and processes are highly interconnected and organized, and thus work together as a coherent system. This personality system develops and functions through reciprocal interactions with the social environment.

Social-cognitive theory explores a variety of personality processes that are central to everyday social behavior. These include (a) modeling, or observational learning; (b) motivation, which involves the self-regulation of behavior as people work toward goals; and (c) the control of impulses, where research on delay of gratification shows that what children pay attention to while trying to control their impulses determines self-control ability.

In the next chapter, we continue to explore contemporary social-cognitive theory. We do so by examining not only the contributions of Bandura and Mischel and their colleagues, but those of other contemporary researchers who contribute to an understanding of social-cognitive processes in personality. We also consider applications of the theoretical ideas to real-world problems, including applications in the psychological clinic.

MAJOR CONCEPTS

Acquisition   The learning of new behaviors, viewed by Bandura as independent of reward and contrasted with performance—which is seen as dependent on reward.

Behavioral signatures   Individually distinctive profiles of situation-behavior relationships.

Cognitive-affective processing system (CAPS)   A theoretical framework developed by Mischel and colleagues in which personality is understood as containing a large set of highly interconnected cognitive and emotional processes; the interconnections cause personality to function in an integrative, coherent way, or as a "system."

Competencies   A structural unit in social-cognitive theory reflecting the individual's ability to solve problems or perform tasks necessary to achieve goals.

Context specificity   The idea that a given personality variable may come into play in some life settings, or contexts, but not others, with the result that a person's behavior may vary systematically across contexts.

Delay of gratification The postponement of pleasure until the optimum or proper time, a concept particularly emphasized in social-cognitive theory in relation to self-regulation.

Direct external consequences In social-cognitive theory, the external events that follow behavior and influence future performance, contrasted with vicarious consequences and self-produced consequences.

Evaluative standards Criteria for evaluating the goodness or worth of a person or thing. In social-cognitive theory, people's standards for evaluating their own actions are seen as being involved in the regulation of behavior and the experience of emotions such as pride, shame, and feelings of satisfaction or dissatisfaction with oneself.

Expectancies In social-cognitive theory, what the individual anticipates or predicts will occur as the result of specific behaviors in specific situations (anticipated consequences).

Goals In social-cognitive theory, desired future events that motivate the person over extended periods of time and enable the person to go beyond momentary influences.

Microanalytic research Bandura's suggested research strategy concerning the concept of self-efficacy in which specific rather than global self-efficacy judgments are recorded.

Observational learning (modeling) Bandura's concept for the process through which people learn merely by observing the behavior of others, called models.

Perceived self-efficacy In social-cognitive theory, the perceived ability to cope with specific situations.

Performance The production of learned behaviors, viewed by Bandura as dependent on rewards, in contrast with the acquisition of new behaviors, which is seen as independent of reward.

Reciprocal determinism The mutual, back-and-forth effects of variables on one another; in social-cognitive theory, a fundamental causal principle in which personal, environmental, and behavioral factors are viewed as causally influencing one another.

Self-evaluative reactions Feelings of dissatisfaction versus satisfaction (pride) in oneself that occur as people reflect on their actions.

Self-produced consequences In social-cognitive theory, the consequences to behavior that are produced personally (internally) by the individual and that play a vital role in self-regulation and self-control.

Self-regulation Psychological processes through which persons motivate their own behavior.

Vicarious conditioning Bandura's concept for the process through which emotional responses are learned through the observation of emotional responses in others.

Vicarious experiencing of consequences In social-cognitive theory, the observed consequences to the behavior of others that influence future performance.

REVIEW

1. Social-cognitive theory centers its analyses of personality on uniquely human-cognitive capacities. Thanks to their ability to think about themselves, their past, and their future, individuals are seen to have the capacity to influence their own experiences and development. Since these thinking processes develop through interaction with the social environment, they are called social-cognitive. Two theorists who have made primary contributions to the development of the social-cognitive approach are Albert Bandura and Walter Mischel.

2. The personality structures emphasized in social-cognitive theory are competencies and skills, expectancies and beliefs, behavioral standards, and personal goals. These four personality variables refer to four distinct classes of cognition; they thus can be seen as distinct subsystems within the overall system of personality. Any given person may have different skills, beliefs, standards, and goals in different situations. Thus, behavior naturally varies across situations in a meaningful manner that reflects the individual's personality characteristics.

3. Social-cognitive theory addresses personality processes in two primary ways. First, the principle of reciprocal determinism captures the back-and-forth influences between personality and the environment. Second, personality is construed as a cognitive-affective processing system. Much research on personality processes from a social-cognitive perspective has explored the phenomena of observational learning, self-regulation, and self-control.

4. The social-cognitive theory analysis of observational learning emphasizes that people's knowledge and skills primarily are acquired by observing others. Observational learning processes include the learning of emotional reactions through observation of models, or "vicarious conditioning." An important distinction is made between *acquiring* patterns of behavior in the absence of rewards and *performing* those behaviors.

5. The social-cognitive theory analysis of motivation emphasizes the role of people's thoughts about themselves. Self-efficacy judgments, or perceptions of one's capability to execute behaviors, are key to motivation; self-efficacy beliefs influence people's selection of goals, effort and persistence toward achieving the goal, emotions prior to and during task performance, and success in coping with stress and negative events. In addition, much work examines processes of goal setting, and the role that people's evaluations of their own actions play in goal-directed motivation.

6. Research on the development of cognitive and behavioral competencies associated with delay in gratification illustrates the social-cognitive approach to questions of both self-control and personality development. Standards for self-control are learned through the observation of models and through reinforcement. The ability to delay gratification involves the development of cognitive competencies, especially involving the control of attention; people who distract themselves from frustrating situations are better able to control their negative emotions and impulses. Research also indicates that individual differences in the capacity to delay gratification are remarkably stable across the course of development.

SOCIAL-COGNITIVE THEORY: APPLICATIONS, RELATED THEORETICAL CONCEPTIONS, AND CONTEMPORARY RESEARCH

13

Chapter Focus

A college senior was trying to work on his medical school applications late one evening, but found himself so paralyzed by anxiety that he could get nothing accomplished. How could he cope with the possibility of not getting accepted anywhere? His family is counting on him to be a doctor! His friends would think he was a big braggart if he didn't get in to a medical school after his years of talk about being pre-med! These thoughts so preoccupied him that he failed to complete his applications by the deadlines. He eventually sent them in, but by being late he significantly worsened his chances of getting into medical school. Thus, his own behavior had increased the likelihood that the unwanted outcome would become a reality.

This young man is doing something that is extremely common. When working on a task, people often think about not only the task at hand (the admissions information, in this case) but about themselves (their goals, hopes, and fears). These thoughts may cause one to do worse; they distract people from the task at hand, create anxiety, and thus undermine performance. A psychologist might say that these thoughts are "dysfunctional": they work (or "function") badly for people, undermining their efforts to succeed.

Basic research in social-cognitive theory has explored the impact of beliefs, goals, and standards on people's emotions and behavior, including negative emotions that undermine performance. In clinical applications of this research, psychologists have developed ways to alter dysfunctional beliefs. These extensions and applications of social-cognitive theory are examined in this chapter. In concluding sections of the chapter, we evaluate social-cognitive theory, in part by comparing it to personality theories you learned about previously in the text.

QUESTIONS TO BE ADDRESSED IN THIS CHAPTER

1. How can the study of knowledge structures, or "schemas," inform the understanding of personality and self-concept?

2. Are there qualitatively different types of goals and standards of self-evaluation that have different effects on a person's motivation and emotional life?

3. How can a social-cognitive analysis of personality contribute to the development of effective psychotherapies?

4. Can psychotherapy rely on cognitive processes alone, or is actual experience a necessary component of therapeutic change?

In Chapter 12, you learned that social-cognitive theory explains personality in terms of basic thinking—or "cognitive"—capacities. The main theorists, Albert Bandura and Walter Mischel, try to understand how people's cognitive capacities develop as people interact with the social world.

As you will recall from the previous chapter, three of these cognitive personality variables were people's

- *beliefs* about the self and the world
- personal aims or *goals*
- *evaluative standards* that people use to judge the goodness or worth of their own actions and those of others.

The basic idea of social-cognitive theory is that beliefs, goals, and standards—as well as competencies for performing behaviors—contribute to the uniqueness and coherence of our personality. These social cognitions, in other words, explain consistent, coherent patterns of emotion and behavior. Consider an example close at hand. Why are you reading this textbook now, when you could be hanging out with friends, listening to music, watching TV, napping, tanning, snacking, and so forth? It probably is because (1) you *believe* that you need to read the book to do well in the personality course in which you're enrolled, (2) you have the *goal* of doing reasonably well in the course, and (3) you know you would *evaluate* yourself negatively (i.e., you'd feel bad about yourself) if you spent your whole day napping, tanning, and snacking instead of working.

These cognitions—beliefs, goals, and evaluative standards—have two important qualities. First, they are socially acquired. If you had been raised by kindly woodland creatures in a forest rather than by people in a human society, you would not have the same beliefs, goals, and standards that you have now. Second, they are enduring; you generally have the same beliefs, goals, and evaluative standards from one day to the next. Beliefs, goals, and evaluative standards thus are "social-cognitive" personality variables that contribute to enduring, consistent patterns of behavior.

In this chapter, we review contemporary research on each of these three social-cognitive components of personality. As you will see, some of the research programs that we review will be ones that were spearheaded by Bandura or Mischel, the primary social-cognitive theorists we discussed in Chapter 12. But others have been initiated by other personality scientists. Numerous researchers analyze personality by examining the role of social-cognitive processes and structures. Their efforts extend and complement the work of Bandura and Mischel and, in so doing, contribute to a broad social-cognitive tradition in contemporary personality psychology.

BELIEFS ABOUT THE SELF AND SELF-SCHEMAS

It is human nature to be self-reflective. People do not merely interact with the world. They reflect on their own interactions and, in so doing, develop beliefs about what they themselves are like. Self-referent beliefs are central to personality functioning. A wide range of phenomena—emotions, motivation, the flow of ideas that constitute our mental life—are affected by our thoughts about our selves. Events elicit emotional reactions and become motivating when they are seen as relevant to our sense of self (Lazarus, 1991).

As we have noted previously, the study of self-concept was relatively neglected during significant portions of psychology's history, particularly in the first three-fourths of the 20th century. But in a remarkable coincidence of timing, the intellectual scene shifted in 1977. A number of scientists, working

COGNITIVE COMPONENTS OF PERSONALITY: BELIEFS, GOALS, AND EVALUATIVE STANDARDS

Hazel Markus

independently, published seminal papers in which aspects of self-concept figured prominently. One such paper was Bandura's (1977a) initial statement of self-efficacy theory, discussed in Chapter 12. Other work included social psychological studies demonstrating that information that is relevant to the self is more memorable than other types of information (Rogers, Kuiper, & Kirker, 1977). Finally, a paper that proved to be of enormous significance to the study of personality, and that we will now discuss, was published by the psychologist Hazel Markus (1977), who explored self-schemas. As a result of these earlier developments, the study of the self now is a flourishing field (Leary & Tangney, 2003).

The idea that the mind contains **schemas** has a long history. The 18th century German philosopher Immanuel Kant recognized that we make sense out of new experiences by interpreting events in terms of preexisting ideas in the mind (Watson, 1963). These preexisting mental structures are what he referred to as schemas. Schemas are knowledge structures that we use to bring order to what otherwise might be a chaotic jumble of stimuli. To illustrate, suppose you listen to a new song on the radio. In terms of the physical stimuli involved, the sound might seem chaotic: There's some banging on a drum, some noises from a synthesizer, a few guitar chords, somebody singing something, somebody else singing something else. And all these different sounds occur at the same time! Chaos! Yet, of course, it isn't chaos. It sounds to you like an ordered, structured, meaningful piece of music. It sounds this way because you have acquired mental schemas for song structures, and these schemas guide your interpretation of the information (i.e., the sounds that comprise the song). The role of schemas becomes clear if you hear music of a musical form with which you are not at all familiar, that is, music for which you are lacking a musical schema. If, for example, you hear music from a different culture or contemporary symphonic music that is not written according to traditional harmonies, rhythms, and melodic structures, it might sound chaotic to you—even though it surely sounds structured and orderly to its composer. This is because you lack the musical schemas that are necessary to make sense of the sounds.

Schemas, then, are structures of the mind that we use to make sense of the world around us. Phrased more technically, schemas are knowledge structures that guide and organize the processing of information. A schema, then, is far more than just a stored list of facts. A schema instead is an organized network of knowledge (Fiske & Taylor, 1991; Smith, 1998) that commonly is of such complexity that it may be impossible for a person to state its contents. For example, you may not be able to state in words all the knowledge of music that you possess (the sounds of instruments, patterns of rhythm and melody, etc.). Yet you surely can use that knowledge to understand and evaluate new songs.

Markus (1977) recognized that many of our most important schemas concern ourselves. In a key step forward in the study of social cognition and personality, she suggested that the self is a concept or category like any other concept or category, and that people form cognitive generalizations about the self just as they do about other things. People, then, develop **self-schemas**. Through interaction with the social world, we develop generalized knowledge structures concerning ourselves. These elements of self-knowledge guide and organize information processing when we encounter new situations.

Importantly, different people—with their different interpersonal, social, and cultural life experiences—develop different self-schemas, that is, schemas with different content. For example, one person might have an independence/dependence self-schema; in other words, she might commonly think of herself as an independent person, might possess a lot of knowledge about this personality characteristic of hers, and might interpret situations according to their relevance to independence. Another person might possess a schema organized around the concept of guilt/innocence, and use this schema to interpret many situations, even though a guilt/innocence schema might not even be present in most other persons. Self-schemas, then, may account for the relatively unique ways in which idiosyncratic individuals think about the world around them.

Self-Schemas and Reaction-Time Methods

An important aspect of Markus's work was that she not only provided theoretical ideas about self-schemas. She also provided methodological tools to study self-schemas. A key research method employed by Markus (1977) was *reaction-time* (or response latency) measures. Reaction-time measures are experimental methods in which an experimenter records not only the content of a person's response (e.g., whether he or she says "yes" or "no" in response to a question), but also how long it takes the person to respond to the question. Reaction-time measures are directly relevant to the central idea associated with the notion of self-schemas. The idea is that schemas guide information processing. People who possess a self-schema with regard to a given domain of social life should, then, be faster in responding to questions regarding that life domain. Reaction-time measures, then, provide the index of speed of response that is necessary to test this theoretical idea.

To illustrate the logic of reaction-time methods, suppose you happen to be someone who spends hours a week doing volunteer service in which you are helpful to other individuals in your community. As a result, you may have developed a self-schema regarding your "helpfulness." Now suppose that both you and another person, who rarely does volunteer service, are in a study in which you are asked the question "Are you a helpful person?" Both of you may say "yes." Even the other person, who only occasionally volunteers, may say that, "yes," he or she is helpful. However, despite your similar "yes" responses, self-schema theory would expect that you would differ in the *speed* with which you make your responses. Compared to the other person, you should be faster to say that, "yes," you are helpful. Your preexisting self-schema regarding helpfulness should speed your information processing.

This is exactly the sort of result that Markus (1977) found and that has been replicated by subsequent investigators. Markus (1977) first identified people who possessed a self-schema regarding independence (the attribute she happened to use in her study). She did this by using a two-step method in which participants (1) rated themselves as high or low on independence and (2) indicated the degree to which the personality characteristic was important to them. Only people who had an extremely high or low self-rating and thought that independence/dependence was important to their personality were judged as being schematic for the attribute; the idea is that we tend to develop schemas about personal attributes that we view as socially important to our lives. Subsequently, participants were asked to rate whether a series of adjectives (some of which were semantically related to independence/dependence) were descriptive of themselves. Exactly as predicted, participants who possessed a schema made these judgments faster. Specifically, independent-schematic participants rated independent adjectives more quickly than dependent adjectives, and dependent-schematic persons identified dependent adjectives faster than independent traits (Markus, 1977).

Research on self-schemas by Markus and others suggests that, once we have developed ways of thinking about ourselves (our self-schemas), there is a strong tendency for them to be maintained. We seem to be biased to pay attention to, to remember, and to judge as being true information that is consistent with our schemas about ourselves. Schemas, then, not only guide the processing of information, but in so doing, they also create self-confirming biases.

An illustration of how self-schemas are not only related to the processing of information but to action as well comes from research on schemas, sexual behavior, and romantic involvement. The researchers tested the idea that women with differing sexual self-schemas would process interpersonal information differently and function differently in their sexual and romantic relationships (Andersen & Cyranowski, 1994). Women were asked to rate themselves on a list of 50 adjectives, 26 of which were used to form a Sexual Self-Schema Scale (e.g., uninhibited, loving, romantic, passionate, direct). They also were asked to respond to measures that asked about sexual experiences and romantic involvement. Clear evidence was found that women with high scores on the Sexual Self-Schema Scale, particularly those with positive sexual self-schemas, were more sexually active, experienced greater sexual arousal and sexual pleasure, and were more able to be involved in romantic love relationships relative to women with low scores on the scale. "Co-schematics," that is, women who had both positive schemas organized around their ability to experience sexual passion and negative schemas involving sexual conservatism or embarrassment, were found to experience high levels of involvement with sexual partners, yet also to experience relatively high levels of sexual anxiety (Cyranowski & Andersen, 1998). These experiences, in turn, could further influence views about the self, creating a self-confirming bias in which schemas contribute to experiences that, in turn, confirm the original schemas.

In this emphasis on the self, it should be clear that any given individual does *not* possess merely one self-schema. Instead, people tend to live complex lives in which they develop a number of different views of themselves. For example, it may not be the case that you are either a hard-working student, or a loyal friend, or a good dancer at parties, or an anxious test-taker. Instead, you well could be all four of these things; that is, you may possess self-schemas concerning all four of these aspects of self. The different self-schemas would tend to come to mind in different settings. Different situational cues may cause different self-schemas to enter working memory and thus, to be part of the **working self-concept** (Markus & Wurf, 1987), that is, the subset of self-concept that is in working memory at any given time (Figure 13.1). Self-concept thus is dynamic; the information about the self that is in consciousness, and guides behavior, at any given time changes dynamically as people interact with the ever-changing events of the social world.

Contemporary research on social cognition and self-concept (e.g., Banaji & Prentice, 1994), then, suggests that the self is not a single, unitary thing. Instead, people commonly possess multiple self-schemas. The different self-schemas frequently are related to one another; for example, using the example above, there may be links between your view of yourself as hard-working and as someone who is anxious when it comes to taking tests, and friendship

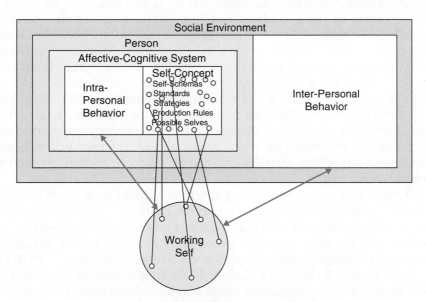

Figure 13.1 *Schematic representation of the Working Self, which consists of a subset of mental representations that make up the overall self-concept. The central idea in this model is that different social circumstances activate different subsets of a person's overall self-knowledge; in other words, different situations bring different information into working memory, creating different "working selves" in different settings. From Markus and Wurf (1987).*

and dancing at parties may provide an important break from the academic routine of college life. Recognizing these relations, investigators have suggested that, rather than a single self-schema, people tend to possess a "family of selves" (Cantor & Kihlstrom, 1987), that is, a collection of self-views that may be as diverse as are different members of the same family, yet that may share some family resemblances. According to this view, you are many things, in many places, with many people. Thus, you have many contextualized selves, each with a set of features. The features of these contextualized selves, this family of selves, will overlap in some ways and be distinctive in others. Each of us, then, has a family of selves, the contents and organization of which are unique. Within this family of selves there may be a prototypic self, a self-concept in relation to which we say, "This is what I am really like." And within this family of selves there may be fuzzy selves, or parts of us that we are not sure how they fit in relation to the other selves.

Self-Based Motives and Motivated Information Processing

Self-schemas do not merely provide information that is used in thinking, in the way that an encyclopedia might provide information that is used in answering a trivia question. Self-schemas also motivate people to process information in particular ways. Motivational processes, then, are often self-based (Banaji & Prentice, 1994; Higgins, 1996, 1997; Kunda, 1990). Two motives in relation to the self have been emphasized in research on social cognition and personality. They are motives for **self-enhancement** and for **self-verification**.

Your intuitions may tell you that people are biased toward seeing themselves in a positive light. For example, when you get a bad grade on an exam, you might be prone to think of how poorly written or unfair the exam was; conversely, when you get a good grade, the professor might seem like an exam-writing genius. Much research is consistent with such intuitions. People often are biased toward positive views of the self (Tesser, Pilkington, & McIntosh, 1989).

These biases can be explained by positing a self-enhancement motive. People may be motivated to establish and maintain a positive self-image. This motive causes us to prefer positive to negative feedback, to overestimate our positive attributes (Dunning. Heath, & Suls, 2004), and to enhance our self-images by selectively comparing ourselves to people who are faring less well than ourselves (Wood, 1989).

Yet a motive to self-enhance may not fully explain motivated features of information processing. People also may be motivated to experience themselves as being consistent and predictable. People like to see themselves as being basically the same person from one day to the next. The psychologist William Swann suggests that people have a self-verification motive (Swann, 1991, 1992; Swann, Rentfrow, & Guinn, 2003), that is, a motive to solicit from others information that confirms aspects of their self-concept. A person who is extraverted, for example, may present herself to others in ways that maintain her extraverted self-concept (e.g., the person might talk about all the outgoing things she did at a wild party last weekend). In this way, the person maintains a stable, predictable sense of self.

This may seem obvious, but the nonobvious part of Swann's view is the suggestion that people even seek self-confirmation when they have negative schemas. That is, a person with a negative self-schema will seek out information

CURRENT APPLICATIONS

SELF-SCHEMAS AND HISTORY OF SEXUAL ABUSE

The first theory of personality discussed in this book, that of Freud, devoted much attention to an experience that is utterly traumatic and unfortunately common: sexual abuse. Given the importance of the topic, you may have expected that subsequent, newer personality theories also would address it in detail. If so, you would have been disappointed. As you have seen from previous chapters, personality theorists working in traditions other that psychodynamic theory devoted much less attention to this problem than Freud did.

Recent work, however, has applied the social-cognitive principles discussed in this chapter—particularly the work of Markus and of Andersen & Cyranowski—to the study of women with a history of sexual abuse. Meston, Rellini, and Heiman (2006), researchers at the University of Texas and at the Kinsey Institute for Sex, Gender, and Reproduction, hypothesized that abuse experiences may alter self-schemas, and do so in a long-lasting manner. To test this idea, they conducted a study whose participants were 48 women with a history of child sexual abuse; these were women who reported coercive sexual activity prior to the age of 16. (The women were, on average, in their late 20s at the time of the study.) They also studied a group of 71 women who had not suffered from abuse experiences and who thus served as control participants. To measure schematic beliefs about the self and sexual behavior—i.e., sexual self-schemas—Meston et al. administered the sexual self-schema scale developed by Anderson and Cyranowski. In this scale, people report on their perceptions of their own sexuality, for example, whether they perceive themselves as romantic, passionate, arousable, inhibited, and so forth.

Their results indicated that women with a history of abuse had different self-schemas than women who were not abused. Specifically, women with a history of abuse believed themselves to be less romantic and passionate; that is, they had lower scores on the romantic/passionate items of the sexual self-schema measure. The childhood abuse experiences, then, did alter people's enduring sense of self.

The researchers also asked women in the study to report on whether they experience negative emotions (fear, anger) during sexual experiences. Data analyses indicated that women who had experienced abuse years earlier had more negative emotional experiences in the present day. Also, among women with abuse experiences, there was a significant association between sexual schemas and emotion: Women with lower romantic/passionate self-schemas reported more negative emotional experiences (Meston et al., 2006). The changes in self-schemas resulting from abuse experiences in childhood, then, were linked to emotions experienced years later.

and social feedback that confirms the negative self-schema, becoming in a sense his or her own worst enemy. For example, depressives who have negative self-schemas can seek out self-verifying information which serves to maintain their negative self-image and their depression (Giesler, Josephs, & Swann, 1996). More generally, in accord with his emphasis on self-verification, Swann presents evidence to the effect that people gravitate toward relationships with people who see them as they see themselves. Thus, not only are persons with positive self-concepts more committed to spouses who think highly of them than to spouses who think poorly of them, but persons with negative self-concepts are more committed to spouses who think poorly of them than to spouses who think well of them (De La Ronde & Swann, 1998; Swann, De La Ronde, & Hixon, 1994). In the words of the comedian Groucho Marx: "I'd never join a club that would have me as a member."

What happens, then, when the two motives conflict? If push comes to shove, do we prefer accurate feedback or positive feedback, the disagreeable truth or what fits our fancy, to be known for who we are or to be adored for who we would like to be (Strube, 1990; Swann, 1991)? In other words, what happens when our cognitive need for consistency or self-verification conflicts with our affective need for self-enhancement, what Swann has called the cognitive-affective crossfire (Swann, Griffin, Predmore, & Gaines, 1987; Swann, Pellham, & Krull, 1989)? A complete answer to this question is not at hand. The evidence to date suggests, however, that generally we prefer positive feedback but prefer negative feedback in relation to negative self-views. In line with this, there is evidence that life events inconsistent with the self-concept can lead to physical illness, even if these events are positive (Brown & McGill, 1989). In other words, positive life events can be bad for one's health if they conflict with a negative self-concept and disrupt one's negative identity. At the same time, there are individual differences in this regard, and we may be more oriented toward self-enhancement in some relationships and self-verification in other relationships. For example, there is evidence that self-enhancement is more important during the early stages of a relationship but self-verification becomes increasingly important as the relationship becomes more intimate (Swann, De La Ronde, & Hixon, 1994).

LEARNING VERSUS PERFORMANCE GOALS

Self-schemas, discussed above, concern people's beliefs about their personal qualities. Other elements of personality that are important to social-cognitive approaches to personality are people's goals for behavior. As we discussed in our previous chapter, goals, which are mental representations of the aim of an action or course of actions, are seen as central to human motivation by social-cognitive personality theorists.

In our previous chapter, we discussed research showing that the presence versus absence of clear goals on a task greatly affects people's motivation (see pages 481–482). Here we discuss contemporary research on a phenomenon that is related, yet slightly different. On any given activity, people may possess different *types of* goals. Different people may think about an activity differently; different thoughts about goals to be achieved may run through people's minds as they perform the same task. These different goals may lead to different patterns of thought, emotion, and behavior; the goals, in other words, may be the cause of what one would interpret as different personality styles. Although a number of useful distinctions among types of goals have been drawn, one particularly valuable distinction differentiates "learning" goals from "performance" goals.

In their social-cognitive theory of personality and achievement motivation, Carol Dweck and her colleagues (Dweck & Leggett, 1988; Grant & Dweck,

Carol Dweck

1999) have differentiated between **learning goals** and **performance goals**. The distinction can perhaps best be understood by reflecting on thoughts that may run through your mind when you are trying to achieve something. Suppose that you are working on a group project in a class that you are taking; perhaps you and a group of people are in a psychology research methods course and you are trying to design an experiment to answer a particular research question. There are at least two ways of thinking about your goals in this situation. On the one hand, you may think about the task and all you can learn from it: the different types of research designs, different ways of analyzing data, conclusions you can draw from the research, and the overall educational experience you will have from this activity. If you are thinking this way, you have what Dweck would refer to as a "learning goal." On the other hand, you might have a very different pattern of thinking. You might have the aim of showing other people in the group how smart you are, of avoiding embarrassment when you don't know some information, of making a good impression on the professor, and so forth. If you are thinking this way, you have what Dweck would call a "performance goal"; that is, you have a goal that involves "putting on a good performance" for other people who may be evaluating you.

People with learning versus performance goals tend to have very different experiences on tasks, particularly if they have doubts about their capabilities or experience setbacks. In an initial experimental test of this idea, Elliott and Dweck (1988) induced learning versus performance goals among grade school students performing a cognitive task. The students were given different information about the task, with the information being designed to induce different types of goals. Some students were told that they were performing a task that would sharpen their mental skills; this was designed to induce learning goals, since the task appeared merely to be one in which people would learn mental skills that might be useful at some later point. Others were told they were performing a task that would be evaluated by experts who would examine how well they were doing; this condition induced performance goals. Students' beliefs in their ability on the task were also manipulated through provision of bogus feedback on a prior activity.

This study (Elliott & Dweck, 1988) yielded two types of results of great interest. First, people who had a combination of performance goals and low

Table 13.1 Percentage of Participants for Whom Task Strategies Improved and Percentage of Participants Who Spontaneously Expressed Negative Affect during a Task, as a Function of Having a Learning versus Performance Goal and Having Low versus High Perceptions of Ability

	Condition			
	Learning Goal		Performance Goal	
	Low Perceived Ability	High Perceived Ability	Low Perceived Ability	High Perceived Ability
Strategy improves	22.2	20.8	8.7	37.0
Negative affect	3.7	0.0	30.4	3.7

beliefs in their ability performed poorly (Table 13.1); specifically, they were less likely than others to develop useful strategies on the task. The second type of finding involved a "think aloud" data-collection procedure, that is, a procedure in which experimenters ask people to think out loud while they are trying to solve a problem. When thinking out loud, most people, of course, voice thoughts about the task they are trying to solve. However, some people think not only about the task, but about themselves and their feelings. For example, Elliott and Dweck (1988) recorded the degree to which people spontaneously expressed negative emotions while working on the task. It turned out that people who had performance goals and low beliefs in their ability were much more likely to make such statements (Table 13.1). Students who had the goal of making a good impression on others (i.e., performance-goal participants) expressed much tension and anxiety when performing the task; for example, one participant, instead of thinking solely about the problems, spontaneously said, "My stomach hurts" (Elliott & Dweck, 1988, p. 10). Learning goals, then, can cause people to have negative thoughts and feelings that interfere with their performance.

This research by Dweck and colleagues provides insight into what we commonly call "test anxiety." As you may know intuitively, some people become highly anxious when taking a test and, as a result, perform more poorly than they would have if they had remained calm. What is so interesting about Dweck's approach to this problem is that she does not hand out a scale of "test anxiety" that describes who might become anxious when taking a test. Instead, she explores a pattern of thinking that is an underlying cause of the emotions and actions that we call "test anxiety." Such an approach is particularly useful if one is interested in developing interventions to help people to become less test anxious. Dweck's social-cognitive analysis suggests that one might intervene by trying to change people's patterns of thinking.

Causes of Learning versus Performance Goals: Implicit Theories

In light of the results we have reviewed, a question that may have crossed your mind is: Why do some people adopt learning goals on tasks, whereas others adopt performance goals? What are the causes of different goal orientations? Fortunately, this question also has crossed the mind of Dweck and colleagues, who have examined this issue systematically. A primary factor they have considered is that different people may have different **implicit theories** about

Test anxiety that occurs when people become concerned with how they are being evaluated by others can lower performance on academic tests.

human attributes, including human abilities, and that these different implicit theories contribute to different goal orientations.

Implicit theories are those we possess, that guide our thinking, but that we may not usually state in words—that is, we usually do not explicitly articulate the ideas. They are "theories" in that they do not involve just simple facts, but more complex ideas about how things work. Clearly, people have many implicit theories. We believe that gravity pulls objects down to earth (even though we may state this explicitly only when taking a physics class). We believe that people have certain fundamental rights (even though we may only state this explicitly when taking a government class).

The particular implicit theories of interest to Dweck and colleagues are theories about whether or not psychological attributes are changeable. In a series of studies, Dweck and her colleagues investigated the implications of children having one or the other of two kinds of beliefs, the two sets of beliefs differing in how malleable or fixed the relevant trait is believed to be (Dweck, 1991, 1999; Dweck, Chiu, & Hong, 1995). According to one set of beliefs, known as an entity theory, a particular characteristic or trait is viewed as fixed. According to the other set of beliefs, known as an incremental theory, a particular characteristic or trait is believed to be malleable or open to change. For example, an entity view of intelligence suggests that intelligence is a fixed trait; in this view, people simply "have" more or less intelligence. On the other hand, an incremental view of intelligence suggests that intelligence is a malleable trait that can be increased; in this view, educational experiences contribute to knowledge and make one a more intelligent person.

Differences in views concerning the nature of a trait such as intelligence have implications for goals that are set and responses to failure (Dweck &

Leggett, 1988). For example, children with an entity view of intelligence tend to set performance goals. If one thinks that intelligence is a fixed entity, then it is only natural to interpret activities as a test of one's intelligence—that is, as a "performance" in which one's intelligence is evaluated. Conversely, children with an incremental view of intelligence tend to set learning goals. If intelligence can be increased, then, it is natural to set the learning goal of acquiring experiences that increase one's intelligence. Different implicit theories, then, lead people to set different goals that, in turn, have different implications for emotion and motivation.

Dweck's analysis does not apply merely to achievement tasks of the sort one encounters in school. It can apply to other characteristics as well; for example, if one sees oneself as being a "lazy" person, one might view this either as a fixed quality or as something that might change for the better over the course of your personal development. Grant and Dweck (1999) use the more general terms "judgment goals" and "development goals" (analogous to performance goals and learning goals, respectively), to capture the fact that any of a variety of characteristics may be viewed as either a fixed trait or as changeable. Bear in mind that they are not asking whether, in reality, the characteristic is fixed or changeable. The personality variable of interest is people's *subjective beliefs about* the degree to which their personality characteristics can change. More recent research has shown that different goal orientations are important not only to achievement tasks, but also to interpersonal behavior (Erdley, Loomis, Cain, & Dumastlines, 1997).

STANDARDS OF EVALUATION

In Chapter 12, you learned that another personality variable important to social-cognitive theory is self-evaluative standards, which are criteria people use to evaluate the goodness or worth of themselves and their actions. Standards are related to, yet differ from, goals (Boldero & Francis, 2002; Cervone, 2004). Goals are aims one hopes to achieve in the future. Standards are criteria used to evaluate events in the present. For example, if you are watching an ice skating performance, you might evaluate the performance as good or bad according to standards you have used for judging the performance of skaters. You might have these standards whether or not you, personally, have the goal of being a figure skater. Goals and standards, then, are psychologically distinct mechanisms. Much work in personality psychology indicates that people regulate their behavior by evaluating whether their actions are consistent with internalized standards for performance (e.g., Baumesiter & Vohs, 2004; Carver & Scheier, 1998; Cervone, Shadel, Smith, & Fiori, 2006).

Our review of the work of Dweck, above, showed that it is valuable to distinguish among qualitatively different types of goals. Similarly, it is valuable to distinguish among qualitatively different types of evaluative standards (Dweck, Higgins, & Grant-Pillow, 2003). An exceptionally fruitful line of theory and research by the psychologist Tory Higgins (1987, 1990, 2006) has expanded the scope of social-cognitive analyses of personality by showing how different types of evaluative standards relate to different types of emotional experiences and motivation. We review that work now.

Self-Standards, Self-Discrepancies, Emotion, and Motivation

The psychological phenomenon of interest to Higgins can be illustrated with an example. Suppose two people are reading in a college library some night late in the semester, are both unhappy with how they have been doing in a course, and are both behind in course readings as the semester draws to a close. And imagine they take a break from their work to discuss how they're doing. "I'm really anxious about this class," one person says tensely, "I wanted an A, but I don't even think I can get a B." "I'm not anxious" says the other, dejectedly, "I'm really *depressed* about this class. I wanted an A, but I don't even think I can get a B."

What's going on here? How can one explain why the two people have different emotional reactions to the same event? Why is one vulnerable to becoming anxious, the other to becoming depressed? Higgins suggests it is because they are evaluating the event with different types of standards. Although they both "want" the same thing, an A, the subjective nature of that standard of performance differs from one person to the other. The critical distinction is the difference between standards that represent "ideals" versus "oughts." Some evaluative standards represent achievement that people *ideally would like* to reach. They represent types of behavior that one values positively. Higgins calls these ideal standards, or aspects of the "ideal self." (In this way, Higgins's analysis is similar to that of Rogers, Chapter 5.) Alternatively, some evaluative standards represent standards of achievement that people feel they *should* or *ought to* achieve. The standards represent duties or responsibilities. These are termed *ought* standards, or elements of the "ought self."

Higgins's analysis is important to the study of personality and individual differences because different individuals may evaluate the same type of behavior using different standards. Recent work demonstrates this point with a behavior of importance to health: smoking. People who are similar in that they all want to quit nonetheless differ in their evaluative standards regarding quitting. Some wish to quit primarily because they ideally would like to be more healthy; smoking for them violates an ideal standard. Other primarily feel a sense of responsibility to others to quit smoking (e.g., to avoid bothering others with cigarette smoke); smoking for them violates an ought standard (Shadel & Cervone, 2006).

Tory Higgins

A key insight of Higgins's is that different types of standards, ought versus ideal, trigger different types of negative emotions (Higgins, 1987, 1996). There are two steps to Higgins's reasoning. (1) People experience negative emotions when they detect a discrepancy between how things really are going for them—or their "actual self"—and a personal standard. These **self-discrepancies** are cognitive mechanisms that contribute to emotional experience. (2) Discrepancies with *different* (ideal versus ought) standards trigger *different* emotions. Discrepancies between the actual and ideal self cause people to feel sad or dejected; failing to meet one's ideal standards is a loss of positive outcomes that brings on sadness. Discrepancies between the actual and ought self cause agitation and anxiety; the possibility of not achieving one's obligations is a potential negative outcome that is threatening.

To test these ideas, Higgins, Bond, Klein, & Strauman (1986) first assessed individual differences in self-discrepancies. They identified one group of people who predominantly have actual/ideal discrepancies, and a second set who predominantly have actual/ought discrepancies. To do this, Higgins and colleagues (1986) employed a simple questionnaire in which people listed attributes they believed they (a) actually possessed, (b) ideally would like to possess, and (c) believed they should, or ought to, possess. In a subsequent experimental session, these people's emotional reactions were assessed as they envisioned themselves experiencing a negative life event. Although all participants envisioned the *same* event, they experienced *different* emotions. People whose self-descriptions featured many actual/ideal discrepancies tended to become sad but not anxious when thinking about the negative outcome. People whose self-described attributes featured mostly actual/ought discrepancies became anxious but not sad.

These findings, then, suggest that self-discrepancies are a cognitive basis for individual differences in emotional experience. However, you might be thinking that the findings are not entirely convincing. They are only correlational; different types of self-discrepancies are correlated with different emotional reactions. As we discussed back in Chapter 2, experimental—rather than merely correlational—research would provide evidence that is more convincing.

A great advantage of Higgins's work is that he is able to provide such experimental evidence. Ought and ideal standards are elements of knowledge, and elements of knowledge can be experimentally primed (that is, made more mentally salient through a procedure that activates the knowledge). A second study, then, experimentally manipulated self-discrepancies through priming. People who possessed both actual/ideal and actual/ought self-discrepancies were assigned at random to conditions that primed either ideal standards or ought standards. Priming alternative standards led to different emotional reactions (Table 13.2). When ideal self-discrepancies were primed, participants felt dejected. When ought standards were primed, they felt agitated. Thus, an experimental manipulation of cognition led to changes in emotion.

Much subsequent research has yielded evidence consistent with Higgins's core idea that discrepancies with ideal versus ought standards lead to different emotional experiences. This includes clinical research with social phobics and clinically depressed patients, who exhibit predominantly actual/ought and actual/ideal discrepancies, respectively (Straumann, 1989). Higher levels of neuroticism and lower levels of subjective well-being are experienced by people

Table 13.2 Mean Change in Dejection Emotions and Agitation Emotions as a Function of Level of Self-Discrepancies and Type of Priming

	Ideal Priming		Ought Priming	
Level of Self-Discrepancies	Dejection Emotions	Agitation Emotions	Dejection Emotions	Agitation Emotions
High actual: ideal and actual: ought discrepancies	3.2	−0.8	0.9	5.1
Low actual: ideal and actual: ought discrepancies	−1.2	0.9	0.3	−2.6

NOTE: Each of 8 dejection emotions and 8 agitation emotions was measured on a 6-point scale from *not at all* to *a great deal*. The more positive the number, the greater the increase in discomfort. SOURCE: Higgins et al., 1986, Study 2.

whose self-descriptions indicate a discrepancy between how they really think they are and how they judge who they think they ought to be (Pavot, Fujita, & Deiner, 1997). The existence of self-discrepancies has health implications, having been found to decrease the effectiveness of the functioning of our immunological system in fighting disease (Strauman, Lemieux, & Coe, 1993). Clinical researchers have begun to develop therapeutic techniques to reduce discrepancies between the actual and ideal self (Strauman et al., 2001).

More recently, Higgins (2006) has emphasized that people's evaluative standards have implications not only for emotional experience, but for motivation. People who evaluate their actions primarily through ideal standards tend to have a "promotion" approach to their activities. In other words, they are motivated toward promoting well-being, which they do by focusing on positive outcomes (either attaining positive outcomes or avoiding their loss once they have been attained). A pre-med student with a promotion focus might dwell on the benefits of a medical career or the importance of not lowering his or her high grade point average. In contrast, a focus on ought standards tends to make one "prevention-focused," that is, focused on preventing the occurrence of (or gaining an absence of) negative outcomes. In our previous example, a prevention-focused pre-med student might focus on the possibility of not being admitted to med school, and might view good class performance primarily as a way in which one avoids this negative outcome. Different motivational processes come into play when one is prevention- versus promotion-focused (Shah & Higgins, 1997), and people's actions feel more natural to them when their activities fit their primary motivational orientation (Higgins, 2006).

A "General Principles" Approach to Personality

Higgins's (1999) analysis of cognition, emotion, and individual differences has a theoretical advantage that is a bit subtle, yet highly significant. It concerns the explanation of consistencies in behavior as opposed to variations in behavior from one situation to another. As we have discussed previously, some personality psychologists treat consistencies in behavior as an indication of an individual's personality, whereas variations are explained in terms of the power of situations to influence behavior. In this approach, "personality variables" explain what people do on average, and "situational factors" explain variations around the average. As Higgins recognizes, this sort of thinking yields a

CURRENT QUESTIONS

PERFECTIONISTIC STANDARDS: GOOD OR BAD?

Much of contemporary society has a hard-driving, motivated quality to it. We value people who achieve. We teach children—in classrooms, on stage, on playing fields, and so forth—to set high standards of achievement. In the language of social-cognitive theory, society models and rewards the adoption of high standards for performance. Our contemporary society promotes high standards—sometimes so high that people evaluate themselves via standards that are "perfectionistic," that is, standards that indicate that anything less than perfect performance is unacceptable.

High standards may cause people to excel. But are extremely high, perfectionistic standards necessarily a good thing? It "astounds me," a contemporary psychologist says, that "people have said that self-oriented perfectionism is adaptive... I don't think needing to be perfect is in any way adaptive." The psychologist Paul Hewitt of the University of British Columbia should know; for years he has studied perfectionism, examining the psychological qualities that are associated with perfectionistic tendencies. Hewitt and colleagues find that perfectionistic standards make people vulnerable to psychological problems: depression, anxiety, eating disorders. People with perfectionistic standards may excel, yet suffer a cost. Hewitt, for example, relates the case of a perfectionistic student who worked so hard on a course that he got an A+, but then became depressed, thinking that if he had been a better student he would have gotten the grade without working so hard!

Research findings are consistent with this anecdotal evidence in suggesting a link between perfectionistic standards and feelings of depression. For example, Flett, Beseer, and Hewitt (2005) studied perfectionism about a group of about 200 adults living in Israel. People completed a perfectionism inventory (a self-report measure of perfectionistic tendencies), rated whether they experienced symptoms of depression, and had close friends rate whether they were experiencing symptoms of depression. People who said that they needed to be perfect to meet the expectations of friends and family rated themselves as being more depressed. Their friends saw them as depressed, too.

An adaptive lifestyle in the contemporary world may be one that mixes high standards of achievement with the capacity to accept oneself—including those aspects of self that are not perfect.

SOURCE: BENSON, 2003; Flett et al., 2005

very unsatisfying science of persons. It is unsatisfying because different, and seemingly unrelated, theoretical principles have to be invoked to explain one versus another behavior by the same person.

In contrast, Higgins's work yields general principles; he describes it as a **general principles approach** to understanding personality and situational influences. People's knowledge—including their ideal and ought standards for performance—explains consistencies in their emotion and behavior, since knowledge is an enduring aspect of personality. But knowledge mechanisms also explain situational influences. Different situations activate different aspects of knowledge and, in so doing, bring about different emotional and motivational patterns. Thus, one obtains an integrated account of personal and situational influences on emotion and behavior in which one set of common, general principles explains both consistency in thought and action that results from personal influences and variability in thought and action that results from situational influences.

Thus far in discussing social-cognitive theory, we primarily have reviewed core theoretical principles and basic research that supports them. We now turn to a key area of application of this theory and research: the psychological clinic. Clinical applications of cognitive theory have been of enormous significance in the past quarter-century. Indeed, in many clinical settings and training programs, the cognitive approach has become the most predominant of all theoretical orientations.

CLINICAL APPLICATIONS

There is no one theory or technique of cognitive therapy. Instead, there are different approaches, often tailored to specific problems, that share some common assumptions:

1. Cognitions (attributions, beliefs, expectancies, memories concerning the self and others) are viewed as critical in determining feelings and behaviors. Thus, there is an interest in what people think and say to themselves.

2. The cognitions of interest tend to be specific to situations or categories of situations, though the importance of some generalized expectancies and beliefs is recognized.

3. Psychopathology is viewed as arising from distorted, incorrect, mal-adaptive cognitions concerning the self, others, and events in the world. Different forms of pathology are viewed as resulting from different cognitions or ways of processing information.

4. Faulty, maladaptive cognitions lead to problematic feelings and behaviors, and these in turn lead to further problematic cognitions. Thus, a self-fulfilling cycle may set in whereby persons act so as to confirm and maintain their distorted beliefs.

5. Cognitive therapy involves a collaborative effort between therapist and patient to determine which distorted, maladaptive cognitions are creating the difficulty and then to replace them with other more realistic, adaptive cognitions. The therapeutic approach tends to be active, structured, and focused on the present.

6. In contrast with other approaches, cognitive approaches do not see the unconscious as important, except insofar as patients may not be aware of their routine, habitual ways of thinking about themselves and life. Further, there is an emphasis on changes in specific problematic cognitions rather than on global personality change.

STRESS AND COPING

The work of cognitively oriented psychologists has been very important in the area of stress, coping, and health (Folkman & Moskowitz, 2004).

Lazarus, whose work has been very influential in this area, suggests that psychological stress depends on cognitions relating to the person and the environment (Lazarus, 1990). In this cognitive approach to stress and coping, stress is viewed as occurring when the person views circumstances as taxing or exceeding his or her resources and endangering well-being. Involved in this are two stages of cognitive appraisal. In primary appraisal, the person evaluates whether there is anything at stake in the encounter, whether there is a threat or danger. For example, is there potential harm or benefit to self-esteem? Is one's personal health or that of a loved one at risk? In secondary appraisal, the person evaluates what, if anything, can be done to overcome harm, prevent harm, or improve the prospects for benefit. In other words, secondary appraisal involves an evaluation of the person's resources to cope with the potential harm or benefit evaluated in the stage of primary appraisal.

There are different ways of coping with any given situation. A key distinction is one that differentiates between **problem-focused coping**, which refers to attempts to cope by altering features of a stressful situation, and **emotion-focused coping**, which refers to coping in which an individual strives to improve his or her internal emotional state, for example, by emotional distancing or the seeking of social support. Research by Folkman, Lazarus, and colleagues has developed a questionnaire to assess coping, the Ways of Coping Scale, and has explored the health implications of different coping strategies.

The experience of stress in daily life can be reduced through cognitive strategies that help people to cope with everyday stressors.

This research suggests the following conclusions (Folkman, Lazarus, Gruen, & DeLongis, 1986; Lazarus, 1993):

1. There is evidence of both stability and variability in the methods individuals use to cope with stressful situations. Although the use of some coping methods appears to be influenced by personality factors, the use of many coping methods appears to be strongly influenced by the situational context.

2. In general, the greater the reported level of stress and efforts to cope, the poorer the physical health and the greater the likelihood of psychological symptoms. In contrast, the greater the sense of mastery, the better is the physical and psychological health.

3. Although the value of a particular form of coping depends on the context in which it is used, in general, planful problem solving ("I made a plan of action and followed it" or "Just concentrate on the next step") is a more adaptive form of coping than escape avoidance ("I hoped a miracle would happen" or "I tried to reduce tension by eating, drinking, or using drugs") or confrontative coping ("I let my feelings out somehow" or "I expressed anger to those who caused the problem").

In addition to this conceptual analysis of stress and coping, the therapist requires practical procedures to reduce stress. Such a procedure has been developed by Don Meichenbaum (1995), whose **stress inoculation training** procedure is based on a cognitive view of stress. In accord with Lazarus's view, Meichenbaum suggests that stress be viewed in cognitive terms; that is, stress involves cognitive appraisals, and individuals under stress often have a variety of self-defeating and interfering thoughts. In addition, such self-defeating cognitions and related behaviors have a built-in self-confirmatory component (e.g., people get others to treat them in an overprotective way). Finally, events are perceived and recalled in ways that are consistent with a negative bias. Meichenbaum's stress inoculation procedure is designed to help individuals cope better with stress and is seen as analogous to medical inoculation against biological disease.

Stress inoculation training involves teaching clients the cognitive nature of stress, followed by instruction in procedures to cope with stress and change faulty cognitions and, finally, training in the application of these procedures in actual situations. In terms of the cognitive nature of stress, the effort is to have the client become aware of such negative, stress-engendering, automatic thoughts as "It is such an effort to do anything" and "There is nothing I can do to control these thoughts or change the situation." The important point here is that the person may not be aware of having these automatic thoughts, and, thus, must be taught to be aware of them and their negative effects. In terms of coping procedures and correction of faulty cognitions, clients are taught relaxation as an active coping skill and taught cognitive strategies such as how to restructure problems so that they appear more manageable. In addition, clients are taught problem-solving strategies, such as how to define problems, generate possible alternative courses of action, evaluate the pros and cons of each proposed solution, and implement the most practicable and desirable one. Clients also are taught to use coping self-statements such as "I can do it," "One step at time," "Focus on the present; what is it I have to

Imagery: Cognitive therapists encourage patients to imagine scenes to determine the nature of their fears and develop positive courses of action.

do?" "I can be pleased with the progress I'm making," and "Keep trying; don't expect perfection or immediate success." Finally, through imagery rehearsal and practice in real-world situations clients are taught to feel comfortable with the use of these procedures. In imagery rehearsal the client imagines various stressful situations and the use of the coping skills and strategies. Practice involves role-playing and modeling involving the therapist as well as practice in real-world situations.

The stress inoculation training procedure is active, focused, structured, and brief. It has been used with medical patients about to undergo surgery, with athletes to help them deal with the stress of competition, with rape victims to help them deal with the trauma of such assaults, and in the work environment to teach workers more efficient coping strategies and to help worker management teams consider organizational change.

PATHOLOGY AND CHANGE

The cognitive, information processing view holds that psychopathology results from unrealistic, maladaptive cognitions. Therapy, then, involves efforts to change such cognitive distortions and replace them with more realistic, adaptive cognitions.

Ellis's Rational-Emotive Therapy

Albert Ellis was a former psychoanalyst who developed a therapeutic system of personality change known as rational emotive-therapy (RET) (Ellis, 1962, 1987; Ellis & Harper, 1975) or, equivalently, rational-emotion behavior theory (REBT; e.g., Ellis & Tafrate, 1997). Ellis's ideas about psychological distress and its treatment have two main parts; that is, there are two primary theses behind Ellis's work.

The first thesis is that people do not respond emotionally to events in the world, but to their *beliefs about* those events. Ellis conveys this idea simply, by suggesting an "ABC" of rational-emotive therapy (Ellis, 1997). An activating (A) event may lead to a consequence (C) such as an emotional reaction. A person unfamiliar with Ellis's analyses may think that the A caused the C, that is, that the activating event is the cause of the emotional consequence. But not so, according to Ellis. "We ... create Beliefs (Bs) between A and C. Our Bs about A largely determine our response to it" (Ellis & Tafrate 1997, p. 31). This first premise of rational-emotive therapy, then, is identical to the central premise of the social-cognitive approach to personality, namely, that people's enduring beliefs systems are immediate determinants of their experiences and actions.

Ellis's second thesis is more unique. It is his claim that the beliefs that cause psychological distress have a particular quality: they are *irrational*. That is, they are beliefs that no rational person would, upon reflection, wish to have because the beliefs are sure to bring about one's own psychological distress.

According to Ellis, then, the causes of psychological difficulties are irrational beliefs or irrational statements we make to ourselves: beliefs, for example, that we *must* do something, that we *have to* feel some way, that other people *always should* treat us in a certain manner. Suppose a person thinks, "If good things happen, bad things must be on the way," or, "If I express my needs, others will reject me." These thoughts are irrational in that persons who think these things are dooming themselves to psychological distress.

Cognitive therapists often distinguish among alternative types of thinking that are maladaptive. The distinctions among them are not terribly important; nonetheless, listing a few can give you an idea of the type of negative thinking that Ellis and similar therapists wish to change in therapy:

Faulty reasoning. "I failed on this effort, so I must be incompetent." "They didn't respond the way I wanted them to, so they must not think much of me."

Dysfunctional expectancies. "If something can go wrong for me, it will." "Catastrophe is just around the corner."

Negative self-views. "I always tend to feel that others are better than me." "Nothing I do ever turns out right."

Maladaptive attributions. "I'm a poor test-taker because I am a nervous person." "When I win, it's luck; when I lose, it's me."

Memory distortions. "Life is horrible now and always has been this way." "I've never succeeded in anything."

Maladaptive attention. "All I can think about is how horrible it will be if I fail." "It's better not to think about things; there's nothing you can do anyway."

Self-defeating strategies. "I'll put myself down before others do." "I'll reject others before they reject me and see if people still like me."

Ellis's therapy techniques are designed to force people to reflect on their own thinking. Rational-emotion therapists try to make people aware of the irrationality of their own thoughts, so they then can replace these thoughts with calm, rational thinking. Therapists use a variety of techniques—logic,

Aaron T. Beck

argument, persuasion, ridicule, humor—in an effort to change the irrational beliefs that cause psychological distress.

Beck's Cognitive Therapy for Depression

Like Albert Ellis, Aaron Beck is a former psychoanalyst who became disenchanted with psychoanalytic techniques and gradually developed a cognitive approach to therapy. His therapy is best known for its relevance to the treatment of depression, but it has relevance to a wider variety of psychological disorders. According to Beck (1987), psychological difficulties are due to automatic thoughts, dysfunctional assumptions, and negative self-statements.

The Cognitive Triad of Depression

Beck's cognitive model of depression emphasizes that a depressed person systematically misevaluates ongoing and past experiences, leading to a view of the self as a loser, the view of the world as frustrating, and the view of the future as bleak. These three negative views are known as the cognitive triad and include negative views of the self such as "I am inadequate, undesirable, worthless," negative views of the world such as "The world makes too many demands on me and life represents constant defeat," and negative views of the future such as "Life will always involve the suffering and deprivation it has for me now." In addition, a depressed person is prone to faulty information processing, such as in magnifying everyday difficulties into disasters and overgeneralizing from a single instance of rejection to the belief that "Nobody likes me." It is these thinking problems, these negative schemas and cognitive errors, that cause depression.

Research on Faulty Cognitions

Considerable research has examined whether faulty cognitions are related to symptoms of depression, as Beck's theory anticipates. Much research in the 1980s and 1990s provided evidence that was consistent with Beck's model (Segal & Dobson, 1992). Compared to nondepressed individuals, depressed persons appeared to focus more on themselves (Wood, Saltzberg, & Goldsamt, 1990), to have more accessible negative self-constructs (Bargh & Tota, 1988; Strauman, 1990), and to have a bias toward pessimism rather than optimism, particularly in relation to the self (Epstein, 1992; Taylor & Brown, 1988).

Much of the early research on cognition and depression employed "concurrent" research designs, that is, research plans in which cognitions and depressive symptoms are measured at the same time. Concurrent designs have a big drawback: It is hard to know if relations between cognition and depression reflect (1) the influence of cognition on depression (as Beck and other cognitive theorists predict), (2) the influence of depressed emotions on cognition, or (3) the influence of some third factor that affects both cognition and depression (e.g., negative life events that affect people's beliefs and emotional experiences). Cognitive theories can be evaluated more convincingly through the use of "prospective" research designs, that is, research in which cognitive factors are measured at one point in time and are used to predict the development of depressive symptoms at later time points.

Fortunately, in recent years investigators have turned to prospective research designs. For example, Hankin, Fraley, and Abela (2005) asked participants, at the outset of a study, to complete a questionnaire that measured their tendencies to engage in negative patterns of thinking that were thought to predispose persons to becoming depressed. They then asked these same research participants to complete a daily diary for a period of 35 days. Individual differences in the tendency to thinking negatively, as assessed at the outset of the study, predicted the subsequent occurrence of depressive symptoms; that is, the cognitive factor predicted depressive symptoms during the following 35 days during which people completed the diary (Hankin et al., 2005).

One of the puzzling questions for psychologists who emphasize the role of faulty cognitions in depression is the following: What happens to the faulty cognitions when the depression has lifted? The reason that this question is important is that once having experienced a serious depression, there is a tendency toward relapse or the likelihood of experiencing another depression. Why should this be the case if the faulty cognitions are gone? There is some evidence that the faulty cognitions that make the person vulnerable to depression are latent and only become manifest under conditions of stress (Alloy, Abramson, & Francis, 1999; Dykman & Johll, 1998; Ingram, Miranda, & Segal, 1998; Wenzlaff & Bates, 1998). For example, people vulnerable to depression may retain negative attitudes toward the self that only become manifest and operational when they experience blows to their self-esteem. The task of therapy, then, is to affect fundamental change in these cognitions as well as to make the person aware of the conditions under which they become operational.

Cognitive Therapy

Cognitive therapy of depression is designed to identify and correct distorted conceptualizations and dysfunctional beliefs (Beck, 1993; Brewin, 1996). Therapy generally consists of 15 to 25 sessions at weekly intervals. The approach is described as involving highly specific learning experiences designed to teach the patient to monitor negative, automatic thoughts, to recognize how these thoughts lead to problematic feelings and behaviors, to examine the evidence for and against these thoughts, and to substitute more reality-oriented interpretations for these biased cognitions. The therapist helps the patient to see that interpretations of events lead to depressed feelings. For example, the following exchange between therapist (T) and patient (P) might occur:

P: I get depressed when things go wrong. Like when I fail a test.

T: How can failing a test make you depressed?

P: Well, if I fail I'll never get into law school.

T: So failing the test means a lot to you. But if failing a test could drive people into clinical depression, wouldn't you expect everyone who failed the test to have a depression? Did everyone who failed get depressed enough to require treatment?

P: No, but it depends on how important the test was to the person.

T: Right, and who decides the importance?

P: I do.

SOURCE: BECK, RUSH, and SHAW, 1979, p. 146.

In addition to the examination of beliefs for their logic, validity, and adaptiveness, behavioral assignments are used to help the patient test certain maladaptive cognitions and assumptions. This may involve the assignment of activities designed to result in success and pleasure. In general, the therapy focuses on specific target cognitions that are seen as contributing to the depression. Beck contrasts cognitive therapy with traditional analytic therapy in terms of the therapist's being continuously active in structuring the therapy, in the focus on the here and now, and in the emphasis on conscious factors.

Beck's cognitive therapy has been expanded to include the treatment of other psychological difficulties, including anxiety, personality disorders, drug abuse, and marital difficulties (Beck, 1988; Beck & Freeman, 1990; Beck, Wright, Newman, & Liese, 1993; Clark, Beck, & Brown, 1989; Epstein & Baucom, 1988; Young, 1990). The idea is that each difficulty is associated with a distinctive pattern of beliefs. Whereas in depression the beliefs concern failure and self-worth, in anxiety, for example, they concern danger. There is evidence for the effectiveness of cognitive therapy (Antonuccio, Thomas, & Danton, 1997; Craighead, Craighead, & Ilardi, 1995; Hollon, Shelton, & Davis, 1993; Robins & Hayes, 1993). Although the distinctive therapeutic features of cognitive therapy and whether changes in beliefs are the key therapeutic ingredients remain to be determined (Dobson & Shaw, 1995; Hollon, De Rubeis, & Evans, 1987), recent evidence suggests that therapeutic change indeed follows cognitive change (Tang & De Rubeis, 1999a, b).

PSYCHOPATHOLOGY: MODELING, SELF-CONCEPTIONS, AND PERCEIVED SELF-EFFICACY

According to social-cognitive theory, maladaptive behavior results from dysfunctional learning. Like all learning, maladaptive responses can be learned as a result of direct experience or as the result of exposure to inadequate or "sick" models. Thus, Bandura suggests that the degree to which parents themselves model forms of aberrant behavior is often a significant causal factor in the development of psychopathology. Again, there is no need to look for traumatic incidents in the early history of the individual or for the underlying conflicts. Nor is it necessary to find a history of reinforcement for the initial acquisition of the pathological behavior. On the other hand, once behaviors have been learned through observational learning, it is quite likely that they have been maintained because of direct and vicarious reinforcement. Recall the research on the vicarious conditioning of emotional responses. Monkeys who observed their parents express a fear of snakes developed a conditioned emotional response that was intense, long-lasting, and generalized beyond the context in which it was first learned. Thus, it is suggested that observational learning and vicarious conditioning may account for a great proportion of human fears and phobias.

Although the learning of specific overt behaviors and emotional reactions is important in psychopathology, increasingly social-cognitive theory has come to emphasize the role of **dysfunctional expectancies** and self-conceptions. People may erroneously expect painful events to follow some events or pain to be associated with specific situations. They then may act so as to avoid certain situations or in a way that creates the very situation they were trying to avoid. An example is the person who fears that closeness will bring pain and then acts in a hostile way, resulting in rejection by others and presumably confirming the expectancy that closeness leads to disappointment and rejection.

Cognitive processes also play a role in psychopathology in terms of **dysfunctional self-evaluations**, in particular in terms of perceived low self-efficacy or perceived inefficacy. Remember that perceived self-efficacy is the perception that one can perform the tasks required by a situation or cope with a situation. In perceived inefficacy, one feels that one cannot perform the necessary tasks or cope with the demands of the situation. Thus, according to social-cognitive theory, it is perceived inefficacy that plays a central role in anxiety and depression (Bandura, 1997).

Self-Efficacy, Anxiety, and Depression

Let us first consider the role of perceived self-efficacy in anxiety. According to social-cognitive theory, people with perceptions of low self-efficacy in relation to potential threats experience high anxiety arousal. It is not the threatening event per se but the perceived inefficacy in coping with it that is fundamental to anxiety. Research indicates that those who believe they cannot manage threatening events experience great distress. They may also develop further dysfunctional cognitions such as a preoccupation with what may happen. In other words, the anxious person may focus attention on the disaster that lies ahead, and on his or her inability to cope with it, rather than focusing on what might be done to cope with the situation. The perception of inability to cope with the situation may then be complicated further by the perceived inability to cope with the anxiety itself, a fear-of-fear response that can lead to panic (Barlow, 1991).

Whereas perceived inefficacy in relation to threatening events leads to anxiety, perceived inefficacy in relation to rewarding outcomes leads to depression; that is, depression represents the response to perceived inability to gain desired rewarding outcomes. Part of the problem with depressives, however, may be their excessively stringent standards. In other words, individuals prone to depression impose upon themselves excessively high goals and standards. When they fall short of these exacting standards, they blame themselves and their lack of ability or competence for what has happened. Excessive self-criticism is, in fact, often a major feature of depression. In sum, although perceived self-inefficacy to fulfill desired goals is fundamental to depression,

**CURRENT
QUESTIONS**

HOW DOES PHYSICAL DISCIPLINE BY PARENTS INFLUENCE CHILDREN?

All parents face the challenge of disciplining their children. The question they have to ask themselves is, "How?" What is the best form of discipline?

One strategy is effective in the short term, but might raise problems in the long run. This is the strategy of physical discipline. Children may not pay attention when you talk to them. But they'll surely notice if you spank them! But maybe spanking has negative consequences. Bandura's analysis of modeling and of the social sources of anxiety suggests that physical discipline may have long-term costs, even if it stops a child from disobeying in the present.

So what are the effects of spanking? Before answering that question, one must pause to recognize that the answer *could* be "it depends." Societies and cultures vary in the degree to which spanking is a typical, expected form of discipline; they vary, in other words, in whether such physical discipline is "normative." Spanking could have different effects depending on whether it is normative in a giving setting.

These questions have been explored in a remarkable cross-cultural study. Researchers studied parents and children from six nations: China, India, Italy, Kenya, the Philippines, and Thailand. In each, they conducted interviews to determine whether individual parents use physical discipline (spanking, grabbing and shaking, etc.) when disciplining their children. They also obtained measures of psychological problems experienced by children, including whether the child is excessively fearful and anxious. Finally, rather than analyzing the data for all parents, from all cultures combined, they determined whether physical discipline occurred frequently (i.e., was normative) in a given culture.

What did they find? It turned out that some influences of physical discipline were the same in *all* cultures, whether or not discipline was normative. In all locations, children who experienced higher levels of physical discipline were found also to experience higher levels of anxiety; the link from

the experience of physical discipline to child anxiety was found in all six nations. Also, in most nations, children who experienced more parental physical disciple were themselves more aggressive with others. Physical discipline may work in the short term, but it appears to have long-term costs wherever you go.

SOURCE: LANSFORD et al., 2005

part of the problem may be the excessive goals themselves. In addition, the low self-efficacy beliefs may contribute to diminished performance, leading to falling even further below standards and additional self-blame (Kavanagh, 1992). Just such a relationship was found in a study of childhood depression. In this study, perceived social and academic inefficacy was found to contribute to depression directly as well as indirectly through problem behaviors that interfered with future social and academic success (Bandura, Pastorelli, Barbaranelli, & Caprara, 1999). Thus, a self-defeating cycle was established wherein low self-efficacy contributed to depression and problem behaviors, which in turn contributed to further perceived inefficacy and depression.

Bandura (1992) raises the interesting point that discrepancies between standards and performance can have varied effects that can lead to greater effort, to apathy, or to depression. What determines which effect will occur? According to Bandura, discrepancies between performance and standards lead to high motivation when people believe they have the efficacy to accomplish the goal. Beliefs that the goals are beyond one's capabilities because they are unrealistic will lead to abandoning the goal and perhaps to apathy, but not to depression. For example, a person may say, "This task is just too hard," and give up, perhaps becoming frustrated and angry, but not depressed. Depression occurs when a person feels ineffective in relation to a goal but believes the goal to be reasonable; therefore that person feels he or she must continue to strive to meet the standard. Thus, the effects of a discrepancy between standards and performance on effort and mood depend on self-efficacy beliefs and whether the standard is perceived to be reasonable, possible to achieve, and important.

The relationships between depressed mood and discrepancies between standards and performance is a two-way street. Not only do these discrepancies create depressed emotions; depressed emotions contribute to the existence of these discrepancies. Evidence on this point comes from research that experimentally manipulates people's moods (Cervone, Kopp, Schaumann, & Scott, 1994; Scott & Cervone, 2002), as well as work that compares depressed and non-depressed persons (Tillema, Cervone, & Scott, 2001). The findings indicate that when people are feeling bad, they tend to have more perfectionistic standards. When in a bad mood, routine outcomes seem less satisfactory; as a result, people are satisfied only with superior attainments. These higher standards for performance commonly exceed the level of performance people think they actually can attain (Cervone et al., 1994).

Self-Efficacy and Health

One of the most active areas of social-cognitive research has been on the relation between self-efficacy beliefs and health (Bandura, 1997). The results of this research can be easily summarized: Strong, positive self-efficacy beliefs are good for your health. Conversely, weak and negative self-efficacy beliefs are bad for your health (Schwarzer, 1992). There are two major ways in which self-efficacy beliefs affect health. These ways are the beliefs' effects on health-related behaviors and their effects on physiological functioning (Contrada, Leventhal, & O'Leary, 1990; Miller, Shoda, & Hurley, 1996). Self-efficacy beliefs affect both the likelihood of developing various illnesses and the process of recovery from illness (O'Leary, 1992).

Self-efficacy beliefs have been related to such varied behaviors as cigarette smoking, alcohol use, and condom use with relation to pregnancy and AIDS. For example, perceptions of self-efficacy to practice safer sexual behavior have been related to the probability of adopting safer sexual practices. Modeling, goal-setting, and other techniques have been used to increase self-efficacy beliefs and thereby reduce risky behavior (O'Leary, 1992). Changes in self-efficacy beliefs also have been found to be of importance in relation to the process of recovery from illness. For example, in recovery from a heart attack it is important to have an appropriate amount of physical activity. That is, sometimes individuals recovering from a heart attack may have unrealistically high self-efficacy beliefs and exercise beyond what is constructive for them. In these cases patients must monitor their self-efficacy beliefs to bring them into more accord with reality and, correspondingly, to bring their exercise into healthier patterns (Ewart, 1992).

Turning to the relation between self-efficacy beliefs and bodily functioning, there is evidence that high self-efficacy beliefs buffer the effects of stress and enhance the functioning of the body's immune (disease-fighting) system.

There is evidence that excessive stress can impair the immune system, whereas reducing stress can enhance its functioning (O'Leary, 1990). In an experiment designed to examine the impact of perceived self-efficacy for controlling stressors on the immune system, Bandura and his associates found that perceived self-efficacy indeed enhanced immune system functioning (Wiedenfeld et al., 1990). In this research, subjects with a phobia (excessive fear of snakes) were tested under three conditions: a baseline control involving no exposure to a snake, a perceived self-efficacy acquisition phase during which subjects were assisted in gaining a sense of coping efficacy, and a perceived maximal self-efficacy phase once they had developed a complete sense of coping efficacy. During these phases, a small amount of blood was drawn from the subjects and analyzed for the presence of cells that are known to help regulate the immune system. For example, the level of helper T cells, known to play a role in destroying cancerous cells and viruses, was measured. These analyses indicated that increases in self-efficacy beliefs were associated with increases in enhanced immune system functioning, as evidenced, for example, by the increased level of helper T cells (Figure 13.2). Thus, although the effects of stress can be negative, the growth of perceived efficacy over stressors can have valuable adaptive properties at the level of immune system functioning.

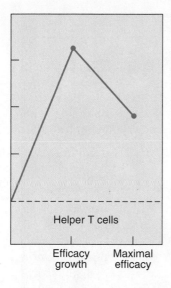

Helper T cells

Efficacy   Maximal
growth   efficacy

Figure 13.2 *Changes in helper T cells during exposure to phobic stressor while acquiring perceived coping self-efficacy and after perceived coping self-efficacy develops to maximal level. (Wiedenfeld et al., 1990) Copyright © 1990 by the American Psychological Association. Adapted by permission.*

Therapeutic Change: Modeling and Guided Mastery

Bringing about beneficial behavior change is a critical goal to Bandura and other social-cognitivists. Bandura pursues this goal while warning that it should be pursued cautiously; therapeutic procedures should be applied clinically only after the basic mechanisms involved are understood and after the effects of the methods have been adequately tested.

According to Bandura, the change process involves not only the acquisition of new patterns of thought and behavior, but also their generalization and maintenance. The social-cognitive view of therapy consequently emphasizes the importance of changes in the sense of efficacy. The treatment approach most emphasized by social-cognitive theory is the acquisition of cognitive and behavioral competencies through modeling and **guided mastery**. In the former, desired activities are demonstrated by various models who experience positive consequences, or at least no adverse consequences. Generally, the complex patterns of behavior to be learned are broken down into subskills and increasingly difficult subtasks so as to ensure optimal progress. In guided mastery the individual not only views a model performing beneficial behaviors, but clients also are assisted in performing the behaviors themselves. The first-hand experience of behavioral success is expected, in social-cognitive theory, to produce the most rapid increases in self-efficacy and performance. In sum, in contrast with therapeutic approaches that emphasize verbal communication, social-cognitive theory prescribes mastery experiences as the principal vehicle of personal change (Bandura, 1997).

Much research on therapeutic modeling and guided participation has been carried out, beginning with work by Bandura and colleagues on the problem of snake phobias (Bandura, 1977). A small percentage of the population suffers from an extreme, irrational fear of snakes that can interfere with their daily life. Bandura hypothesized that therapeutic treatments would help people to overcome their fears only if they increased people's self-perceptions of their personal capability to cope with the situation that makes them afraid. The

*Guided Mastery: Bandura emphasizes the role of modeling and guided participation
in behavior change. Here, individuals afraid of snakes are helped to overcome their
fear by a therapist who models the desired behavior.*

hypothesized psychological mechanism that is key to change, in other words,
is perceived self-efficacy.

Bandura and colleagues tested this hypothesis through their microanalytic
research strategy. They conducted an experiment in which chronic snake
phobics were assigned to one of three conditions: participant modeling (the
therapist models the threatening activities and subjects gradually perform the
tasks, with therapist assistance, until they can be performed alone); modeling
(subjects observe the therapist perform the tasks but do not engage in them);
and a control condition (Bandura, Adams, & Beyer, 1977). Both before and
after these conditions, the subjects were tested on a Behavioral Avoidance Test
(BAT), consisting of 29 performance tasks requiring increasingly threatening
interactions with a red-tailed boa constrictor. The final task involved letting
the snake crawl in their laps while holding their hands at their sides. To
determine the generality of change, subjects were also tested after treatment
with a dissimilar threat—a corn snake. To test the role of perceived self-
efficacy, the researchers conducted a highly detailed assessment in which they
measured snake phobics' perceived self-efficacy for performing each of a series
of increasingly challenging behaviors with a snake (e.g., walking to within
five feet of a snake, touching a snake, picking up a snake, etc.). The self-
efficacy assessments were taken before treatment, after treatment but before
the second administration of the BAT, following the second administration of
the BAT, and again one month following the completion of treatment.

The results indicated that, as expected, participant modeling produced the
strongest changes in behavior (Figure 13.3). More important, for the study
of perceived self-efficacy, changes in self-efficacy perceptions and changes in

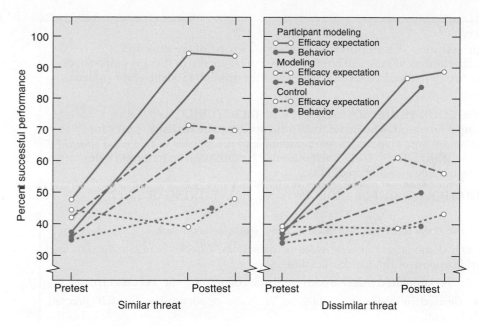

Figure 13.3   *Level of Self-Efficacy and Approach Behavior Displayed by Subjects Toward Different Threats after Receiving Vicarious (Modeling) or Performance-based Participant Modeling Treatments or No Treatment. (In the posttest phase, level of self-efficacy was measured prior to and after the behavioral avoidance tests with the two subjects.) (Bandura, Adams, & Beyer, 1977). Copyright © 1977 American Psychological Association. Reprinted by permission.*

behavior were extremely closely related. This was true at both the between-group level (i.e., one experimental group versus another) and the within-group level (i.e., one individual versus another, within the same experimental condition). At the between-group level, the groups that achieve the greatest changes in self-efficacy perceptions also achieved the greatest changes in behavior (Figure 13.3). At the individual level, self-efficacy judgments (before the second BAT) were uniformly accurate predictors of performance; that is, strong self-efficacy judgments were associated with higher probabilities of successful task performance. The self-efficacy/behavior relations were remarkably large; Bandura and colleagues (1977) report a correlation of .84 between level of self-efficacy and subsequent approach behavior. Self-efficacy expectations were even better predictors of future performance than was past performance! Follow-up data indicated that the subjects not only maintained their gains in self-efficacy and approach behavior but achieved further improvements. In sum, the data supported the utility of guided participation and the social-cognitive view that treatments improve performance because they raise expectations of personal efficacy (also see Bandura & Adams, 1977; Bandura, Adams, & Beyer, 1977; Bandura, Reese, & Adams, 1982; Williams, 1992).

This social-cognitive approach subsequently has been used in the treatment of a wide variety of difficulties. For example, studies have demonstrated the utility of developing coping skills and increased self-efficacy in handling test anxiety (Smith, 1989) and of vulnerability to assault in women (Ozer & Bandura, 1990; Weitlauf, Cervone, & Smith, 2001). In the latter case, women

GENERAL VIEW

Psychological procedures, whatever their format, serve as ways of creating and strengthening expectations of personal effectiveness. Social-cognitive therapy emphasizes the acquisition of cognitive and behavioral competencies through modeling and guided participation.

ATTRIBUTES OF GOOD MODELS: RELEVANCE AND CREDIBILITY

Models who compel attention, who instill trust, who appear to be realistic figures for self-comparison, and whose standards seem reasonable to the learner will be good sources for therapeutic modeling effects. These attributes may be summarized in terms of the positive functions of relevance and credibility.

SOME ILLUSTRATIVE RULES FOR INDUCING AND MAINTAINING DESIRED CHANGES

1. Structure the tasks to be learned in an orderly, stepwise sequence.

2. Explain and demonstrate general rules or principles. Check client's understanding and provide opportunities for clarification.

3. Provide guided simulated practice with feedback concerning success and error.

4. Once the desired behavior is established, increase opportunities for self-directed accomplishment.

5. Test newly acquired skills in the natural environment under conditions likely to produce favorable results.

6. Test skills in increasingly more demanding situations until a satisfactory level of competence and self-efficacy has been obtained.

7. Provide opportunity for therapist consultation and feedback during periods of increased independent mastery.

THERAPEUTIC EFFECTS OF MODELING

1. *Development of New Skills.* Through observing models and through guided participation people acquire new patterns of behavior and new coping strategies. For example, submissive clients learn to model assertive behavior.

2. *Changes in Inhibitions about Self-Expression.* As a result of modeling, responses already available to the person may be weakened or strengthened. For example, inhibitory effects can occur as a result of observing models receive negative consequences for certain behaviors. Disinhibitory effects, which are more common in therapy, result from observing models perform behaviors without adverse consequences or with positive consequences. Fears may be overcome in this way.

3. *Facilitation of Preexisting Patterns of Behavior.* Behaviors already available to the person and that are not associated with anxiety may occur more often as a result of modeling influences. For example, learners may be aided to become more skillful conversationalists.

4. *Adoption of More Realistic Standards for Judging One's Own Performance.* Observing models reward themselves for varying levels of performance can affect the learner's self-standards. For example, rigid self-demands characteristic of depressed people can be relaxed as a result of modeling.

CONCLUSION

"A burgeoning literature confirms the value of modeling treatments for redressing deficits in social and cognitive skills, and for helping to remove defensive avoidance behavior."

Figure 13.4 *Summary of Social-Cognitive Therapy. (Rosenthal & Bandura, 1978, p. 622)*

who participated in a modeling program in which they mastered the physical skills needed to defend themselves against unarmed sexual assailants gained increased freedom of action and decreased avoidant behavior. Fundamental to all of these studies is the experience of mastery that leads to a therapeutic increase in perceived self-efficacy (Figure 13.4)

It is important to determine whether positive effects of therapy endure and generalize to multiple aspects of a person's functioning. Skeptics of modeling and guided mastery approaches might expect there to be little evidence of enduring change or of generalization beyond, for example, the specific phobia treated. However, research suggests that the effects often are enduring and transfer to self-efficacy beliefs in other areas as well (Cervone & Scott, 1995; Williams, 1992). Bandura describes such effects as follows:

> Psychological treatments have traditionally attempted to change human behavior by talk. In the sociocognitive view, human functioning can be enhanced more dependably and fundamentally by mastery experiences than by conversation. In translating this notion to therapeutic practice for phobic disorders, my students and I evolved a powerful guided mastery treatment. It eradicates phobic behavior and biochemical stress reactions, eliminates phobic ruminations and recurrent nightmares, and creates positive attitudes toward formerly dreaded threats. These striking changes are achieved by everyone in a brief period. The changes endure. In follow-up assessments we discovered that the participants not only maintained their therapeutic gains, but made notable improvements in domains of functioning quite unrelated to the treated dysfunction.
>
> SOURCE: BANDURA, as quoted in PERVIN, 1996, p. 82.

THE CASE OF JIM

Twenty years ago Jim was assessed from various theoretical points of view: psychoanalytic, phenomenological, personal construct, and trait. At the time, social-cognitive theory was just beginning to evolve, and thus he was not considered from this standpoint. Later, however, it was possible to gather at least some data from this theoretical standpoint as well. Although comparisons with earlier data may be problematic because of the time lapse, we can gain at least some insight into Jim's personality from this theoretical point of view. We do so by considering Jim's goals, reinforcers he experiences, and his self-efficacy beliefs.

Jim was asked about his goals for the immediate future and for the long-range future. He felt that his immediate and long-term goals were pretty much the same: (1) getting to know his son and being a good parent, (2) becoming more accepting and less critical of his wife and others, and (3) feeling good about his professional work as a consultant. Generally he feels that there is a good chance of achieving these goals but he is guarded in that estimate, with some uncertainty about just how much he will be able to "get out of myself" and thereby be more able to give to his wife and child.

Jim also was asked about positive and aversive reinforcers, things that were important to him that he found rewarding or unpleasant.

Concerning positive reinforcers, Jim reported that money was "a biggie." In addition he emphasized time with loved ones, the glamor of going to an opening night, and generally going to the theater or movies. He had a difficult time thinking of aversive reinforcers. He described writing as a struggle and then noted, "I'm having trouble with this."

Jim also discussed another social-cognitive variable, his competencies or skills (both intellectual and social). He reported that he considered himself to be very bright and functioning at a very high intellectual level. He felt that he writes well from the standpoint of a clear, organized presentation, but he had not written anything that is innovative or creative. Jim also felt that he was very skilled socially: "I do it naturally, easily, well. I can pull off anything and have a lot of confidence in myself socially. I am at ease with both men and women, in both professional and social contexts." The one social concern noted was his constant struggle with "how egocentric I should be, how personally to take things." He felt that sometimes he takes things too personally: "My security is based on how I'm doing with others. I put a lot of energy into friendships, and when I'm relating well I feel good."

In terms of self-efficacy beliefs, Jim had many positive views of himself. He believes that he does most things well; he is a good athlete, a competent consultant, bright, and socially skilled. Does he have areas of low self-efficacy? Jim mentioned three: that he does not genuinely accept his wife; a difficulty "getting out of myself so that I can be genuinely devoted to others"; and, thirdly, creativity: "I know I'm not good at being creative, so I don't try it."

It also was informative to consider irrational beliefs, dysfunctional thoughts, and cognitive distortions. Jim described his tendency to overpersonalize: "This is a problem of mine. If someone doesn't call, I attribute it to a feeling state in relation to me. I can feel terribly injured at times." In his responses to the Automatic Thoughts Questionnaire (Hollon & Kendall, 1980) he reported having the following thoughts frequently: "I've let people down," "I wish I were a better person," "I'm disappointed in myself," and "I can't stand this." These frequent thoughts have to do with his not being as loving or generous as he would like, his being very demanding of himself professionally and in athletics, his obsession about things that might go wrong, and his intolerance of things not going his way. For example, he cannot stand to be in traffic and will say: "I can't stand this. This is intolerable." Jim did not think much of Ellis's work and an interview suggested that he didn't have many irrational beliefs, yet on a questionnaire he checked four out of nine items as frequent thoughts of his: "I must have love or approval," "When people act badly, I blame them," "I tend to view it as a catastrophe when I get seriously frustrated or feel rejected," and "I tend to get preoccupied with things that seem fearsome." He also described his tendency to catastrophize if he is going to be late for a movie: "It's a calamity if I'm going to be one minute late. It becomes a life and death emergency. I go through red lights, honk the horn, and pound on the wheel." This is in contrast to his own tendency to be at least a few minutes late for virtually all appointments, though rarely by more than a few minutes.

In some ways the social-cognitive data on Jim are more limited than those associated with the previous theories of personality. We learn about important aspects of Jim's life, but clearly there also are major gaps. There are two reasons for this. First, only a limited amount of time was available for assessment. Second, and perhaps more important, social-cognitive theorists have not developed comprehensive personality assessment tests; only recently have social-cognitive investigators turned their attention explicitly to questions of personality assessment (Cervone, Shadel, & Jencius, 2001). In part, the previous lack of attention reflected social-cognitive theory's conviction that systematic research and the testing of hypotheses, rather than the in-depth study of individuals, is critical to building a scientifically valid personality theory. It perhaps also reflected the social-cognitive criticism of traditional approaches to assessment that emphasize broad personality consistencies across many domains. In this regard, it is interesting that Jim had difficulty articulating out differences in his functioning in various areas. In this sense, he functions much more like a traditional personality theorist than like a social-cognitive theorist, although with further questioning he probably would have been able to specify ways in which his goals, reinforcers, competencies, and self-efficacy beliefs varied from context to context.

From a social-cognitive perspective, what can be said about Jim as he approaches midlife? We see that in general Jim has a strong sense of self-efficacy in relation to intellectual and social skills, though he feels less efficacious in relation to creative thought and the ability to be loving, generous, and giving to people who are dear to him. He values money and financial success but has settled more on family intimacy and the quality of his work as a consultant as goals for the future. He has a strong sense of individual responsibility and belief in personal control over events. His attributions tend to be internal, stable, and global, and there is a streak of pessimism and depression to him. He is bothered by concerns about the approval of others, by his perfectionism and impatience, and by a tendency to worry about things. He tends to be self-controlled in coping with stress rather than avoiding problems or escaping from them. Generally he sees himself as a competent person and is guardedly optimistic about his chances of achieving his goals in the future.

SCIENTIFIC OBSERVATION: THE DATABASE

CRITICAL EVALUATION

We turn now to a critical evaluation of this last of the personality theories we present, social-cognitive theory (Table 13.3). As in our prior evaluations, we first assess the quality of the scientific observations that furnish the database on which the theory rests.

On this criterion, social-cognitive theory excels. Bandura, Mischel, and colleagues have built their theory on a systematic accumulation of objective scientific evidence. A particularly outstanding feature of this database is its

Table 13.3   Summary of Strengths and Limitations of Social-Cognitive Theory

Strengths	*Limitations*
1. Has impressive research record.	1. Is not a systematic, unified theory.
2. Considers important phenomena.	2. Contains potential problems associated with the use of verbal self-report.
3. Shows consistent development and elaboration as a theory.	3. Requires more exploration and development in certain areas (e.g., motivation, affect, system properties of personality organization).
4. Focuses attention on important theoretical issues.	4. Provides findings concerning therapy that are tentative rather than conclusive.

diversity. To test claims that social-cognitive processes causally influence personality functioning, social-cognitivists have run controlled laboratory experiments. To study the development of individual differences, they have run correlational studies and employed longitudinal methods. To study behavior change, they have conducted clinical outcome studies. The participants in their studies have been diverse: children, adolescents, and adults; people suffering from psychological distress; high-functioning members of the population at large. They have employed a variety of research methods: self-report questionnaires; parental and peer reports of personality; direct observations of behavior in natural settings; measures of cognitive processes in the laboratory.

Of all the approaches to personality, social-cognitive theory and the trait theories are built on the largest and most systematic sets of scientific evidence. This surely is why they long have been the two most influential frameworks in modern personality science (Cervone, 1991).

THEORY: SYSTEMATIC?

Social-cognitive theory has many strengths. But its ability to provide a theory that is systematic—that is, in which all theoretical elements are coherently interrelated—is not one of them. Social-cognitive theory does not provide an overarching network of assumptions that coherently ties together all elements of the theoretical perspective. The approach sometimes functions more as a strategy or framework for studying personality than a fully specified theory. Mischel (2004, p. 13) has described his CAPS framework as a "meta-theory" rather than a complete theory of the person.

The absence of a fully complete and systematic theory becomes evident if one imagines the task of comprehensively assessing personality from a social-cognitive perspective. The theory indicates the *sort of* things one should assess: beliefs about the self, including self-efficacy beliefs; goals and standards for behavior; competencies; and so forth. But there is no simple yet comprehensive assessment scheme of the type provided by the trait theories. (Of course, the social-cognitive theorist would argue that the trait theorists' schemes are *too* simple and thus would reject their approach.) This is because there is no simple yet comprehensive theoretical depiction of the whole person.

Recent years have seen greater efforts at systematization, including work that endeavors to specify the overall nature, or "architecture," of social-cognitive personality systems (Cervone, 2004; see Chapter 14).

THEORY: TESTABLE?

Social-cognitive theorists unquestionably have succeeded in providing a personality theory that is testable. This is evident if one reflects on the research studies we have reviewed in the past two chapters. They could have come out differently; the social-cognitive hypotheses could have been proven wrong. It is possible that participant modeling would not have been such a success, or that attentional factors would not have been so important to delay of gratification, or that self-efficacy beliefs would have been unrelated to behavior once one controlled for "third variables." In these and numerous other cases, social-cognitive theorists defined their constructs with clarity and provided measurement tools and experimental methods that enabled their ideas to be tested. On this criterion, social-cognitive theory gets high marks.

THEORY: COMPREHENSIVE?

Social-cognitive theory is quite comprehensive. Theorists have addressed questions of motivation, development, self-concept, self-control, and behavioral change. The approach even addresses a topic that is skipped in most other personality theories: the learning of social skills and other behavioral competencies.

Yet there also are ways in which social-cognitive theory lacks comprehensiveness. Some aspects of the human experience simply have received little attention from social-cognitive theorists. For example, biological forces of maturation would appear important to people's experiences of the world; sexual feelings in adolescence or a desire for parenting in adulthood may reflect biological rather than social and cognitive features of personality. But these maturational factors receive relatively little formal attention in social-cognitive theory. Inherited temperament may interact with social experience in the development of social-cognitive systems, but these interactions have received less attention in research than they deserve. Other important types of experience—for example, mental conflict, feelings of alienation or anomie, existential concerns about death—similarly have not been systematically targeted in social-cognitive theorizing. Social-cognitive theory has expanded gradually over the years. Expansions that include topics such as those listed here are a challenge for future work.

APPLICATIONS

Social-cognitive theorists have succeeded admirably in applying their theory to the solution of social problems and the alleviation of psychological distress. Indeed, no personality theory exceeds the social-cognitive theorists' level of success on this point. Both Bandura and Mischel were trained as clinicians,

Social-Cognitive Theory at a Glance

Theorist or Theory	Structure	Process
Social-Cognitive Theory	Competencies, Beliefs, Goals, Evaluative Standards	Cognitive and affective processing system functions in reciprocal interaction with the social environment, especially in observational learning, self-regulated motivation, and self-control

and this surely heightened their awareness of the need to apply basic theory to practical concerns.

Two features contribute greatly to social-cognitive theorists' success in relating theory to practice. One is that they did not artificially separate "basic" and "clinical" research. Instead, they pursued basic research questions in clinical contexts; for example, the first experimental tests of self-efficacy theory were done in a clinical setting (with snake phobics). The other is that the social-cognitive theorists wrote books that were central to the professional training of many other psychologists who, in turn, advanced psychological applications. Bandura's (1969) volume on behavior therapy was used as a textbook by many clinicians who advanced cognitive-behavioral therapy in the last third of the 20th century. Mischel's (1968) volume on personality assessment and prediction taught, to applied psychologists, lessons about the limitations of behavioral predictions based on traditional psychodynamic or trait-theoretic assessments.

MAJOR CONTRIBUTIONS AND SUMMARY

Social-cognitive theory is a current favorite among academic personality psychologists. Many clinicians also would label themselves social-cognitive psychologists. The two main social-cognitive theorists, Bandura and Mischel, are two of the most eminent figures to be found in any branch of the psychological sciences. Numerous factors have contributed to the success of the approach. Some were cited above: its large and systematic database, the testability of its formulations, the applicability of its theoretical principles. Yet one last meritorious feature should be noted. It is that social-cognitive theorists have been open to change. They have incorporated ongoing scientific advances into their theory, modifying features of the work as facts dictate. A comparison of *Social Learning and Personality Development* (1963) by Bandura and Walters with the latest formulations of social-cognitive theory (Bandura, 2006; Mischel & Morf, 2002) testifies to the rapid evolution of the approach. The early work is described by the authors themselves as a "socio-behavioristic approach" (Bandura & Walter, 1963, p. 1). The recent work is miles from behaviorism, with theorists now explicating the

Growth and Development	Pathology	Change
Social learning through observation and direct experience; development of self-efficacy judgments and standards for self-regulation	Learned response patterns; excessive self-standards; problems in self-efficacy	Modeling; guided mastery; increased self-efficacy

uniquely human cognitive capabilities that are the basis of human agency. We anticipate that social-cognitive theory will continue to evolve in the years ahead.

MAJOR CONCEPTS

Dysfunctional expectancies   In social-cognitive theory, maladaptive expectations concerning the consequences of specific behaviors.

Dysfunctional self-evaluations   In social-cognitive theory, maladaptive standards for self-reward that have important implications for psychopathology.

Emotion-focused coping   Coping in which an individual strives to improve his or her internal emotional state, for example, by emotional distancing or the seeking of social support.

General principles approach   Higgins's term for an analysis of personal and situational influences on thought and action in which a common set of causal principles is used to explain both cross-situational consistency in thought and action that results from personal influences and variability in thought and action that results from situational influences.

Guided mastery   A treatment approach emphasized in social-cognitive theory in which a person is assisted in performing modeled behaviors.

Implicit theories   Broad, generalizable beliefs that we may not be able to state explicitly in words, yet that influence our thinking.

Learning goals   In Dweck's social-cognitive analysis of personality and motivation, a goal of trying to enhance one's knowledge and personal mastery of a task.

Performance goals   In Dweck's social-cognitive analysis of personality and motivation, a goal of trying to make a good impression on other people who may evaluate you.

Problem-focused coping   Attempts to cope by altering features of a stressful situation.

Schemas   Complex cognitive structures that guide information processing.

Self-discrepancies   In theoretical analyses of Higgins, incongruities between beliefs about one's current psychological attributes (the actual self) and desired attributes that represent valued standards or guides.

Self-enhancement   A motive to maintain or enhance positive views of the self.

Stress inoculation training   A procedure to reduce stress developed by Meichenbaum in which clients are taught to become aware of such negative, stress-inducing cognitions.

Self-schemas   Cognitive generalizations about the self that guide a person's information processing.

Self-verification   A motive to obtain information that is consistent with one's self-concept.

Working self-concept   The subset of self-concept that is in working memory at any given time; the theoretical idea that different social circumstances may activate different aspects of self-concept.

REVIEW

1. Much research in the social-cognitive tradition has explored three cognitive components of personality: beliefs, goals, and evaluative standards. The study of beliefs has included research on the role of cognitive generalizations about the self, or self-schemas. Research on goals has explored differences between types of goals, including learning versus performance goals. Work on evaluative standards has explored discrepancies between people's views of their actual self and standards representing ideals versus oughts, or obligations.

2. Research has established that people's thoughts about the causes of significant life events, or attributions about the events, significantly influence motivation and emotional reactions.

3. In clinical applications, social-cognitive theory rejects the medical symptom/disease model of psychopathology, emphasizing instead the dysfunctional learning of behaviors, expectancies, standards for self-reward, and, most significantly, self-efficacy beliefs. Dysfunctional learning can occur through the observation of models, in particular through vicarious conditioning, or through direct experience.

4. According to social-cognitive theory, there are two key points in bringing about psychological change in therapy. One is that low levels of perceived self-efficacy contribute to a wide variety of psychological dysfunctions, including anxiety and depression. The other is that self-efficacy perceptions can be increased therapeutically, especially through modeling and guided mastery therapies. In modeling, models demonstrate the skills and subskills necessary in specific situations. In guided participation, the person is assisted in performing these modeled behaviors. Research supports the use of these procedures in raising the perception of self-efficacy.

5. In relation to the theories considered previously, social-cognitive theory emphasizes (a) conscious cognitive processes and experimental data as opposed to the psychoanalytic emphasis on unconscious processes and clinical data; (b) the role of social context and contextual variability in cognition and action, as opposed to the global self-conceptions emphasized by Rogers; and (c) personal capabilities for action, including people's potential to control and alter their own typical patterns of behavior, rather than the stable dispositional tendencies emphasized in the trait conceptions of personality.

6. Social-cognitive theory's strengths include its ability to bring systematic research to bear on important problems of personality functioning and social behavior. Its primary limit is that it is not yet a wholly unified, systematic theory. A primary challenge to social-cognitive theory is to relate the development of social-cognitive structures to inherited biological qualities that contribute to individual differences.

PERSONALITY IN CONTEXT: INTERPERSONAL RELATIONS, CULTURE, AND DEVELOPMENT ACROSS THE COURSE OF LIFE

14

"I wish I was like you. You're always so optimistic about everything."

"Yeah, right. I just broke up with Pete."

"Oh no! What happened?"

"Well, I thought for sure that he was going to break up with me, so I challenged him on it, and we had a big fight."

"What made you think you'd break up?"

"That's what always happens, isn't it?"

"No. I mean, I've been with Sam for two years, and I'm sure we're going to stick together."

"Well, then you're the optimist I guess. Except for how weird you get about exams."

"I'm telling you, I'm going to fail the final in this personality class."

"That's ridiculous. You said the same thing before the mid-term and then you got an A!"

Are both of these people "optimists"? Or are both "pessimists"? Or might there be a deeper lesson to be learned from this dialogue?

To many contemporary personality psychologists, the lesson is that personality must be understood "in context." We learn about someone's personality as we observe them interact with the social situations—the "contexts"—of their life. Even if the two people in the dialogue above are both "moderately optimistic" on average, this characterization does not tell you much about the differences in their personalities. A deeper understanding is obtained only if one explores how they cope with the different situations of their lives. The nature of their uniqueness and of the differences between them cannot be discovered by yanking their personality out of the life contexts in which they live—for example, by asking them how they tend to act in general, irrespective of context, or by requiring them to perform some laboratory puzzles that bear no relation to the textures of their everyday life. Instead, we can only understand *who* they are by asking *where* they are when they display the distinctive patterns of experience and action that are the hallmarks of their personality.

This chapter, then, considers the question of personality in context. We address a range of issues: interpersonal relationships, socioeconomic contexts within which persons develop, personality development across the life span and the ways in which one's stage of life serves as a context that influences social motives, interactions among personality and culture, and the possibility that principles of personality theory can foster beneficial social change. Although the topics will vary, as you read the chapter you will detect a consistent theme. In each case, scientific progress in understanding persons is made through a careful study of both persons and the contexts of their lives.

Why are personality psychologists interested in social context? It is not because they are "closet social psychologists" or "closet sociologists."

Instead, the interest is driven, to a large degree, by a different consideration. It is that personality functioning involves processes of meaning construction. People make sense of—that is, construct meaning out of—the social and personal events they encounter. As you read the pages of this book, your mental life cannot be characterized merely in terms of perceptual information processing (e.g., "your visual system detects lines, curves, and angles on a white background," etc.). Instead, you are engaged also in an activity imbued with social meaning; you are "cramming for a final exam," perhaps "to graduate on time," so that "your family doesn't think you're a big failure," or maybe so that "you can achieve your dream of a college degree" and "move on to a job where you finally earn some real money." This sort of "imposition of meaning on life is the major end and primary condition of human existence" (Geertz, 1973, p. 434). What does meaning construction have to do with "personality in context"? Processes of meaning construction inherently involve social context. We rarely sit around thinking "things are OK in general" or "I'm very disappointed, but not with anything in particular." Instead, our thoughts are directed to the world. We are preoccupied with specific persons, situations, relationships, and life challenges. Personality, then, involves psychological systems through which people assign meaning to the significant contexts of their lives.

In terms of the personality theories, in this chapter we draw significantly on the social-cognitive approaches of Bandura, Mischel, and related investigators that were discussed in Chapters 12 and 13. Yet we take an even broader view by capitalizing on a variety of research traditions in contemporary personality psychology that address the ways in which people make sense of their social world.

1. Why do some people experience anxiety about the relationship even when it seems to be going well?

2. In what ways does personality involve strategies for coping with life challenges, and how might people differ in the strategies they invoke?

3. How does people's knowledge about themselves and about social situations contribute to consistent styles of response that are evidenced across social contexts?

4. How is personality development influenced by socioeconomic conditions—and how does it influence them?

5. Through what personality processes are older adults able to maintain a strong sense of psychological well-being in the later years of life?

6. What is the nature of the relation between personality and culture?

7. Can personality theory contribute to widespread, beneficial social change?

QUESTIONS TO BE ADDRESSED IN THIS CHAPTER

Two of the chapters of this textbook—9 and the present chapter, 14—differ from the others. The other chapters (after our introductory ones, Chapters 1 and 2) introduced you to a given personality theory. We presented a theoretical view and then reviewed research and applications related to that theory. However, in this book on *Personality: Theory and Research* our goal is to introduce you not only to the theories of personality but also to research findings in the contemporary field of personality science. Many of these findings are associated with one versus another theoretical framework, and thus were presented in association with their most relevant theory in the previous chapters. Yet some research findings stand apart from any one theory, in that they provide information that is important to *all* personality psychologists, no matter what their theoretical views.

One such set of these findings was reviewed in Chapter 9: research exploring the biological foundations of personality. In comparison to Chapter 9, the work reviewed here is the "flip side of the coin": research exploring cultural, social, and interpersonal foundations of personality.

Readers with a biological bent may be inclined to think that biological foundations are basic elements of personality, with sociocultural factors being more peripheral to questions of human nature. Anyone inclined to such a view should consider the sage advice of philosophers of psychology, who have admonished that a science of personality "should treat people, for scientific purposes, as if they were human beings" (Harré & Secord, 1972, p. 87). Yes, humans are lumps of biomass whose evolutionary ancestry can be traced to non-human origins. But they also are self-reflective beings who live in social and cultural settings. Without sociocultural experiences, no person would be fully human. Understanding how persons develop in interaction with the sociocultural settings of their lives thus is no less basic to a science of personality than is a study of personality's biological foundations. This chapter, then, reviews recent research in personality psychology that illustrates how personality develops and functions in interpersonal and sociocultural contexts.

INTERPERSONAL RELATIONSHIPS

The most significant contexts in most people's lives are ones that involve other people. Although individuals face many financial, professional, and academic demands, challenges that involve relationships with others—friends, family, romantic partners, ex-romantic partners, prospective romantics partners—have a particular power. They capture our attention. They bring us joy and make us heartsick. "Close relationships provide the most central context for our daily lives" (Cooper, 2002, p. 758). In exploring personality-in-context, then, the first context we consider is that of interpersonal relationships—an aspect of life that has received increasing attention from personality scientists in recent years (e.g., Baldwin, 2005; Chen, Boucher, and Parker-Tapais, 2006).

Relationships are two-way streets; there are two people who influence one another. The role of personality factors thus must be considered from each of two directions. On the one hand, personality characteristics may lead a person to do things that are helpful or harmful to a relationship. One might, for example, insult his partner's appearance, start an argument, or start a relationship with a different partner—or, more happily, do things that support and strengthen the relationship. On the other hand, personality qualities may influence someone's *interpretation of* the partner's behavior *irrespective of* what the partner actually does. People's perceptions of their partner may not be accurate. Biases in perception may cause a person erroneously to think that his or her partner said something insulting, or was trying to start an argument, or was interested in a different relationship partner.

Research shows how this two-way impact of personality on relationships can work. When investigators study the interactions of relationship partners in detail (Gable, Reis, & Downey, 2003) they do find that positive behaviors (e.g., being affectionate) and negative behaviors (e.g., being critical or inattentive) have positive and negative effects, respectively, on a partner's satisfaction and happiness with the relationship. This much is obvious. However, they also find that influences run in the opposite direction; specifically, inaccurate perceptions of one's partner affect relationship outcomes. People are less satisfied with their relationship when they infer that their partner has engaged in a negative behavior toward them—even in circumstances in which the partner reports that he or she never did the behavior in the first place (Gable et al., 2003). The importance of people's subjective perceptions of their relationship partners is vividly illustrated in research on a personality quality known as rejection sensitivity.

REJECTION SENSITIVITY

Consider again the dialogue that opened this chapter. One of the speakers—the one who broke up with Pete—displayed a style of personality-in-context known as **rejection sensitivity**.

As studied by the psychologist Geraldine Downey and her colleagues (e.g., Downey and Feldman, 1996; see also Ayduk, Mischel, & Downey, 2002; Downey, Mougios, Ayduk, London, & Shoda, 2004; Pietrzak, Downey, & Ayduk, 2005), rejection sensitivity refers to a particular style of thinking. It is characterized by anxious expectations of rejection in interpersonal relationships. Some people seem particularly prone to expect that a relationship—even a relationship that is going quite well—will break up. Such persons dwell on, and become anxious about, the possibility that they will be rejected.

This thinking style is particularly important because it can harm a good relationship. Even if they are not grounded in fact, anxious expectations create interpersonal tension that can make a strong relationship less strong. Expectations of rejection, then, can be a self-fulfilling prophecy.

Downey and Feldman (1996) assess individual differences in rejection sensitivity through the *Rejection Sensitivity Questionnaire (RSQ)*. Respondents are presented with a list of interpersonal requests (e.g., asking a boyfriend/girlfriend to move in with you, asking someone out on a date). For each circumstance, they indicate their subjective sense of the likelihood that their relationship partner would accept versus reject their request (i.e., the request of moving in, going out on a date, etc.). They also indicate how concerned or anxious they would be regarding the other person's response in each circumstance. People who frequently say that there is a high likelihood of their being rejected, and also that they would be very anxious about being rejected, are classified as high in rejection sensitivity.

The potential impact of rejection sensitivity on interpersonal relationships has been documented in research involving first-year college students (Downey

Research on rejection sensitivity reveals that some people are particularly concerned that relationships they are in will break up—even when the relationship appears to be going very well.

& Feldman, 1996). This was a longitudinal study, with key measures taken at two different points in time. First, participants completed the RSQ early in an academic year. Four months later, the researchers identified a subset of people who had begun a romantic relationship only *after* completing the RSQ. These individuals were asked to report on their new, current relationship; specifically, they completed a measure tapping attributions of hurtful intent in the new relationship. People were presented with hypothetical acts that could have a number of different causes (e.g., your boyfriend/girl friend begins spending less time with you) and were asked whether each act was an indication that the relationship partner was being intentionally hurtful. By designing the research in this manner, with the relationship occurring only after the RSQ was completed, the researchers could be sure that RSQ responses were not themselves a reaction to the specific relationship that people reported on four months into the academic year. Thus, this research design enabled Downey and Feldman to determine whether rejection sensitivity would *contribute to* thoughts about the subsequent relationship.

Findings revealed that rejection sensitivity indeed did predict beliefs about the new relationship (Table 14.1, left column). People who were higher in rejection sensitivity before their relationship began were more likely to infer hostile intent on the part of their partner after the relationship was underway. Since the thought that "my partner is intentionally being hostile to me" obviously can be bad for the health of a relationship, this implies that the personality characteristic of rejection sensitivity can be consequential to the quality and longevity of relationships.

A second feature of the results reported in Table 14.1 speaks to the overall theme of this chapter: the importance of studying personality in context.

Table 14.1   Correlations between Dispositional Variables and Rejection Sensitivity Questionnaire (RSQ) and Attributions of Hurtful Intent for the Behavior of a Subsequent Romantic Partner

Dispositional Variables	Correlation of RSQ with Attributions Partialling Out the Dispositional Variable	Correlation of Dispositional Variable with Attributions
Neuroticism	.34*	.06
Introversion	.35*	.08
Self-esteem	.34*	−.13
Social avoidance	.30*	.17
Social distress	.31*	.16
Interpersonal sensitivity	.35**	.06
Secure attachment	.40**	.04
Resistant attachment	.42**	−.12
Avoidant attachment	.43**	−.07

*$p < .05$, **$p < .01$

NOTE: "Partialling out" a variable refers to a statistical technique in which one examines the relation between two variables while controlling statistically for the effects of a third variable. The significant correlations in the center column thus indicate that RSQ scores are significantly correlated with attributions of hurtful intent even after one controls for the effects of the dispositional variables listed in the left column of the table.
SOURCE: Downey & Feldman, 1996

Rejection sensitivity is a *contextual* personality variable. It refers to a pattern of thinking (anxious expectations) that occurs in a specific context: interpersonal settings in which there is some possibility of not being socially accepted by someone you care about. Contrast this to *decontextual* or "global" personality variables such as "neuroticism" (see Chapters 7 and 8). Neuroticism refers to a a generalized, overall tendency to experience anxiety and related psychological distress.

Downey and Feldman (1996) related their contextualized variable, rejection sensitivity, to global trait variables in the following way. They determined whether rejection sensitivity predicted thoughts about hostility *after accounting for* the relation between these thoughts and a variety of global personality constructs. (This is accomplished through statistical procedures that determine the degree to which two variables are related while controlling statistically for the impact of a third variable.) As you can see from the left column of Table 14.1, the contextualized variable, rejection sensitivity, did predict thoughts about hostility after controlling for the effects of global trait variables. In contrast, none of the global trait variables uniquely predicted people's thoughts about their relationships. This result clearly highlights the value of studying personality in context.

Subsequent findings indicate that individual differences in rejection sensitivity are related not only to attributions of hostility, but to long-term relationship outcomes. Both rejection-sensitive individuals and their romantic partners have been found to experience less satisfaction with their relationships, as compared to persons low in rejection sensitivity (Downey & Feldman, 1996). As one might suspect, the relationships of people who are high in rejection sensitivity also are more likely to break up than are the relationships of people who are not prone to anxious expectations of rejection (Downey, Freitas, Michaelis, & Khouri, 1998).

"Hot" and "Cool" Focus

Ideally, personality psychologists would not only describe the fact that people high and low in rejection sensitivity have different experiences in relationships, they also would identify psychological processes through which people can gain control over their relationship experiences.

Researchers have taken up this challenge by exploring people's "cognitive strategies," that is, strategic ways of thinking that, when executed properly, can give people control over their behavior and emotional life. Particularly important cognitive strategies are ones that involve attention. In any complex social situation, there are lots of different things that one might pay attention to. Some of these things are emotionally neutral, whereas others stir one's emotions; psychologists describe this by saying that different aspects of a situation are "cool" versus "hot" (Metcalfe & Mischel, 1999).

Ayduk, Mischel, and Downey (2002) have explored the influence of **hot versus cool attentional focus** on emotions associated with interpersonal rejection. In their research, participants were asked to recall an experience from their past that had made them feel rejected by another person. Then, depending on the experimental condition to which they were assigned, participants were asked to think about this rejection experience in different ways. In a hot-focus condition, they thought about their emotions during the rejection experience (e.g., "How did your heart beat? How did your face feel"). In a cool-focus condition, participants' attention was directed to features of the situation that did not involve emotional experience, such as the physical setting in which the experience occurred (e.g., "Where were you standing with respect to the people and the objects around you?" Ayduk et al., 2002, p. 445).

Focusing attention on "hot" versus "cool" aspects of the past experience had a variety of effects (Ayduk et al., 2002). When asked to describe their mood after thinking about the rejection experience, people who focused on "cool" aspects of the experience described themselves as being less angry than people in the hot-focus condition or people in a control condition in which there were no "hot" or "cool" instructions. When participants wrote an essay describing their thoughts and feelings while thinking about the experience, cool-focus participants composed essays featuring less angry, emotional content. A third dependent measure in the experiment involved reaction-time measures (see Chapter 13). All participants engaged in a lexical decision task, which is a task in which both words and strings of letters that do not form words are presented on a computer screen and the research participant is asked to decide, as quickly as possible, whether a given letter string actually is a word. In this research (Ayduk et al., 2002), participants were presented with some words that related to hostility (e.g., "enraged," "vengeance"). Participants who earlier had focused their attention on "hot" features of their past interpersonal rejection were found to be the quickest to recognize that the hostility words were, in fact, words. The interpretation of this finding is that focusing attention on one's emotional reactions ("How did your heart beat?", etc.) activated thoughts about hostility, with that greater activation being revealed in the fast reaction times of the hot-focus participants. In summary, then, people who thought about the same type of interpersonal encounter but who focused their attention on *different aspects of* the encounter had substantially different psychological experiences.

More recent work sheds light on the biological bases of these different experiences. Among people high in rejection sensitivity, circumstances related to rejection activate a specific biologically-based motivational system, namely, a defensive motivational system that appears to have been evolutionarily adapted to protect people from environmental danger and threats (Downey et al., 2004).

As Ayduk and colleagues (2002) note, the ability to identify a specific psychological process, attentional focus, that contributes to hostile reactions has a significant applied implication. People who are particularly vulnerable to experiencing hostile emotions that interfere with their interpersonal relationships could be taught "cooling strategies." In principle, psychological interventions could teach people to gain greater control over their emotional life by focusing their attention on "cool" rather than "hot" aspects of interpersonal encounters.

TRANSFERENCE IN INTERPERSONAL RELATIONSHIPS

Have you ever met a person who vaguely reminded you of someone from your past? Have you ever had the intuition that your reactions toward someone were identical to your reactions toward someone else who you have known? In Chapter 4, we learned that this possibility was of much interest to psychoanalysts. They felt that patients repeat, in therapy, attitudes and styles of interaction they first experienced with significant figures from their past. This experience of attitudes toward the analyst that are based in attitudes toward such figures was called "transference."

Contemporary experimental research suggests that transference processes may not be limited to the therapeutic setting. Many of our everyday reactions to people we meet may be influenced by a key contextual factor: the degree to which the new person we meet happens to resemble significant people in our past.

Highly informative research on this topic has been done by Susan Andersen and her colleagues. They have developed a social-cognitive analysis of transference in interpersonal relationships (Andersen & Chen, 2002). In other words, although Andersen is interested in the same phenomenon as was Freud, she tries to explain the phenomenon using contemporary social-cognitive theory and methods, rather than the theoretical model employed by Freud.

Andersen suggests that the phenomenon of transference is a natural by-product of basic social-cognitive processes of the sort we reviewed in our previous two chapters. The specific idea is the following. Much research already established two facts about individuals' interpretations of people and events (Higgins, 1996). First, we interpret events by using previously stored knowledge. For example, if we see someone standing in the street wearing blue pants and a blue shirt and blowing a whistle, we interpret this person as being "a police officer" thanks to the fact that we already have, stored in our head, knowledge about police officers. Our thoughts and expectations about the person are then guided by our preexisting knowledge about police officers.

Second, we use a given piece of stored knowledge to interpret an event when that knowledge overlaps with information in the situation we are interpreting. In our example, if there had been less overlap between our knowledge of police officers and the person in the street—for example, if he had not been wearing blue pants and a blue shirt—then we might not have interpreted the person as a police officer, but merely as some nut standing in the street blowing a whistle.

Andersen and Chen (2002) recognize that these basic processes of social-cognition might explain the phenomenon that Freud had recognized as transference. Suppose you meet a new person who happens to have qualities that resemble those of someone you have known well in your past. For example, the person might have a similar hairstyle or manner of speaking, or a similar set of interests and hobbies. This informational overlap between the new person and your past acquaintance may activate knowledge about the individual in your past. This activated knowledge about the past acquaintance may then influence your thoughts and feelings toward the new individual. You may assume—even without realizing that you are doing so—that the new individual possesses qualities that actually are those that were possessed by your past acquaintance. In other words, you will "transfer" your beliefs from your past acquaintance to the new person.

Anderson and colleagues have developed strategies for studying transference experimentally. In an initial experimental session, participants write a description of a person with whom they have had a personally significant relationship. In a subsequent session, participants are asked to read descriptions of various target persons. Some of these descriptions include information that overlaps with their earlier description of their significant other. Later, participants are asked to try to recall information from the descriptions. The key dependent measure is "false positives," that is, the "remembering" of information about the target person that was not actually in the description of the target person, but was a characteristic of the significant other; these false-positive memories are the evidence of the transference of information from the past relationships to the new person. What do they find? People indeed are more likely to exhibit false-positive memories when target persons resemble significant others from their past (Andersen & Cole, 1990; Andersen, Glassman, Chen, & Cole, 1995). Transference processes influence not only memory, but emotional reactions and desires to establish a close relationship with a new acquaintance (Andersen & Baum, 1994; Andersen, Reznik, & Manzella, 1996). People are found to react differently to a new acquaintance when the new person has qualities that overlap with someone from their past.

Like the work on rejection sensitivity reviewed earlier, research on social-cognitive processes in transference also illustrates this chapter's theme. In this case, the key contextual variable in understanding "personality in context" is the relation between the attributes of an old and a new acquaintance. When these attributes overlap, a person's experiences and actions cannot be explained in terms of their general, average behavioral tendencies. Instead, they must be understood in terms of context-specific thoughts that link an old and a new acquaintance. Thanks to these transference processes, then, even after you break up with a person, that person may "live on in your head" and influence your future relationships.

Research on rejection sensitivity sounds a theme that one hears often: People who have negative thoughts about an upcoming situation may "shoot themselves in the foot"; their negative expectations may cause them to do less well. But is this always the case? One important line of research suggests that the answer is no. The psychologists Nancy Cantor, Julie Norem, and their colleagues find that, for some people, thinking "bad" is a good thing. There is, for some, "positive power" in "negative thinking" (Norem, 2001). These people are called defensive pessimists.

STRATEGIES FOR MEETING ACADEMIC AND SOCIAL CHALLENGES: OPTIMISTIC STRATEGIES AND DEFENSIVE PESSIMISM

Defensive pessimism is a cognitive personality variable, that is, a personality variable that involves styles of thinking. Defensive pessimists think about life challenges in a different manner than do others; specifically, they differ from people referred to as "optimists." **Optimists** hold relatively realistic expectations about their capabilities. If they have the skills to handle a challenge, they generally will say so. Defensive pessimists, in contrast, often think negatively. Even when it seems like they might have the skills to succeed, they express doubts and expect the worst.

A key idea in research on defensive pessimism is that, for people who typically think in this way, pessimism may not be all that bad a thing. For some people, negative thinking may be an effective coping strategy that enables them to motivate themselves to attain high levels of performance.

Research on strategic optimism and defensive pessimism (Cantor et al., 1987) has examined a life transition that is of relevance to many readers of this text: the transition from high school to college. In the senior year of high school, people often settle into comfortable routines. They have well-established friendship patterns, know many of the school's teachers and administrators, and have figured out how to achieve decent grades. Moving on to college, in contrast, presents novel challenges. meeting new friends, staying in touch with old friends, keeping up with academics, becoming involved in social activities on campus. These hectic life transitions are of much interest to the personality psychologist. Because they are challenging, they are revealing of individual differences in coping skills and strategies. Just as challenging IQ-test items are more revealing of differences in analytic intelligence than the question "What is $2 + 2$?" challenging social situations are more revealing of individual differences in "social intelligence" (Cantor & Kihlstrom, 1987).

In this research, investigators studied college students throughout their freshman year (Cantor et al., 1987). At the beginning of the year, students completed a questionnaire measuring their optimism versus defensive pessimism when thinking about various life challenges. During the year, they assessed other variables of potential importance to academic performance, including expectations about one's GPA and "self-discrepancies," that is, discrepancies between one's actual self and one's ideal self-image in the domain of academics (Higgins, 1987; see Chapter 13). Finally, students' GPA at the end of the year was recorded.

Academic optimists and defensive pessimists did equally well at school. Yet they differed in another way. They appeared to travel along different psychological paths to academic success (Cantor et al., 1987). This is revealed by the way personality variables predicted GPA in the two groups (Figure 14.1). Among academic optimists, academic success was predicted by positive thinking;

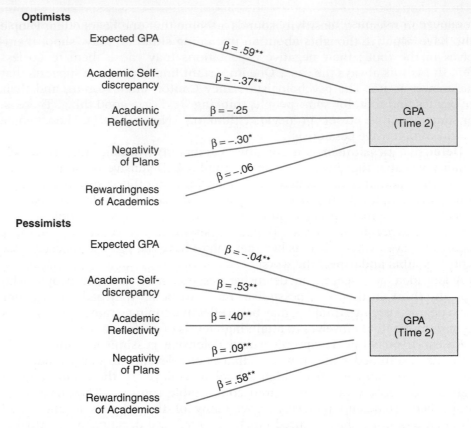

Optimists

Expected GPA — $\beta = .59^{**}$

Academic Self-discrepancy — $\beta = -.37^{**}$

Academic Reflectivity — $\beta = -.25$

Negativity of Plans — $\beta = -.30^{*}$

Rewardingness of Academics — $\beta = -.06$

GPA (Time 2)

Pessimists

Expected GPA — $\beta = -.04^{**}$

Academic Self-discrepancy — $\beta = .53^{**}$

Academic Reflectivity — $\beta = .40^{**}$

Negativity of Plans — $\beta = .09^{**}$

Rewardingness of Academics — $\beta = .58^{**}$

GPA (Time 2)

Figure 14.1   *Variables that predicted grade point average among two groups of people: academic optimists and academic defensive pessimists. The same personality variables predicted performance differently for the two groups. From Cantor et al. (1987).*

people who expected to do well and who experienced relatively few self-discrepancies at the beginning of the academic year earned higher grades. But among defensive pessimists, expectations about academic performance at the beginning of the year were *un*related to end-of-year grades. If the defensive pessimist said, "I'm going to get a low GPA," this did *not* predict low levels of subsequent performance. Furthermore, among defensive pessimists, large actual-ideal self-discrepancies predicted *higher*, not lower, academic attainment. Negative thinking was good, not bad.

Another feature of these results highlights the importance of studying personality in context. Optimism versus pessimism did not turn out to be a generalized variable that was evident in all aspects of a given student's life. Instead, many students who were pessimists with regard to getting good grades were optimists in other life contexts. Cantor and colleagues (1987) studied academic optimists' and pessimists' cognitions in two contexts: grade attainment and making new friends. In the domain of grade attainment, the groups differed enormously on cognitive factors such as their perceptions of the difficulty, controllability, and stress associated with academics. But when contemplating the challenge of making friends, they did not differ at all!

When asked about the difficulty, controllability, and stress associated with the challenge of establishing new friendships, academic optimists and pessimists did not differ.

Starting in Chapter 1 of this text, you have learned that a defining feature of personality is that people display consistent patterns of experience and action across different life contexts. This cross-context (or cross-situational) consistency was so important that it was part of the very definition of "personality," which refers to consistent styles of experience and behavior. A central challenge for personality psychology, then, is to identify and explain the patterns of cross-situational consistency that distinguish people from one another.

To get a sense of the nature of this challenge, and how one might address it, consider the following four situations: telling a joke at a party, jogging with friends, taking an exam for this class, and talking with people about political issues during lunch. To most people the situations may seem unrelated. But now imagine someone who sees himself or herself as being extremely competitive. To this person, the situations might be highly related; each might be viewed as a form of competition (to tell the best joke, run the fastest, get the best grade, make the best arguments).

The general point is that people may hold beliefs about their personal qualities that influence the meaning of the situations they experience. Situations that superficially may appear unrelated could be highly interrelated for some people, namely, people who think that the situations all are relevant to an important personal quality of theirs. People's beliefs about themselves, then, may contribute to the consistent patterns of experience and action that are defining of "personality."

This possibility has been addressed in a recently formulated theoretical model that is known as a **knowledge-and-appraisal personality architecture (KAPA**; Cervone, 2004, 2005; Cervone, Caldwell, & Orom, in press). Since that phrase is a mouthful, we will explain it in parts. **Personality architecture** refers to the overall design of those mental systems (emotional and cognitive) that contribute to personality functioning. "Knowledge and appraisal" means that, to understand the mental systems of personality, one must distinguish between two aspects of thinking: knowledge and appraisal (Lazarus, 1991). Knowledge refers to stored information that we carry around with us: information about our personal characteristics, our goals, other people's personal characteristics, their goals, objects in the world, types of social situations, and so on. Knowledge is relatively consistent across time; we usually have the same basic knowledge of our personal qualities and of the world around us from one day (or month or year) to the next. Appraisals are evaluations of the relationship between ourselves and some particular situation. As we live our lives, we almost continuously evaluate the situations we are in: whether they are good or bad for us, whether and how we can cope with them, and so forth. These evaluations may shift from one moment or situation to the next.

Now let us return to the example above, with this knowledge/appraisal distinction in mind. Our competitive person presumably carries around with him knowledge about competitiveness. This knowledge might, for example, include enduring goals for exceeding other people and self-schemas involving

PERSONALITY CONSISTENCY IN CONTEXT

the self as a competitor. When thinking about each of the situations, the person may categorize the situation in terms of this competition-related knowledge. As a result the person would appraise the core mean of each situation as involving competition against others, and respond in a similar style across the different contexts.

Knowledge and appraisal processes have been studied in research (Cervone, 1997, 2004; Cervone et al., 2001, Cervone, Orom, et al., in press). To assess people's knowledge about themselves, or self-schemas (cf. Chapter 13), participants write brief narratives describing their most central personal qualities, including characteristics that are personal strengths and weaknesses. To assess subjective beliefs about social situations, they judge how relevant each of the variety of situations is to each of their self-schemas. In later experimental sessions, participants are asked to make appraisals about a large series of different situations they may encounter. The appraisals are ones that are familiar to you from Chapter 12; people appraise their self-efficacy (Bandura, 2006) for executing a particular challenging behavior in each of the situations. The question is whether, and where, people display consistent high and low self-efficacy appraisals across different situations.

Data from one research participant illustrates the results that these methods yield (Figure 14.2). This person's self-schemas included the belief that she is a "responsible" person. The situations that she believed to be related to the characteristic of responsibility were interesting in that they were idiosyncratic. Some of them were typical of the traditional definition of the term (e.g., saving money). However, this person judged that a circumstance that might be construed as a negative, calculating act—making friends with someone who "looks smart" so you can get their lecture notes—was an instance of "responsible" action for a college student. In contrast, a potentially prototypic act of responsibility—speaking to a professor if one is lost in a course—was judged as irrelevant to this attribute by Participant 37.

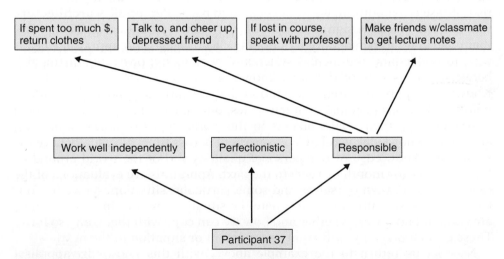

Figure 14.2 *Diagram displays three self-schemas of a research participant and situations that the person related to one of these self-schemas, namely, her belief that she is a "Responsible" person. From Cervone (2004).*

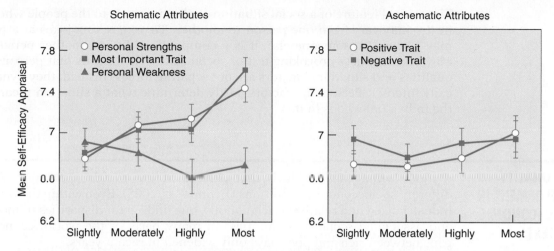

Figure 14.3   *Mean self-efficacy appraisals plotted as a function of type of personality attribute (self-schemas versus non-schematic, or aschematic, attributes) and situational knowledge (i.e., participants' beliefs about the relevance of the attribute to situations). From Cervone (2004).*

What about the self-efficacy judgments? As Figure 14.3 illustrates, very large differences in self-efficacy appraisal were found across situations that participants believed to be highly related to positive versus negative self-schemas. Thus, schematic self-knowledge indeed appeared to influence self-efficacy appraisals, with positive self-knowledge bringing about consistently high appraisals of self-efficacy. It is also of relevance that, as predicted by the KAPA model, null results were found when participants made the same ratings but with traits for which they were not schematic, that is, for which they did not have a significant degree of self-knowledge.

Note that these results turn the tables on the typical arguments of the "person-situation controversy" (Chapters 8 and 12). Originally, social-cognitive theorists were thought to have expected merely cross-situational variability in action, whereas trait theorists expected consistency. Yet these results (Cervone, 2004) show that social-cognitive processes can cause people to group seemingly different situations together, and thus to respond to the situations in a consistent manner.

More generally, the results highlight something that is critical to understanding personality in context. It concerns how one thinks about context. In the physical sciences, contextual factors can be thought of as having fixed properties. If we heat different substances to 50 degrees centigrade and ask if they melt, the contextual factor of temperature can be seen as being the same from one substance to another. If we drop a series of objects to see how fast they fall, the force of gravity is fixed; it is the same from one object to another. Situational factors can be viewed as distinct from objects that exist in the given situation, and the situational factors can be viewed as having properties that are fixed, or constant, from the vantage point of one versus another object in that environment. In the study of personality, however, things are different. This is because people generally must interpret situations in order to respond to them. They have to figure out what the situation means. Once one recognizes this fact, it is clear that a great many situations do not have a fixed meaning.

The critical feature of a social situation—what it means to the people who are in it—may vary from one person to another. To you, telling jokes at a party may be fun. To someone else, it is a competition. To yet another person, it may be an anxiety-provoking test of social skills. This means that personality qualities and situational factors are not separate forces. Instead, they dynamically interact. Personality factors partly determine what a situation means to the individual who is in it.

PERSONALITY DEVELOPMENT IN SOCIOECONOMIC CONTEXT

A fundamental fact of life is that citizens of the world experience widely different socioeconomic conditions (Economist, 2005). Even within the world's industrialized and relatively rich nations, one finds great disparities in income and associated social opportunities. In many parts of the world, economic gaps between rich and poor have only widened in recent years.

Of what relevance are socioeconomic circumstances to the development of personality? Based on what you have learned about personality psychology so far, you might think that the answer is "little relevance." Historically, personality theorists have devoted relatively little attention to the socioeconomic conditions of the persons about whom they are theorizing. Theorists working in psychoanalytic, behavioral, and trait-theory traditions explicitly have sought to identify general principles of personality functioning that would transcend particular social circumstances (in the same way that, for example, a biologist might try to identify basic principles of human anatomy and physiology that transcend social circumstances). Recent work, however, suggests that this traditional approach to the study of personality might be inadequate. Specifically, different personality attributes appear to have different implications for the individual in different socioeconomic settings. Important advances on this topic come from the work of Caspi, Elder, and their colleagues (Caspi, 2002; Caspi, Bem, & Elder, 1989).

Consider a seemingly simple question: What are the implications of individual differences in impulsivity for social development? For example, if we identify adolescents who differ in the degree to which they are impulsive, will we find that more impulsive individuals experience more problems of social development, such as delinquency? One possibility is that adolescents who are less able to control their emotional impulses (i.e., "high impulsivity" adolescents) inevitably will experience more social difficulties in their teenage years; this might occur because the avoidance of such problems (e.g., drug and alcohol use, physical aggression, vandalism) requires that one control one's impulses. However, another possibility is that the effects of impulsivity are not inevitable. Instead, the implications of high versus low impulsivity perhaps can only be understood by examining personality in its socioeconomic context. In poor neighborhoods, adolescents may experience a relatively large number of circumstances that have the potential to trigger antisocial acts while, at the same time, benefiting from relatively few community structures that might help them to develop self-control skills. In contrast, in affluent neighborhoods, there are fewer opportunities for delinquency and there are more social supports.

Findings indicate that these differences between affluent and poor neighborhoods are highly consequential. The relation between impulsivity and

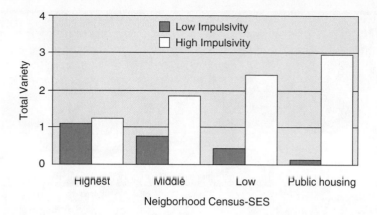

Figure 14.4 *The relation between impulsivity and a measure of delinquency (vertical axis) in neighborhoods of varying socioeconomic status. From Caspi et al. (2000).*

delinquency is found to vary in the different socioeconomic contexts. Lynam and colleagues (2000) studied a large sample of 13-year-olds in Pittsburgh, Pennsylvania. These individuals lived in widely varying socioeconomic circumstances that ranged from neighborhoods high in socioeconomic status (SES) to neighborhoods that were poverty-stricken, including ones in which people lived in public housing that featured many factors that might foster delinquency. Using various laboratory measures that were administered when research participants were 13 years of age, the researchers determined whether each participant was high or low in impulsivity. With measures of both impulsivity and socioeconomic circumstances, Lynam and colleagues could determine whether the personality factor had different implications in different circumstances. It did. Among adolescents living in poor neighborhoods, high-impulsive individuals were more likely than low-impulsive individuals to become involved in delinquent behaviors (Figure 14.4). In contrast, in the affluent neighborhoods, adolescents who were either high or low in impulsivity did not differ in delinquency. Community resources in affluent neighborhoods appeared to buffer the potentially negative effects of the personality characteristic.

CAUSES AND EFFECTS OF PERSONALITY ATTRIBUTES

Other work has examined an issue that is particularly important, yet also particularly difficult to "untangle." It commonly is found that people living in lower-class neighborhoods experience higher levels of psychological distress (e.g., anxiety, depression). If, at this point in your education in personality, you are "thinking like a psychologist," you will immediately recognize that such a finding is ambiguous: It is not clear whether people's personality characteristics cause them to end up in lower-class neighborhoods or if, conversely, living in lower-class neighborhoods causes psychological distress.

Caspi (2002) and colleagues have been able to study this issue by working with a very large sample of persons who are studied at multiple points in time.

Some personality characteristics have a particularly large impact on life outcomes among people who live in lower socioeconomic conditions.

This research setting enables the personality scientist to use statistical methods that can disentangle the different potential causal influences. Specifically, Caspi and colleagues have worked with data from the Dunedin study, which is a project that has carefully followed the lives of 1000 individuals living in Dunedin, New Zealand, over a 30-year period. This project has yielded evidence of importance not only to applied concerns regarding psychological distress, but to core issues in personality theory. A key finding is that questions about cause-and-effect relationships (i.e., is personality a causal influence on social class, or vice versa?) *vary* from one personality characteristic to another. For example, anxiety and social circumstances were closely related. Children who grew up in low-SES families became relatively more anxious adolescents. Furthermore, adolescents who received relatively less education became more anxious adults. Life conditions, then, causally influenced levels of anxiety, but anxiety did not causally appear to influence social class outcomes. In contrast, analyses of antisocial disorders yielded a different result. Engaging in antisocial conduct did have an effect on social class. People who engaged in antisocial behavior experienced more academic failure that, in turn, contributed to lower-class economic outcomes (Caspi, 2002). The general point is that the contemporary researcher can, in fact, disentangle the back-and-forth influences of personality and social class, but only by specifying the exact personality characteristics of interest and studying the development of persons over time.

PERSONALITY, GENDER, AND HISTORICAL CONTEXT

Caspi, Bem, and Elder (1989) provide related research on the interplay between personality and socioeconomic conditions. These investigators analyzed data describing the lives of American research participants who grew up during the Great Depression. In the late 1940s these people reached the age at which one might enter the workforce.

A personality characteristic of particular interest in this group was ill-temperedness, which is the tendency to display uncontrolled bouts of anger, including temper tantrums, verbal outbursts, and aggression. Ill-temperedness was assessed in childhood using interviews with mothers who described their child's emotional tendencies. The researchers then related high versus low ill-temperedness to later life outcomes.

Findings revealed that high versus low ill-temperedness was significantly related to economic outcomes in adulthood (Caspi et al., 1989). Importantly, results differed for male and female research participants. Male research participants who were ill-tempered as children were found to have lower occupational status at age 40. Amazingly, the effects of the personality variable were as large as the effects of a key socioeconomic variable, namely, the economic class in which people grew up as children. In general, people who grow up in higher-class households tend to end up with higher occupational status in adulthood. In the data analyzed by the Caspi group (1989), this typical result did hold among men who were low in ill-temperedness; in this group, men from higher-class backgrounds had higher-status jobs as adults. However, among men who were high in ill-temperedness, things were different. Ill-tempered men from higher social-class backgrounds essentially lost the advantages of their social class. Their occupational status in adulthood was no higher than that of men from lower-class backgrounds. Additional results indicated why this happened. Ill-tempered men tended to have lower educational achievement, and educational achievement, in turn, affected adult occupational status (Caspi et al., 1989).

Note that these results were obtained when examining the lives of men. Among women, ill-temperedness was unrelated to occupational status. If one considers historical circumstances, this result is not surprising. In the United States during the 1940s women had limited job opportunities, so personal qualities that might potentially affect job status under other circumstances would have little effect. However, among women, high versus low ill-temperedness still was consequential. It was related to the occupational status of women's husbands. Women who were *low* in ill-temperedness were more likely to marry men with *higher* occupational status. In other words, women who were *high* in ill-temperedness in childhood "fared less well in the marriage market" (Caspi et al., 1989, p. 388). Note that they fared less well in a particular marriage market, namely, that of mid-20th century America. As Caspi and colleagues emphasize, different results might be obtained in different sociohistorical contexts during which women had greater economic opportunities. The work of Caspi, Elder, and colleagues suggests, then, that the historical period during which one conducts a study can itself function as an important context for understanding personality and its consequences.

PERSONALITY FUNCTIONING ACROSS THE LIFE SPAN

Research in psychology has focused to a very large degree on the young. In the study of personality, the historical tradition established by Freud (Chapter 3) suggested that personality structure was established in the first few years of life. In the study of cognition, much effort has been directed to understanding the growth of cognitive functions in children (e.g., Flavell, 1999). Critics of psychological research commonly have complained that a disproportionately large amount of the field's research involves young adults in college.

In many respects, a focus on childhood, adolescence, and young adulthood is quite reasonable. These are critical periods of personal development. However, this focus does conflict with a basic fact of 21st-century life: The world contains ever-larger percentages of older adults. Thanks to advances in medicine, people are living much longer than in the past. The changes in life span are quite dramatic. Historians remind us that "before the nineteenth century, wherever he lived, man could only count on a short expectation of life, with a few extra years in the case of the rich" (Braudel, 1981, p. 90). The life span was so much shorter centuries ago that it apparently was not an unusual event when a ruler of France in the 14th century took the throne at age 17 and abdicated it at age 42 while holding the reputation of a wise elder statesman (Braudel, 1981). Today, of course, large numbers of people in the industrialized world live into their 70s, 80s, and beyond. This is a circumstance unknown in prior human history.

PSYCHOLOGICAL RESILIENCE IN THE LATER YEARS

The growth of older-adult populations suggests a new research agenda for psychology: the study of personality functioning later in life. In the past decade, psychologists have responded to this agenda. Extensive research programs have examined psychological functioning in the later years of life (e.g., Baltes & Mayer, 1999).

A repeated finding in this area of research is one that is somewhat surprising. Since old age is accompanied by many difficulties and challenges—retirement, physical declines, the death of peers and same-generation family members—one might expect that the psychological experience of older adults would be primarily negative. However, this is not the case. On objective measures of self-esteem, a sense of personal control, and psychological well-being versus depression, researchers commonly find that older adults are *not* worse off than middle-aged and younger adults (Baltes & Graf, 1996; Brändtstadter & Wentura, 1995). Rather than being characterized by despondency, in the later years of life individuals commonly report deeply satisfying, rich positive emotional experiences (Carstensen & Charles, 2003).

Older adults, then, exhibit much psychological resilience. They commonly are able to withstand the difficulties that accompany the later years and to maintain a remarkably strong sense of self and personal well-being. A challenge for the personality scientist, then, is to understand the processes through which many older adults maintain a positive sense of self.

A core insight into this issue came from the work of the German psychologist Paul Baltes and his associates (Baltes, 1997; Baltes & Baltes, 1990; Baltes & Staudinger, 2000). They recognized that development inherently involves trade-offs. When moving from one stage of life to another, people lose some psychological qualities but gain others. For example, early in life children gain logical reasoning capacities but may lose some capacities for fantasy life. In the later years, older adults may experience a decline in some basic cognitive functions yet may gain in personal wisdom (Baltes & Staudinger, 2000). The gains in knowledge and wisdom that people acquire with age often enable them to compensate for any losses in cognitive capacities.

The analysis by Baltes suggests a general model of psychological development and resilience in the later years of life (Baltes, 1997). In the Baltes model, people can maintain psychological well-being by selecting particular domains of life on which they focus their energies and knowledge. Although it may be difficult for the older adult to maintain a diverse array of life activities—work, clubs, athletic pursuits, hobbies, the development of new social networks, and so forth—he or she may be extremely capable of maintaining high levels of functioning and well-being within selected life domains. By focusing their energies on a few important aspects of life, older adults may be able to compensate for physical or cognitive declines and maintain a high sense of well-being.

Evidence of the beneficial impact of wise selection processes comes from a very large-scale study of adults in Berlin (Freund & Baltes, 1998). Participants completed a self-report questionnaire that assessed the degree to which they engaged in selection processes to optimize their functioning in the face of physical declines in old age. This questionnaire measured people's tendency to select a small number of significant life goals on which to concentrate their energies, as well as their capacity to draw on family and social-network resources to cope with life challenges. Even after controlling for other personality variables, people who more frequently employed these strategies for social living were found to have a higher sense of personal well-being and to experience more positive emotions in their daily life (Freund & Baltes, 1998).

EMOTIONAL LIFE IN OLDER ADULTHOOD: SOCIOEMOTIONAL SELECTIVITY

One illustration of selection processes comes from the research of Laura Carstensen and her colleagues (Carstensen, 1995; 1998; Carstensen, Isaacowitz, & Charles, 1999). Carstensen's **socioemotional selectivity theory** examines the ways in which social motivations shift across the course of life. The basic idea is that people are aware of the opportunities and constraints associated with different points in the life course. For example, a 20-year-old likely recognizes that many decades of family and professional life lie ahead, whereas an 85-year-old recognizes that he or she is likely entering, or already in, the last decade of life. This awareness of time influences one's life goals. For the younger adult, it makes sense to focus on the future, investing energy in long-term goals that involve the acquisition of information and skills that will prove useful in the decades ahead (e.g., skills of the sort acquired in college) or the development of one's self and sense of identity. In contrast, if one sees oneself as being near the end of life, it makes little sense to focus on such long-term goals. Instead, it is more reasonable to select one or two goals that have an immediate positive impact on one's life, and to focus one's energies on them. Thus, socioemotional selectivity theory predicts that goals involving meaningful emotional experiences become relatively more important in older adulthood. The older adult is predicted to be relatively less motivated

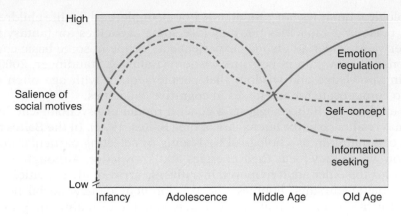

Figure 14.5 *Schematic representation of socioemotional selectivity theory's predictions about variations in social motives across the life course. From Carstensen (1995).*

to gain information about the world and to start new social networks, and relatively more motivated to have positive emotional experiences, which may be achieved by maintaining personally meaningful relationships with family and long-term friends (Figure 14.5). In sum, Carstensen's theory predicts that the older adult will be more likely than the younger adult to invest energy into a small, select set of social relationships that enhance emotional experience.

Research supports this hypothesis. For example, Carstensen and Fredrickson (1998) tested socioemotional selectivity theory in a study involving a large and ethnically diverse sample of adults ranging in age from 18 to 88. Their goal was to test the hypothesis that older adults would focus their attention on the enhancement of current emotional experiences, whereas younger adults would focus on possibilities for the future, such as meeting new people from whom new things about the world could be learned. To test this idea, they gave younger- and older-adult research participants a long list of different types of people (e.g., a long-time close friend, the author of a book you have just read). They asked the participants to make ratings that would reveal the dimensions (i.e., the features that differentiated the individuals in the list) that were most important to them as they thought about the different people on the list. As predicted, older adults seemed to focus their thoughts on the emotional qualities of the people on the list, and to pay less attention to whether a meeting with a given person might provide information that would be valuable in the future. In contrast, younger adults focused less on people's emotional qualities and more on the possibility of informative meetings with new people—whether or not those meetings involved experiences that were emotionally positive. Older adults, recognizing that they are in the latter years of life, thus seemed to be far more attentive to social experiences that would bring immediate emotional rewards. Interestingly, a subsequent study found similar results among HIV-positive men with symptoms of AIDS; though not elderly, these men faced the possibility of a limited life span and, in a manner similar to older adults, focused heavily on the immediate emotional qualities of social relationships (Carstensen & Fredricksen, 1998).

   In previous sections of this chapter on personality in context, the contexts we have examined have primarily been social settings. The work of Baltes, Carstensen, and colleagues indicates that age, and especially the number of years that one feels one has remaining in life, is another critical context for personality functioning.

There is no such thing as a human nature independent of culture. Men without culture would not be clever savages... nature's noblemen [or] intrinsically talented apes who had somehow failed to find themselves. They would be unworkable monstrosities with very few useful instincts, fewer recognizable sentiments, and no intellect: mental basket cases. As our central nervous system—and most particularly its crowning curse and glory, the neocortex—grew up in great part in interaction with culture, it is incapable of directing our behavior or organizing our experience without the guidance provided by systems of significant symbols.

SOURCE: GEERTZ, 1973, p. 49

PERSONS IN CULTURES

TWO STRATEGIES FOR THINKING ABOUT PERSONALITY AND CULTURE

Strategy #1: Personality... and Culture?

There are two strategies for thinking about personality and culture. The first is one that you already have seen a number of times in this text. It is a strategy that begins with a particular theoretical conception or theory-driven hypothesis, and then asks whether the idea happens to apply across cultures. Since so much of 20th-century psychological science was a product of the Western world (the United States and Europe), in practice this strategy is one in which (1) a personality scientist starts with an idea about human nature that is based in Western culture and that reflects research findings or clinical experiences involving U.S. or European citizens, and then (2) asks whether this conception of personality receives support when research is conducted in non-Western cultures. You saw this strategy back in Chapter 6, when learning about the phenomenological theory of personality and self developed by the American psychologist Carl Rogers. After reviewing his theory, we summarized contemporary research on the question of whether Rogerian self-processes occur in Asian cultures. You saw this strategy again in Chapter 8, where we asked whether the Big Five model of personality traits (another product of Western personality psychology) replicates cross-culturally.

   In this strategy for thinking about personality and culture, questions of culture and personality boil down to what the research psychologist calls questions of "generalizability." The issue is whether a given psychological finding holds, or generalizes, from one setting to another. Just as one can ask whether a given research result generalizes across genders, socioeconomic circumstances, or age groups, one can ask whether it generalizes across cultures.

   It is important to determine whether research findings generalize across cultures. This first strategy, then, is a good one. But it is not good enough. It has two significant limitations. First, it may fail to identify aspects of personality that are important in other cultures but not in one's own. If researchers simply import a Western conception of personality into a non-Western culture, they may completely overlook aspects of personhood that are key features in the non-Western culture but are relatively unimportant in their own. As an example, consider the efforts of researchers studying the Big Five model of personality (Chapter 8) to characterize the basic units of language that individuals use to describe themselves and other persons. When researchers import the five-factor structure to non-Western cultures, they indeed do obtain evidence that these personality dimensions are recognized by members of these cultures as significant ways that individuals differ (McCrae & Costa, 1997); it should be noted, however, that significant culture variations in the language of individual differences are also found (Saucier & Goldberg, 2001). Yet this research still could be overlooking important aspects of other cultures' language of human nature. For example, consider Buddhist cultures. In this cultural context, a primary term for thinking about persons and their actions is *karma*, which refers to the positive and negative effects of actions on one's stream of consciousness, where that consciousness can extend from one physical lifetime to another through reincarnation (Chodron, 1990). This conception of karma is not prevalent in the Western cultures in which the Big Five were first studied. Questionnaires designed to measure the five personality dimensions thus do not contain many (if any) items that are directly relevant to the conception of karma. As a result, if these Western-world, English-language questionnaires are imported to a Buddhist culture, researchers probably will fail to "find karma." The notion of karma will be overlooked, despite the fact that it is important to the non-Western culture, because it is not a component of the Western-world research instrument.

There is a second limitation to the strategy of asking merely whether a given research finding generalizes from one cultural context to another. It is that, implicitly, it treats culture as peripheral to the study of human nature. It implies that the personality theorist first can develop a culture-free model of core aspects of personality and individual differences, and then—as a kind of afterthought—can ask whether the model has to be "tweaked" here or there to account for cultural variation. Such an approach treats issues of culture as an optional supplement to personality psychology's core concern with basic human nature.

The quote that opened this section of our chapter, from the anthropologist Clifford Geertz, suggests that this way of thinking is backwards. To Geertz's thinking, there is no culture-free personality in the first place. Instead, psychological functioning is inherently cultural. People think about the world using languages and related communication systems that they acquire from their culture and that are themselves the products of generations of cultural experience. The things that people think about—other people, social settings, future possibilities, themselves—take on personal significance within meaning systems that are based on cultural and social practices, where those practices might vary from one cultural context to another.

Strategy #2: Culture and Personality

This way of thinking suggests a different strategy for conceptualizing personality and culture. In this alternative approach, culture is not on the periphery of personality psychology. It is at the core. Persons are seen as acquiring their sense of personhood through interactions with their culture.

This way of thinking about personality–culture relations has important implications for how one thinks not only about personality, but culture as well. Cultures consist of those very same persons who acquired their sense of personhood from that culture. Culture and personality, in other words, "make each other up" (Shweder & Sullivan, 1990, p. 399). "The practices and meanings of culture, and the psychological processes and structures of each member of the culture, are *mutually constitutive*" (Kitayama & Markus, 1999, p. 250).

In this view, then, there is no culture-free personality on the one hand and person-free culture on the other. Instead, there are persons who function psychologically by using cultural tools, including language and related meaning systems. And there are cultures whose practices are maintained by those very same people who inhibit them. For more than a decade, this way of thinking has been advanced within a field known as cultural psychology (Shweder & Sullivan, 1993). Cultural psychology is concerned with whether research findings generalize from one culture to another (the main question of what we have called Strategy #1). Yet it asks deeper questions about human nature, with a particular focus on the human capacity to use conscious reflection to make sense of the world of experience (Shweder & Sullivan, 1990).

The argument that one should view human experience through a cultural lens is made compelling by examples in which people of a given culture seem to lead lives that differ deeply from one's own. Consider, first, your own experiences and actions in a setting in which you meet a new acquaintance, for example at a party. If you are a member of the Western world, you are likely to introduce yourself by stating your name, and if the conversation continues and the two of you want to get to know each other better, you are likely to talk about your own interests, hobbies, personal background, or goals in life. If, the next day, you describe your new acquaintance to an old friend, you are likely to use personality trait terms that describe personal qualities that differentiate the individual from others (you might see your new acquaintance as "somewhat extraverted," "very open-minded," etc.). This probably strikes you as obvious. Isn't it always like this? Don't people present themselves and talk about each other in this manner no matter where in the world you go? Apparently not. Detailed analyses of personhood within traditional culture on the island of Bali (Geertz, 1973) indicate that our own ways of being a person are not universal.

In Bali, the label that people use to describe themselves is not a unique, personal name. Personal names are treated as very private; they are "treated as though they are military secrets" (Geertz, 1973, p. 375). Instead, people are differentiated using labels that make reference to the individual's place within family and community systems. Terms for referring to people make reference to family members (a person is "Mother-of-_____"), social status (which strongly defines how the person should be treated), or social roles (e.g., village chief). This system reflects a broader cultural conception in which persons are not primarily thought of as unique, idiosyncratic individuals, but as elements of a larger, eternal social order. Their cultural practices "[mute] the more idiosyncratic, merely biographical, and, consequently, transient aspects of... existence as a human being (what, in our more egoistic framework, we call

Social practices in Bali suggest that Balinese culture emphasizes the relations among a person and the generations of his or her family, rather than highlighting the distinctive, unique features of the isolated individual, as is more common in Western cultures.

"personality") in favor of some rather more typical, highly conventionalized, and, consequently, enduring ones" (Geertz, 1973, p. 370).

PERSONALITY AND SELF AS SOCIALLY CONSTRUCTED WITHIN CULTURE

The implications of cultural psychology for the study of personality are vividly illustrated by research on conceptions of self in American and Japanese culture conducted by Shinobu Kitayama and Hazel Markus (Cross & Markus, 1999; Kitayama & Markus, 1999; Markus et al., 2006). A central idea in this work is that there may be variations from culture to culture in people's implicit conceptions of self (Markus & Kitayama, 1991; Triandis, 1995). People's beliefs about what it is to be a "self" or a person may not be the same throughout the world. Different cultures may feature different beliefs about the rights, duties, possibilities, and most central features associated with personhood. Note that such beliefs are not necessarily explicit; in other words, it might be that many members of a culture do not explicitly put into words these culturally shared beliefs about the nature of personality. Yet, even if they do not stop to think about it explicitly, everyone does have conceptions about the most basic aspects of personality. It is these conceptions that appear to differ across cultures.

Independent and Interdependent Views of Self

Specifically, differences are found when contrasting European-American and East Asian cultures. In European-American cultures, the self is primarily construed as being **independent**. In an independent view, the individual is

Research suggests that individuals in Asian cultures are more likely than are persons in Western cultures to possess interdependent views of self that highlight the interrelations among members of a community, as well as individuals' obligations to family and society.

viewed as possessing a set of psychological qualities (personality traits, goals, etc.) that are distinct from, or independent of, those of other people. Individuals also are construed in terms of independent rights, such as the right to pursue personal happiness. In an independent view of self, then, a person is an entity that can be characterized as a kind of "container" within which are stored a collection of psychological traits that are the cause of the person's actions.

This perspective contrasts with a view of self found in East Asian cultures (Markus & Kitayama, 1991; Triandis, 1995). Here one finds an **interdependent** conception of self. In an interdependent view, people are construed in terms of their roles with family and social relationships. The cultural system emphasizes the responsibilities that are inherent in one's position within these relationships, rather than highlighting the individual person's self-centered pursuit of happiness. In interdependent cultures, behavior is not explained in terms of autonomous mental traits that reside in the person's head. Instead, people explain behavior in terms of networks of social obligations. It is the person's location within such social systems that is seen as the cause of behavior. For example, a person's chronic expression of "conscientious" behavior might be explained in terms of social obligations that compel the person to act conscientiously, rather than by saying that the person possesses a trait of conscientiousness.

How might these different conceptions of self have developed historically? How are they maintained in the contemporary world? Kitayama and Markus (1999) address these questions through a "collective-constructionist theory" of the self (Figure 14.6). This theory addresses three interlocking factors:

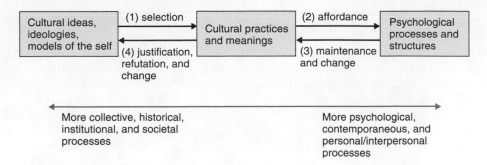

Figure 14.6   *Representation of the "collective-constructionist theory" of the self. From Kitayama & Markus (1999).*

broad philosophical traditions that arise in a given culture and that provide a framework within which social groups and individuals function; social practices that are characteristic of a given culture and that take on meaning within that cultural system; and psychological processes and structures of the individual person, which develop through interaction with those social practices. Note that the paths of influence in this theory (Figure 14.6) run in two directions. Just as personality develops through social practices that occur within a cultural context, culture itself is maintained by social practices that are enacted by persons.

In this theory, the existence of independent versus interdependent conceptions of self is understood in terms of broad historical trends that have characterized European-American versus East Asian cultures. Drawing on the work of the social theorist Max Weber, Kitayama and Markus note that the history of the West includes a Protestant ethic in which individuals pursue a "calling," with industrious pursuit of this calling being a course of action that is thought to increase the glory of God. This belief system fosters a capitalistic set of social practices in which individuals work industriously to maximize their personal gain. Once these practices are in place, they become self-maintaining; in other words, social practices involving the industrious pursuit of wealth continue even when they no longer have any connection to their religious origins. Finally, individual people develop through engagement with these social practices. When social practices concern the maximization of personal gain, individuals tend to set goals for personal achievement, to think of life's possibilities in terms of costs and benefits, and to be concerned with personal qualities such as individual conscientiousness, which relates to personal achievement.

In contrast, in the East, social practices have their origin in a different ethos. Confucionism, Taoism, and Zen Buddhism provide a philosophical backdrop that differs markedly from the Protestant ethic (Kitayama & Markus, 1999). Within Japanese culture, these philosophical systems function to highlight hierarchies in the social order, the interconnectedness of individuals within and across those hierarchies, and feelings of compassion toward others (Figure 14.6, bottom panel). This cultural context fosters two types of social practices. In formal or official social settings (or the "official frame"), strict social hierarchies dictate rules of acceptable behavior. In informal, personal settings (or the "personal frame"), empathic emotions such as sympathy and compassion figure centrally in social relations. The individual who develops within this two-part system of social practices develops two aspects of self-concept. One, which comes into play in the official frame, centers on a motive for self-improvement and feelings of self-criticism when one's actions do not contribute sufficiently to the welfare of society. The other, which is pertinent to the personal frame, centers on feelings of empathy toward others.

The notion that Eastern and Western cultures feature interdependent and independent senses of self is consistent with a range of empirical findings. As we reviewed in Chapter 6, psychological processes involving self-esteem differ from one cultural to another. East Asians are less likely to make efforts to maintain a high sense of personal esteem (Heine et al., 1999). Instead, self criticism functions as a salient motive (Kitayama et al., 1997). Unlike findings in the Western world, in East Asia people are not more intrinsically motivated to engage in tasks when they choose them personally; instead, they experience greater intrinsic motivation when choices are made by authority figures or trusted peers (Iyengar & Lepper, 1999). Consistent with the notion that Western conceptions of the self draw attention to internal personal qualities that function as causes of behavior, Americans are found to over-attribute the causes of action to personal rather than situational factors (Ross, 1977). People in Japan, India, and China are less likely to exhibit this attributional bias (Kitayama & Masuda, 1997; Miller, 1984; Morris & Peng, 1994). Studies of subjective well-being also reveal interesting cross-cultural variations. When predicting people's ratings of satisfaction with their life, the pleasantness of everyday emotional experiences is a stronger predictor in Western than in Eastern cultures (Suh, Diener, Oishi, & Triandis, 1998). Each of these findings, then, is consistent with the contention that people in Eastern versus Western cultures have different, interdependent versus independent, construals of self.

The interplay of culture and personality also is revealed in studies of people who move from one cultural context to another. For example, consider what happens when people move from an Eastern culture to the West. Western social practices, more than Eastern ones, emphasize the asserting of one's personal attributes. Becoming engaged in these new social practices should cause people to become more extraverted, as they learn to fit in with their new culture. There is evidence that this does indeed occur. McCrae, Yik, Trapnell, Bond, & Paulhus (1998) studied Chinese students enrolled in a Canadian university. Some of these students had been in North America for many years, whereas others had immigrated only a few years before the study was conducted. People who had longer exposure to Canadian culture tended to have higher extraversion scores (McCrae et al., 1998).

The role of cognitive processes in these cultural differences is further revealed by studies of bicultural individuals. These are persons who have lived long enough in each of two different cultures that they have internalized the belief systems of both (Hong, Morris, Chiu, & Martinez, 2000). Such people are capable of "frame switching"; they can change the culturally grounded framework through which they interpret any given event. Interestingly, stimuli that cognitively prime one versus another cultural frame can thereby influence the bicultural individual's subsequent thinking processes. Cultural frameworks have been primed by exposing people to symbols representative of Chinese versus American culture (e.g., an American flag, a picture of a

Chinese dragon). Compared to when they view Chinese symbols, bicultural individuals are more likely to attribute the causes of actions to internal causes after viewing symbols of American culture (Hong et al., 2000). Such findings suggest that cultural variations in cognition can be understood within the general theoretical framework provided by social-cognitive analyses (Chapters 12 and 13).

PERSONALITY PROCESSES AND SOCIAL CHANGE

With the end of our coverage of personality theories on the horizon, we, the authors of this text, hope that you have become intellectually engaged with the field's theoretical issues. Twenty-first century personality psychologists address theoretical puzzles about human nature that have intrigued humankind since at least fourth-century B.C. Athens. The ability to think deeply and systematically about these issues is perhaps the most basic intellectual skill that you should have acquired in your course on personality. Even after you have forgotten the names of all the factors of the Big Five trait model or the results of some experiment testing Freud's ideas about the unconscious, you should retain the ability to ask critical questions about theoretical conceptions of human nature put forth by social scientists, philosophers, and public intellectuals.

Yet many readers may also have a practical bent. "Sure, I can evaluate these theories," you may be thinking to yourself, "but I have a different question: What can one *do* with these theories? Is there anything practical that can be achieved?"

If you are in fact asking this, then to you we would say, "Congratulations!" This question is appropriate and enormously important. One of the most important ways of evaluating a theory or set of theories is not by scrutinizing their theoretical elegance, but by asking what practical goals they can achieve. This practical criterion becomes particularly important in light of contemporary critiques of the nature of theorizing. The personality theorist hopes to discover truths about human nature. Yet he or she inherently is engaged in a task in which the discovery of eternal truths may be so unlikely that "truth-seeking" is not even the best way to characterize the activity of theory construction. Scholars recognize that theorists in any scientific field work with a set of constraints (Gergen, 2001). They employ whatever knowledge, languages, and ways of thinking happen to be available to them at the particular historical time and social place in which they live. These cognitive systems are the theorists' tools. It is very unlikely that, at any particular point in history, these tools will be perfect, enabling the theorist to construct a scientific model that perfectly mirrors reality. All theories, then, will be limited by the intellectual tools available at the time that the theory is constructed. At best, then, one can hope that a scientific theory will provide a good model of some aspects of the world, while recognizing that it may provide a poor model of other aspects and may fail even to address some issues of importance (Giere, 1999).

If the entire odyssey of theory constructing is limited in this manner, then that is all the more reason for asking a practical, here-and-now question: "Sure, these theories may not be perfect, yet is there anything practical that one can do with them?"

We have, of course, addressed this question at numerous points earlier in the text. We generally have done so by reviewing clinical applications. As you have seen, there is no shortage of cases in which theoretical insights have been translated into clinical applications of practical significance.

Yet you may rightly ask whether there is anything more that the personality psychologist can do. The citizens of the world face incredible challenges: a large percentage of the world continues to live in poverty (3 billion people live on $2 or less a day), much of the world receives little formal education (e.g., in 35 African and South Asian nations, half of current teenagers from poor households never completed even the first grade), and the spread of HIV/AIDS is a medical catastrophe of incredible proportions (the disease strikes 14,000 new persons a *day*, with more than 60 million cases of HIV worldwide) (all figures from United Nations Population Fund, 2002). Admittedly, many of the causes of these problems involve socioeconomic and political factors that are beyond the reach of the personality psychologist. Yet other problems have significant behavioral components. HIV/AIDS rates, for example, can be lowered through avoidance of high-risk behaviors. Behavioral change similarly can influence the risk of medical maladies such as cancer and heart disease.

A challenge for personality theorists, then, is to show how their theorizing might contribute to society-wide changes in behavior that are of widespread benefit. How could this be done? In an ideal world, one might first identify a theory that could be applied to issues of social change. One then would design an intervention that is based on the principles of this theory. Next (the hard part) one would have to figure out a way for *large* numbers of people—tens or hundreds of thousands of people in a community, geographic region, or nation—to be exposed to the intervention. Finally, a systematic statistical analysis of the behavior of the population in the study would have to be conducted to see if the intervention beneficially changed the behavior of the population. In short, one would have to run a giant theory-based psychology experiment. Sound like science fiction? It's not. It's science. Such experiments already have been conducted, and with great success.

MEDIA MODELING OF PROSOCIAL BEHAVIOR

Numerous investigators, working in different parts of the world, have drawn upon the principle of Bandura's social-cognitive theory when designing interventions for social change (Smith, October 2002). As you learned earlier (Chapter 12), social-cognitive theory highlights the influence of psychological models on people's thoughts and actions. By observing other people, we acquire skills, learn about features of the social world, and develop attitudes and expectations about the benefits of alternative courses of action. As you also learned (Chapter 13), psychologists already have devised modeling-based interventions to change behavior; these interventions generally have been applied in the treatment of individual clients or in studies with small groups of people.

The problem, then, is to figure out a way to bring well-established interventions based on social-cognitive theory to large populations of persons. The solution: television. The same medium that brings us professional wrestling and infomercials can also deliver entertainment that fosters beneficial society-wide change.

Literacy

As summarized by Bandura (2002; also see Smith, October 2002), the first individual who recognized this potential and implemented it for social good was the Mexican television executive Miguel Sabido. Sabido's goal was to increase adult literacy in his nation. Although the Mexican government had designed adult literacy programs and established centers at which citizens could obtain literacy booklets, these efforts initially proved insufficient. The educational program itself was fine; the problem was that insufficient numbers of people were taking advantage of the program. What was needed was an intervention that would motivate individuals to go to the literacy center, acquire the educational materials, and invest the considerable effort that is required to develop literacy in adulthood. Obstacles in the way of this goal included people being unaware of exactly how to obtain the educational materials, lacking a sense of self-efficacy for becoming literate, and in some cases not feeling worthy of having an educated government official devote time to their own educational development (Bandura, 2002).

Sabido's tool for overcoming these obstacles was a televised soap opera. A year-long televised drama depicted the lives of characters who were participating in a literacy study group. Using social-cognitive theory principles regarding the effects of different types of psychological models (Bandura, 1986), Sabido made the program's message relevant to the widest possible audience by including in the show characters who represented persons of varying social status, age, and language skills. To provide concrete information about the government's literacy program, the show's characters were shown picking up actual literacy materials in actual distribution centers in Mexico City. As the weeks and months of programming unfolded, then, characters modeled the possibility of attaining literacy, the motivation and effort required to do so, and the benefits that literacy brings. Such modeling has the potential of shifting social norms, making it seem more appropriate and socially acceptable to embark on literacy education later in life.

Sabido's intervention proved to be a huge success. The show had millions of viewers, and they responded to the program's message. Although fewer than 100,000 people had enrolled in the Mexican government's literacy program in the year prior to the programming, after Sabido's program was viewed more than 800,000 people enrolled during a one-year period (Bandura, 1986, 2002). Sabido, then, had done it: He created an intervention based on the social-cognitive theory of personality, applied that intervention to a huge audience, and produced a widespread, beneficial social change.

HIV/AIDS Prevention

In addition to using modeling to bring about social change among formerly non-literate citizens of Mexico, Sabido proved himself to be a role model to other psychological researchers. In the years since Sabido initiated education-entertainment broadcasting based on principles of social-cognitive theory, many others have followed in his footsteps. A particularly critical application has aimed to reduce the prevalence HIV/AIDS in the East African nation of Tanzania (Vaughn, Rogers, Singhal, & Swalehe, 2000; Mohammed, 2001).

For more than five years, from 1993 to 1999, citizens of Tanzania were able to hear a radio soap opera entitled *Twende na Wakati (Let's Go with the*

Times). In some ways, this was a typical entertainment series, with multiple characters whose lives unfolded gradually over the course of the drama. Yet the program had another element. It was designed by the Tanzanian government, working in collaboration with a non-profit organization called Population Communications International (PCI), to provide not only entertainment but education about HIV/AIDS risk behaviors.

Such education was particularly critical in this nation. Before the program began, the nation's citizens were relatively uninformed about the actual causes of HIV infection. The majority did not know how to prevent HIV. Many people suffered from misinformation as a result of rumors such as that the young could not contract the disease, that condoms were ineffective, and that it was possible by casual observation to determine whether a potential sexual partner had the virus (Vaughn et al., 2000). The society also suffers from a gender imbalance, with women being less likely to receive HIV/AIDS counseling and testing than men (United Nations Population Fund, 2002). The context for all these concerns is that Tanzania also suffers from one of the world's highest rates of HIV infection, with the vast majority of infections being caused by unprotected sexual intercourse (Vaughn et al., 2000).

Since radio is a particularly important source of information in Tanzania, investigators chose to use an education-entertainment radio broadcast in an attempt to foster behaviors in the population that would reduce the prevalence of HIV/AIDS. To this end *Twende na Wakati* featured characters who modeled the full range of positive and negative possibilities regarding HIV/AIDS, so that listeners would be aware not only of the benefits of taking HIV-preventive steps but the costs of not taking them. Negative models (e.g., a promiscuous truck driver who failed to use condoms and acquired HIV) exemplified the consequences of high-risk behavior. Positive models provided medically accurate information and counseling to other characters. Perhaps most important, the show featured "transitional" models. These were characters who, at first, were not engaging in safe-sex behaviors but who gradually adopted those behaviors as a result of the interventions of other characters. Social-cognitive theory and research (Bandura, 1986, 1997) indicate that such transitional models are particularly important in building a high sense of self-efficacy, since listeners can first identify with the character and his or her struggles and then, after this sense of identification, can observe the person succeeding.

The Tanzanian government took the remarkably valuable step not only of broadcasting this series, but of conducting an experiment to determine precisely whether the broadcast had its intended effect on the adoption of safe-sex practices. From 1993 to 1995, the program was broadcast in some regions of the country but not others; it subsequently was broadcast nationwide. The different regions could then be compared to gauge the effectiveness of the program. This was done through interview/surveys that asked people about their practice of specific behaviors that prevent HIV infection (Vaughn et al., 2000).

The broadcasting of *Twende na Wakati* proved to have a number of beneficial effects. Based on listener self-reports in a survey that was conducted, people engaged in more interpersonal communication about HIV risks as a result of listening to the program (Vaughn et al., 2000); analyses indicate that these communications are quite important, with part of the overall effect of the program being due to its influence of people's tendency to discuss more openly

Photos depict researchers and radio actors who, working with the organization Population Communications International, are developing and recording radio dramas that are designed to foster beneficial social change.

the problem of HIV/AIDS prevention (Mohammed, 2001). The program also affected attitudes and beliefs about HIV/AIDS. A valuable indication of this examined the percentage of people who reported having one or more HIV/AIDS risk factors (e.g., multiple sexual partners, unprotected sex), yet who felt that they personally were not at risk for getting the infection. During the 1993–1995 period, the percentage of such people in the region in which *Twende na Wakati* was broadcast fell from 21 percent to 10 percent; in contrast, in the region in which the show was not broadcast, the percentage of people who believed they were not at risk increased during the same period (Vaughn et al., 2000). Thus, the radio broadcast significantly influenced this critical HIV-related belief. Most importantly, the modeling of safe-sex practices on the radio show significantly affected people's actual sexual practices. In the broadcast region, both men and women reported declines in their number of sexual partners during the years 1993 to 1995. (People in the region in which the show initially was not broadcast showed such declines after the show was beamed to their area.) Further, condom use increased in the broadcast regions more rapidly than it did in the regions that were not exposed to the radio soap opera (Vaughn et al., 2000).

In summary, the broadcast had its intended effect. By applying principles of social-cognitive theory to the design of an intervention that can bring about behavioral change, and by devising a way of delivering that intervention to large numbers of persons, the researchers were able to bring about societal-wide changes in HIV/AIDS risk behaviors. To anyone asking whether psychologists actually can do something socially useful with their theories of personality, the work in Tanzania and Mexico provides a resounding yes.

SUMMARY

In this chapter, you have learned about a series of research programs in contemporary personality psychology. The research topics were diverse. Yet they illustrated a common theme. Each concerned the interaction between persons and the social contexts in which they live. Questions about interpersonal relations, cross-situational coherence in experience and action, personality development in its socioeconomic context, development across the life span, personality and culture, and personality processes and social change were answered by research strategies that attended carefully both to personality and to social context.

At a very general level, this chapter's tour of contemporary research on personality in context conveys a message about the scientific field. It illustrates advances that have been made over the years in the scientific study of personality. A generation ago, many investigators construed persons and situations as two separate, independent forces. Each presumably exerted a separate effect—a person effect and a situation effect—on behavior. As you saw in our coverage of the person-situation controversy, investigators debated the relative size of person and situation effects (Chapter 8), sometimes computing statistical indices of the size of each separate factor (e.g., Funder & Ozer, 1983).

The research reviewed in this chapter shows how much the science of personality has advanced since that earlier era. Current research findings indicate that "person" and "context" are not independent forces. Instead, persons and contexts interact dynamically. They "make each other up" (Shweder & Sullivan, 1990, p. 399). Contexts are comprised primarily of persons, and the meaning of a social situation is constructed by the people who are in it. This may seem like an abstract theoretical point. Yet, as we have seen, recognizing it has practical advantages. It opens the door to a psychology of personality that can shed light on how people try to cope with the everyday challenges of their lives—and that can help them to do so.

MAJOR CONCEPTS

Defensive pessimism   A coping strategy in which people use negative thinking as a way of coping with stress.

Hot versus cool attentional focus   The focusing of one thought on emotionally arousing (hot) versus less arousing (cool) aspects of a situation or stimulus.

Independent versus interdependent construals of self   Alternative implicit beliefs about self-concept in which the self is viewed either as possessing a set of psychological qualities that are distinct of other people (independent self) or is viewed in terms of roles in family, social, and community relationships (interdependent self).

Knowledge-and-appraisal personality architecture (KAPA)   Theoretical analysis of personality architecture that distinguishes two aspects of

cognition in personality functioning: enduring knowledge and dynamic appraisals of the meaning of encounters for the self.

Optimism   A coping strategy that features relatively realistic expectations about one's capabilities.

Personality architecture   A term to describe the overall design and operating characteristics of those psychological systems that underlie personality functioning.

Rejection sensitivity   A thinking style characterized by anxious expectations of rejection in interpersonal relationships.

Socioemotional selectivity theory   Theoretical analysis by Carstensen that examines the ways in which social motivations shift across the course of life.

REVIEW

1. Contemporary research shows how personality can be understood by examining interactions between persons and the contexts in which they live. The first example of this general point involved interpersonal relations, which in the context of romantic relationships was seen to elicit negative, pessimistic, and ultimately self-defeating thoughts among a group of people with the personality characteristic of rejection sensitivity. Other research showed how people may transfer thoughts and feelings from a past relationship onto a new relationship partner.

2. Research on the coping strategies of optimism and defensive pessimism showed how people may address the same social stressor with very different yet sometimes equally effective strategies that involve optimistic versus pessimistic styles of thinking.

3. Research on knowledge, appraisal, and cross-situational coherence illustrated how a given aspect of knowledge may come into play across seemingly diverse contexts, and thus produce consistent self-appraisals in the different settings.

4. Work on personality development in context illustrated how socioeconomic circumstances can affect personality development. Findings included research showing how a given personality characteristic can have different implications for development in economically affluent versus poor contexts.

5. Research on personality and culture shows how the meaning of personality and of the self may vary from one culture to another; major differences involve self-construals that are independent versus interdependent.

6. Principles from social-cognitive theory have been applied to bring about large-scale social change. Research applying modeling techniques to enhance literacy and HIV/AIDS prevention were reviewed.

ASSESSING PERSONALITY THEORY AND RESEARCH

15

Chapter Focus

In this last of our chapters, we broaden our focus. Rather than considering theories one at a time, we address them as a whole. How did they do? How successful were the personality theorists in achieving the five goals we have considered throughout this text: (1) basing a theory on an objective, reliable, and diverse body of scientific observations; developing a theory that is (2) systematic, (3) testable, and (4) comprehensive; and (5) devising theory-based applications that benefit individual and social welfare?

QUESTIONS TO BE ADDRESSED IN THIS CHAPTER

1. How successful were the theories of personality in achieving the goals for the field that we discussed in Chapter 1?

2. Why did the theories differ so much? How can we understand their development of such different units of analysis for understanding personality structure and processes?

3. How can we capitalize on the most useful features of the personality theories, even as we struggle to reconcile their differences?

HOW DID THEY DO? A CRITICAL EVALUATION OF PERSONALITY THEORIES AND RESEARCH

Once upon a time, you read Chapter 1 of this text. It opened with a series of personality sketches written by people just like you—or just like you *were*: Students in a class on personality psychology, writing on the very first day of the course. The sophistication of these sketches prompted us to ask what the professional psychologists could possibly be accomplishing that is not already accomplished by the insightful non-professional who observes and reflects upon persons and the differences among them.

We answered this question by outlining five activities that are unique to the professional personality psychologist. In "Critical Evaluation" sections in subsequent chapters we used these five as criteria for evaluating each of the theories. This proved revealing. The theories differed strikingly. Some were comprehensive but were not consistently testable. Others were testable but not comprehensive. Some theorists built their frameworks on a mountain of evidence. Others built them on observations of a small number of clients. These five criteria highlighted the relative strengths and limits of the individual theories.

We begin this chapter by taking a broader view. Rather than reviewing individual theories one at a time, we treat them as a whole and ask, "How did they do?" How successful was personality psychology as a whole in meeting these five goals?

We pose this question to two different readerships. Most of you reading this text will not enter the field of psychology. Nonetheless, personality psychology may prove relevant to you in the future. You may have a friend with a mental health problem and want to know how the person can be helped. You may be running a business, selecting employees, and trying to predict which job applicants will prove reliable, trustworthy, and hard working. You may have

572

children and worry if their psychological development is "normal." You may be in sales for a multi-national corporation and wonder if the motives and thinking styles of overseas clients differ from your own. Do you have to just take your best guess? Or were the ideas and research findings of personality psychology of sufficiently high quality that they can inform your decisions?

The other readership is those of you who may go into the field. We hope that, when learning about personality psychology's strengths and weaknesses, some of you will have the same thought about the field that moved us, the authors, to go into it: that it is important yet imperfect and that maybe one can make it better.

SCIENTIFIC OBSERVATION: THE DATABASE

Ideally, the personality theories would have been built on a database of scientific observations that is large and diverse, that employed measures that were objective and reliable, and that included research methods that shed light on specific cognitive, affective, and biological systems of personality. How close was the field as a whole to this ideal?

One cannot help but be impressed by the diversity of research methods that scientists have brought to bear on questions about personality. Consider the range of research techniques we reviewed in previous chapters. Personality psychologists employed diverse research strategies: correlational studies of individual differences; laboratory experiments that manipulate specific social, cognitive, and emotional processes; and case studies that provide detailed portraits of the individual. They also employed diverse scientific measures: psychometrically sophisticated questionnaires; reaction-time measures that drew from research in cognitive psychology; molecular genetic and brain imaging methods that capitalized on advances in the biological sciences; studies of culture that drew on ideas and methods developed in allied social sciences, such as anthropology. It is true that individual theorists commonly relied on only a subset of the available research techniques; most of the individual theories, then, rested on databases that were limited in some significant way. But the field as a whole can be applauded for the diversity and objectivity of its large and ever-growing database.

How could the field have done better? Perhaps the largest disappointment is the relative absence of idiographic research methods in the mainstream research field. Drawing on ideas developed by European scholars since the late 19th century, Allport (1937) encouraged personality psychologists to complement their studies of individual differences with research methods that illuminated the organization of psychological qualities within the individual (Hurlburt & Knapp, 2006). That was a long time ago. It is reasonable at this point to look back and see how well the field has done in heeding Allport's call. When it comes to formulating theory, it has done well. The theories of personality we reviewed primarily were systematic theoretical accounts of the organization of personality structures and dynamics within the individual. (The significant exceptions were behaviorism, which tried to explain behavior without speculating about inner mental structures and dynamics, and the lexical Big Five trait model, which viewed itself as a taxonomy of individual differences in the population, not as a model of within-the-head psychological structures.) But when it comes to executing research, they have done less well. In practice, the field's research sometimes fails to match its theorizing. Kelly, Rogers, Bandura, and Mischel explained, theoretically, how multiple within-person psychological structures develop and function as the individual interacts with the social world. One might have expected to see, then, research programs in which these multiple psychological systems were assessed, over time and in context and in detail, for each of a series of individuals whom one learned about in depth. But you did not see much of that. Instead, researchers primarily invoked simpler research strategies. They selected one or two variables from a given theory and conducted traditional correlational or experimental studies. This work was highly informative. Yet one can be disappointed at the relative absence of objective, reliable methods for studying individual persons in depth, across time, in context. One can, however, be hopeful that the growth of novel technologies for assessing psychological experience within the everyday contexts of people's lives (Bolger et al., 2003) will rectify this shortcoming in the years ahead.

THEORY: SYSTEMATIC?

Did personality psychologists provide systematic, coherent accounts of the individual? If one looks at the field, does one find that investigators were able to move from a set of disconnected insights about human nature to an integrated theory of the person?

It is harder to answer this question about the field. This is because the answer depends on "when" you look, that is, the historical era one assesses. Professional psychologists generally say that personality psychology experienced a period of "grand theories" in the middle of the 20th century. This phrase seems correct in two respects. The theories of the time were grand in scope; theorists attempted to address all aspects of psychological functioning and development. They also were "grand" in another meaning of the word: "wonderful," "excellent." Freud, Jung, Eysenck, Cattell, and Kelly, for example, provided sweeping accounts of personality that were highly systematic, and in this way were outstanding examples of theory construction.

Later in the 20th century, personality theory experienced a shift in thinking that reflected broader intellectual trends. Psychologists became skeptical of grand theories. They saw them as "armchair" speculations rather than as contributions to a science of persons. This shift in thinking had some major advantages. Psychologists began to ground their theories in particularly large and systematic bodies of data. Their conclusions thus were more convincing. The data-driven evolution of the Big Five trait model and of social-cognitive theory throughout the last quarter of the 20th century testifies to the virtues of this scientifically cautious strategy of theory construction. But caution has its costs. The field's more contemporary theories are less systematic. It is easy to pose questions that the theories do not answer. Why is the number of "big" factors five and not, for example, eight? Are there functional relations between one's level of extraversion and one's level of neuroticism (e.g., are some people less extraverted because they are neurotically anxious)? Or, turning to social-cognitive theory: Would the chronic adoption of "ought" versus "ideal" standards of self-evaluation cause a person to develop a high versus low sense of self-efficacy? Is the child who is better able to delay gratification more likely to develop learning or performance goals? Not only is it difficult to answer these questions empirically, but it is difficult even to derive *potential* answers that are grounded in well-specified trait or social-cognitive theory. This suggests that contemporary theories may be insufficiently systematic.

THEORY: TESTABLE?

Of all our five criteria for evaluating theories, the criterion of testability is the one on which personality psychology does the best. Early psychodynamic theorists may have formulated their ideas in a manner that was difficult to test. But virtually all subsequent personality theorists ensured that their theoretical statements possessed a clarity that enabled them to be tested unambiguously. Time and again in the chapters of this book, you read about research in which investigators were able to derive specific predictions from one of the theories and to put those predictions to the test.

Personality psychology's success reflects the overall standards of contemporary psychological science. Theories are not considered to be valuable unless they make predictions that can be tested unambiguously. Research reports are not accepted for publication in scientific journals unless they provide convincing tests of hypotheses. Personality psychology thus has been a data-driven field for decades. One might question whether the theories are sufficiently systematic and comprehensive. But one cannot doubt that they yield numerous testable predictions that can be, and have been, evaluated via objective evidence.

One indirect sign of the fact that personality theorists have been sensitive to the need for testable theories is the relatively small number of theories we presented in this text. Many other psychologists, not discussed in this text, have tried to develop comprehensive frameworks for studying persons during the past century. Our primary consideration when deciding whether to include a given theory involved the criterion of testability. We included those theories that are open to empirical test, have received significant support, and remain of importance to the contemporary field of psychological research.

THEORY: COMPREHENSIVE?

Taken individually, the theories we reviewed generally were less comprehensive than would be ideal. Freud and Skinner did extend their theories to an exceptionally broad range of phenomena. But they were nearly unique in this regard and most contemporary investigators would severely question the validity of many of their extensions. Among the more contemporary theorists we reviewed only Bandura (1986), who has applied his social-cognitive theory to an exceptional breadth of personal and social phenomena, could claim to have achieved a level of comprehensiveness similar to that of Freud and Skinner. Yet even his social cognitive theory does not directly confront some seemingly important aspects of the human experience, as we noted in evaluating the social-cognitive perspective.

However, if one's focus shifts from individual theories to the field as a whole, the range of topics addressed is impressively comprehensive. It is difficult to formulate questions about personality that were not at least addressed by the work presented here, even if all questions could not be answered convincingly. Our topics in this book included human development from infancy (e.g., the temperament research of Kagan, Chapter 9) to older adulthood (the analyses of Baltes and Carstensen, Chapter 14). It included determinants of personality ranging from the evolutionary past to the sociocultural present. Theory and research addressed unconscious cognitive structures and conscious phenomenological experience; impulsive emotions and rational self-control strategies; individual differences that are stable over time and patterns of social behavior that vary across context.

Some topics that did not receive much coverage are ones that, by general consensus among personality psychologists, fall outside of the field. For example, important questions about human behavior include questions of ethics: What is "right" and "wrong"? Are there universal ethical principles? How should individual rights be balanced against the rights of society? One might argue that personality psychology lacked comprehensiveness in that it did not address these important questions. But these are questions that research psychologists intentionally have left to the philosopher because they are not questions of fact that can be resolved by reference to scientific evidence.

One topic that, in retrospect, received less attention than it deserves in a comprehensive account of psychological functioning is the ecology of human action. By that, we mean the systematic study of social settings, including analysis of the types of psychological experiences and action that a given setting fosters and inhibits. We illustrate the importance of social ecology with a simple example. In the class meetings you have attended throughout your course in personality psychology, the person who did the most talking in class probably was not any one of the students. In all likelihood, it was your course instructor. But this may tell one nothing about the personality of the instructor (his or her traits, or construct systems, or unconscious conflicts, or self-efficacy beliefs). Instead it tells us about the social setting. A classroom is a setting with well-defined roles (instructor, student, teaching assistant), each of which has distinct social norms for action. In principle, personality psychologists could attend more carefully to the ecology of social settings when seeking to explain the personality functioning of the individual. In doing so, they would not have to start "from scratch." Psychologists in other branches of the field, such as community psychology, already have made headway in characterizing the opportunities and constraints on personal development that are available in social settings (Kelly, 2006). Some personality psychologists have already analyzed personality dynamics from a social ecological perspective (Little, 2000, 2006). A deeper understanding of the social contexts within which people develop and act may, in turn, enable deeper insight into the structures and dynamics of personality.

More generally, there is worry that, in their search for scientific laws of cognition and behavior that generalize across time and place, research psychologists may have lost touch with the textures of everyday experience. Some scholars express concern that the general principles put forth by most theories fail to touch base with the specific everyday details of life—details that explain much of everyday social experience and action. These include details such as the culturally-specific norms and obligations associated with one's relation to another person (family member, friend, boss, subordinate); implicit rules of action that characterize a particular social setting (a party, a funeral, an elevator); beliefs that are shared by members of a group (a business, a club, a religion) that possesses a particular history within its society; deep emotions that people share merely by looking each other in the eye. Scheibe (2000, p. 2), for example, calls for a "quotidian psychology," that is, a psychology of everyday acts, experiences, and social contexts. Rather than search for generalized laws of behavior, he analyzes specific actions and experiences of life: conversations that are "serious" rather than lighthearted and joking; the function of styles of dress, cosmetics, and costumes; motives involving financial greed; feelings of compassion and piety. When the personality theories treat these topics, they usually just subsume them under some general law or principle. But if the general principles fail to address the social rules, roles, norms, and constraints within which people act in a given point in time, one may end up with a psychology that "is not generally successful in offering convincing and satisfactory accounts of a wide range of events in our everyday lives" (Scheiebe, 2000, p. 2). Such a psychology would not be comprehensive.

APPLICATIONS

Our last criterion, translating basic theory into practical applications, is another one which personality theorists and researchers can rightly claim to have made significant progress. You have seen these applications throughout this text. They have ranged from one-on-one encounters with patients and clients (starting with Freud in Chapter 3) to programs for social change (Chapter 14). A substantial percentage of this overall field of study actually is

A sports psychologist at work. The enhancement of athletic performance is one of many domains in which psychologists put the principles of personality theory into practice.

an applied enterprise. Personality assessors work in organizational and educational settings. Students of personality and health work in medical centers. Rogerian principles are put into play in counseling centers. Social-cognitive principles of behavior change are put into practice by cognitive-behavioral therapists.

The range of applications of personality psychology does not stem merely from the "good will" of theorists and researchers. It reflects two additional factors. First, most of the primary personality theorists began as practitioners. They were trained as clinical psychologists or as physicians. Thus they really did not have to move "from theory to practice." They started with the "practice," which was in place prior to their development of the theory. If one moves from practice to theory, then one inevitably ends up not only with abstract theory, but practical applications. The second consideration involves the fact that research is expensive. It thus requires funding. Much of this funding comes from governmental institutions. Such institutions commonly are most interested in research that can be applied—directly and immediately—to the benefit of those citizens whose taxpayer dollars are being used to fund the research. There thus is more money available for applied research than for laboratory investigations of basic psychological processes. In the United States, for example, the National Institute of Mental Health recently reorganized its funding priorities to emphasize "translational" research, that is, research whose findings can be translated quickly from the lab to the alleviation of physical or psychological distress. The proliferation of applied studies thus reflects the practical constraints and opportunities faced by the personality psychologist, who is more able to obtain funding for applied investigations than for studies that primarily advance basic theory—even though the theoretical advance may, in the long run, have substantial applied benefits.

In applauding the magnitude of attention given to applied concerns, we do not mean to imply that the applications have always been fully successful or that they do not need improvement. Therapies commonly are less successful than one would hope—particularly when one considers the problem of relapse. Predictions based on personality testing commonly are less accurate than one would hope—particularly when one tries to predict real-world behaviors performed in social contexts. In developing applications, personality theorists and researchers deserve an "A for effort" even if one could not assign that grade every time one evaluated the success of their efforts.

ON STRUCTURES, PROCESSES, DEVELOPMENT, AND THERAPEUTIC CHANGE

Four substantive elements of the personality theories were discussed repeatedly in this book: their treatment of (1) personality structure, (2) personality processes, (3) personality development and growth, and (4) the alleviation of psychological distress via therapy. We return to these four topics now, as a way of reviewing the ground we have covered and comparing the theories to one another.

PERSONALITY STRUCTURE

The personality theories differed greatly in their approach to modeling personality structure. The primary difference is the one we highlighted throughout:

WHY SO MUCH WEST, SO LITTLE EAST?

Our book has reviewed ideas about persons that originated in the West, particularly in Europe and North America. All of the primary theorists were Europeans or North Americans of European ancestry. What about the rest of the world? This is a particularly important question since "the rest of the world," the peoples outside of Europe and North America, of course is the large majority of the world's population. Why was there so little impact of non-Western ideas in a textbook on personality theory and research?

The answer to this question is *not* that these ideas lack intellectual sophistication or that they are substantively irrelevant to the issues discussed in personality psychology. Scholars in non-Western traditions have provided sophisticated accounts of topics discussed in this text. Indeed, they often provided those accounts centuries before the topics were addressed in the Western tradition. Twentieth-century behaviorists, as you learned, grappled with the question of whether there can be free will in a deterministic world. Centuries earlier, Islamic scholars addressed precisely this same question. They asked how humans could be said to choose freely courses of action when, as the Koran explains, God is in command of the world (Harré, 2000). Contemporary researchers in the social-cognitive tradition examine how people's beliefs about themselves and appraisals of the world determine their own emotional experiences. Exactly this question was addressed, in great detail, in systematic treatises on psychology in the Buddhist tradition that were composed in the 18th century and whose logic is grounded in the works of the Buddha, who was born more than 2,500 years ago

The Islamic scholar Averroes (or Ibn Rushd) who, building on the works of Aristotle, wrote extensively on questions of the mind and human nature in the 12th century.

(Guenther & Kawamura, 1975). Why did we review so little of this work? Why, in other words, have the diverse and intellectually rich philosophical and religious traditions of non-Western cultures—as well as the Judeo-Christian religious tradition that has been dominant in the West—not been a significant part of personality science, and thus not a significant part of our text?

The answer to this question is found in the criteria we have used to evaluate the theories of personality throughout this text. The unique feature of the work of the personality theorists we have reviewed is not that they have grappled with questions of human nature and individual differences. Scholars throughout the world have done that for as long as the world's societies have been able to support scholars. The unique feature is that contemporary personality psychologists have tried to base their theories on observations that qualify as scientific and have tried to ensure that these ideas can be tested via the accumulation of further scientific evidence. The personality theorists generally confined themselves to claims that can be modified or rejected via scientific test. They avoided metaphysical claims that are completely beyond the bounds of science. Is there a god who is in command of the universe? Is there an afterlife? Are our minds reincarnated from one life to the next? Philosophical and religious systems—non-Western and Western—have raised these questions throughout the ages. They have based views of human nature on their answers. And this is precisely why these other traditions have not been covered in our text. Answers to questions about a creator and an afterlife must be posited on faith, not on scientific evidence. It is this "on faith" quality that places many of the world's great intellectual and religious traditions outside of the class of ideas that constitute the theories of personality. Nonetheless, as we reach the end of this text, we should recall that many of the issues addressed by the personality theorists also have received careful treatment in philosophical and religious thought throughout the centuries.

They employed qualitatively different units of analysis. The basic variables of the theories differed in type from one theory to the next. Psychodynamic theorists inferred the existence of conscious and unconscious mental systems that conflicted with one another. Trait theorists (especially the Big Five or five-factor theorists), by contrast, did not discuss mental conflict and, strictly speaking, did not even infer mental systems. Instead, the structural variables in their theories were dispositional tendencies, that is, overt tendencies to perform actions, and have emotional experiences, or one versus another sort. Behaviorists inferred neither trait structures nor psychodynamic structures. Instead, they suggested that persons possess different response strengths as a result of their history of classic and operant conditioning. The structural variables in the theories of Rogers, Kelly, Bandura, and Mischel were similar to one another in significant ways, while differing from the psychodynamic, trait, and behaviorist approaches. These latter theorists each emphasized conscious thinking processes, enduring beliefs about the self, and the social contexts in which these beliefs develop and function. When scanning the full range of theories, one finds enormous substantive differences in the structural variables employed.

In addition to these substantive differences, there is a more subtle difference. The theorists differed in the degree to which they abstracted away from their data when positing structural variables. Some theories were concrete. Their variables directly represented the data about personality that were observed by the theorist. Other theories were abstract. Theorists posited unseen psychological structures that, in some cases, were only indirectly related to the features of personality that were observed.

These differences in levels of abstraction reflect beliefs about how science should be conducted. In the early and middle parts of the 20th century, many psychological scientists embraced a view known as logical positivism (see, e.g., Suppe, 1977). This view argued that scientific theories should discuss only observable events. One should search for regularities in events that are observed, and confine one's theories to statements of laws that correspond to those regularities. Positivism most directly influenced the behaviorists, whose "theories" were little more than statements about observable relations between external stimuli and subsequent responses. Positivism appears also to have influenced the trait theories. Five-factor theory, for example, observes recurring individual differences, posits variables that correspond to those differences (the five-factor trait variables), and avoids speculation about any specific psychological or biological systems that underlie the factors. These theorists judge that "sticking to the data" is the best way to build a scientific theory.

By the end of the 1960s, the main tenets of logical positivism had been "repudiated" (Suppe, 1977, p. 618) by philosophers of science, who increasingly recognized that science often makes progress by being speculative. Scientists speculate about what the world may be like by creating conceptual models of unseen systems that underlie observed events (Giere, 1999; Harré, 2002, Morgan & Morrison, 1999). Darwin, for example, speculated about evolutionary processes of natural selection that he himself could not directly observe. Einstein created theoretical models of elements of the universe that were unseen by him. Positivism, in retrospect, was a well-intentioned mistake.

Some of the personality theorists clearly were not positivistic in their thinking. Freud freely speculated about unseen mental systems. Rogers and Kelly repudiated behaviorism and, in so doing, largely repudiated positivistic thinking. They moved far beyond directly observable data when positing a self system and a system of personal constructs. Social-cognitive theorists strike a kind of middle ground. They generally have tried to tie their theorizing closely to observed data. Bandura (1977), for example, did not merely speculate about dynamic changes in self-efficacy perceptions that occurred in therapy; he provided self-report measures of self-efficacy beliefs and observed changes in these measures. Nonetheless, with the advantage of working in a post-positivistic era, social-cognitive theorists are able to speculate productively about personality structures underlying observed behavior. Mischel and Shoda's (1995) CAPS model is one example of this form of thinking. Other recent approaches similarly provide conceptual models of mental systems that underlie, and potentially account for, the data of personality that are observed (e.g., Cervone, 2004; Cloninger, 2004; Kuhl, 2000). The optimist can look forward to a future that might again be marked by "grand theories."

PROCESS

Our review of process aspects of personality theories—the parts of the theories that addressed the "why" of behavior—revealed much diversity. For Freud, the individual's efforts are directed toward expressing the sexual and aggressive instincts and, thereby, toward the reduction of the tension associated with these instincts. For Rogers, the individual is more forward looking, seeking growth and self-actualization even at the cost of increased tension. Rogers also places emphasis on a third motivational force: consistency. The particular kind of consistency emphasized by Rogers is a congruence between self and experience. For Kelly, who also emphasizes consistency, the relevant variables are different. According to Kelly, it is important that the individual's constructs be consistent with one another, so that the predictions from one do not cancel out the predictions from another. It is also important that predictions be consistent with experiences, in other words, that events confirm and validate the construct system. For Skinner, processes of personality involved reinforcements. He found no use for concepts of drive or tension. Social-cognitive theory similarly did not invoke drive variables, but instead saw dynamic cognitive processes, particularly involving goals and the self, as being central to human motivation.

Notice that these motivational models conflict with one another only if we assume that all behavior must follow the same motivational principles. In relation to structure, we need not assume that an individual only has drives, that one only has a concept of the self, or that one only has personal constructs. In the same way, we need not assume that an individual is always reducing tension, or always striving toward actualization, or always seeking consistency. It may be that all three models of motivation are relevant to human behavior. An individual may at some points be functioning to reduce tension, at other times to actualize his or her self, and at yet other times to achieve cognitive consistency. Another possibility is that, at one time, two kinds of motivation are operating, but they are in conflict with one another. For example, an individual may seek to relieve aggressive urges by hitting someone, but he or she may also like the person involved and view this behavior as out of character. A third possibility is that two kinds of motivation may combine to support one another. Thus, to make love to someone can represent the reduction of tension from sexual urges, an actualizing expression of the self, and an act consistent with the self-concept and with predictions from one's construct system. If room is left for more than one process model, it becomes the task of psychologists to define the conditions under which each type of motivation will occur and the ways in which the different types of motivation can combine to determine behavior

Why was there so much diversity in the theories' treatment of personality processes? Again a historical perspective is illuminating. Different theories were developed in different historical eras that, in turn, featured different perspectives on mind and behavior. The individual theorists inevitably were affected by the surrounding ideas of their times. Freud began his career in an era that featured deterministic, energy-based models of the physical universe. He thus developed an energy-based model of personality processes. Rogers's intellectual era was influenced by existential philosophers. He thus focused on people's experience when contemplating their own existence. Had Freud and Rogers "switched" historical eras, they would have developed different theories of motivation. Social-cognitive theory was developed subsequent to the growth of information-processing models of the mind. These models led social-cognitivists to focus on cognition—expectations, goals, cognitive skills—as basic elements in a theory of personality processes.

GROWTH AND DEVELOPMENT

As a general rule, the theories we covered commonly devoted less attention to personality growth and development than would have been ideal. There were happy exceptions. Trait theorists have done important work on the influences of heredity and environment, and on age trends in personality development. Psychoanalytic theorists attended carefully to questions of personality development at the level of theory, but, with the exception of attachment theorists, engaged in relatively little direct observation of the developing child. It is disappointing that Rogers and Kelly did not have more to say about specific processes of development. The behaviorists devoted little attention to biological factors in development; in retrospect, their work contributed little to an understanding of the development of persons. Progress has been made by social-cognitive theorists such as Bandura, who has long explored the role of modeling in personality development, and Mischel, who has explored longitudinal consistency in delay of gratification. Nonetheless, the personality theories did not capitalize on, or contribute to, research in developmental psychology to quite the degree that one might have hoped.

To be clear, the research domain of personality development is a vibrant area of study (e.g., Bergman, Magnusson, & El-Khouri, 2003; Pulkkinen & Caspi, 2002). The concern is that the classic personality theories have not incorporated a developmental perspective as fully as would be optimal.

In considering the theorists covered in this text, differences concerning two questions about development become apparent. The first concerns the utility of the concept of stages of development, and the second concerns the importance of early experiences for later personality development. Psychoanalytic theory attaches great importance to the early years and to the concept of stages of development. When discussing the early years, they emphasize the psychological impact of experiences within the family. By contrast, trait theorists do not posit developmental stages, and emphasize the influence of heredity rather than the family environment. The psychoanalytic emphasis can be contrasted as well with the social-cognitive criticism of the concept of stages of development and of suggestions that personality is relatively fixed by developments during the early years. Social-cognitive theorists emphasize, instead, the potential for different parts of personality to develop in different ways and much greater potential for change as a result of later experience.

PSYCHOPATHOLOGY

The forces producing psychopathology are interpreted differently by the theorists. However, the concept of conflict is essential to a number of them. This is most clearly the case in psychoanalytic theory. According to Freud, psychopathology occurs when the instinctive urges of the id come into conflict with the functioning of the ego. Although Rogers does not emphasize the importance of conflict, one can interpret the problem of incongruence in terms of a conflict between experience and the self-concept. Learning theory offers a number of explanations for psychopathology, and at least one of these explanations emphasizes the importance of approach avoidance conflicts. And although cognitive theorists do not emphasize the importance of conflict, one can think of the implications of goal conflicts and conflicting beliefs or expectancies. In addition, as cognitive theorists consider motivational questions, they come to recognize the potential for conflict between the motives for self-verification and self-enhancement.

Many complex questions concerning psychopathology remain unanswered. For example, we know that cultures vary in the incidence of various forms of psychopathology. Depression is rare in Africa but is common in the United States. Why? Conversion symptoms, such as hysterical paralysis of the arm or leg, were quite common in Freud's time but are observed much less frequently today. Why? Are there important differences in the problems that people in different cultures face? Or do they face the same problems but cope with them differently? Or is it just that some problems are more likely to be reported than others and that this pattern varies with the culture? If people today are more concerned with problems of identity than with problems of guilt, if they are more concerned with the problem of finding meaning than of relieving sexual urges, what are the implications for psychoanalysis and the other theories of personality?

Psychopathology is a major concern for clinical theories of personality. In Kelly's terms, this is a major focus of convenience for these theories. However, we have seen that interpretations of the nature of psychopathology vary considerably among them. And although other theories of personality are derived from observations outside the therapeutic setting, they have nonetheless recognized the importance of explaining psychopathology. The issue here is not whether personality theory should offer some understanding of psychopathology, but rather how central this topic is for the theory and the variables that are emphasized. It is fascinating to observe how each theory of personality, with its own set of structural units and process concepts, can come up with such varying interpretations of the same phenomena.

There were, of course, major differences in the theories concerning the potential for deep psychological change. At one extreme, psychoanalytic theory suggested that fundamental personality change is quite difficult and some versions of trait theory contended that traits are relatively unchanged by environmental experience. However, as we have seen, research findings provide new evidence of change. Recognizing this, various theorists now pursue the exciting challenge of explaining the how's and why's of personality change across the life course. In considering the question of how people change, we again recognize the extent to which theories of personality emphasize different processes of change, different conditions for change, and change in different aspects of personality functioning. Some of these differences may well represent competing and conflicting points of view, and others merely various terms for similar processes. Finally, some differences may result from attending to different aspects of the person. Sorting these out is a task for both students and professionals in the field.

As a final review, some of the major concepts deriving from each theory are given in Table 15.1.

Table 15.1   Summary of Major Theoretical Concepts

Theorist, Theory, or Approach	Structure	Process	Growth and Development	Pathology	Change
Freud	Id, ego, superego; unconscious, preconscious, conscious	Sexual and aggressive instincts; anxiety and the mechanisms of defense	Erogenous zones; oral, anal, phallic stages of development; Oedipus complex	Infantile sexuality; fixation and regression; conflict; symptoms	Transference; conflict resolution; "Where id was, ego shall be"
Rogers	Self; ideal self	Self-actualization; congruence of self and experience; incongruence and defensive distortion and denial	Congruence and self-actualization versus incongruence and defensiveness	Defensive maintenance of self; incongruence	Therapeutic atmosphere: congruence, unconditional positive regard, empathic understanding
Trait Approaches	Traits	Dynamic traits; motives associated with traits	Contributions of heredity and environment to traits	Extreme scores on trait dimensions (e.g., neuroticism)	(No formal model)
Learning Approaches	Response	Classical conditioning; instrumental conditioning; operant conditioning	Schedules of reinforcement and successive approximations	Maladaptive learned response patterns	Extinction; discrimination learning; counterconditioning; positive reinforcement; systematic desensitization; behavior modification
Kelly	Constructs	Processes channelized by anticipation of events	Increased complexity and definition to construct system	Disordered functioning of construct system	Psychological reconstruction of life; invitational mood; fixed-role therapy
Social Cognitive Theory	Beliefs; standards; goals; competencies	Observational learning; vicarious conditioning; self-evaluative and self-regulatory processes	Social learning through observation and direct experience; development of self-efficacy judgments and standards for self-regulation	Learned response patterns; excessive self-standards; problems in self-efficacy	Modeling; guided participation; increased self-efficacy; cognitive therapy

THE CASE OF JIM

The case of Jim gave us an opportunity to compare clinical assessments based on different theories of personality. What emerged from these comparisons?

On the one hand, some psychological themes were evident across assessment methods. When Jim was in his college years, all of the tests show evidence of tension, insecurity, and anxiety. Different forms of assessment indicated difficulties in relating to women, plus more general interpersonal difficulties involving the experience and expression of warmth. Finally, the tests consistently depicted Jim as rigid, inhibited, compulsive, and as having difficulty in being creative.

In other respects the pictures that emerged from different approaches differed. They reveal qualitatively different aspects of Jim's personality, rather than providing information that conflicted. Vampire and "Count Dracula sucking blood" images on the Rorschach can be interpreted as evidence of sadism. This differed from Jim's self-reports of problems in interpersonal relationships. The projectives also highlighted some of his conflicts and defenses. The 16 P.F. indicated somatic complaints and mood swings. Interview data revealed his perception of himself as deep, sensitive, kind, and basically good.

Jim was given access to the results of his personality testing. What did he think of the tests and personality sketches? Jim felt that the projective data did a good job of pointing out his conflicts and defenses, but that they overemphasized psychological insecurities. He believed that phenomenological and personal construct data (semantic differential, Rep test) gave an accurate picture of his personality at the time he was tested. Jim felt that the trait approach also captured a part of him that was present at the time of testing. Jim felt that different assessment methods and approaches to therapy could be useful with different people.

There is much merit to Jim's conclusion. Different aspects of personality studied are revealed with greater or lesser ease with different assessment devices. Each theory and associated form of assessment appears to have its own special contribution to make, as well as its own potential for sources of error or bias. Thus, if we limit ourselves to one approach to research or assessment, we may restrict our observations to phenomena directly relevant to a specific theoretical position. Alternatively, we can appreciate the contributions that different theories, research procedures, and assessment devices can make to our understanding of human behavior. Like Jim, we can consider the possibility that each approach captures a glimpse of the person, highlighting different aspects of personality while picking up common themes.

A FINAL SUMMING UP: THEORIES AS TOOLKITS

Those of you with particularly good powers of memory will recall that, back in Chapter 1, we suggested a metaphor. It was that theories are toolkits. Each theory provides "tools" for doing jobs faced by the psychologist. The tools, we now have seen, are of three sorts: (1) theoretical concepts, (2) procedures for personality assessment, and (3) techniques for psychological change. They can be used on tasks that are both basic (understanding personality structure, processes, development, and individual differences) and applied (predicting outcomes of interest, alleviating personal and social problems).

Our goal in presenting the toolkit metaphor was to prompt you to ask questions that are more nuanced than "Which theory was right?" As you now have seen, each theory provided uniquely useful tools. Psychodynamic theorists provided conceptual tools for thinking about symbolism, dreams, and the unconscious that cannot be found in any of the other toolkits. Rogerian tools can be put to work on the basic-science task of understanding phenomenological experience and self-concept, plus the applied task of developing rapport with clients in therapy. If your job requires you to classify and measure individual differences, then you had better pull something out of the trait-theoretical tool box. Behaviorists furnished uniquely effective tools for bringing about behavioral change. Yet Kelly found their toolkit to be barren, lacking implements for understanding the complex thinking capacities of persons. Social-cognitivists employed some tools that were forged originally by Kelly. Yet they felt they needed to devise more in order to understand the development of skills and self-regulatory capacities, and to maximize the effectiveness of therapy.

To readers who now move on to fields of study and professions outside of psychology we express our hope that, when life presents jobs that require the tools of a psychologist, you will recall the diversity of devices that the theories of personality provide. To readers who continue in our field, we express our hope that you do so with creativity. We could always use some more tools.

REVIEW

1. The field of personality psychology as a whole can be evaluated by considering its success in meeting a series of goals that have been discussed throughout this text. As a way of reviewing the material of the book, this chapter evaluated the field's success in achieving the goals of developing (a) systematic, (b) testable, (c) comprehensive models of personality that were (d) based on sound scientific evidence and that (e) fostered useful applications.

2. The chapter also reviewed the material of the text by commenting, in retrospect, on how the different theories of personality treated four main topics: personality structure, personality process, growth and development, and psychopathology.

3. It is suggested that the theories be considered as conceptual "tools" that help psychologists to solve the problems they face, and that each of the theories we reviewed provides unique tools of unique value to basic and applied personality scientists.

GLOSSARY

ABA research design A Skinnerian variant of the experimental method consisting of exposing one subject to three experimental phases: (A) a baseline period, (B) introduction of reinforcers to change the frequency of specific behaviors, and (A) withdrawal of reinforcement and observation of whether the behaviors return to their earlier frequency (baseline period).

ABC assessment In behavioral assessment, an emphasis on the identification of antecedent (A) events and the consequences (C) of behavior, and (B) a functional analysis of behavior involving identification of the environmental conditions that regulate specific behaviors.

Ability, temperament, and dynamic traits In Cattell's trait theory, these categories of traits capture the major aspects of personality.

Acquisition The learning of new behaviors, viewed by Bandura as independent of reward and contrasted with performance—which is seen as dependent on reward.

Adoption studies An approach to establishing genetic behavior relationships through the comparison of biological siblings reared together with biological siblings reared apart through adoption. Generally combined with twin studies.

Anal personality Freud's concept of a personality type that expresses a fixation at the anal stage of development and related to the world in terms of the wish for control or power.

Anal stage Freud's concept for that period of life during which the major center of bodily excitation or tension is the anus.

Anxiety In psychoanalytic theory, a painful emotional experience that signals or alerts the ego to danger.

Attachment behavioral system (ABS) Bowlby's concept emphasizing the early formation of a bond between infant and caregiver, generally the mother.

Attributions Beliefs about the causes of events.

Authenticity The extent to which the person behaves in accord with his or her self as opposed to behaving in terms of roles that foster false self-presentations.

Behavioral assessment The emphasis in assessment on specific behaviors that are tied to defined situational characteristics (e.g., ABC approach).

Behavioral genetics The study of genetic contributions to behaviors of interest to psychologists, mainly through the comparison of degrees of similarity among individuals of varying degrees of biological-genetic similarity.

Behavioral signatures Individually distinctive profiles of situation-behavior relationships.

Big Five In trait factor theory, the five major trait categories including emotionality, activity, and sociability factors.

Bivariate method Cattell's description of the method of personality study that follows the classic experimental design of manipulating an independent variable and observing the effects on a dependent variable.

Cardinal trait Allport's concept for a disposition that is so pervasive and outstanding in a person's life that virtually every act is traceable to its influence.

Case studies An approach to research in which one studies an individual person in great detail. This strategy commonly is associated with clinical research, that is, research conducted by a therapist in the course of in-depth experiences with a client.

Catharsis The release and freeing of emotion through talking about one's problems.

Castration anxiety Freud's concept of the boy's fear, experienced during the phallic stage, that the father will cut off the son's penis because of their sexual rivalry for the mother.

Central trait Allport's concept for a disposition to behave in a particular way in a range of situations.

Classical conditioning A process, emphasized by Pavlov, in which a previously neutral stimulus becomes capable of eliciting a response because of its association with a stimulus that automatically produces the same or a similar response.

Client-centered therapy Rogers's term for his earlier approach to therapy in which the counselor's attitude is one of interest in the ways in which the client experiences the self and the world.

Clinical methods Cattell's description of the method of personality study in which there is an interest in complex patterns of behavior as they occur in life but variables are not assessed in a systematic way.

Cognitive-affective processing system (CAPS) A theoretical framework developed by Mischel and colleagues in which personality is understood as containing a large set of highly interconnected cognitive and emotional processes; the interconnections cause personality to function in an integrate, coherent way, or as a "system."

Cognitive complexity/simplicity An aspect of a person's cognitive functioning that is defined at one end by the use of many constructs with many relationships to one another (complexity) and at the other end by the use of few constructs with limited relationships to one another (simplicity).

Collective unconscious Carl Jung's term for inherited, universal unconscious features of mental life that reflect the evolutionary experiences of the human species.

Competencies A structural unit in social-cognitive theory reflecting the individual's ability to solve problems or perform tasks necessary to achieve goals.

Conditioned emotional reaction Watson and Rayner's term for the development of an emotional reaction to a previously neutral stimulus, as in Little Albert's fear of rats.

Congruence Roger's concept expressing an absence of conflict between the perceived self and experience. Also one of three conditions suggested as essential for growth and therapeutic progress.

Context specificity The idea that a given personality variable may come into play in some life settings, or contexts, but not others, with the result that a person's behavior may vary systematically across contexts.

Conscious Those thoughts, experiences, and feelings of which we are aware.

Construct In Kelly's theory, a way of perceiving, construing, or interpreting events.

Constructive alternativism Kelly's view that there is no objective reality or absolute truth, but only alternative ways of construing events.

Contingencies of self-worth The positive and negative events on which one's feelings of self-esteem depend.

Contrast pole In Kelly's personal construct theory, the contrast pole of a construct is defined by the way in which a third element is perceived as different from two other elements that are used to form a similarity pole.

Core construct In Kelly's personal construct theory, a construct that is basic to the person's construct system and cannot be altered without serious consequences for the rest of the system.

Correlational coefficient A numerical index that summarizes the degree to which two variables are related linearly.

Correlational research An approach to research in which existing individual differences are measured and related to one another, rather than being manipulated as in experimental research.

Counterconditioning The learning (or conditioning) of a new response that is incompatible with an existing response to a stimulus.

Death instinct Freud's concept for drives or sources of energy directed towards death or a return to an inorganic state.

Defense mechanisms Freud's concept for those mental strategies used by the person to reduce anxiety. They function to exclude from awareness of some thought, wish, or feeling.

Defensive pessimism A coping strategy in which people use negative thinking as a way of coping with stress.

Delay of gratification The postponement of pleasure until the optimum or proper time, a concept particularly emphasized in social-cognitive theory in relation to self-regulation.

Demand characteristics Cues that are implicit (hidden) in the experimental setting and influence the subject's behavior.

Denial A defense mechanism, emphasized by both Freud and Rogers, in which threatening feelings are not allowed into awareness.

Determinism The belief that people's behavior is caused in a lawful scientific manner; determinism opposes a belief in "free will."

Direct external consequences In social-cognitive theory, the external events that follow behavior and influence future performance, contrasted with vicarious consequences and self-produced consequences.

Discrimination In conditioning, the differential response to stimuli depending on whether they have been associated with pleasure, pain, or neutral events.

Distortion According to Rogers, a defensive process in which experience is changed so as to be brought into awareness in a form that is consistent with the self.

Dysfunctional expectancies In social-cognitive theory, maladaptive expectations concerning the consequences of specific behaviors.

Dysfunctional self-evaluations In social-cognitive theory, maladaptive standards for self-reward that have important implications for psychopathology.

Effortful control A temperament quality involving the capacity to control one's actions by stopping one activity (a dominant response) in order to do another.

Ego   Freud's structural concept for the part of the personality that attempts to satisfy drives (instincts) in accordance with reality and the person's moral values.

Emotion-focused coping   Coping in which an individual stresses to improve his or her internal emotional state, for example, by emotional distancing or the seeking of social support.

Empathic understanding   Rogers's term for the ability to perceive experiences and feelings and their meanings from the standpoint of another person. One of three therapist conditions essential for therapeutic progress.

Energy system   Freud's view of personality as involving the interplay among various forces (e.g., drives, instincts) or sources of energy.

Erogenous zones   According to Freud, those parts of the body that are the sources of tension or excitation.

Evaluative standards   Criteria for evaluating the goodness or worth of a person or thing. In social-cognitive theory, people's standards for evaluating their own actions are seen as being involved in the regulation of behavior and the experience of emotions such as pride, shame, and feelings of satisfaction or dissatisfaction with oneself.

Evolved psychological mechanisms   In evolutionary psychology, psychological mechanisms that are the result of evolution by selection, that is, they exist and have endured because they have been adaptive to survival and reproductive success.

Existentialism   An approach to understanding people and conducting therapy, associated with the human potential movement, that emphasizes phenomenology and concerns inherent in existing as a person. Derived from a more general movement in philosophy.

Expectancies   In social-cognitive theory, what the individual anticipates or predicts will occur as the result of specific behaviors in specific situations (anticipated consequences).

Experimenter expectancy effects   Unintended experimenter effects involving behaviors that lead subjects to respond in accordance with the experimenter's hypothesis.

Experimental research   An approach to research in which the experimenter manipulates a variable of interest, usually by assigning different research participants, at random, to different experimental conditions.

Extinction   In conditioning, the progressive weakening of the association between a stimulus and a response; in classical conditioning because the conditioned stimulus is no longer followed by the unconditioned stimulus; and in operant conditioning because the response is no longer followed by reinforcement.

Extraversion   In Eysenck's theory, one end of the introversion-extraversion dimension of personality characterized by a disposition to be sociable, friendly, impulsive, and risk taking.

Facets   The more specific traits (or components) that make up each of the broad Big Five factors. For example, facets of extraversion are activity level, assertiveness, excitement seeking, positive emotions, gregariousness, and warmth.

Factor analysis   A statistical method for analyzing correlations among a set of personality tests or test items in order to determine those variables or test responses that increase or decrease together. Used in the development of personality tests and of some trait theories (e.g., Cattell, Eysenck).

Fear   In Kelly's personal construct theory, fear occurs when a new construct is about to enter the person's construct system.

Five-factor model   An emerging consensus among trait theorists suggesting five basic factors to human personality: neuroticism, extraversion, openness, agreeableness, and conscientiousness.

Fixation   Freud's concept expressing a developmental arrest or stoppage at some point in the person's psychosexual development.

Fixed (schedules of reinforcement)   Schedules of reinforcement in which the relation of behaviors to reinforcers remains constant.

Fixed-role therapy   Kelly's therapeutic technique that makes use of scripts or roles for people to try out, thereby encouraging people to behave in new ways and to perceive themselves in new ways.

fMRI (functional magnetic resonance imaging)   A brain imaging technique that identifies specific regions of the brain that are involved in the processing of a given stimulus or the performance of a given task; the technique relies on recordings of changes in blood flow in the brain.

Focus of convenience   In Kelly's personal construct theory, those events or phenomena that are best covered by a construct or by the construct system.

Free association   In psychoanalysis, the patient's reporting to the analyst of every thought that comes to mind.

Functional analysis   In behavioral approaches, particularly Skinnerian, the identification of the environmental stimuli that control behavior.

Functional autonomy   Allport's concept that a motive may become independent of its origins; in particular, motives in adults may become independent of their earlier basis in tension reduction.

Fundamental lexical hypothesis   The hypothesis that over time the most important individual differences in human interaction have been encoded as single terms in language.

Generalization   In conditioning, the association of a response with stimuli similar to the stimulus to which the response was originally conditioned or attached.

Generalized reinforcer   In Skinner's operant conditioning theory, a reinforcer that provides access to many other reinforcers (e.g., money).

General principles approach   Higgins's term for an analysis of personal and situational influences on thought and action in which a common set of causal principles is used to explain both cross-situational consistency in thought and action that results from personal influences and variability in thought and action that results from situational influences.

Genital stage   In psychoanalytic theory, the stage of development associated with the onset of puberty.

Goals   In social-cognitive theory, desired future events that motivate the person over extended periods of time and enable the person to go beyond momentary influences.

Guided mastery   A treatment approach emphasized in social-cognitive theory in which a person is assisted in performing modeled behaviors.

Heritability   The proportion of observed variance in scores in a specific population that can be attributed to genetic factors.

Hierarchy   A relation between entities in which one of them is an example of, or serves the purpose of, the other. In any given personality theory, different variables often are related hierarchically.

Hot versus cool attentional focus   The focusing of one thought on emotionally arousing (hot) versus less arousing (cool) aspects of a situation or stimulus.

Human potential movement   A group of psychologists, represented by Rogers and Maslow, who emphasize the actualization or fulfillment of individual potential, including an openness to experience.

Id   Freud's structural concept for the source of the instincts or all of the drive energy in people.

Ideal self   The self-concept the individual would most like to possess. A key concept in Rogers's theory.

Identification   The acquisition, as characteristics of the self, of personality characteristics perceived to be part of others (e.g., parents).

Idiographic (strategies)   Strategies of assessment and research in which the primary goal is to obtain a portrait of the potentially unique, idiosyncratic individual.

Implicit theories   Broad, generalized beliefs that we may not be able to state explicitly in words, yet that influence our thinking.

Incongruence   Rogers's concept of the existence of a discrepancy or conflict between the perceived self and experience.

Independent versus interdependent construals of self   Alternative implicit beliefs about self-concept in which the self is viewed either as possessing a set of psychological qualities that are distinct of other people (independent self) or is viewed in terms of roles in family, social, and community relationships (interdependent self).

Inhibited-uninhibited temperaments   Relative to the uninhibited child, the inhibited child reacts to unfamiliar persons or events with restraint, avoidance, and distress, takes a longer time to relax in new situations, and has more unusual fears and phobias. The uninhibited child seems to enjoy these very same situations that seem so stressful to the inhibited child. The uninhibited child responds with spontaneity in novel situations, laughing and smiling easily.

Internal working model   Bowlby's concept for the mental representation (images) of the self and others that develop during the early years of development, in particular in interaction with the primary caretaker.

Introversion   In Eysenck's theory, one end of the introversion-extraversion dimension of personality characterized by a disposition to be quiet, reserved, reflective, and risk avoiding.

Isolation   The defense mechanism in which emotion is isolated from the content of a painful impulse or memory.

Knowledge-and-appraisal personality architecture (KAPA)   Theoretical analysis of personality architecture that distinguishes two aspects of cognition in personality functioning: enduring knowledge and dynamic appraisals of the meaning of encounters for the self.

Latency stage   In psychoanalytic theory, the stage following the phallic stage in which there is a decrease in sexual urges and interest.

Learning goals   In Dweck's social-cognitive analysis of personality and motivation, a goal of trying to enhance one's knowledge and personal mastery of a task.

L-data   Life record data or information concerning the person that can be obtained from his or her life history or life record.

Libido The psychoanalytic term for the energy associated first with the sexual instincts and later with the life instincts.

Life instinct Freud's concept for drives or sources of energy (libido) directed towards the preservation of life and sexual gratification.

Maladaptive response In the Skinnerian view of psychopathology, the learning of a response that is maladaptive or not considered acceptable by people in the environment.

Mechanism An intellectual movement of the 19th century which argued that basic principles of natural science could explain not only the behavior of physical objects, but human thought and action.

Microanalytic research Bandura's suggested research strategy concerning the concept of self-efficacy in which specific rather than global self-efficacy judgments are recorded.

Multivariate method Cattell's description of the method of personality study, favored by him, in which there is study of interrelationships among many variables at once.

NEO-PI-R A personality questionnaire designed to measure people's standing on each of the factors of the five-factor model, as well as on facets of each factor.

Neuroticism In Eysenck's theory, a dimension of personality defined by stability and low anxiety at one end and by instability and high anxiety at the other end.

Neurotransmitters Chemical substances that transmit information from one neuron to another (e.g., dopamine and serotonin).

Nomothetic (strategies) Strategies of assessment and research in which the primary goal is to identify a common set of principles or laws that apply to all members of a population of persons.

Observational learning (modeling) Bandura's concept for the process through which people learn merely by observing the behavior of others, called models.

OCEAN The acronym for the five basic traits: openness, conscientiousness, extraversion, agreeableness, and neuroticism.

O-data Observer data or information provided by knowledgeable observers such as parents, friends, or teachers.

Oedipus complex Freud's concept expressing a boy's sexual attraction to the mother and fear of castration by the father, who is seen as a rival.

Operant conditioning Skinner's term for the process through which the characteristics of a response are determined by its consequences.

Operants In Skinner's theory, behaviors that appear (are emitted) without being specifically associated with any prior (eliciting) stimuli and are studied in relation to the reinforcing events that follow them.

Optimism A coping strategy that features relatively realistic expectations about one's capabilities.

Oral personality Freud's concept of a personality type that expresses a fixation at the oral stage of development and relates to the world in terms of the wish to be fed or to swallow.

Oral stage Freud's concept for that period of life during which the major center of bodily excitation or tension is the mouth.

OT-data In Cattell's theory, objective test data or information about personality obtained from observing behavior in miniature situations.

Parental investment theory The view that women have a greater parental investment in offspring than do men because women pass their genes onto fewer offspring.

Penis envy In psychoanalytic theory, the female's envy of the male's possession of a penis.

Perceived self-efficacy In social-cognitive theory, the perceived ability to cope with specific situations.

Perception without awareness Unconscious perception or perception of a stimulus without conscious awareness of such perception.

Perceptual defense The process by which an individual defends (unconsciously) against awareness of a threatening stimulus.

Performance The production of learned behaviors, viewed by Bandura as dependent on rewards, in contrast with the acquisition of new behaviors, which is seen as independent of reward.

Performance goals In Dweck's social-cognitive analysis of personality and motivation, a goal of trying to make a good impression on other people who may evaluate you.

Peripheral construct In Kelly's personal construct theory, a construct that is not basic to the construct system and can be altered without serious consequences for the rest of the system.

Personality Those characteristics of the person that account for consistent patterns of experience and action.

Personality architecture A term to describe the overall design and operating characteristics of those psychological systems that underlie personality functioning.

Person-situation controversy A controversy between psychologists who emphasize the importance of personal (internal) variables in determining behavior and those who emphasize the importance of situational (external) influences.

Phallic character   Freud's concept of a personality type that expresses a fixation at the phallic stage of development and strives for success in competition with others.

Phallic stage   Freud's concept for that period of life during which excitation or tension begins to be centered in the genitals and during which there is an attraction to the parent of the opposite sex.

Phenomenal field   The individual's way of perceiving and experiencing his or her world.

Phenomenology   The study of human experience; in personality psychology, an approach to personality theory that focuses on how the person perceives and experiences the self and the world.

Phrenology   The early 19th century attempt to locate areas of the brain responsible for various aspects of emotional and behavioral functioning. Developed by Gall, it was discredited as quackery and superstition.

Plasticity   The ability of parts of the neurobiological system to change, temporarily and for extended periods of time, within limits set by genes, to meet current adaptive demands and as a result of experience.

Pleasure principle   According to Freud, psychological functioning based on the pursuit of pleasure and the avoidance of pain.

Positive regard, need for   Rogers's concept expressing the need for warmth, liking, respect, and acceptance from others.

Preverbal construct   In Kelly's personal construct theory, a construct that is used but cannot be expressed in words.

Problem-focused coping   Attempts to cope by altering features of a stressful situation.

Process   In personality theory, the concept that refers to the motivational aspects of personality.

Projective test   A test that generally involves vague, ambiguous stimuli and allows subjects to reveal their personalities in terms of their distinctive responses (e.g., Rorschach Inkblot Test, Thematic Appreciation Test).

Proximate causes   Explanations for behavior associated with current biological processes in the organism.

Psychoticism   In Eysenck's theory, a dimension of personality defined by a tendency to be solitary and insensitive at one end and to accept social custom and care about others at the other end.

Punishment   An aversive stimulus that follows a response.

Q-data   In Cattell's theory, personality data obtained from questionnaires.

Q-sort   An assessment device in which the subjects sorts statements into categories following a normal distribution. Used by Rogers as a measure of statements regarding the self and the ideal self.

Range of convenience   In Kelly's personal construct theory, those events or phenomena that are covered by a construct or by the construct system.

Reaction formation   The defense mechanism in which the opposite of an unacceptable impulse is expressed.

Reality principle   According to Freud, psychological functioning based on reality in which pleasure is delayed until an optimum time.

Reciprocal determinism   The mutual, back-and-forth effects of variables on one another; in social-cognitive theory, a fundamental causal principle in which personal, environmental, and behavioral factors are viewed as causally influencing one another.

Regression   Freud's concept expressing a person's return to ways of relating to the world and the self that were part of an earlier stage of development.

Reinforcer   An event (stimulus) that follows a response and increases the probability of its occurrence.

Rejection sensitivity   A thinking style that is characterized by anxious expectations of rejection in interpersonal relationships.

Reliability   The extent to which observations are stable, dependable, and can be replicated.

Repression   The primary defense mechanism in which a thought, idea, or wish is dismissed from consciousness.

Response style   The tendency of some subjects to respond to test items in a consistent, patterned way that has to do with the form of the questions or answers rather than with their content.

Role   Behavior considered to be appropriate for a person's place or status in society. Emphasized by Cattell as one of a number of variables that limit the influence of personality variables on behavior relative to situational variables.

Role construct repertory test (Rep test)   Kelly's test to determine the constructs used by a person, the relationships among constructs, and how the constructs are applied to specific people.

Sample approach   Mischel's description of assessment approaches in which there is an interest in the behavior itself and its relation to environmental conditions, in contrast to sign approaches that infer personality from test behavior.

Schedule of reinforcement   In Skinner's operant conditioning theory, the rate and interval of reinforcement of responses (e.g., response ratio schedule and time intervals).

Schemas   Complex cognitive structures that guide information processing.

S-data   Self-report data or information provided by the subject.

Secondary disposition   Allport's concept for a disposition to behave in a particular way that is relevant to few situations.

Secondary process   In psychoanalytic theory, a form of thinking that is governed by reality and associated with the development of the ego.

Selective breeding   An approach to establishing genetic-behavior relationships through the breeding of successive generations with a particular characteristic.

Self-actualization   The fundamental tendency of the organism to actualize, maintain, enhance itself, and fulfill its potential. A concept emphasized by Rogers and other members of the human potential movement.

Self-concept   (or the "Self") The perceptions and meaning associated with the self, me, or I.

Self-consistency   Rogers's concept expressing an absence of conflict among perceptions of the self.

Self-discrepancies   In theoretical analyses of Higgins, incongruities between beliefs about one's current psychological attributes (the actual self) and desired attributes that represent valued standards or guides.

Self-enhancement   A motive to maintain or enhance positive views of the self.

Self-evaluative reactions   Feelings of dissatisfaction versus satisfaction (pride) in oneself that occur as people reflect on their actions.

Self-experience discrepancy   Rogers's emphasis on the potential for conflict between the concept of self and experience—the basis for psychopathology.

Self-guides   Tory Higgins's term for self-evaluative standards that serve to motivate and direct one's behavior.

Self-produced consequences   In social-cognitive theory, the consequences of behavior that are produced personally (internally) by the individual and that play a vital role in self-regulation and self-control.

Self-regulation   Psychological processes through which persons motivate their own behavior.

Self-schemas   Cognitive generalizations about the self that guide a person's information processing.

Self-verification   A motive to obtain information that is consistent with one's self-concept.

Shaping   In Skinner's operant conditioning theory, the process through which organisms learn complex behavior through a step-by-step process in which behavior increasingly approximates a full, target response.

Shared and nonshared environments   The comparison in behavior genetics research of the effects of siblings growing up in the same or different environments. Particular attention is given to whether siblings reared in the same family share the same family environment.

Sign approach   Mischel's description of assessment approaches that infer personality from test behavior, in contrast with sample approaches to assessment.

Similarity pole   In Kelly's personal construct theory, the similarity pole of a construct is defined by the way in which two elements are perceived to be similar.

Situational specificity   The emphasis on behavior as varying according to the situation, as opposed to the emphasis by trait theorists on consistency in behavior across situations.

Socioemotional selectivity theory   Theoretical analysis by Carstensen that examines that ways in which social motivations shift across the course of life.

Source trait   In Cattell's theory, behaviors that vary together to form an independent dimension of personality, which is discovered through the use of factor analysis.

State   Emotional and mood changes (e.g., anxiety, depression, fatigue) that Cattell suggested may influence the behavior of a person at a given time. The assessment of both traits and states is suggested to predict behavior.

Stress inoculation training   A procedure to reduce stress developed by Meichenbaum in which clients are taught to become aware of such negative, stress-inducing cognitions.

Structure   In personality theory, the concept that refers to the more enduring and stable aspects of personality.

Subception   A process emphasized by Rogers in which a stimulus is experienced without being brought into awareness.

Submerged construct   In Kelly's personal construct theory, a construct that once could be expressed in words, but now either one or both poles of the construct cannot be verbalized.

Subordinate construct   In Kelly's personal construct theory, a construct that is lower in the construct system and is thereby included in the context of another (superordinate) construct.

Successive approximation In Skinner's operant conditioning theory, the development of complex behaviors through the reinforcement of behaviors that increasingly resemble the final form of behavior to be produced.

Superfactor A higher-order or secondary factor representing a higher level of organization of traits than the initial factors derived from factor analysis.

Superordinate construct In Kelly's personal construct theory, a construct that is higher in the construct system and thereby includes other constructs within its context.

Surface trait In Cattell's theory, behaviors that appear to be linked to one another, but do not in fact increase and decrease together.

Sublimation The defense mechanism in which the original expression of the instinct is replaced by a higher cultural goal.

Subliminal psychodynamic activation The research procedure associated with psychoanalytic theory in which stimuli are presented below the perceptual threshold (subliminally) to stimulate unconscious wishes and fears.

Superego Freud's structural concept for the part of personality that expresses our ideals and moral values.

Symptom In psychopathology, the expression of psychological conflict or disordered psychological functioning. For Freud, a disguised expression of a repressed impulse.

System A collection of highly interconnected parts that function together; in the study of personality, distinct psychological mechanisms may function together as a system that produces the psychological phenomena of personality.

Systematic desensitization A technique in behavior therapy in which a competing response (relaxation) is conditioned to stimuli that previously aroused anxiety.

Target behaviors (target response) In behavioral assessment, the identification of specific behaviors to be observed and measured in relation to changes in environmental events.

T-data Test data or information obtained from experimental procedures or standardized tests.

Temperament Biologically based emotional and behavioral tendencies that are evident in early childhood.

Threat In Kelly's personal construct theory, threat occurs when the person is aware of an imminent, comprehensive change in his or her construct system.

Three-dimensional temperament model The three superfactors describing individual differences in temperament: Positive Emotionality (PE), Negative Emotionality (NE), and Disinhibition vs. Constraint (DvC).

Token economy Following Skinner's operant conditioning theory, an environment in which individuals are rewarded with tokens for desirable behaviors.

Trait An enduring psychological characteristic of an individual; or a type of psychological construct (a "trait construct") that refers to such characteristics.

Transference In psychoanalysis, the patient's development towards the analyst of attitudes and feelings rooted in past experiences with parental figures.

Twin studies An approach to establishing genetic-behavior relationships through the comparison of degree of similarity among identical twins, fraternal twins, and nontwin siblings. Generally combined with adoption studies.

Type A cluster of personality traits that may constitute a qualitatively distinct category of persons (i.e., a personality type).

Unconditional positive regard Rogers's term for the acceptance of a person in a total, unconditional way. One of three therapist conditions suggested as essential for growth and therapeutic progress.

Unconscious Those thoughts, experiences, and feelings of which we are unaware. According to Freud, this unawareness is the result of repression.

Undoing The defense mechanism in which one magically undoes an act or wish associated with anxiety.

Units of analysis A concept that refers to the basic variables of a theory; different personality theories invoke different types of variables, or different basic units of analysis, in conceptualizing personality structure.

Validity The extent to which observations reflect the phenomena or constructs of interest to us (also "construct validity").

Variable (schedules of reinforcement) Schedules of reinforcement in which the relation of behaviors to reinforcers changes unpredictably.

Vicarious conditioning Bandura's concept for the process through which emotional responses are learned through the observation of emotional responses in others.

Vicarious experiencing of consequences In social-cognitive theory, the observed consequences to the behavior of others that influence future performance.

REFERENCES

ADAMS-WEBBER, J.R. (1979). *Personal construct theory: Concepts and applications.* New York: Wiley.

ADAMS-WEBBER, J.R. (1982). Assimilation and contrast in personal judgment: The dichotomy corollary. In J.C. Mancuso & J.R. Adams-Webber (Eds.), *The construing person* (pp. 96–112). New York: Praeger.

ADAMS-WEBBER, J.R. (1998). Differentiation and sociality in terms of elicited and provided constructs. *American Psychological Society, 9,* 499–501.

ADLER, A. (1927). *Understanding human nature.* New York: Garden City Publishing.

AINSWORTH, A., BLEHER, M., WATERS, E., & WALL, S. (1978). *Patterns of attachment: A psychological study of the strange situation.* Hillsdale, NJ: Erlbaum.

AINSWORTH, M.D.S., & BOWLBY, J. (1991). An ethological approach to personality development. *American Psychologist, 46,* 333–341.

ALEXANDER, F., & FRENCH, T.M. (1946). *Psychoanalytic therapy.* New York: Ronald.

ALLEN, J.J., IACONO, W.G., DEPUE, R.A., & ARBISI, P. (1993). Regional electroencephalographic asymmetries in bipolar seasonal affective disorder before and after exposure to bright light. *Biological Psychiatry, 33,* 642–646.

ALLOY, L.B., ABRAMSON, L.Y., & FRANCIS, E.L. (1999). Do negative cognitive styles confer vulnerability to depression? *Current Directions in Psychological Science, 8,* 128–132.

ALLPORT, F.H., & ALLPORT, G.W. (1921). Personality traits: Their classification and measurement. *Journal of Abnormal and Social Psychology, 16,* 1–40.

ALLPORT, G.W. (1937). *Personality: A psychological interpretation.* New York: Holt, Rinehart & Winston.

ALLPORT, G.W. (1961). *Pattern and growth in personality.* New York: Holt, Rinehart, & Winston.

ALLPORT, G.W. (1967). Autobiography. In E.G. Boring & G. Lindzey (Eds.), *A history of psychology in autobiography* (pp. 1–26). New York: Appleton-Century-Crofts.

ALLPORT, G.W., & ODBERT, H.S. (1936). Trait-names: A psycholexical study. *Psychological Monographs, 47* (Whole No. 211).

American Psychological Association. Ethical Principles of Psychologists. (1981). *American Psychologist, 36,* 633–638.

ANDERSON, A.K., & PHELPS, E.A. (2002). Is the human amygdala critical for the subjective experience of emotion? Evidence of intact dispositional affect in patients with amygdala lesions. *Journal of Cognitive Neuroscience, 14,* 709–720.

ANDERSEN, B.L., & CYRANOWSKI, J.M. (1994). Women's sexual self-schema. *Journal of Personality and Social Psychology, 67,* 1079–1100.

ANDERSEN, S.M., & CHEN, S. (2002). The relational self: An interpersonal social-cognitive theory. *Psychological Review, 109,* 619–645.

ANDERSEN, S.M., & COLE, S.W. (1990). "Do I know you?": The role of significant others in general social perception. *Journal of Personality & Social Psychology, 59,* 384–399.

ANDERSEN, S.M., GLASSMAN, N.S., CHEN, S., & COLE, S.W. (1995). Transference in social perception: The role of chronic accessibility in significant-other representations. *Journal of Personality & Social Psychology, 69,* 41–57.

ANDERSEN, S.M., REZNIK, I., & MANZELLA, L.M. (1996). Eliciting facial affect, motivation, and expectancies in transference: Significant-other representations in social relations. *Journal of Personality & Social Psychology, 71,* 1108–1129.

ANDERSON, C.A., & BUSHMAN, B.J. (2001). Effects of violent video games on aggressive behavior, aggressive cognition, aggressive affect, physiological arousal, and prosocial behavior: A meta-analytic review of the scientific literature. *Psychological Science, 12,* 353–359.

ANDERSON, N., & ONES, D.S. (2003). The construct validity of three entry level personality inventories used in the UK: Cautionary findings from a multiple inventory investigation. *European Journal of Personality, 17,* S39–S66.

ANTONUCCIO, D.O., THOMAS, M., & DANTON, W.G. (1997). A cost-effectiveness analysis of cognitive behavior therapy and fluoxetine (Prozac) in the treatment of depression. *Behavior Therapy, 28,* 187–210.

APA MONITOR. (1982). The spreading case of fraud, 13, 1.

ARONSON, E., & METTEE, D.R. (1968). Dishonest behavior as a function of differential levels of induced self-esteem. *Journal of Personality and Social Psychology, 9,* 121–127.

ASENDORPF, J.B., BANSE, R., & MÜCKE, D. (2002). Double dissociation between implicit and explicit personality self-concept: The case of shy behavior. *Journal of Personality and Social Psychology, 83*, 380–393.

ASHTON, M.C., LEE, K., & PAUNONEN, S.V. (2002). What is the central feature of extraversion? Social attention versus reward sensitivity. *Journal of Personality and Social Psychology, 83*, 245–252.

ASPINWALL, L.G., & STAUDINGER, U.M. (Eds.) (2002). *A psychology of human strengths: Perspectives on an emerging field*. Washington, DC: American Psychological Association.

AYDUK, O., MISCHEL, W., & DOWNEY, G. (2002). Attentional mechanisms linking rejection to hostile reactivity: The role of "hot" versus "cool" focus. *Psychological Science, 13*, 443–448.

AYLLON, T., & AZRIN, H.H. (1965). The measurement and reinforcement of behavior of psychotics. *Journal of the Experimental Analysis of Behavior, 8*, 357–383.

BACCUS, J.R., BALDWIN, M.W., & PACKER, D.J. (2004). Increasing implicit self-esteem through classical conditioning. *Psychological Science, 15*, 498–502.

BAKERMANS-KRANENBURG, M.J., & VAN IZENDOORN, M.H. (1993). A psychometric study of the Adult Attachment Interview: Reliability and discriminant validity. *Developmental Psychology, 29*, 870–879.

BALAY, J., & SHEVRIN, H. (1988). The subliminal psychodynamic activation method. *American Psychologist, 43*, 161–174.

BALAY, J., & SHEVRIN, H. (1989). SPA is subliminal, but is it psychodynamically activating? *American Psychologist, 44*, 1423–1426.

BALDWIN, A.L. (1949). The effect of home environment on nursery school behavior. *Child Development, 20*, 49–61.

BALDWIN, M.W. (1999). Relational schemas: Research into social-cognitive aspects of interpersonal experience. In D. Cervone & Y. Shoda (Eds.), *The coherence of personality: Social-cognitive bases of consistency, variability, and organization* (pp. 127–154). New York: Guilford Press.

BALDWIN, M.W. (Ed.) (2005). *Interpersonal cognition*. New York: Guilford Press.

BALTES, P.B. (1997). On the incomplete architecture of human ontogeny: Selection, optimization, and, compensation as foundation of developmental theory. *American Psychologist, 52*, 366–380.

BALTES, P.B., & BALTES, M.M., (1990). *Successful aging. Perspective from the Behavioral Sciences*. Cambridge, UK: Cambridge University Press.

BALTES, P.B., & GRAF, P. (1996). Psychological aspects of aging: Facts and frontiers. In D. Magnusson (Ed.), *The lifespan development of individuals: Behavioral, neurobiological, and psychosocial perspectives* (pp. 427–460). Cambridge, UK: Cambridge University Press.

BALTES, P.B., & MAYER, K.U. (1999). *The Berlin aging study: Aging from 70 to 100*. Cambridge, UK: Cambridge University Press.

BALTES, P.B., & STAUDINGER, U.M. (2000). Wisdom: A methateuristic (pragmatic) to orchestrate mind and virtue toward excellence. *American Psychologist, 55*, 122–136.

BALTES, P.B., STAUDINGER, U.M., & LINDENBERGER, U. (1999). Lifespan psychology: Theory and application to intellectual functioning. *Annual Review of Psychology, 50*, 471–507.

BANAJI, M., & PRENTICE, D.A. (1994). The self in social contexts. *Annual Review of Psychology, 45*, 297–332.

BANDURA, A. (1965). Influence of models' reinforcement contingencies on the acquisition of imitative responses. *Journal of Personality and Social Psychology, 1*, 589–595.

BANDURA, A. (1969). *Principles of behavior modification*. New York: Holt, Rinehart and Winston.

BANDURA, A. (1977a). Self-efficacy: Toward a unifying theory of behavioral change. *Psychological Review, 84*, 191–215.

BANDURA, A. (1986). *Social foundations of thought and action: A social cognitive theory*. Englewood Cliffs, NJ: Prentice Hall.

BANDURA, A. (1989a). Social cognitive theory. *Annals of Child Development, 6*, 1–60.

BANDURA, A. (1989b). Self-regulation of motivation and action through internal standards and goal systems. In L.A. Pervin (Ed.), *Goal concepts in personality and social psychology* (pp. 19–85). Hillsdale, NJ: Erlbaum.

BANDURA, A. (1990). Self-regulation of motivation through anticipatory and self-reactive mechanisms. *Nebraska Symposium on Motivation, 38*, 69–164.

BANDURA, A. (1992). Self-efficacy mechanism in psychobiologic functioning. In R. Schwarzer (Ed.), *Self-efficacy: Thought control of action* (pp. 335–394). Washington, DC: Hemisphere.

BANDURA, A. (1997). *Self-efficacy: The exercise of control*. New York: Freeman.

BANDURA, A. (1999). Social cognitive theory of personality. In L.A. Pervin & O.P. John (Eds.), *Handbook of personality: Theory and research* (pp. 154–196). New York: Guilford.

BANDURA, A. (2001). Social cognitive theory: An agentic perspective. *Annual Review of Psychology, 52,* 1–26.

BANDURA, A. (2002). Environmental sustainability by sociocognitive deceleration of population growth. In P. Schmuch & W. Schultz (Eds.), *The psychology of sustainable development* (pp. 209–238). Dordrecht, The Netherlands: Kluwer.

BANDURA, A. (2006). Toward a psychology of human agency. *Perspectives on Psychological Science, 1,* 164–180.

BANDURA, A., & ADAMS, N.E. (1977). Analysis of self efficacy theory of behavioral change. *Cognitive Therapy and Research, 1,* 287–310.

BANDURA, A., ADAMS, N.E., & BEYER, J. (1977). Cognitive processes mediating behavioral change. *Journal of Personality and Social Psychology, 35,* 125–139.

BANDURA, A., & CERVONE, D. (1983). Self-evaluative and self-efficacy mechanisms governing the motivational effect of goal systems. *Journal of Personality and Social Psychology, 45,* 1017–1028.

BANDURA, A., GRUSEC, J.E., & MENLOVE, F.L. (1967). Some social determinants of self-monitoring reinforcement systems. *Journal of Personality and Social Psychology, 5,* 449–455.

BANDURA, A., & KUPERS, C.J. (1964). Transmission of patterns of self-reinforcement through modeling. *Journal of Abnormal and Social Psychology, 69,* 1–9.

BANDURA, A., & LOCKE, E.A., (2003). Negative self-efficacy and goal effects revisited. *Journal of Applied Psychology, 88,* 87–99.

BANDURA, A., & MISCHEL, W. (1965). Modification of self-imposed delay of reward through exposure to live and symbolic models. *Journal of Personality and Social Psychology, 2,* 698–705.

BANDURA, A., PASTORELLI, C., BARBARANELLI, C., & CAPRARA, G.V. (1999). Self-efficacy pathways to childhood depression. *Journal of Personality and Social Psychology, 76,* 258–269.

BANDURA, A., REESE, L., & ADAMS, N.E. (1982). Microanalysis of action and fear arousal as a function of differential levels of perceived self-efficacy. *Journal of Personality and Social Psychology, 43,* 5–21.

BANDURA, A., & ROSENTHAL, T.L. (1966). Vicarious classical conditioning as a function of arousal level. *Journal of Personality and Social Psychology, 3,* 54–62.

BANDURA, A., ROSS, D., & ROSS, S. (1963). Imitation of film-mediated aggressive models. *Journal of Abnormal and Social Psychology, 66,* 3–11.

BANDURA, A., & SCHUNK, D.H. (1981). Cultivating competence, self-efficacy, and intrinsic interest. *Journal of Personality and Social Psychology, 41,* 586–598.

BANDURA, A., & WALTERS, R.H. (1959). *Adolescent aggression.* New York: Ronald.

BANDURA, A., & WALTERS, R.H. (1963). *Social learning and personality development.* New York: Holt, Rinehart, & Winston.

BARGH, J.A. (1997). The automaticity of everyday life. In R.S. Wyer, Jr. (Ed.), *Advances in social cognition* (Vol. 10, pp. 1–61). Mahwah, NJ: Erlbaum.

BARGH, J.A. (2004). Being here now: Is consciousness necessary for human freedom? In J. Greenberg, S.L. Koole, & T. Pyszczynski (Eds.), *Handbook of experimental existential psychology* (pp. 385–397). New York: Guilford Press.

BARGH, J.A., & BARNDOLLAR, K. (1996). Automaticity in action: The unconscious as a repository of chronic goals and motives. In P.M. Gollwitzer & J.A. Bargh (Eds.), *The psychology of action* (pp. 457–481). New York: Guilford.

BARGH, J.A., & FERGUSON, M.J. (2000). Beyond behaviorism: On the automaticity of higher mental processes. *Psychological Bulletin, 126,* 925–945.

BARGH, J.A., & GOLLWITZER, P.M. (1994). Environmental control of goal-directed action: Automatic and strategic contingencies between situations and behavior. In W.D. Spaulding (Ed.), *Nebraska symposium on motivation: Vol. 41. Integrative views of motivation, cognition, and emotion* (pp. 71–124). Lincoln, NE: University of Nebraska Press.

BARGH, J.A., & TOTA, M.E. (1988). Context-dependent automatic processing in depression: Accessibility of negative constructs with regard to self but not others. *Journal of Personality and Social Psychology, 54,* 925–939.

BARLOW, D.H. (1991). Disorders of emotion. *Psychological Inquiry, 2,* 58–71.

BARONDES, S.H. (1998). *Mood genes: Hunting for the origins of mania and depression.* New York: W.H. Freeman.

BARRICK, M.R., & MOUNT, M.K. (1991). The Big Five personality dimensions and job performance: A meta-analysis. *Personnel Psychology, 44,* 1–26.

BARSALOU, L.W., SIMMONS, W.K., BARBEY, A.K., & WILSON, C.D. (2003). Grounding conceptual knowledge in modality-specific systems. *Trends in Cognitive Sciences, 7,* 84–91.

BARTHOLOMEW, K., & HOROWITZ, L.K. (1991). Attachment styles among young adults: A test of a four-category model. *Journal of Personality and Social Psychology, 61,* 226–244.

BASEN-ENGQUIST, K. (1994). Evaluation of theory based HIV prevention intervention in college students. *AIDS Education and Prevention, 6,* 412–424.

BAUMEISTER, R.F. (Ed.) (1991). *Escaping the self.* New York: Basic Books.

BAUMEISTER, R.F. (1999). On the interface between personality and social psychology. In L.A. Pervin & O.P. John (Eds.), *Handbook of personality: Theory and research* (pp. 367–377). New York: Guilford.

BAUMEISTER, R.F., CAMPBELL, J.D., KRUEGER, J.I., & VOHS, K.D. (2003). Does high self-esteem cause better performance, interpersonal success, happiness, or healthier lifestyles? *Psychological Science in the Public Interest, 4,* Whole Issue (Supplement to Psychological Science).

BAUMEISTER, R.F., & VOHS, K.D. (Eds.) (2004). *Handbook of self-regulation: Research, theory, and applications.* New York: Guilford Press.

BECHARA, A., DAMASIO, H., & DAMASIO, A.R. (2000). Emotion, decision making and the orbitofrontal cortex. *Cerebral Cortex, 10,* 295–307.

BECK, A.T. (1987). Cognitive models of depression. *Journal of Cognitive Psychotherapy, 1,* 2–27.

BECK, A.T. (1988). *Love is never enough.* New York: Harper & Row.

BECK, A.T. (1993). Cognitive therapy: Past, present, and future. *Journal of Consulting and Clinical Psychology, 61,* 194–198.

BECK, A.T., FREEMAN, A., & ASSOCIATES. (1990). *Cognitive therapy of personality disorders.* New York: Guilford Press.

BECK, A.T., WRIGHT, F.D., NEWMAN, C.D., & LIESE, B.S. (1993). *Cognitive therapy of drug abuse.* New York: Guilford Press.

BENET-MARTINEZ, V., & JOHN, O.P. (1998). Los Cinco Grandes across cultures and ethnic groups: Multitrait multimethod analyses of the Big Five in Spanish and English. *Journal of Personality and Social Psychology, 75,* 729–750.

BENJAMIN, J., LIN, L., PATTERSON, C., GREENBERG, B.D., MURPHY, D.L., & HAMER, D.H. (1996). Population and familial association between the D4 dopamine receptor gene and measures of novelty seeking. *Nature Genetics, 12,* 81–84.

BENSON, E. (2003). The many faces of perfectionism. *Monitor on Psychology, 34,* Retrieved Oct. 9, 2004 http://www.apa.org/monitor/nov03/manyfaces.html

BENSON, E.S. (2004). Behavioral genetics: Meet molecular biology. *Monitor on Psychology, 35,* 42–45.

BERGMAN, L.R., MAGNUSSON, D., & EL-KHOURI, B.M. (2003). *Studying individual development in an interindividual context: A process-oriented approach.* Mahwah, NJ: Erlbaum.

BERKOWITZ, L., & DONNERSTEIN, E. (1982). External validity is more than skin deep. *American Psychologist, 37,* 245–257.

BERNDT, T.J. (2002). Friendship quality and social development. *Current Directions in Psychological Science, 11,* 7–10.

BIERI, J. (1955). Cognitive complexity-simplicity and predictive behavior. *Journal of Abnormal and Social Psychology, 51,* 263–268.

BIERI, J. (1986). Beyond the grid principle. *Contemporary Psychology, 31,* 672–673.

BLOCK, J. (1971). *Lives through time.* Berkeley, CA: Bancroft Books.

BLOCK, J. (1993). Studying personality the long way. In D.C. Funder, R.D. Parke, C. Tomlinson-Keasey, & K. Widaman (Eds.), *Studying lives through time,* (pp. 9–41). Washington, DC: American Psychological Association.

BOGAERT, A.F. (2006). Biological versus nonbiological older brothers and men's sexual orientation. *Proceedings of the National Academy of Sciences, 103,* 10771–10774.

BOLDERO, J., & FRANCIS, J. (2002). Goals, standards, and the self: Reference values serving different functions. *Personality & Social Psychology Review, 6,* 232–241.

BOLGER, N., DAVIS, A., & RAFAELI, E. (2003). Diary methods: Capturing life as it is lived. *Annual Review of Psychology, 54,* 579–616.

BORKENAU, P., & OSTENDORF, F. (1998). The big five as states: How useful is the five-factor model to describe intraindividual variations over time? *Journal of Research in Personality, 32,* 202–221.

BORNSTEIN, R.F., & MASLING, J.M. (1998). *Empirical perspectives on the psychoanalytic unconscious.* Washington, DC: American Psychological Association.

BORSBOOM, D., MELLENBERGH, G.J., & VAN HEERDEN, J. (2003). The theoretical status of latent variables. *Psychological Review, 110,* 203–219.

BOUCHARD, T.J., JR., LYKKEN, D.T., MCGUE, M., SEGAL, N.L., & TELLEGEN, A. (1990). Sources of human psychological differences: The Minnesota study of twins reared apart. *Science, 250,* 223–228.

BOZARTH, J.D. (1992, October). Coterminous intermingling of doing and being in person-centered therapy. *The Person-Centered Journal: An International Journal Published by the Association for The Development of The Person-Centered Approach.* Retrieved October 9, 2004 http://www.adpca.org/Journal/vol1_1/indexpage.htm.

BRADLEY, R.H., & CORWYN, R.F. (2002). Socioeconomic status and child development. *Annual Review of Psychology, 53,* 371–399.

BRAMEL, D., & FRIEND, R. (1981). Hawthorne, the myth of the docile worker, and the class bias in psychology. *American Psychologist, 36,* 867–878.

BRÄNDTSTADTER, J., & WENTURA, D. (1995). Adjustment to shifting possibility frontiers in later life: Complementary adaptive modes. In R.A. Dixon & L.

BÄCKMAN (Eds.), *Compensating for psychological deficits and declines: Managing losses and promoting gains.* Mahwah, NJ: Erlbaum.

BRAUDEL, F. (1981). *The structures of everyday life: Civilization and capitalism, 15th–18th century* (Vol. 1). New York: Harper & Row.

BRESSLER, S.L. (2002). Understanding cognition through large-scale cortical networks. *Current Directions in Psychological Science, 11,* 58–61.

BRETHERTON, I. (1992). The origins of attachment theory: John Bowlby and Mary Ainsworth. *Developmental Psychology, 28,* 759–775.

BREWIN, C.R. (1996). Theoretical foundations of cognitive- behavior therapy for anxiety and depression. *Annual Review of Psychology, 47,* 33–57.

BROWN, J.D. (1998). *The self.* New York: McGraw-Hill.

BRUNER, J.S. (1956). You are your constructs. *Contemporary Psychology, 1,* 355–356.

BULLER, D.J. (2005). *Adapting minds: Evolutionary psychology and the persistent quest for human nature.* Cambridge, MA: MIT Press.

BUSHMAN, B.J., & ANDERSON, C.A. (2002). Violent video games and hostile expectations: A test of the general aggression model. *Personality & Social Psychology Bulletin, 28,* 1679–1686.

BUSS, A.H. (1989). Personality as traits. *American Psychologist, 44,* 1378–1388.

BUSS, A.H., & PLOMIN, R. (1975). *A temperament theory of personality development.* New York: Wiley Interscience.

BUSS, A.H., & PLOMIN, R. (1984). *Temperament: Early-developing personality traits.* Hillsdale, NJ: Erlbaum,

BUSS, D.M. (1989). Sex differences in human mate preferences : Evolutionary hypotheses tested in 37 cultures. *Behavioral and Brain Sciences, 12,* 1–14 .

BUSS, D.M. (1991). Evolutionary personality psychology. *Annual Review of Psychology, 42,* 459–492.

BUSS, D.M. (1995). Evolutionary psychology: A new paradigm for psychological science. *Psychological Inquiry, 6,* 1–30.

BUSS, D.M. (1999). Human nature and individual differences: The evolution of human personality. In L.A. Pervin & O.P. John (Eds.), *Handbook of personality: Theory and Research* (pp. 31–56). New York: Guilford.

BUSS, D.M. (2000). The evolution of happiness. *American Psychologist, 55,* 15–23.

BUSS, D.M. (Ed.) (2005). *The handbook of evolutionary psychology.* Hoboken, NJ: Wiley.

BUSS, D.M., & KENRICK, D.T. (1998). Evolutionary social psychology. In D.T. Gilbert, S.T. Fiske, & Lindzey, G. (EDS.), *The handbook of social psychology* (4th ed.). New York: McGraw- Hill.

BUSS, D.M., LARSEN, R., WESTEN, D., & SEMMELROTH, J. (1992). Sex differences in jealousy: Evolution, physiology and psychology. *Psychological Science, 3,* 251–255.

BUSSEY, K., & BANDURA, A. (1999). Social cognitive theory of gender development and differentiation. *Psychological Bulletin, 106,* 676–713.

CAMPBELL, J.B., & HAWLEY, C.W. (1982). Study habits and Eysenck's theory of extroversion-introversion. *Journal of Research in Personality, 16,* 139–146.

CAMPBELL, R.S., & PENNEBAKER, J.W. (2003). The secret life of pronouns. *Psychological Science, 14,* 60–65.

CAMPBELL, W.K. (1999). Narcissism and romantic attraction. *Journal of Personality and Social Psychology, 77,* 1254–1270.

CANTOR, N. (1990). From thought to behavior: "Having" and "doing" in the study of personality and cognition. *American Psychologist, 45,* 735–750.

CANTOR, N. & KIHLSTROM, J.F. (1987). *Personality and social intelligence.* Englewood Cliffs, NJ: Prentice Hall.

CANTOR, N., NOREM, J.K., NEIDENTHAL, P.M., LANGSTON, C.A., & BROWER, A.M. (1987). Life tasks, self-concept ideals, and cognitive strategies in a life transition. *Journal of Personality and Social Psychology, 53,* 1178–1191.

CAPORAEL, L.R. (2001). Evolutionary psychology: Toward a unifying theory and a hybrid science. *Annual Review of Psychology, 52,* 706–628.

CAPRARA, G.V., & CERVONE, D. (2000). *Personality: Determinants, dynamics, and potentials.* New York: Cambridge University Press.

CAPRARA, G.V., & PERUGINI, M. (1994). Personality described by adjective: The generalizability of the Big Five to the Italian lexical context. *European Journal of Personality, 8,* 351–369.

CARNELLEY, K.B., PIETROMONACO, P.R., & JAFFE, K. (1994). Depression, working models of others, and relationships functioning. *Journal of Personality and Social Psychology, 66,* 127–140.

CARSTENSEN, L.L. (1995). Evidence for a life-span theory of socioemotional selectivity. *Current Directions in Psychological Science, 4,* 151–156.

CARSTENSEN, L.L. (1998). A life-span approach to social motivation. In J. Heckhausen & C. Dweck (Eds.), *Motivation and self-regulation across the life span* (pp. 341–364). New York: Cambridge University Press.

CARSTENSEN, L.L., & CHARLES, S.T. (2003). Human aging: Why is even good news taken as bad? In L.G. Aspinwall & U.M. Staudinger (Eds.), *A psychology of human strengths: Perspectives on an emerging field* (pp. 75–86). Washington, DC: American Psychological Association.

CARSTENSEN, L.L., & FREDRICKSON, B.L. (1998). Influence of HIV status and age on cognitive representations of others. *Health Psychology 17,* 494–503.

CARSTENSEN, L.L., ISAACOWITZ, D.M., & CHARLES, S.T. (1999). Taking time seriously: A theory of socioemotional selectivity. *American Psychologist, 54,* 165–181.

CARTWRIGHT, D.S. (1956). Self-consistency as a factor affecting immediate recall. *Journal of Abnormal and Social Psychology, 52,* 212–218.

CARVER, C.S., & BAIRD, E. (1998). The American dream revisited: Is it what or why you want it that matters? *Psychological Science, 9,* 289–292.

CARVER, C.S., & SCHEIER, M.F. (1998). *On the self-regulation of behavior.* New York: Cambridge University Press.

CASPI, A. (2000). The child is father of the man: Personality correlates from childhood to adulthood. *Journal of Personality and Social Psychology, 78,* 158–172.

CASPI, A. (2002). Social selection, social causation, and developmental pathways: Empirical strategies for better understanding how individuals and environments are linked across the life course. In L. Pulkkinen and A. Caspi (Eds.), *Paths to successful development; Personality in the life course* (pp. 281–301). Cambridge, UK: Cambridge University Press.

CASPI, A., & BEM, D.J. (1990). Personality continuity and change across the life course. In L.A. Pervin (Ed.), *Handbook of personality: Theory and research* (pp. 549–575). New York: Guilford Press.

CASPI, A., BEM, D.J., & ELDER, G.H. (1989). Continuities and consequences of interactional styles across the life course. *Journal of Personality, 57,* 375–406.

CASPI, A., & ROBERTS, B. (1999). Personality continuity and change across the life course. In L.A. Pervin & O.P. John (Eds.), *Handbook of personality: Theory and research* (pp. 300–326). New York: Guilford.

CASPI, A., SUGDEN, K., MOFFITT, T.E., TAYLOR, A., CRAIG, I.W., HARRINGTON, H., et al. (2003). Influence of life stress on depression: Moderation by a polymorphism in the 5-HTT gene. *Science, 301,* 386–389.

CASSIDY, J., & SHAVER, P.R. (Eds.) (1999). *Handbook of attachment theory and research.* New York: Guilford.

CATTELL, R.B. (1965). *The scientific analysis of personality.* Baltimore: Penguin.

CATTELL, R.B. (1979). *Personality and learning theory.* New York: Springer.

CAVALLI-SFORZA, L.L., & CAVALLI-SFORZA, F. (1995). *The great human diasporas: The history of diversity and evolution.* Reading, MA: Addison-Wesley.

CERVONE, D. (1991). The two disciplines of personality psychology. *Psychological Science, 6,* 371–377.

CERVONE, D. (1997). Social-cognitive mechanisms and personality coherence: Self-knowledge, situational beliefs, and cross-situational coherence in perceived self-efficacy. *Psychological Science, 8,* 43–50.

CERVONE, D. (2000). Evolutionary psychology and explanation in personality psychology: How do we know which module to invoke? [Special issue on Evolutionary Psychology (J. Heckhausen & P. Boyer, Eds.)], *American Behavioral Scientist, 6,* 1001–1014.

CERVONE, D. (2004). The architecture of personality. *Psychological Review,* 111.

CERVONE, D. (2005). Personality architecture: Within-person structures and processes. *Annual Review of Psychology,* 56, 423–452.

CERVONE, D., CALDWELL, T.L., & OROM, H. (in press). Beyond person and situation effects: Intraindividual personality architecture and its implications. In A. Kruglanski & J. Forgas (Series Eds.) & F. Rhodewalt (Volume Ed.), *Frontiers of social psychology: Personality and Social behavior.* Psychology Press.

CERVONE, D., & CAPRARA, G.V. (2001). Personality assessment. In N.J. Smelser & P.B. Baltes (Eds.), *International encyclopedia of the social and behavioral sciences* (pp. 11281–11287). Oxford, UK: Elsevier.

CERVONE, D., KOPP, D.A., SCHAUMANN, L., & SCOTT, W.D. (1994). Mood, self-efficacy, and performance standards: Lower moods induce higher standards for performance. *Journal of Personality and Social Psychology, 67,* 499–512.

CERVONE, D., & MISCHEL, W. (2002). Personality science. In D. Cervone & W. Mischel (Eds.), *Advances in personality science* (pp. 1–26). New York: Guilford.

CERVONE, D., OROM, H., ARTISTICO, D., SHADEL, W.G., & KASSEL, J. (in press). Using a knowledge-and-appraisal model of personality architecture to understand consistency and variability in smokers' self-efficacy appraisals in high-risk situations. *Psychology of Addictive Behaviors.*

CERVONE, D., & PEAKE, P.K. (1986). Anchoring, efficacy, and action: The influence of judgmental heuristics on self-efficacy judgments and behavior. *Journal of Personality and Social Psychology, 50,* 492–501.

CERVONE, D., & SCOTT, W.D. (1995). Self-efficacy theory of behavioral change: Foundations, conceptual issues, and therapeutic implications. In W. O'Donohue & L. Krasner (Eds.), *Theories in behavior therapy.* Washington, DC: American Psychological Association.

CERVONE, D., & SHADEL, W.G. (2003). Idiographic methods. In R. Ferdandez-Ballasteros (Ed.), *Encyclopedia of psychological assessment* (pp. 456–461). London: Sage.

CERVONE, D., SHADEL, W.G., & JENCIUS, S. (2001). Social-cognitive theory of personality assessment. *Personality and Social Psychology Review, 5,* 33–51.

CERVONE, D., SHADEL, W.G., SMITH, R.E., & FIORI, M. (2006). Self-regulation: Reminders and suggestions from personality science. *Applied Psychology: An International Review, 55,* 333–385.

CERVONE, D., & WILLIAMS, S.L. (1992). Social cognitive theory and personality. In G. Caprara & G.L. Van Heck (Eds.), *Modern personality psychology* (pp. 200–252). New York: Harvester Wheatsheaf.

CHAPLIN, W.F., JOHN, O.P. & GOLDBERG, L.R. (1988). Conceptions of states and traits: Dimensional attributes with ideals as prototypes. *Journal of Personality and Social Psychology, 54,* 541–557.

CHEN, S., BOUCHER, H.C., & PARKER-TAPIAS, M. (2006). The relational self revealed: integrative conceptualization and implications for interpersonal life. *Psychological Bulletin, 132,* 151–179.

CHEUNG, F.M., LEUNG, K., FAN, R.M., SONG, W.Z., ZHANG, J.X., & ZHANG, J.P. (1996). Development of the Chinese Personality Assessment Inventory. *Journal of Cross-Cultural Psychology, 27,* 181–199.

CHODORKOFF, B. (1954). Self perception, perceptual defense, and adjustment. *Journal of Abnormal and Social Psychology, 49,* 508–512.

CHODRON, T. (1990). *Open heart, clear mind.* Ithaca, NY: Snow Lion.

CHOMSKY, N. (1959). A review of B.F. Skinner's *Verbal Behavior. Language, 35,* 26–58.

CHOMSKY, N. (1987). Psychology and ideology. In J. Peck (Ed.), *The Chomsky reader* (pp. 157–182). New York: Pantheon Books.

CHURCHLAND, P.S. (2002). *Brain-wise: Studies in neurophilosophy.* Cambridge, MA: MIT Press.

CLARK, D.A., BECK, A.T., & BROWN, G. (1989). Cognitive mediation in general psychiatric outpatients: A test of the content-specificity hypothesis. *Journal of Personality and Social Psychology, 56,* 958–964.

CLARK, L.A., & WATSON, D. (1999). Temperament: A new paradigm for trait psychology. In L.A. Pervin & O.P. John (Eds.), *Handbook of personality: Theory and research* (pp. 399–423). New York: Guilford.

CLONINGER, C.R., SVRAKIC, D.M., & PRZBECK, T.R. (1993). A psychobiological model of temperament and character. *Archives of General Psychiatry, 50,* 975–990.

CLONINGER, C.R. (2004). *The science of well-being.* New York: Oxford University Press.

COLVIN, C.R. (1993). "Judgable" people: Personality, behavior, and competing explanations. *Journal of Personality and Social Psychology, 64,* 861–873.

COLVIN, C.R., BLOCK, J., & FUNDER, D.C. (1995). Overly positive self-evaluations and personality: Negative implications for mental health. *Journal of Personality and Social Psychology, 68,* 1152–1162.

CONLEY, J.J. (1985). Longitudinal stability of personality traits: A multitrait-multimethod-multioccasion analysis. *Journal of Personality and Social Psychology, 49,* 1266–1282.

CONTRADA, R.J., LEVENTHAL, H., & O'LEARY, A. (1990). Personality and health. In L.A. Pervin (Ed.), *Handbook of personality: Theory and research* (pp. 638–669). New York: Guilford Press.

CONWAY, M.A., & PLEYDELL-PEARCE, C.W. (2000). The construction of autobiographical memories in the self memory system. *Psychological Review, 107,* 261–288.

COOPER, M.L. (2002). Personality and close relationships: Embedding people in important social contexts. *Journal of Personality, 70,* 757–782.

COOPER, R.M., & ZUBEK, J.P. (1958). Effects of enriched and restricted early environments on the learning ability of bright and dull rats. *Canadian Journal of Psychology, 12,* 159–164.

COOPERSMITH, S. (1967). *The antecedents of self-esteem.* San Francisco: Freeman.

COSMIDES, L. (1989). The logic of social exchange: Has natural selection shaped how humans reason? Studies with the Wason selection task. *Cognition, 31,* 187–276.

COSTA, P.T., JR., & MCCRAE, R.R. (1985). *The NEO Personality Inventory manual.* Odessa, FL: Psychological Assessment Resources.

COSTA, P.T., JR., & MCCRAE, R.R. (1989). *The NEOPI/ NEO-FFI manual supplement.* Odessa, FL: Psychological Assessment Resources.

COSTA, P.T., JR., & MCCRAE, R.R. (1992). *NEO-PI-R: Professional manual*. Odessa, FL: Psychological Assessment Resources.

COSTA, P.T., JR., & MCCRAE, R.R. (1994). Stability and change in personality from adolescence through adulthood. In C.F. Halverson, Jr., G.A. Kohnstamm, & Roy P. Martin (Eds.), *The developing structure of temperament and personality from infancy to adulthood* (pp. 139–155). Hillsdale, NJ: Erlbaum.

COSTA, P.T., JR., & MCCRAE, R.R. (1995). Primary traits of Eysenck's PEN system: Three- and five-factor solutions. *Journal of Personality and Social Psychology, 69*, 308–317.

COSTA, P.T., JR., & MCCRAE, R.R., (1998). Trait Theories of Personality. in Barone, D.F., Hersen, M., & van Hasselt, V.B. (Eds.), *Advanced Personality* (pp. 103–121). New York: Plenum.

COSTA, P.T., JR., & MCCRAE, R.R. (2001). A theoretical context for adult temperament. In T.D. Wachs & G.A. Kohnstamm (Eds.), *Temperament in context* (pp. 1–22). Mahwah, NJ: Erlbaum.

COSTA, P.T. JR., & MCCRAE, R.R. (2002). Looking backward: Changes in the mean levels of personality traits from 80 to 12. In D, Cervone & W. Mischel (Eds.), *Advances in personality science* (pp. 219–237). New York: Guilford Press.

COSTA, P.T., & WIDIGER, T.A. (Eds.) (1994). *Personality disorders and the five factor model of personality*. Washington, DC: American Psychological Association.

COSTA, P.T. JR., & WIDIGER, T.A. (2001). *Personality disorders and the five-factor model of personality* (2nd ed.). Washington, DC: American Psychological Association.

COYNE, J.C. (1994). Self-reported distress: Analog or ersatz depression? *Psychological Bulletin, 116*, 29–45.

COZZARELLI, C. (1993). Personality and self-efficacy as predictors of coping with abortion. *Journal of Personality and Social Psychology, 65*, 1224–1236.

CRAIGHEAD, W.E., CRAIGHEAD, L.W., & ILARDI, S.S. (1995). Behavior therapies in historical perspective. In B. Bongar & L.E. Bentler (Eds.), *Comprehensive textbook of psychotherapy* (pp. 64–83). New York: Oxford University Press.

CRAMER, P. (1991). *The development of defense mechanisms: Theory, research and assessment*. New York: Springer-Verlag.

CRAMER, P. (1996). *Storytelling, narrative, and the Thematic Apperception Test*. New York: Guilford.

CRAMER, P. (2003). Personality change in later adulthood is predicted by defense mechanism use in early adulthood. *Journal of Research in Personality, 37*, 76–104.

CRAMER, P., & BLOCK, J. (1998). Preschool antecedents of defense mechanism use in young adults: A longitudinal study. *Journal of Personality and Social Psychology, 74*, 159–169.

CREWS, F. (1993). The unknown Freud. *The New York Review of Books*, November 18, 55–66.

CREWS, F. (1998). (Ed.). *Unauthorized Freud: Doubters confront a legend*. New York: Penguin Books.

CROCKER, J., & KNIGHT, K.M. (2005). Contingencies of self-worth. *Current Directions inPsychological Science, 14*, 200–203.

CROCKER, J., SOMMERS, S.R., & LUHTANEN, R.K. (2002). Hopes dashed and dreams fulfilled: Contingencies of self-worth and graduate school admissions. *Personality & Social Psychology Bulletin, 28*, 1275–1286.

CROCKER, J., & WOLFE, C.T. (2001). Contingencies of self-worth. *Psychological Review, 108*, 593–623.

CROCKETT, W.H. (1982). The organization of construct systems: The organization corollary. In J.C. Mancuso & J.R. Adams-Webber (Eds.), *The construing person* (pp. 62–95). New York: Praeger.

CRONBACH, L.J., & MEEHL, P.E. (1955). Construct validity in psychological tests. *Psychological Bulletin, 52*, 281–302.

CROSS, H.J. (1966). The relationship of parental training conditions to conceptual level in adolescent boys. *Journal of Personality, 34*, 348–365.

CROSS, S.E., & MARKUS, H.R. (1999). The cultural constitution of personality. In L.A. Pervin & O.P. John (Eds.), *Handbook of personality: Theory and research* (2nd ed., pp. 378–396). New York: Guilford Press.

CURTIS, R.C., & MILLER, K. (1986). Believing another likes or dislikes you: Behaviors making the beliefs come true. *Journal of Personality and Social Psychology, 51*, 284–290.

CYRANOWSKI, J.M., & ANDERSEN, B.L. (1998). Schemas, sexuality, and romantic attachment. *Journal of Personality and Social Psychology, 74*, 1364–1379.

DABBS, J.M., JR. (2000). *Heroes, rogues and lovers: Outcroppings of testosterone*. New York: McGraw-Hill.

DAMASIO, A.R. (1994). *Descartes' error*. New York: Avon.

DANNER, D.D., SNOWDON, D.A., & FRIESEN, W.V. (2001). Positive emotions in early life and longevity: Findings from the nun study. *Journal of Personality & Social Psychology, 80*, 804–813.

DARLEY, J.M., & FAZIO, R. (1980). Expectancy confirmation processes arising in the social interaction sequence. *American Psychologist, 35,* 867–881.

DARWIN, C. (1859). *The origin of the species.* London: Murray.

DARWIN, C. (1872). *The expression of the emotions in man and animals.* London: Murray.

DAVIDSON, R.J. (1994). Asymmetric brain function, affective style, and psychopathology. *Development and Psychopathology, 66,* 486–498.

DAVIDSON, R.J. (1995). Cerebral asymmetry, emotion, and affective style. In R.J. Davidson & K. Hugdahl (Eds.), *Brain asymmetry* (pp. 361–387). Cambridge, MA: Massachusetts Institute of Technology.

DAVIDSON, R.J. (1998). Affective style and affective disorders: Perspectives from affective neuroscience. *Cognition and Emotion, 12,* 307–330.

DAVIDSON, R.J., & FOX, N.A. (1989). Frontal brain asymmetry predicts infants' response to maternal separation. *Journal of Abnormal Psychology, 98,* 127–131.

DAWES, R.M. (1994). *House of cards: Psychology and psychotherapy built on myth.* New York: The Free Press.

DECI, E.L., & RYAN, R.M. (1985). *Intrinsic motivation and self determination in human behavior.* New York: Plenum.

DECI, E.L., & RYAN, R.M. (1991). A motivational approach to self: Integration in personality. *Nebraska Symposium on Motivation, 38,* 237–288.

DE FRUYT, F., & SALGADO, J.F. (Eds.) (2003). Personality and industrial, work and organizational applications. *European Journal of Personality, 17* (whole issue).

DE LA RONDE, C., & SWANN, W.B., JR. (1998). Partner verification: Restoring shattered images of our intimates. *Journal of Personality and Social Psychology, 75,* 374–382.

DENES-RAJ, V., & EPSTEIN, S. (1994). Conflict between intuitive and rational processing: When people behave against their better judgment. *Journal of Personality and Social Psychology, 66,* 819–829.

DENNETT, D.C. (1984). *Elbow room: The varieties of free will worth wanting.* Cambridge, MA: MIT Press.

DENNETT, D.C. (2003). *Freedom evolves.* New York: Viking.

DEPUE, R.A. (1995). Neurobiological factors in personality and depression. *European Journal of Personality, 9,* 413–439.

DEPUE, R.A. (1996). A neurobiological framework for the structure of personality and emotion: Implications for personality disorders. In J. Clarkin & M. Lenzenweger (Eds.), *Major theories of personality disorders* (pp. 347–390). New York: Guilford.

DEPUE, R.A., & COLLINS, P.F. (1999). Neurobiology of the structure of personality: Dopamine, facilitation of incentive motivation, and extraversion. *Behavioral and Brain Sciences, 22,* 491–517.

DE RAAD, B. (2005). Situations that matter to personality. In A. Eliasz, S.E. Hampson, & B. de Raad (Eds.), *Advances in personality psychology* (Vol. 2, pp. 179–204). Philadelphia, PA: Psychology Press.

DESTENO, D., BARTLETT, M.Y., BRAVERMAN, J., & SALOVEY, P. (2002). Sex differences in jealousy: Evolutionary mechanism or artifact of measurement? *Journal of Personality and Social Psychology, 83,* 1103–1116.

DEWSBURY, D.A. (1997). In celebration of the centennial of Ivan P. Pavlov's (1897/1902) *The Work of the Digestive Glands. American Psychologist, 52,* 933–935.

DI BLAS, L., & FORZI, M. (1999). Refining a descriptive structure of personality attributes in the Italian language: The abridged big three circumplex structure. *Journal of Personality and Social Psychology, 76,* 451–481.

DOBSON, K.S., & SHAW, B.F. (1995). Cognitive therapies in practice. In B. Bongar & L.E. Bentler (Eds.), *Comprehensive textbook of psychotherapy* (pp. 159–172). New York: Oxford University Press.

DOLNICK, E. (1998). *Madness on the couch: Blaming the victim in the heyday of psychoanalysis.* New York: Simon & Schuster.

DOMJAN, M. (2005). Pavlovian conditioning: A functional perspective. *Annual Review of Psychology, 56,* 179–206.

DONAHUE, E.M. (1994). Do children use the Big Five, too? Content and structural form in personality descriptions. *Journal of Personality, 62,* 45–66.

DOWNEY, G., & FELDMAN, S.I. (1996). Implications of rejection sensitivity for intimate relationships. *Journal of Personality and Social Psychology, 70,* 1327–1343.

DOWNEY, G., FREITAS, A.L., MICHAELIS, B., & KHOURI, H. (1998). The self-fulfilling prophecy in close relationships: Rejection sensitivity and rejection by romantic partners. *Journal of Personality and Social Psychology, 75,* 545–560.

DRAGANSKI, B., GASER, C., BUSCH, V., SCHUIERER, G., BOGDAHN, I., & MAY, A. (2004). Changes in grey matter induced by training. *Nature, 427,* 311–312.

DUNNING, D., HEATH, C., & SULS, J.M. (2004). Flawed self-assessment: Implications for health, education, and the workplace. *Psychological Science in the Public Interest, 5,* 69–106.

DUCK, S. (1982). Two individuals in search of agreement: The commonality corollary. In J.C. Mancuso

& J.R. Adams-Webber (Eds.), *The construing person* (pp. 222–234). New York: Praeger.

DUNN, J., & PLOMIN, R. (1990). *Separate lives: Why siblings are so different.* New York: Basic Books.

DUTTON, K.A., & BROWN, J.D. (1997). Global self esteem and specific self-views as determinants of people's reactions to success and failure. *Journal of Personality and Social Psychology, 73,* 139–148.

DWECK, C.S. (1991). Self-theories and goals: Their role in motivation, personality, and development. In R.D. Dienstbier (Ed.), *Nebraska Symposium on Motivation* (pp. 199–235). Lincoln, NE: University of Nebraska Press.

DWECK, C.S. (1999). *Self-theories: Their role in motivation, personality, and development.* Philadelphia: Psychology Press/Taylor & Francis.

DWECK, C.S., CHIU, C., & HONG, Y. (1995). Implicit theories and their role in judgments and reactions: A world from two perspectives. *Psychological Inquiry, 6,* 267–285.

DWECK, C.S., HIGGINS, E.T., & GRANT-PILLOW, H. (2003). Self-systems give unique meaning to self variables. In M.R. Leary & J.P. Tangney (Eds.), *Handbook of self and identity* (pp. 239–252). New York: Guilford Press.

DWECK, C., & LEGGETT, E. (1988). A social-cognitive approach to motivation in personality. *Psychological Review, 95,* 256–273.

DYKMAN, B.M. (1998). Integrating cognitive and motivational factors in depression: Initial tests of a goal orientation approach. *Journal of Personality and Social Psychology, 74,* 139–158.

DYKMAN, B.M., & JOHLL, M. (1998). Dysfunctional attitudes and vulnerability to depressive symptoms: A 14-week longitudinal study. *Cognitive Therapy and Research, 22,* 337–352.

EAGLE, M., WOLITZKY, D.L., & KLEIN, G.S. (1966). Imagery: Effect of a concealed figure in a stimulus. *Science, 18,* 837–839.

EAGLY, A.H., & WOOD, W. (1999). The origins of sex differences in human behavior. *American Psychologist, 54,* 408–423.

EBSTEIN, R.P. NOVICK, O. UMANSKY, R., PRIEL, B., OSHER, Y., BLAINE, D., et al. (1996). Dopamine D4 receptor (D4DR) exon III polymorphism associated with the human personality trait of novelty seeking. *Nature Genetics, 12,* 78–80.

THE ECONOMIST (2005). *Pocket World in Figures* (2005 Ed.). Profile Books: London.

EDELMAN, G.M., & TONONI, G. (2000). *A universe of consciousness: How matter becomes imagination.* New York: Basic Books.

EDELSON, M. (1984). *Hypothesis and evidence in psychoanalysis.* Chicago: University of Chicago Press.

EHRLICH, P.R. (2000). *Human natures: Genes, cultures, and the human prospect.* Washington, DC: Island Press.

EISENBERG, N., FABES, R.A., GUTHRIE, I.K., & REISER, M. (2000). Dispositional emotionality and regulation: Their role in predicting quality of social functioning. *Journal of Personality and Social Psychology, 78,* 136–157.

EKMAN, P. (1992). An argument for basic emotions. *Cognition and Emotion, 6,* 169–200.

EKMAN, P. (1993). Facial expression and emotion. *American Psychologist, 48,* 384–392.

EKMAN, P. (1994). Strong evidence for universals in facial expressions: A reply to Russell's mistaken critique. *Psychological Bulletin, 115,* 268–287.

ELFENBEIN, H.A., & AMBADY, N. (2002). On the universality and cultural specificity of emotion recognition: A meta-analysis. *Psychological Bulletin, 128,* 203–235.

ELLIOTT, A.J., & DWECK, C.S. (1988). Goals: An approach to motivation and achievement. *Journal of Personality and Social Psychology, 54,* 5–12.

ELLIOT, A.J., & SHELDON, K.M. (1998). Avoidance personal goals and the personality-illness relationship. *Journal of Personality and Social Psychology, 75,* 1282–1299.

ELLIOT, A.J., SHELDON, K.M., & CHURCH, M.A. (1997). Avoidance personal goals and subjective well-being. *Personality and Social Psychology Bulletin, 9,* 915–927.

ELLIS, A. (1962). *Reason and emotion in psychotherapy.* Secaucus, NJ: Lyle Stuart.

ELLIS, A. (1987). The impossibility of achieving consistently good mental health. *American Psychologist, 42,* 364–375.

ELLIS, A., & HARPER, R.A. (1975). *A new guide to rational living.* North Hollywood, CA: Wilshire.

ELLIS, A., & TAFRATE, R.C. (1997). *How to control your anger before it controls you.* New York: Citadel Press.

EMMONS, R.A. (1987). Narcissism: Theory and measurement. *Journal of Personality and Social Psychology, 52,* 11–17.

EPEL, E.S., BLACKBURN, E.H., LIN, J., DHABHAR, F.S., ADLER, N.E., MORROW, J.D., & CAWTHON, R.M. (2004). Accelerated telomere shortening in response to life stress. *Proceedings National Academy of Sciences, 101,* 17312–17315.

EPSTEIN, N., & BAUCOM, N. (1988). *Cognitive-behavioral marital therapy.* New York: Springer.

EPSTEIN, S. (1979). The stability of behavior: I. On predicting most of the people much of the time. *Journal of Personality and Social Psychology, 37,* 1092–1126.

EPSTEIN, S. (1983). A research paradigm for the study of personality and emotions. In M.M. Page (Ed.), *Personality: Current theory and research* (pp. 91–154). Lincoln, NE: University of Nebraska Press.

EPSTEIN, S. (1992). The cognitive self, the psychoanalytic self, and the forgotten selves. *Psychological Inquiry, 3,* 34–37.

EPSTEIN, S. (1994). Integration of the cognitive and the psychodynamic unconscious. *American Psychologist, 49,* 709–724.

EPTING, F.R., & ELIOT, M. (2006). A constructive understanding of the person: George Kelly and humanistic psychology. *The Humanistic Psychologist, 34,* 21–37.

ERDELYI, M. (1984). *Psychoanalysis: Freud's cognitive psychology.* New York: Freeman.

ERDLEY, C.A., LOOMIS, C.C., CAIN, K.M., & DUMASHINES, F. (1997). Relations among children's social goals, implicit personality theories, and responses to social failure. *Developmental Psychology, 33,* 263–272.

ERICSSON, K.A., & SIMON, H.A. (1993). *Protocol analysis: Verbal reports as data.* Cambridge, MA: MIT Press.

ERIKSON, E. (1950). *Childhood and society.* New York: Norton.

ERIKSON, E.H. (1982). *The life cycle completed: A review.* New York: Norton.

ESTERSON, A. (1993). *Seductive mirage: An exploration of the work of Sigmund Freud.* New York: Open Court.

EVANS, R.I. (1976). *The making of psychology.* New York: Knopf.

EWART, C.K. (1992). The role of physical self-efficacy in recovery from heart attack. In R. Schwarzer (Ed.), *Self-efficacy: Thought control of action* (pp. 287–304). Washington, DC: Hemisphere.

EXNER, J.E. (1986). The Rorschach: A comprehensive system: Basic foundations (Volume 1, 2nd ed.). New York: Wiley.

EYSENCK, H.J. (1953). *Uses and abuses of psychology.* London: Penguin.

EYSENCK, H.J. (1970). *The structure of personality.* (3rd edition). London: Methuen

EYSENCK, H.J. (1982). *Personality genetics and behavior.* New York: Praeger.

EYSENCK, H.J. (1990). Biological dimensions of personality. In L.A. Pervin (Ed.), *Handbook of personality: Theory and research* (pp. 244–276). New York: Guilford Press.

FARBER, I.E. (1964). A framework for the study of personality as a behavioral science. In P. Worchel & D. Byrne (Eds.), *Personality change* (pp. 3–37). New York: Wiley.

FAZIO, R.H., & OLSON, M.A. (2003). Implicit measures in social cognition research: Their meaning and use. *Annual Review of Psychology, 54,* 297–327.

FEENEY, J.A., & NOLLER, P. (1990). Attachment style as a predictor of adult romantic relationships. *Journal of Personality and Social Psychology, 58,* 281–291.

FERSTER, C.B. (1973). A functional analysis of depression. *American Psychologist, 28,* 857- 870.

FERSTER, C.B., & SKINNER, B.F. (1957). *Schedules of reinforcement.* New York: Appleton-Century-Crofts.

FISKE, A.P., KITAYAMA, S., MARKUS, H.R., & NISBETT, R.E. (1998). The cultural matrix of social psychology. In D.T. Gilbert, S.T. Fiske, & G. Lindzey (Eds.) (1998). *The handbook of social psychology* (4th ed.) (pp. 915–981). New York: McGraw-Hill.

FISKE, S.T., & TAYLOR, S.E. (1991). *Social Cognition.* New York: McGraw-Hill.

FLAVELL, J.H. (1999). Cognitive development: Children's knowledge about the mind. *Annual Review of Psychology, 50,* 21–45.

FLEESON, W. (2001). Toward a Structure- and Process- Integrated View of Personality: Traits as Density Distributions of States *Journal of Personality and Social Psychology, 80,* 1011–1027.

FLEESON, W., & LEICHT, C. (2006). On delineating and integrating the study of variability and stability in personality psychology: Interpersonal trust as illustration. *Journal of Research in Personality, 40,* 5–20.

FLETT, G.L., BESSER, A., & HEWITT, P.L. (2005). Perfectionism, ego defense styles, and depression: A comparison of self-reports versus informant ratings. *Journal of Personality, 73,* 1355–1396.

FODOR, J.A. (1983). *The modularity of mind: An essay on faculty psychology.* Cambridge, MA: MIT Press.

FORGAS, J. (1995). Mood and judgment: The affect Infusion model. *Psychological Bulletin, 117,* 39–66.

FOLKMAN, S., LAZARUS, R.S., GRUEN, R.J., & DELONGIS, A. (1986). Appraisal, coping, health status, and psychological symptoms. *Journal of Personality and Social Psychology, 50,* 571–579.

FOLKMAN, S., & MOSKOWITZ, J.T. (2004). Coping: Pitfalls and promises. *Annual Review of Psychology, 55,* 745–774.

FOX, N.A., HENDERSON, H.A., MARSHALL, P.J., NICHOLS, K.E., & GHERA, M.A. (2005). Behavioral inhibition: Linking biology and behavior within a developmental framework. *Annual Review of Psychology, 56,* 235–262.

FRALEY, R.C. (1999). *Attachment continuity from infancy to adulthood: Meta-analysis and dynamic modeling of developmental mechanisms.* Unpublished manuscript, University of California, Davis.

FRALEY, R.C. (2002). Attachment stability from infancy to adulthood: Meta-analysis and dynamic modeling of developmental mechanisms. *Personality and Social Psychology Review, 6*, 123–151.

FRALEY, R.C., & ROBERTS, B.W. (2005). Patterns of continuity: A dynamic model for conceptualizing the stability of individual differences in psychological constructs across the life course. *Psychological Review, 112*, 60–74.

FRALEY, R.C., & SHAVER, P.R. (1998). Airport separations: A naturalistic study of adult attachment dynamics in separating couples. *Journal of Personality and Social Psychology, 75*, 1198–1212.

FRALEY, R.C., & SPIEKER, S.J. (2003). Are infant attachment patterns continuously or categorically distributed? A taxometric analysis of strange situation behavior. *Developmental Psychology.*

FRANKL, V.E. (1955). *The doctor and the soul.* New York: Knopf.

FRANKL, V.E. (1958). On logotherapy and existential analysis. *American Journal of Psychoanalysis, 18*, 28–37.

FREUD, S. (1915/1970). Instincts and their vicissitudes. In W.A. Russell (Ed.), *Milestones in motivation: Contributions to the psychology of drive and purpose* (pp. 324–331). New York: Appleton-Century-Crofts.

FREUD, S. (1949). *Civilization and its discontents.* London: Hogarth Press. (Original Edition, 1930.)

FREUD, S. (1953). The interpretation of dreams. In *Standard edition*, Vols. 4 & 5. London: Hogarth Press. (First German Edition, 1900.)

FREUD, S. (1959). Analysis of a phobia in a five-yearold boy. In *Standard edition*, Vol. 10. London: Hogarth Press. (First German Edition, 1909.)

FREUND, A.M., & BALTES, P.B. (1998). Selection, optimization, and compensation as strategies of life management: Correlations with subjective indicators of successful aging. *Psychology and Aging, 13*, 531–543.

FRIEDMAN, H.S., TUCKER, J.S., SCHWARTZ, J.E., MARTIN, L.R., TOMLINSON-KEASY, C., WINGARD, D.L., & CRIQUI, M.H. (1995b). Childhood conscientiousness and longevity: Health behaviors and cause of death. *Journal of Personality and Social Psychology, 68*, 696–703.

FRIEDMAN, H.S., TUCKER, J.S., SCHWARTZ, J.E., TOMLINSON-KEASY, C., MARTIN, L.R., WINGARD, D.L., & CRIQUI, M.H. (1995). Psychosocial and behavioral predictors of longevity: The aging and death of the "Termites." *American Psychologist, 50*, 69–78.

FROMM, E. (1959). *Sigmund Freud's mission.* New York: Harper.

FUNDER, D.C. (1989). Accuracy in personality judgment and the dancing bear. In D.M. Buss & N. Cantor (Eds.), *Personality psychology: Recent trends and emerging directions* (pp. 210–223). New York: Springer-Verlag.

FUNDER, D.C. (1993). Judgments of personality and personality itself. In K.H. Craik, R. Hogan, & R.N. Wolfe (Eds.), *Fifty years of personality psychology* (pp. 207–214). New York: Plenum.

FUNDER, D.C. (1995). On the accuracy of personality judgment: A realistic approach. *Psychological Review, 102*, 652–670.

FUNDER, D.C., KOLAR, D.C., & BLACKMAN, M.C. (1995). Agreement among judges of personality: Interpersonal relations, similarity, and acquaintanceship. *Journal of Personality and Social Psychology, 69*, 656–672.

FUNDER, D.C., & OZER, D.J. (1983). Behavior as a function of the situation. *Journal of Personality and Social Psychology, 44*, 107–112.

GABLE, S.L., REIS, H.T., & DOWNEY, G. (2003). He said, she said: A quasi-signal detection analysis of daily interactions between close relationship partners. *Psychological Science, 14*, 100–105.

GAENSBAUER, T.J. (1982). The differentiation of discrete affects. *Psychoanalytic Study of the Child, 37*, 29–66.

GALATZER-LEVY, R.M., BACHRACH, H., SKOLNIKOFF, A., & WALDRON, S., JR. (2000). *Does psychoanalysis work?* New Haven: Yale University Press.

GALLO, L.C., & MATTHEWS, K.A. (2003). Understanding the association between socioeconomic status and physical health: Do negative emotions play a role?*Psychological Bulletin, 129*, 10–51.

GAY, P. (1998). *Freud: A life for our time.* New York: Norton.

GEEN, R.G. (1984). Preferred stimulation levels in introverts and extroverts: Effects on arousal and performance. *Journal of Personality and Social Psychology, 46*, 1303–1312.

GEEN, R.G. (1997). Psychophysiological approaches to personality. In R. Hogan, J.A. Johnson, & S.R. Briggs (Eds.), *Handbook of Personality Psychology* (pp. 387–414). San Diego: Academic Press.

GEERTZ, C. (1973). *The interpretation of cultures.* New York: Basic Books.

GEERTZ, C. (2000). *Available light: Anthropological reflections on philosophical topics.* Princeton, NJ: Princeton University Press.

GEISLER, C. (1986). The use of subliminal psychodynamic activation in the study of repression. *Journal of Personality and Social Psychology, 51*, 844–851.

GERARD, H.B., KUPPER, D.A., & NGUYEN, L. (1993). The causal link between depression and bulimia. In J.M. Masling & R.F. Bornstein (Eds.), *Psychoanalytic perspectives in psychopathology* (pp. 225–252). Washington, DC: American Psychological Association.

GERGEN, K.J. (2001). Psychological science in a postmodern context. *American Psychologist, 56,* 803–813.

GIERE, R.N. (1999). *Science without laws.* Chicago: University of Chicago Press.

GIESLER, R.B., JOSEPHS, R.A., & SWANN, W.B., JR. (1996). Self-verification in clinical depression: The desire for negative evaluation. *Journal of Abnormal Psychology, 105,* 358–368.

GLADUE, B.A., BOECHLER, M., & MCCAUL, D.D. (1989). Hormonal response to competition in human males. *Aggressive Behavior, 15,* 409–422.

GOBLE, F. (1970). *The third force: The psychology of Abraham Maslow.* New York: Grossman.

GOLDBERG, L.R. (1981). Language and individual differences: The search for universals in personality lexicons. In L. Wheeler (Ed.), *Review of personality and social psychology* (pp. 141–165). Beverly Hills, CA: Sage.

GOLDBERG, L.R. (1990). An alternative "description of personality": The Big-Five factor structure. *Journal of Personality and Social Psychology, 59,* 1216–1229.

GOLDBERG, L. (1992). The development of markers for the Big-Five factor structure. *Psychological Assessment, 4,* 26–42.

GOLDBERG, L.R., & ROSOLACK, T.K. (1994). The Big Five factor structure as an integrative framework: An empirical comparison with Eysenck's P-E-N model. In C.F. Halverson, Jr., G.A. Kohnstamm, & R.P. Martin (Eds.), *The developing structure of temperament and personality from infancy to adulthood* (pp. 7–35). New York: Erlbaum.

GOLDSMITH, H.H., & CAMPOS, J.J. (1982). Toward a theory of infant temperament: In R.M. Emde and R.J. Harmon (Eds.), *The development of attachment and affiliative systems* (pp. 161–193). New York: Plenum.

GOLDSTEIN, K. (1939). *The organism.* New York: American Book.

GOSLING, S.D., & JOHN, O.P. (1998, May). Personality dimensions in dogs, cats, and hyenas. Paper presented at the annual meeting of the American Psychological Society, Washington, DC.

GOSLING, S.D., & JOHN, O.P. (1999). Personality dimensions in nonhuman animals: A cross-species review. *Contemporary Directions in Psychological Science, 8,* 69–75.

GOSLING, S.D., JOHN, O.P., CRAIK, K.H., & ROBINS, R.W. (1998). Do people know how they behave? Self reported act frequencies compared with on-line codings by observers. *Journal of Personality and Social Psychology, 74,* 1337–1349.

GOSLING, S.D., KO, S.J., MANNARELLI, T., & MORRIS, M.E. (2002). A Room with a cue: Judgments of personality based on offices and bedrooms. *Journal of Personality and Social Psychology, 82,* 379–398.

GOTTLIEB, G. (1998). Normally occurring environmental and behavioral influences on gene activity: From central dogma to probabilistic epigenesis. *Psychological Review, 105,* 792–802.

GOULD, E., REEVES, A.J., GRAZIANO, M.S. A., & GROSS, C.G. (1999). Neurogenesis in the neocortex of adult primates. *Science, 286,* 548–552.

GOULD, S.J. (1981). *The mismeasure of man.* New York: Norton.

GRANT, H., & DWECK, C. (1999). A goal analysis of personality and personality coherence. In D. Cervone & Y. Shoda (Eds.), *The coherence of personality: Social cognitive bases of consistency, variability, and organization* (pp. 345–371). New York: Guilford Press.

GRAY, J.A. (1987). *The psychology of fear and stress.* Cambridge, UK: Cambridge University Press.

GRAY, J.A. (1990). A critique of Eysenck's theory of personality. In H.J. Eysenck (Ed.), *A model for personality,* (2nd ed.) Berlin: Springer-Verlag.

GRAY, J.A. (1991). Neural systems, emotion and personality. In J. Madden IV (Ed.), *Neurobiology of learning, emotion and affect.* New York: Raven Press.

GREENBERG, J.R., & MITCHELL, S.A. (1983). *Object relations in psychoanalytic theory.* Cambridge, MA: Harvard University Press.

GREENE, B. (2004). *The fabric of the cosmos: Space, time, and the texture of reality.* New York: Knopf.

GREENE, J.D., SOMMERVILLE, R.B., NYSTROM, L.E., DARLEY, J.M., & COHEN, J.D. (2001). An fMRI investigation of emotional engagement in moral judgment. *Science, 293,* 2105–2108.

GREENWALD, A.G., & BANAJI, M.R. (1995). Implicit social cognition: Attitudes, self-esteem, and stereotypes. *Psychological Review, 102,* 4–27.

GREENWALD, A.G., BANAJI, M.R., RUDMAN, L.A., FARNHAM, S.D., NOSEK, B.A., & MELLOT, D.S. (2002). A unified theory of implicit attitudes, stereotypes, self-esteem, and self-concept. *Psychological Review, 109,* 3–25.

GRICE, J.W. (2004). Bridging the idiographic-nomothetic divide in ratings of self and others on the big five. *Journal of Personality, 72,* 203–241.

GRIFFIN, D., & BARTHOLOMEW, K. (1994). Models of the self and other: Fundamental dimensions underlying measures of adult attachment. *Journal of Personality and Social Psychology, 67*, 430–445.

GRIGORENKO, E.L. (2002). In search of the genetic engram of personality. In D. Cervone & W. Mischel (Eds.), *Advances in personality science* (pp. 29–82). New York: Guilford Press.

GRODDECK, G. (1961). *The book of the it*. New York: Vintage. (ORIGINAL EDITION, 1923.)

GROSS, J.L. (1999). Emotion and emotion regulation. In L.A. Pervin & O.P. John (Eds.), *Handbook of personality: Theory and research* (pp. 525–552). New York: Guilford.

GRUNBAUM, A. (1984). *Foundations of psychoanalysis: A philosophical critique*. Berkeley: University of California Press.

GRUNBAUM, A. (1993). *Validation in the clinical theory of psychoanalysis: A study in the philosophy of psychoanalysis*. Madison, CT: International Universities Press.

GUENTHER, H.V., & KAWAMURA, L.S. (1975). *Mind in Buddhist Psychology*. Berkeley, CA: Dharma Press.

HAGGBLOOM, S.J., WARNICK, R., WARNICK, J.E., JONES, V.K., YARBROUGH, G.L., RUSSELL, T.M., et al. (2002). The 100 most eminent psychologists of the 20th century. *Review of General Psychology, 6*, 139–152.

HALL, C.S. (1954). *A primer of Freudian psychology*. New York: Mentor.

HALVERSON, C.F., KOHNSTAMM, G.A., & MARTIN, R.P. (Eds.) (1994). *The developing structure of temperament and personality from infancy to adulthood*. Hillsdale, NJ: Erlbaum.

HAMER, D. (1997). The search for personality genes: Adventures of a molecular biologist. *Current Directions in Psychological Science, 6*, 111–114.

HAMER, D., & COPELAND, P. (1998). *Living with our genes*. New York: Doubleday.

HAMPSON, S.E., GOLDBERG, S.E., VOGT, T.M., & DUBANOSKI, J.P. (2006). Forty Years on: Teachers' assessments of children's personality traits predict self-reported health behaviors and outcomes at midlife. *Health Psychology, 25*, 57–64.

HAMPSON, S.E., GOLDBERG, S.E., VOGT, T.M., & DUBANOSKI, J.P. (in press). Mechanisms by which childhood personality traits influence adult health status: educational attainment and healthy behaviors. *Health Psychology*.

HANKIN, B.L., FRALEY, R.C., & ABELA, J.R. Z. (2005). Daily depression and cognitions about stress: Evidence for a trait like depressogenic cognitive style and the prediction of depressive symptoms in a prospective daily diary study. *Journal of Personality and Social Psychology, 88*, 673–685.

HARARY, K., & DONAHUE, E. (1994). *Who do you think you are?* San Francisco: Harper.

HARKNESS, A.R., & LILIENFELD, S.O. (1997). Individual differences science for treatment planning: Personality traits. *Psychological Assessment, 9*, 349–360.

HARRÉ, R. (1998). *The singular self: An introduction to the psychology of personhood*. London: Sage.

HARRÉ, R. (2002). *Cognitive Science: A philosophical introduction*. London Sage.

HARRÉ, R., & SECORD, P.F. (1972). *The explanation of social behaviour*. Oxford, UK: Blackwell.

HARRINGTON, D.M., BLOCK, J.H., & BLOCK, J. (1987). Testing aspects of Carl Rogers's theory of creative environments: Child-rearing antecedents of creative potential in young adolescents. *Journal of Personality and Social Psychology, 52*, 851–856.

HARRIS, B. (1979). Whatever happened to Little Albert? *American Psychologist, 34*, 151–160.

HARRIS, C.R. (2000). Psychophysiological responses to imagined infidelity: The specific innate modular view of jealousy reconsidered. *Journal of Personality and Social Psychology, 78*, 1082–1091.

HARRIS, C.R. (2002). Sexual and romantic jealousy in heterosexual and homosexual adults. *Psychological Science, 13*, 7–12.

HARRIS, J.R. (1995). Where is the child's environment? A group socialization theory of development. *Psychological Review, 102*, 458–489.

HARRIS, J.R. (1998). *The nurture assumption: Why children turn out the way they do*. New York: Free Press.

HARRIS, J.R. (2000). Context-specific learning, personality, and birth order. *Current Directions in Psychological Science, 9*, 174–177.

HARTSHORNE, H., & MAY, M.A. (1928). *Studies in the nature of character. Vol.1: Studies in deceit*. New York: Macmillen.

HAWKINS, R.P., PETERSON, R.F., SCHWEID, E., & BIJOU, S.W. (1966). Behavior therapy in the home: Amelioration of problem parent-child relations with the parent in a therapeutic role. *Journal of Experimental Child Psychology, 4*, 99–107.

HAYDEN, B.C. (1982). Experience—A case for possible change: The modulation corollary. In J.C. Mancuso & J.R. Adams-Webber (Eds.), *The construing person* (pp. 170–197). New York: Praeger.

HAZAN, C., & SHAVER, P. (1987). Romantic love conceptualized as an attachment process. *Journal of Personality and Social Psychology, 52*, 511–524.

HAZAN, C., & SHAVER, P. (1990). Love and work: An attachment-theoretical perspective. *Journal of Personality and Social Psychology, 59*, 270–280.

HEILBRONER, R.L. (1986). *The worldly philosophers: The lives, times and ideas of the great economic thinkers.* New York: Simon and Schuster.

HEIMPEL, S.A., WOOD, J.V., MARSHALL, M.A., & BROWN, J.D. (2002). Do people with low self-esteem really want to feel better? Self-esteem differences in motivation to repair negative moods. *Journal of Personality & Social Psychology, 82*, 128–147.

HEINE, S.J., LEHMAN, D.R., MARKUS, H.R., & KITAYAMA, S. (1999). Is there a universal need for positive self-regard? *Psychological Review, 106*, 766–794.

HELLER, W., SCHMIDTKE, J.I., NITSCHKE, J.B., KOVEN, N.S., & MILLER, G.A. (2002). States, traits, and symptoms: Investigating the neural correlates of emotion, personality, and psychopathology. In D. Cervone & W. Mischel (Eds.), *Advances in personality science* (pp. 106–126). New York: Guilford Press.

HELSON, R., & KWAN, V.S.Y. (2000). Personality change in adulthood: The broad picture and processes in one longitudinal study. In S. Hampson (Ed.), *Advances in personality psychology* (Vol. 1), (pp. 77–106). East Sussex, UK: Psychology Press, Ltd.

HELSON, R., KWAN, V.S.Y., JOHN, O.P., & JONES, C. (2002). The growth of evidence for personality change in adulthood: Findings from research with personality inventories. *Journal of Research in Personality, 36*, 287–306.

HERMANS, H.J.M. (2001). The construction of a personal position repertoire: Method and practice. *Culture and Psychology, 7*, 323–365.

HESSE, H. (1951). *Siddhartha.* New York: New Directions.

HIGGINS, E.T. (1987). Self-discrepancy: A theory relating self and affect. *Psychological Review, 94*, 319–340.

HIGGINS, E.T. (1990). Personality, social psychology, and person-situation relations: Standards and knowledge activation as a common language. In L.A. Pervin (Ed.), *Handbook of Personality: Theory and Research* (pp. 301–338). New York: Guilford.

HIGGINS, E.T. (1996). Knowledge activation: Accessibility, applicability, and salience. In E.T. Higgins & A.W. Kruglanski (Eds.), *Social psychology: Handbook of basic principles* (pp. 133–168). New York: Guilford.

HIGGINS, E.T. (1997). Beyond pleasure and pain. *American Psychologist, 52*, 1280–1300.

HIGGINS, E.T. (1999). Persons and situations: Unique explanatory principles or variability in general principles? In D. Cervone & Y. Shoda (Eds.), *The coherence of personality* (pp. 61–93). New York: Guilford.

HIGGINS, E.T. (2006). Value from regulatory fit. *Current Directions in Psychological Science, 14*, 209–213.

HIGGINS, E.T., BOND, R.N., KLEIN, R., & STRAUMAN, T. (1986). Self-discrepancies and emotional vulnerability: How magnitude, accessibility, and type of discrepancy influence affect. *Journal of Personality and Social Psychology, 51*, 5–15.

HIGGINS, E.T., KING, G.A., & MAVIN, G.H. (1982). Individual construct accessibility and subjective impressions and recall. *Journal of Personality and Social Psychology, 43*, 35–47.

HOFSTEE, W.K. B. (1994). Who should own the definition of personality? *European Journal of Personality, 8*, 149–162.

HOFSTEE, W.K.B., KIERS, H.A., DERAAD, B., GOLDBERG, L.R., & OSTENDORF, F. (1997). A comparison of Big Five structures of personality traits in Dutch, English, and German. *European Journal of Personality, 11*, 15–31.

HOGAN, J, & ONES, D.S. (1997). Conscientiousness and integrity at work. In R. Hogan, J. Johnson & S. Briggs (Eds.), *Handbook of personality psychology* (pp. 849–870). San Diego, CA: Academic Press.

HOLENDER, D. (1986). Semantic activation without conscious identification in dichotic listening, paraforeal vision, and visual masking: A survey and appraisal. *Behavioral and Brain Sciences, 9*, 1–66.

HOLLAND, J.L. (1985). *Making vocational choices: A theory of vocational personality and work environments.* Englewood Cliffs, NJ: Prentice-Hall.

HOLLON, S.D., DE RUBEIS, R.J., & EVANS, M.D. (1987). Causal mediation of change in treatment for depression: Discriminating between nonspecificity and noncausality. *Psychological Bulletin, 102*, 139–149.

HOLLON, S.D., & KENDALL, P.C. (1980). Cognitive self statements in depression: Development of an Automatic Thoughts Questionnaire. *Cognitive Therapy and Research, 4*, 383–395.

HOLLON, S.D., SHELTON, R.C., & DAVIS, D.D. (1993). Cognitive therapy for depression: Conceptual issues and clinical efficacy. *Journal of Consulting and Clinical Psychology, 61*, 270–275.

HOLT, R.R. (1978). *Methods in clinical psychology.* New York: Plenum.

HONG, Y., MORRIS, M.W., CHIU, C., & MARTINEZ, V. (2000). Multicultural minds: A dynamic constructivist approach to culture and cognition. *American Psychologist, 55*, 709–720.

HORNEY, K. (1937). *The neurotic personality of our time.* New York: Norton.

HORNEY, K. (1945). *Our inner conflicts.* New York: Norton.

HORNEY, K. (1973). *Feminine psychology.* New York: Norton.

HOUGH, L.M., & OSWALD, F.L. (2000). Personal selection: Looking toward the future—Remembering the past. *Annual Review of Psychology, 51,* 631–664.

HUESMANN, L.R., MOISE-TITUS, J., PODOLSKI, C., & ERON, L.D. (2003). Longitudinal relations between children's exposure to TV violence and their aggressive and violent behavior in young adulthood: 1977–1992. *Developmental Psychology, 39,* 201–221.

HULL, J.G., YOUNG, R.D., & JOURILES, E. (1986). Applications of the self-awareness model of alcohol consumption: Predicting patterns of use and abuse. *Journal of Personality and Social Psychology, 51,* 790–796.

HURLBURT, R.T., & KNAPP, T.J. (2006). Münsterberg in 1898, not Allport in 1937, introduced the terms 'idiographic' and 'nomothetic' to American psychology. *Theory and Psychology, 16,* 287–293.

HYMAN, S. (1999). Susceptibility and "second hits." In R. Conlan (Ed.), *States of mind* (pp. 24–28). New York: Wiley.

INGRAM, R.E., MIRANDA, J., & SEGAL, Z.V. (1998). *Cognitive vulnerability to depression.* New York: Guilford.

IYENGAR, S.S., & LEPPER, M.R. (1999). Rethinking the value of choice: A cultural perspective on intrinsic motivation. *Journal of Personality and Social Psychology, 76,* 349–366.

IZARD, C.E. (1991). *The psychology of emotion.* New York: Plenum.

IZARD, C.E. (1994). Innate and universal facial expressions: Evidence from developmental and cross-cultural research. *Psychological Bulletin, 115,* 288–299.

JACKSON, D.N., & PAUNONEN, S.V. (1985). Construct validity and the predictability of behavior. *Journal of Personality and Social Psychology, 49,* 554–570.

JACOBY, L.L., LINDSAY, D.S., & TOTH, J.P. (1992). Unconscious influences revealed. *American Psychologist, 47,* 802–809.

JAMES, W. (1890). *Principles of psychology.* New York: Holt.

JANKOWICZ, A.D. (1987). Whatever became of George Kelly? *American Psychologist, 42,* 481–487.

JENSEN, M.R. (1987). Psychobiological factors predicting the course of breast cancer. *Journal of Personality, 55,* 317–342.

JOHN, O.P. (1990). The "Big Five" factor taxonomy: Dimensions of personality in the natural language and in questionnaires. In L.A. Pervin (Ed.), *Handbook of personality: Theory and research* (pp. 66–100). New York: Guilford Press.

JOHN, O.P., ANGLEITNER, A., & OSTENDORF, F. (1988). The lexical approach to personality: A historical review of trait taxonomic research. *European Journal of Personality, 2,* 171–203.

JOHN, O.P., CASPI, A., ROBINS, R.W., MOFFITT, T.E., & STOUTHAMER-LOEBER, M. (1994). The "Little Five": Exploring the nomological network of the Five-Factor model of personality in adolescent boys. *Child Development, 65,* 160–178.

JOHN, O.P., HAMPSON, S.E., & GOLDBERG, L.R. (1991). The basic level in personality-trait hierarchies: Studies of trait use and accessibility in different contexts. *Journal of Personality & Social Psychology, 60,* 348–361.

JOHN, O.P., & ROBINS, R.W. (1993). Gordon Allport: Father and critic of the Five-Factor model. In K.H. Craik, R.T. Hogan, & R.N. Wolfe (Eds.), *Fifty years of personality psychology* (pp. 215–236). New York: Plenum.

JOHN, O.P., & ROBINS, R.W. (1994). Accuracy and bias in self-perception: Individual differences in self enhancement and the role of narcissism. *Journal of Personality and Social Psychology, 66,* 206–219.

JOHN, O.P., & SRIVASTAVA, S. (1999). The Big Five: History, measurement, and development. In L.A. Pervin & O.P. John (Eds.), *Handbook of personality: Theory and research* (pp. 102–138). New York: Guilford.

JONAS, E., & GREENBERG, J. (2004). Terror management and political attitudes: The influence of mortality salience on Germans' defence of the German reunification. *European Journal of Social Psychology, 34,* 1–9.

JONES, A., & CRANDALL, R. (1986). Validation of a short index of self-actualization. *Personality and Social Psychology Bulletin, 12,* 63–73.

JONES, M.C. (1924). A laboratory study of fear. The case of Peter. *Pedagogical Seminar, 31,* 308–315.

JOST, J.T., GLASER, J., KRUGLANSKI, A.W., & SULLOWAY, F.J. (2003). Political conservatism as motivated social cognition. *Psychological Bulletin, 129,* 339–375.

JOURARD, S.M., & REMY, R.M. (1955). Perceived parental attitudes, the self, and security. *Journal of Consulting Psychology, 19,* 364–366.

JUNG, C.G. (1939). *The integration of the personality.* New York: Farrar & Rinehart.

JUNG, C.G. & COLLABORATORS (1964). *Man and his symbols.* New York: Doubleday & Company

KAGAN, J. (1994). *Galen's prophecy: Temperament in human nature*. New York: Basic Books.

KAGAN, J. (1998). *Three seductive ideas*. Cambridge, MA: Harvard University Press.

KAGAN, J. (1999). Born to be shy? In R. Conlan (Ed.), *States of mind* (pp. 29–51). New York: Wiley.

KAGAN, J. (2002). *Surprise, uncertainty, and mental structures*. Cambridge: Harvard University Press.

KAGAN, J. (2003). Biology, context, and developmental inquiry. *Annual Review of Psychology, 54*, 1–23.

KAGAN, J., ARCUS, D., & SNIDMAN, N. (1993). The idea of temperament: Where do we go from here? In R. Plomin & G.E. McClearn (Eds.), *Nature, nurture and psychology* (pp. 197–210). Washington, DC: American Psychological Association.

KANDEL, E.R. (2000). Autobiography. Retrieved August 28, 2002 from http://www.nobel.se/medicine/laureates/2000/kandel-autobio.html.

KANFER, F.H., & SASLOW, G. (1965). Behavioral analysis: An alternative to diagnostic classification. *Archives of General Psychiatry, 12*, 519–538.

KASSER, T., & RYAN, R.M. (1996). Further examining the American dream: Differential correlates of intrinsic and extrinsic goals. *Personality and Social Psychology Bulletin, 22*, 280–287.

KAVANAGH, D. (1992). Self-efficacy as a resource factor in stress appraisal processes. In R. Schwarzer (Ed.), *Self-efficacy: Thought control of action* (pp. 177–194). Washington, DC: Hemisphere.

KAZDIN, A.E. (1977). *The token economy: A review and evaluation*. New York: Plenum.

KELLER, H., & ZACH, U. (2002). Gender and birth order as determinants of parental behaviour. *International Journal of Behavioral Development, 26*, 177–184.

KELLEY, W.M., MACRAE, C.N., WYLAND, C.L., CAGLAR, S., INATI, S., & HEATHERTON, T.F. (2002). Finding the self? An event-related fMRI study. *Journal of Cognitive Neuroscience, 14*, 785–794.

KELLY, G.A. (1955). *The psychology of personal constructs*. New York: Norton.

KELLY, G.A. (1964). The language of hypothesis: Man's psychological instrument. *Journal of Individual Psychology, 20*, 137–152.

KELLY, J.G. (2006). *Becoming ecological: An expedition into community psychology*. New York: Oxford University Press.

KELTNER, D., GRUENFELD, D.H., & ANDERSON, C. (2003). Power, approach, and inhibition. *Psychological Review, 110*, 265–284.

KENNY, D.A. (1994). *Interpersonal perception*. New York: Guilford.

KENNY, D.A., ALBRIGHT, L., MALLOY, T.E., & KASHY, D. A. (1994). Consensus in interpersonal perception: Acquaintance and the Big Five. *Psychological Bulletin, 116*, 245–258.

KENRICK, D.T. (1994). Evolutionary social psychology: From sexual selection to social cognition. *Advances in Experimental Social Psychology, 26*, 75–121.

KIHLSTROM, J.F. (1990). The psychological unconscious. In L.A. Pervin (Ed.), *Handbook of personality: Theory and research* (pp. 445–464). New York: Guilford Press.

KIHLSTROM, J.F. (1999). The psychological unconscious. In L. A. Pervin & O. P. John (Eds.), *Handbook of personality: Theory and research* (pp. 424–442). New York: Guilford.

KIHLSTROM, J.F., BARNHARDT, T.M., & TATARYN, D.J. (1992). The cognitive perspective. In R.F. Bornstein & T.S. Pittman (Eds.), *Perception without awareness*, (pp. 17–54). New York: Guilford Press.

KING, J.E., & FIGUEREDO, A.J. (1997). The Five-Factor Model plus dominance in chimpanzee personality. *Journal of Research in Personality, 31*, 257–271.

KIRKPATRICK, L.A. (1998). God as a substitute attachment figure: A longitudinal study of adult attachment style and religious change in college students. *Personality and Social Psychology Bulletin, 9*, 961–973.

KIRKPATRICK, L.A., & DAVIS, K.E. (1994). Attachment style, gender, and relationship stability: A longitudinal analysis. *Journal of Personality and Social Psychology, 66*, 502–512.

KIRSCHENBAUM, H. (1979). *On becoming Carl Rogers*. New York: Delacorte.

KIRSCHENBAUM, H., & JOURDAN, A. (2005). The current status of Carl Rogers and the person-centered approach. *Psychotherapy: Theory, Research, Practice, Training, 42*, 37–51.

KITAYAMA, S., & MARKUS, H.R. (1999). Yin and Yang of the Japanese self: The cultural psychology of personality coherence. In D. Cervone & Y. Shoda (Eds.), *The coherence of personality: Social-cognitive bases of consistency, variability, and organization* (pp 242–302). New York: Guilford.

KITAYAMA, S., MARKUS, H.R., MATSUMOTO, H., & NORASAKKUNIT, V. (1997). Individual and collective processes of self-esteem management: Self-enhancement in the United States and self-depreciation in Japan. *Journal of Personality and Social Psychology, 72*, 1245–1267.

KITAYAMA, S., & MASUDA, T. (1997). [A cultural mediation model of social inference: Correspondence bias in Japan.] In K. Kashiwagi, S. Kitayama. & H. Azuma (Eds.), [*Cultural psychology: Theory and research*] (pp. 109–127). Tokyo: University of Tokyo

Press. (In Japanese; Cited in Kitayama & Markus, 1999)

KLINGER, M.R., & GREENWALD, A.G. (1995). Unconscious priming of association judgments. *Journal of Experimental Psychology: Learning, Memory, and Cognition, 21*, 569–581.

KNUTSON, B., WOLKOWITZ, O.M., COLE, S.W., CHAN, T., MOORE, E.A., JOHNSON, R.C., et al. (1998). Selective alteration of personality and social behavior by serotonergic intervention. *American Journal of Psychiatry, 155*, 373–378.

KOESTNER, R., LEKES, N., POWERS, T.A., & CHICOINE, E. (2002). Attaining personal goals: Concordance plus implementation intentions equals success. *Journal of Personality and Social Psychology, 83*, 231–244.

KRANTZ, D.S., & MANUCK, S.B. (1984). Acute psychophysiologic reactivity and risk of cardiovascular disease: A review and methodologic critique. *Psychological Bulletin, 96*, 435–464.

KRASNER, L. (1971). The operant approach in behavior therapy. In A.E. Bergin & S.L. Garfield (Eds.), *Handbook of psychotherapy and behavior change* (pp. 612–652). New York: Wiley.

KROSNICK, J.A., BETZ, A.L., JUSSIM, L.J., & LYNN, A.R. (1992). Subliminal conditioning of attitudes. *Journal of Personality and Social Psychology, 18*, 152–162.

KUHL, J. (2000). A functional-design approach to motivation and volition: The dynamics of personality systems interactions. In M. Boekaerts, P.R. Pintrich, & M. Zeidner (Eds.), *Self-regulation: Directions and challenges for future research* (pp. 111–169). New York: Academic Press.

KUHL, J., & KOOLE, S.L. (2004). Workings of the will: A functional approach. In J. Greenberg, S.L. Koole, & T. Pyszczynski (Eds.), *Handbook of experimental existential psychology* (pp. 411–430). New York: Guilford Press.

KUNDA, Z. (1990). The case for motivated reasoning. *Psychological Bulletin, 108*, 480–498.

LAKOFF, G., & Johnson. M. (1999). *Philosophy in the flesh: The embodied mind and its challenge to Western thought*. New York: Basic Books.

LANDFIELD, A.W. (1971). *Personal construct systems in psychotherapy*. Chicago: Rand McNally.

LANDFIELD, A.W. (1982). A construction of fragmentation and unity. In J.C. Mancuso & J.R. Adams-Webber (Eds.), *The construing person* (pp. 198–221). New York: Praeger.

LANSFORD, J.E., et al. (2005). Physical discipline and children's adjustment: Cultural normativeness as a moderator. *Child Development, 76*, 1234–1246.

LAVINE, T.Z. (1984). *From Socrates to Sartre: The philosophic quest*. New York: Bantam Books.

LAZARUS, A.A. (1965). Behavior therapy, incomplete treatment and symptom substitution. *Journal of Nervous and Mental Disease, 140*, 80–86.

LAZARUS, R.S. (1990). Theory-based stress measurement. *Psychological Inquiry, 1*, 3–13.

LAZARUS, R.S. (1991). *Emotion and adaptation*. New York: Oxford University Press.

LAZARUS, R.S. (1993). From psychological stress to the emotions: A history of changing outlooks. *Annual Review of Psychology, 44*, 1–21.

LEARY, M.R., & TANGNEY, J.P. (2002). (Eds.). *Handbook of self and identity*. New York: Guilford Press.

LECKY, P. (1945). *Self-consistency: A theory of personality*. New York: Island.

LEDOUX, J.L. (1995). Emotion: Clues from the brain. *Annual Review of Psychology, 46*, 209–235.

LEDOUX, J. (1999). The power of emotions. In R. Conlan (Ed.), *States of mind* (pp. 123–149). New York: Wiley.

LEWIS, M. (2002). Models of development. Cervone, D. & Mischel, W. (EDS.), *Advances in personality science* (pp. 153–176). New York: Guilford Press.

LEWIS, M., FEIRING, C., MCGUFFOG, C., & JASKIR, J. (1984). Predicting psychopathology in six year olds from early social relations. *Child Development, 55*, 123–136.

LEWONTIN, R. (2000). *The triple helix: Gene, organism, and environment*. Cambridge, MA: Harvard University Press.

LILIENFELD, S.O., WOOD, J.M., & GARB, H.N. (2000). The scientific status of projective techniques. *Psychological Science in the Public Interest, 1*, (whole issue).

LINVILLE, P. (1985). Self-complexity and affective extremity: Don't put all your eggs in one basket. *Social Cognition, 3*, 94–120.

LINVILLE, P. (1987). Self-complexity as a cognitive buffer against stress-related illness and depression. *Journal of Personality and Social Psychology, 52*, 663–676.

LITTLE, B.R. (1999). Personality and motivation: Personal action and the conative revolution. In L.A. Pervin & O.P. John (Eds.), *Handbook of personality: Theory and research* (pp. 501–524). New York: Guilford.

LITTLE, B.R. (2000). Free traits and personal contexts: Expanding a social ecological model of well-being. In W.B. Walsh, K.H. Craik, & R. Price (Eds.), *Person environment psychology* (2nd edition, pp. 87–116). New York: Guilford.

LITTLE, B.R. (2006). Personality science and self-regulation: Personal projects as integrative units.

Applied Psychology: An International Review, 55, 419–427.

LOCKE, E.A., & LATHAM, G.P. (1990). *A theory of goal setting and task performance.* Englewood Cliffs, NJ: Prentice-Hall.

LOCKE, E.A., & LATHAM, G.P. (2002). Building a practically useful theory of goal setting and task motivation: A 35–year odyssey. *American Psychologist, 57*, 705–717.

LOEHLIN, J.C. (1982). Rhapsody in G. *Contemporary Psychology, 27*, 623.

LOEHLIN, J.C. (1992). *Genes and environment in personality development.* Newbury Park, CA: Sage.

LOEHLIN, J.C., MCCRAE, R.R., COSTA, P.T., & JOHN, O. P. (1998). Heritabilities of common and measure specific components of the Big Five personality factors. *Journal of Research in Personality, 32*, 431–453.

LOEHLIN, J.C., & NICHOLS, R.C. (1976). *Heredity, environment, and personality: A study of 850 sets of twins.* Austin, TX: University of Texas Press.

LOEVINGER, J. (1993). Measurement in personality: True or false. *Psychological Inquiry, 4*, 1–16.

LUCAS, R.E., DIENER, E., GROB, A., SUH, E.M., & SHAO, L. (2000). Cross-cultural evidence for the fundamental features of extraversion. *Journal of Personality and Social Psychology, 79*, 452–468.

LYKKEN, D.T., BOUCHARD, T.J., JR., MCGUE, M., & TELLEGEN, A. (1993). Heritability of interests: A twin study. *Journal of Applied Psychology, 78*, 649–661.

LYNAM, D.R., CASPI, A., MOFFIT, T.E., WIKSTROEM, P., LOEBER, R., & NOVAK, S. (2000). The interaction between impulsivity and neighborhood context on offending: The effects of impulsivity are stronger in poorer neighborhoods. *Journal of Abnormal Psychology, 109*, 563–574.

MACKENZIE, K.R. (1994). Using personality measurements in clinical practice. In P.T. Costa, Jr. & T.A. Widiger (Eds.), *Personality disorders and the five-factor model of personality* (pp. 237–250). Washington, DC: American Psychological Association.

MAGNUSSON, D. (1999). Holistic interactionism: A perspective for research on personality development. In L.A. Pervin & O.P. John (Eds.), *Handbook of personality: Theory and research* (pp. 219–247). New York: Guilford.

MANCUSO, J.C., & ADAMS-WEBBER, J.R. (Eds.). (1982). *The construing person.* New York: Praeger.

MANUCK, S.B., BLEIL, M.E., PETERSEN, K.L., FLORY, J.D., MANN, J.J., FERRELL, R.E., & MULDOON, M.F. (2005). The socio-economic status of communities predicts variation in brain serotonergic responsivity. *Psychological Medicine, 35*, 519–528.

MARCIA, J. (1994). Ego identity and object relations. In J.M. Masling & R.F. Bornstein (Eds.), *Empirical perspectives on object relations theory*, (pp. 59–104). Washington, DC: American Psychological Association.

MARKUS, H. (1977). Self-schemata and processing information about the self. *Journal of Personality and Social Psychology, 35*, 63–78.

MARKUS, H. (1983). Self-knowledge: An expanded view. *Journal of Personality, 51*, 543–565.

MARKUS, H., & KITAYAMA, S. (1991). Culture and the self: Implications for cognition, emotion, and motivation. *Psychological Review, 98*, 224–253.

MARKUS, H.R., UCHIDA, Y., OMOREGIE, H., TOWNSEND, S.S. M., & KITAYAMA, S. (2006). Going for the gold: Models of agency in Japanese and American contexts. *Psychological Science, 17*, 103–112.

MARKUS, H., & WURF, E. (1987). The dynamic self-concept: A social psychological perspective. *Annual Review of Psychology, 38*, 299–337.

MASLOW, A.H. (1954). *Motivation and personality.* New York: Harper.

MASLOW, A.H. (1968). *Toward a psychology of being.* Princeton, NJ: Van Nostrand.

MASLOW, A.H. (1971). *The farther reaches of human nature.* New York: Viking.

MATTHEWS, G. (1997). The Big Five as a framework for personality assessment. In N. Anderson & P. Herriot (Eds.), *International handbook of selection and assessment*, (pp. 475–492). Chichester, UK: Wiley.

MAY, E.R., & ZELIKOW, P.D. (1997). (Eds.). *The Kennedy tapes: Inside the White House during the Cuban missile crisis.* Cambridge, MA: Harvard University Press.

MAYO, C.W., & CROCKETT, W.H. (1964). Cognitive complexity and primacy; recency effects in impression formation. *Journal of Abnormal and Social Psychology, 68*, 335–338.

MCADAMS, D.P. (1994). A psychology of the stranger. *Psychological Inquiry, 5*, 145–148

MCADAMS, D.P. (2006). *The redemptive self: Stories Americans live by.* Oxford University Press.

MCCAUL, K.D., GLADUE, B.A., & JOPPE, M. (1992). Winning, losing, mood, and testosterone. *Hormones and Behavior, 26*, 486–504.

MCCLELLAND, D., KOESTNER, R., & WEINBERGER, J. (1989). How do self-attributed and implicit motives differ? *Psychological Review, 96*, 690–702.

MCCOY, M.M. (1981). Positive and negative emotion: A personal construct theory interpretation. In H. Bonarius, R. Holland, & S. Rosenberg (Eds.), *Personal construct psychology: Recent advances in theory and practice* (pp. 96–104). London: Macmillan.

MCCRAE, R.R. (1996). Social consequences of experiential openness. *Psychological Bulletin, 120,* 323–337.

MCCRAE, R. (2002). The maturation of personality psychology: Adult personality development and psychological well-being. *Journal of Research in Personality, 36,* 307–317.

MCCRAE, R.R., & COSTA, P.T. (1987). Validation of the five-factor model of personality across instruments and observers. *Journal of Personality and Social Psychology, 52,* 81–90.

MCCRAE, R.R., & COSTA, P.T., JR. (1990). *Personality in adulthood.* New York: Guilford Press.

MCCRAE, R.R., & COSTA, P.T., JR. (1994). The stability of personality: Observations and evaluations. *Current Directions in Psychological Science, 3,* 173–175.

MCCRAE, R.R., & COSTA, P.T. (1996). Toward a new generation of personality theories: theoretical contexts for the five-factor model. In J.S. Wiggins (Ed.), *The five-factor model of personality. Theoretical perspectives* (pp. 51–87). New York: Guilford.

MCCRAE, R.R., & COSTA, P.T. (1997). Personality trait structure as a human universal. *American Psychologist, 52,* 509–516.

MCCRAE, R.R., & COSTA, P.T., JR., (1999). A Five-factor Theory of Personality. In L.A. Pervin & O.P. John (Eds.), *Handbook of Personality: Theory and Research* (pp. 139–153). New York: Guilford.

MCCRAE, R.R., COSTA, P.T., OSTENDORF, F., ANGLEITNER, A., HREBICKOVA, M., AVIA, M.D., et al. (2000). Nature over nurture: Temperament, personality, and lifespan development. *Journal of Personality and Social Psychology, 78,* 173–186.

MCCRAE, R.R., YIK, S.M., TRAPNELL, P.D., BOND, M. H., & PAULHUS, D.L. (1998). Interpreting personality profiles across cultures: Bilingual, acculturation, and peer rating studies of Chinese undergraduates. *Journal of Personality and Social Psychology, 74,* 1041–1055.

MCGREGOR, I., & LITTLE, B.R. (1998). Personal projects, happiness, and meaning: On doing well and being yourself. *Journal of Personality and Social Psychology, 74,* 494–512.

MCGINNIES, E. (1949). Emotionality and perceptual defense. *Psychological Review, 56,* 244–251.

MCMILLAN, M. (2004). *The person-centred approach to therapeutic change.* London: Sage.

MEDINNUS, G.R., & CURTIS, F.J. (1963). The relation between maternal self-acceptance and child acceptance. *Journal of Consulting Psychology, 27,* 542–544.

MEEHL, P. (1992). Factors and taxa, traits and types, differences of degree and differences in kind. *Journal of Personality, 60,* 117–174.

MEICHENBAUM, D. (1995). Cognitive-behavioral therapy in historical perspective. In B. Bongar & L.E. Bentler (Eds.), *Comprehensive textbook of psychotherapy.* (pp. 140–158). New York: Oxford University Press.

MENAND, L. (2002). *The metaphysical club: A story of ideas in America.* New York: Farrar, Straus, & Giroux.

MENAND, L. (Nov. 25, 2002). What comes naturally: Does evolution explain who we are? *The New Yorker.*

MENDEL, G. (1865/1966). Experiments on plant hybrids. In C. Stern & E.R. Sherwood (Eds.), *The origin of genetics: A Mendel source book.* San Francisco: Freeman.

MESTON, C.M., RELLINI, A.H., & HEIMAN, J.R. (2006). Women's history of sexual abuse, their sexuality, and sexual self-schemas. *Journal of Consulting and Clinical Psychology, 74,* 229–236.

METCALFE, J., & MISCHEL, W. (1999). A hot/cool-system analysis of delay of gratification: Dynamics of willpower. *Psychological Review, 106,* 3–19.

MILGRAM, S. (1965). Some conditions of obedience and disobedience to authority. *Human Relations, 18,* 57–76.

MILLER, J.G. (1984). Culture and the development of everyday social explanation. *Journal of Personality and Social Psychology, 46,* 961–978.

MILLER, L.C., PUTCHA-BHAGAVATULA, A., & PEDERSEN, W.C. (2002). Men's and women's mating preferences: Distinct evolutionary mechanisms? *Current Directions in Psychological Science, 11,* 88–93.

MILLER, S.M., SHODA, Y., & HURLEY, K. (1996). Applying cognitive-social theory to health-protective behavior: Breast self-examination in cancer screening. *Psychological Bulletin, 119,* 70–94.

MILLER, T.R. (1991). Personality: A clinician's experience. *Journal of Personality Assessment, 57,* 415–433.

MINEKA, S., DAVIDSON, M., COOK, M., & KLEIR, R. (1984). Observational conditioning of snake fear in rhesus monkeys. *Journal of Abnormal Psychology, 93,* 355–372.

MISCHEL, W. (1968). *Personality and assessment.* New York: Wiley.

MISCHEL, W. (1971). *Introduction to personality.* New York: Holt, Rinehart & Winston.

MISCHEL, W. (1973). Toward a cognitive social learning reconceptualization of personality. *Psychological Review, 80,* 252–283.

MISCHEL, W. (1974). Processes in delay of gratification. In L. Berkowitz (Ed.), *Advances in experimental social psychology* (Vol. 7, pp. 249–292). San Diego, CA: Academic Press.

MISCHEL, W. (1976). *Introduction to personality*. New York: Holt, Rinehart & Winston.

MISCHEL, W. (1990). Personality dispositions revisited and revised: A view after three decades. In L.A. Pervin (Ed.), *Handbook of personality: Theory and research* (pp. 111–134). New York: Guilford Press.

MISCHEL, W. (1999). Personality coherence and dispositions in a cognitive-affective processing system (CAPS) approach. In D. Cervone and Y. Shoda (Eds.), *The coherence of personality: Social-cognitive bases of consistency, variability, and organization* (pp. 37–60). New York: Guilford Press.

MISCHEL, W., & BAKER, N. (1975). Cognitive transformations of reward objects through instructions. *Journal of Personality and Social Psychology, 31,* 254–261.

MISCHEL, W., & EBBESEN, E.B. (1970). Attention in delay of gratification. *Journal of Personality and Social Psychology, 16,* 239–337.

MISCHEL, W., & LIEBERT, R.M. (1966). Effects of discrepancies between observed and imposed reward criteria on their acquisition and transmission. *Journal of Personality and Social Psychology, 3,* 45–53.

MISCHEL, W., & MOORE, B. (1973). Effects of attention to symbolically-presented rewards on self-control. *Journal of Personality and Social Psychology, 28,* 172–197.

MISCHEL, W., & MORF, C. (2002). The self as a psychosocial dynamic processing system: a meta-perspective on a century of the self in psychology. In M.R. Leary & J.P. Tangney (Eds.), *Handbook of self and identity* (pp. 15–43). New York: Guilford.

MISCHEL, W., & PEAKE, P.K. (1983). Analyzing the construction of consistency in personality. In M.M. Page (Ed.), *Personality: Current theory and research* (pp. 233–262). Lincoln, NE: University of Nebraska Press.

MISCHEL, W., & SHODA, Y. (1995). A cognitive-affective system theory of personality: Reconceptualizing the invariances in personality and the role of situations. *Psychological Review, 102,* 246–286.

MISCHEL, W., & SHODA, Y. (1998). Reconciling processing dynamics and personality dispositions. *Annual Review of Psychology, 49,* 229–258.

MISCHEL, W., & SHODA, Y. (1999). Integrating dispositions and processing dynamics within a unified theory of personality: The cognitive-affective personality system. In L.A. Pervin, & O.P. John (Eds.), *Handbook of personality: Theory and research* (pp. 197–218). New York: Guilford.

MOHAMMED, S. (2001). Personal communication networks and the effects of an entertainment-education radio soap opera in Tanzania. *Journal of Health Communication, 6,* 137–154.

MOORE, B., MISCHEL, W., & ZEISS, A.R. (1976). Comparative effects of the reward stimulus and its cognitive representation in voluntary delay. *Journal of Personality and Social Psychology, 34,* 419–424.

MOORE, M.K., & NEIMEYER, R.A. (1991). A confirmatory factor analysis of the threat index. *Journal of Personality and Social Psychology, 60,* 122–129.

MORF, C.C., & RHODEWALT, F. (2001). Unraveling the paradoxes of narcissism: A dynamic self-regulatory processing model. *Psychological Inquiry, 12,* 177–196.

MORGAN, M. (1985). Self-monitoring of attained subgoals in private study. *Journal of Educational Psychology, 77,* 623–630.

MORGAN, M., & MORRISON, M. (Eds.) (1999). *Models as mediators*. New York: Cambridge University Press.

MORRIS, M.W., & PENG, K. (1994). Culture and cause: American and Chinese attributions for social and physical events. *Journal of Personality and Social Psychology, 67,* 949–971.

MORRISON, J.K., & COMETA, M.C. (1982). Variations in developing construct systems: The experience corollary. In J.C. Mancusco & J.R. Adams-Webber (Eds.), The construing person (pp. 152–169). New York: Praeger.

MOSKOWITZ, D.S., & HERSCHBERGER, S.L. (Eds.) (2002). *Modeling intraindividual variability with repeated measures data: Methods and applications*. Mahwah, NJ: Lawrence Erlbaum Associates.

MOSKOWITZ, D.S., & ZUROFF, D.C. (2005). Robust predictors of flux, pulse, and spin. *Journal of Research in Personality, 39,* 130–147.

MOSS, P.D., & MCEVEDY, C.P. (1966). An epidemic of over-breathing among school-girls. *British Medical Journal, 2,* 1295–1300.

MURPHY, G. (1958). *Human potentialities*. New York: Basic Books.

MURRAY, H.A. (1938). *Explorations in personality*. New York: Oxford University Press.

NASH, M. (1999). The psychological unconscious. In V. J. Derlega. B.A. Winstead, & W.H. Jones, (Eds.), *Personality: Contemporary theory and research* (pp. 197–228). Chicago: Nelson-Hall.

NEIMEYER, G.J. (1992). Back to the future with the psychology of personal constructs. *Contemporary Psychology, 37,* 994–997.

NEIMEYER, R.A. (1994). *Death anxiety handbook: Research, instrumentation, and application*. Washington, DC: Taylor & Francis.

NEIMEYER, R.A., & NEIMEYER, G.J. (Eds.) (1992). *Advances in personal construct psychology* (Vol. 2). Greenwich, CT: JAI Press.

NESSELROADE, J.R., & DELHEES, K.H. (1966). Methods and findings in experimentally based personality theory. In R.B. Cattell (Ed.), *Handbook of multivariate experimental psychology* (pp. 563–610). Chicago: Rand McNally. Newsweek Magazine (March 27, 2006). Freud is *not* dead. (Cover story headline.)

NICHOLSON, I.A. M. (2002). *Inventing personality: Gordon Allport and the science of selfhood*. Washington, D C: American Psychological Society.

NIEDENTHAL, P.M., BARSALOU, L., WINKIELMAN, P., KRAUTH-GRUBER, S., & RIC, F. (2005). Embodiment in attitudes, social perception, and emotion. *Personality and Social Psychology Review, 9*, 184–211.

NISBETT, R. (2003). *The geography of thought: How Asians and Westerners think differently*. New York: Free Press.

NISBETT, R.E., PENG, K., CHOI, I., & NORENZAYAN, A. (2001). Culture and systems of thought: Holistic versus analytic cognition. *Psychological Review, 108*, 291–310.

NISBETT, R., & ROSS, L. (1980). *Human inference: Strategies and shortcomings of social judgment*. Englewood Cliffs, NJ: Prentice Hall.

NISBETT, R.E., & WILSON, T.D. (1977). Telling more than we know: Verbal reports on mental processes. Psychological Review, 84, 231–279.

NOREM, J.K. (2001). *The positive power of negative thinking: Using defensive pessimism to manage anxiety and perform at your peak*. New York: Basic Books.

NORMAN, W.T. (1963). Toward an adequate taxonomy of personality attributes. *Journal of Abnormal and Social Psychology, 66*, 574–583.

NOWAK, A., VALLACHER, R.R., & ZOCHOWSKI, M. (2002). The emergence of personality: Personality stability through interpersonal synchronization. In D. Cervone & W. Mischel (eds.), *Advances in personality science* (pp. 292–331). New York: Guilford.

NOZICK, R. (1981). *Philosophical explanations*. Cambridge, MA: Belknap Press of Harvard University Press.

OHMAN, A., & SOARES, J.F. (1993). On the automaticity of phobic fear: Conditional skin conductance responses to masked phobic stimuli. *Journal of Abnormal Psychology, 102*, 121–132.

O'LEARY, A. (1990). Stress, emotion, and human immune function. *Psychological Bulletin, 108*, 363–382.

O'LEARY, A. (1992). Self-efficacy and health: Behavioral and stress-physiological mediation. *Cognitive Therapy and Research, 16*, 229–245.

O'LEARY, K.D. (1972). The assessment of psychopathology in children. In H.C. Quay & J.S. Werry (Eds.), *Psychopathological disorders of childhood* (pp. 234–272). New York: Wiley.

ORNE, M.T. (1962). On the social psychology of the psychological experiment: With particular reference to demand characteristics and their implications. *American Psychologist, 17*, 776–783.

ORR, H.A. (Feb. 27, 2003). Darwinian storytelling. *The New York Review of Books, 50*, 17–20.

OSGOOD, C.E., & LURIA, Z. (1954). A blind analysis of a case of multiple personality using the semantic differential. *Journal of Abnormal and Social Psychology, 49*, 579–591.

OSGOOD, C.E., SUCI, G.J., & TANNENBAUM, P.H. (1957). *The measurement of meaning*. Urbana, IL: University of Illinois Press.

OSOFSKY, M.J., BANDURA, A., & ZIMBARDO, P. (2005). The role of moral disengagement in the execution process. *Law and Human Behavior, 29*, 371–393.

OZER, D.J. (1999). Four principles for personality assessment. In L.A. Pervin & O.P. John (Eds.), *Handbook of personality: Theory and research* (pp. 671–686). New York: Guilford.

OZER, E., & BANDURA, A. (1990). Mechanisms governing empowerment effects: A self-efficacy analysis. *Journal of Personality and Social Psychology, 58*, 472–486.

PARANJPE, A.C. (1998). *Self and identity in modern psychology and Indian thought*. New Nork: Plenum.

PARK, R. (2004). Development in the family. *Annual Review of Psychology, 55*, 365–399.

PAULHUS, D.L., FRIDHANDLER, B., & HAYES, S. (1997). Psychological defense: Contemporary theory and research (pp. 544–579). In R. Hogan, J. Johnson., & S. Briggs (Eds.), *Handbook of personality psychology* (pp. 543–579). San Diego, CA: Academic Press.

PAULHUS, D.L., TRAPNELL, P.D., & CHEN, D. (1999). Birth order effects on personality and achievement within families. *Psychological Science, 10*, 482–488.

PAVLOV, I.P. (1927). *Conditioned reflexes*. London: Oxford University Press.

PAVOT, W., FUJITA, F., & DIENER, E. (1997). The relation between self-aspect congruence, personality and subjective well-being. *Personality & Individual Differences, 22*, 183–191.

PENNEBAKER, J.W. (1985). Traumatic experience and psychosomatic disease: Exploring the roles of behavioral inhibition, obsession, and confiding. *Canadian Psychology, 26*, 82–95.

PENNEBAKER, J.W. (1990). *Opening up: The healing powers of confiding in others*. New York: Morrow.

PERVIN, L.A. (1964). Predictive strategies and the need to confirm them: Some notes on pathological types of decisions. *Psychological Reports, 15*, 99–105.

PERVIN, L.A. (1967a). A twenty-college study of student/college interaction using TAPE (Transactional Analysis of Personality and Environment): Rationale, reliability, and validity. *Journal of Educational Psychology, 58,* 290–302.

PERVIN, L.A. (1967b). Satisfaction and perceived self environment similarity: A semantic differential study of student-college interaction. *Journal of Personality, 35,* 623–634.

PERVIN, L.A. (1983). Idiographic approaches to personality. In J. McV. Hunt & N. Endler (Eds.), *Personality and the behavior disorders* (pp. 261–282). New York: Wiley.

PERVIN, L.A. (1994). A critical analysis of current trait theory. *Psychological Inquiry, 5,* 103–113.

PERVIN, L.A. (1999). Epilogue: Constancy and change in personality theory and research. In L.A. Pervin & O.P. John (Eds.), *Handbook of personality: Theory and research* (pp. 689–704). New York: Guilford.

PERVIN, L.A. (2003). *The science of personality* (2nd ed.). London: Oxford University Press.

PETRIE, K.J., BOOTH, R.J., & PENNEBAKER, J.W. (1998). The immunological effects of thought suppression. *Journal of Personality and Social Psychology, 75,* 1264–1272.

PFUNGST, O. (1911). *Clever Hans: A contribution to experimental, animal, and human psychology.* New York: Holt, Rinehart & Winston.

PICKERING, A.D., & GRAY, J.A. (1999). The neuroscience of personality. In L.A. Pervin & O.P. John (Eds.), *Handbook of personality: Theory and research* (pp. 277–299). New York: Guilford.

PIETRZAK, J., DOWNEY, G., & AYDUK, O. (2005). Rejection sensitivity as an interpersonal vulnerability. In M.W. Baldwin (Ed.), *Interpersonal cognition* (pp. 62–84). New York: Guilford Press.

PINKER, S. (1997). *How the mind works.* New York: Norton.

PINKER, S. (1999). *Words and rules: The ingredients of language.* New York: Basic Books.

PINKER, S. (2002). *The blank slate: The modern denial of human nature.* New York: Viking.

PLAUT, V.C., MARKUS, H.R., & LACHMAN, M.E. (2002). Place matters: Consensual features and regional variation in American well-being and self. *Journal of Personality and Social Psychology, 83,* 160–184.

PLOMIN, R. (1990). *Nature and nurture.* Pacific Grove, CA: Brooks/Cole.

PLOMIN, R. (1994). *Genetics and experience: The interplay between nature and nurture.* Newbury Park, CA: Sage.

PLOMIN, R., & CASPI, A. (1999). Behavioral genetics and personality. In L.A. Pervin & O.P. John (Eds.),

Handbook of personality: Theory and research (pp. 251–276). New York: Guilford.

PLOMIN, R., CHIPUER, H.M., & LOEHLIN, J.C. (1990). Behavioral genetics and personality. In L.A. Pervin (Ed.), *Handbook of personality: Theory and research* (pp. 225–243). New York: Guilford Press.

PLOMIN, R., & DANIELS, D. (1987). Why are children in the same family so different from each other? *Behavioral and Brain Sciences, 10,* 1–16.

PLOMIN, R., & NEIDERHISER, J.M. (1992). Genetics and experience. *Current Directions in Psychological Science, 1,* 160–163.

PLOTNIK, J.M., de WAAL, F.B.M., & Reiss, D (2006). Self-recognition in an Asian elephant. *Proceedings of the National Academy of Sciences, 103,* 17053–17057.

POLKINGHORNE, D. (1988). *Narrative knowing and the human sciences.* Albany, NY: State University of New York Press.

PONOMAREV, I., & CRABBE, J.C. (1999). Genetic association between chronic ethanol withdrawal severity and acoustic startle parameters in WSP and WSR mice. *Alcoholism: Clinical & Experimental Research, 23,* 1730–1735.

POWELL, R.A., & BOER, D.P. (1994). Did Freud mislead patients to confabulate memories of abuse? *Psychological Reports, 74,* 1283–1298.

PROCTOR, R.W., & CAPALDI E.J. (2001). Empirical evaluation and justification of methodologies in psychological science. *Psychological Bulletin, 127,* 759–772.

PULKKINEN, L., & CASPI, A. (Eds.) (2002). *Paths to successful development: Personality in the life course.* New York: Cambridge University Press.

RAFAELI-MOR, E., & STEINBERG, J. (2002). Self-complexity and well-being: A Review and Research Synthesis. *Personality and Social Psychology Review, 6,* 31–58.

RÄIKKÖNON, K., MATTHEWS, K.A., & SALOMON, K. (2003). Hostility predicts metabolic syndrome risk factors in children and adolescents. *Health Psychology, 22,* 279–286.

RALEIGH, M.J., & MCGUIRE, M.T. (1991). Bidirectional relationships between tryptophan and social behavior in vervet monkeys. *Advances in Experimental Medicine and Biology, 294,* 289–298.

RASKIN, R., & HALL, C.S. (1979). A narcissistic personality inventory. *Psychological Reports, 45,* 590.

RASKIN, R., & HALL, C.S. (1981). The Narcissistic Personality Inventory: Alternate form reliability and further evidence of construct validity. *Journal of Personality Assessment, 45,* 159–162.

RASKIN, R., & SHAW, R. (1987). *Narcissism and the use of personal pronouns.* Unpublished manuscript.

RASKIN, R., & TERRY, H. (1987). *A factor-analytic study of the Narcissistic Personality Inventory and further evidence of its construct validity.* Unpublished manuscript.

REISS, D. (1997). Mechanisms linking genetic and social influences in adolescent development: Beginning a collaborative search. *Current Directions in Psychological Science, 6*, 100–105.

REISS, D., NEIDERHISER, J., HETHERINGTON, E.M., & PLOMIN, R. (1999). *The relationship code: Deciphering genetic and social patterns in adolescent development.* Cambridge, MA: Harvard University Press.

REYNOLDS, G.S. (1968). *A primer of operant conditioning.* Glenview, IL: Scott, Foresman.

RHODEWALT, F., & MORF, C.C. (1995). Self and interpersonal correlates of the Narcissistic Personality Inventory: A review and new findings. *Journal of Research in Personality, 29*, 1–23.

RHODEWALT, F., & SORROW, D.L. (2002). Interpersonal self-regulation: Lessons from the study of narcissism. In M.R. Leary & J.P. Tangney (Eds.), *Handbook of self and identity* (pp. 519–535). New York: Guilford.

RICOEUR, P. (1970). *Freud and philosophy.* (D. Savage, trans.). New Haven: Yale University Press.

RIDLEY, M. (2003). *Nature via nurture: Genes, experience, and what makes us human.* New York: Harper Collins.

RIEMANN, R., ANGLEITNER, A., & STRELAU, J. (1997). Genetic and environmental influences on personality: A study of twins reared together using the self and peer report NEO-FFI scales. *Journal of Personality, 65*, 449–476.

ROBERTS, B.W. (1997). Plaster or plasticity: Are adult work experiences associated with personality change in women? *Journal of Personality, 65*, 205–232.

ROBERTS, B.W., & CHAPMAN, C.N. (2000). Change in dispositional well-being and its relation to role quality: A 30–year longitudinal study. *Journal of Research in Personality, 34*, 26–41.

ROBERTS, B.W., & DEL VECCHIO, W.F. (2000). The rank-order consistency of personality traits from childhood to old age: A quantitative review of longitudinal studies. *Psychological Bulletin, 126*, 3–25.

ROBERTS, B.W., & HOGAN, R. (Eds.). (2001). *Personality in the workplace.* Washington, DC: American Psychological Association.

ROBERTS, J.A., GOTLIB, I.H., & KASSEL, I.D. (1996). Adult attachment security and symptoms of depression: The mediating roles of dysfunctional attitudes and low self-esteem. *Journal of Personality and Social Psychology, 70*, 310–320.

ROBINS, C.J., & HAYES, A.M. (1993). An appraisal of cognitive therapy. *Journal of Consulting and Clinical Psychology, 61*, 205–214.

ROBINS, R.W., & JOHN, O.P. (1997). Self-perception, visual perspective, and narcissism: Is seeing believing? *Psychological Science, 8*, 37–42.

ROBINS, R.W., NOREM, J.K., & CHEEK, J.M. (1999). Naturalizing the self. In L.A. Pervin & O.P. John (Eds.), *Handbook of personality: Theory and research* (pp. 443–477). New York: Guilford.

ROBINSON, R.G., & DOWNHILL, J.E. (1995). Lateralization of psychopathology in response to focal brain injury. In R.J. Davidson & K. Hugdahl (Eds.), *Brain asymmetry* (pp. 693–711). Cambridge, MA: MIT Press.

ROCCAS, S., & BREWER, M. (2002). Social identity complexity. *Personality & Social Psychology Review, 6*, 88–106.

ROGERS, C.R. (1951). *Client-centered therapy.* Boston: Houghton Mifflin.

ROGERS, C.R. (1954). The case of Mrs. Oak: A research analysis. In C.R. Rogers & R.F. Dymond (Eds.), *Psychotherapy and personality change* (pp. 259–348). Chicago: University of Chicago Press.

ROGERS, C.R. (1956). Some issues concerning the control of human behavior. *Science, 124*, 1057–1066.

ROGERS, C.R. (1959). A theory of therapy, personality, and interpersonal relationships as developed in the client-centered framework. In S. Koch (Ed.), *Psychology: A study of science* (pp. 184–256). New York: McGraw-Hill.

ROGERS, C.R. (1963). The actualizing tendency in relation to "motives" and to consciousness. In M.R. Jones (Ed.), *Nebraska symposium on motivation* (pp. 1–24). Lincoln, NE: University of Nebraska Press.

ROGERS, C.R. (1964). Toward a science of the person. In T.W. Wann (Ed.), *Behaviorism and phenomenology* (pp. 109–133). Chicago: University of Chicago Press.

ROGERS, C.R. (1966). Client-centered therapy. In S. Arieti (Ed.), *American handbook of psychiatry* (pp. 183–200). New York: Basic Books.

ROGERS, C.R. (1970). *On encounter groups.* New York: Harper.

ROGERS, C.R. (1977). *Carl Rogers on personal power.* New York: Delacorte Press.

ROGERS, C.R. (1980). *A way of being.* Boston: Houghton Mifflin.

ROGERS, T.B., KUIPER, N.A., & KIRKER, W.S. (1977). Self-reference and the encoding of personal information. *Journal of Personality and Social Psychology, 35*, 677–688.

RORER, L.G. (1990). Personality assessment: A conceptual survey. In L.A. Pervin (Ed.), *Handbook of Personality: Theory and Research* (pp. 693–720). New York: Guilford.

ROSENBERG, S. (1980). A theory in search of its zeitgeist. *Contemporary Psychology, 25,* 898–900.

ROSENTHAL, R. (1994). Interpersonal expectancy effects: A 30–year perspective. *Current Directions in Psychological Science, 3,* 176–179.

ROSENTHAL, R., & RUBIN, D. (1978). Interpersonal expectancy effects: The first 345 studies. *Behavioral and Brain Sciences, 3,* 377–415.

ROSENTHAL, T., & BANDURA, A. (1978). Psychological modeling: Theory and practice. In S.L. Garfield & A. E. Bergin (Eds.), *Handbook of psychotherapy and behavior change* (pp. 621–658). New York: Wiley.

ROTHBARD, J.C. & SHAVER, P.R. (1994). Continuity of attachment across the life-span. In M. B, Sperling & W.H. Berman (Eds.), *Attachment in adults: Clinical and developmental perspectives* (pp. 31–71). New York: Guilford Press.

ROTHBART, M.K., AHADI, S.A., & EVANS, D.E. (2000). Temperament and personality: Origins and outcomes. *Journal of Personality and Social Psychology, 78,* 122–135.

ROTHBART, M.K., & BATES, J.E. (1998). Temperament. In W. Damon (Ed.), *Handbook of child psychology: Vol. 3. Social, emotional, and personality development* (5th ed., pp. 105–176). New York: Wiley.

ROTHBART, M.K., ELLIS, L.K., RUEDA, M.R., & POSNER, M.I. (2003). Developing mechanisms of temperamental effortful control. *Journal of Personality, 71,* 1113–1143.

ROWE, D.C. (1999). Heredity. In V.J. Derlega, B.A. Winstead, & Jones, W.H. (EDS.), *Personality: Contemporary theory and research* (pp. 66–100). Chicago: Nelson-Hall.

ROZIN, P., & ZELLNER, D. (1985). The role of Pavlovian conditioning in the acquisition of food likes and dislikes. *Annals of the New York Academy of Sciences, 443,* 189–202.

RUGGIERO, K.M., & MARX, D.M. (2001). "Less pain and more to gain: Why high-status group members blame their failure on discrimination": Retraction. *Journal of Personality & Social Psychology, 81,* 178.

RYAN, R.M. (1993). Agency and organization: Intrinsic motivation, autonomy, and the self in psychological development. In J. Jacobs (Ed.), *Nebraska symposium on motivation.*(Vol. 40). (pp. 1–56). Lincoln, NE: University of Nebraska Press.

RYAN, R.M., & DECI, E.L. (2000). Self-determination theory and the facilitation of intrinsic motivation, social development, and well-being. *American Psychologist, 55,* 68–78.

RYFF, C.D. (1995). Psychological well-being in adult life. *Current Directions in Psychological Science, 4,* 99–104.

RYFF, C.D., & SINGER, B. (1998). The contours of positive human health. *Psychological Inquiry, 9,* 1–28.

RYFF, C.D., & SINGER, B. (2000). Interpersonal flourishing: A positive health agenda for the new millennium. *Personality and Social Psychology Review, 4,* 30–44.

SANDERSON, C., & CLARKIN, J.F. (1994). Use of the NEO-PI personality dimensions in differential treatment planning. In P.T. Costa, Jr. & T.A. Widiger (Eds.), *Personality disorders and the five-factor model of personality* (pp. 219–236). Washington, DC: American Psychological Association.

SANFREY, A.G., RILLING, J.K., ARONSON, J.A., NYSTROM, L.E., & COHEN, J.D. (2003). The neural basis of economic decision-making in the Ultimatum game. *Science, 300,* 1755–1758.

SAPOLSKY, R.M. (1994). *Why zebras don't get ulcers.* New York: W.H. Freeman.

SAUCIER, G. (1997). Effects of variable selection on the factor structure of person descriptors. *Journal of Personality & Social Psychology, 73,* 1296–1312.

SAUCIER, G., & GOLDBERG, L.R. (1996). Evidence for the Big Five in analyses of familiar English personality adjectives. *European Journal of Personality, 10,* 61–77.

SAUCIER, G., & GOLDBERG, L.R. (2001). Lexical studies of undigenous personality factors: Premises, products, and prospects. *Journal of Personality, 69,* 847–880.

SAUCIER, G., HAMPSON, S.E., & GOLDBERG, L.R. (2000). Cross-language studies of lexical personality factors. In S.E. Hampson (Ed.), *Advances in personality psychology* (Vol. 1, p. 1–36). East Sussex, UK: Psychology Press, Ltd.

SAUDINO, K. (1997). Moving beyond the heritability question: New directions in behavioral genetic studies of personality. *Current Directions in Psychological Science, 6,* 86–90.

SCHAFER, R. (1954). *Psychoanalytic interpretation in Rorschach testing.* New York: Grune & Stratton.

SCHEIER, M.F., & CARVER, C.S. (1985). Optimism, coping, and health: Assessment and implications of generalized outcome expectancies. *Health Psychology, 4,* 219–247.

SCHMIDT, L.A., & FOX, N.A. (2002). Individual differences in childhood shyness: Origins, malleability, and developmental course. In D. Cervone & W. Mischel (Eds.), *Advances in personality science* (pp. 83–105). New York: Guilford Press.

SCHNEIDER, D.J. (1982). Personal construct psychology: An international menu. *Contemporary Psychology, 27,* 712–713.

SCHUNK, D.H., & COX, P.D. (1986). Strategy training and attributional feedback with learning disabled students. *Journal of Educational Psychology, 1986, 78,* 201–209.

SCHWARTZ, C.E., WRIGHT, C.I., SHIN, L.M., KAGAN, J., & RAUCH, S.L. (2003). Inhibited and uninhibited children "grown up": Amygdalar response to novelty. *Science, 300,* 1952–1953.

SCHWARZ, N. (1999). Self-reports: How the questions shape the answers. *American Psychologist, 54,* 93–105.

SCHWARZER, R. (Ed.) (1992). *Self-efficacy: Thought control of action.* Washington, DC: Hemisphere.

SCOTT, J.P., & FULLER, J.L. (1965). *Genetics and the social behavior of the dog.* Chicago: University of Chicago Press.

SCOTT, W.D., & CERVONE, D. (2002). The impact of negative affect on performance standards: Evidence for an affect-as-information mechanism. *Cognitive Therapy and Research, 26,* 19–37.

SECHREST, L. (1963). The psychology of personal constructs. In J.M. Wepman & R.W. Heine (Eds.), *Concepts of personality* (pp. 206–233). Chicago: Aldine.

SECHREST, L., & JACKSON, D.N. (1961). Social intelligence and accuracy of interpersonal predictions. *Journal of Personality, 29,* 167–182.

SEGAL, Z.V., & DOBSON, K.S. (1992). Cognitive models of depression: Report from a consensus development conference. *Psychological Inquiry, 3,* 219–224.

SELIGMAN, M.E.P., & CSIKSZENTMIHALYI, M. (2000). Positive psychology. *American Psychologist, 55,* 5–14.

SHADEL, W.G., & CERVONE, D. (2006). Evaluating social cognitive mechanisms that regulate self-efficacy in response to provocative smoking, to resist smoking in high risk situations: An experimental investigation. *Psychology of Addictive Behaviors, 20,* 91–96.

SHAH, J., & HIGGINS, E.T. (1997). Expectancy x value effects: Regulatory focus as a determinant of magnitude and direction. *Journal of Personality and Social Psychology, 73,* 447–458.

SHAVER, P.R., & MIKULINCER, M. (2005). Attachment theory and research: Resurrection of the psychodynamic approach to personality. *Journal of Research in Personality, 39,* 22–45.

SHEDLER, J., MAYMAN, M., & MANIS, M. (1993). The illusion of mental health. *American Psychologist, 48,* 1117–1131.

SHELDON, K.M., & ELLIOT, A.J. (1999). Goal striving, need satisfaction, and longitudinal well-being: The self-concordance model. *Journal of Personality and Social Psychology, 76,* 482–497.

SHELDON, K.M., RYAN, R.M., RAWSTHORNE, L.J., & ILARDI, B. (1997). Trait self and true self: Cross-role variation in the Big-Five personality traits and its relations with psychological authenticity and subjective well-being. *Journal of Personality and Social Psychology, 73,* 1380–1393.

SHELDON, W.H. (1940). *The varieties of human physique.* New York: Harper.

SHELDON, W.H. (1942). *Varieties of temperament.* New York: Harper.

SHINER, R.L. (1998). How shall we speak of children's personalities in middle childhood? A preliminary taxonomy. *Psychological Review, 124,* 308–332.

SHODA, Y. (1999). Behavioral expressions of a personality system: Generation and perception of behavioral signatures. In D. Cervone & Y. Shoda (Eds.), *The coherence of personality: Social-cognitive bases of consistency, variability, and organization* (pp. 155–181). New York: Guilford Press.

SHODA, Y., MISCHEL, W., & PEAKE, P.K. (1990). Predicting adolescent cognitive and self-regulatory competencies from preschool delay of gratification: Identifying diagnostic conditions. *Developmental Psychology, 26,* 978–986.

SHODA, Y., MISCHEL, W., & WRIGHT, J.C. (1994). Intraindividual stability in the organization and patterning of behavior: Incorporating psychological situations into the idiographic analysis of personality. *Journal of Personality and Social Psychology, 67,* 674–687.

SHOWERS, C.J. (2002). Integration and compartmentalization: A model of self-structure and self-change. In D. Cervone & W. Mischel (Eds.), *Advances in personality science* (pp. 271–291). New York: Guilford Press.

SHUMYATSKY, G P., MALLERET, G., SHIN, R., TAKIZAWA, S., TULLY, K., TSVETKOV, E., et al. (2005). *Stathmin,* a gene enriched in the amygdala, controls both learned and innate fear. *Cell, 123,* 697–709.

SHWEDER, R. A & SULLIVAN, M.A. (1990). The semiotic subject of cultural psychology. In L. Pervin (Ed.) *Handbook of Personality* (pp. 399–416). New York: Guilford.

SHWEDER, R.A., & SULLIVAN, M.A. (1993). Cultural psychology: Who needs it? *Annual Review of Psychology. 44* 1993, 497–523.

SIEGEL, S. (1984). Pavlovian conditioning and heroin overdose: Reports by overdose victims. *Bulletin of the Psychonomic Society, 22,* 428–430.

SIEGEL, S., HINSON, R.E., KRANK, M.D., & MCCULY, J. (1982). Heroin "overdose" death: Contribution of drug-associated environmental cues. *Science, 216,* 436–437.

SIGEL, I.E. (1981). Social experience in the development of representational thought: Distancing theory. In I.E. Sigel, D. Brodzinsky, & R. Golinkoff (Eds.), *New directions in Piagetian theory and practice* (pp. 203–217). Hillsdale, NJ: Erlbaum.

SILVERMAN, L.H. (1976). Psychoanalytic theory: The reports of its death are greatly exaggerated. *American Psychologist, 31,* 621–637.

SILVERMAN, L.H. (1982). A comment on two subliminal psychodynamic activation studies. *Journal of Abnormal Psychology, 91,* 126–130.

SILVERMAN, L.H., ROSS, D.L., ADLER, J.M., & LUSTIG, D.A. (1978). Simple research paradigm for demonstrating subliminal psychodynamic activation: Effects of oedipal stimuli on dart-throwing accuracy in college men. *Journal of Abnormal Psychology, 87,* 341–357.

SIMPSON, B., LARGE, B., & O'BRIEN, M. (2004). Bridging difference through dialogue: A constructivist perspective. *Journal of Constructivist Psychology,* 17, 45–59.

SIMPSON, J.A., & RHOLES, W.S. (1998). (Eds.) *Attachment theory and close relationships.* New York: Guilford.

SKINNER, B.F. (1948). *Walden two.* New York: Macmillan.

SKINNER, B.F. (1953). *Science and human behavior.* New York: Macmillan.

SKINNER, B.F. (1956). A case history in the scientific method. *American Psychologist, 11,* 221–233.

SKINNER, B.F. (1959). *Cumulative record.* New York: Appleton-Century-Crofts.

SKINNER, B.F. (1967). Autobiography. In E.G. Boring & G. Lindzey (Eds.), *A history of psychology in autobiography* (pp. 385–414).

SKINNER, B.F. (1971). *Beyond freedom and dignity.* New York: Knopf.

SKINNER, B.F. (1974). *About behaviorism.* New York: Knopf.

SMITH, D. (October, 2002). The theory heard 'round the world: Albert Bandura's social cognitive theory is the foundation of television and radio shows that have changed the lives of millions. APA *Monitor on Psychology, 33.*

SMITH, D. (January, 2003). Five principles for research ethics: Cover your bases with these ethical strategies. *Monitor on Psychology, 34,* 56.

SMITH, E.R. (1998). Mental representations and memory. In D.T. Gilbert, S.T. Fiske, & G. Lindzey (Eds.), *The handbook of social psychology* (4th ed.), (Vol. 1), (pp. 391–445). Boston: McGraw-Hill.

SMITH, R.E. (1989). Effects of coping skills training on generalized self-efficacy and locus of control. *Journal of Personality and Social Psychology, 56,* 228–233.

SOLOMON, R.C., & HIGGINS, K.M. (1996). *A short history of philosophy.* New York: Oxford university Press.

SOMER, O., & GOLDBERG, L.R. (1999). The structure of Turkish trait-descriptive adjectives. *Journal of Personality and Social Psychology, 76,* 431–450.

SPENCER, S.J., STEELE, C.M., & QUINN, D.M. (1999). Stereotype threat and women's math performance. *Journal of Experimental Social Psychology, 35,* 4–28.

SPERLING, M.B., & BERMAN, W.H. (Eds.) (1994). *Attachment in adults: Clinical and developmental perspectives.* New York: Guilford Press.

SPINOZA, B. (1677/1952). *Ethics.* (W.H. White, translator). Chicago: Encyclopedia Britannica.

SRIVASTAVA, S., JOHN, O.P., GOSLING, S.D., & POTTER, J. (2003). Development of personality in early and middle adulthood: Set like plaster or persistent change? *Journal of Personality and Social Psychology, 84,* 1041–1053.

SROUFE, L.A., CARLSON, E., & SHULMAN, S. (1993). Individuals in relationships: Development from infancy. In D.C. FUNDER, R.D. Parke, C. Tomlinson-Keasey, & K. Widaman (Eds.), *Studying lives through time* (pp. 315–342). Washington, DC: American Psychological Association.

STADDON, J.E. R., & CERUTTI, D.T. (2003). Operant conditioning. *Annual Review of Psychology, 54,* 115–144.

STAJKOVIC, A.D., & LUTHANS, F. (1998). Self-efficacy and work-related performance: A meta-analysis. *Psychological Bulletin, 124,* 240–261.

ST. CLAIR, M. (1986). *Object relations and self psychology: An introduction.* Monterey, CA: Brooks Cole.

STEELE, C.M. (1997). A threat in the air: How stereotypes shape intellectual identity and performance. *American Psychologist, 52,* 613–629.

STEINER. J.F. (1966). *Treblinka.* New York: Simon & Schuster.

STEPHENSON, W. (1953). *The study of behavior.* Chicago: University of Chicago Press.

STOCK, J., & CERVONE, D. (1990). Proximal goal-setting and self-regulatory processes. *Cognitive Therapy and Research, 14,* 483–498.

STONE, V.E., COSMIDES, L., TOOBY, J., KROLL, N., & KNIGHT, R.T. (2002). Selective impairment of reasoning about social exchange in a patient with bilateral limbic system damage. *Processing of the National Academy of Sciences, 99*, 11531–11536.

STRAUMAN, T.J. (1989). Self-discrepancies in clinical depression and social phobia: Cognitive structures that underlie emotional disorders? *Journal of Abnormal Psychology, 98*, 14–22.

STRAUMAN, T.J. (1990). Self-guides and emotionally significant childhood memories: A study of retrieval efficiency and incidental negative emotional content. *Journal of Personality and Social Psychology, 59*, 869–880.

STRAUMAN, T.J., KOLDEN, G.G., STROMQUIST, V., DAVIS, N., KWAPIL, L., HEEREY, E., & SCHNEIDER, K. (2001). The effects of treatments for depression on perceived failure in self-regulation. *Cognitive Therapy and Research, 25*, 693–712.

STRAUMAN, T.J., LEMIEUX, A.M., & COE, C.L. (1993). Self-discrepancy and natural killer cell activity: Immunological consequences of negative self-evaluation. *Journal of Personality and Social Psychology, 64*, 1042–1052.

STRELAU, J. (1997). The contribution of Pavlov's typology of CNS properties to personality research. *European Psychologist, 2*, 125–138.

STRELAU, J. (1998). *Temperament: A psychological perspective*. New York: Plenum Press.

STRUBE, M.J. (1990). In search of self: Balancing the good and the true. *Personality and Social Psychology Bulletin, 16*, 699–704.

SUEDFELD, P., & TETLOCK, P.E. (Eds.). (1991). *Psychology and social policy*. New York: Hemisphere.

SUGIYAMA, L.S., TOOBY, J., & COSMIDES, L. (2002). Cross-cultural evidence of cognitive adaptations for social exchange among the Shiwiar of Ecuadorian Amazonia. *Processing of the National Academy of Sciences, 99*, 11537–11542.

SUH, E., DIENER, E., OISHI, S., & TRIANDIS, H.C. (1998). The shifting basis of life satisfaction judgments across cultures: Emotions versus norms. *Journal of Personality and Social Psychology, 74*, 482–493.

SUINN, R.M., OSBORNE, D., & WINFREE, P. (1962). The self concept and accuracy of recall of inconsistent self-related information. *Journal of Clinical Psychology, 18*, 473–474.

SULLIVAN, H.S. (1953). *The interpersonal theory of psychiatry*. New York: Norton.

SULLOWAY, F.J. (1979). *Freud: Biologist of the mind*. New York: Basic Books.

SULLOWAY, F.J. (1991). Reassessing Freud's case histories. ISIS, *82*, 245–275.

SULLOWAY, F.J. (1996). *Born to rebel: Birth order, family dynamics, and creative lives*. New York: Pantheon.

SUOMI, S. (1999, June). Jumpy monkeys. Address presented at the annual meeting of the American Psychological Association, Denver, CO.

SUPPE, F. (1977). (Ed.) *The structure of scientific theories*. Urbana, IL: University of Illinois Press.

SWANN, W.B., JR. (1991). To be adored or to be known? The interplay of self-enhancement and self-verification. In E.T. Higgins & R.M. Sorrentino (Eds.), *Handbook of motivation and cognition* (pp. 408–450). New York: Guilford Press.

SWANN, W.B., JR. (1992). Seeking "truth," finding despair: Some unhappy consequences of a negative self-concept. *Current Directions in Psychological Science, 1*, 15–18.

SWANN, W.B. JR., DE LA RONDE, C., & HIXON, J.G. (1994). Authenticity and positivity strivings in marriage and courtship. *Journal of Personality and Social Psychology, 66*, 857–869.

SWANN, W.B., JR., GRIFFIN, J.J., JR., PREDMORE, S.C., & GAINES, B. (1987). The cognitive-affective crossfire: When self-consistency confronts self-enhancement. *Journal of Personality and Social Psychology, 52*, 881–889.

SWANN, W.B., JR., PELHAM, B.W., & KRULL, D.S. (1989). Agreeable fancy or disagreeable truth? Reconciling self-enhancement and self-verification. *Journal of Personality and Social Psychology, 57*, 782–791.

SWANN, W.B., JR., RENTFROW, P.J., & GUINN, J.S. (2003). Self-verification: The search for coherence. In M.R. Leary & J.P. Tangney (Eds.), *Handbook of self and identity* (pp. 367–383). New York: Guilford Press.

TANG, T.Z., & DE RUBEIS, R.J. (1999a). Reconsidering rapid early response in cognitive behavioral therapy for depression. *Clinical Psychology: Science and Practice, 6*, 283–288.

TANG, T.Z., & DE RUBEIS, R.J. (1999b). Sudden gains and critical sessions in cognitive-behavioral therapy for depression. *Journal of Consulting and Clinical Psychology, 67*, 894–904.

TAYLOR, C. (1985). *Human agency and language: Philosophical papers I*. Cambridge, UK: Cambridge University Press.

TAYLOR, S.E. (1989). *Positive illusions: Creative self deception and the healthy mind*. New York: Basic Books.

TAYLOR, S.E., & BROWN, J.D. (1988). Illusion and wellbeing: Where two roads meet. *Psychological Bulletin, 103*, 193–210.

TELLEGEN, A. (1985). Structures of mood and personality and their relevance to assessing anxiety, with an emphasis on self-report. In A.H. Tuma & J.D.

Maser (Eds.), *Anxiety and the anxiety disorders* (pp. 681–706). Mahwah, NJ: Erlbaum.

TEMOSHOK, L. (1985). The relationship of psychosocial factors to prognostic indicators in cutaneous malignant melanoma. *Journal of Psychosomatic Research, 29*, 139–153.

TEMOSHOK, L. (1991). Assessing the assessment of psychosocial factors. *Psychological Inquiry, 2*, 276–280.

TESSER, A., PILKINGTON, C.J., & MCINTOSH, W.D. (1989). Self-evaluation maintenance and the mediational role of emotion: The perception of friends and strangers. *Journal of Personality and Social Psychology, 57*, 442–456.

TETLOCK, P.E., PETERSON, R.S., & BERRY, J.M. (1993). Flattering and unflattering personality portraits of integratively simple and complex managers. *Journal of Personality & Social Psychology, 64*, 500–511.

THOMAS, A., & CHESS, S. (1977). *Temperament and development.* New York: Brunner/Mazel.

THOMPSON, R.A. (1998). Early socialization and personality development. In N. Eisenberg (Ed.), *Handbook of child psychology* (5th ed., Vol. 3, pp. 25–104). New York: Wiley.

TILLEMA, J., CERVONE, D., & SCOTT, W.D. (2001). Dysphoric mood, perceived self-efficacy, and personal standards for performance: The effects of attributional cues on self-defeating patterns of cognition. *Cognitive Therapy and Research, 25*, 535–549.

TOBACYK, J.J., & DOWNS, A. (1986). Personal construct threat and irrational beliefs as cognitive predictors of increases in musical performance anxiety. *Journal of Personality and Social Psychology, 51*, 779–782.

TONINI, G., & EDELMAN, G.M. (1998). Consciousness and complexity. *Science, 282*, 1846–1851.

TOOBY, J., & COSMIDES, L. (1992). The psychological foundations of culture. In J.H. Barkow, L. Cosmides, & J. Tooby (Eds.), *The adapted mind: Evolutionary psychology and the generation of culture.* New York: Oxford University Press.

TOOBY, J., & COSMIDES, L. (2005). Conceptual foundations of evolutionary psychology. In D.M. Buss (Ed.), *The handbook of evolutionary psychology* (pp. 5–67). Hoboken, NJ: Wiley.

TOULMIN, S. (1961). *Foresight and understanding: An enquiry into the aims of science.* Bloomington, IN: Indiana University Press.

TRIANDIS, H. (1995). *Individualism and collectivism.* Boulder, CO: Westview Press.

TRIVERS, R. (1972). Parental investment and sexual selection. In B. Campbell (Ed.), *Sexual selection and the descent of man: 1871–1971* (pp. 136–179). Chicago: Aldine.

TRIVERS, R. (1976). Foreword. R. Dawkins, *The selfish gene.* New York: Oxford University Press.

TVERSKY, A., & KAHNEMAN, D. (1974). Judgment under uncertainty: Heuristics and biases. *Science, 185*, 1124–1131.

TWENGE, J. (2002). Birth cohort, social change, and personality: The interplay of dysphoria and individualism in the 20th century. D. Cervone & W. Mischel (Eds.), *Advances in personality science* (pp. 196–218). New York: Guilford.

UNITED NATIONS POPULATION FUND (2002). *State of World Population 2002: People, Poverty, and Possibilities.* New York: United Nations.

VAN IJZENDOORN, M.H., & KROONENBERG, P. (1988). Cross-cultural patterns of attachment: A meta-analysis of the strange situation. *Child Development, 59*, 147–156.

VAN LIESHOUT, C.F., & HASELAGER, G.J. (1994). The Big Five personality factors in Q-sort descriptions of children and adolescents. In C.F. Halverson, G.A. Kohnstamm, & R.P. Martin (Eds.), *The developing structure of temperament and personality from infancy to childhood,* (pp. 293–318). Hillsdale, NJ: Erlbaum.

VAUGHN, P.W., ROGERS, E.M., SINGHAL, A., & SWALEHE, R.M. (2000). Entertainment-education and HIV/AIDS prevention: A field study in Tanzania. *Journal of Health Communication, 5* (Supplement), 81–200.

WALLER, N.G., & SHAVER, P.R. (1994). The importance of nongenetic influences on romantic love styles. *Psychological Science, 5*, 268–274.

WALTERS, R.H., & PARKE, R.D. (1964). Influence of the response consequences to a social model on resistance to deviation. *Journal of Experimental Child Psychology, 1*, 269–280.

WATSON, D. (2000). *Mood and temperament.* New York: Guilford.

WATSON, D., & CLARK, L.A. (1997). Extraversion and its positive emotional core. In R. Hogan, J. Johnson, & S. Briggs (Eds.), *Handbook of personality psychology* (pp. 681–710). San Diego, CA: Academic Press.

WATSON, D., & TELLEGEN, A. (1999). Issues in the dimensional structure of affect-effects of descriptors, measurement error, and response formats: Comment on Russell and Carroll. *Psychological Bulletin, 125*, 601–610.

WATSON, D., WIESE, D., VAIDYA, J., & TELLEGEN, A. (1999). The two general activation systems of affect: Structural findings, evolutionary considerations, and psychobiological evidence. *Journal of Personality and Social Psychology, 76*, 820–838.

WATSON, J.B. (1919). *Psychology from the standpoint of a behaviorist*. Philadelphia: Lippincott.

WATSON, J.B. (1924). *Behaviorism*. New York: People's Institute Publishing.

WATSON, J.B. (1936). Autobiography. In C. Murchison (Ed.), *A history of psychology in autobiography* (pp. 271–282). Worcester, MA: Clark University Press.

WATSON, J.B., & RAYNER, R. (1920). Conditioned emotional reactions. *Journal of Experimental Psychology, 3,* 1–14.

WATSON, M.W., & GETZ, K. (1990). The relationship between Oedipal behaviors and children's family role concepts. *Merrill-Palmer Quarterly, 36,* 487–506.

WATSON, R.I. (1963). *The great psychologists: From Aristotle to Freud*. Philadelphia: Lippincott.

WEAVER, I.C. G., MEANEY, M.J., & SZYF, M. (2006). Maternal care effects on the hippocampal transcriptome and anxiety-mediated behaviors in the offspring that are reversible in adulthood. *Proceedings of the National Academy of Sciences, 103,* 3480–3485.

WEBER, S.J., & COOK, T.D. (1972). Subject effects in laboratory research: An examination of subject roles, demand characteristics, and valid inference. *Psychological Bulletin, 77,* 273–295.

WEGNER, D.M. (2002). *The illusion of conscious will*. Cambridge, MA: MIT Press.

WEGNER, D. (2003). The mind's best trick: How we experience conscious will. *Trends in Cognitive Science, 7,* 65–69.

WEINBERGER, D.A., SCHWARTZ, G., & DAVISON, R.J. (1979). Low-anxious, high-anxious, and repressive coping styles: Psychometric patterns and behavioral and psychological responses to stress. *Journal of Abnormal Psychology, 88,* 369–380.

WEINBERGER, J. (1992). Validating and demystifying subliminal psychodynamic activation. In R.F. Bornstein & T.S. Pittman (Eds.), *Perception without awareness* (pp. 170–188). New York: Guilford Press.

WEINER, B. (1979). A theory of motivation for some classroom experiences. *Journal of Educational Psychology, 71,* 3–25.

WEITLAUF, J., CERVONE, D., & SMITH, R.E. (2001). Assessing generalization in perceived self- efficacy: Multidomain and global assessments of the effects of self-defense training for women. *Personality and Social Psychology Bulletin, 27,* 1683–1691.

WENZLAFF, R.M., & BATES, D.E. (1998). Unmasking a cognitive vulnerability to depression: How lapses in mental control reveal depressive thinking. *Journal of Personality and Social Psychology, 75,* 1559–1571.

WEST, S.G., & FINCH, J.F. (1997). Personality measurement: Reliability and validity issues. In R. Hogan, J. Johnson, & S. Briggs (Eds.), *Handbook of personality psychology* (pp. 143–165). San Diego, CA: Academic Press.

WESTEN, D. (1991). Clinical assessment of object relations using the TAT. *Journal of Personality Assessment, 56,* 56–74.

WESTEN, D., & GABBARD, G.O. (1999). Psychoanalytic approaches to personality. In L.A. Pervin & O.P. John (Eds.), *Handbook of personality: Theory and research* (pp. 57–101). New York: Guilford.

WHITE, P. (1980). Limitations of verbal reports of internal events: A refutation of Nisbett and Wilson and of Bem. *Psychological Review, 87,* 105–112.

WIDIGER, T.A. (1993). The DSM-III-R categorical personality disorder diagnoses: A critique and an alternative. *Psychological Inquiry, 4,* 75–90.

WIDIGER, T.A., VERHEUL, R., & VAN DEN BRINK, W. (1999). Personality and psychopathology. In L.A. Pervin & O.P. John (Eds.), *Handbook of personality: Theory and research* (pp. 347–366). New York: Guilford.

WIEDENFELD, S.A., BANDURA, A., LEVINE, S., O'LEARY, A., BROWN, S., & RASKA, K. (1990). Impact of perceived self-efficacy in coping with stressors in components of the immune system. *Journal of Personality and Social Psychology, 59,* 1082–1094.

WIGGINS, J.S. (1984). Cattell's system from the perspective of mainstream personality theory. *Multivariate Behavioral Research, 19,* 176–190.

WILLIAMS, S.L. (1992). Perceived self-efficacy and phobic disability. In R. Schwarzer (Ed.), *Self-efficacy: Thought control of action* (pp. 149–176). Washington, DC: Hemisphere.

WILSON, T.D. (1994). The proper protocol: Validity and completeness of verbal reports. *Psychological Science, 5,* 249–252.

WILSON, T.D., HULL, J.G., & JOHNSON, J. (1981). Awareness and self-perception: Verbal reports on internal states. *Journal of Personality and Social Psychology, 40,* 53–71.

WINTER, D.G. (1992). Content analysis of archival productions, personal documents, and everyday verbal productions. In C.P. Smith (Ed.), *Motivation and personality: Handbook of thematic content analysis* (pp. 110–125). Cambridge, UK: Cambridge University Press.

WISE, R.A. (1996). Addictive drugs and brain stimulation reward. *Annual Review of Neuroscience, 19,* 319–340.

WITTGENSTEIN, L. (1953). *Philosophical investigations* (G.E. M. Anscombe, Trans.). Oxford, UK: Blackwell.

WOIKE, B.A. (1995). Most-memorable experiences: Evidence for a link between implicit and explicit motives and social cognitive processes in everyday life. *Journal of Personality and Social Psychology, 68,* 1081–1091.

WOIKE, B.A., GERSHKOVICH, I., PIORKOWSKI, R. & POLO, M. (1999). The role of motives in the content and structure of autobiographical memory. *Journal of Personality and Social Psychology, 76,* 600–612.

WOIKE, B., & POLO, M. (2001). Motive-related memories: Content, structure, and affect. *Journal of Personality, 69,* 391–415.

WOLPE, J. (1961). The systematic desensitization treatment of neuroses. *Journal of Nervous and Mental Disorders, 132,* 189–203.

WOLPE, J., & RACHMAN, S. (1960). Psychoanalytic "evidence." A critique based on Freud's case of Little Hans. *Journal of Nervous and Mental Disease, 130,* 135–148.

WOOD, J.V. (1989). Theory and research concerning social comparison of personal attributes. *Psychological Bulletin, 106,* 231–248.

WOOD, J.V., SALTZBERG, J.A., & GOLDSAMT, L.A. (1990). Does affect induce self-focused attention? *Journal of Personality and Social Psychology, 58,* 899–908.

WOOD, W., & EAGLY, A.H. (2002). A cross-cultural analysis of the behavior of women and men: Implications for the origins of sex differences. *Psychological Bulletin, 128,* 699–727.

WOODWARD, S.A., LENZENWEGER, M.F., KAGAN, J., SNIDMAN, N., & ARCUS, D. (2000). Taxonic structure of infant reactivity: Evidence from a taxometric perspective. *Psychological Science. 11,* 296–301.

ZIMBARDO, P.G. (1973). On the ethics of intervention in human psychological research: With special reference to the Stanford prison experiment. *Cognition, 2,* 243–256.

ZUCKERMAN, M. (1991). *Psychobiology of personality.* New York: Cambridge University Press.

ZUCKERMAN, M. (1995). Good and bad humors: Biochemical bases of personality and its disorders. *Psychological Science, 6,* 325–332.

ZUCKERMAN, M. (1996). The psychobiological model for impulsive unsocialized sensation seeking: A comparative approach. *Neuropsychobiology, 34,* 125–129.

PHOTO CREDITS

Office. Page 322: Sean Cayton/The Image Works. Page 328: Courtesy Grazyna Kochanska. Page 329: Courtesy Grazyna Kochanska. Page 338: Alistair Berg/Photo Disc/Getty Images. Page 345: AFP/Corbis Images. Page 353: Courtesy Robert Plomin. Page 354: Corbis Stock Market. Page 367: Corbis Stock Market.

CHAPTER 10

Page 379: Corbis-Bettmann. Page 380: ©Bettmann/Corbis. Page 384: Benjamin Harris. Page 386: Courtesy Psychology Today. Page 392: Courtesy B.F. Skinner, 1956. Page 391: Courtesy Julie S. Vargas. Reproduced with permission. Page 387: Sidney Harris. Page 396: Corbis Collection/Alamy Images. Page 398: Dion Ogust/The Image Works.

CHAPTER 11

Page 414: Courtesy Brandeis University. Page 422: Marianne Gontarz/Jeroboam. Page 423: Bruce Ayres/Stone/Getty Images. Page 429: Jed Jacobsohn/Getty Images News and Sport Services. Page 432: Bruno Barbey/Magnum Photos, Inc. Page 434: Martha Stewart/The Picture Cube/Index Stock. Page 437: Drawing by Lippman; ©1972 The New Yorker Magazine by cartoonbank.com. All Rights Reserved.

CHAPTER 12

Page 453: Courtesy of Albert Bandura. Page 454: Courtesy of Walter Mischel. Page 460: John Bazemore/ΠAP/Wide World Photos. Page 468: Reuters/Fabrizio Bensch/Landov LLC. Page 475: Etta Hulme; reprinted by permission of NEA, Inc. Page 478: Andrew Lichtenstein/The Image Works. Page 486: Based on Mischel W., Ebbesen, E.B., & Zeiss, A.R. (1972). Cognitive and attentional mechanisms in delay of gratification. Journal of Personality and Social Psychology, 21, 204–218.

CHAPTER 13

Page 496: Courtesy of Hazel Markus. Page 503: Courtesy of Carol Dweck. Page 505: Ellen Senisi/The Image Works. Page 507: Courtesy of Tory Higgins. Page 512: Fred Goldstein/iStockphoto. Page 514: ©NYT Co./Gil Eisner. Page 516: Courtesy Dr. Aaron T. Beck. Page 520: Spencer Grant/PhotoEdit. Page 524: Michael Newman/PhotoEdit.

CHAPTER 14

Page 540: iStockphoto. Page 552: iStockphoto. Page 560: Lindsay Hebberd/Corbis Images. Page 561: Alain Nogues/Corbis Sygma. Page 568 (left): Courtesy of PCI. Page 568 (right): Courtesy of PCI.

CHAPTER 15

Page 577: Gautam Singh/ΠAP/Wide World Photos. Page 579: Alamy Images.

NAME INDEX

SUBJECT INDEX

process, 85–95
strength/limitations, summarized, 157
structure, 74–85
superego, 83
thinking processes, 106–107
unconscious, 76–82
Psychoanalytic theory of psychopathology, 120–124
Psychobiology. *See* Biological foundations of personality
Psychodynamic theory. *See* Psychoanalytic theory
Psychodynamics, 112
Psychological freedom, 186
Psychological resilience, 554–555
Psychological safety, 186
Psychology from the Standpoint of a Behaviorist (Watson), 379
Psychology of Personal Constructs, The (Kelly), 445
Psychopathology
behavior change, 20
behaviorism/learning approaches, 376, 383, 397–398
concluding remarks, 583–584
personal construct theory, 435–436
social-cognitive theory, 514, 518–527
unanswered questions, 584
Psychosexual stages of development, 98–101
Psychoticism (P), 259, 260
Punishment, 397

Q

Q-data, 250–252
Q-sort technique, 171, 172
Quantum physics, 239
Quotidian psychology, 577

R

Racial differences, 16
Radio soap opera and social change, 566–568
Random assignment, 53, 54
Range of convenience, 416
Rational-emotion behavior theory (REBT), 514
Rational emotive theory (RET), 514–516
Rational thinking, 107
Rationalization, 91
Reaction formation, 91
Reality orientation, 88
Reality principle, 84
REBT, 514
Reciprocal determinism, 470–471
Recovered memories, 96–97
Regression, 121
Reinforcer, 394

Rejection sensitivity, 539–542
Rejection sensitivity questionnaire (RSQ), 539–540
Relationship schema, 441
Relaxation, 513
Reliability, 41
Rep test, 423–425
Repression, 92–95
Repressive coping style, 93
Research, 33–36
case studies/clinical research, 44–47, 56–57
data, 35–40
ethics, 42–44
laboratory research/experimental research, 51–56, 59–61
personality theory, and, 63–64
questionnaires/correlational research, 48–51, 58–59
reliability, 41
validity, 41–42
verbal reports, 61–62
Resistance, 152
Response styles, 58
RET, 514–516
Right vs. left hemisphere dominance, 358–359
Rogers's person-centered theory, 161–189. *See also* Post-Rogerian phenomenological theory
applications, 232
authenticity, 166–167
conditions of worth, 183
conditions precedent required for change, 196–198, 200
congruence, 177–178
critical evaluation, 228–233
denial, 178
distortion, 178
effectiveness, 198–202
growth and development, 183–188
hermeneutics, 169–170
human motivation, 167
major contributions, 232–233
need for positive regard, 182–183
parent-child relationships, 184–187
phenomenological perspective, 167–168
presence, 200, 202
process, 175–183
psychological change, 194–198
Q-sort technique, 171, 172
Rogers at a glance, 233–234
Rogers's 14 principles, 165
Rogers's view of person, 166–168
Rogers's view of science of personality, 168–170
self, 170–171
self-actualization, 175–176
self-consistency, 177

self-esteem, 185–187
self-experience discrepancy, 194
semantic differential, 173, 175
shift to groups, 205
social acceptance, 187–188
strength/limitations, summarized, 233
subception, 178
Role, 253
Role Construct Repertory Test (Rep test), 423–425
Rorschach inkblot test, 114–116
RSQ, 539–540

S

S-data, 36
Sample approach, 401
Schedules of reinforcement, 395
Schema, 441
Schizophrenia, 359
Science of personality, 25–26
Scientific fraud, 43
Scientific observation, 4
Scientific study of people. *See* Research
Secondary disposition, 244
Secondary process thinking, 107
Secure, 149–151, 153
Selective breeding studies, 344
Self
brain, and, 366–367
concept of, 24
feared, 195
ideal, 171, 195, 218
independent vs. interdependent view, 560–563
ought, 218, 507
Rogers, 170–171
self-efficacy beliefs, 460–462
variable vs. consistent view, 179
Self-actualization, 175–176
Self-concept, 45–46, 47, 170. *See also* Self
Self-conceptions, 519
Self-concordant, 223
Self-consistency, 177
Self-deception, 89
Self-defeating strategies, 515
Self-determination theory, 222
Self-directed mirror behavior, 172
Self-discrepancies, 219
Self-efficacy, anxiety, depression, 519–521
Self-efficacy and condom use, 465
Self-efficacy and health, 522
Self-efficacy and performance, 462–464
Self-efficacy appraisal, 548, 549
Self-efficacy beliefs, 460–462, 483, 522
Self-efficacy expectations, 461, 525